D1599657

The World Book Health & Medical Annual

1989

World Book, Inc./Chicago • London • Sydney • Toronto
a Scott Fetzer company

Staff

Publisher
William H. Nault

Editor in Chief
Robert O. Zeleny

Editorial

Executive Editor
A. Richard Harmet

Managing Editor
Wayne Wille

Associate Editor
Joan Stephenson

Senior Editors
David L. Dreier
Robin Goldman
Jinger Hoop
Mary A. Krier
Barbara A. Mayes
Jay Myers
Rod Such

Contributing Editors
Sara Dreyfuss
Darlene R. Stille

Research Editor
Irene B. Keller

Index Editor
Claire Bolton

Cartographic Services
H. George Stoll, Head
Wayne K. Pichler

Editorial Assistant
Ethel Matthews

Art

Art Director
Alfred de Simone

Senior Artist, Health & Medical Annual
Melanie J. Lawson

Senior Artists
Nikki Conner
Lucy Smith

Artists
Alice Dole
Deirdre Wroblewski

Photographs

Photography Director
John S. Marshall

Senior Photographs Editor
Sandra M. Ozanick

Photographs Editors
Barbara A. Bennett
Geralyn Swietek

Research Services

Director
Mary Norton

Library Services
Mary Kayaian, Head

Product Production

Executive Director
Peter Mollman

Director of Manufacturing
Henry Koval

Manufacturing, Manager
Sandra Van den Broucke

Pre-Press Services
Jerry Stack, Director
Lori Frankel
Barbara Podczerwinski
Randi Park

Proofreaders
Anne Dillon
Marguerite Hoye
Esther Johns
Daniel Marotta

ISBN 0-7166-1189-9
ISSN 0890-4480
Library of Congress Catalog Card Number: 87-648075
Printed in the United States of America

IMPORTANT NOTE: The information contained in *The World Book Health & Medical Annual* is not intended to take the place of the care and attention of a physician or other medical or health-care professional. The information contained in *The World Book Health & Medical Annual* is believed to be accurate, but cannot be warranted. On any matters related to health, always consult a physician or other appropriate health-care professional.

Editorial Advisory Board

Joseph R. Christian, M.D., is Professor Emeritus of Pediatrics, Rush Medical College, and Consultant Emeritus to the Department of Pediatrics, Rush-Presbyterian-St. Luke's Medical Center. Dr. Christian received the Associate of Arts degree from the University of Chicago in 1940 and the M.D. degree from Loyola University School of Medicine in 1944. He is Emeritus Fellow of the American Academy of Pediatrics, the American Pediatric Society, the American College of Physicians, and the American College of Chest Physicians.

C. Anderson Hedberg, M.D., is Associate Professor of Medicine, Rush Medical College, and Attending Physician, Rush-Presbyterian-St. Luke's Medical Center. Dr. Hedberg received the Bachelor of Arts degree from Harvard College in 1957 and the M.D. degree from Cornell University Medical College in 1961. He is a Fellow of the American College of Physicians and a member of the American Gastroenterology Association, the Institute of Medicine of Chicago, the Chicago Society of Internal Medicine, and the Chicago Society of Gastroenterology.

James V. McConnell, Ph.D., is Professor of Psychology at The University of Michigan. He received the B.A. degree from Louisiana State University in 1947 and the M.A. and Ph.D. degrees from the University of Texas in 1954 and 1956. His research has included the biochemistry of memory, with emphasis on memory transfer. He is the author of *Understanding Human Behavior,* the leading college textbook on introductory psychology, which is in its fifth edition.

June E. Osborn, M.D., is Dean of the School of Public Health at The University of Michigan, and was trained as a pediatrician and as a virologist. Dr. Osborn received the B.A. degree from Oberlin College in 1957 and the M.D. degree from Case Western Reserve University in 1961. She has been an adviser to the U.S. government and is a member of the World Health Organization's Global Commission on AIDS. She is a Fellow of the American Academy of Pediatrics and a member of the Institute of Medicine of the National Academy of Sciences.

Robert E. Rakel, M.D., is Associate Dean for Academic and Clinical Affairs and Chairman of the Department of Family Medicine at Baylor College of Medicine. Dr. Rakel received the B.S. and M.D. degrees from the University of Cincinnati in 1954 and 1958. He is a charter Diplomate of the American Board of Family Practice and was a member of its Board of Directors from 1973 to 1979. His widely used *Textbook of Family Practice* went into its third edition in 1984.

Contents

Special Reports

Fifteen articles present in-depth information about topics of current importance in the fields of health and medicine.

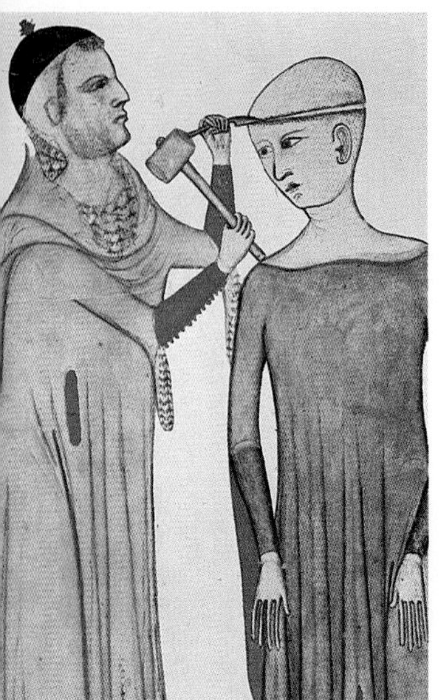

See page 20.

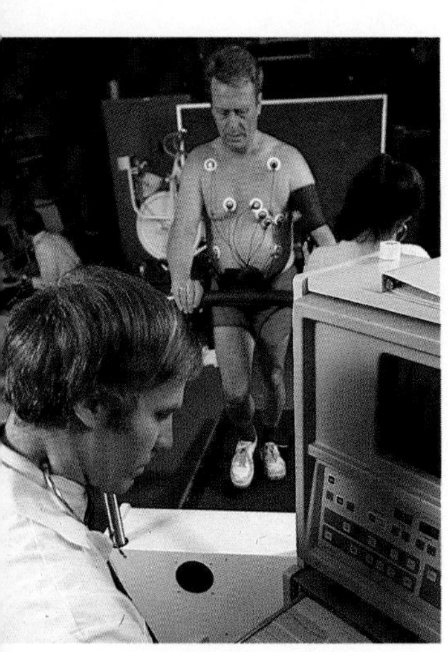

See page 71.

A tear-out page of cross-reference tabs for insertion in *The World Book Encyclopedia* appears after page 384.

See page 212.

See page 349.

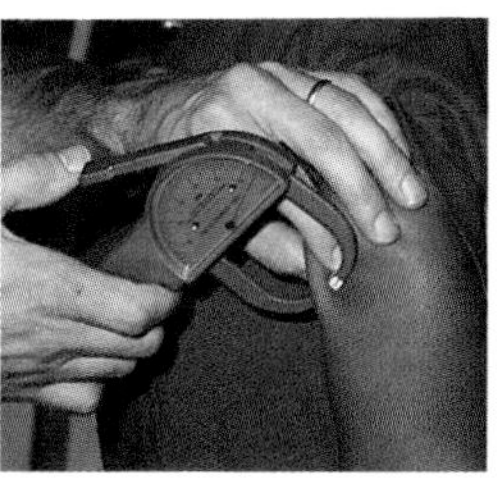

See page 370.

Contributors

Allen, William H., B.S., M.A., B.S.J.
Senior Editor, University of Illinois News Bureau.
[Special Report, *Conquering the Summertime Terror*; *Diabetes*; *Smoking*]

Balk, Robert A., M.D.
Director of Medical Intensive Care Unit and Director of Respiratory Therapy, Rush-Presbyterian-St. Luke's Medical Center.
[*Respiratory System*]

Barger-Lux, M. Janet, M.S.
Research Associate, Department of Medicine, Creighton University.
[Special Report, *Bone Up Now for Stronger Bones Later*]

Barone, Jeanine, M.S.
Nutritionist and Exercise Physiologist,
American Health Foundation.
[*Nutrition*]

Baum, John, M.D.
Professor of Medicine and Pediatrics and of Preventive Family and Rehabilitation Medicine, University of Rochester School of Medicine.
[*Arthritis and Connective Tissue Disorders*]

Birnbaum, Gary, M.D.
Professor of Neurology, University of Minnesota.
[*Brain and Nervous System*]

Brownell, Kelly D., Ph.D.
Professor, Department of Psychiatry,
University of Pennsylvania School of Medicine.
[Health Studies, *Weight Control and Your Health*]

Cates, Willard, Jr., M.D., M.P.H.
Director, Division of Sexually Transmitted Diseases, Centers for Disease Control.
[*Sexually Transmitted Diseases*]

Cohen, Edward P., M.D.
Professor of Microbiology, University of Illinois.
[*Allergies and Immunology*; *Infectious Diseases*]

Cormier, Frank, B.S., M.S.
Free-Lance Writer.
[People in Health Care, *Family Doctor to America*]

Cormier, Margot, B.A., M.S.
Free-Lance Writer.
[People in Health Care, *Family Doctor to America*]

Crawford, Michael H., M.D.
Professor of Medicine, University of Texas Health Science Center.
[*Heart and Blood Vessels*]

Dover, Jeffrey S., M.D., F.R.C.P. (C)
Chief, Division of Dermatology, Harvard Medical School.
[*Skin*]

Doyle, Larry
Free-Lance Writer.
[Special Report, *When Someone Aged Needs Your Support*]

Franklin, James L., M.D.
Associate Professor, Rush-Presbyterian-St. Luke's Medical Center.
[*Digestive System*]

Friedman, Emily Ann, B.A.
Contributing Editor,
Hospitals.
[*Financing Medical Care*; *Hospitals*]

Gartland, John J., M.D.
Chairman Emeritus, Orthopaedic Surgery, Jefferson Medical College.
[*Bone Disorders*]

Heaney, Robert Proulx, M.D.
John A. Creighton University Professor,
Creighton University.
[Special Report, *Bone Up Now for Stronger Bones Later*]

Hussar, Daniel A., B.S., Ph.D.
Remington Professor of Pharmacy,
Philadelphia College of Pharmacy and Science.
[*Drugs*]

Jubiz, William, M.D.
Director, Medical Service, Veterans Administration.
[*Glands and Hormones*]

Korbet, Stephen M., M.D., F.A.C.P.
Clinical Nephrologist, Rush-Presbyterian-St. Luke's Medical Center.
[*Kidney*]

Lake, Laura M., B.A., M.A., Ph.D.
Adjunct Assistant Professor of Environmental Science and Engineering, School of Public Health, University of California at Los Angeles.
[*Environmental Health*]

Lane, Thomas J., B.S., D.V.M.
Extension Veterinarian, University of Florida.
[*Veterinary Medicine*]

Maugh, Thomas H., II, Ph.D.
Science Writer,
Los Angeles Times.
[People in Health Care, *A Place to Heal*]

McInerney, Joseph D., B.S., M.S., M.A.
Director, Biological Sciences Curriculum Study, The Colorado College.
[*Genetics*]

Merz, Beverly, A.B.
Associate Editor,
Journal of the American Medical Association.
[Special Report, *Taking Steps to Better Foot Care*; *Eye and Vision*; *Stroke*; *Dentistry* (Close-Up)]

Newman-Horm, Patricia A., B.A.
Chief, Reports Section,
Office of Cancer Communications,
National Cancer Institute.
[Special Report, *The Cancer You Can See*; *Cancer*]

Nozetz, Stephen P., M.D.
Endocrinology and Metabolism Specialist.
[*Weight Control*]

Ovitsky, Margaret Moore, A.M.L.S.
Information Services Librarian,
Library of the Health Sciences,
University of Illinois at Chicago.
[*Books of Health and Medicine*]

Pessis, Dennis A., M.D.
Associate Attending and Assistant Professor of Urology,
Rush-Presbyterian-St. Luke's Medical Center.
[*Urology*]

Phillips, Tania, M.B., M.R.C.P.
Dermatology Fellow,
Boston University School of Medicine.
[*Skin*]

Powers, Robert D., M.D.
Acting Director,
Emergency Medical Services,
University of Virginia Medical Center.
[*Emergency Medicine*]

Raymond, Chris Anne, B.A., M.A., Ph.D.
Associate Editor,
Journal of the American Medical Association.
[Special Report, *Food's Hidden Hazard*; *Infectious Diseases* (Close-Up)]

Rowse, Arthur E., I.A., M.B.A.
President, Consumer News, Inc.
[*Safety*; *Safety* (Close-Up)]

Saper, Joel R., M.D., F.A.C.P.
Director, Michigan Headache and Neurological Institute;
Clinical Associate Professor of Neurology,
Michigan State University.
[Special Report, *Portrait of a Migraine*]

Satz, Paul, Ph.D.
Professor and Chief,
Neuropsychology Program,
Neuropsychiatric Institute,
University of California at Los Angeles.
[Special Report, *A Look at Left-Handers*]

Schaenman, Philip S., B.S., B.S.E.E., M.S.E.E.
President,
TriData Corporation.
[Special Report, *Fire!*]

Schommer, Nancy, B.S.
Free-Lance Writer.
[Special Report, *Fiber: A Recipe for Good Health?*]

Silberner, Joanne, B.A., M.A.
Associate Editor,
U.S. News and World Report.
[Special Report, *Reducing the Risk of Heart Disease*]

Simmons, Mark S., B.A., B.S., D.D.S., M.A.
Director, General Practice Residency Program, University of Minnesota School of Dentistry.
[*Dentistry*]

Skinner, James S., Ph.D.
Director, Exercise and Sport Research Institute, and
Professor, Department of Health and Physical Education,
Arizona State University.
[*Exercise and Fitness*]

Spivak, Jerry L., M.D.
Director, Division of Hematology,
Johns Hopkins School of Medicine.
[*Blood*]

Trotter, Robert J., B.S.
Managing and Executive Editor,
Psychology Today magazine.
[*Child Development*; *Mental and Behavioral Disorders*]

Trubo, Richard, B.A., M.A.
Contributing Editor,
Medical World News.
[Special Report, *Cosmetic Surgery: New Trends, Old Concerns*; *AIDS*]

Turner, Deborah Ann, M.D.
Assistant Professor,
Department of Obstetrics and Gynecology,
University of Iowa.
[*Pregnancy and Childbirth*]

Tyrer, Louise B., M.D.
Vice President for Medical Affairs, Planned Parenthood Federation.
[*Birth Control*]

Wallace, Joseph, B.A.
Free-Lance Writer.
[Special Report, *Solving the Mystery of Lyme Disease*]

Williams, T. Franklin, M.D.
Director, National Institute on Aging.
[*Aging*]

Wolinsky, Howard, B.S., M.S.
Medical Writer,
Chicago Sun-Times.
[Special Report, *Hope for the Hyperactive Child*]

Woods, Michael, B.S.
Science Editor, *Toledo Blade.*
[Special Report, *The High Cost of Quackery*]

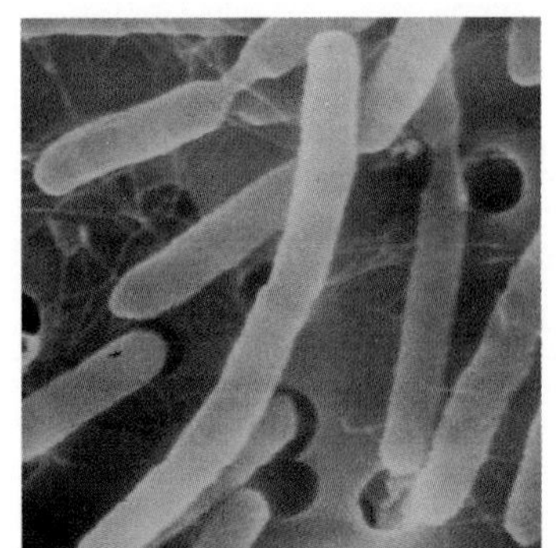

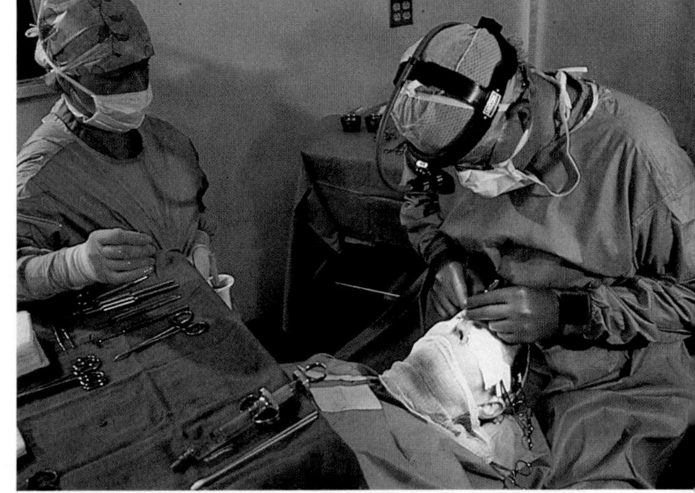

Special Reports

Fifteen Special Reports present in-depth information about topics of current importance in health and medicine.

A noted headache specialist describes the bizarre, painful symptoms of migraine, as well as its diagnosis and treatment.

Portrait of a Migraine

By Joel R. Saper

"*I . . . went to school and later to work in spite of it, sat through lectures in Middle English and presentations to advisers with involuntary tears running down the right side of my face, threw up in washrooms, stumbled home by instinct, emptied ice trays onto my bed and tried to freeze the pain in my right temple, wished only for a neurosurgeon who would do a lobotomy on house call. . . .* "*

Chances are good that about 20 per cent of the readers of this article have firsthand experience of the illness that author Joan Didion describes above. The rest may be surprised to learn that the source of her suffering was not a brain tumor, a stroke, or some exotic ailment of the nervous system—but *migraine*, a common form of headache.

No one dies of migraine; in fact, it causes no lasting harm to the body. But its symptoms—severe head pain, stomach and bowel upsets, and, in some cases, hallucinations—exact a high cost. Without treatment, migraine sufferers such as Didion are at the mercy of unpredictable migraine attacks that force them to abandon their day's plans and flee to quiet, darkened rooms, where they hope for sleep to shut out their agony. Not surprisingly, recurring migraine often brings loneliness and desperation along with the pain.

The symptoms of migraine are bizarre, the cause or causes elusive, and the treatment far from clear cut. It is no wonder that the ailment has presented an absorbing puzzle to those of us involved in headache research. Sufferers—along with their

Opposite page: An artist's rendering depicts the searing pain and visual disturbances of migraine. All the paintings reproduced in this article were created by migraine sufferers for entry in a British health association's art competition.

*From "In Bed" from *The White Album* by Joan Didion. Copyright © 1979 by Joan Didion.

families, who often do not understand why a simple headache should be so incapacitating—have long shared our perplexity. Fortunately, migraine research has made an exciting leap forward in the 1980's. Not only have we found several new and effective treatments, but our growing knowledge of brain function is leading us to a more complete understanding of this strange and punishing ailment.

Migraine headaches, which involve a complex and variable group of symptoms, are quite unlike the familiar *tension headache,* the dull pain affecting both sides of the head that almost everyone has experienced at one time or another. *Common migraine,* which affects the majority of *migraineurs* (migraine sufferers), does not always begin with head pain. Instead, the first sign may be blurred vision, a strange "metallic" taste in the mouth, a sudden food craving, thirst, constipation, confusion, or a change in mood. Hours to days later, the headache begins, sometimes rousing the sleeping migraineur in the middle of the night.

In more than two-thirds of common migraine attacks, the pain is felt on only one side of the head at a time, often radiating from the eye or the forehead. The ache, dull at first, usually progresses to a throbbing pain that is intensified by lifting, bending, or straining.

The pain can grow much more severe. A sufferer may soon feel as if the head is being pierced, crushed, or split in two.

The headache is usually accompanied by other symptoms that may, in some cases, be more troublesome than the pain. More than half of those who have common migraine become nauseated and vomit during the attack, and up to one-fifth have diarrhea. Queasiness, lack of appetite, and abdominal cramping are so common that migraines have long been called "sick headaches." In addition, the senses can become alarmingly heightened. The migraineur may experience an exaggerated and painful sensitivity to light called *photophobia,* or find that everyday noises such as the clatter of dishes being put away seem excruciatingly loud. Finally, some people become confused or disoriented—or even lose consciousness—during an attack.

Untreated, the migraine may last from several hours to more than a day, leaving the sufferer weak and fuzzy-headed. Depending on the individual, the next migraine may come in a day, a week, or a month or more.

About 1 of every 7 migraineurs has *classic migraine,* in which the symptoms of common migraine are preceded by an *aura,* a group of bizarre neurological disturbances caused by temporary brain impairment. Lasting 15 to 30 minutes, the aura sometimes produces weakness, numbness, garbled speech,

The author:

Joel R. Saper is director of the Michigan Headache and Neurological Institute in Ann Arbor and clinical associate professor of neurology at Michigan State University in East Lansing.

Piercing, stabbing, or throbbing pain characterizes some migraine attacks. The pain is typically concentrated in one side of the head and can become so severe that the migraine sufferer, or *migraineur,* is incapable of continuing daily activities.

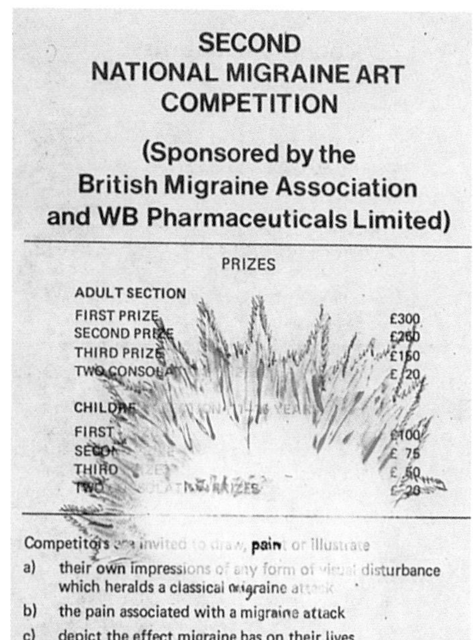

Bizarre visual disturbances that may precede a migraine attack in some people include the "doughnut effect," *top*, which obliterates the center of the field of vision, and the "fortification spectrum," *above*, a hallucinatory barrier consisting of geometric shapes and zigzag lines.

and coordination problems—symptoms that can lead observers to believe that the migraine sufferer is drunk. The most distinctive of the many symptoms of aura, however, are bizarre visual disturbances. One such disturbance has been called the "doughnut effect," the absence of sight in the center of the field of vision. While suffering from this visual disorder, the migraineur may look into a mirror and see only part of a reflection—the hair, shoulders, and neck, but a blank spot instead of the face.

The aura can also make the body of the migraine sufferer seem to shrink, grow, change shape, or turn colors. This disturbance is called the *Alice-in-Wonderland syndrome,* named for the fantastic happenings in *Alice's Adventures in Wonderland,* by Lewis Carroll, who was himself a migraine sufferer.

Another common symptom is the *fortification spectrum,* an eerie image of glittering zigzag lines and geometric shapes that blocks the field of vision like a wall. Interestingly, the fortification spectrum affects some totally blind migraine sufferers. A blind migraine victim can "see" the zigzag lines because this visual disturbance, like all the neurological symptoms of migraine, arises from *inside* the brain—not something actually sensed by the eyes, but a hallucination.

Surprisingly, not all migraine sufferers have head pain. Just as some people have migraine without an aura, a few have migraine without a headache—something we call a *migraine equivalent.* Most of these people have one of the symptoms of the aura and may also have stomach upsets, nausea, or vomiting. Their sense of balance may be disturbed, making them light-headed or dizzy. More children than adults suffer from migraine equivalents. Their symptoms are frequently misdiagnosed as evidence of flu or another ailment, but as the attacks recur, they can be properly attributed to migraine.

Most people with migraine have at least one parent or close relative who also suffered from the headaches, which has led us to conclude that migraine is a hereditary illness. Often, but not always, the hereditary trait seems to be passed to children from their mother rather than their father. One's first migraine can strike at any age—it has been diagnosed in children as young as 2 years old—but most patients suffer their first attack between the teens and the 30's.

In childhood, both boys and girls are equally affected by the ailment, but many children stop having migraines before they reach adulthood. Among adult migraineurs, however, women outnumber men 3 to 1. About 15 to 19 per cent of all males and 25 to 29 per cent of all females will have at least one migraine attack in their lifetime.

For decades, most researchers and physicians believed that migraine was caused by alterations in the diameter of the brain's blood vessels. They thought that the aura was caused by an extreme *constriction* (narrowing) of blood vessels that starved the brain of oxygen. When blood vessels then *dilated* (widened), they put pressure on nerves or stretched them, causing throbbing head pain.

But new research has led me and many of my colleagues to believe that blood vessel constriction and dilation alone cannot explain most of the symptoms of migraine. We think that something in the brain tissue itself causes both the blood vessel changes and the other symptoms. Central to our new concepts are *neurotransmitters*, brain chemicals that control many functions, including the perception of pain, and *receptors*, areas of nerves to which neurotransmitters attach. We suspect that changes in the levels of neurotransmitters or in the function of receptors may be at the root of the problem.

Our theory proposes that a disturbance of receptors and neurotransmitters in two parts of the brain can cause migraine. These two areas are the *brain stem*, the stalk of the brain that connects the two brain hemispheres with the spinal cord, and the *hypothalamus*, a kind of command center for many of the body's functions that is located behind the eyes. The brain stem appears to have a control over pain perception, while the hypothalamus not only directs blood vessel dilation and constriction but also influences bodily rhythms, hormonal function, appetite, and the body's reactions to emotions, among many other functions. Thus, if our theory is correct, an impaired pain-control system—which could be the result of an inherited defect, disease, or head injury—could by itself result in pain.

Although the underlying cause of migraine is not entirely understood, we—along with most migraine sufferers—know that certain events and substances can provoke attacks in people who are already prone to migraine. We call such provoking factors *migraine triggers*.

While many people believe that stress and the emotional strain it brings are triggers that underlie most migraine attacks, authorities now believe that stress is *not* the common denominator among all migraineurs. In fact, most migraines can be linked to internal bodily cycles rather than anything the migraineur did or felt.

A more important trigger than stress is the "letdown" period following a sudden decrease in stress levels. For example, many attacks come during a vacation, after an important examination at school, or on the weekend after a stressful week. Any change from one physical, mental, or emotional state to another can be headache-provoking.

For women, changes in hormone levels are actually the most common and predictable migraine triggers. Generally, migraine worsens when hormone levels change and improves when the levels stabilize. As many as 60 per cent of female migraineurs report attacks just before, during, or after their menstrual periods—a time when there is a drop in the level of *estrogen,* a sex hormone that plays an important role in sexual development in females. Up to 14 per cent of female migraine sufferers can link all their attacks to menstruation, and many had their first migraine during their first period.

Pregnancy, another event involving dramatic changes in hormone levels, has a variable effect on migraine. Most women find that migraine attacks intensify during the first three months of pregnancy but lessen during the rest of the term, when hormone levels stabilize. After the baby is born, migraine attacks may return, with the first migraine often occurring minutes after delivery.

In the same manner, birth control pills, which contain hormones, usually increase the frequency and severity of migraine. Half of the migraine sufferers who take birth control pills never had an attack before going on the pill. Although a few women report that oral contraceptives improved their condition, migraine specialists generally advise female migraineurs to use an alternative method of birth control.

Another time of hormone fluctuation that may trigger migraine attacks is *menopause,* the time of life, usually between the ages of 45 to 50, when a woman's menstrual periods cease. Some women have their first migraine attack at this time. Those who already had migraine may find that their condition either improves or intensifies at menopause. Unfortunately, the estrogen supplements that doctors often prescribe for women

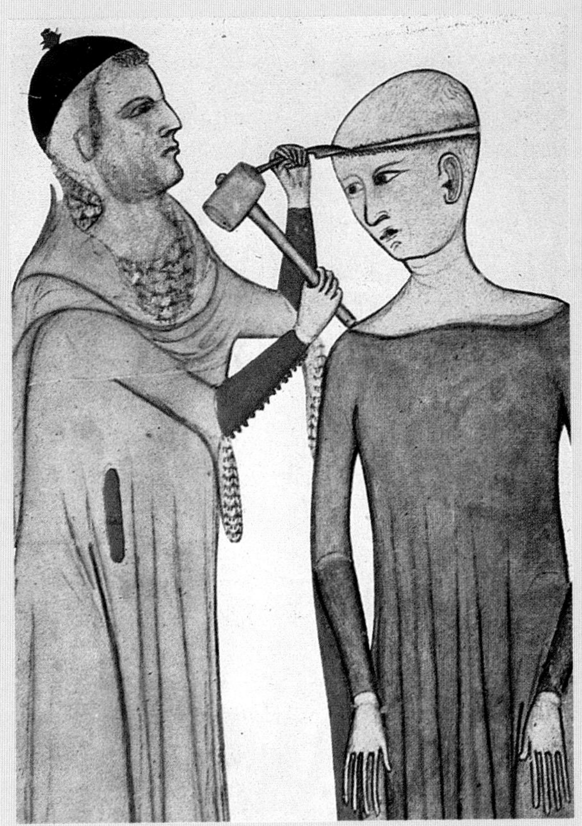

An age-old malady

Migraine headaches have afflicted people for thousands of years. The early Greeks called the headache *hemikranios,* which means *half the head,* and the Romans used the term *hemicranium* with the same meaning. The modern word *migraine* is derived from the second and third syllables of this Latin word.

Famous migraine sufferers include Julius Caesar, Saint Paul, Miguel de Cervantes, Thomas Jefferson, Charles Darwin, Frédéric Chopin, Leo Tolstoy, Peter Ilich Tchaikovsky, Sigmund Freud, Virginia Woolf, C. Everett Koop, and Kareem Abdul-Jabbar.

Extreme pain led migraineurs in ancient and medieval times to try extreme remedies. During the Middle Ages (500 to 1450), such treatments included covering the head with rags soaked in vinegar and cow dung, dripping cocoa juice onto the area of pain, or massaging the head with various parts of animal carcasses.

The most drastic treatment, *left,* was *trepanning*—cutting open the skull to release "evil spirits." That patients would consent to such treatment in the days before anesthesia is a testament to the severity of their pain.

after the menopause may make migraine worse. Whether or not to continue the estrogen supplements, which ward off the development of *osteoporosis* (a potentially serious disorder involving thinning of bone), is a difficult decision for doctor and patient (see the Special Report BONE UP NOW FOR STRONGER BONES LATER).

Certain foods and other consumables such as red wines, ripened cheeses, citrus fruits, monosodium glutamate (MSG), and milk can also be migraine triggers. But such foods do not affect everyone with migraine and often have a variable and inconsistent effect. Sometimes a specific food provokes migraine only when combined with another trigger. Oddly, fasting or missing meals also appears to be a trigger. We are not certain why this is so, except to say that when people routinely eat their meals at the same time each day, the body seems to learn to "expect" food at those predictable times. When a meal is missed, the body's response to this disruption—a response we call "disappointed anticipation"—may provoke a migraine attack.

Disruption of another routine activity—one's sleep schedule—can cause a similar disappointed anticipation. Although

More serious than a migraine

Most headaches are not symptoms of serious disease, but sometimes a headache can be a sign of life-threatening illness. Seek immediate medical attention if the head pain fits one of the following descriptions.

- **The headache is accompanied by fever and stiff neck.**
  This may be a sign of *meningitis,* a potentially fatal inflammation of the membranes covering the brain and spinal cord.
- **The headache is linked to an impairment such as loss of speech or paralysis.**
  There may be a blood clot, abscess, or bleeding within the brain.
- **The headache strikes as suddenly and powerfully as a thunderclap.**
  This can be a sign of bleeding inside the skull.
- **The headache slowly worsens over a period of days or weeks.**
  Such head pain may indicate the presence of a brain tumor or blood clot.
- **The headache is centered in the temple of someone over 60.**
  This could be a symptom of *cranial arteritis,* a condition that, without treatment, can lead to blindness.

sleep can relieve migraine once an attack has begun, sleeping later than normal, taking an unaccustomed nap, or in other ways deviating from routine sleeping and waking times may provoke migraine in some people.

Numerous other factors can be triggers, among them the sight of flickering or dazzling light. Even a change in weather can trigger an attack. Studies by researchers in Israel suggest that weather changes may subtly alter body chemistry in some crucial way. The term *ill winds* is thought to have been coined to describe this phenomenon.

But perhaps the most important point to make is that we do not fully understand the role of triggers, though I and many other headache specialists tend to think that the most important triggers are disruptions in natural body rhythms. Consistent daily, monthly, and yearly cycles—including those of sleep, menstruation, and body temperature rise and fall—are necessary for good health. As the list of triggers indicates, migraine attacks seem to come on the heels of an abrupt change in one of these cycles. The body may also be more sensitive to triggers at certain points in its cycles.

Because the symptoms of migraine are so variable and its cause has yet to be pinpointed, diagnosis of the disease is not easy. Migraine itself is not life threatening, but its symptoms can mimic those of stroke, brain tumors, or *meningitis,* an inflammation of the membranes covering the brain and spinal cord—all of which are deadly. For this reason, it is vitally important for anyone who has an unusual or severe headache to seek medical attention.

Family physicians may diagnose and treat most migraine patients but refer those with more complicated symptoms to a *neurologist,* a physician with special training in brain illnesses, or to a *headache specialist,* a doctor who has become particularly adept at evaluating and treating headache problems. In addition, since 1979, about two dozen reputable centers for headache diagnosis and treatment have been founded in the United States to help patients with particularly troublesome headache problems. These centers are directed by headache specialists, who oversee a group of trained medical and nonmedical professionals. The best centers are eligible for national accreditation by the Commission for Accreditation of Rehabilitation Facilities and offer a variety of evaluation and treatment methods. Some of these are private medical centers and others are associated with major universities.

Whether the patient seeks help from a headache center or a family physician, diagnosis begins with a discussion of the patient's personal and family medical history, followed by a physical exam, including special tests of the nervous system and brain as well as the eyes, ears, nose, and throat. Severe jaw disorders, allergies, infections, or sinus blockages can aggravate or, in rare cases, be the sole cause of the headaches. The doctor may also ask questions about the patient's mental and emotional health.

Laboratory tests are sometimes a necessary part of migraine diagnosis, especially if the patient's case is not typical. Blood tests to detect changes in blood chemistry should usually be done. An *electroencephalogram* (EEG) and other tests of the electrical activity of the brain help determine if the brain is working normally. *Computerized axial tomography* (CAT or CT scanning) and *magnetic resonance imaging* (MRI)—ways of taking pictures of the brain—can show whether a headache is being caused by a brain tumor, a serious defect in the brain's blood vessels, or another abnormality.

Sometimes the diagnosis of migraine must be made by a process of elimination. For most patients with migraine, the results of all tests are normal. This is good news—though many of my patients are frustrated by normal test results in the face of their severe, recurring pain. But once the possibility of life-threatening disease is ruled out, treatment for migraine can begin. It is worth emphasizing that migraine is a disease that, like heart disease, high blood pressure, diabetes, and other chronic illnesses, can be controlled though it cannot be cured. As many as 85 per cent of sufferers are eventually relieved of most of their symptoms.

Migraine prevention and treatment

One of the first steps in controlling migraine is keeping a headache diary, *right,* in which the migraineur records the frequency and severity of the headaches. The diary can help the migraine sufferer pinpoint and avoid foods or drinks or events that trigger the migraine attacks.

Migraines triggered by disruptions in daily routines can be avoided by maintaining regular times for sleeping, eating, and exercising—and adhering to the schedule even on weekends and during vacations.

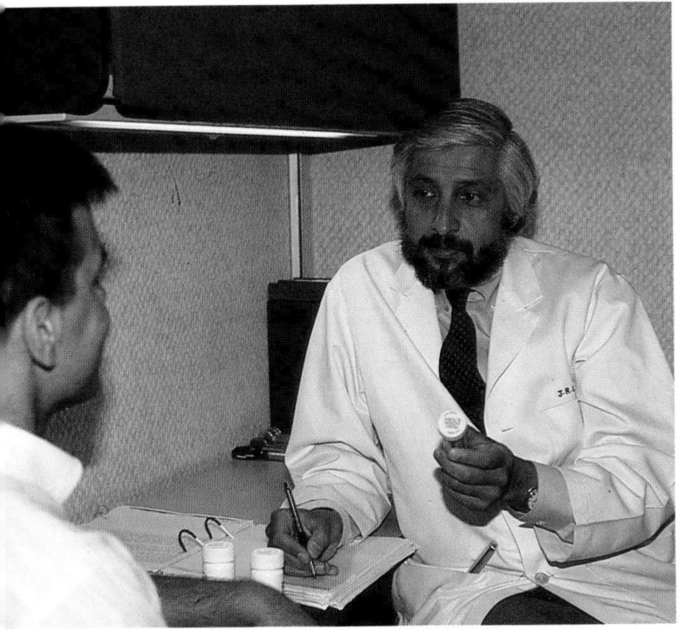

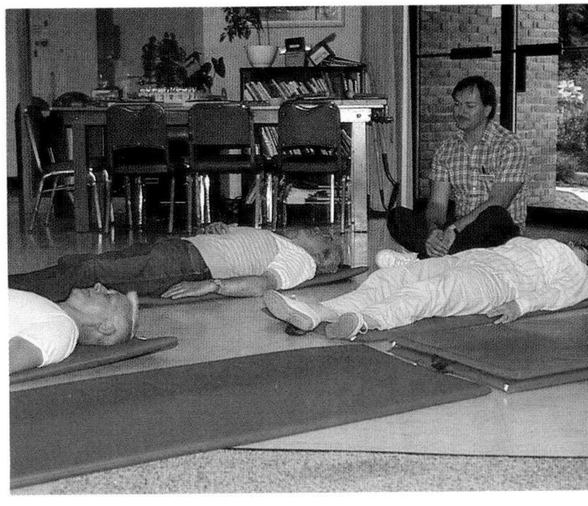

Physicians and headache clinics offer migraineurs professional treatment with a high degree of success. The author, *left,* prescribes one of the many drugs used to treat migraine, while patients at a headache clinic, *above,* learn relaxation techniques that may help them avoid some attacks.

The simplest treatment is to eliminate the patient's migraine triggers. The patient can identify these triggers by keeping a daily headache diary that records what happened before the headache occurred, including what the patient was doing, eating, and feeling. The diary can then be used to track the pattern of attacks and see if there are any recurring provoking agents.

Maintaining regular body functions and daily activities will eliminate some triggers and may be a far more important way to control migraine than we used to think. I advise my patients to awaken at about the same time each day and go to bed at approximately the same time at night—even on weekends and during vacations, when sleeping patterns are usually changed and when migraine attacks seem to be more frequent. I also suggest that patients stick to regular mealtimes and try to make their daily schedule of physical—and even emotional—activities as predictable as possible.

If migraine seems to be triggered by stress or emotional upset, getting help in the form of *psychotherapy* (treatment of mental or emotional disorders) or *biofeedback*—together with other forms of treatment—may go a long way toward gaining relief. Biofeedback is a process of learning to mentally control certain bodily processes such as heartbeat, blood pressure, brain waves, or skin temperature—processes that ordinarily cannot be controlled voluntarily. The patient is connected to electronic equipment that continuously monitors the bodily process to be controlled. The equipment gives signals such as rising or falling tones as the bodily process changes. This enables the patient to learn which thoughts result in the sought-after effect.

Interestingly, it does not seem to matter which bodily process migraine patients use biofeedback to control; the mental exercise alone seems to improve the condition in some people. We do not know why biofeedback appears to improve migraine, but my personal theory is that regular use of these techniques may somehow help maintain the body's natural rhythms.

For some people, eliminating food triggers may prove valuable in reducing migraine. But for others, this sometimes difficult task may be of no benefit. I do not recommend severely limiting the diet or extensive food-allergy testing for most of my patients. Regular exercise and adequate relaxation, however, seem to help almost everyone, and migraine patients are no exception. Finally, laughter may also be good for the migraineur's health. Laughing entails certain nervous-system reflexes that appear related to the mechanism of pain reduction.

When migraine persists despite these self-help measures, medication may be necessary. *Symptomatic medicines* can relieve a migraine attack after it has begun, and *preventive medicines,* as the name suggests, can forestall migraines. Doctors take several factors into account before recommending one of the two types of medication—including the patient's overall health and the frequency, intensity, and duration of the migraine attacks. We prescribe symptomatic medicines most often, generally reserving preventive medicines for patients who have very frequent migraines or who cannot take symptomatic medication. On occasion, the two therapies are combined.

Symptomatic migraine medications range from substances that affect the brain's pain-control centers and blood vessels to painkillers that simply mask the pain as the migraine runs its course. These drugs are usually available in pill form, which can be a problem because most patients' digestive tracts do not absorb food or medicine efficiently during a migraine attack. To circumvent the problem, some symptomatic medicines are taken by injection or as a rectal suppository.

For more than 50 years, a drug called *ergotamine tartrate* has been the favored symptomatic treatment, providing relief for most patients. It is most effective when taken by injection or rectal suppository, but the drug is also available in pill form. Its side effects—including abdominal cramps, chest pain, and a tingling in the limbs—prevent some patients from using it. In addition, overuse of the drug causes *ergotism,* a progressive and severe constriction of blood vessels that decreases circulation throughout the body, and can lead to stroke, kidney damage, and other medical emergencies.

In 1980, a few of my colleagues and I noted another consequence of too-frequent usage of ergotamine tartrate. Most patients who take the drug more than twice a week become dependent on it and develop seriously incapacitating and prolonged headaches when they stop using the ergotamine tartrate. We treat this condition, known as *rebounding*, by immediately discontinuing the use of the drug—a measure which often requires hospitalization and painkilling medication.

There are alternatives to ergotamine tartrate, however. *Midrin* is a less powerful symptomatic medicine that has few side effects. Certain arthritis medications called *nonsteroidal anti-inflammatory drugs* can also stop migraine attacks in some people. Finally, painkilling drugs called *analgesics* can be used to mask the pain.

Because all symptomatic medicines can cause rebounding or other unpleasant side effects, they can be used only occasionally. Patients who have migraine attacks more than one or two times per week are given preventive medications, which are taken daily to stop migraine attacks before they begin.

The safest and most effective preventives are *beta-blockers*, a group of drugs originally used for the treatment of *angina* (chest pain caused by coronary artery disease) and high blood pressure. For people who cannot take beta-blockers, a range of other preventive medicines is available. All preventive medications should be discontinued from time to time. Some people stop having migraine attacks naturally, and only by withholding the medication temporarily can we see if it is still needed.

One of these forms of treatment will stop the agony of most migraine sufferers. Joan Didion, for example, found relief with symptomatic medication. For the small percentage whose symptoms cannot be controlled by currently available treatments, the future looks bright. Today, major scientific efforts are aimed at understanding migraine, and a growing network of support, evaluation, and treatment—from the family doctor to the staff at a headache center—is becoming available. All of us are working toward helping migraineurs find what Didion calls the "pleasant convalescent euphoria" that comes when the pain finally ceases.

For further reading:

Lance, James W. *Migraine and Other Headaches*. Scribners, 1986.

Sacks, Oliver. *Migraine*. University of California Press, 1985.

Saper, Joel R. *Help for Headaches*. Warner, 1987.

The Cancer You Can See

By Patricia A. Newman-Horm

Skin cancer—the most common malignancy—is also the most curable. The key is to look for its early signs.

Years of sun exposure, *above left*, may eventually lead to the discovery of skin cancer, *above*.

"The tests indicate that you have cancer."

Who hasn't dreaded hearing those words? Which of us hasn't worried over the prospect of developing breast cancer, or prostate cancer, or colon cancer—or any of the more than 100 other diseases called cancer? Among modern health anxieties, fear of cancer ranks high. Except, perhaps, in the case of skin cancer.

Skin cancer, it seems, is one form of the disease that few people worry about. Perhaps this is because almost everyone knows of someone who developed a skin tumor and then had it removed, quite easily, in the doctor's office. It is true that more than 90 per cent of all skin cancers are completely curable if treated in the early stages. But, like other cancers, skin cancer in any of its three forms—basal cell carcinoma, squamous cell carcinoma, or malignant melanoma—can be a serious disease. When ignored, it can cause disfigurement and death.

Skin cancer is also the most common form of cancer in the United States—1 out of 7 Americans will develop it—and the incidence is growing. The Skin Cancer Foundation in New York City, using data provided by the National Cancer Institute, estimated that more than 500,000 cases of skin cancer were diagnosed in the United States in 1987 and predicted that the number will double by the year 2012.

The incidence of malignant melanoma, the most serious but least common of the three major forms of skin cancer, has been increasing steadily—at about 6 per cent annually since 1973. This growth rate is greater than the increase in any other form of cancer except lung cancer in women. In 1930, about 1 person in 1,500 developed malignant melanoma in his or her lifetime. Today, the odds stand at a startling 1 in 135.

Sunlight is a direct cause of most skin cancers, and many experts believe that the rising incidence is probably the result of the popularity of sunbathing, which became a fashionable leisure-time activity in the 1950's. Because of an increase in outdoor leisure activities such as sunbathing, skin cancer is no longer confined almost solely to people over 50 and to those who work outdoors. Today, it strikes an increasing number of young people. Luckily, most skin cancers progress slowly, and prevention can begin at any age.

In the United States every year, at least 400,000 people develop *basal cell carcinoma,* the single most common form of skin cancer. (Their ranks were joined in the mid-1980's by U.S. President Ronald Reagan, first lady Nancy Reagan, Senator Edward M. Kennedy [D., Mass.], and television journalist Ted Koppel.) The disease involves the abnormal, uncontrolled growth of *basal cells,* which are found in the thin, outer layer of skin called the *epidermis.* The cancerous cells form a tumor that in most cases appears as a small, smooth, translucent or pearly growth on sun-damaged or exposed skin. It usually develops on the face, ears, neck, or back of the hand, with the nose being the most common site.

Basal cell carcinomas are generally slow-growing. If left untreated, the tumor may form an open sore that never completely heals. It may alternately bleed and crust over, however. The tumor can eventually become dangerous and destroy a considerable amount of skin and may invade other nearby organs such as the eye, ear, bone, or brain. Fortunately, *metastasis* (spread of the cancer to distant sites in the body) is very rare in this form of skin cancer.

Squamous cell carcinoma is a slightly more dangerous form of skin cancer but it occurs much less frequently, affecting about 100,000 persons in the United States each year. Squamous cell tumors arise from the uncontrolled growth of cells

The author:

Patricia A. Newman-Horm is chief of the Reports Section of the Office of Cancer Communications at the National Cancer Institute in Bethesda, Md.

The most common cancer

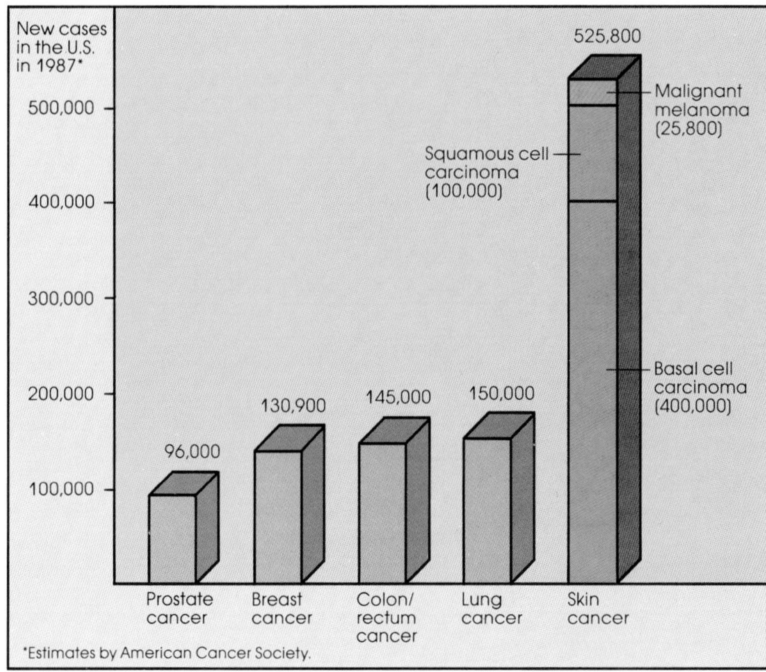

Skin cancer is by far the most prevalent type of cancer. About 1 in 7 Americans will eventually develop the disease.

called *keratinocytes* in the epidermis. When the tumor does not spread to the lower layers of skin, this cancer is also called *Bowen's disease.*

The appearance of squamous cell tumors is highly variable, but they often begin as opaque pink lesions with a scaly or crusted surface. They may grow into ulcers or wartlike bumps. The tumor edges may be yellow, red, or brown, and the normal tissue around the tumor is often reddened. Most such cancers develop on exposed areas of the body, such as the lower lip, ear, and back of the hand, but they can occur anywhere.

Because squamous cell carcinoma sometimes looks like basal cell carcinoma, a doctor must usually perform a *biopsy* (removal of all or part of the growth for analysis under a microscope) before making a diagnosis. Squamous cell carcinoma grows more quickly than basal cell carcinoma and can cause extensive damage to surrounding tissues. Squamous cell cancer can metastasize, and does so more often with tumors that are large, that have been present for many years, or that form on a scar or on the site of past X-ray treatment.

Malignant melanoma, the most deadly but least common form of skin cancer, begins in cells called *melanocytes,* which produce *melanin,* the pigment that gives skin its color. In the United States, about 26,000 new cases of malignant melanoma

Recognizing skin cancer

Skin cancer tumors of all three types—basal cell carcinoma, squamous cell carcinoma, and malignant melanoma—have a widely varying appearance. Any new growth or unusually colored patch of skin—even if it does not match one of those shown below—should be examined by a doctor.

Basal cell carcinoma, shown below, is the most common type of skin cancer. It often appears as a smooth growth that may crust and bleed. The tumor usually forms on sun-damaged skin, with the face, neck, and back of the hand being the most common sites.

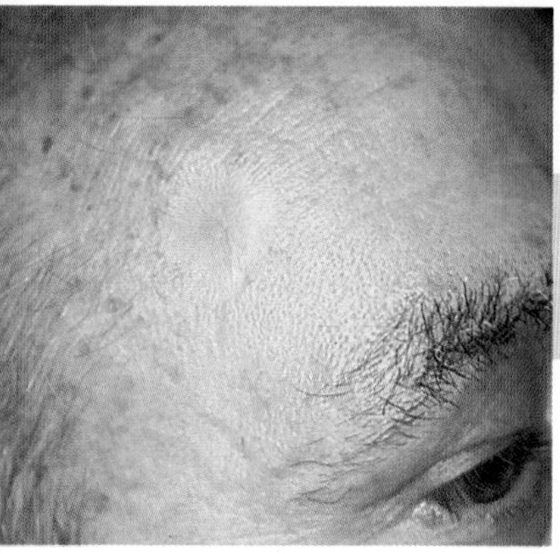

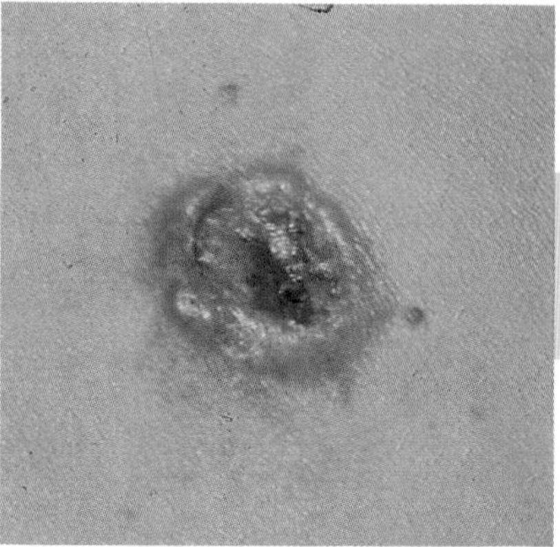

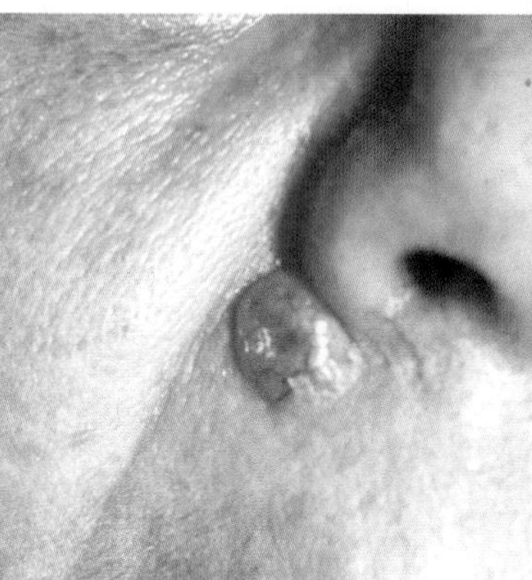

Squamous cell carcinoma, *below,* can be hard to distinguish from basal cell carcinoma. The tumor may be a scaly, crusted lesion, an ulcer, or a wartlike bump. The lower lip, ear, and back of the hand are common locations for squamous cell tumors.

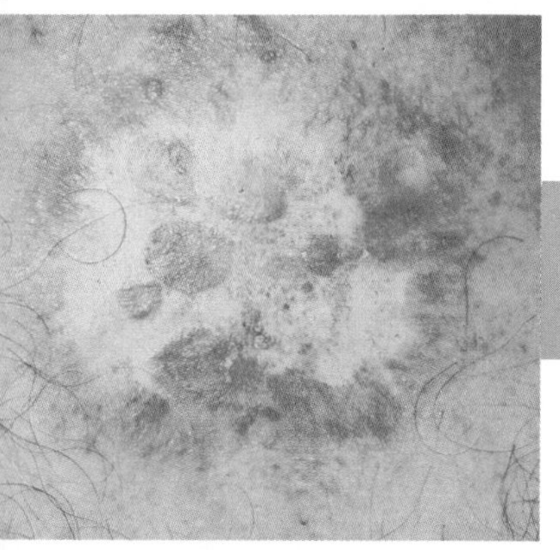

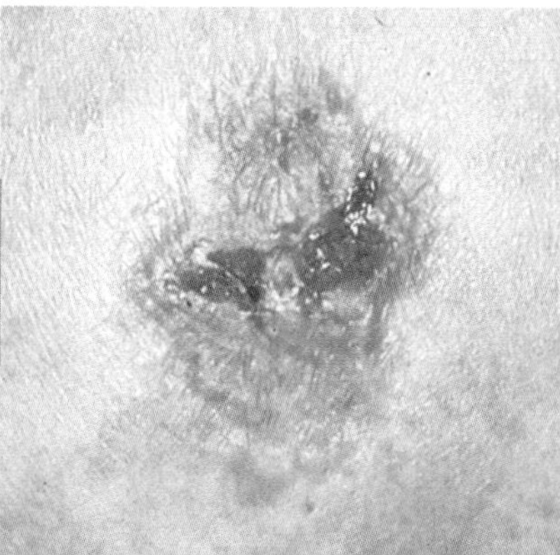

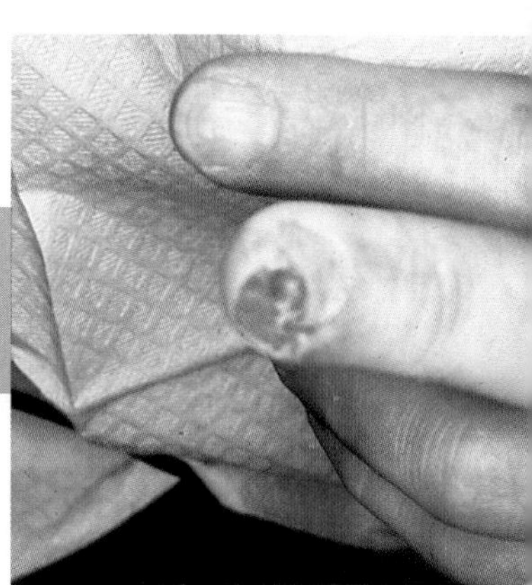

Malignant melanoma, *below,* can form anywhere on the skin. It may appear as a changing mole or a new, unusually colored patch of skin. You should see a doctor at the very first sign of melanoma. Tumors as thick as the one at far right usually prove fatal.

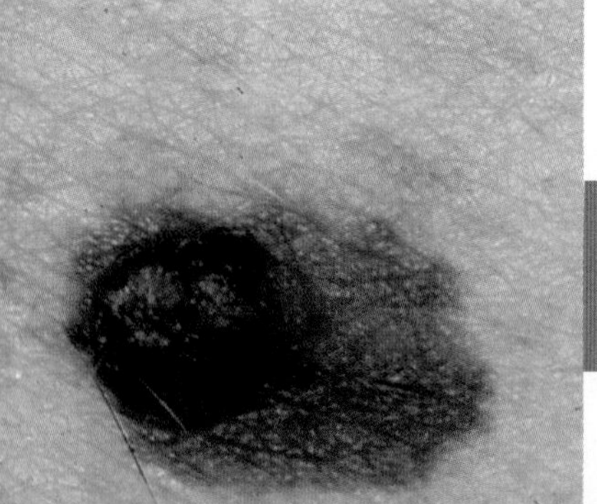

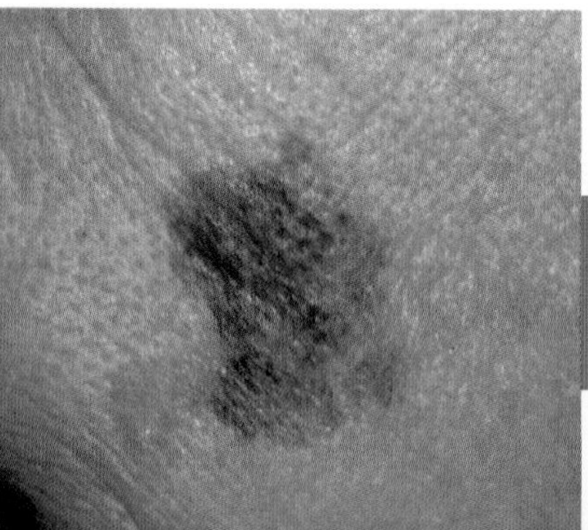

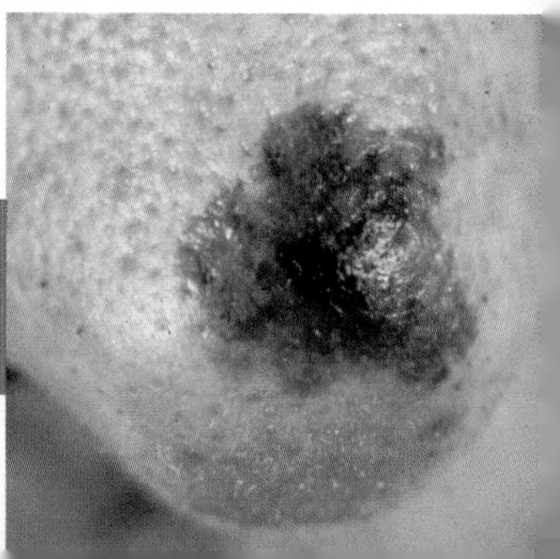

and about 6,000 deaths due to this disease are reported annually.

The most frequent melanoma symptom is the increase in size or change in color of a birthmark or of a mole, freckle, or other colored patch of skin that has been present for many years. In some people, however, the melanoma begins as a new molelike growth. The tumor is usually a slightly raised patch of skin that may be unusual in color, containing shades of brown, white, red, black, or even blue. Its surface is uneven, and its border is scalloped or irregular. Occasionally, a malignant melanoma bleeds or appears infected. The surrounding skin may become red and swollen, and the tumor may feel itchy, tender, or painful.

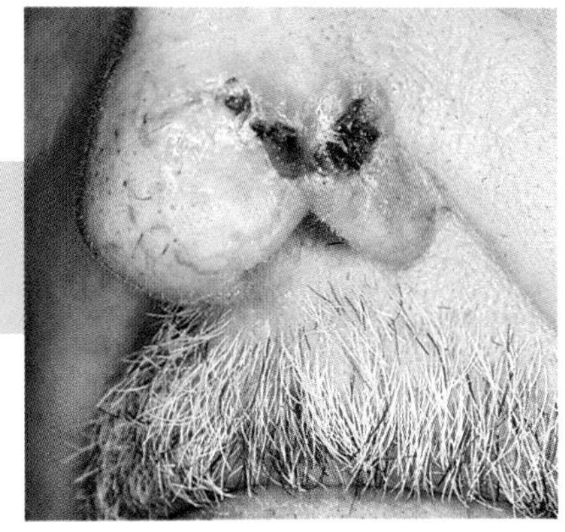

Malignant melanomas can appear anywhere on the skin. Among whites, the most common locations are the torso (especially the back), head, neck, arm, and, in women, the lower leg. Among blacks, who have a smaller risk of all skin cancers than whites, malignant melanomas usually develop under a nail, inside the mouth, or on the palm of the hand or sole of the foot.

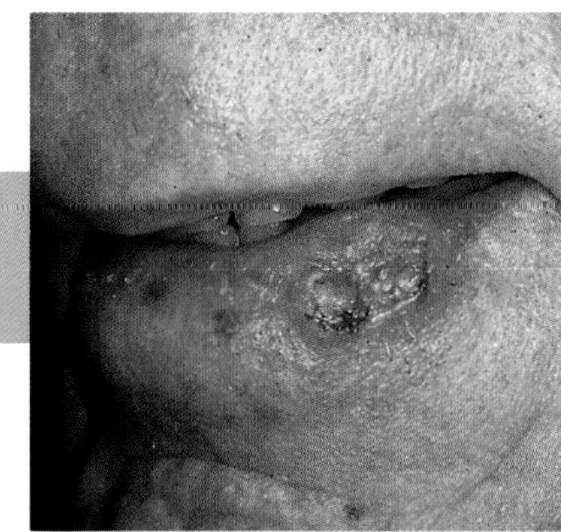

Because this type of skin cancer readily metastasizes, early diagnosis and treatment are essential. Scientists have found that they can estimate the survival rate of melanoma patients by the thickness of the tumor. If a tumor is removed early, before the cancer spreads beyond the top layers of the skin, the patient has an excellent chance of cure.

Researchers first began to understand the causes of skin cancer in the late 1800's, when physicians noted that some fair-skinned people were highly sensitive to sunlight and were more likely to develop skin cancer than dark-skinned people, who appeared to be protected from the sun's damaging effects. In 1928, scientists induced skin cancer in mice exposed to ultraviolet (UV) radiation, which makes up about 5 per cent of sunlight. During the next 30 years, scientists established that two wavelengths of UV radiation—UV-B and, in combination with UV-B, UV-A—are the precise com-

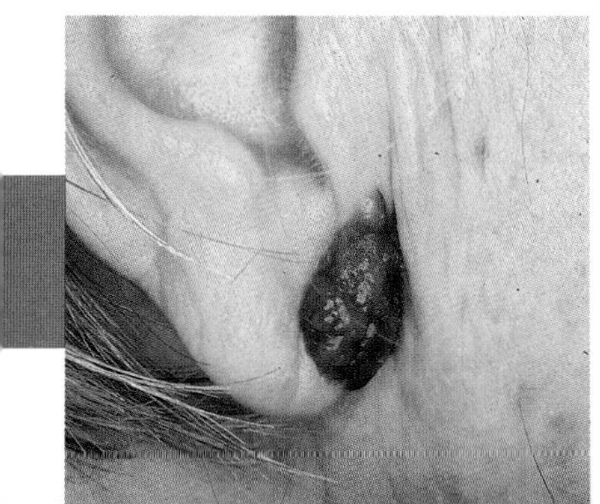

Skin type and skin cancer risk

Fair skin is especially vulnerable to the sun's cancer-causing rays, while deeply pigmented skin is well protected. Skin type is only one of several risk factors, however, and people with a family or personal history of skin cancer or a high level of sun exposure will be at risk no matter what their skin type.

Skin type: I
Coloring: Very fair, freckled
Ease of tanning: Never tans, always burns
Average skin cancer risk: High

Skin type: II
Coloring: Fair
Ease of tanning: Tans minimally, burns easily
Average skin cancer risk: High

Skin type: III
Coloring: Medium
Ease of tanning: Tans easily, seldom burns
Average skin cancer risk: Moderate to high

Skin type: IV
Coloring: Medium to olive
Ease of tanning: Always tans, burns minimally
Average skin cancer risk: Moderate to low

Skin type: V
Coloring: Brown
Ease of tanning: Tans profusely, rarely burns
Average skin cancer risk: Low

Skin type: VI
Coloring: Black
Ease of tanning: Tans darkly, never burns
Average skin cancer risk: Very low

ponents of sunlight that cause skin cancer. Research on the link between sunlight and skin cancer continues today. A 1988 study of 900 Maryland men conducted by scientists at Johns Hopkins University in Baltimore provided some of the first evidence that a person's risk of squamous cell carcinoma is directly related to the amount of UV-B radiation he or she is exposed to over a lifetime.

Although some exposure to sunlight is essential for good health because it helps the body synthesize vitamin D, chronic, extended exposure to UV-A and UV-B radiation can alter a skin cell's genes, causing it to grow abnormally. UV radiation can also damage the body's disease-fighting immune system so that skin cancer cells are not efficiently rejected.

A healthy person's risk of developing skin cancer is related to his or her lifetime exposure to UV radiation. For most people, UV damage begins with the hours spent outdoors during childhood. In general, the damage slowly accumulates through childhood and adulthood, with the majority of skin cancers appearing after age 50. People at higher than normal risk include those who spend more than two hours per day outdoors for 10 or more years, as well as people who work indoors but regularly spend weekends and holidays in the sun.

Skin coloring, which determines the amount of UV radiation the skin can safely absorb before burning, is one of the most important risk factors—especially for basal and squamous cell carcinomas. Fair-complexioned people who sunburn and freckle easily but tan poorly are in general more likely to develop skin cancer than are people with darker skin. To evaluate a person's susceptibility, dermatologists developed a system to classify skin types—from type I (greatest risk) to type VI (smallest risk)—based on the tendency to sunburn. Type I skin sunburns very quickly, after only 15 to 30 minutes of exposure to UV-B radiation. Type II skin burns in 25 to 35 minutes; type III in 30 to 50 minutes; type IV in 45 to 60 minutes; type V in 60 to 100 minutes; and type VI in 100 to 200 minutes.

Where a person lives or habitually vacations is another risk factor. Different global latitudes receive different intensities of UV radiation. For this reason, skin cancer is more common among whites living at latitudes near the equator than among whites living closer to the North or South pole. In addition, high altitudes receive more intense UV radiation than do low altitudes.

A few studies have suggested that blistering sunburns in childhood or adolescence play an especially important role in the development of malignant melanoma. In 1983, researchers at Massachusetts General Hospital in Boston discovered that melanoma patients were more likely to recall being painfully

Skin cancer self-exam
The Skin Cancer Foundation and the American Academy of Dermatology recommend that everyone—especially those with a personal or family history of skin cancer—thoroughly examine the skin every month. Look for changing moles, new growths, or oddly colored patches of skin.

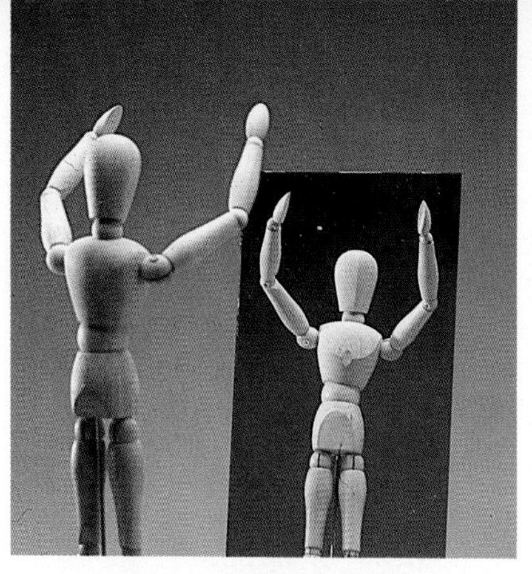
With arms raised, examine the front of the body in a full-length mirror. Turn and check sides and back.

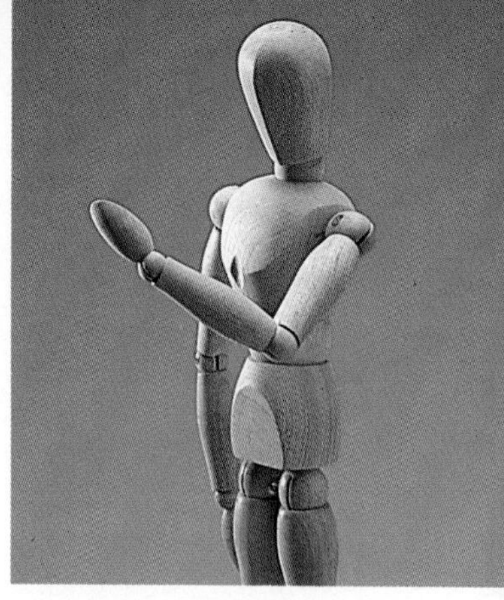
Check each arm, including the upper underarms, and examine the backs of the hands and the palms.

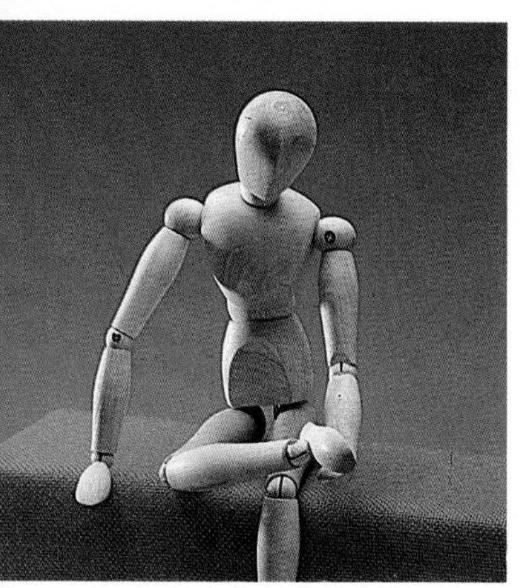
While seated, check the backs of the legs and the feet—including the soles and between the toes.

Using a hand mirror, check the back of the neck and the scalp. A blow dryer can help part the hair.

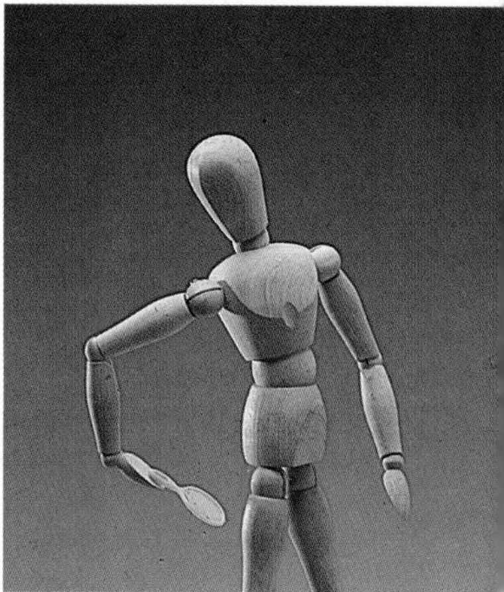
Examine the buttocks, lower back, and backs of the thighs, using a hand mirror.

sunburned during adolescence than were patients who did not have melanoma. A 1985 study by medical researchers at the University of Queensland in Australia supported this finding and reported that six or more severe sunburns during childhood seemed to double a person's risk of developing malignant melanoma.

Malignant melanoma risk is also linked to family history. The cancer occurs more frequently in families with an inherited condition called *dysplastic nevus* (unusual mole) *syndrome.* Some members of affected families develop moles that are unusually large, numerous, and variegated in color. People with this syndrome who also have two or more relatives who developed malignant melanoma have a very high lifetime melanoma risk—about 1,500 times that of the general population, according to a 1987 study by researchers at the New York University

School of Medicine in New York City. In addition, if a person has had any type of skin cancer, that is a strong indicator that other skin cancers may develop in the future.

X-ray treatments were at one time a significant cause of skin cancer, but modern X-ray techniques reduce the risk. On-the-job exposure to radiation or to chemicals such as coal tar, pitch, creosote, arsenic compounds, and radium is yet another cause of skin cancer. Limiting workers' exposure to these chemicals has made this a relatively insignificant factor.

Many Americans are aware of the most important cause of skin cancer, according to a 1987 survey conducted for the American Academy of Dermatology in Evanston, Ill. Nearly all the adults interviewed knew that exposure to sunlight damages the skin, and more than half knew that sunbathing is linked to skin cancer. But the notion that tanned skin is "healthy" and attractive persists. One-third of the adults surveyed said they work on getting a tan every summer, and one-fourth said they did not use any kind of sunscreen while sunbathing.

Deep tans may become less fashionable, however, and simple precautions will lead to the truly healthy look of well-protected skin. Because the summer sun is most intense between 11 A.M. and 3 P.M., those who are outside during these hours should cover up. Wearing long-sleeved shirts and long pants is advisable, particularly for people with skin types I, II, or III. Tightly woven, colored fabrics are most effective in blocking UV radiation. Broad-brimmed hats help shield the scalp, ears, nose, and cheeks.

Using sunscreen lotions and creams formulated to protect against the absorption of UV-B and, in some cases, UV-A radiation will also reduce the risk of developing skin cancer. These products should not be confused with suntan lotions, which do little to protect the skin from UV damage. A good sunscreen contains one of the more than 20 chemicals approved by the U.S. Food and Drug Administration (FDA) as safe and effective for filtering out UV-B radiation. The most common filtering ingredients are para-aminobenzoic acid (PABA) and its chemical relatives.

The protective quality of a sunscreen is measured in terms of its sun protection factor (SPF). SPF-15, for example, allows the user to spend 15 hours in the sun while absorbing the amount of UV-B radiation he or she would receive in only 1 hour without the sunscreen. Most sunscreens have SPF's ranging from 2 to 25. A person's sensitivity to sunlight, the activity being engaged in, and the season, altitude, latitude, and time of day all influence the choice of sunscreen. The key is to select a sunscreen with an SPF high enough to prevent sunburn.

It is a good idea to test a small area of skin for an allergic reaction before using any sunscreen. People who are allergic to PABA may be able to use a product containing cinnamate as its active ingredient. Swimmers should use waterproof sunscreens, and all sunscreens should be reapplied every hour or two.

Children should be especially well protected from sunburn because of the possibility that severe burns will increase their risk of later developing malignant melanoma. Sunscreens may not be safe for infants younger than 6 months, so babies should be carefully shielded by clothing and shade. Young children, along with fair-skinned adults who are constantly exposed to the sun, may need to use sun blocks, such as zinc oxide, in addition to sunscreens. Sun blocks, which are usually opaque white creams, contain particulates that reflect and scatter UV radiation. They should be applied to areas that need extra protection, such as the bridge and tip of the nose, the back of the neck, the shoulders, the lips, and the tops of the ears.

Medical researchers suggest avoiding the use of tanning salons and personal tanning equipment—even though some salon operators claim they provide a safe way to tan. Such assertions are usually based on the fact that most modern tanning lamps produce only UV-A radiation, which is less likely to cause sunburn than is UV-B radiation. Researchers concerned about the long-term effects of UV-A exposure dispute such claims of safety, however.

Although UV-A radiation burns skin less quickly than UV-B, it burns more deeply. In tests on laboratory animals, UV-A enhanced the cancer-causing potential of UV-B. In people with skin allergies and other sun-sensitive conditions, short-term effects of UV-A exposure include swelling, blistering, rashes, and genetic damage to skin cells. Because of its ability to damage genes and its disruptive effects on the immune system, UV-A radiation may also have serious long-term effects. In view of the scientific evidence, the FDA said in 1987 that UV-A sunlamps—especially new, high-powered versions—may cause skin burns, eye burns, cataracts, premature aging of the skin, and skin cancer, though those effects may not be as readily apparent as UV-B damage.

Early detection of skin cancer is as crucial as prevention. The American Cancer Society urges all adults to examine their skin every month for new growths, sores that do not heal, changes in moles or birthmarks, and patches of unusual pigmentation. Using a hand mirror and a full-length mirror, one can check every inch of skin from the scalp to the soles of the feet. Because malignant melanoma often develops from a mole, the

Skin cancer and the ozone layer

Some 15 miles (24 kilometers) above the surface of the earth lies the stratosphere, a layer of atmospheric gas that plays a major role in protecting all life on earth from solar radiation damage—including skin cancer in humans. This layer contains ozone (O_3), a form of molecular oxygen made up of three atoms instead of the two atoms that comprise the molecular oxygen (O_2) we breathe. This ozone layer absorbs much of the ultraviolet (UV) radiation and allows only small amounts of UV-B to reach the earth's atmosphere, preventing it from saturating the planet and damaging all living things.

Since 1985, atmospheric scientists have noticed that the stratospheric ozone layer above Antarctica becomes dramatically thinner during the Antarctic spring. In 1987, ozone levels during September and October were the lowest since monitoring began in the late 1950's. The sharp decline has fueled scientific discussion over both the cause of this "hole" in the ozone layer and the effects of reduced ozone or changed ozone distribution on the earth's climate and environment, and on skin cancer rates.

The ozone layer is relatively diffuse to begin with, representing only a tiny fraction of the total composition of the atmosphere. Complex natural forces continually create and break down ozone in the atmosphere, producing a natural balance between atomic oxygen (0), O_2, and O_3.

The balance can be disturbed, however, by *chlorofluorocarbons* (CFC's), a group of gaseous chemicals first manufactured in the 1930's. CFC's can drift up into the atmosphere and release chlorine atoms, each of which can destroy up to about 100,000 ozone molecules during a cycle of chemical reactions. Other manufactured chemicals may also be cause for concern.

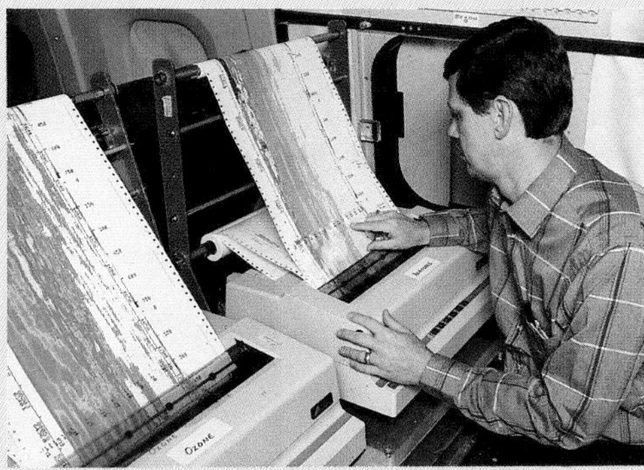

A research scientist examines computerized data showing the amount of aerosols and atmospheric ozone in the stratosphere above Antarctica.

Although scientists have relatively little information about how and to what extent these chemicals are affecting the ozone layer, many fear that the chemicals may be responsible for the ozone hole. This position was strengthened in 1986, when scientists in Antarctica discovered an increase in atmospheric chlorine that correlated with the springtime loss of ozone.

The ozone hole may be an indicator of how CFC's may affect the ozone layer above more densely populated areas of the earth. The relationship between depletion of the ozone layer and recent skin cancer rates is unclear, however. Some scientists have predicted that a 1 per cent decrease in global ozone levels will cause an increase of about 2 per cent in the amount of solar radiation reaching the earth. According to estimates by the U.S. Environmental Protection Agency, this might result in 20,000 additional cases of skin cancer in the United States each year.

But the work of biostatistician Joseph Scotto and other scientists at the National Cancer Institute in Bethesda, Md., suggests that other meteorological factors in addition to ozone may absorb UV-B radiation before it reaches earth, and they are working to identify them. Scotto and his colleagues have worked with skin cancer experts and weather scientists since 1974 to monitor the levels of UV-B radiation reaching the ground at several sites throughout the United States. Their results, published in February 1988, showed no increase in UV-B levels in some urban areas in the United States, though satellite instruments indicated some global depletion of the ozone layer.

Despite the scientific uncertainty, leaders of several nations believe the ozone layer is being depleted too rapidly to allow any delay in corrective action. In September 1987, 24 nations signed the first worldwide agreement designed to protect the ozone layer by making a 50 per cent reduction in the production and consumption of ozone-damaging chemicals by 1999. United States President Ronald Reagan in December 1987 sent the agreement to the Senate, which ratified the treaty in March 1988. [P. N.-H.]

You can protect against skin cancer and still enjoy the outdoors. Wear a hat or scarf, pants, and long sleeves, and generously apply sunscreen to exposed areas such as the face, hands, and feet for additional protection.

cancer society created a simple "ABCD" rule for distinguishing a melanoma from a harmless mole:

- *A* is for *asymmetry*; one-half of the growth usually does not match the other half.
- *B* is for *border irregularity*; the edges of the tumor are ragged, notched, or blurred.
- *C* is for *color*; the tumor's pigmentation is not uniform.
- *D* is for *diameter*; the width of a malignant melanoma is often greater than ¼ inch (6 millimeters), or the size of a pencil eraser, and sudden or continuing growth is of special concern.

People who have a personal history of skin cancer and those who have a family history of melanoma should have a doctor examine their skin regularly, perhaps every six months. Those with *actinic keratosis*, a precancerous skin condition characterized by scaly, reddish spots on weather-beaten skin, should also be monitored by a doctor.

Anyone who discovers a suspicious lesion should promptly seek a physician's advice. In most cases, the doctor will surgically remove the entire growth, and then analyze it for the presence of cancerous or precancerous cells. The majority of growths are harmless, but if cancer cells are found, more extensive removal or tests to see if the cancer has metastasized may be necessary.

Dermatologists (physicians who specialize in skin diseases) use one of four methods to treat early-stage skin cancer: surgery, *electrodesiccation* (tissue destruction by heat), *cryosurgery* (tissue destruction by freezing), or radiation therapy. Treatment for basal or squamous cell carcinoma is determined by the tumor's appearance, size, and site, and by the findings of the biopsy report.

To remove small tumors, dermatologists commonly use a special type of surgery called *curettage.* After injecting a local anesthetic to numb the area, the doctor scoops out the cancer with a *curette,* a tiny, sharp, spoon-shaped instrument. The doctor may then treat the area with electrodesiccation—using an electrified needle to burn the edges of the wound, thus controlling bleeding and killing any remaining cancer cells.

People undergoing a recurrence of skin cancer and those with tumors whose shape and depth are hard to determine may be treated with *Mohs' chemosurgery,* a specialized technique in which a trained dermatologist or plastic surgeon removes a thin horizontal slice of the tumor and immediately examines it under a microscope for the presence of cancer cells. The doctor repeats the process until all of the cancer cells have been shaved off. President Reagan underwent this type of surgery in 1987 for his second recurrence of basal cell carcinoma. Although the technique may be unnecessarily painstaking for many skin cancers, it has a very high cure rate.

To destroy abnormal cells by freezing them, physicians spray extremely cold liquid nitrogen on tumors or precancerous skin lesions. When it thaws, the abnormal tissue falls off. More than one such cryosurgery treatment may be needed. A final technique, radiation therapy, is occasionally used to destroy skin cancer tumors, especially when the patient is not strong enough to undergo surgery or when the tumor is on the eyelid or in other areas of the body that are difficult to treat surgically.

Treatment plans for malignant melanoma depend on the thickness of the tumor. Melanomas less than 0.03 inch (0.76 millimeter) deep can usually be completely cured by surgery. Thicker, more advanced melanomas call for extensive surgery—sometimes followed by a skin graft—and possibly *chemotherapy* (the use of anticancer drugs) to destroy cancer cells that may have spread to other parts of the body.

Medical researchers throughout the United States are investigating new approaches to malignant melanoma treatment. Especially promising is the use of chemicals such as interferon and interleukin-2, which are produced by the human body and which enlist the body's immune system to fight metastasized cells. Scientists are also trying to find new ways to help prevent skin cancer in people known to be at high risk for the disease, such as those who have already had skin cancer. While the research continues, the best approach for individuals is close attention to prevention and early detection. You cannot undo skin damage acquired in the past, but you can reduce your future cancer risk.

In 1975, a baffling illness struck the people of Lyme, Conn. A team of medical detectives set out to uncover the cause of the mystery malady.

Solving the Mystery of Lyme Disease

By Joseph Wallace

When the first few residents of Lyme, Conn., were stricken with a mysterious illness, no one suspected that the handful of seemingly unrelated cases hinted of a danger within the community. A small town along the eastern bank of the Connecticut River, Lyme is a place of affluence, comfort, and order. The landscape is dotted with farms and vacation cottages, and many of the community's well-tended homes are nestled in brushy, wooded areas where white-tailed deer graze. All in all, the peaceful New England town seems an unlikely setting for the appearance of a baffling new disease.

The Murrays were one of the first families to be stricken.

In the fall of 1974, Sandy Murray, an athletic high school senior, developed a stiff neck and excruciating pain in his thigh. Although he seemed fully recovered after a week in bed, repeated attacks of joint pain and inflammation—often severe enough to put him on crutches—continued to plague him.

Then other members of the Murray family became ill. In June 1975, 11-year-old Todd Murray developed severe headaches and an odd skin rash—a raised, red ring on one arm, soon followed by others. Later, his knee became so swollen he could not walk. His condition was diagnosed as *juvenile rheumatoid arthritis* (JRA), a potentially crippling illness that can last for years.

The boys' parents were not spared either. Days after Todd's attack, Gillis Murray, the boys' father, became ill. And their mother, Polly Murray, recalled that puzzling attacks of joint pain, fever, and rashes had troubled her since 1971.

After the doctors said that Todd had JRA, Polly Murray read up on the disease. She learned that JRA is fairly rare and that it is not contagious. Yet Murray knew that most of her family had suffered arthritis symptoms for years. What, she wondered, were the odds that several members of one family would contract the same uncommon, noncontagious disease?

Murray quizzed friends and neighbors and discovered that four students in one local school had recently been diagnosed as having JRA. She then heard about an 8-year-old girl named Anne Mensch, who had been hospitalized when her knee became so swollen she could barely walk. The diagnosis: JRA.

The girl's mother, Judith Mensch, shared Polly Murray's skepticism about the diagnosis of JRA. The Mensch family lived in a heavily wooded area of Lyme, just a few miles from the Murrays. Mensch knew that three other children on her street also had been stricken with arthritis—too much of a coincidence, thought Mensch. Like Murray, she investigated and put together a list of people suffering from arthritis symptoms.

Positive that the town was in the grip of some strange arthritislike epidemic, the two amateur investigators independently decided to alert professional medical sleuths at the Connecticut State Department of Health in Hartford, Conn. Health depart-

The author:

Joseph Wallace is a New York-based writer.

The artist:

Bob Fuller is an artist based in Denver.

ment officials at first resisted the idea of an arthritis epidemic in Lyme. They assured the two women that JRA and its adult counterpart, rheumatoid arthritis, were not infectious diseases.

But both women persisted, convinced that the Lyme victims were suffering from something other than conventional arthritis. In November 1975, they found a more receptive listener—David Snydman, then acting director of preventable diseases at the state health department.

Snydman listened to the two women with interest. Fortunately for Polly Murray and Judith Mensch, Snydman had been trained as a "disease detective" at the Centers for Disease Control (CDC) in Atlanta, Ga. The CDC is a federal health agency that investigates outbreaks of disease the way Scotland Yard tracks down criminals. CDC investigators have learned from experience that an unusual outbreak of illness in a community might point to a larger problem. Agents of the CDC's Epidemic Intelligence Service—physicians like David Snydman—are posted around the country to help local health departments look into such outbreaks.

The mystery begins . . . When residents of Lyme, Conn., were first stricken with severe, crippling joint pain in the early to mid-1970's, they had no idea that a mysterious new disease had surfaced in their town.

One typical CDC responsibility is the investigation of disease "clusters"—instances where an unexpectedly large number of people in a small geographical area become ill with the same disease. When a disease cluster turns up, health experts may begin an epidemiological investigation, searching for the basic details of the cause and distribution of the illness. Many disease clusters, particularly those involving chronic diseases such as various forms of cancer, apparently occur by chance. But medical sleuthing occasionally unearths a factor that all the victims have in common, such as exposure to a toxin or an infectious microorganism.

Snydman was intrigued with the suggestion of a cluster of arthritis cases. "I didn't know what it was, but it sounded interesting," Snydman told a reporter from *The New York Times*. The two mothers gave Snydman lists of people they thought had the same illness, and he went to work.

After Snydman phoned everyone on the lists and put together quick medical histories, he drove to Lyme and talked to some of the patients, as well as to local physicians and school nurses. Sure enough, an usually large number of people had symptoms resembling those of rheumatoid arthritis.

The concern of the two Lyme women appeared to be justified, but the cause of the strange outbreak of arthritis was a complete mystery. Perhaps some pollutant was poisoning people in Lyme, or perhaps a previously unknown disease had gained a foothold there. Snydman decided to enlist some help in investigating Lyme's mysterious malady. He contacted a colleague, physician Allen C. Steere of Yale University School of Medicine in New Haven, Conn.

The Lyme mystery seemed tailor-made for someone with Steere's background. For one thing, Steere is a *rheumatologist,* a doctor who specializes in arthritis and other disorders characterized by inflamed, stiff, and sometimes swollen joints and muscles. And Steere, like Snydman, had been trained in epidemiological field work at the CDC.

Steere regarded a cluster of arthritis victims as an exciting find because no one knows the exact cause of either JRA or rheumatoid arthritis, though there is evidence that a malfunctioning immune system plays a role in both illnesses. "We saw the possibility of learning a great deal about these diseases," recalls Steere, who is now at Tufts University's New England Medical Center in Boston.

But the Lyme outbreak was also baffling, because no one had ever before reported a cluster of arthritis cases. "So we thought we might be studying something we hadn't seen before," says Steere. "But what was it?"

To answer this and other questions, Steere and his fellow medical sleuths immediately launched an epidemiological investigation, an effort that would span the next seven years. The first step was to interview hundreds of people in the Lyme community, from physicians to arthritis patients and their families and neighbors.

Amateur detectives
Some Lyme residents, alarmed when family members and neighbors were diagnosed as having a relatively rare form of arthritis, decided in 1975 to do some amateur detective work, quizzing townspeople about their health, *above.* Their efforts turned up additional victims of the mysterious ailment.

From the start, the interviews yielded a variety of fascinating clues. The medical detectives quickly found that the outbreak of what came to be called *Lyme arthritis* (later renamed *Lyme disease,* in recognition of its wider effects on its victims) was limited to three adjacent towns on the east bank of the Connecticut River—Lyme, Old Lyme, and East Haddam. JRA normally affects only about 1 in 100,000 children, as well as some adults. But in the three Connecticut towns, with a total population of only about 12,000 people, 39 children and 12 adults had been diagnosed as

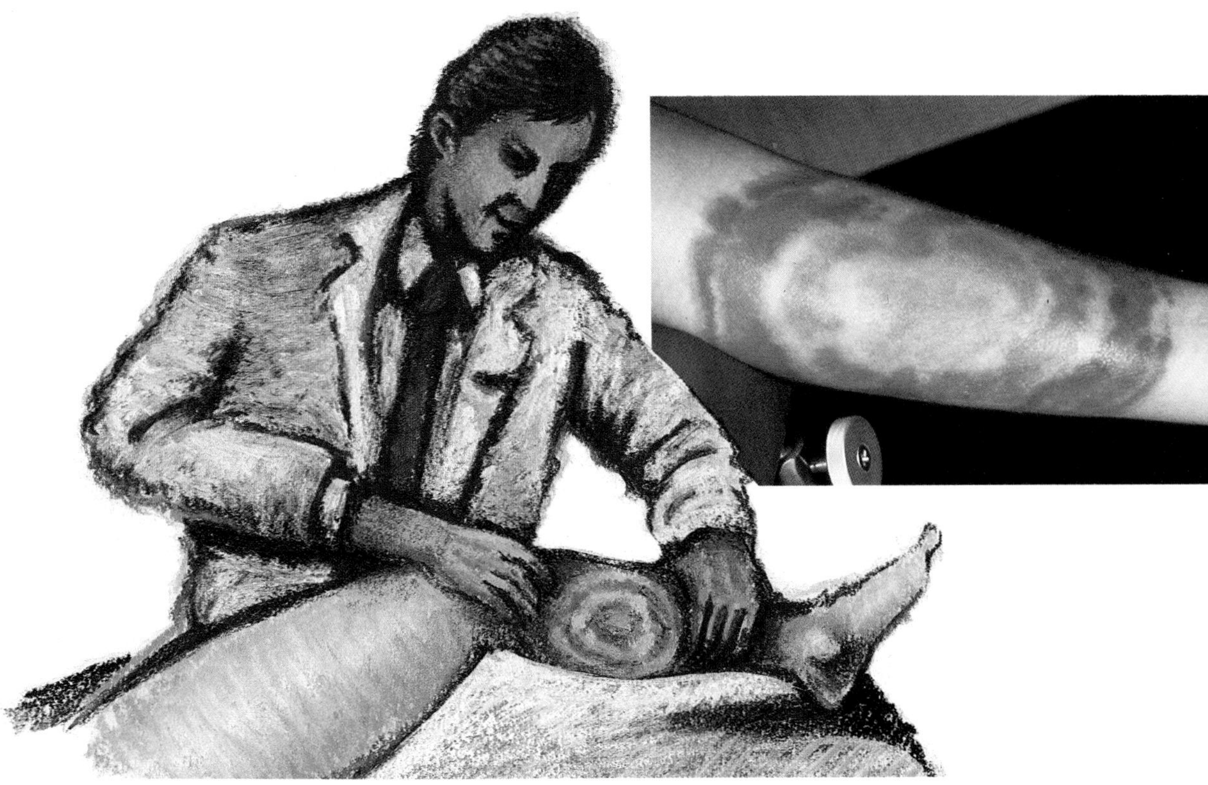

An early clue
Researchers learned that for many victims of Lyme disease, the first symptom of the illness was a skin rash shaped like a bull's-eye, *above*—a rash that might have been caused by the bite of an insect, spider, or tick.

having JRA—a huge number of cases compared with the expected rate of incidence.

A careful look at where the victims lived provided even more compelling evidence that the dramatic number of cases represented more than a chance occurrence. Although a few victims resided in the town centers, most lived in wooded areas. In fact, the homes of half the victims in Old Lyme and East Haddam were located on just four roads.

"In these clusters, as many as 1 in 10 children—and many adults—were told they had arthritis," says Steere. "That was a frequency 10,000 times higher than normal—far too high for it to be true arthritis."

Rumors swept through the affected areas. Some people were worried that radiation had leaked from a nearby nuclear power plant. Others feared that the local water supply had been contaminated by toxic pollutants or germs.

But the epidemiological detective work began to turn up clues that suggested to Steere and his team that the culprit was neither radiation nor contaminated water. "Every outbreak of disease has an epidemiological 'fingerprint,' a set of details that help identify its cause," he explains.

Steere's investigation turned up several such significant details. First, the highest incidence of illness occurred among people who lived in heavily wooded areas. Second, most patients first experienced symptoms during the summer months, June through September. And third, some of the patients remembered that one to several weeks before the onset of the arthritis symptoms they had developed a strange skin rash—a small red bump that expanded to form a bull's-eye, white in the center and red on the outside.

To Steere and his team, these clues suggested that the illness was spread by an *arthropod*—an insect, spider, or tick. In such infections, the arthropod functions as a *vector*, a carrier that transmits a bacterium or virus to human beings and other animals without being affected itself.

What type of arthropod might be responsible for the Lyme illness? Because the bull's-eye rash usually appeared on a patient's chest, abdomen, or back, Steere suspected that some crawling arthropod, such as a tick or spider, had inflicted the bite, rather than a fly or mosquito. Aside from this educated guess, however, Steere and his team had no specific suspect in mind. Finding the carrier was crucial to the next stage of the investigation—uncovering the identity of the bacterium or virus that was the actual cause of the disease.

Just a few months into the investigation, Steere had a lucky break. Tipped off by a Scandinavian physician, he learned that European doctors had reported seeing patients with a skin rash similar to the bull's-eye rash of Lyme patients. Following up on this piece of information, Steere then turned up a 1909 medical study from Europe. In the article, a Swedish doctor named Arvid Afzelius reported that patients bitten by a certain tick called *Ixodes ricinus* often developed a strange, slowly spreading red rash. Afzelius called the rash *erythema chronicum migrans* (ECM), which means "chronic migrating rash."

Here was a tantalizing clue, indeed. Not only did Afzelius' slowly spreading red rash sound very much like the rash reported by the Lyme victims, the Swedish physician's report also linked the symptom to a tick. Steere greeted this finding with guarded excitement; he had followed false leads before. He suspected that ECM and the Lyme illness might be closely related illnesses, but he needed proof of the existence of a North American tick vector.

For the next two years, as the number of victims of the Lyme illness continued to climb, Steere searched for clues to the identities of the vector and the germ it carried. He tested the blood of Lyme patients for the presence of more than 200 diseases known to be carried by ticks and other arthropods. These

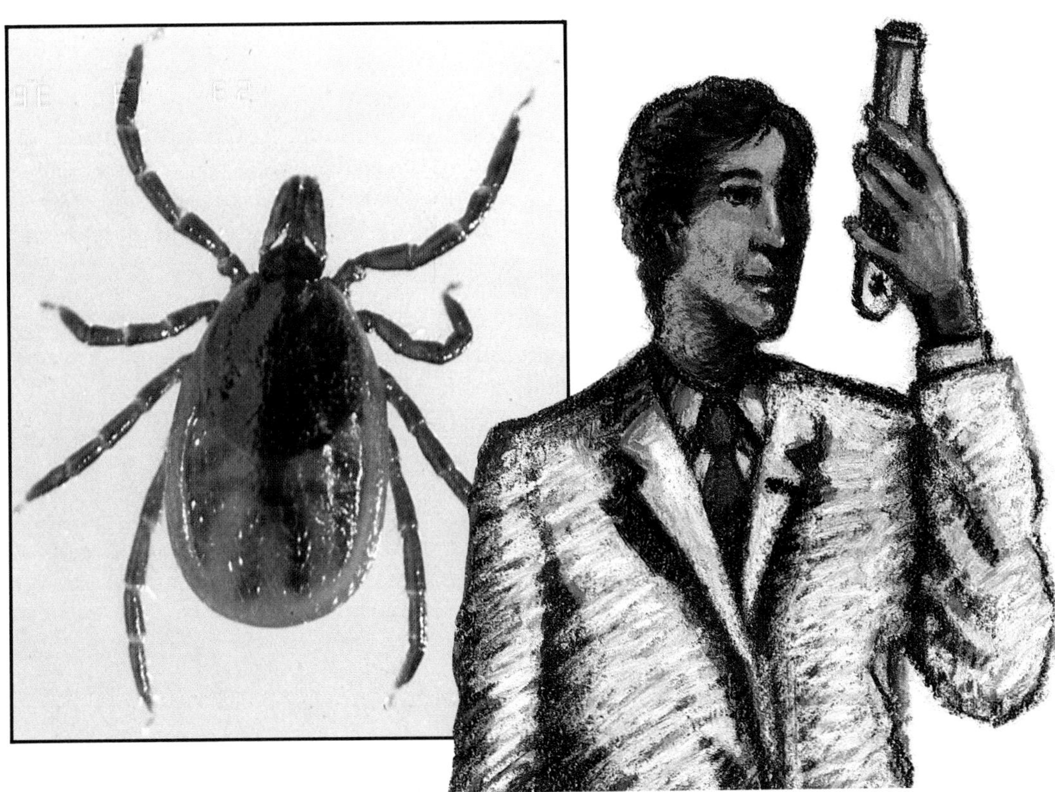

Prime suspect
In 1977, a patient handed the medical sleuths a major clue—a tick, *above* (shown in the drawing actual size), that had bitten him shortly before he became ill. The researchers soon learned that the tiny tick, *Ixodes dammini, above left,* is the carrier of Lyme disease.

tests were designed to reveal the presence of disease-fighting proteins called *antibodies* that might have been produced by the body in response to a bacterium or virus. A positive antibody test in all the patients might suggest that a particular agent was causing the illness. But the tests of the Lyme patients all proved negative, and it seemed as if the cause of their misery might never be found.

Finally, late in the summer of 1977, a crucial piece of evidence turned up. Nine Lyme disease patients remembered having been bitten by a tick at the site of the rash before becoming ill. One enterprising individual had even removed the tick and saved it.

At last, about two years after he had begun his search for the elusive carrier of the disease, Steere had a prime suspect. It was a brown tick about the size of a match head, so tiny that it was easily missed even by those experienced in spotting the much larger dog tick common in rural and suburban Connecticut. He turned the precious specimen over to medical entomologist Andrew Spielman of the Harvard School of Public Health, who identified it as a previously unknown species that is a close relative of the European tick that spreads ECM.

The investigators' next job was to confirm that the tick, named *Ixodes dammini,* was the vector for Lyme disease. To tighten the net of circumstantial evidence around the tiny brown tick, the research team set out animal traps on both sides of the Connecticut River to see if the distribution of *I. dammini* corresponded to the outbreaks of Lyme disease.

They were elated by what they found. The dog tick was equally common on both sides of the river, but *I. dammini* was 12 times more abundant on the east side of the river—near the three towns where Lyme disease had erupted. The investigators were confident they had identified the vector for Lyme disease.

The mystery solved
In 1981, an expert in tick-borne diseases spotted an unfamiliar kind of bacteria on a slide prepared from a tick specimen, *above.* He suspected that the corkscrew-shaped bacterium, *top* (greatly magnified), might be the long-sought cause of Lyme disease—a suspicion that was soon confirmed.

Having found the probable carrier of the illness, the researchers sought details about the arthropod. Soon, a vivid picture emerged of the tick's life, which depends greatly on the presence of a variety of mammals that serve as a combination of host and food supply. *I. dammini* lives for about two years, though it is inactive during the winter. The tick begins life as a tiny larva, nearly invisible to the unaided eye, which emerges from an egg during the summer. During this phase, the tick must feed for about two days on the blood of a host, usually the common white-footed mouse.

After its first winter, the larva *molts* (sheds its skin) and enters a second phase, called the *nymphal* phase. The nymphs are little larger than a speck of dust, and once again they must feed on blood. The white-footed mouse is again a prime target, but so are human beings and other mammals, including beef and dairy cattle, horses, dogs, and cats. Unfortunately, the tiny nymphal tick is easily overlooked or mistaken for a mole or other skin blemish.

At the end of its second summer, the tick molts again and enters its adult phase. The adult tick requires a third blood meal. This time, the tick's most common host is the white-tailed deer, a familiar sight to anyone who lives in wooded areas in the Northeastern United States. Again, human beings, livestock, or pets may be a target. The male and female ticks mate while on this final host. The female lays her eggs—probably in brushy areas near the ground—and they hatch into larvae the following spring.

Despite this wealth of information about the

tick and its hosts, the researchers still lacked a vital piece of the puzzle: the identity of the tick-borne microbe that causes the disease. Because no bacteria had turned up in fluid removed from the joints of Lyme disease patients, Steere thought that the culprit could be a virus—a guess that ultimately proved to be wrong.

For four frustrating years, Steere and others searched in vain for the elusive organism that they felt sure was carried by *I. dammini*. Microscopic examination of the internal organs of the tick failed to uncover the sought-after microbe. And the investigators had no better luck when they examined cultures of tick cells grown in the laboratory. Meanwhile, the disease continued to spread from its first home in Lyme to many other areas in the Northeastern United States.

Finally, in 1981, at the Rocky Mountain Laboratories in Hamilton, Mont., a crucial piece of evidence turned up under the microscope of Willy Burgdorfer, a Swiss-born entomologist and an expert in tick-borne diseases. Burgdorfer was examining an *I. dammini* specimen collected in New York, looking for signs of the microbe that causes Rocky Mountain spotted fever, a serious tick-borne illness. Scanning a microscope slide that contained cells from the gut of the tick, he saw no sign of the Rocky Mountain spotted fever microbe.

Instead, he was surprised to find the slide teeming with unfamiliar bacteria of a type known as a *spirochete*, a minuscule, corkscrew-shaped organism. Burgdorfer had heard about the search for the tick-borne microbe that causes Lyme disease. Could this tiny organism be that long-sought microbe?

It was an exciting possibility, but only further work could confirm whether the spirochete was the creature that had caused such distress to the residents of Lyme and other areas. First, Burgdorfer examined blood samples from New York patients infected with Lyme disease, looking for the presence of antibodies against the new-found spirochete. The blood tests were positive, indicating that the patients had indeed been infected with the organism.

Researchers moved quickly to confirm the spirochete's identity as the cause of Lyme disease. To track down their prey in the human body, they relied on laboratory-made antibodies that specifically recognize and attach to the spirochete. Tagged with a fluorescent molecule, the antibodies function as chemical bloodhounds. They attach to the bacteria and emit a glow when viewed under ultraviolet light, enabling researchers to track down even a few spirochetes in tissue samples from a Lyme disease patient.

Animal accomplices
Ticks infected with Lyme disease bacteria need animal hosts, usually deer or mice, to survive, *above.* As a result, Lyme disease is a problem in areas where these animals are common. Migratory birds also may help spread Lyme disease by carrying infected ticks into new areas.

By the summer of 1982, investigators at the New York State Department of Health and at Yale had found the suspect spirochete in the tissues of Lyme disease patients. The long search for the germ that causes Lyme disease was finally over.

Researchers at the University of Minnesota Medical School determined that the spirochete was a previously unknown species related to the spirochete that causes syphilis. Details about the bacterium, named *Borrelia burgdorferi* to honor Burgdorfer, its discoverer, soon emerged. The spirochete is extremely small—about 0.001 inch long (roughly 0.030 millimeter)—and is normally found in very low numbers in the tissue of an infected animal. In retrospect, it was not surprising that Steere and others had had so much difficulty finding the bacterium in the tissues of Lyme disease patients and in *I. dammini.*

The spirochetes enter the host's bloodstream while the tick is attached to the host. Then, as the bacteria multiply, they may invade the joints, the heart and other internal organs, and the brain and spinal cord. If the infection is not treated, Lyme disease's long-term effects can be painful and debilitating.

We now know that Lyme disease is also a veterinary problem. At an international meeting on Lyme disease held in New York City in September 1987, researchers reported that dairy cattle in Wisconsin and race horses and show dogs in New Jersey were disabled with joint problems linked to infection with the Lyme disease spirochete.

Health experts have divided the ailment's course into three stages, though symptoms vary enormously. The first stage of Lyme disease, most famous for the bull's-eye rash, may feature such symptoms as excruciating headaches, fever and other flulike symptoms, and overwhelming lethargy. These symptoms usually begin from 2 to 30 days after an individual has been bitten by a tick. But no one symptom appears in every case; in fact, about 30 per cent of infected individuals do not even develop the rash.

Rounding up the guilty
A researcher collects ticks by sweeping a cloth across the ground, *above.* Both infected ticks and cases of Lyme disease are now found in many areas; by mid-1988, the disease had been reported in 35 states, *above left.*

The second and more serious stage, which begins weeks or months later, may include the first signs of joint pain. Again, some patients are symptom-free during this phase of the infection, but others experience such neurological problems as short-term memory loss or *Bell's palsy* (a facial paralysis), caused by inflammation of the nervous system. In about 10 per cent of the patients, the heart is affected, and some develop problems that may require the implantation of a temporary pacemaker to regulate the heartbeat.

Finally, the devastating arthritis that gave the disease its original name develops during the third stage of Lyme disease. Arthritis symptoms, which usually begin within two years after a person becomes infected, may last from weeks to months, and recur intermittently for years. About 60 per cent of Lyme disease patients develop joint problems.

Lyme disease is rarely life-threatening, though at least two deaths have been traced to the infection. The first case, as Steere and other doctors reported in 1985, involved a man from Nantucket, Mass., who suddenly died from heart failure—the result of the spirochete's effects on his heart muscle. The second fatality, reported in 1988, involved a woman who suf-

Caution: ticks at large
A sign warns of danger in an area where tick-borne infections are a health problem, *above.* Wearing long-sleeved shirts and tucking pants into socks will help protect against tick bites, *right.*

fered lung damage that was believed to be a complication of Lyme disease.

Fortunately, if Lyme disease is properly diagnosed, it is usually easy to treat with a variety of antibiotics, including tetracycline, penicillin, and erythromycin. Drug treatments are most successful when the disease is diagnosed early. Even in the later stages, patients usually respond well to antibiotic therapy, though hospitalization may be necessary. But symptoms may recur in some patients not treated until the later stages. Unfortunately, recovered Lyme disease patients apparently do not develop immunity against future infection.

With the discovery of the vector, potential hosts, and the spirochete responsible for the disease, Steere and other medical detectives had successfully completed the epidemiological investigation that began in 1975. But scientists have no intention of abandoning the study of Lyme disease. "We still have an enormous amount to learn about diagnosis, treatment, and control," Steere says.

Early diagnosis of the disease is a particularly tricky problem because the spirochete is so difficult to find and no single symptom appears in all cases. Until recently, physicians have depended on a blood test that detects antibodies produced by the body in response to the spirochete. Unfortunately, this method of detecting the disease is far from certain; some Lyme disease patients never develop detectable levels of antibodies.

Experts say that improved diagnostic tests are on the horizon. A blood test that gives results in less than an hour was expected to be available for veterinary use in 1988 and for human use in 1989, according to researchers at Tufts University School of Veterinary Medicine's laboratory in Jamaica Plain, Mass. And scientists at the University of Minnesota in Minneapolis are developing a urine test for Lyme disease that will actually detect the spirochete itself—a quicker, easier, and more effective method for identifying the infection. The urine test may be available sometime in 1989, according to Russell C. Johnson, professor of microbiology at the University of Minnesota.

But no matter how precise a diagnostic test is, it is useless if the disease is not even considered. Patients may experience years of needless suffering and expense if their illness is not promptly diagnosed and treated.

"Educating doctors is one of our biggest challenges," Johnson says. "Lyme disease can look like so many other conditions—arthritis, the flu, even Alzheimer's disease—that misdiagnosis is very common."

Misdiagnosis is particularly common, he adds, in areas where the disease has not received much publicity. For example, physicians who practice in urban areas or in parts of the United States where the disease is a recent arrival often fail to recognize the infection. In contrast, most doctors in Connecticut are quick to consider the disease when weighing their patients' symptoms.

In fact, all physicians and veterinarians should keep the infection in mind when examining patients. For one thing, even people who live in the heart of a big city—where the ticks that carry Lyme disease are virtually unknown—are vulnerable if they visit regions where the infection is common. Furthermore, Lyme disease is continuing to spread into new areas throughout the United States. By the end of 1987, it had been found in more than 30 states. In addition to an area extending along the eastern coast of the United States, from Massachusetts to North Carolina, "hot spots" have developed in Minnesota, Wisconsin, California, and Oregon.

"We think that it is spread by migrating birds, which may mean that the ticks will eventually reach every state," warns Johnson. "The only limits on their spread will be the population of such hosts as the white-tailed deer and the field mouse." In fact, Lyme disease is shaping up as a global problem; cases have turned up in Europe and elsewhere.

Nearly 1,500 cases were reported annually in the United

How to remove a tick

What should you do if you find a tick on your body? If it has not yet attached itself by embedding its barbed mouthparts into your skin, simply lift it off. Avoid touching the tick; use a tissue or tweezers to handle it.

If the tick has already dug into the skin, health experts warn *against* trying any of the popular home remedies for removing ticks, such as smearing the tick with petroleum jelly, alcohol, or lighter fluid, or trying to burn it out with a match or glowing cigarette. Instead, using needle-point tweezers, grasp the tick firmly—as close to the mouthparts as possible, to make sure you remove the entire tick—and pull straight out.

Seal the tick inside a jar containing some alcohol, and save it to show your doctor if any symptoms appear. Finally, wash your hands and apply antiseptic to the bite.

States during the late 1980's—up from about 600 cases in 1983 and 226 in 1980. Just north of New York City in New York's Westchester County, doctors reported more than 500 cases of Lyme disease in 1987—the highest total ever for the county. And experts warn that these numbers probably represent only one-quarter to one-half of the number of cases that were actually diagnosed, because many physicians still neglect to report the disease to local health departments.

Scientists predicted that an even larger number of cases would be reported in 1988. In fact, no one has any idea when the disease will reach a peak, says entomologist Richard Falco of the Westchester County Health Department. The reason for this is simple: There are a lot of infected ticks out there.

How many? No one knows for sure, but some recent studies paint a grim picture. Researchers examining a single dog tallied an astounding 401 ticks following the dog's daily exercise. The dog's owner also was found to be infested with the tiny ticks, many of which harbored *B. burgdorferi*. If such a large number of ticks managed to hitch a ride on the dog after a single day, there is a strong likelihood that the animal—and its owner—will become infected with Lyme disease.

To make matters worse, *I. dammini* is not choosy about where it lives. At first, experts believed that the tick preferred brushy, unmowed areas like weedy fields and wood lots. But even people who stay in the supposed safety of their yards are apparently enjoying a false sense of security. Falco and his colleagues took a tick census of a lawn in Westchester County, collecting the tiny ticks by sweeping a cloth across the grass. Assuming that the area they swept was a representative sample, the lawn, which measured about 840 square yards (700 square meters), harbored more than 600 ticks.

"Clearly, the ticks are quite at home in cut grass," says Falco. In fact, studies show that more than 60 per cent of all tick bites take place in the victim's backyard.

One obvious solution to eliminating the risk of Lyme disease is to get rid of the ticks. But widespread spraying of insecticides would be extremely expensive, and would not be possible in areas with dense populations. Chemical sprays might also do great harm to many insects and other animals that have nothing to do with Lyme disease.

As an alternative, many people have suggested eliminating the common hosts of the tick from Lyme disease areas. "But eliminating deer really means shooting them, which would cause a huge furor," says Falco. Exterminating another major host of the ticks, the white-footed mouse, is also an unlikely option. Finding and destroying all the tiny, well-hidden mouse burrows would be a hopeless task.

Although eliminating the mice was ruled out, a team of Harvard scientists developed an ingenious scheme to exploit the mice to help them kill ticks. On an island off Cape Cod, the researchers set out open-ended tubes containing cotton, an irresistible sight to any mouse seeking soft, warm material for its burrow. Though dry to the touch, the cotton contained *permethrin,* a poison known to kill the ticks.

As expected, the mice raided the tubes, carrying the cotton off to their burrows. And when mice from these sites were examined, they were found to carry far fewer ticks than mice from untreated burrows; nearly 75 per cent were tick-free. If used on a larger scale, this technique might someday significantly reduce the number of ticks in selected areas.

Tick-fighting tactic
Scientists have found that mice will remove cotton from cardboard tubes and carry the soft material to their nests. Putting insecticide in the cotton can help keep the nests—and the mice—tick-free.

Nevertheless, reducing the number of ticks and their hosts merely decreases the chances of becoming infected with Lyme disease. The best preventive measure of all would be a vaccine that would protect people, pets, and livestock from infection. In 1987, Johnson and the University of Minnesota received a patent for a potential vaccine. Testing is underway on dogs, and if the animal tests are successful, tests on human beings will follow.

But widespread availability of such a vaccine is most likely years away. For now, experts stress that the best way to minimize your chances of contracting Lyme disease is to be aware of the threat, particularly during the peak months between May and September.

"Try to avoid tick-infested areas, even your backyard," says Falco. "If you can't do that, then take other precautions." Such precautions include using strong insect repellents, wearing long-sleeved shirts and long pants, tucking pants into socks or boots, and inspecting yourself—and any pets that spend time outside—for ticks every night.

If you or a member of your family get bitten by a tick in spite of taking precautions, remove the tick if it is still on your skin (see box on opposite page) and consult a physician if any symptoms appear. If you have been infected, early treatment with antibiotics can prevent the more serious and debilitating effects of Lyme disease.

Thanks to the medical detectives, the mystery of Lyme disease has been solved. Today we know what causes the infection, how it is transmitted, and how to treat it. But until we can curtail the spread of Lyme disease or develop a vaccine to prevent infection, a walk in the woods or a backyard barbecue—at least for people living in high-risk areas—should be approached with caution.

Some simple precautions can help prevent the crippling bone disorder called osteoporosis.

Bone Up Now for Stronger Bones Later

By Robert Proulx Heaney and M. Janet Barger-Lux

Louise was an energetic 62-year-old woman who prided herself on her appearance and on dressing well. Gardening was her special passion. One Saturday morning, while lifting a sack of fertilizer, she felt a stab of pain in her upper back. When she finally saw a physician several days later, the pain between her shoulder blades was still intense. She was stunned to learn that she had fractured her spine. Even more alarming was the news that she was at great risk of suffering additional fractures. "From now on," her doctor said, "you must never forget that your body is very, very fragile. Be careful in everything you do."

Eight years later, Louise remained remarkably energetic, but her back was permanently deformed. Clothes no longer fitted well, and she was troubled that her figure had become lumpy and bowed. She was nearly 5 inches (13 centimeters) shorter and had been afraid to go back to her gardening.

Louise is the victim of a crippling, disfiguring bone disorder called *osteoporosis*, and she is far from unique. Experts estimate that, in the United States alone, osteoporosis affects 15 million to 20 million people, nearly all of them women, and that it causes about 1.3 million new fractures each year.

A silent crippler

Osteoporosis develops silently and gradually over many years. In most cases, the condition is discovered only after the victim suffers a fracture during ordinary activities or as a result of a minor fall that would not injure normal bones. Once the diagnosis is made, treatment can slow the ravages of osteoporosis but cannot reverse the damage. For these reasons, health professionals stress lifelong prevention, including regular exercise and a calcium-rich diet, as the only real answer.

The typical fractures caused by osteoporosis affect different portions of the skeleton at different ages. The earliest type of fracture generally recognized as osteoporotic is a fracture of the lower forearm or wrist. The incidence of this fracture peaks in women in their 50's.

Women in their 60's have a high incidence of compression fractures of the spine, the injury Louise suffered. No one knows how many of these fractures happen in any given year. Some women are seriously incapacitated, but others are unaware that a fracture has occurred. These spinal fractures accumulate gradually over a period of years, and sometimes extensive damage occurs before the victim seeks medical help.

Nearly 250,000 of the osteoporotic injuries reported each year in the United States are hip fractures, typically happening to women in their 70's or 80's. As many as 1 in 5 of these women die within three months of pneumonia, blood clots, or other complications of hip surgery. About half of those who

The authors:

Robert Proulx Heaney is John A. Creighton University Professor at Creighton University in Omaha, Nebr. M. Janet Barger-Lux is a research associate in the Department of Medicine at Creighton.

survive need long-term custodial care, and many others never regain their independence.

Besides extracting a heavy toll in human suffering, osteoporosis is a public health problem of major proportions. Experts estimate the yearly cost in the United States of hip fractures alone at $7 billion to $10 billion.

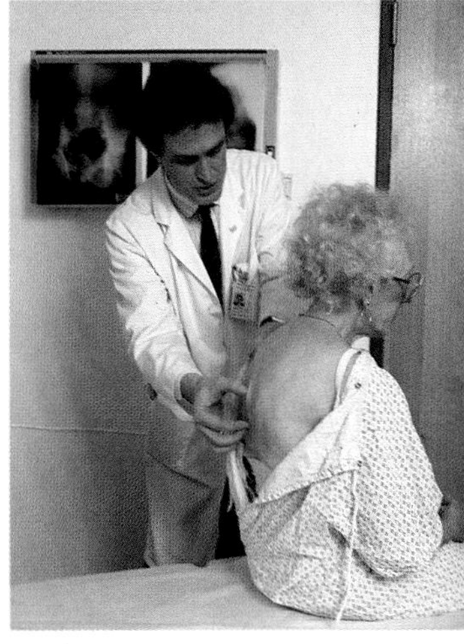

A typical result of osteoporosis is the back deformity known as a *dowager's hump,* which results when the spinal column collapses due to a series of small fractures.

How osteoporosis weakens bones

A bone weakened to the breaking point by osteoporosis can be compared to a bridge collapsing or a building crumbling. Structures, whether bones or buildings, fail for three main reasons. One is that the structure contains too little building material. Another is that the materials used are poor quality, either originally or because they have developed defects with use. Still another is that the materials, though adequate in quantity and quality, are assembled poorly, or that some of their connections have come apart with use.

All three of these factors apply to osteoporosis. The first factor—an insufficient quantity of bone, due to a gradual loss of bone over time—is the one that has given its name to the problem. The term *osteoporosis* comes from two Greek words meaning *porous bones*. In other words, the bones contain less bony material than do healthy bones of the same size and shape. But a loss of bone, though it has dominated the attention of medical science for the past 50 years, is not the only cause of bony fragility. Physicians have recently realized the importance of two other factors—defects in the quality of the bone and flaws in its structural connections.

Defects in the quality of the bony material occur after repeated use has weakened the structure. When such weakening affects a building, structural engineers refer to it as *fatigue damage*. Fatigue damage is simply a pattern of microscopic cracks that reduce the structure's strength. Fatigue damage is what causes a piece of metal or plastic to break after you bend it repeatedly. The same type of damage occurs in human bone. Every time we use our bones, we bend them ever so slightly. After we do this thousands of times, tiny cracks develop and the material gradually weakens.

The third cause of weakness, defective structural connections, especially affects a type of bone called *trabecular* (pronounced *truh BEHK yuh luhr*). Trabecular bone makes up about 20 per cent of the human skeleton. Bones with much trabecular bone include the spine, the hips, and the wrists.

Unlike solid bone, trabecular bone consists of intersecting structural members, somewhat resembling a honeycomb, with

Parts of a bone

Most bones have honeycombed *trabecular bone* (also called *cancellous bone*) on the inside and solid *cortical bone* (also known as *compact bone*) on the outside. The bone's hollow center, the *medullary cavity,* is filled with a soft substance called *marrow.* Trabecular and cortical bone occur in different proportions in different parts of the skeleton. There is much trabecular bone, for example, at the ends of long bones such as the *femur* (thighbone).

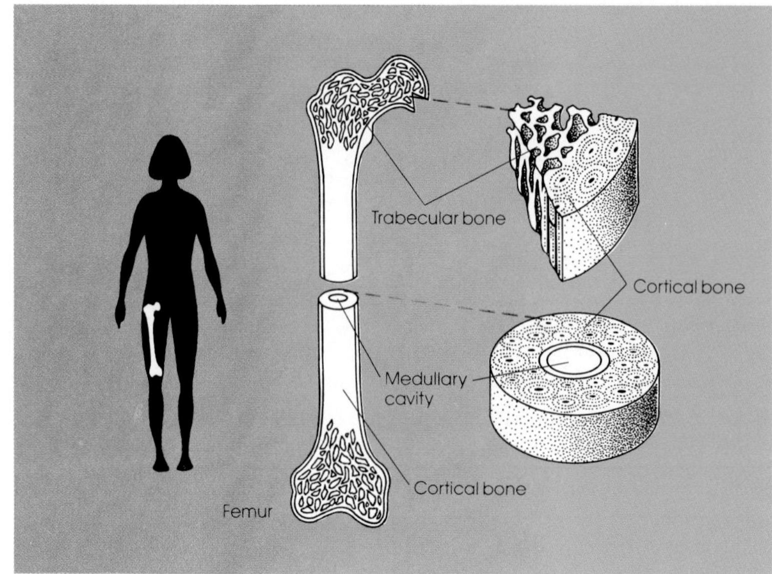

marrow filling the spaces between. Such structures are normally lightweight and extremely strong. But that strength depends upon the integrity of all the connections. In normal trabecular bone, vertical and horizontal members brace one another like the girders and crossbeams of a building and keep the members in either direction from bending too much. Disconnect the horizontal members, and the vertical ones become flimsy. Researchers have determined that this process occurs in many people who suffer fractures due to osteoporosis.

Whether a woman ever develops an osteoporotic fracture depends not only upon the amount of bone she has but also upon the amount of fatigue damage that has accumulated in that bone and upon the structural integrity of the connections that give the bone its strength. As might be expected, all three factors interact. A decrease in the amount of bony material allows the bone to bend more and thus causes more fatigue damage. So, too, flimsiness of the bony material aggravates the problem of defective structural connections.

Rather than a single disease, osteoporosis is a group of related disorders that have in common only the fact that the bones are fragile. As a result, there is no single prevention or treatment.

The recognition that there are multiple causes of fragility also helps explain why bone scanning—the use of gamma rays or X rays to measure bone density—is of limited use in the early detection of osteoporosis. Bone scans measure only one of the reasons bones become fragile—a decrease in mass—but tell nothing about fatigue damage or structural connections.

How bone renews itself

Bone undergoes a constant process of renewal in which old bone is digested and removed—in an operation called *resorption*—and replaced by new bone in a process called *formation*. In healthy bone, this renewal keeps the bony material strong and resilient. Osteoporosis results when bone formation fails to make enough new bone or when renewal fails to repair damaged structures.

Bone resorption

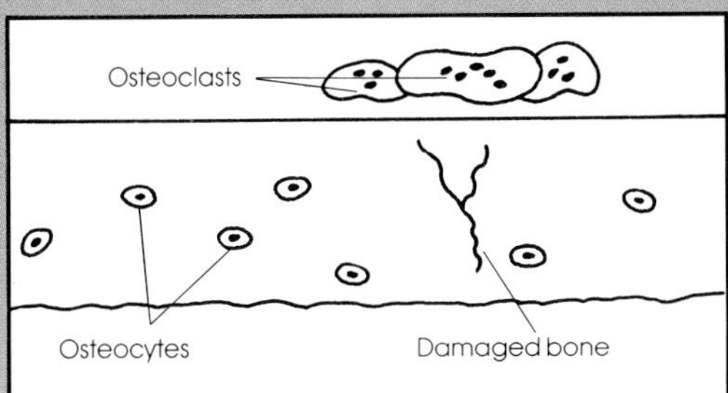

Bone resorption begins when large cells called *osteoclasts,* each with numerous nuclei, attach themselves to the site of damaged bone. A single osteoclast is shown greatly magnified below.

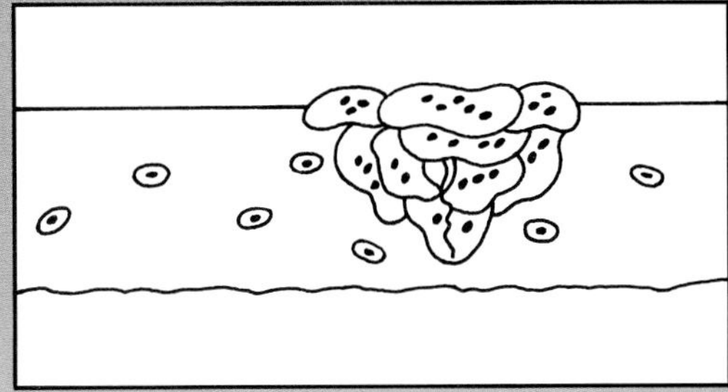

The osteoclasts produce chemicals that digest the old bone, releasing the calcium and other minerals in the bone and leaving a crater with a rough, unfinished surface, shown greatly magnified below.

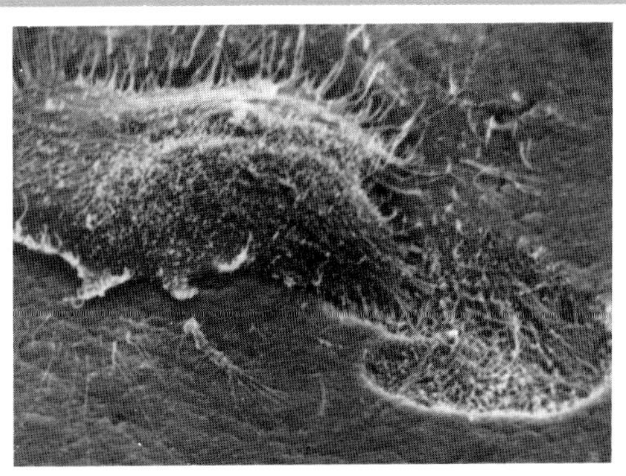

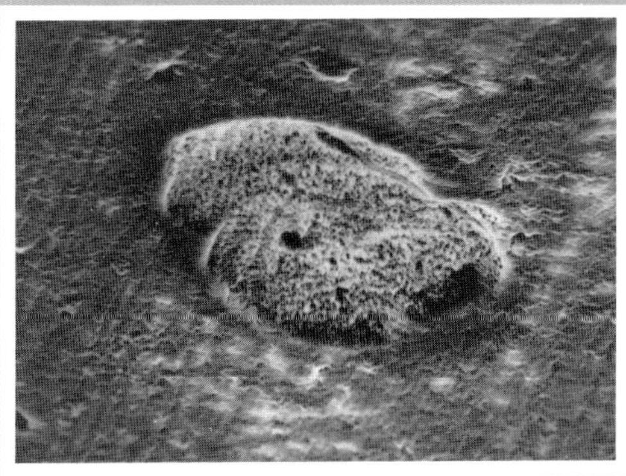

Bone formation

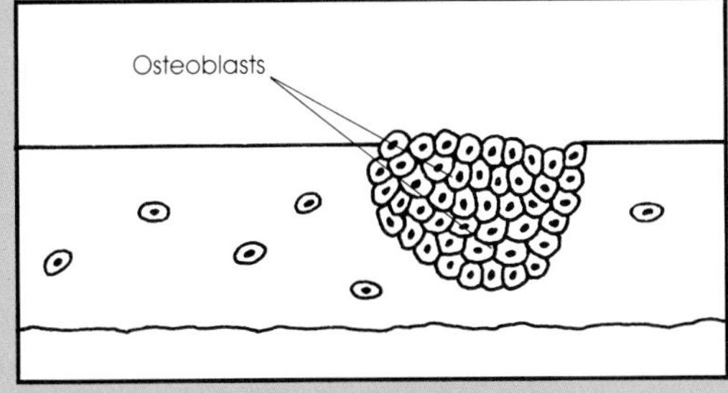

Bone-forming cells called *osteoblasts* move to the cavity left by the osteoclasts and begin rebuilding the bony tissue.

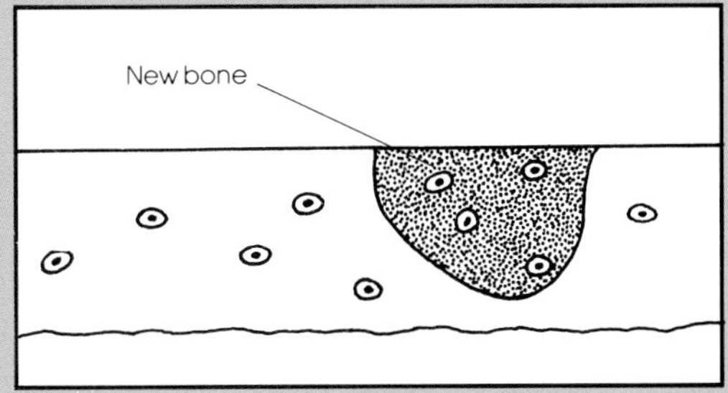

While forming bone, osteoblasts become trapped in the bone they manufacture and change into cells called *osteocytes,* which live embedded in the bone for many years.

Results of osteoporosis

A healthy spine, in a computer-enhanced image, *a*, is straight and sturdy. In an osteoporotic spine, *b*, the vertebrae have collapsed due to repeated fractures, resulting in curvature of the spine. Compared under a microscope with normal bone, *c*, osteoporotic bone, *d*, has less bony material. And certain critical connections that give strength to the bony structure may be missing, as shown in the circle.

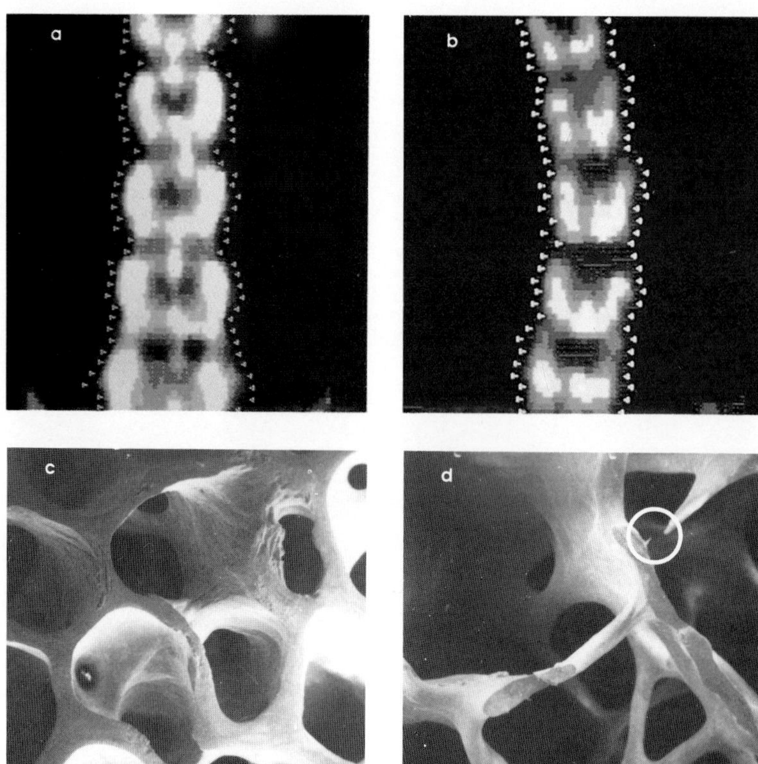

Nevertheless, bone mass is important. People with heavy, dense skeletons can tolerate more fatigue damage and structural disconnection than can those with lightweight skeletons. Furthermore, bone mass is the only component of osteoporosis that medical science knows much about. As a result, current efforts to prevent the disorder all concentrate on factors that influence the amount of bone a person has.

How bone is renewed

Like the other tissues in our body, bone undergoes a constant process of renewal. Throughout life, old bony tissue is torn down and replaced by new bone. This process, called *remodeling*, keeps the skeleton strong and resilient.

The process of bone remodeling is similar to the renovation of a run-down urban area. First, demolition cells called *osteoclasts* remove the old material, creating an excavation with a raw, unfinished surface. Later, cells called *osteoblasts* move into that site and fill in the excavation with new bone. The first process, the destructive one, is called *bone resorption*, and the second, *bone formation*.

There are several ways in which defects in remodeling can lead to osteoporosis. The first way—one that has been studied for many years—occurs when the osteoblasts fail to form as much bone as was taken out by the osteoclasts. If this failure occurs repeatedly, bone mass decreases and the bones get progressively more flimsy.

Another way the remodeling process can go wrong occurs when the body fails to detect fatigue damage or when the remodeling process becomes too sluggish to keep up with the damage. Uncorrected, the fatigue damage accumulates and spreads.

Finally, defective remodeling can lead to fragility if it severs some of the connections between the horizontal and vertical beams. With those links gone, the strength of the internal bony

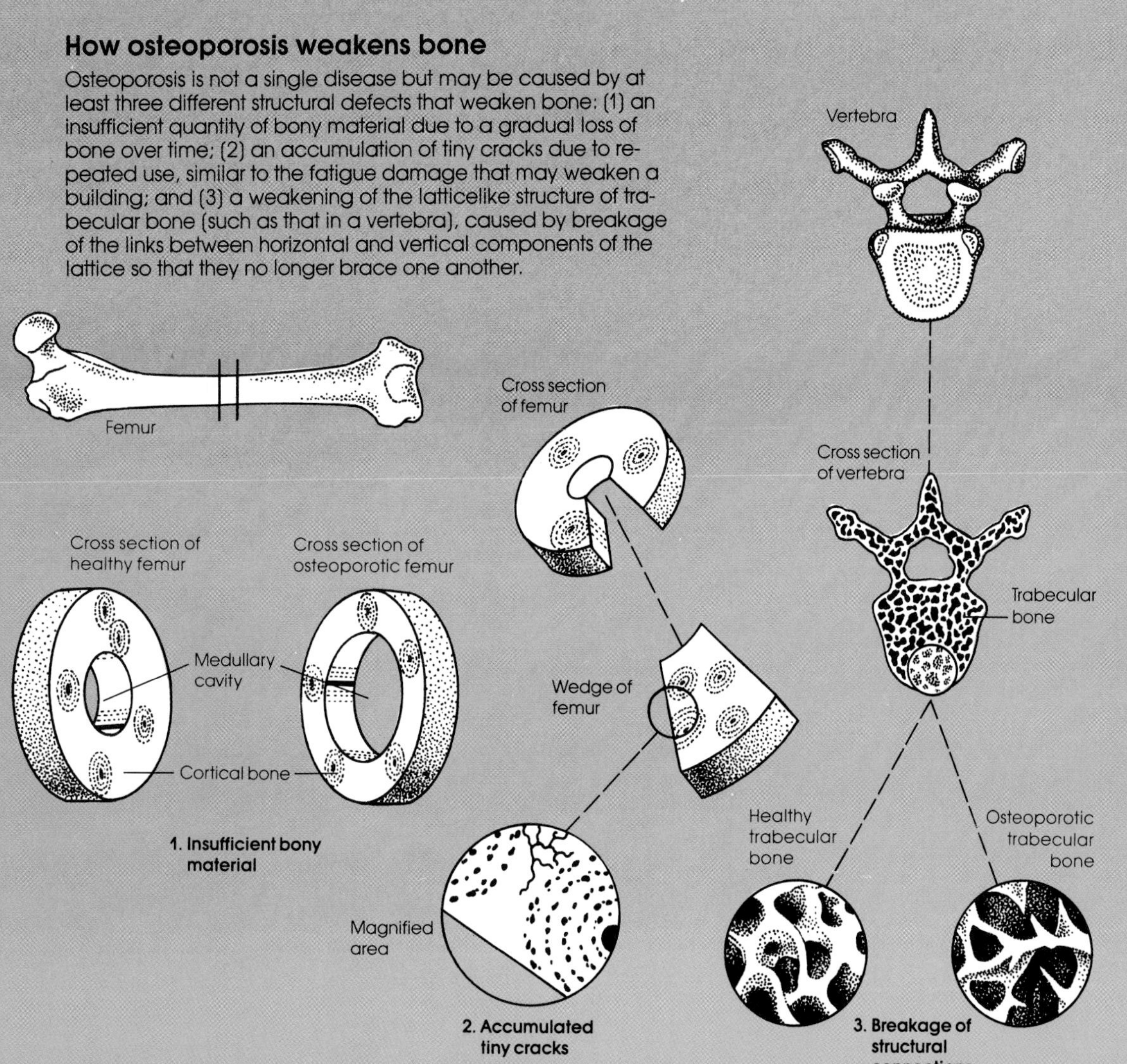

How osteoporosis weakens bone

Osteoporosis is not a single disease but may be caused by at least three different structural defects that weaken bone: (1) an insufficient quantity of bony material due to a gradual loss of bone over time; (2) an accumulation of tiny cracks due to repeated use, similar to the fatigue damage that may weaken a building; and (3) a weakening of the latticelike structure of trabecular bone (such as that in a vertebra), caused by breakage of the links between horizontal and vertical components of the lattice so that they no longer brace one another.

Are you at risk for osteoporosis?

This table shows the principal risk factors that increase the odds of developing osteoporosis according to the age when they begin to affect the bones. The table illustrates how women accumulate an increasing burden of risk throughout life—and how they can minimize it.

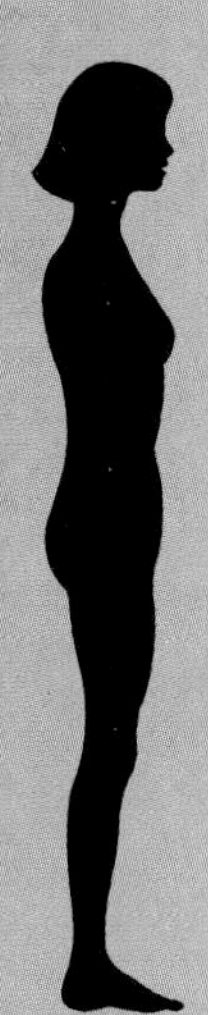

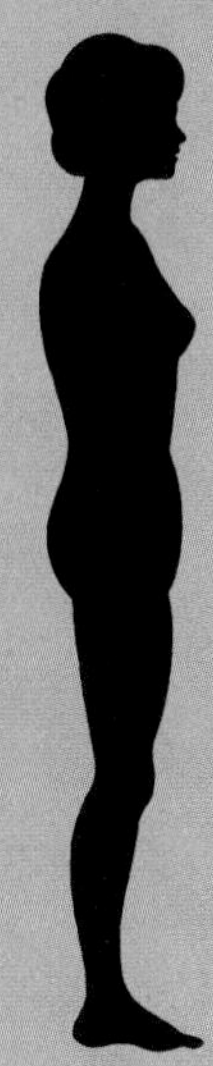

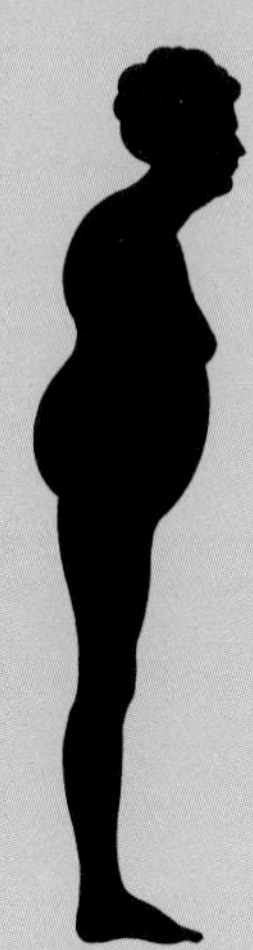

Adolescent girls
(aged 12 to 19)

Hereditary and medical risk factors

- A female relative (such as a grandmother or aunt on either side of the family) who lost more than 2 inches (5 centimeters) in height as she got older.
- A female relative who had a broken hip before age 85.
- Slender or small-boned build.
- Fair-skinned and blonde with little body hair.
- First menstrual period after age 14.
- *Anorexia nervosa*, an eating disorder involving drastic restriction of food intake and leading to extreme thinness and interruption of menstrual cycles.
- Long-term use of *anticonvulsant drugs* (medications given to control epilepsy).

Life-style risk factors

- Smoking.
- Frequent use of alcohol.
- Low calcium intake, often associated with substituting soft drinks for milk.
- Little or no vigorous physical activity.
- Extreme thinness, sometimes associated with training for dance or competitive sports.

Women in the childbearing years and nearing menopause
(aged 20 to 54)

All the earlier risk factors, plus:

Medical risk factors

- Health problems such as kidney stones that require a diet low in calcium.
- Chronic diarrhea, which in some instances leads to excessive loss of calcium from the body.
- Loss of menstrual cycles in a woman who is neither pregnant nor breast-feeding.
- Premature menopause, often stemming from surgical removal of the ovaries, without estrogen replacement.
- Long-term use of *corticosteroid drugs* (anti-inflammatory medications given to control rheumatoid arthritis, asthma, and other serious diseases).
- *Lactose intolerance*, a lack of the enzyme necessary to digest the milk sugar *lactose*, resulting in intestinal gas and diarrhea after drinking milk—and consequent avoidance of dairy products.

Life-style risk factors

- Chronic alcohol abuse.
- Persistent thinness.
- Avoidance of dairy products.
- Few or no pregnancies carried to term.
- Habitual use of laxatives or of antacids containing aluminum. (Other antacids can be good sources of calcium.)

Women past menopause
(aged 55 and older)

All the earlier risk factors, plus:

Medical risk factors

- Inability to replace the female hormone estrogen after menopause for medical reasons, especially in a woman with other risk factors.
- Illness or injury that restricts mobility for a month or more.

Life-style risk factors

- A deficiency of vitamin D, often due to lack of exposure to sunlight.

scaffolding is severely reduced. What is worse, the loss of connections removes the platform the osteoblasts need to make their repairs, so the damage becomes irreversible.

Causes of bone loss

Why does bone remodeling sometimes fail to put back as much bone as it removes? All the answers are not known, but three major reasons are recognized as important: (1) physical inactivity; (2) a loss of sex hormones, particularly—in women—the decreased production of a female hormone called *estrogen*; and (3) an inadequate amount of basic nutrients, mainly calcium, in the diet.

Physical activity is just as important for bone as it is for muscle. When we are inactive, our muscles become flabby, we are weak, and we have little endurance. Exactly the same thing happens to bones. If we exercise vigorously and regularly, we maintain strong bones. If we are physically inactive, our bones become weak.

A loss of sex hormones is unusual in men but occurs normally in women at *menopause*, the time in a woman's life—usually between the ages of 45 and 50—when the ovaries decrease their production of estrogen and menstruation stops. In both sexes, hormone loss results in bone loss. A woman can lose from 10 to 20 per cent of the bone in critical areas of her skeleton in the 10 to 15 years following menopause. Estrogen-like hormones have proved effective in preventing this loss of bone.

Nutritional deficiency, particularly a lack of calcium, also reduces bone mass. The mineral component of bone is made up mostly of calcium, phosphate, and carbonate. Phosphate and carbonate are almost never in short supply in the human body, but calcium often is. Calcium deficiency results in bone loss simply because the body treats bone as a reservoir of calcium, drawing upon it to support the necessary level of calcium in the blood and other vital body fluids.

If our diet does not provide enough calcium, then our body turns to the bones as a backup source of calcium. The body scavenges the calcium that is released by the osteoclasts during the destructive first phase of bone remodeling. When the remodeled region moves into its forming phase, it needs calcium. If the diet is still inadequate, then enough calcium may not be available to replace the bone earlier removed. In that case, the body goes back to the "bone bank" for yet another "loan"—a type of refinancing in which the calcium debt gets progressively larger. An adequate calcium intake throughout life helps prevent this problem.

Bad habits for bones
Life-style factors that increase the risk of osteoporosis include smoking, drinking, physical inactivity, and poor nutrition—especially low intake of dairy products and other calcium-rich foods.

Inactivity, reduced estrogen levels, and calcium deficiency are the major causes of bone loss, but there are other causes that are probably also important. One is inadequate intake of trace nutrients such as manganese, zinc, and copper. In November 1987, researchers at the United States Department of Agriculture reported that the element boron also may be an important nutrient. Tiny amounts of boron may help prevent osteoporosis by helping the body conserve calcium and even reinforcing the calcium-conserving effect of the sex hormones.

Besides these nutritional factors, smoking results in accelerated bone loss. Alcohol abuse does the same. Certain medicines—particularly a family of drugs called *corticosteroids*, which are used to control rheumatoid arthritis, asthma, and other serious diseases—may produce severe osteoporosis. Finally, osteoporosis may result from several other diseases, including thyroid disorders and diseases that interfere with the body's absorption of nutrients.

Although the typical victim of an osteoporotic fracture is middle-aged or older, osteoporosis risk begins much earlier. The roots of the problem usually go back to adolescence. Certain conditions, called *risk factors*, increase a person's odds of developing osteoporosis (see ARE YOU AT RISK FOR OSTEOPOROSIS? on page 62). Many risk factors are hereditary or medical conditions that people cannot control. For example, the greatest risk factor for osteoporosis is being female. The women who are most prone to osteoporosis are slender, small-boned, and of northern European ancestry. Life-style factors, however, are

How to build strong bones
Measures that protect against osteoporosis include regular vigorous exercise, moderate exposure to sunlight, good nutrition—especially an adequate calcium intake—and, after *menopause* (the time in a woman's life when menstruation stops), *hormone replacement therapy,* in which a physician prescribes synthetic hormones to compensate for the hormone loss that occurs with menopause.

particularly important because people can choose to change them. Some simple precautions can substantially reduce the risk of osteoporosis.

How young women can protect themselves

The best time to protect yourself from the ravages of osteoporosis is while you are young, when your body is still building its skeleton. Skeleton growth is especially rapid during adolescence but continues until about age 35. During those years, there are three key steps to building and maintaining a strong skeleton. The first is a generous calcium intake, the second is the development of lifelong habits of vigorous exercise, and the third is adequate total nutrition, which helps maintain normal hormone levels. It is also important to avoid smoking and excessive drinking.

The calcium intake recommended for adolescents by the National Research Council, the research arm of the National Academy of Sciences in Washington, D.C., is 1,200 milligrams per day. Surveys show that most young boys have no trouble meeting the 1,200-milligram requirement but that most adolescent girls fall far short of this standard—largely, it seems, because female teen-agers consume soft drinks and other beverages instead of milk. A typical girl enters adolescence with a calcium intake in the range of 800 milligrams per day, and by the time she is 16, it has dropped to less than 600 milligrams per day.

The best way for healthy people to get calcium is from food, especially dairy products. Milk, yogurt, and hard cheeses contain from 150 to 450 milligrams of calcium per serving, and an adolescent needs three such servings per day in addition to the calcium provided by other foods.

Another good way to ensure an adequate calcium intake is to use calcium-fortified foods. Since the mid-1980's, food manufacturers have introduced various calcium-fortified products, including bread, beverages, and breakfast cereals. Parents concerned about their children's calcium intake—or their own—should look for calcium-fortified foods when they shop.

Exercise helps build strong bones early in life and helps preserve them later. Some experts recommend upright, weight-bearing exercise such as jogging or racquet sports, but there is no evidence that such exercise has more value than other activities, such as bicycling or swimming. Almost any exercise is better than none. It is particularly important for a woman to choose an activity that she can stick with for life.

The calcium intake recommended for adolescents is 1,200 milligrams per day. Adult women need about 1,000 milligrams daily before menopause and about 1,500 milligrams per day after menopause to reduce the risk of osteoporosis.

Foods that are good sources of calcium

Food	Serving size	Calcium content
Low-fat yogurt	1 cup (240 milliliters)	350-450 milligrams (Plain yogurt contains slightly more than yogurt with fruit.)
Sardines with bones	3 ounces (85 grams)	350-450 milligrams
Milk	1 cup (240 milliliters)	250-350 milligrams (Skim and low-fat milk contain slightly more than whole milk.)
Swiss or Gruyère cheese	1 ounce (28 grams)	250-350 milligrams
Other hard cheeses such as Cheddar or Edam	1 ounce (28 grams)	150-250 milligrams
Salmon with bones	3 ounces (85 grams)	150-250 milligrams
Collard greens	1/2 cup (120 milliliters)	150-250 milligrams
Soft cheeses such as blue cheese, feta, and mozzarella	1 ounce (28 grams)	50-150 milligrams
Broccoli	1/2 cup (120 milliliters)	50-150 milligrams
Ice cream	1/2 cup (120 milliliters)	50-150 milligrams
Turnip greens	1/2 cup (120 milliliters)	50-150 milligrams
Cottage cheese	1/2 cup (120 milliliters)	50-150 milligrams
Cream cheese	1 ounce (28 grams)	20-50 milligrams

Source: U.S. Department of Agriculture.

The third step a young woman can take is to maintain a normal hormone status. Many young women become so thin through strenuous exercise or severe dieting that their female hormone production shuts down and they stop having menstrual periods. When that happens, their bones start to weaken, just like the bones of a woman who has gone through menopause.

How mature women can protect themselves

After age 35, there no longer is much chance to build a stronger skeleton. The emphasis then must be on maintaining the strength of the skeleton and holding additional bone loss to a minimum.

An adequate calcium intake remains important; in fact, it becomes more important because absorption of calcium is less efficient later in life. The National Institutes of Health (NIH) in Bethesda, Md., in 1984 recommended that women near menopause should consume 1,000 milligrams of calcium per day. After menopause, the NIH says, women should consume 1,500 milligrams per day.

For older women as well as for younger women, dairy products and calcium-fortified foods are the preferred sources of calcium. Calcium pills can be taken if adequate calcium cannot be obtained from the diet. Bone health is a complicated problem, however, and taking a calcium tablet is no insurance against inadequate intake of other nutrients. Moreover, nutritionists and other health professionals warn that pill-taking probably will not be sustained for the many years required.

An adequate amount of vitamin D is especially important for the mature woman. Vitamin D is normally manufactured in the skin when the body is exposed to sunlight. Vitamin D promotes the body's absorption of calcium from foods and the health of the bone remodeling system.

Although excessive tanning is harmful to the skin, a few minutes exposure to the sun each day provides the necessary vitamin D and will not cause skin cancer (see the Special Report THE CANCER YOU CAN SEE). Lacking such exposure to sunshine, a woman should take a vitamin supplement that contains the recommended dietary allowance (RDA) of vitamin D. Drinking milk helps because each glass contains about 25 per cent of the RDA of vitamin D.

Getting enough vitamin D is rarely a problem for young people, who generally spend much time outdoors and wear clothing that exposes a lot of skin. But many elderly people are housebound or institutionalized and rarely get outdoors. The result is that an aged person may lack vitamin D.

It is important to maintain a vigorous pattern of exercise in midlife and beyond. Most people, however, decrease the amount of exercise they do as they reach midlife. And because our bones adjust to the amount of work we ask them to do, a reduction in the loads placed on our skeleton results in a corresponding reduction in bone mass.

A final consideration of major importance to the mature woman is *estrogen replacement therapy* (ERT), in which a physician prescribes natural or synthetic estrogen to compensate for the hormone loss that occurs after menopause. Women who begin ERT at menopause lose bone only at the same slow rate as men their age. Furthermore, women who have used ERT for several years are less likely to suffer bone fractures later in life.

Estrogen replacement is the most powerful weapon we have in the war against osteoporosis. It is estimated that ERT could prevent about half of all fractures due to osteoporosis.

There are several reasons, however, why ERT is not more widely used. One is that ERT increases the risk of developing cancer of the lining of the uterus. This risk can be decreased or eliminated by the simultaneous use of another hormone called a *progestagen,* a synthetic version of the female hormone progesterone. The combination of estrogen and progestagen is known as *hormone replacement therapy* (HRT). Most physicians today recommend HRT rather than ERT.

Some women find HRT objectionable because they continue to have monthly menstrual periods while on the therapy, though HRT does not prolong fertility. In addition, many women object to a treatment that seems to turn a normal life event—menopause—into a medical condition to be managed.

Coping with osteoporosis

Older women who suspect that they have osteoporosis should remain as physically active as possible. Inactivity is the enemy of the osteoporotic woman because it leads to further bone loss.

To reduce the risk of falls, the elderly should eliminate hazards from their surroundings. These include furniture and loose throw rugs on slippery hardwood floors that might make an elderly person trip. It is important to maintain adequate night lighting, and to install handrails in the bathroom.

A doctor probably will prescribe several types of treatment for a patient who has suffered a fracture due to osteoporosis. Pain control is particularly important to help the woman get back on her feet quickly, which is vital if she is to avoid further bone loss. Second, physical therapy can be extremely helpful. It should include a program of muscle training, with emphasis on strengthening the back muscles.

In addition, a variety of drug therapies may be used for osteoporosis. Calcium, of course, is a mainstay of virtually every treatment program because there is not much hope of slowing bone loss without a generous supply of calcium in the diet. The amount of calcium required in such cases is too large to get easily from food, so most patients require calcium supplements. Many doctors also prescribe estrogen at this stage. Estrogen by itself does not add new bone; like calcium, it helps primarily by slowing further bone loss.

By contrast, a chemical called *fluoride* can substantially increase the amount of trabecular bone in such regions as the spine and hip. Fluoride is the same chemical used in the fluoridation of water supplies to prevent tooth decay, but the doses used to treat osteoporosis are much higher and there are uncomfortable side effects in some patients. Fluoride treatment is still experimental and has not yet been approved by the federal government for this use. But of the treatments now being studied, it seems the most promising.

What about Louise?

Louise was lucky. A physical therapist designed a program of exercises to strengthen her back, and Louise followed it vigorously. As a result, today she is relatively free from pain. She still regrets the changes in her figure but has learned how to dress stylishly in spite of them. She now works as a volunteer at a local osteoporosis center to help other women learn to cope with this disorder. Louise has even returned, cautiously, to her gardening.

For further reading:

Hausman, Patricia. *The Calcium Bible: How to Have Better Bones All Your Life*. Warner Books, 1985.

Heaney, Robert P., and Barger-Lux, M. Janet. *Calcium and Common Sense*. Doubleday, 1988.

Osteoporosis: Cause, Treatment, Prevention. National Institutes of Health, 1986.

For more information about osteoporosis, write to the National Osteoporosis Foundation, 1625 I Street NW, Suite 1011, Washington, DC 20006.

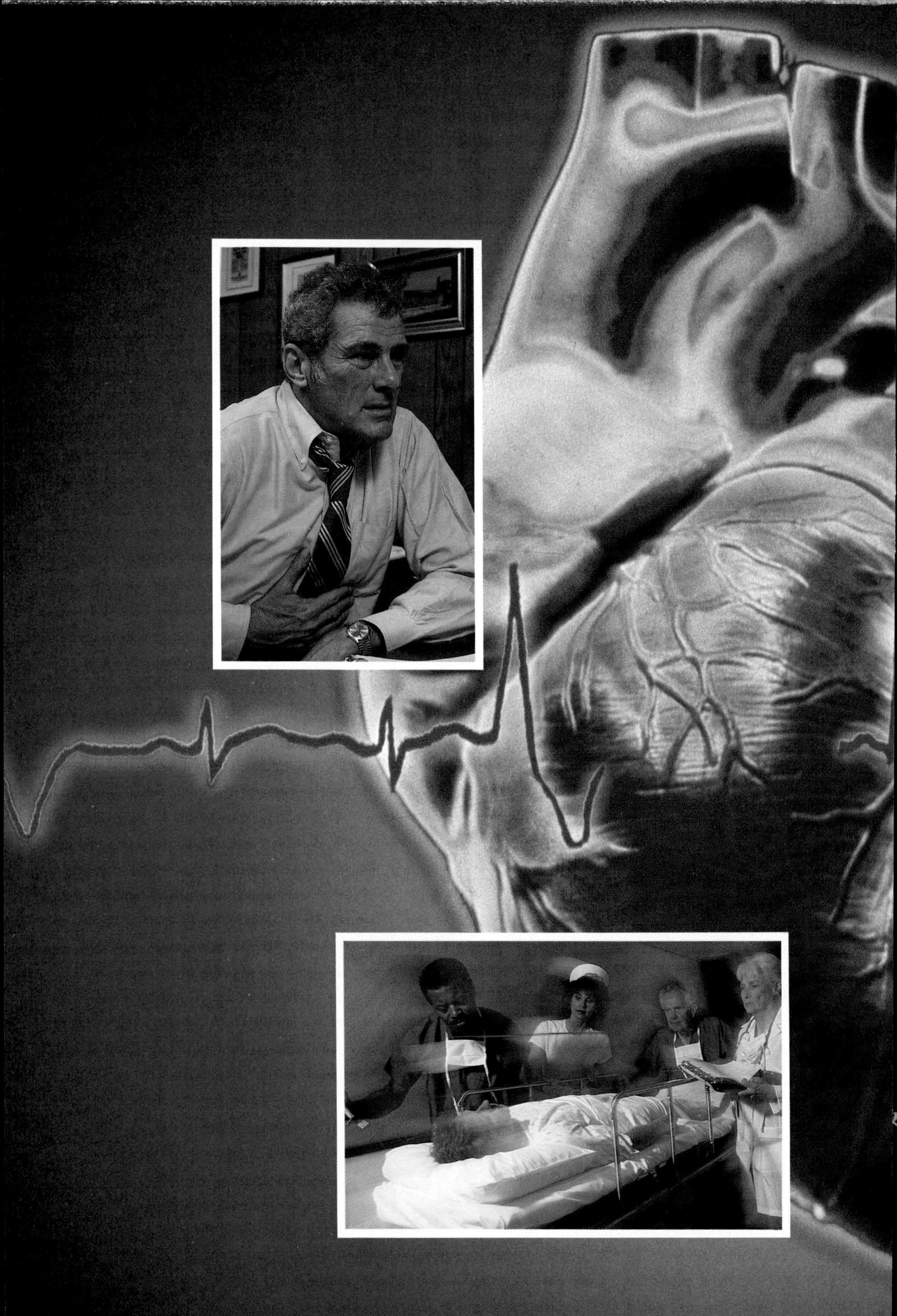

Reducing the Risk of Heart Disease

By Joanne Silberner

New drugs and surgical procedures can help treat coronary artery disease, but making wise life-style decisions is the best way to prevent this dangerous health problem.

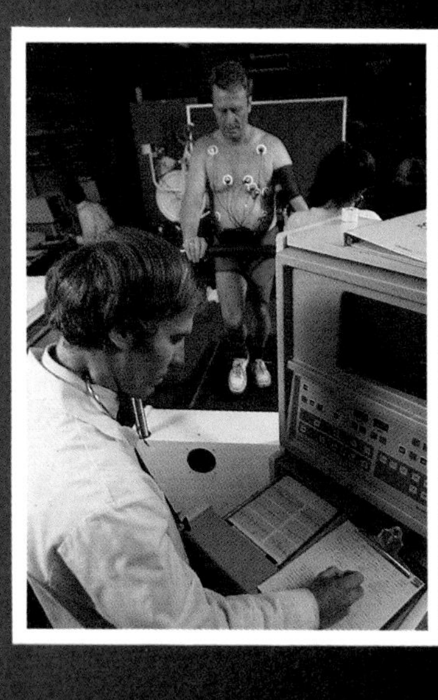

Albert took a deep breath, threw the tennis ball high into the air, and slammed it with his racquet just as the ball began its descent. Pretty good for a 45-year-old, he thought. All his opponent saw was a yellow blur flying across the net. Game, set, match.

Albert and his opponent moved to the side of the court to cool off after their game. They sat quietly, watching the next pair begin to play. But Albert did not seem to be cooling down. His chest, shoulder, neck, and arms ached, and he was still breathing heavily 15 minutes after he stopped playing. He nervously lit a cigarette. The flash of the match reminded him of his brother Don, who taught him how to smoke 30 years ago. It also brought back memories of the fatal heart attack Don suffered at the age of 50. Suddenly uneasy, Albert put out his cigarette and asked his friend to take him to the hospital.

When they arrived at the emergency room, Albert was admitted for observation and tests. The next day, the doctor came into Albert's hospital room. "You're lucky," she told him. "You did not have a heart attack. What you experienced was a temporary stop in the flow of blood to one section of your heart. Fortunately, the flow of blood resumed before any heart muscle was damaged. This type of warning attack is most often caused by a condition called coronary artery disease. If you're willing to make a few changes in the way you live, we can try to prevent another episode like the one you experienced yesterday."

The first thing the doctor told Albert to do was to stop smoking. Although he was not grossly overweight, he had the start of a potbelly, and the doctor suggested he shed a few pounds and switch to a low-fat diet. To reduce stress on the heart, she recommended that Albert curtail very strenuous activities and take a brisk walk three times a week instead. She also prescribed medication to improve the flow of blood to his heart.

Albert was lucky. His symptoms, though frightening, served as a valuable warning that he was one of millions of Americans who suffer from coronary artery disease (CAD)—a progressive narrowing or blockage of the coronary arteries, the blood vessels that feed oxygen-rich blood to the heart muscle. Untreated, the consequences of CAD can include a fatal condition called *myocardial infarction*, commonly called a heart attack.

CAD is the most common cause of death in the United States. The American Heart Association (AHA) in Dallas reports that every year more than 1.5 million people in the United States suffer heart attacks and more than 500,000 die. For most of these victims, CAD set the stage for their attacks.

A heart attack—which involves the death of heart tissue—is usually launched when a blood clot or a spasm in the wall of a blood vessel occurs in an already narrowed coronary artery, completely cutting off the flow of blood through that vessel. As

The author:

Joanne Silberner is an associate editor of *U.S. News & World Report*.

a result, the part of the heart muscle served by that artery is deprived of oxygen. If the flow of blood is not restored quickly, the deprived section of the heart tissue dies. It is important, therefore, for people who suffer a heart attack to get treatment as soon as possible.

A heart attack may be fatal if the damage interferes with the tissue that produces the electrical impulses that regulate the heartbeat, or if the damaged tissue begins to beat abnormally. In very severe attacks, the patient may go into *shock* (a condition in which so much of the heart's function is lost that not enough blood can be pumped to keep the body functioning normally). In addition, damage left by an attack may cause a serious condition called *congestive heart failure,* in which the heart is unable to pump the normal amount of blood through the body, resulting in the build-up of blood and other fluids in the lungs, liver, legs, and even the tissues under the skin.

A heart attack is accompanied by a variety of symptoms. An uncomfortable pressure, squeezing, or pain in the center of the chest that lasts for two minutes or longer could signal a heart attack. Pain may also be felt in the shoulder, neck, or arms. A heart attack victim may feel dizzy, faint, or nauseated, and may begin to sweat and have difficulty breathing. Because these symptoms are common to many ailments, people who experience a mild heart attack may think they are suffering from indigestion, gas, or stress. But any one of these symptoms could signal a heart attack and medical help should be sought immediately.

The heart
The heart is a fist-sized muscle that pumps oxygen-rich blood throughout the body. Because the heart also needs oxygen to function, blood vessels called coronary arteries feed blood to the heart muscle. Coronary artery disease causes these arteries to become narrow or completely blocked.

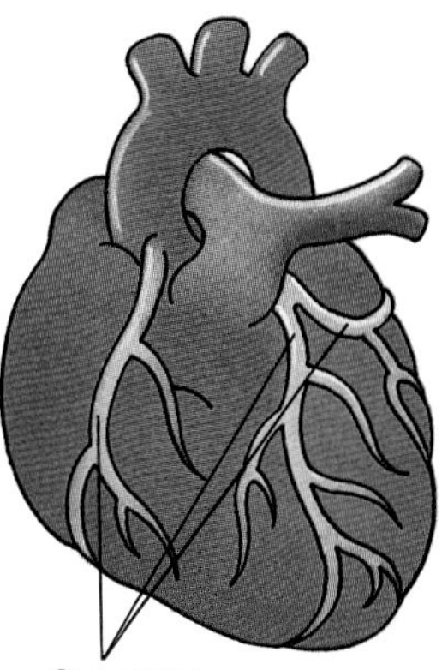

Angina and heart attack: the heart's cry for help

Two results of coronary artery disease are angina pectoris and heart attack. Both cause chest pain, but a heart attack lasts longer than an angina attack and is more severe. A heart attack also can cause permanent damage to the heart muscle.

Angina usually occurs during periods of stress or exercise when a narrowed coronary artery cannot carry enough blood and oxygen to the heart. Rest and medication can relieve the pain. The symptoms of angina are:

- Pain or heaviness in the chest, upper body, and sometimes the left arm, that usually lasts from 30 seconds to 15 minutes
- In some cases, sweating and difficulty in breathing.

Heart attack occurs when a blood clot or spasm in the wall of a narrowed coronary artery deprives part of the heart muscle of oxygen. If the flow of blood is not restored quickly, the muscle tissue will die. A combination of any of the following symptoms may signal a heart attack:

- Severe pressure, squeezing pain, or heaviness in the chest or upper body that lasts two minutes or longer
- Difficulty in breathing
- Sweating
- Nausea
- Dizziness or faintness.

CAD causes other serious conditions besides heart attack. The AHA estimates that 2.5 million Americans suffer from *angina pectoris,* chest pain that is similar to that of a heart attack but is milder and does not last as long. Angina occurs when a narrowed artery is unable to carry enough blood—and oxygen—to a part of the heart muscle, especially during periods of exercise or stress when the body's demands on the heart increase. Angina can also occur when a person is at rest if a coronary artery goes into spasm and constricts the flow of blood. For most people, an episode of angina, which usually lasts a few minutes, causes no damage to the heart muscle. But people who have severe angina run the risk of suffering a heart attack if the narrowing of their arteries grows worse or if a blood clot forms at a narrowed part of an artery.

The AHA also reports that up to 4 million Americans may suffer from *silent ischemia,* another condition caused by CAD. Silent ischemia is a temporary stoppage in the flow of blood to the heart. It is similar to angina, but it causes no pain or other warning symptoms.

What is CAD?

CAD is caused by *atherosclerosis,* a build-up of fatty deposits along the inner walls of blood vessels. This build-up can occur in blood vessels throughout the body, but when atherosclerosis affects the coronary arteries, the condition is called CAD.

Most medical experts believe that atherosclerosis results from an injury to the lining of the inner walls of the blood vessels. They suspect that atherosclerosis is triggered by damage to the wall of a blood vessel due to such conditions as high blood pressure, carbon monoxide from tobacco smoke, or some unknown factors. According to this theory, the body's disease-fighting immune system sends white blood cells to the damaged area, where they stick to the vessel wall, and cells in the damaged lining begin to divide. *Plaques*—deposits of cholesterol (a white, fatlike substance), calcium, and other substances—start to collect along the inner wall at the site of the injury. As a result, the vessel wall becomes thick and rough and the opening through which the blood flows becomes narrow.

The damaged inner vessel wall also attracts *platelets,* disk-shaped structures in the blood. Platelets normally help repair cut or broken blood vessels or tissue by sticking to the damaged surface, binding to each other, and releasing substances that start the process of blood clotting. But if a blood clot forms at a narrowed section of a blood vessel, this can cut off the supply of blood and oxygen to the heart, causing a heart attack.

Who is at risk?

Scientists have found that people who suffer from CAD share certain characteristics, or risk factors. Some risk factors cannot be controlled. For example, someone with a close relative who has had CAD is at higher risk than someone with no family history of the disease. Age is another uncontrollable factor; atherosclerosis is most often associated with the elderly. According to the AHA, 55 per cent of heart attack victims are 65 years old or older, though scientists believe that some signs of atherosclerosis can be found by the time most people reach their 20's.

Sex, race, and the presence of other ailments appear to increase the risk of CAD. For reasons that are not understood, men run a greater risk of developing heart disease than women. Women over 35 who take birth control pills increase their risk somewhat, and the risk of death due to CAD increases for all women after *menopause* (the time in a woman's life when menstruation stops). But in either instance, the risk is never as great as it is for men. Also, blacks are more likely to suffer from heart disease than people of other races, possibly because high blood pressure, or *hypertension,* is more common in blacks. People with *diabetes* (a condition in which the body cannot use sugar properly) or certain types of kidney disease are more likely to develop CAD than those without these disorders.

Fortunately, other risk factors for CAD can be reduced or eliminated. These include high blood pressure, high blood cholesterol, cigarette smoking, obesity, and, perhaps, stress.

High blood pressure. Blood pressure, the pressure exerted by the blood against the inner walls of the blood vessels, is necessary to circulate your blood. High blood pressure, however, can damage blood vessels by injuring these inner walls. Scientists do not know what causes hypertension, but they suspect that stress, smoking, excessive alcohol and salt consumption, and obesity play contributing roles in some people who have an inherited tendency to develop it. Most physicians diagnose hypertension if a patient has a persistent

How arteries become narrowed and clogged

Scientists believe that when the inner wall of a blood vessel is injured by conditions such as high blood pressure, deposits of *cholesterol* (a fatlike substance) and other fatty materials begin to build up along the artery's inner wall. This process, called *atherosclerosis,* is the cause of coronary artery disease.

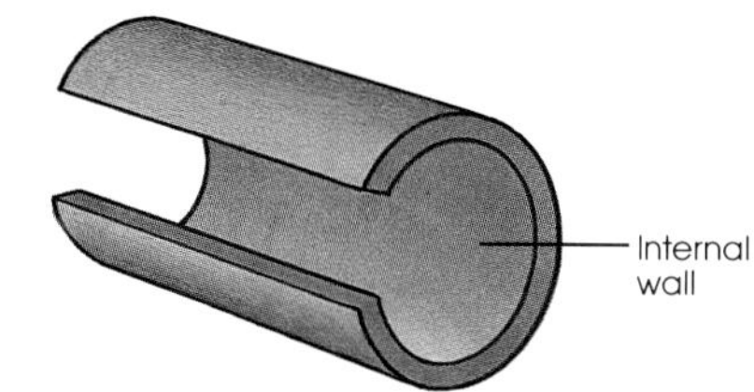

A normal artery has a smooth inner lining.

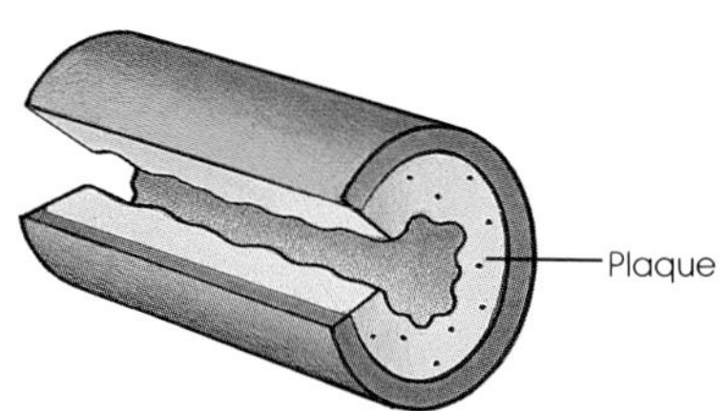

When the artery's inner wall is damaged, the body sends white blood cells to the area, where they stick to and enter the inner lining. Cells in the lining also begin to divide. The artery is further narrowed by *plaques,* deposits of cholesterol and other substances, which collect along the artery's inner wall.

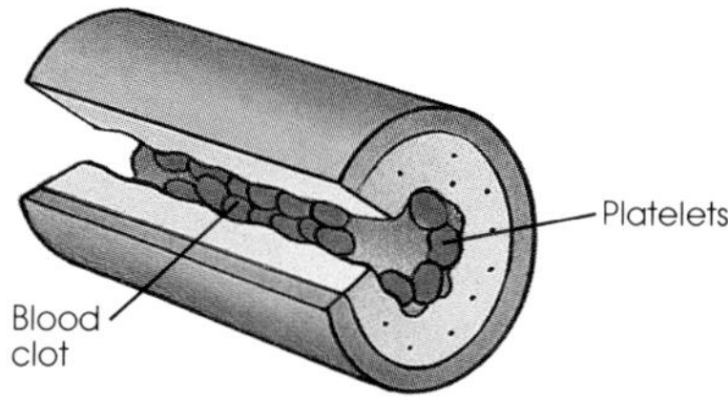

At the same time, the damaged area also attracts *platelets,* structures in the blood that stick to the artery lining where they release a substance that promotes blood clotting. If a clot forms at a narrowed part of a coronary artery and stops the flow of blood to the heart, a heart attack can occur.

blood-pressure reading of 140/95 or higher. (The first number in a blood-pressure reading represents the blood pressure when the heart is contracting; the second number represents the blood pressure when the heart is relaxing. Normal blood pressure is a persistent reading between 100/60 to 140/90.) In most cases, high blood pressure causes no symptoms until dangerous complications occur. Therefore, it is important that people of all ages have their blood pressure measured regularly.

High blood cholesterol. If high blood pressure helps set the stage for coronary artery disease by injuring blood vessel walls, high blood cholesterol continues the process by providing the body with the raw material of CAD. Cholesterol, which is produced by the liver, is important to good health. It is part of the membranes of all the cells in the body, and it plays an important role in the production of certain hormones. Cholesterol also is the chief ingredient in *bile*, a substance made by the liver that is necessary for digestion. The body obtains additional cholesterol from animal foods, such as meat, eggs, and milk and other dairy products.

Cholesterol is carried through the bloodstream by special molecules called *lipoproteins*. *High-density lipoproteins* (HDL's) are beneficial because they remove cholesterol from cells and from the bloodstream and carry it to the liver, where it is processed into harmless substances. But *low-density lipoproteins* (LDL's) help deposit cholesterol in cells, including the cells that line the walls of the blood vessels. For this reason, LDL cholesterol (cholesterol carried by LDL's) is considered a primary cause of atherosclerosis.

High levels of blood cholesterol occur if the liver produces too much LDL cholesterol or if a person consumes a diet rich in cholesterol or *saturated fats* (fats that tend to increase cholesterol in the blood). Blood cholesterol is measured in milligrams of cholesterol per deciliter of blood. A safe cholesterol level for adults is one under 200 milligrams per deciliter, according to the AHA and the National Heart, Lung, and Blood Institute (NHLBI) in Bethesda, Md. People who have cholesterol levels between 200 and 240 milligrams run a moderate risk of developing CAD. But people who have cholesterol levels of 240 milligrams or higher markedly increase their risk of developing the disease.

Genetic defects also are a factor in high blood levels of cholesterol. People who suffer from *familial hypercholesterolemia* (FH) have cells that lack —or have defective—*receptors* (special molecules on the surface of cells) that attach to LDL cholesterol. Without these receptors, liver cells cannot draw harmful cholesterol from the blood. As a result, people with FH have extremely high blood cholesterol levels, and many of them have heart attacks early in life.

Smoking. Cigarette smoking plays an important role in CAD as well. A person who smokes runs more than twice the average risk of having a heart attack. But this is not because smoking causes CAD. Researchers suspect that the nicotine and carbon monoxide from tobacco smoke, which are absorbed into the blood when a person smokes, promote the formation of blood clots.

Obesity. People who are obese also run a significantly greater risk of developing coronary artery disease. Studies have revealed that obesity can cause hypertension and high blood cholesterol. Furthermore, having to pump blood through extra body tissue increases the burden on the heart, intensifying both of these problems.

Stress. Scientists are less certain about the role of stress in CAD because levels of stress are difficult to measure. Nevertheless, most medical experts believe that stress may be a significant factor in CAD because symptoms of stress include increased heart rate and high blood pressure, which put an additional strain on the heart.

Diagnosing CAD

Early diagnosis of CAD is crucial. The sooner atherosclerosis is detected, the better the chance that this destructive process can be halted.

Even before symptoms of CAD become apparent, a physician may periodically monitor the cholesterol levels of all patients, including those who have a family history of CAD. This can be done by a *fingerstick test,* which will show if cholesterol in the blood is at a high level. In this test, the physician or medical assistant pricks the patient's fingertip with a small needle to produce a drop of blood that is analyzed in a laboratory or with a portable measuring device. Sometimes a blood sample is drawn from the vein in a patient's arm.

The physician may also order a test called an *electrocardiogram* (ECG or EKG), a printed record of the electric currents produced by the heart. These electric signals are picked up by *electrodes* (small metal plates that conduct electricity) taped to the patient's chest, arms, and legs. If the heart muscle has been damaged by a previous heart attack—or other heart disorder—the recorded electric signals are abnormal.

A *resting ECG*—an ECG taken while a patient is lying down—takes only a few minutes. If the test does not reveal any problems, but the patient has symptoms of CAD, such as an-

Diagnosing coronary artery disease

Early diagnosis of atherosclerosis increases the chance of halting this deadly process. Physicians may prescribe one or both of the diagnostic tests below to patients suspected of having coronary artery disease.

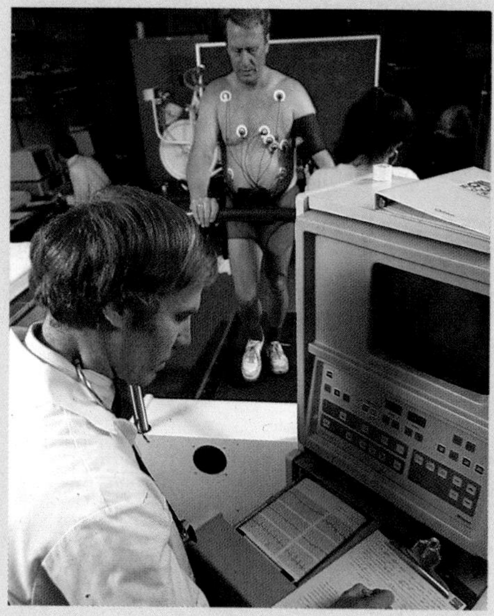

Electrocardiogram: capturing the heart's beat

Some patients may be given an *electrocardiogram* (ECG) so the doctor can obtain a printed record of the electrical signals produced by the heart. If the heart has been damaged by a heart attack or other heart disorder, the electric signals will be abnormal. One type of ECG, the *stress ECG* shown at left, is taken while a patient walks on a slanted treadmill or performs some other type of controlled exercise. Electrodes are taped to the patient's body to pick up the heart's signals, which are then monitored by medical personnel. Stress ECG's reveal the state of a patient's heart and arteries by creating a condition that increases the heart's demand for oxygen-rich blood.

Angiography: portrait of an artery

Patients suspected of having serious coronary artery disease may undergo a procedure called *coronary angiography* to determine where the arteries are narrowed by atherosclerosis.

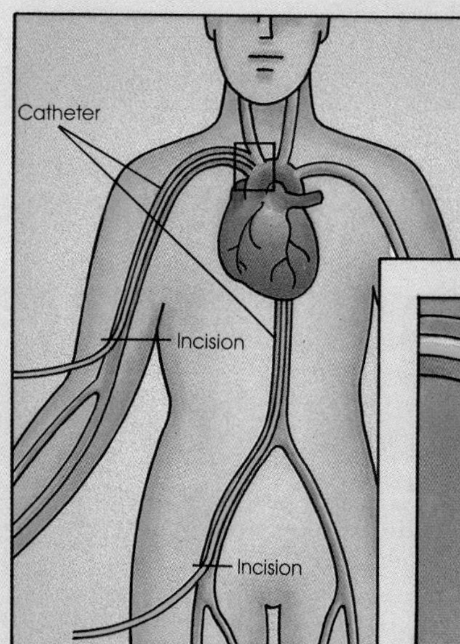

During angiography, a thin tube called a *catheter* is threaded into the blood vessels through an incision made in the patient's arm or thigh.

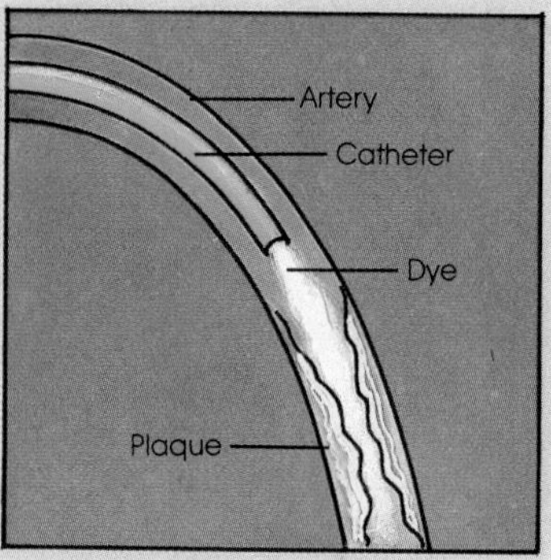

The catheter is guided into a coronary artery. A dye is injected through the catheter, and an X-ray photograph called an *angiogram* is made.

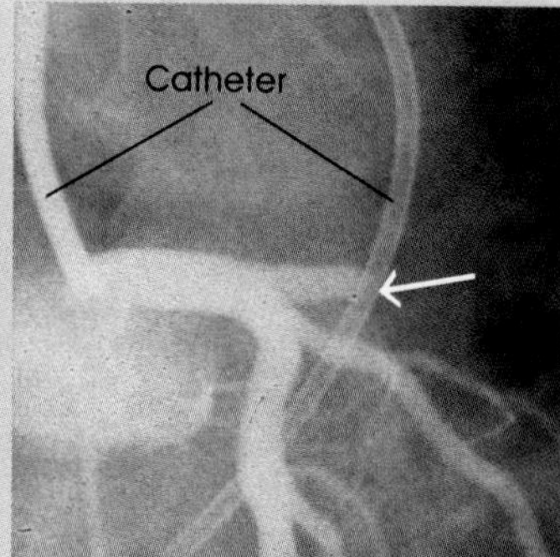

On an angiogram, unblocked arteries outlined by dye resemble white threadlike strands. This angiogram shows an artery that is totally blocked by plaque (arrow).

gina, the doctor might prescribe a *stress ECG*. A stress ECG—or an exercise-tolerance or stress test—is taken while a patient engages in controlled exercise, such as walking on a slanted treadmill or riding a stationary bike. Stress ECG's provide more specific information on the condition of the heart and coronary arteries by indicating whether the heart receives enough oxygen during exercise. This type of ECG usually takes about 30 to 45 minutes.

ECG's are not foolproof, however. They may indicate whether there is something wrong with the heart, but they do not always define a problem or indicate its extent. If CAD has not yet damaged a person's heart, a resting ECG can be normal. And a stress ECG may be normal even though the patient may have CAD.

If an ECG indicates serious damage to the heart or other symptoms of CAD are present, a more complicated procedure called *coronary angiography* (also called *arteriography*) may be performed. Angiography allows the physician to determine precisely where the arteries are blocked by atherosclerosis. After administering a mild sedative and a local anesthetic, the physician threads a long, thin, flexible tube called a *catheter* into the patient's blood vessels through a small incision made in the thigh or arm. The catheter is carefully guided up to the coronary arteries, where a dye that will show up on X rays is injected through the catheter and into the arteries. Then an *angiogram* (an X-ray photograph) is taken so that the doctor can see which arteries are narrowed.

Angiography usually requires a one-day hospital stay. The patient remains awake during the procedure. Coronary angiography may disturb the rhythm of the heart or the heart muscle, which, in rare cases, may cause a heart attack. Because of this, doctors use this procedure only when they are sure or strongly suspect atherosclerosis exists and they need to know its location and extent in order to treat the patient.

Detecting CAD is difficult in people who have no symptoms of the disease. In fact, many people have extensive CAD—and may even have a mild heart attack—without knowing it. Sometimes their doctors will be able to detect the condition by taking a blood test, an ECG, or an angiogram. But for many individuals, a serious heart attack may be the first indication the patient has of CAD.

Treating CAD

Fortunately, there are measures that people with CAD can take to help prevent a heart attack or episodes of angina. These include life-style changes, drugs, and surgery.

Life-style changes. The first line of attack in preventing and treating CAD is lowering fat and cholesterol in the diet. The

AHA advises that people consume no more than 300 milligrams of cholesterol a day and no more than three egg yolks—including yolks used in cooking—each week. The AHA also recommends a diet in which no more than 30 per cent of a person's total daily calories come from fat.

Medical experts recommend that people reduce or eliminate animal fat from their diet by substituting lean fish and poultry for fatty meats, and by drinking skim or low-fat milk instead of whole milk. People should also avoid the saturated fats found in butter and in certain plant oils, such as coconut oil and palm oil. Instead, doctors recommend safflower oil, liquid corn oil, or other oils that contain *polyunsaturated fats,* which seem to lower blood cholesterol levels. Blood cholesterol levels can be reduced by 10 to 15 per cent simply by modifying one's diet. And although it does not help everyone, medical experts recommend people limit their salt intake as a way of reducing high blood pressure.

People who smoke can make another life-style change to cut the risk of heart attack: They can stop smoking. Studies show that the risk of a heart attack—which is twice as high for smokers as for nonsmokers—begins to decrease as soon as a person stops smoking. Ten years after quitting the habit, people who formerly smoked a pack of cigarettes a day have reduced their risk of heart attack to almost the level of nonsmokers.

Another life-style change that may be prescribed to reduce the risk of coronary artery disease is regular exercise. Exercise helps strengthen the heart and lower blood pressure. Regular exercise also helps lower cholesterol levels by increasing the amount of the beneficial HDL's in the blood. Before starting an exercise program, however, people should consult their physician, especially if they are over the age of 35 and have not exercised for some time.

Drug treatment. When changes in life style fail to reduce high blood cholesterol and hypertension, doctors may prescribe drugs to lower cholesterol and high blood pressure. In addition, other medications may be prescribed to treat symptoms of CAD and to prevent episodes of angina and reduce the chance of a heart attack.

There are many cholesterol-lowering drugs available, but six are the most widely used—cholestipol, cholestyramine, nicotinic acid, gemfibrozil, probucol, and lovastatin. All these medications lower blood cholesterol, but they are not miracle drugs. Some can cause gastrointestinal problems and other side effects. Others, such as lovastatin, which was approved by the U.S. Food and Drug Administration in September 1987, are so

Reducing the risk of coronary artery disease

The best way for most healthy people to prevent coronary artery disease is to make wise life-style choices, according to medical experts. Doctors also prescribe changes in diet and life style to treat many people who already have been diagnosed as having this disease.

Stop smoking
Smoking promotes and intensifies the symptoms of atherosclerosis. By quitting the habit, smokers can significantly reduce their risk of a heart attack.

Control hypertension
Because hypertension can damage blood vessels, blood pressure should be lowered by losing weight, reducing stress and salt intake, or by taking medication.

Eat right
Because foods high in cholesterol, such as meat and dairy products, can promote atherosclerosis, doctors recommend reducing consumption of these foods.

Exercise regularly
Regular exercise can strengthen the heart, lower blood pressure, and even help lower cholesterol levels.

new that not all of their long-term side effects are known.

There are also drugs that help relieve the symptoms of CAD. For more than 100 years, *nitroglycerin* (a chemical based on compounds called *nitrates*) has been used to treat angina pain. A nitroglycerin pill placed under the tongue quickly reduces the strain on the heart by lowering the blood pressure and dilating the arteries so that more blood can reach the heart muscle. But nitroglycerin is quickly broken down by the body, so the drug's beneficial effects do not last. To remedy this, scientists have developed other, longer-lasting nitrate-based drugs that are administered orally or in the form of a skin patch. Nitrates have some drawbacks, however. They can increase the heart rate and sometimes lower blood pressure too much. People can also develop a tolerance to nitrates so that increasingly larger doses are required to produce the same results.

Beta-blockers are a group of drugs often prescribed to prevent repeated attacks of angina or stave off second heart attacks. These drugs slow the heart rate and the force with which the heart beats, so that the amount of work the heart must do—as well as the patient's blood pressure—is decreased. Beta-blockers can cause fatigue, however, and can slow down the heart too much. They also may aggravate asthma or heart failure in people who have these conditions.

Calcium blockers, another class of drugs, increase the flow of blood to the heart by preventing calcium from entering muscle cells in the walls of coronary arteries. Blocking the channels through which calcium moves causes narrowed arteries to expand, preventing angina caused by spasms in the walls of these arteries. Potential side effects of calcium blockers include heart palpitations, headaches, and constipation.

The latest addition to the list of drugs that treat the symptoms of CAD is aspirin. Aspirin does not cure coronary artery disease, but many medical experts believe it can cut the risk of heart attack in healthy men by preventing the formation of blood clots that can lodge in narrowed arteries. In January 1988, researchers at Harvard Medical School and Brigham and Women's Hospital in Boston reported that 22,071 healthy men between the ages of 40 and 84 who took an aspirin tablet every other day for more than four years reduced the risk of heart attack by 47 per cent.

But these results do not mean that everyone should begin taking aspirin. For one thing, the study did not explore the benefits or risks of aspirin for women. Even more important, the researchers found that there was a small increase in *hemorrhagic strokes* (strokes that result from bleeding in the brain) among the men who took aspirin. Because of this, physicians strongly warn people to check with a doctor before beginning an aspirin regimen. See Close-Up on page 296, ASPIRIN—A ROLE IN PREVENTING HEART ATTACKS?

Finally, there is a new group of drugs developed in the 1980's that help reduce the damage caused by a heart attack. These drugs—tissue plasminogen activator (t-PA), urokinase, and streptokinase—do not prevent heart attacks or treat the symptoms of CAD. Instead, they quickly dissolve the blood clots that cause heart attacks, reducing the damage to the heart muscle. Although studies have found these drugs—popularly called "clotbusters"—to be effective in treating heart attack patients, they have their drawbacks. They must be administered within a few hours of the attack to save heart muscle. And they can generate some serious side effects, such as internal bleeding and allergic reactions.

Surgical treatment of CAD. People who have angina attacks that do not improve with life-style changes or angina that grows progressively worse, may require surgery. One surgical procedure used to treat CAD is *coronary artery by-pass surgery.* In by-pass surgery, a team of surgeons take a portion of a vein

Surgical treatments for coronary artery disease

Patients with severe coronary artery disease may require either coronary artery by-pass surgery or balloon angioplasty—a relatively new procedure developed in the 1980's. Both treatments help restore blood flow to the heart muscle.

Coronary by-pass surgery

In this procedure, a portion of a blood vessel that is free from atherosclerosis is taken from the patient's leg or chest and is grafted or sewn onto the heart above and below the clogged part of the coronary artery. Blood flows through the healthy grafted vessel, detouring the clogged artery.

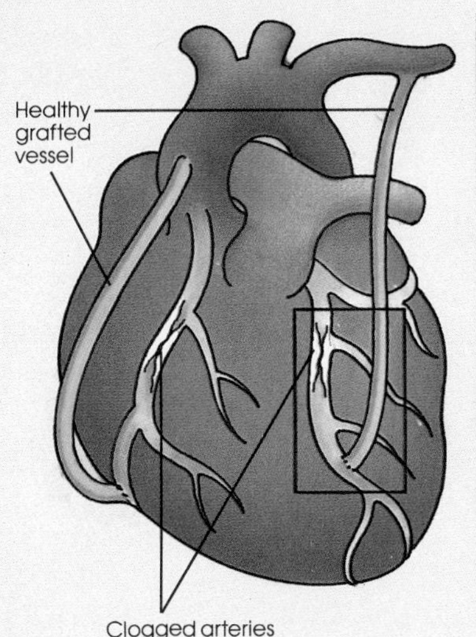

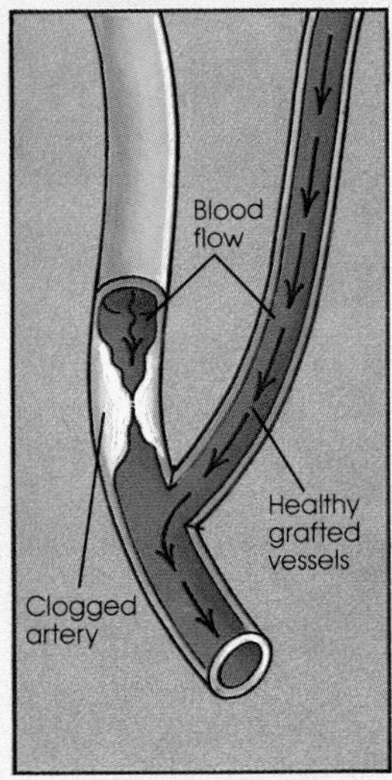

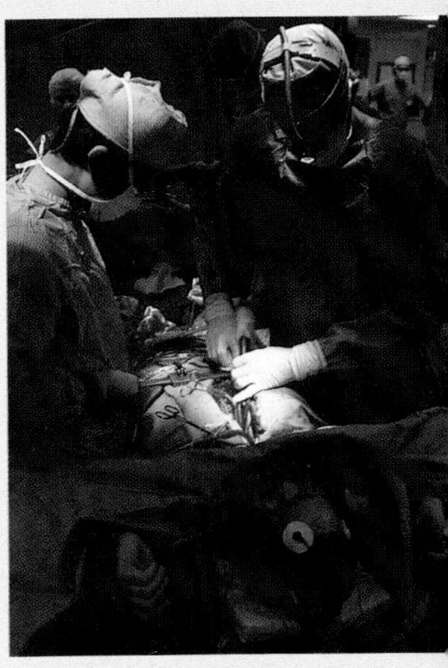

Balloon angioplasty

In this procedure, a catheter is threaded through the patient's blood vessels to a narrowed artery. A second catheter with a tiny balloon at its tip is pushed through the center of the first catheter. When the second catheter reaches the narrowed section, the balloon is inflated with a fluid. The balloon compresses the plaque along the inner wall of the clogged artery, expanding the narrowed section and improving the flow of blood through the artery.

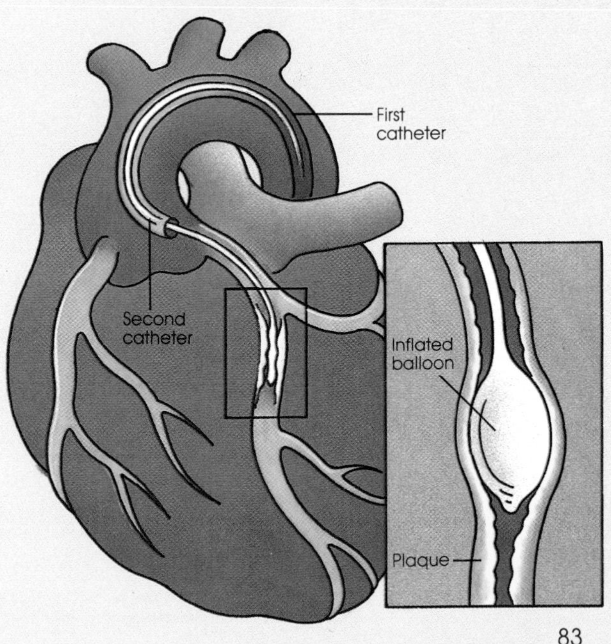

that is free of atherosclerosis from the patient's leg—or an artery from the chest wall—and sew it above and below the clogged part of a coronary artery. The grafted healthy vessel detours the blood flow around the clogged artery. A patient may have as many as five arteries by-passed at one time if necessary. Because by-pass surgery is a major operation, it has its risks, but the health of most patients is significantly improved by this procedure.

In the early 1980's, several studies suggested that by-pass surgery is overused in the United States and that many people who underwent by-pass operations could have been treated just as successfully with drugs. The medical community is still debating who should receive by-pass operations and when. In 1985, the NHLBI reported on a study that provides some rough guidelines. It found that patients who experience severe heart pain and have three or more arteries blocked by atherosclerosis or who have a severe blockage in a major coronary artery tend to do better with surgery. Patients who have only one or two blocked arteries and suffer little angina pain can sometimes be treated just as effectively with medication.

Another method that helps bring more blood to the heart is *balloon angioplasty*, a technique developed in the early 1980's. A catheter is threaded through a patient's blood vessels to a narrowed portion of a coronary artery. A second catheter, which has a tiny balloon at its tip, is pushed through the hollow center of the first catheter. When it reaches the narrowed section, the doctor inflates the balloon with a fluid and the balloon compresses the plaque along the inner wall of the vessel. As a result, the narrow opening in the blood vessel is expanded.

Angioplasty is simpler than a by-pass operation. Patients are given a mild sedative, but remain awake during the procedure. There may be some chest pain when the balloon is inflated, but most patients are up the next day. Balloon angioplasty is not for everyone, however. The narrowed vessel must be in an area that can be reached by a catheter and must also be wide enough to accommodate the catheter.

Researchers quickly discovered one problem with balloon angioplasty: About 25 to 30 per cent of angioplasty-treated arteries close within a year. In most of these cases, however, angioplasty can be performed a second time, and often with more success.

Scientists are working on another way to prevent angioplasty-treated blood vessels from narrowing again. Swiss and

French researchers developed a device called a *stent*—a tiny metal brace that is slipped into the newly widened artery to keep the vessel walls apart. In 1987, the FDA approved research studies of this experimental device in animals and human beings.

Another potential treatment for CAD uses *lasers* (narrow and intense beams of light). After learning how to use lasers to burn out plaques in blood vessels of the legs in the early 1980's, researchers have moved on to the coronary arteries. But they are progressing cautiously, because the stakes are high with lasers: If the laser beam burns through an artery wall, it can cause serious complications and even death. It will take years to determine if laser treatment can be widely used.

Prevention: the best strategy

Considerable strides have been made in diagnosing and treating CAD. But while drug therapy and surgical procedures save lives, they merely treat the problem; they do not prevent it from occurring. The message from heart specialists is clear. For most people, the best way to avoid CAD is to make wise life-style decisions. Keep your blood pressure under control. Choose foods that contain less fat. Maintain the weight that is proper for your height. Don't smoke. Exercise regularly.

People have been listening. The incidence of death from CAD has dropped more than 20 per cent since 1976, according to the AHA. But as long as CAD remains the major killer in the United States, more of us need to take the message to heart.

For more information:

The American Heart Association publishes a pamphlet called *Heart Facts* and has established guidelines for a healthy diet. You can obtain this material by contacting the American Heart Association branch in your area.

Evidence is mounting that a high-fiber diet may have a beneficial effect on a variety of ailments—from diabetes to heart disease.

Fiber: A Recipe for Good Health?

By Nancy Schommer

Whether you're grocery shopping, watching television, or reading your favorite magazine, it's difficult to avoid the nutritional buzz word of the 1980's—fiber. Stroll down the supermarket aisle and you'll find breakfast cereals that boast "high fiber with great taste" or "more fiber than any other cereal." Turn on the TV set and you'll see commercials that tout the high content of fiber in a variety of breads, fruits, and vegetables. Thumb through magazines or newspapers and you'll discover articles suggesting that a high-fiber diet can help protect against a number of diseases. And, as many of these articles point out, the American Cancer Society and the National Cancer Institute recommend that Americans consume adequate amounts of fiber.

As a result of all the alleged "good news" about fiber, many people are trying to increase their daily intake of dietary fiber—apparently convinced that fiber can prevent or cure a host of maladies ranging from cancer to heart disease to constipation. And in so doing, these health-conscious individuals are reversing a decades-old trend of reduced fiber consumption among Americans.

Medical professionals have known about the benefits of fiber for centuries. In 430 B.C., the Greek physician Hippocrates wrote about the laxative effects of coarse wheat. The new trend toward increased fiber consumption, however, began in the 1970's, triggered largely by the work of Denis Burkitt, a British physician and *epidemiologist* (a scientist who studies the causes, distribution, and control of disease). In 1969, Burkitt reported that rural Africans who eat a high-fiber diet rarely develop cancer of the colon and certain other disorders, including heart disease, *hemorrhoids* (enlargement of the veins of the rectum), and *gallstones* (deposits that form in the gall bladder). These disorders are common in the United States and Europe, where the typical diet is low in fiber.

Although Burkitt was criticized because he did not take into account other possible explanations for the Africans' health—for example, they neither smoked cigarettes nor drank alcohol—his work has had far-reaching effects. It has inspired other researchers to conduct epidemiological studies, animal experiments, and human clinical trials on the effects of fiber in the diet and has revived interest in fiber among those who are concerned about their health.

What is fiber?

The author:

Nancy Schommer is a free-lance writer based in Sag Harbor, N.Y.

Your grandparents simply called it *roughage*, meaning the coarser parts of food. But dietary fiber, which is found only in plant foods—fruits, vegetables, and grains—is more complicated than that. The term *dietary fiber* usually refers to those substances that cannot be broken down by the enzymes in a person's digestive tract. Such substances are found in a plant's cell walls, in the "glue" that holds plant cells together, and in the secretions a plant produces to heal an injury.

Actually, there are many different kinds of dietary fiber, each with different properties. But all fiber can be classified into two groups, *soluble* and *insoluble*. Nearly every plant food contains a mixture of these two fiber types.

Soluble fiber dissolves in water. Plant substances that fall into this group—*pectin, gum,* and *mucilage*—are found primarily in fruits, vegetables, dried beans and peas, barley, and oats. Apples and pears, for example, contain pectin, a fibrous substance that thickens when it is cooked. Oats and dried beans contain various types of gum. Gum is the material that causes cooked oatmeal to become sticky. Mucilage is found in cells that form the outer layer of certain seeds. Soluble fibers are also found in the cell walls of certain seaweeds. These seaweed-derived fibers—*alginates, carrageenin,* and *agar*—are often used as thickeners in processed foods.

Insoluble fiber does not dissolve in water. This type of fiber is found primarily in whole cereal and grains, as well as in peas and beans, apples, and root vegetables, such as sweet potatoes. The fibrous components in these foods include *cellulose* and *hemicellulose,* the main components of plant cell walls; *lignin,* a substance that holds plant cells together; and *cutin,* a waxy substance that makes up the outer skin of many plants.

Food plants vary not only in their ratios of the different types of fiber but also in the total amount of fiber they contain. For example, ½ cup (118 milliliters) of cooked kidney beans contains about 2.5 grams of soluble fiber—as much as four bananas. A mere 2 tablespoons (29 milliliters) of wheat germ supply roughly 2.1 grams of insoluble fiber—as much as two slices of whole-wheat bread.

Fiber content also may vary according to a plant's variety, the environment in which it is grown, how it was stored, and how it is cooked. The richest sources of fiber are plants that are eaten raw. In fact, even peeling fruits and vegetables reduces their fiber content somewhat. Foods that are not highly processed or refined yield more fiber than foods that undergo such treatment. For example, unrefined whole-grain foods still contain *bran,* the firm, fiber-rich outer coat of cereal grain kernels. Bran is usually separated from the kernel when grain is milled.

Fiber's role in a healthy diet

Dietary fiber—unlike fats, proteins, carbohydrates, vitamins, and minerals—is not considered an essential nutrient. Human beings do not need fiber to survive, and they apparently do not

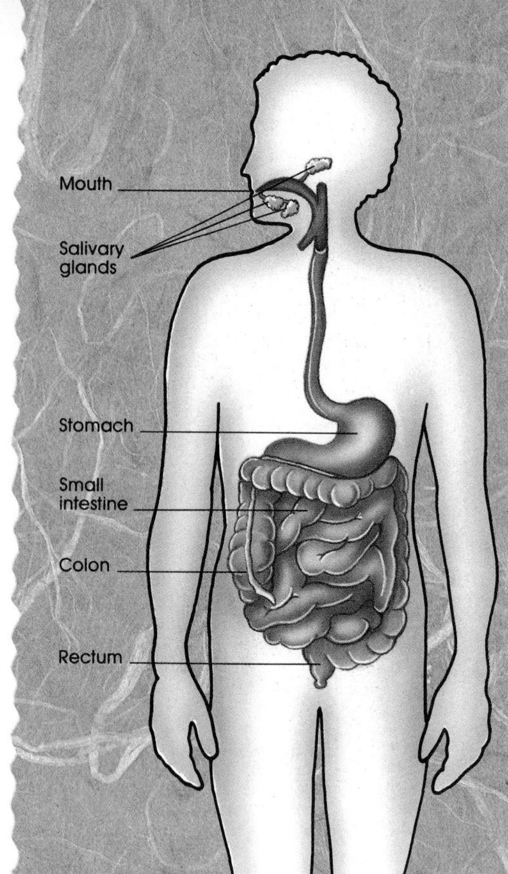

How the body digests fiber

Foods that come from plants—such as fruits, vegetables, and grains—contain a substance called *fiber.* As fiber passes through the body, it slows digestion in the stomach, but speeds the elimination of feces through the intestines and rectum.

In the mouth, fibrous food takes longer to chew, triggering the salivary glands to produce more saliva. This makes the food moister and easier to swallow.

In the stomach, gastric juices are unable to break down fiber. As a result, fiber adds bulk to the stomach, making a person feel full longer. Fiber also slows down the amount of time it takes for the contents of the stomach to empty into the small intestine.

In the small intestine, bacteria break down that part of the fiber that is *soluble* (can be dissolved in water) into substances such as fatty acids. These substances pass through the intestinal wall and are absorbed by the body's cells.

In the colon, the remaining fiber, which is *insoluble* (does not dissolve in water), acts like a sponge and absorbs water, making feces softer and easier to push through the rectum.

develop deficiency diseases when their diet includes little fiber or no fiber at all.

Nevertheless, fiber does have important physiological effects on the body. The first noticeable effect occurs when we chew a food that contains fiber. It takes a relatively long time to break up the food in our mouth, and it requires some effort to do so. During chewing, our salivary glands produce more saliva, which is absorbed by the fiber, making the food moist and easier to swallow.

After we swallow our food, its fiber content passes through our stomach and small intestine pretty much untouched. In the stomach, fiber resists breakdown by gastric juices and consequently adds bulk and thickness to the contents of the stomach. As a result, fiber may increase the time it takes for food to empty out of the stomach into the small intestine, making us feel full or satisfied for a longer time after eating. Fiber also adds bulk to the contents of the intestines. But here the added bulk speeds up the movement of the food, thus decreasing the time it takes for food to be processed and its waste products eliminated by the body.

By the time fiber moves through the stomach and small intestine and reaches the large intestine or *colon,* the soluble portion has been broken down. The end products of this process include fatty acids, which may pass through the intestinal wall and into the body's cells, where they serve as fuel. Thus, soluble fiber actually provides the body with a small amount of energy. In the colon, most of the insoluble fiber acts like a sponge and absorbs water. This increases the bulk of—and softens—the feces, making it easier for the intestines to push wastes through the rectum and out of the body.

Because fiber's physiological role seems limited—it provides a small amount of energy and helps speed the movement of solid wastes out of the body—people long regarded it as a "bit player" in the cast of dietary substances. But the observations of Burkitt and other researchers have brought increasing interest in fiber's possible role in preventing, relieving, or treating certain disorders and diseases.

Effects on gastrointestinal disorders

More than any other gastrointestinal disorder, constipation seems to be the one most positively—and conclusively—affected by the amount of fiber in the diet. Many studies have shown that fiber acts as a natural laxative because it behaves like a sponge in the large intestine, absorbing water and making the feces larger, softer, and easier to pass. Researchers have found that people who consume high-fiber diets have larger stools and eliminate their wastes more rapidly after eating. Because it creates softer stools, a high-fiber diet may also benefit those who suffer from hemorrhoids, though researchers have not yet proved this benefit.

Researchers have, however, found convincing evidence of fiber's beneficial effect on *diverticulosis*, a disorder in which pouches, called *diverticula*, form along weakened areas of the colon wall. Diverticulosis can develop into *diverticulitis*, a disease in which one or more diverticula become inflamed, leading to abdominal pain and fever.

In March 1979, a group of researchers at the University of Oxford in England compared the incidence of diverticulosis between two groups of volunteers—vegetarians and nonvegetarians. The scientists found that 12 per cent of the vegetarians, who consumed an average of 41.5 grams of fiber per day, had diverticulosis. Among the nonvegetarians, who consumed about half that amount of fiber per day, 33 per cent had the disorder. Moreover, when the researchers analyzed the amount of fiber consumed by both groups, they found that individuals without diverticulosis—whether vegetarians or nonvegetarians—consumed more fiber than those who had developed the condition.

The results of the Oxford study were based solely on records of the patients' diets and, therefore, merely suggest a connection between fiber intake and diverticulosis. But other studies involving treatment of diverticulosis patients with fiber have shown relatively conclusive evidence. In a clinical study reported in 1973, British researchers at the Hastings Hospital Group in Hastings and the Energen Food Company in Ashford, found that 71 per cent of their diverticulitis patients were relieved of symptoms of the disorder when they ate six slices of high-fiber bread each day.

Based on these studies, experts conclude that a diet low in fiber, which results in firm, compact stools, forces the colon to exert high pressure to move the feces toward the rectum. This high pressure can cause the inner membrane of the colon to bulge out through weak points in the intestinal lining, thus creating diverticula. Armed with this knowledge, physicians advise patients with diverticulitis to include more fiber in their diet. Yet just 25 years ago, doctors gave such patients the opposite advice, on the mistaken assumption that high-fiber intake would aggravate the condition.

The colon cancer connection

Colorectal cancer (cancer of the colon or rectum) is the second leading cause of cancer deaths in the United States after lung cancer. Colorectal cancer takes an estimated 60,000 lives each year in the United States. It is not surprising, therefore, that scientists are still seeking to validate Burkitt's theory that increased fiber intake may prevent this dreaded disease. According to one theory, fiber—particularly insoluble fiber—decreases the time that *carcinogens* (cancer-causing substances) found in some foods stay in the colon and rectum, thus reducing a person's chances of developing cancer. It has also been suggested that increasing one's intake of fiber decreases the time it takes for feces to move through the colon and rectum, thereby reducing the activity of bacterial enzymes that may convert digestive chemicals called *bile acids* into potential carcinogens. In addition, fiber stimulates the secretion of mucus that coats the wall of the colon. Researchers suspect that the mucus may provide a barrier that keeps toxic substances, including cancer-causing agents, from reaching the cells in the wall of the colon.

Until now, most of the evidence that fiber protects against colon cancer has come from epidemiologists. Although Burkitt's study of rural Africans was among the first to suggest that fiber helps prevent cancer, evidence from recent studies continues to accumulate, suggesting that appropriate amounts of fiber may indeed have such a preventive effect.

Because the rural population of Finland has one of the lowest rates of colon cancer in Europe, several researchers have

Fiber and your health

High-fiber diets have been advocated as a way to protect against a variety of diseases. Some of these claims are supported by research. Other claims, however, still lack solid scientific evidence.

Fiber and diverticulosis
Scientific evidence supports the claim that high-fiber diets can help relieve symptoms of diverticulosis, a disorder of the colon.

Fiber and obesity
Scientists have been unable to prove that eating fibrous foods, which add bulk to the stomach, prevents overeating and reduces weight.

Fiber and colon cancer
Since the 1960's, some health experts have promoted fiber as a preventive for colon cancer. But though many studies have been conducted, there is no solid evidence that proves fiber prevents colon cancer.

Fiber and heart disease
Scientists have found that a high-fiber diet seems to reduce the risk of heart attack by lowering the level of cholesterol in the blood.

Fiber and diabetes
Many studies have shown fiber to help treat diabetes. Since 1979, the American Diabetes Association has recommended that diabetics—under strict medical supervision—eat a diet high in fiber and carbohydrates.

sought to find out whether the Finns' intake of dietary fiber plays a role in preventing the disease. In a study reported in July 1977, members of the Intestinal Microecology Group of the International Agency for Research on Cancer in Albany, N.Y., compared the diets of Finns living in the rural town of Kuopio with the diets of city dwellers in Copenhagen, Denmark. In another study, reported in January 1978 by the Naylor Dana Institute for Disease Prevention in Valhalla, N.Y., researchers studied the dietary characteristics of another group of rural Finns in Kuopio and compared them with residents of the New York City area. In each of these studies, the researchers reported that the higher the fiber intake the lower the incidence of colon cancer. The studies revealed that the Finns' intake of fiber was significantly higher than that of the groups in Copenhagen and New York City. The key difference between the Finns and the other groups appeared to be in their consumption of insoluble fiber found in whole-grain foods.

Although scores of other epidemiological studies have shown

a similar inverse relationship between the incidence of colon cancer and the intake of fiber, the evidence is still more suggestive than conclusive. There are, at present, no data proving that a high-fiber diet protects against *any* cancer, according to Victor Herbert, chief of the Hematology and Nutrition Laboratory at the Veterans Administration Medical Center in the Bronx—a borough, or section, of New York City. Epidemiological studies show an association between high-fiber intake and a low frequency of cancer, but this coincidence does not establish a cause-and-effect relationship. Epidemiological evidence is subject to many possible interpretations, Herbert notes. For example, in cases where two groups are compared, there are always several differences between the groups—some differences are dietary; some are related to life-style activities, such as smoking cigarettes or drinking alcohol; and some are genetic.

Fiber and diabetes

Medical professionals have known for years that diet and exercise can benefit individuals who suffer from diabetes, and new evidence is emerging that dietary fiber may play a key role in the treatment of the disease. Diabetes affects the way the human body processes fats, proteins, and carbohydrates. It occurs when the body fails to produce enough of the hormone *insulin* or cannot use it properly, which interferes with the process by which energy-yielding sugar molecules enter the body's cells. When this happens, the level of sugar in the blood rises and the cells are deprived of necessary fuel. A serious complication of diabetes, damage to the blood vessels, can lead to blindness, kidney failure, and heart disease. Many diabetics must take insulin injections or oral drugs that help the body process blood sugar more efficiently. Some researchers believe that because diabetes runs in certain families, the disease may be caused in some cases by genetic factors.

Since the early 1960's, a number of epidemiological studies have indicated that a low-fiber diet may be associated with diabetes. Research has shown, for example, that diabetes is rare among certain African populations who consume high-fiber diets. One study, reported by researchers at the University of Oklahoma School of Medicine in Oklahoma City in 1971, compared the nutritional factors with the prevalence of diabetes in 11 countries of Asia, South America, and Central America, and in Bangor, Pa. The scientists found that the highest prevalence of diabetes occurred in the Pennsylvania area, while the lowest prevalence of the disease occurred in East Pakistan. Other researchers who analyzed the University of Oklahoma study pointed out that in Bangor low-fiber white bread made up 30 per cent of the calories consumed by residents. In East Pakistan, however, wheat, whole meal, legumes, and vegetables

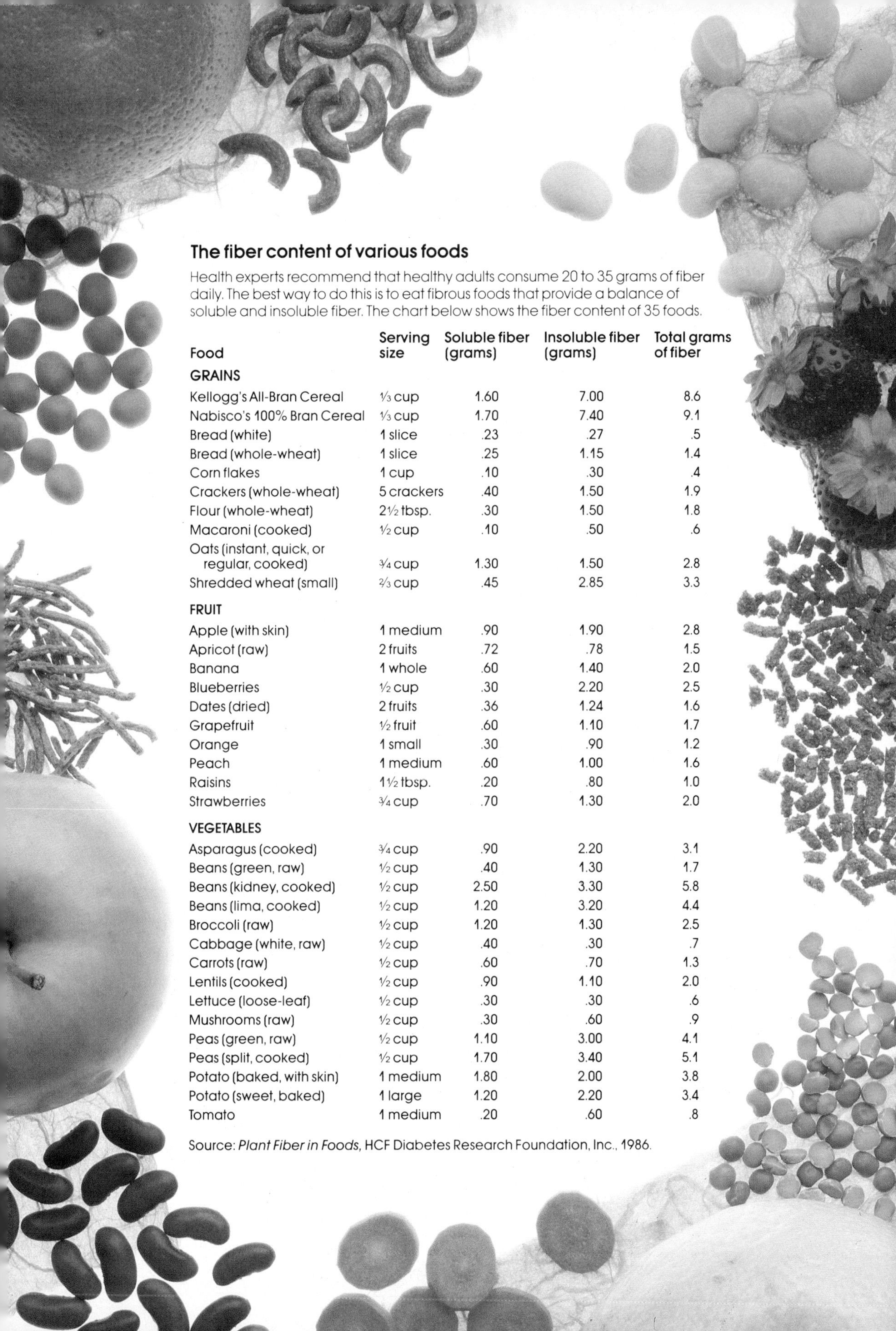

The fiber content of various foods

Health experts recommend that healthy adults consume 20 to 35 grams of fiber daily. The best way to do this is to eat fibrous foods that provide a balance of soluble and insoluble fiber. The chart below shows the fiber content of 35 foods.

Food	Serving size	Soluble fiber (grams)	Insoluble fiber (grams)	Total grams of fiber
GRAINS				
Kellogg's All-Bran Cereal	⅓ cup	1.60	7.00	8.6
Nabisco's 100% Bran Cereal	⅓ cup	1.70	7.40	9.1
Bread (white)	1 slice	.23	.27	.5
Bread (whole-wheat)	1 slice	.25	1.15	1.4
Corn flakes	1 cup	.10	.30	.4
Crackers (whole-wheat)	5 crackers	.40	1.50	1.9
Flour (whole-wheat)	2½ tbsp.	.30	1.50	1.8
Macaroni (cooked)	½ cup	.10	.50	.6
Oats (instant, quick, or regular, cooked)	¾ cup	1.30	1.50	2.8
Shredded wheat (small)	⅔ cup	.45	2.85	3.3
FRUIT				
Apple (with skin)	1 medium	.90	1.90	2.8
Apricot (raw)	2 fruits	.72	.78	1.5
Banana	1 whole	.60	1.40	2.0
Blueberries	½ cup	.30	2.20	2.5
Dates (dried)	2 fruits	.36	1.24	1.6
Grapefruit	½ fruit	.60	1.10	1.7
Orange	1 small	.30	.90	1.2
Peach	1 medium	.60	1.00	1.6
Raisins	1½ tbsp.	.20	.80	1.0
Strawberries	¾ cup	.70	1.30	2.0
VEGETABLES				
Asparagus (cooked)	¾ cup	.90	2.20	3.1
Beans (green, raw)	½ cup	.40	1.30	1.7
Beans (kidney, cooked)	½ cup	2.50	3.30	5.8
Beans (lima, cooked)	½ cup	1.20	3.20	4.4
Broccoli (raw)	½ cup	1.20	1.30	2.5
Cabbage (white, raw)	½ cup	.40	.30	.7
Carrots (raw)	½ cup	.60	.70	1.3
Lentils (cooked)	½ cup	.90	1.10	2.0
Lettuce (loose-leaf)	½ cup	.30	.30	.6
Mushrooms (raw)	½ cup	.30	.60	.9
Peas (green, raw)	½ cup	1.10	3.00	4.1
Peas (split, cooked)	½ cup	1.70	3.40	5.1
Potato (baked, with skin)	1 medium	1.80	2.00	3.8
Potato (sweet, baked)	1 large	1.20	2.20	3.4
Tomato	1 medium	.20	.60	.8

Source: *Plant Fiber in Foods,* HCF Diabetes Research Foundation, Inc., 1986.

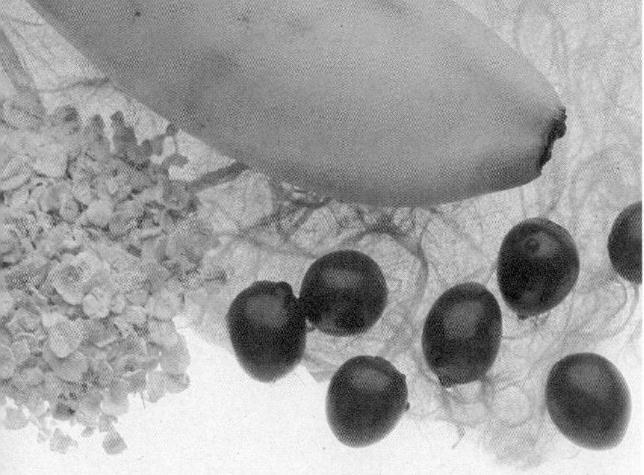

Recipes with a fiber difference

Foods made with high-fiber ingredients, such as oats, bananas, and kidney beans, can be tasty and good for you, too. The recipes below and on the opposite page were developed by WORLD BOOK under a nutritionist's supervision.

Banana-berry muffins

- 1 c. quick-cooking oats
- 1 c. whole-wheat flour
- ¾ c. all-purpose flour
- 1 tbsp. baking powder
- 1½ tsp. cinnamon
- ½ tsp. nutmeg
- ¼ tsp. salt
- 2 large ripe bananas
- 1 large egg
- ½ c. orange juice
- ⅓ c. honey
- ¼ c. vegetable oil
- 1 tsp. vanilla
- 1 c. cranberries, coarsely chopped or 1¼ c. fresh or thawed frozen blueberries

Preheat oven to 400°F. Grease twelve 2¾-inch muffin cups. In large bowl, mix oats, flours, baking powder, spices, and salt until well blended. In medium bowl, mash bananas with fork; beat in egg. Stir in juice, honey, oil, and vanilla. Make a well in center of dry ingredients; pour banana mixture into well. Stir just until dry ingredients are moistened. Do not overmix; batter will be lumpy. Blend in berries. Spoon batter evenly into prepared muffin cups. (Muffin cups will be almost full.) Bake 18 to 20 minutes or until golden brown. Remove to wire racks. Makes 2 dozen muffins.

made up nearly 70 per cent of the typical diet.

While this study suggested a relationship between low-fiber intake and diabetes, recent clinical trials are providing actual evidence that diabetics may benefit from a high-fiber diet. In clinical studies at the Veterans Administration (VA) Medical Center in Lexington, Ky., endocrinologist James W. Anderson found that appropriate amounts of dietary fiber enabled some diabetics to reduce or even eliminate their need for insulin or oral antidiabetic drugs while under medical supervision. In 1979, Anderson observed that some diabetics who consumed diets containing high-fiber food and food high in complex carbohydrates, such as bread and corn, were able to reduce their insulin medication by 50 per cent. In addition, some diabetics whose treatment programs included a relatively low dose of insulin were able to stop taking the hormone when they included appropriate amounts of fiber and carbohydrates in their daily diet.

Several researchers have suggested that the combination of fiber and complex carbohydrates influences the level of sugar in the blood, allowing patients to reduce their intake of insulin. For reasons not completely understood, the fiber appears to slow the absorption of carbohydrates. This seems to occur because fiber delays the passage of food from the stomach to the intestines, thus reducing the body's need for a sudden large output of insulin. Some scientists suspect that this action may be linked to other benefits experienced by diabetics on high-fiber and high-carbohydrate diets, such as lower blood pressure. Indeed, because of the many benefits that diabetics seem to derive from diets that include appropriate amounts of fiber, the American Diabetes Association in 1979 began recommending that diabetics—under medical supervision—consume diets rich in certain high-fiber, high-complex carbohydrate foods.

What about heart disease?

Although hypertension, cigarette smoking, diabetes, and even genetic factors have been linked to heart disease, increasing evidence has shown that the food we eat—particularly if it is high in fat and cholesterol—can play a role in causing *atherosclerosis,* a disease in which cholesterol deposits narrow and harden the arteries, leading to a heart attack or stroke. Since the 1970's, however, scientists have learned that a substantial amount of soluble fiber in the diet may lower the cholesterol level in the blood.

In the body, cholesterol, which is essential for many body functions, is transported through the blood by molecules called lipoproteins. *High-density lipoproteins* (HDL's) tend to remove cholesterol from artery walls and carry it to the liver, where it is excreted in the bile. *Low-density lipoproteins* (LDL's), on the other hand, tend to deposit cholesterol along artery walls. When a person's body manufactures excessive amounts of cholesterol or uses it poorly, or when a person's diet is too rich in saturated fat and cholesterol, blood cholesterol levels rise. As a result, the inner walls of the arteries can become coated with *plaques*—deposits of cholesterol, calcium, and other material. As a plaque thickens, it narrows and eventually blocks the opening of the artery, cutting off the blood flow. When this happens in one of the arteries that nourish the heart, a heart attack—and death—can result.

A number of epidemiological studies have shown that in populations where fiber intake is high, blood cholesterol levels—and the incidence of heart disease—are low. Encouraged by such reports, a number of researchers have tried to determine, in clinical experiments, whether fiber can be used to lower cholesterol levels.

In most of these clinical trials, researchers added soluble fiber to subjects' diets. Apparently, soluble fiber binds cholesterol-rich bile components in the large intestine, drawing them into the feces so that they cannot be reabsorbed by the body and become part of the body's cholesterol supply.

Studies have revealed that guar gum, a fi-

7-vegetable minestrone

1	tbsp. vegetable oil
1	large onion, chopped
2	cloves garlic, minced
3	medium carrots, coarsely chopped
2	tsp. dried basil
1½	tsp. dried oregano
5	c. beef broth
2	(15½ oz.) cans kidney beans, undrained
1	(16 oz.) can whole tomatoes, coarsely chopped, undrained
1	(15 oz.) can tomato purée
1	medium zucchini, halved lengthwise, sliced
1	c. sliced fresh mushrooms
¼	c. chopped fresh parsley
2 to 3	tbsp. honey (optional)
¼	tsp. pepper
1	(10 oz.) package frozen peas

In 6-qt. Dutch oven, heat oil over medium-high heat. Add onion, garlic, carrots, basil, and oregano. Cook, stirring occasionally, for 3 minutes or until vegetables are crisp-tender. Stir in broth, kidney beans, tomatoes, tomato purée, zucchini, mushrooms, parsley, honey, and pepper. Bring to a boil. Reduce heat and simmer, covered, for 10 minutes, stirring occasionally. Stir in frozen peas. Simmer, covered, for 15 minutes. Makes about 3½ qts. Note: Recipe may be cut in half.

brous substance found in beans, is particularly effective in lowering cholesterol. Several experiments showed that subjects whose diets were supplemented with about 8 to 15 grams of guar gum per day had a decrease of 10 to 15 per cent in their blood levels of LDL. At the VA Medical Center in Lexington, researchers found that oat bran, which contains guar gum, not only lowers cholesterol levels in the blood but also reduces blood levels of *triglycerides,* fatty substances that have also been linked to heart disease.

Fiber and obesity

The news media and some health professionals have touted a fiber-rich diet as a relatively easy way for overweight individuals to lose weight. Theoretically, this should be true for a variety of reasons. Fiber adds bulk to the stomach and gives one a feeling of fullness, which can prevent overeating. By itself, fiber contains few, if any, calories, and foods that contain fiber—fruits and vegetables, for example—are generally low in calories. In addition, high-fiber foods also require more time to chew. This slows the eating process and creates the impression that the amount of food eaten is substantial.

Nevertheless, few studies have shown that dietary fiber promotes significant weight reduction. In fact, in the majority of studies, weight loss has been modest at best. Moreover, no follow-up studies have been done to determine whether individuals on high-fiber diets can maintain their weight loss. A June 1987 report prepared for the U.S. Food and Drug Administration said that dietary fiber may have a limited role in treating obesity, but that controlled, long-term clinical trials are needed before this role can be established.

What the experts say

Despite the uncertainty regarding fiber's role in disease prevention, there is enough evidence to suggest that Americans, who on average consume only about 10 grams of dietary fiber per day, should increase their intake of high-fiber foods. Indeed, several agencies—including the National Cancer Institute, the American Cancer Society, and the National Research Council—recommend that healthy adults consume between 20 and 35 grams of fiber every day. A recommended range of daily fiber intake for children and the elderly has not yet been determined.

How much dietary fiber should be derived from soluble fiber and how much from insoluble fiber? No one knows for sure. But according to the National Cancer Institute, the fiber we consume should come from a variety of food sources—whole grains, legumes, fruits, and vegetables.

Experts caution against switching abruptly from a low-fiber diet to one high in fiber. Some people who do so experience flatulence, because fiber increases the formation of intestinal gases. Others suffer from bloating or diarrhea—conditions caused, in part, by the tendency of fiber to absorb water. To avoid these adverse side effects, most medical professionals recommend that people gradually increase their fiber intake daily over several weeks. Although the best way to do this is by eating high-fiber foods, many experts recommend the use of fiber supplements as a way to increase one's daily intake of fiber. To avoid adverse side effects, these supplements should be taken according to directions on the label—or under a physician's supervision. Studies have shown that bran tablets or cellulose powders, for example, may cause bloating, excess stomach gas, and, in rare cases, intestinal obstruction.

Of greater concern is fiber's potential to interfere with the absorption of certain nutrients. Studies have shown that *phytate,* a substance found in certain cereal fibers, interferes with the absorption of the mineral zinc. Other research has suggested that fibrous foods may also adversely affect the absorption of other minerals, including calcium, magnesium, and iron. In most of these studies, however, the nutrients lost due to fiber did not seem to affect the subjects' overall mineral balance. Apparently, people on high-fiber diets receive enough of these minerals to compensate for the losses. Because most Americans consume excess amounts of many nutrients in their diet, there is little reason to worry that an increased intake of fiber will cause any dietary deficiency.

Although a great deal still remains to be learned about dietary fiber and its role in health, researchers have made significant progress in unraveling the truth about fiber in the diet. Increased awareness of the benefits of fiber in a well-balanced diet, together with efforts to increase exercise and decrease use of alcohol and tobacco, may ensure a healthier future for us all.

For further reading:

Burkitt, Denis. *Don't Forget Fiber in Your Diet.* Arco Publishing, 1984.

"The Fiber Furor." *Consumer Reports,* October 1986.

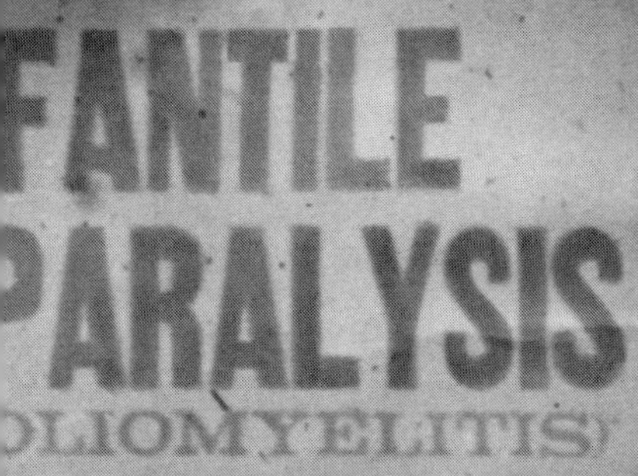
FANTILE
PARALYSIS
OLIOMYELITIS)
ANTILE PARALYSIS IS VERY PREV-
IN THIS PART OF THE CITY. ON
STREETS MANY CHILDREN ARE ILL
HIS IS ONE OF THE STREETS
P OFF THIS STREET

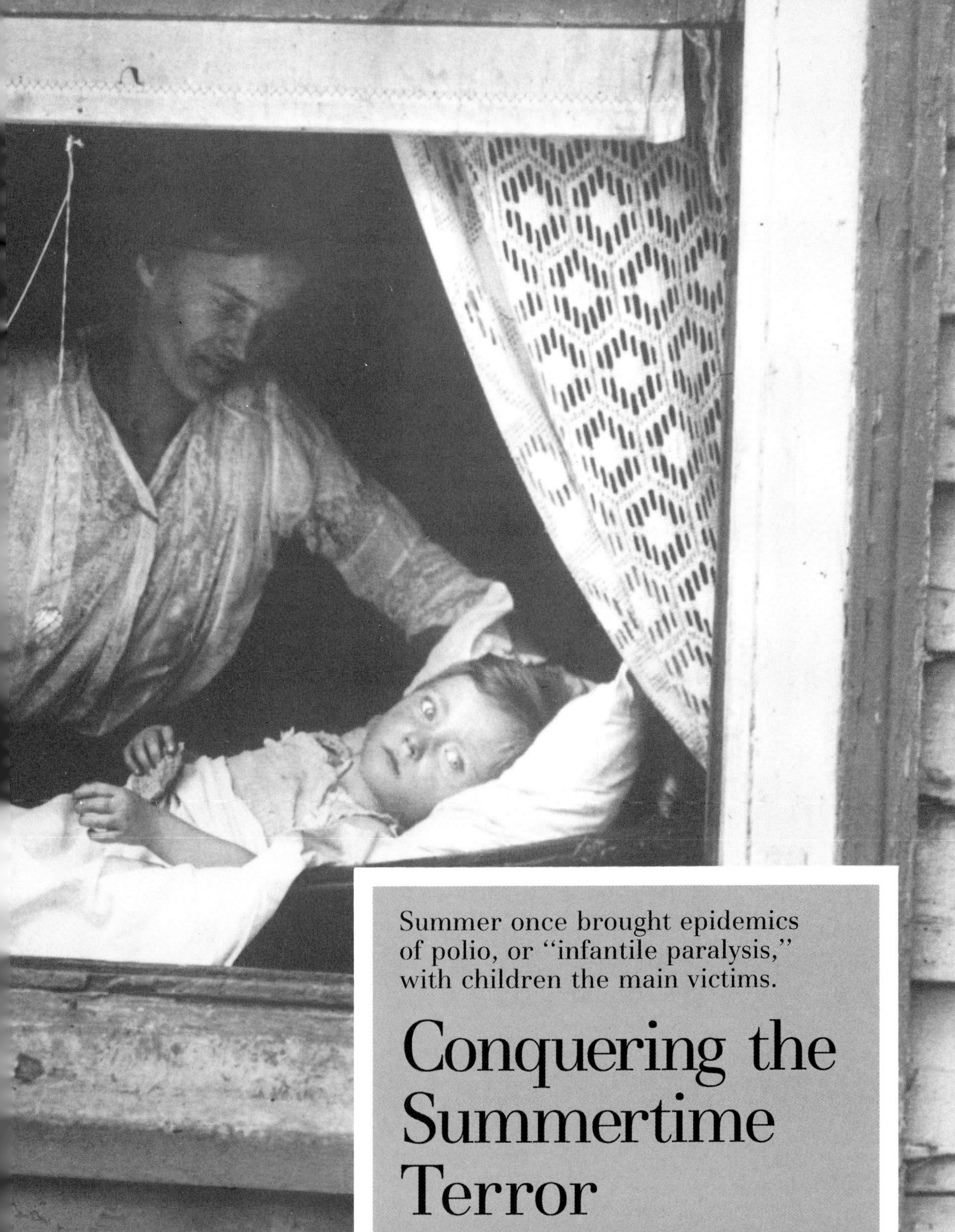

Summer once brought epidemics of polio, or "infantile paralysis," with children the main victims.

Conquering the Summertime Terror

By William H. Allen

Previous pages: A quarantine sign in New York City told the story of the devastating U.S. polio epidemic of 1916: "Infantile Paralysis (Poliomyelitis). Infantile paralysis is very prevalent in this part of the city. On some streets many children are ill. This is one of the streets. Keep off this street."

The author:

William H. Allen is a free-lance writer specializing in scientific and medical topics.

In the summer of 1916, while World War I raged in Europe, the United States became a battleground for a different kind of devastation. In the nation's cities, millions of people were contracting *poliomyelitis*, a terrifying illness often called *infantile paralysis* because of its reputation as a crippler of children in particular.

Highly contagious in the summer months, the illness passed from child to child on playgrounds, beaches—anywhere young people congregated. While most infected children easily shook off the infection without becoming ill, some developed headache, sore throat, nausea, and fever. The muscles of those afflicted went into spasms that could be followed by permanent paralysis of one or both legs and arms. In some cases, the disease then attacked the base of the brain, impairing nerves that control muscles used in breathing or causing delirium, coma, and death.

Polio continued to terrorize parents for decades after that 1916 outbreak, and even today it remains the chief cause of lameness in developing nations. But the summer of 1916 was significant because during those months the United States was in the grip of the worst known polio epidemic the world had yet endured. According to public health records kept in 20 states, more than 27,000 people were paralyzed by polio that summer, and 7,179 died. But these cases were only a fraction of the entire epidemic. For every child whose nervous system was affected, 5 others suffered mild cases of polio that caused no permanent damage and another 95 contracted the illness but had no symptoms. All of those infected—the very ill and the symptom-free alike—could pass the disease to others.

New York City was hardest hit. Many families spent an anxious, isolated summer almost entirely within their homes. Quacks appeared on street corners selling fraudulent polio "cures" made of alcohol, so-called "radium water," or ox blood. Whenever a child contracted the disease, the city's public health officials quarantined the entire household, and, as the epidemic worsened, they restricted travel out of the city. Thousands of families fled anyway, but the citizens of outlying communities turned them back, often at gunpoint. By the end of the summer, 2,448 residents of New York City—almost all of them children—were dead.

In the autumn, the epidemic and the hysteria diminished. But parents, aware of the lack of a medication to prevent or cure the little-understood disease, feared that there would be more polio epidemics in the summers to come. Unfortunately, their fears were realized.

People have suffered from polio for centuries, though isolated cases were far more common than epidemics until the 1800's. An Egyptian stone carving dating from 1580 to 1350 B.C. depicts a crippled man with a withered leg who is thought to be

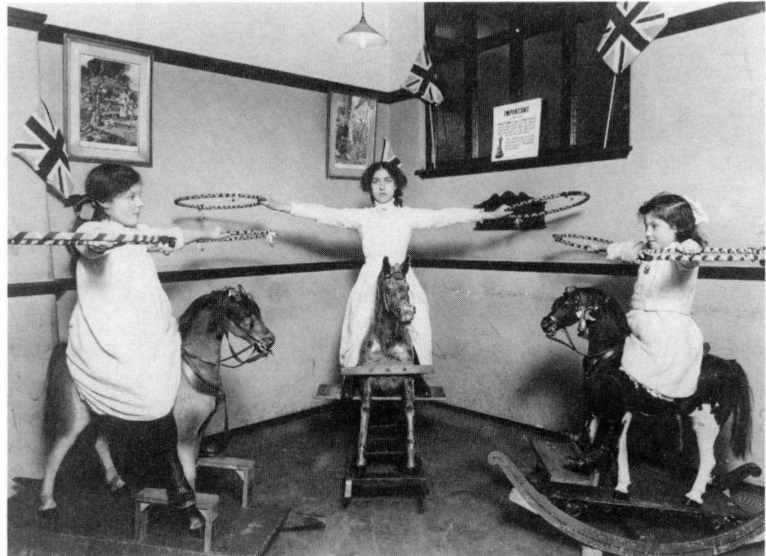

At a British polio treatment center in the early 1900's, quaintly named The Tiny Tim Guild, polio victims with paralyzed legs employed a "scientific use of music and rhythm" to exercise their undamaged muscles.

a survivor of polio. Victims of what could have been polio are also mentioned in early Christian literature and that of ancient Greece and Rome.

Historians do not know what, if any, treatments early physicians used for polio. The first written medical description of the disease did not appear until 1789. The author was a British physician named Michael Underwood, who gave the illness its first recorded name, *debility of the lower extremities*. Its present scientific name, *poliomyelitis*—which was derived from the Greek words *polios* (gray) and *myelos* (marrow) and refers to the grayish tissue in the spinal cord that becomes inflamed during the course of the illness—did not come into widespread use until the 1900's.

Before then, few physicians thought the ailment was contagious. In fact, reports of polio outbreaks were rare until the late 1830's and 1840's, when clusters of cases were reported in England, the South Atlantic island of St. Helena, and Louisiana. The first sizable U.S. epidemic occurred in 1894 in Vermont, with 132 cases reported. From that time on, polio epidemics became more common and more severe. Polio hit New York City in 1907; Mason City, Iowa, in 1910; and Cincinnati, Ohio, in 1911.

These outbreaks convinced physicians that polio was caused by a disease-causing microbe that could be passed from one person to another. Several medical experts proposed that a bacterium—one type of microbe—was the culprit, but they were unable to prove it. In 1908, Karl Landsteiner, an Austrian

Children in Louisville, Ky., were barred from a swimming pool during that city's 1935 polio scare. Health officials sometimes prohibited group play in an effort to halt the rapid spread of the polio virus.

pathologist and *immunologist* (specialist in the study of disease and in the function of the immune system) tried a different approach. Landsteiner and his assistant, Erwin Popper, injected two monkeys with cells taken from the spinal cord of a boy who had died of polio. No bacteria could be found in the cells, but both of the monkeys developed the disease. The explanation, Landsteiner said, was that the monkeys' polio was caused by an "invisible virus" present in the boy's spinal cord.

Polio is indeed caused by a *virus*, an extremely small disease-causing organism. The polio virus usually enters the body through the mouth or nose, then invades cells in the digestive tract, where it begins to multiply. In the vast majority of cases, the body's disease-fighting immune system kills the virus while it is in the digestive tract or in nearby *lymph nodes* (glands that filter harmful microscopic organisms from *lymph*, a colorless fluid that bathes the body's cells). In such cases, the infected person suffers few, if any, symptoms. But if the polio virus is unusually strong or if the victim's immune system is weak, the virus travels to the central nervous system. There it multiplies in the nerve tissues of the brain and spinal cord. In one form of the disease, *spinal paralytic poliomyelitis,* the virus kills or damages nerve cells in the spinal cord that control movement. In the most deadly form of polio, *bulbar paralysis,* the virus also attacks nerve cells in the brain stem.

Although polio strikes most people in childhood, people of any age can be infected, and even infected persons who have no symptoms can unknowingly spread polio to others through coughing, sneezing, or, most commonly, fecal contamination. No one knows for certain why the number of cases of polio increases in the summer months.

Why, if the disease is contagious, were polio epidemics unheard of until modern times? Ironically, outbreaks were indirectly caused by the same improvements in hygiene and sanitation that helped curb the spread of such infectious disease as typhoid fever and cholera around the turn of the century. Experts believe that before today's industrialized nations adopted sanitary sewage disposal and other hygienic practices in the 1800's, the polio virus was so abundant in densely populated areas that many people first encountered it in infancy.

Such early exposure to the disease actually can be beneficial. Very young infants are temporarily protected against many diseases by *maternal antibodies,* germ-killing proteins that pass to the child from the mother before birth and during breast-feeding. These antibodies presumably kept infected babies from succumbing to the disease, while early exposure to the virus in the environment caused their own immune systems to create antibodies that would protect them against the polio virus later in life.

By the early 1900's, improved sanitation had produced a less hospitable environment for the polio virus, making the virus less prevalent so that people rarely encountered it. When people did, they tended to be older and no longer protected by maternal antibodies. If they had not been exposed to the virus before, they had no antibodies of their own and thus were more likely to become ill. And, because a large percentage of the people in contact with an infected individual had never been exposed to the polio virus, they, too, were likely to be infected and become ill, leading to an ever-widening circle of infected people—an epidemic.

As outbreaks occurred summer after summer throughout the

Two of the strongest warriors in the battle against polio, President Franklin D. Roosevelt, *below left,* seated at left, and Basil O'Connor, president of the National Foundation for Infantile Paralysis, met with Sister Elizabeth Kenny in 1943. Kenny, *below,* helped revolutionize the rehabilitation of polio patients by encouraging them to exercise their impaired limbs.

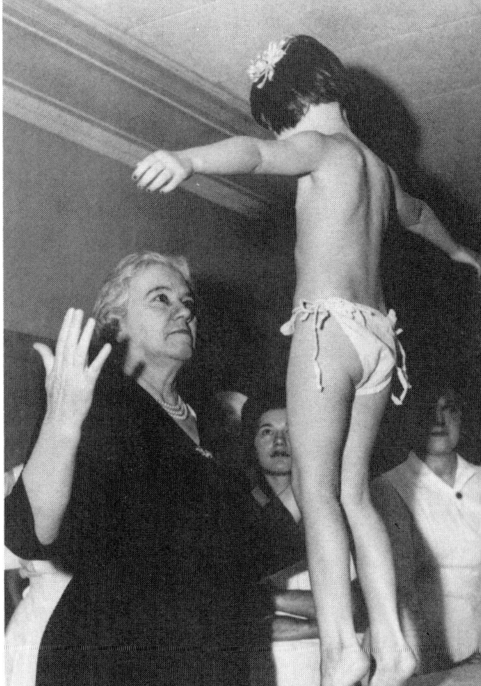

early 1900's, research physicians hunted for ways to cure, prevent, or treat the disease. In 1928, medical researchers Philip Drinker and Louis A. Shaw of the Harvard University School of Public Health in Boston invented the iron lung, a device designed to save the lives of polio survivors left with paralysis so severe that they were unable to breathe. A metal tank that enclosed the entire body of the patient except the head, the iron lung worked like a bellows; air repeatedly filled the tank and then was pumped out. As the tank was filled, the air pressed down on the patient's body, forcing the patient to exhale. As the tank emptied, the patient's chest expanded, causing air to flow into the lungs.

Iron lungs kept some patients alive until their breathing muscles regained enough strength to operate alone. Many people, however, were confined to iron lungs for all or part of every day for the rest of their lives.

Treatment for survivors whose breathing was unimpaired but whose limbs were paralyzed remained unchanged for decades. Doctors typically advised their patients to rest, and some physicians favored complete immobilization of the patient, often enclosing the paralyzed limbs in plaster casts. But in 1940, such notions were challenged by a nurse named Elizabeth Kenny.

A vigorous Australian, Sister Kenny (as she was called after she had achieved the status of head nurse) had traveled to the United States to promote her controversial view that survivors of paralytic polio should be encouraged to exercise their weakened limbs. To traditionalists, this was like ordering people recovering from pneumonia to sit outside in the dead of winter. But Kenny's methods were successful in some patients, proving that exercise can strengthen and retrain many muscles paralyzed by polio. The U.S. medical establishment was eventually won over, and her methods are, with some modification, still used today.

While people like Drinker, Shaw, and Kenny were developing ways to treat polio patients, others sought a polio vaccine to prevent the disease. But in 1935, testing of a crudely concocted vaccine developed by a scientist at Temple University in Philadelphia killed six children and left three paralyzed. The scientific community was appalled, and the search for a vaccine was virtually stopped.

This began to change when U.S. President Franklin D. Roosevelt—whose legs had been paralyzed in a 1921 bout with polio—launched a series of annual fund drives to fight paralytic polio and support a therapy center he established at Warm Springs, Ga. Motivated by an understandably keen desire to wipe out polio, Roosevelt founded the National Foundation for

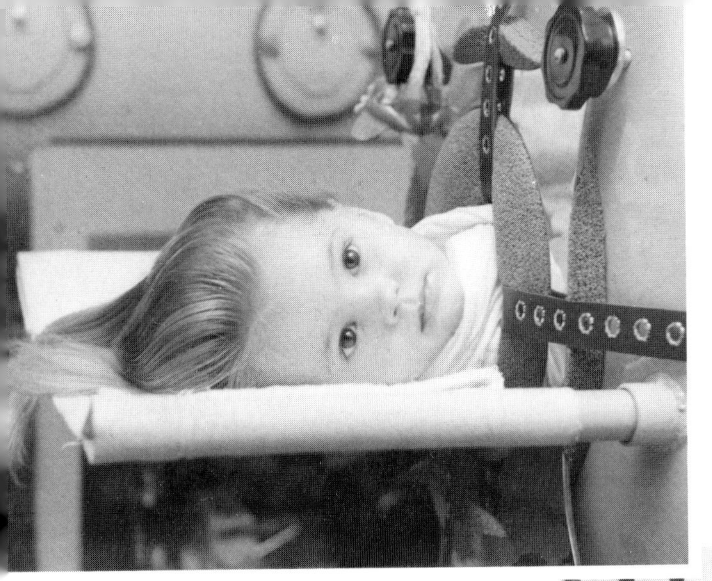

Helping polio victims breathe

Every parent's worst fears were evoked by images of polio-stricken children whose breathing muscles, as well as limbs, were paralyzed. Only the use of respirators prevented such patients from suffocating. A portable chest respirator aided a 3-year-old boy, *below,* and two young girls, *left* and *bottom left,* were assisted by "iron lungs," respirators that encased the entire body, leaving only the head exposed. As the polio epidemics worsened in the 1950's, polio victims in iron lungs filled some hospital wards, *bottom right.*

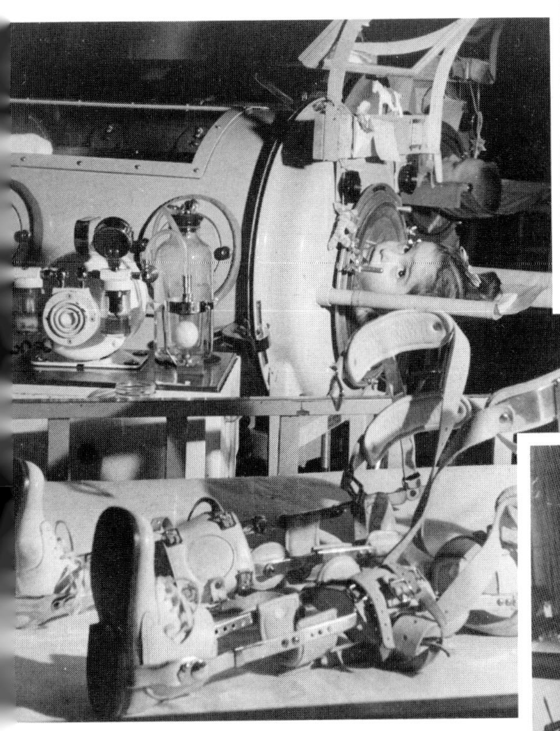

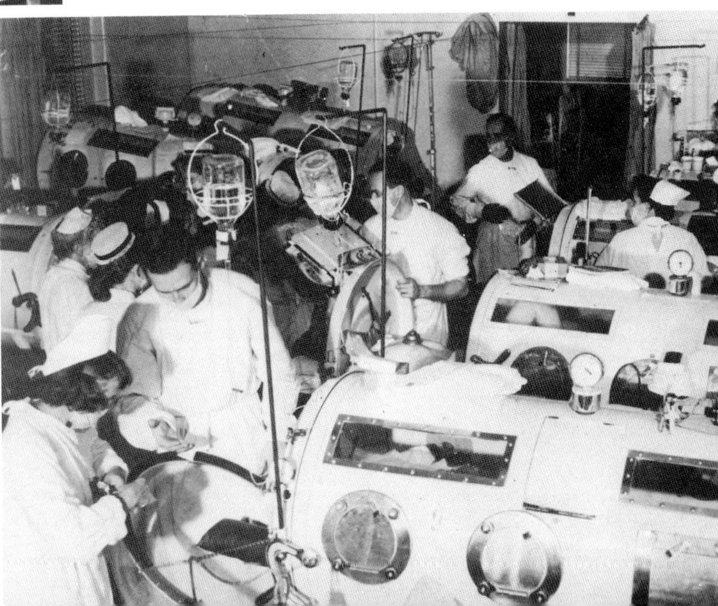

Rivals in the race to find a vaccine
Albert B. Sabin, *right,* thought a polio vaccine should contain living polio viruses—while Jonas E. Salk, *far right,* advocated using killed viruses. The scientific debate they began in the 1950's still continues today.

Infantile Paralysis in 1938 "to lead, direct, and unify the fight on every phase of this sickness."

The foundation asked people to send dimes directly to the White House to help in the fight against the disease—a fund-raising tactic known as the *March of Dimes.* (The organization would in 1958 take the slogan as its name.) Public response to the foundation's drives was enormous. In the first 15 years of the organization's existence, more than 100 million U.S. citizens contributed money.

Under the leadership of Basil O'Connor, an influential lawyer and Roosevelt confidant, the foundation greatly increased medical assistance to polio patients and provided for the education of polio experts and technicians. It established iron lung centers and organized teams of specialists to rush to the scene of polio outbreaks. And most important, the foundation flooded the stagnant research field with financial support, calling for a renewed search for a cure or preventive.

Rather than strike out blindly in search of a vaccine, the foundation decided to emphasize long-term basic studies that would discover exactly how the polio virus affected the human body. The foundation also organized a costly and painstakingly detailed study to determine how many types of the virus existed, information that would be crucial to developing a vaccine that gave complete immunity. Success on this front came in 1949, when a medical researcher named David Bodian and his co-workers at Johns Hopkins University in Baltimore found three distinct types of the virus, all of them capable of causing paralysis and death. Lab techniques were quickly developed for producing and studying the three types of the polio virus.

In 1952, Bodian and Dorothy M. Horstmann, a *pediatrician* (specialist in childhood diseases) at Yale University in New Haven, Conn., independently discovered that the virus invaded the bloodstream shortly after it infected the digestive tract. This meant that vaccine-induced antibodies circulating in the bloodstream could overcome the virus before it invaded the spinal cord and caused permanent damage.

As the search for a vaccine intensified, a rivalry arose over what would be the best type of vaccine to pursue. Albert B. Sabin, then a University of Cincinnati medical researcher, was a vocal proponent of the widely held theory that a polio vaccine should contain living, though weakened, polio viruses. In theory, the weakened viruses would not cause disease but would nonetheless prompt the body to manufacture antibodies, thus giving protection from polio.

Sabin's intellectual opponent was Jonas E. Salk, a medical researcher then working at the University of Pittsburgh. Salk, who during World War II helped develop a flu vaccine made from a virus that had been killed with chemicals, feared that a weakened but living virus could *mutate* (change) into a stronger, more dangerous polio virus as it multiplied in the body. Salk believed that a safer vaccine could be made from killed polio viruses. Sabin, on the other hand, rejected Salk's approach in the belief that a killed-virus vaccine would not be potent enough to give effective, long-lasting protection.

By the early 1950's, while the rivals labored out of the public eye, ordinary citizens endured the terror of the annual polio epidemics. The mood of the times was in some ways similar to that of the 1980's—except that today AIDS (acquired immune deficiency syndrome) is the infectious disease claiming

An effective vaccine at last

Salk's killed-virus vaccine was tested on nearly 2 million schoolchildren during field trials in 1954, *below left.* When the federal government approved the vaccine for widespread use, relieved Americans poured out their thanks in speeches, letters, telegrams—and hand-lettered signs, *below.*

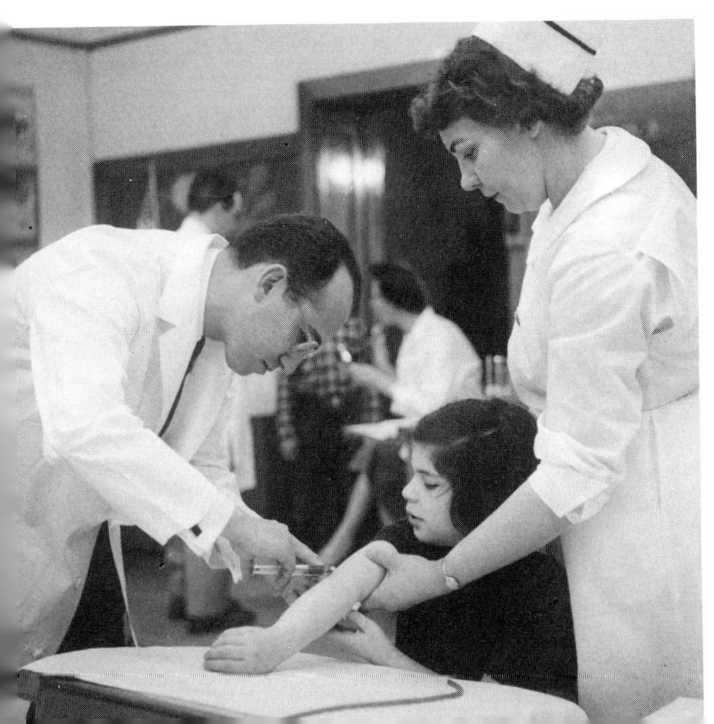

New Yorkers lined up for free polio vaccination shots in 1959 after a resurgence of polio cases prompted health officials in many cities to step up the drive to get everyone vaccinated.

attention. Both periods saw thousands of Americans struck down by a viral disease while the medical community scrambled to fight it.

Although AIDS is more often fatal than polio, polio is much more easily spread and, throughout the early 1950's, parents wondered whether this would be the year their child fell victim. In some communities, polio outbreaks prompted authorities to ban children from theaters, restaurants, and candy stores and from any kind of group play. Some summer camps, beaches, and swimming pools stayed closed all summer.

A brief glimmer of hope appeared in 1953, when the public learned that injections of *gamma globulin,* an antibody-containing preparation made from human blood, might help combat polio. Gamma globulin extracts can provide temporary immunity—similar to the protection afforded by maternal antibodies—to certain infections, including a form of viral hepatitis, a liver ailment.

Special health clinics stayed open late into the night distributing their limited supplies of the preparation. As gamma globulin became scarce, the parents of some polio victims bribed health officials to obtain it, and in New York City, a noisy mob of parents laid siege to the city's Health Department. The hysteria was founded on nothing but faint hope, however. Gamma globulin was effective against polio only in people who had not yet developed symptoms, and it produced immunity for only a few weeks. People continued to pray for a real breakthrough in polio research.

Later in 1953, that breakthrough finally came. In March, Salk had reported that he had developed a vaccine that, in limited tests, successfully protected children and young adults against polio. Called *inactivated poliovirus vaccine* (IPV), the vaccine contained viruses that had been chemically killed yet could trigger production of antibodies against all three types of the virus. A medical advisory committee reviewed the results of Salk's tests and in December agreed that IPV should be tested more extensively.

In 1954, Salk's vaccine was tested in the largest medical field trial in U.S. history—a test involving nearly 2 million schoolchildren, conducted by the University of Michigan School of Public Health under the direction of Thomas Francis, Jr., an *epidemiologist* (specialist in the study of epidemics). A Gallup Poll conducted that year showed that more Americans knew about the field trial than could remember then-President Dwight David Eisenhower's full name.

On April 12, 1955, amid much fanfare and in front of dozens of television cameras and radio microphones, Francis announced that the trials proved that the Salk vaccine was safe and effective and could indeed prevent paralytic polio. Hailed as "the most spectacular new medical product since penicillin," IPV would be licensed by the government immediately, in time for the upcoming polio season.

The announcement inspired almost as much jubilation as a cure for cancer or AIDS would cause today. Americans honked horns, fired salutes, and rang bells. Schools were closed in honor of the occasion. Salk received truckloads of mail and a 208-foot-long telegram. Tearful women kissed his hands, and Congress gave him a medal. President Eisenhower's voice broke with emotion as he told the sudden celebrity, "I have no words to thank you. I am very, very happy."

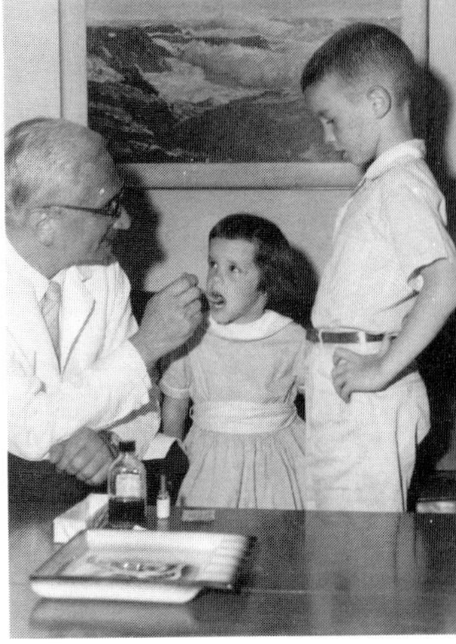

Sabin, shown giving a child a dose of his live-virus vaccine, found that his preparation soon became the vaccine of choice in the United States after it was federally licensed in 1961.

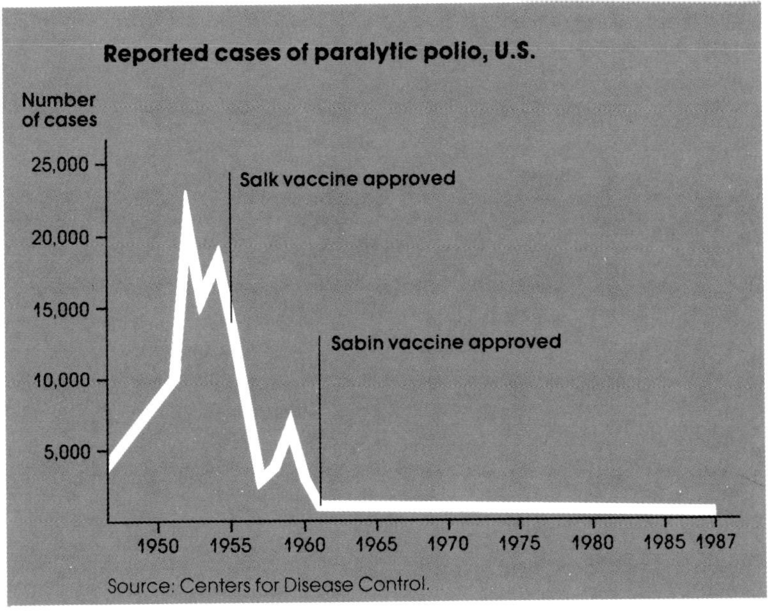

One of medicine's greatest success stories is dramatically shown by the sharp decline in the number of cases of the paralytic form of polio. In 1952, there were 21,269 cases in the United States; in 1987, none.

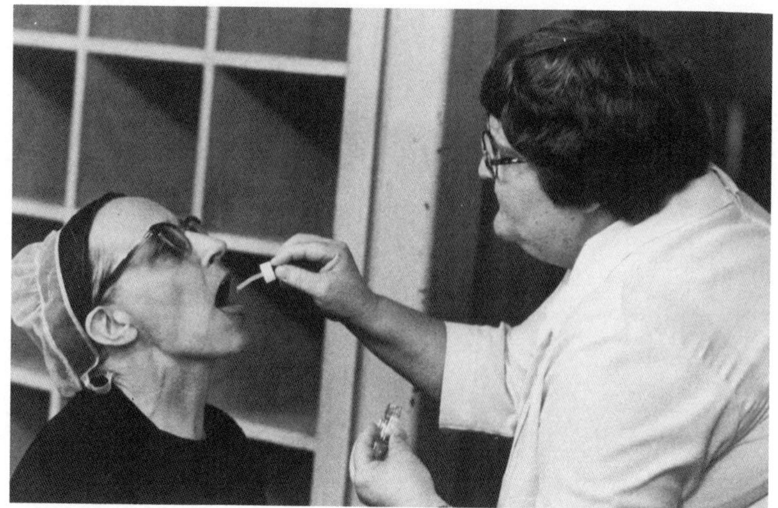

An Amish woman was among many who received live-virus vaccine during a 1979 polio outbreak among Canadian and U.S. members of the religious group. Epidemiologists traced the source of infection to foreign travelers who inadvertently brought the polio virus to the Amish communities. There it was easily spread because many Amish avoided vaccination as an intrusion of outside society.

The public celebration—and a nationwide vaccination program—were quickly cut short. A bad batch of vaccine manufactured by one of the many pharmaceutical firms producing IPV apparently caused 260 cases of polio and 11 deaths. By the end of May, however, the U.S. Public Health Service issued stricter manufacturing guidelines and, despite moderately dampened public zeal, vaccination resumed.

In 1955, 10 million children were injected with the Salk vaccine, and the number of polio cases dropped by 25 per cent from the previous year. By 1957, more than half of all U.S. citizens under age 40 had received at least one of the three doses of vaccine needed for protection against all three types of the polio virus. By 1961, the incidence of polio had been reduced by 96 per cent from levels of the early 1950's.

Meanwhile, Sabin had continued working on a live-virus vaccine. In 1961, the federal government approved his *oral poliovirus vaccine* (OPV), which contained weakened, living polio viruses. It could be given as a few drops of liquid placed in the mouth or on a sugar cube to be eaten.

In 1962, OPV was introduced to the public through a massive publicity campaign funded by drug companies, the American Medical Association, the U.S. Public Health Service, and state and local health services and medical societies. New mass vaccination programs were launched, and in the United States, the Sabin vaccine quickly replaced Salk's IPV as the polio preventive of choice. Some developed nations, especially the Scandinavian countries, saw no need to abandon IPV, however, and never made the switch.

Both vaccines can be credited with one of medicine's greatest successes. In the four years before the polio vaccine was first used, an average of 16,000 cases of paralytic polio were reported in the United States each year. By the early 1980's, the figure had dropped to 10.

But the killed-virus versus live-virus debate is far from dead. Modern proponents of OPV list several advantages for a live vaccine: It is easier to administer than IPV, and, because it is given orally, it causes the body to produce antibodies in the digestive system and not solely in the bloodstream. Another advantage—known as the "herd effect"—is that the harmless virus lives in the digestive tract long enough to be spread to other people, immunizing them as well.

Those who back the use of IPV argue that there is no substantial evidence to prove that the two vaccines differ in their ability to provide protection against polio. They also question the importance of OPV's ability to produce antibodies in the digestive tract and pass the virus to others.

But the weightiest argument of those who favor IPV is a phenomenon that most researchers acknowledge as fact—that most of the 10 or so annual cases of paralytic polio in the United States today are actually caused by OPV. As Salk had predicted, the weakened virus sometimes—though rarely—mutates into a more dangerous form. Indeed, in recent legal cases, drug companies have been ordered to pay huge sums of money to polio sufferers who claimed to have contracted the disease after they—or someone close to them—received an OPV vaccination.

Nevertheless, OPV-associated paralytic polio is rare, amounting to 1 case for every 2.6 million doses of vaccine. Certain peo-

Reported cases of polio worldwide*

Region	Cases
Africa	1,847
North, Central, and South Americas	865
Asia and Western Pacific Islands	23,310
Middle East	3,604
Europe	264

*1985, latest available statistics.

Source: World Health Organization.

Polio continues to cripple thousands of people every year in nonindustrial nations. The World Health Organization estimates that 10 times more cases actually occur than are reported.

Nearly 90 per cent of the children in the African country of Somalia were immunized during a recent World Health Organization campaign. The child shown at the left in 1986 received a dose of live-virus polio vaccine.

Vaccination is still a necessity to protect against a recurrence of polio epidemics. Doctors recommend that parents adhere to the inoculation schedule shown here so that children are completely immunized.

Recommended polio vaccination schedule for children*

	Vaccine type	
	OPV (live virus)	**IPV (killed virus)**
First dose	Age 6 to 12 weeks	Age 6 to 12 weeks
Second dose	6 to 8 weeks after first dose	4 to 8 weeks after first dose
Third dose	At least 6 weeks after second dose, usually at age 8 to 12 months	4 to 8 weeks after second dose
Fourth dose	None	6 to 12 months after third dose
Booster	Age 4 to 6 years	Age 4 to 6 years, then every five years until age 18
Risks	Extremely small risk that the child or contacts will develop paralytic polio	Possible allergic reaction in children who are sensitive to streptomycin and neomycin, two vaccine ingredients

*Unvaccinated adults should follow an immunization schedule recommended by their doctors.
Source: Centers for Disease Control.

ple are more vulnerable than others. For example, children suffering from AIDS and other diseases involving an impaired immune system have a much greater risk of developing vaccine-associated polio than healthy children. Thus, the Centers for Disease Control in Atlanta, Ga., has recommended that IPV rather than OPV be given to children and young adults who have AIDS or other immune-deficiency diseases. The agency also warns against giving OPV to healthy children living in a household with an AIDS patient because vaccine viruses shed by the child could infect the AIDS patient with polio.

In light of this problem, in 1988 a panel of medical experts organized by the U.S. Public Health Service began discussing whether to recommend that physicians use a newly developed, more potent formulation of IPV instead of OPV. In May, the panel recommended that physicians continue to use OPV for most children in the United States, but suggested that parents be given the option of having their children vaccinated with IPV instead.

It would be wrong to suggest that polio's widespread devastation has ended, however. In the early 1980's, physicians noted another continuing problem associated with polio. Survivors of this century's polio epidemics had begun developing strange new symptoms, including fatigue, muscle weakness and pain, and breathing difficulties. Many of those who had worked hard to regain muscular strength once again developed trouble walking, climbing stairs, dressing, or getting in and out of wheelchairs. Some polio survivors have had to be hospitalized.

These symptoms are now known as *postpolio syndrome*. About 1 in 4 of the 300,000 U.S. survivors of paralytic polio have been affected. The cause of these delayed effects may be that the polio virus remains in the spinal cord, slowly destroying nerve cells for years after the initial infection, according to a report published in May 1988 by researchers at two federal health agencies.

Physicians are treating these patients with extra rest, painkillers, and the use of respirators if breathing becomes difficult. New research into the syndrome is supported by the federal government and various philanthropic organizations.

And polio is still with us in an even more tragic way. Despite the fact that the naturally occurring polio virus has been virtually wiped out in the United States, Canada, Japan, Australia, New Zealand, and most of Europe, developing nations are still in the thick of the battle against the disease. Each year polio strikes about 275,000 people in Africa, Asia, and Latin America. Only 1 in 200 of those infected displays polio symptoms, but among those who do, 1 in 10 dies. The situation is especially tragic given the existence of two effective vaccines.

In 1977, the World Health Organization (WHO), an agency of the United Nations, launched a global campaign to vaccinate all children in developing nations against polio and five other diseases by 1990. Currently, $500 million is spent on this campaign each year. In Brazil, Cuba, and Mexico, massive polio vaccination drives, usually with OPV, have met with success. In many other countries, however, inadequate programs and the difficulty of keeping vaccine preparations cool during transport and storage continue to hamper the effort. In these areas, polio epidemics are common.

Nonetheless, the goal of eradicating polio from the face of the earth is within reach. Like smallpox, another dread disease that once devastated humanity—but which was completely eliminated by vaccination in the late 1970's—polio should eventually succumb to the skill, hard work, sacrifice, and genius of generations of people.

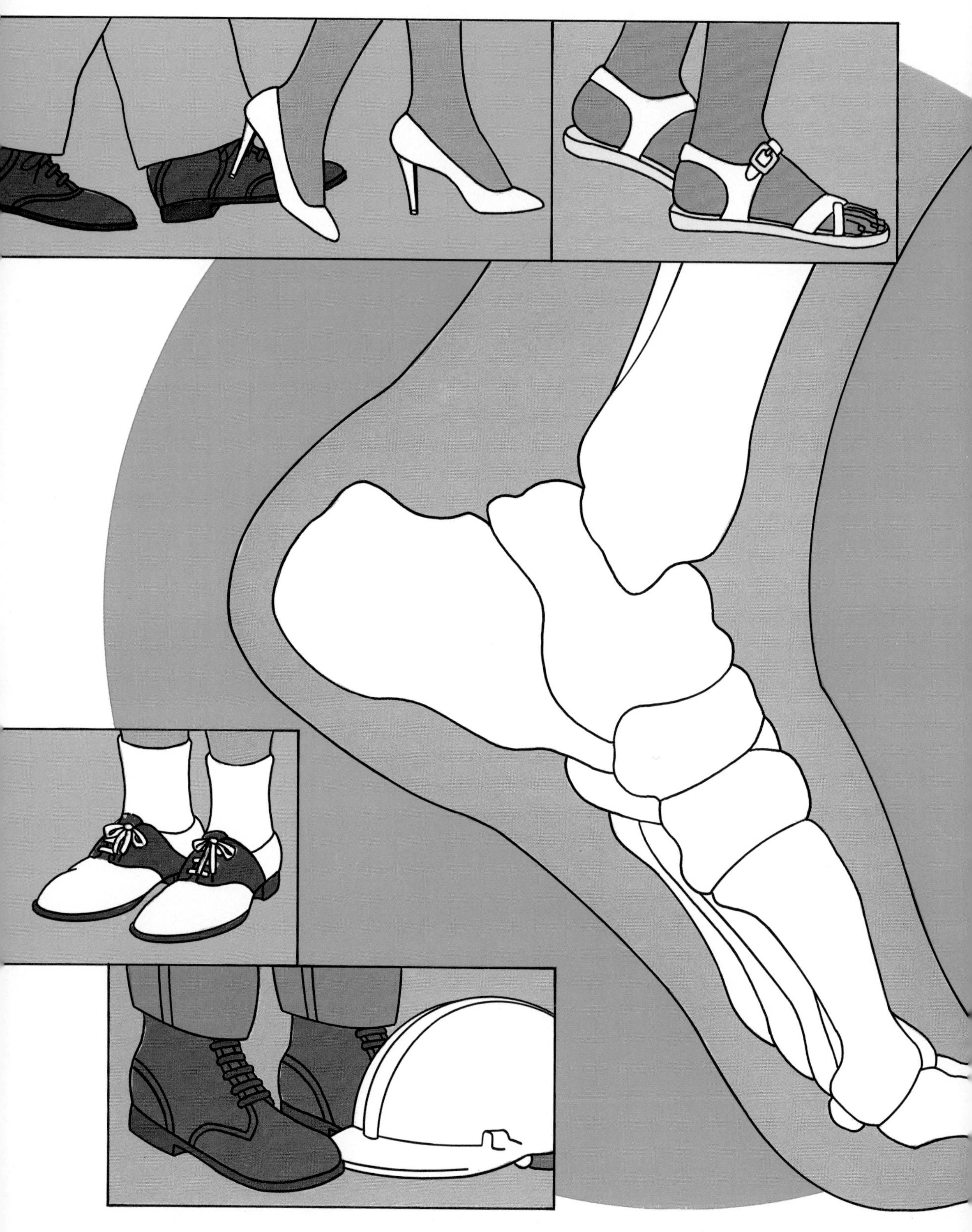

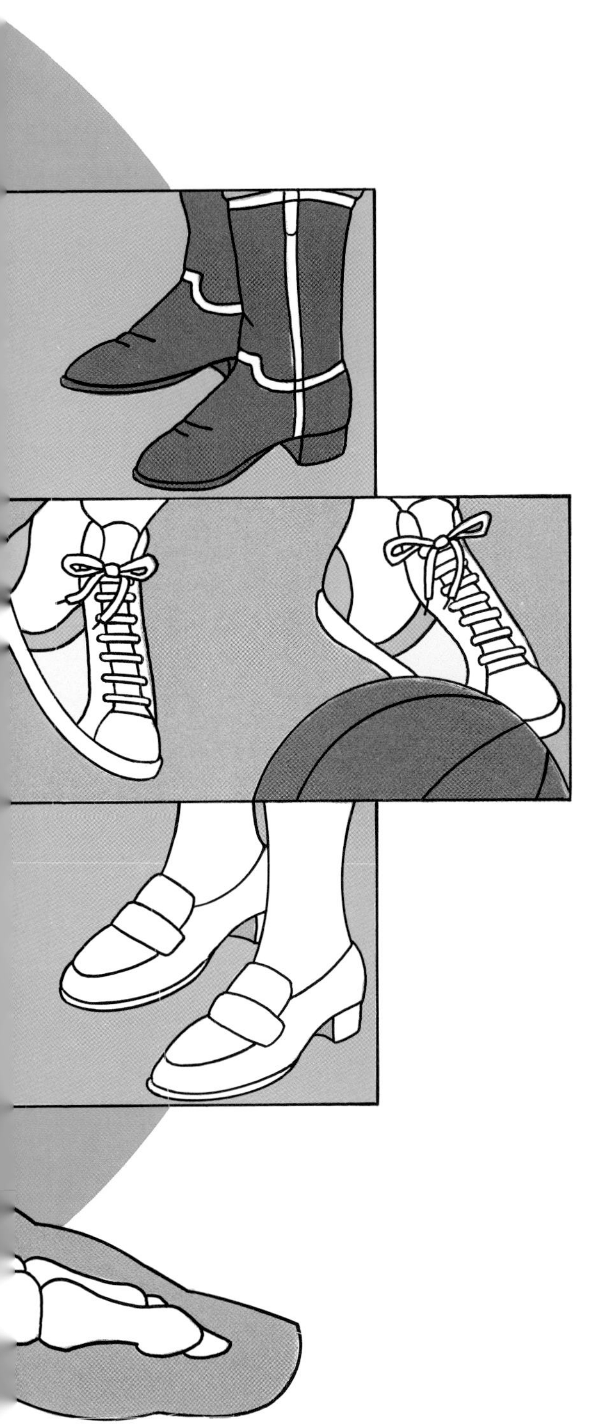

Most of us suffer from foot problems at some time in our lives. Proper care and the right shoes can help prevent some common ailments.

Taking Steps to Better Foot Care

By Beverly Merz

In a familiar Aesop's fable, the Greek slave Androcles removes a thorn from the paw of a lion, who later spares the man's life when the two face each other in combat in the Roman arena. The official moral of the story is, "Gratitude is the sign of noble souls." It might just as well have been, "Few things are more aggravating than a sore foot."

Aesop established aching feet as a symbol of distress 2,500 years ago, and millions of people through the ages have learned firsthand that feet take a lot of punishment. Each day, our feet hit the ground 15,000 to 20,000 times as we sprint to catch a bus, charge up a flight of stairs, or simply walk around in the house or at work. In a lifetime, our feet log a distance equal to four treks around the world.

Fortunately, the human foot is usually equal to such demands. More than 400 years ago, the great Italian painter and scientist Leonardo da Vinci, one of the first to analyze its structure, pronounced it "a masterpiece of engineering and a work of art." What Leonardo found was a scaffold of 26 bones hinged at 33 joints, linked by 107 bands of tissue called *ligaments*, and powered by 19 muscles.

But because the foot is so complex, any number of things can go wrong with it. In fact, up to 80 per cent of Americans seek medical care for foot complaints at some point in their lives. And the cost of relief adds up; Americans spend an estimated $350 million on over-the-counter remedies and $4 billion on foot surgery in a single year.

A brief look at foot anatomy

Unfortunately, many of us are victims of our anatomy, born with a tendency to develop certain foot problems. Various structural malformations, such as bones that do not align properly or connective tissues that are too short or too elastic, are at the root of many common foot complaints.

The human foot contains nearly one-fourth of the total number of bones in the body. The hind foot or back part of the foot consists of two of the foot's seven *tarsal* bones; these are the anklebone, or *talus*, and the foot's largest bone, the heel bone, or *calcaneus*. The middle section of the foot is composed of the remaining five tarsal bones, which together form the rear part of the instep, the portion of the human foot between the hind foot and the toes. The front part of the instep consists of five *metatarsal bones*, which join the 14 toe bones, or *phalanges*, to form the ball of the foot. The big toe has two phalanges, and each of the remaining toes has three.

The bones of the foot are joined to form three arches, which provide the natural spring of the foot during walking, running, or jumping. The main arch, called the *longitudinal*, *plantar*, or *medial arch*, runs lengthwise along the inside of the foot, from the heel to the ball. A second, less pronounced arch called the *lateral* arch runs along the outside of the foot, parallel to the longitudinal arch. The third arch, the *transverse* or *metatarsal* arch, runs across the ball of the foot.

The arches are supported by ligaments, in much the same way as cables support a bridge. These ligaments, which expand and contract like elastic bands, absorb the impact as the foot strikes the ground. A layer of fat cushions the sole, or *plantar side*, of the foot. The skin on the sole, 10 times thicker than the skin on the rest of the body, adds further protection.

The structure of the foot determines how each step affects other parts of the body. For example, people with high-arched feet may be bothered by back, hip, and knee pains because high arches are poor shock absorbers. Low arches distribute

The author:

Beverly Merz is an associate editor of *The Journal of the American Medical Association.*

Boning up on foot anatomy

Twenty-six bones make up the basic supporting structure of the foot, *below*. They include 14 toe bones (phalanges) and 5 metatarsal bones in the front of the foot, 5 tarsal bones in the middle of the foot, and 2 tarsal bones—the ankle bone (talus) and heel bone (calcaneus)—in the back of the foot. Phalanges are shown in green, metatarsals are shown in purple, and tarsals are shown in blue.

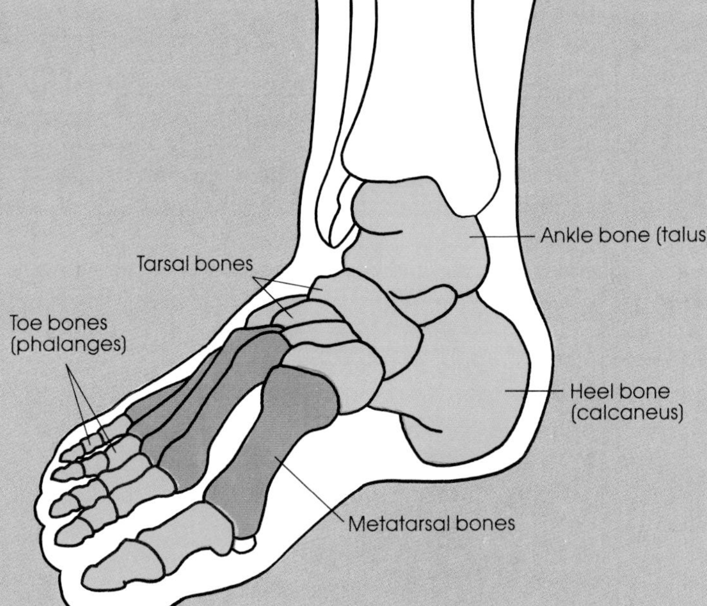

The body's weight is primarily distributed on two areas of the foot, the ball and heel of the foot, *below*.

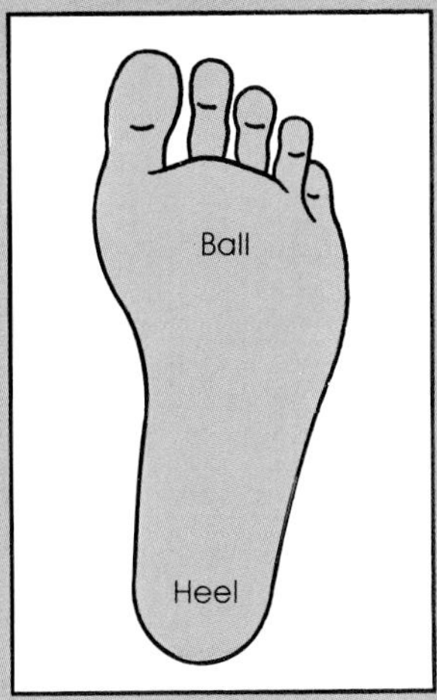

the impact evenly, but do not provide much spring to the step. For that reason, people with low arches may be spared leg and back pain, but they are unlikely to excel at sports that require a great deal of mobility.

Structural disorders: flat feet and other complaints

Not surprisingly, in addition to causing back, hip, and knee pain, structural malformations of the foot can lead to painful disorders of the foot itself. Common structural problems include fallen arches, bunions, and hammertoes.

Fallen arches. *Pronated arches*—popularly called flat feet or

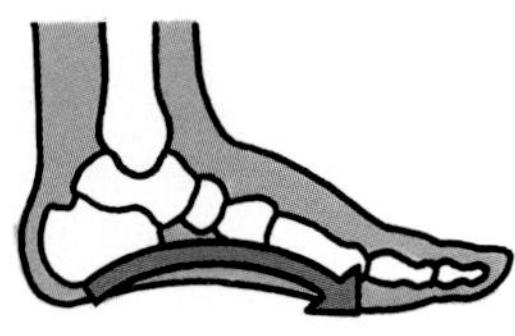

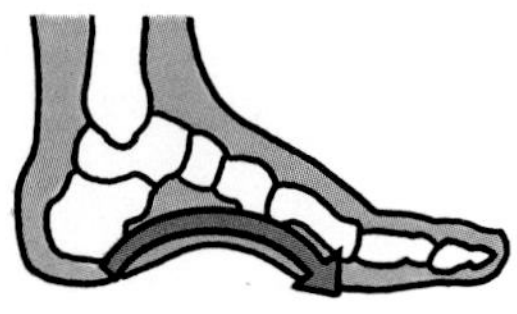

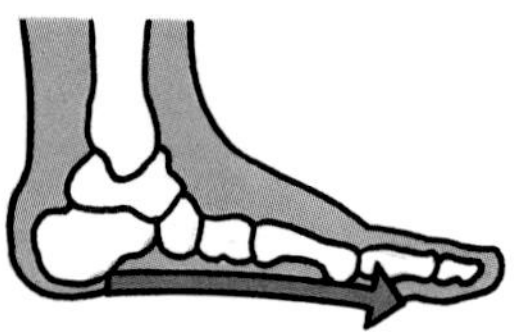

About arches
The bones of the foot are joined to form the longitudinal arch, *top* (indicated by red arrow). The longitudinal arch and two smaller arches provide the natural spring in the step. High-arched feet, *middle*, are poor shock absorbers and may lead to back, hip, and knee pain. Low, relaxed arches, called fallen arches, *bottom*, may bring on pain in the feet, legs, and back.

fallen arches—result when the tissues that normally support the arches are too weak to distribute the body's weight properly on the ball and heel of the foot. Instead, the ligaments stretch too far, causing the longitudinal arch to collapse rather than merely flatten.

People with severe fallen arches walk with their feet turned out and their ankles turned in—rather like children learning to ice-skate. Although some people with fallen arches experience little discomfort, others find that walking or even standing produces pain in the feet, legs, and lower back.

Severe fallen arches may require surgery to tighten the ligaments and realign the bones, but most cases can be treated with custom-designed shoe inserts made of rigid plastic, leather, or a foamlike material. These inserts, called *orthotics*, redistribute the body's weight on the foot. Because orthotics are custom-fitted and handmade, they may cost hundreds of dollars.

Bunions. Fallen arches, as well as an improper alignment of the metatarsals, may lead to a *bunion*—a bony protrusion along the inside edge of the foot at the base of the big toe. A similar bony prominence, called a *bunionette*, can occur at the outside edge of the foot, at the base of the fifth toe.

A bunion develops when the metatarsal bone that connects to the big toe shifts toward the inner side of the foot, forcing the big toe toward the center of the foot. Eventually, the head of the metatarsal creates a bump on the side of the foot—the bunion—and the big toe begins to crowd the second toe.

Some people appear to have an inherited tendency to develop bunions. Bunions also may develop with arthritis. And poorly fitting shoes can hasten the development of bunions and aggravate the problem in bunion-prone individuals. Shoes that are too narrow can press against a bunion and irritate the *bursa*, the sac of fluid that cushions the joint. The bunion then becomes red, swollen, and painful, a condition called *bursitis*. If the swelling persists, it may be necessary to drain the bursa by drawing off fluid with a needle and syringe.

People with small bunions or bunionettes may find relief by selecting shoes that do not rub against the protrusion or by wearing orthotics that straighten the misaligned joint somewhat. Prescription shoes with an extra wide forefoot (front of the shoe) also may help. While these approaches do not eliminate bunions or bunionettes, they can make it easier to live with them and help avoid more drastic measures.

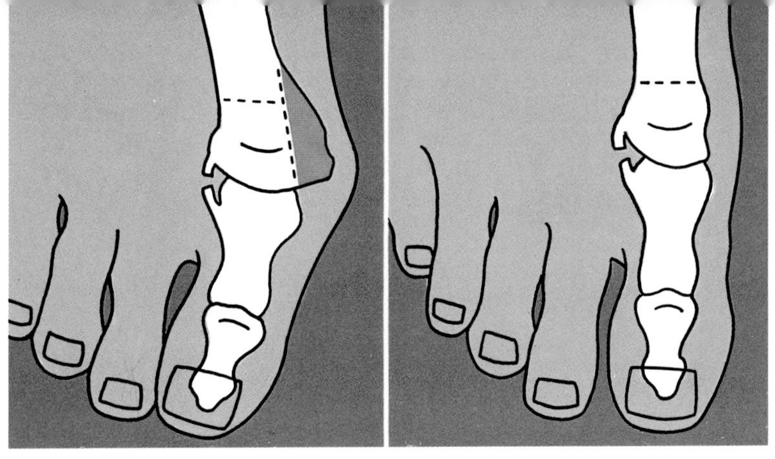

Bunion
A bunion, *far left*, is a bony protrusion (area shaded in purple) along the inside of the foot, at the base of the big toe. In a bunion, the bones are misaligned so that the big toe is forced toward the center of the foot. Severe bunions may cause pain and swelling, and may require surgery to bring relief. In this operation, the surgeon usually removes the bony protrusion and cuts a bone (indicated by dotted line) to realign the big toe, *left*.

When nonsurgical methods fail to bring relief, an operation called a *bunionectomy* may be performed. With mild bunions, the surgeon may perform a simple procedure that involves grinding down the bony protrusion through a small incision. But when the misalignment is severe, extensive surgery to realign the bones may be necessary.

Hammertoes are abnormalities in which the smaller toes buckle up, creating clawlike digits. The first joint of a hammertoe—the joint at the base of the toe—is raised, and the end joints bend down. Although hammertoes usually don't affect balance or walking, they may rub against the shoe, producing thickenings of the skin called *corns* and *calluses*.

Most hammertoes develop because some of the foot's *tendons*—thick, strong bands of tissue that attach muscle to bone—are too short. As a result of this defect, the phalanges of the affected toe are pulled too tightly together, causing the bones to bunch up in a clawlike manner. Permanent correction of a hammertoe requires an operation in which the surgeon snips a tendon or two and removes wedges of bone underlying the joint to flatten the toe.

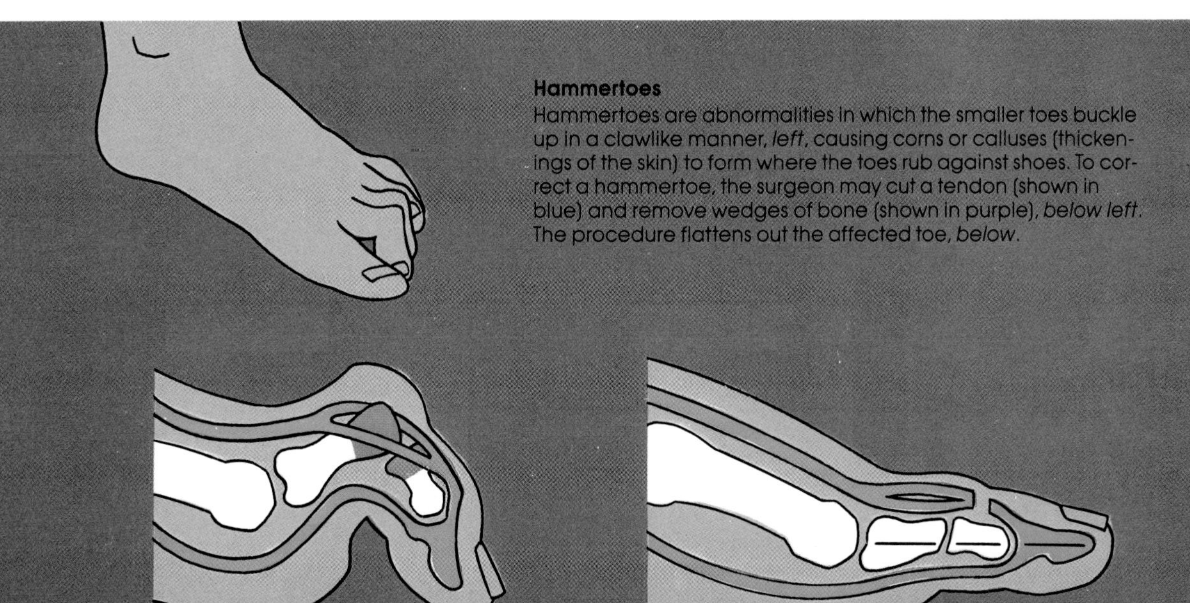

Hammertoes
Hammertoes are abnormalities in which the smaller toes buckle up in a clawlike manner, *left*, causing corns or calluses (thickenings of the skin) to form where the toes rub against shoes. To correct a hammertoe, the surgeon may cut a tendon (shown in blue) and remove wedges of bone (shown in purple), *below left*. The procedure flattens out the affected toe, *below*.

Skin disorders of the foot

Corns and calluses are thickenings of skin caused by rubbing or pressure from shoes. A corn, *below left*, forms on the toes; a callus, *below right*, develops on the heel or ball of the foot. Self-treatment for corns and calluses includes: soaking the area in warm water (1), rubbing it with ointment or oil (2), and gently sanding the area with a pumice stone or a special file designed for foot care (3). People with diabetes or poor circulation should consult a physician.

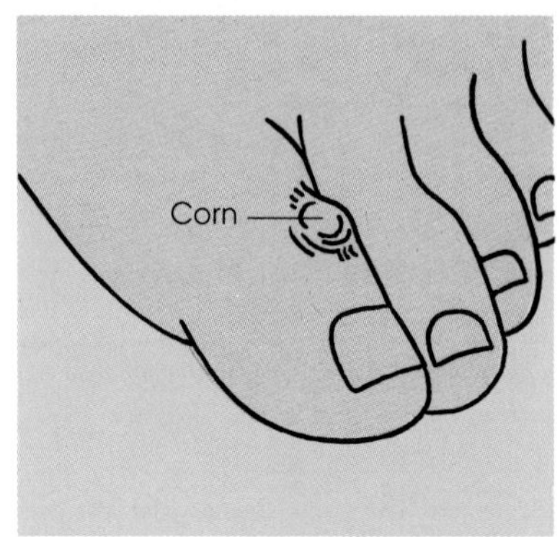

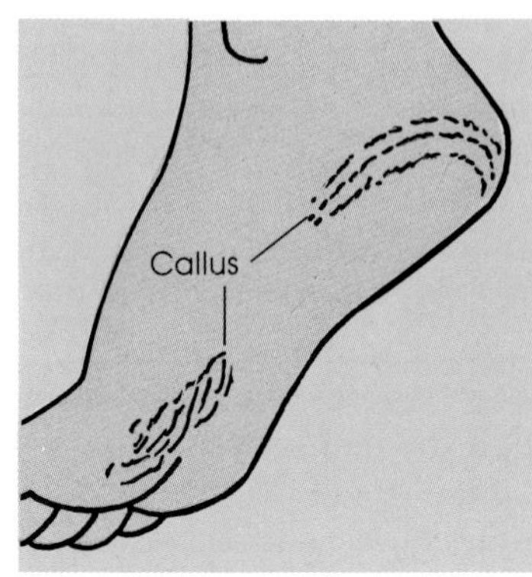

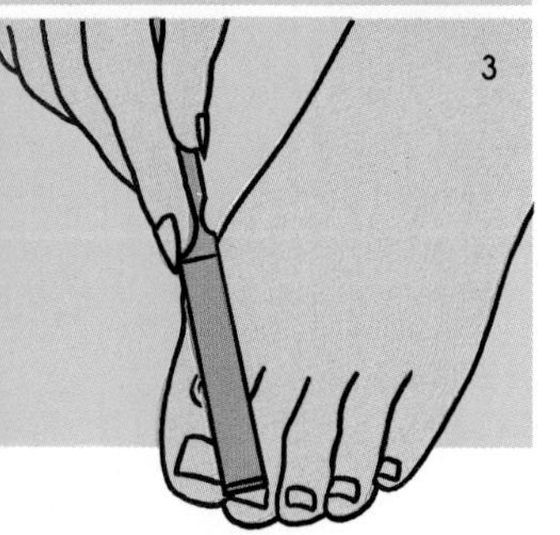

Skin disorders: there's the rub

Skin disorders of the foot—including corns, calluses, and ingrown toenails—are more common, though generally less serious, than structural disorders. Fortunately, most of these skin disorders can be prevented by wearing properly fitting shoes and practicing good foot care.

A corn is a thickening of skin on the toe that develops as a protective response to rubbing or pressure from a shoe. But as the corn grows larger and harder, it becomes a source of pain, like a pebble wedged between the toe and the shoe.

One long-standing piece of medical lore—that corns are often particularly painful before and during storms—is not just a popular misconception. Small sacs of fluid, which often develop beneath corns to cushion the bones from outside friction, can transform corns into crude storm-warning devices. As the barometric pressure drops in response to a passing storm front, the fluid in the sac expands, causing the sac to press painfully against the base of the corn.

Experts advise against trying to cut away a corn or attempting to dissolve it with an over-the-counter acid preparation. Such self-treatment can lead to infection of the bones and joints. Instead, doctors recommend soaking the toe in warm water for 10 minutes, drying it thoroughly, and rubbing some ointment or vegetable oil into it to further soften the skin. Then the corn should be gently sanded with a pumice stone or file. After most of the dead skin has been removed, the area should be covered with a doughnut-shaped corn pad, with the hole placed over the center of the corn. Nonmedicated corn pads should be used because the chemicals in medicated pads may damage the tissue. (People—especially diabetics and others with impaired blood circulation—should check with a medical doctor or a podiatrist before trying this procedure.)

The best way to keep corns from reappearing is to remove the source of irritation, which in most cases is a shoe that is too short or too narrow. But occasionally, corns may be caused by bone spurs or stray bonelike fragments called calcium deposits that rub against a shoe that is otherwise a good fit. For example, *soft corns,* thickenings of skin between two toes, are caused by pressure from a bone spur. Such bone abnormalities often require surgery to remove the source of the irritation and thus prevent corns from recurring.

Calluses, like corns, are thickenings of skin that develop where shoes press or rub. But because calluses grow in response to pressure spread out over a greater area of the foot, they are larger and flatter than corns. They develop most often on the heel and ball of the foot—the areas that bear the most body weight.

Most calluses can be treated with the softening and sanding procedure recommended for corns. In some cases, better-fitting shoes will prevent calluses from forming. Calluses that are caused by a misalignment of the bones rather than the fit of a shoe are more difficult to prevent, though padding shoes with orthotics or special foam inserts may help. If these measures fail, however, surgical correction of the bone abnormalities may be necessary.

Ingrown toenails. An ingrown toenail is a painful disorder usually caused by improper nail trimming—cutting the nail so that it is rounded, angled, or too short. Then, as the nail grows up from the base, its sides are pushed downward, into the skin. Tight shoes can aggravate the process by pressing down against the nail. Eventually, skin grows up over the sides of the nail, embedding the nail's sharp edges in the fleshy toe.

Fortunately, it is often possible to rescue a toe from an ingrown nail in the early stages. The best approach is to soak the foot in warm water to soften the nail, lift the nail slightly at the tip, and insert a few strands of sterile cotton under the nail at the edges. The cotton relieves the pressure and forms a barrier between the nail and the skin, allowing the nail to grow out.

Ingrown toenails

An ingrown toenail is a painful condition—usually the result of improper nail trimming—in which the sides of the nail become embedded in the surrounding skin, *below left.* Minor surgery may be necessary to correct the condition, a procedure that involves removal of a narrow slice of the toenail, *below center.* Proper nail trimming—cutting the nail straight across, leaving it long enough to extend to the tip of the toe, *below right*—will help prevent an ingrown toenail from developing.

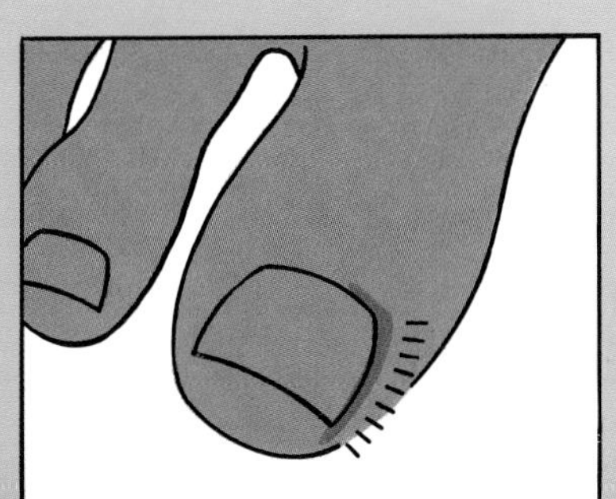

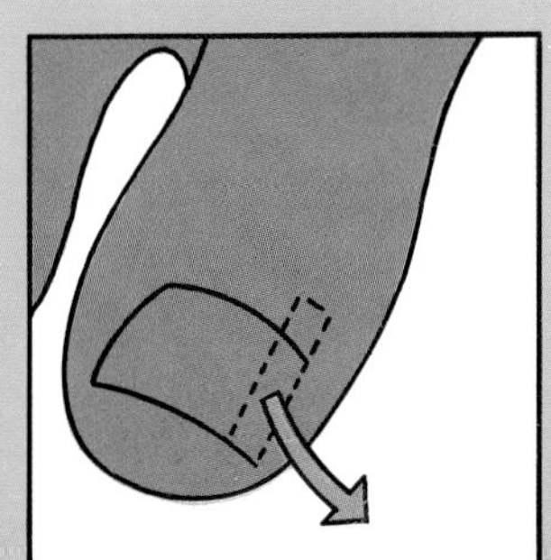

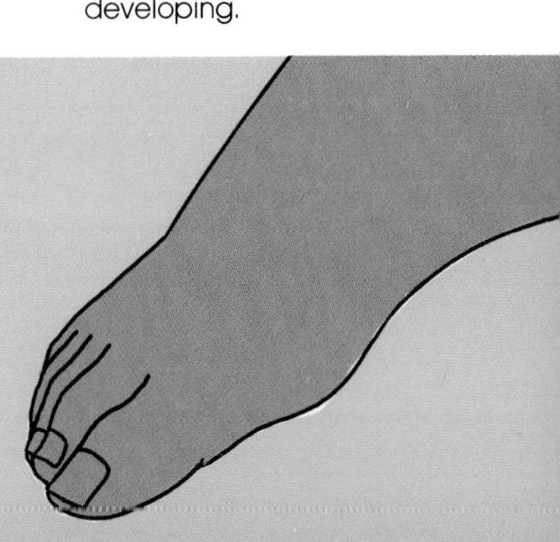

Plantar warts

Plantar warts develop on the sole of the foot, *above,* and may occur as a single wart or as a cluster of warts. Because they are located on a weight-bearing part of the body, plantar warts are pushed inward beneath the surface of the skin and are covered with thickened callus tissue, as shown in the cross-section view of a plantar wart. The underlying wart is pinkish-white and dotted with tiny blood vessels.

If an ingrown nail is not treated in the early stages, bacteria can move into the damaged tissue. The sides of the toe then become red, swollen, and painful.

Correcting an advanced ingrown nail usually requires minor surgery. The surgeon injects the toe with a local anesthetic and then cuts away a narrow slice of the ingrown nail, all the way to the base of the nail. The surgeon then applies acid to the base, to prevent the nail segment from growing back—leaving the patient with a narrower, but healthy, toenail.

Preventing ingrown toenails through proper trimming is much simpler than treating them. Experts offer a simple prescription: Trim the nail straight across, leaving it long enough to extend to the tip of the toe.

Foot infections: warts and all

Unfortunately, our feet are an inviting target for various infections, including plantar warts and athlete's foot and other fungal infections. Encased in shoes and socks, the feet provide a warm, moist environment that encourages the growth of the viruses and fungi that infect the foot.

Plantar warts, noncancerous tumors that occur on the sole of the foot, are caused by a virus that thrives in warm, moist conditions. The virus enters the sole through pores in the skin. Once inside, the virus reproduces, often giving rise to clusters of warts that measure 1 inch (2.5 centimeters) or more across. Plantar warts are smooth, pinkish-white, and dotted with tiny blood vessels. When they develop on areas of the sole that are subject to great pressure, these warts can be painful. The virus also may spread beyond the foot, producing warts on the fingers and other parts of the body. Because corns, calluses, and skin cancers are sometimes mistakenly identified as plantar warts, it is a good idea to have them diagnosed by a doctor.

Although plantar warts may disappear without treatment, many people choose to have them removed, particularly if the warts are painful or unsightly. There are several methods for removing plantar warts, including killing the cells of the wart by freezing them with dry ice, burning them with an electric needle, or destroying them with acid. Deep-seated warts may be cut out with a scalpel or destroyed by a laser device, which uses highly focused light energy to vaporize the tissue. Experts advise against using over-the-counter preparations to dissolve a plantar wart, because these substances can damage healthy tissue surrounding the wart.

The best way to prevent plantar warts is to keep the virus from entering the foot in the first place. Important preventive measures include keeping the feet dry and wearing shoes or sandals around swimming pools and in public showers.

Athlete's foot and other fungal infections. Although bacteria and viruses account for most of the body's infections, a fungus is responsible for the most common skin disease in the United States—athlete's foot. This itching misery can be caused by any one of 20 different types of single-celled fungi that digest skin tissue and thrive in the warm, moist environment of the feet.

The infection often starts between the toes, from where it may spread to the rest of the foot. Most cases begin with small blisters that are usually followed by burning itching between the toes, cracked and peeling skin between the toes and on the soles of the feet, and, in some cases, thickening of the toenails.

Athlete's foot not only spreads easily from one part of the foot to another but also is transmitted readily from person to person. Infected individuals shed the fungi, which can then be picked up by healthy feet, particularly in such places as locker rooms and showers.

Mild cases of athlete's foot often respond to nonprescription powders and ointments containing fungicides such as tolnaftate or miconazole nitrate. In treating a severe case, the doctor may remove a small sample of infected skin to determine what type of fungus has invaded the foot. The results—available in 7 to 10 days—enable the physician to determine the appropriate medication, usually a prescription fungicidal powder or ointment. Particularly severe infections may require an oral medication—a fungicide such as griseofulvin, which is taken by mouth and then enters the bloodstream.

The best way to prevent athlete's foot is to make the foot an

Shoe business

Poorly fitting shoes—particularly shoes with cramped, narrow toes or very high heels—can cause or aggravate many foot problems. Choose a shoe that neither pinches nor slips at the heel, has a roomy *toe box* (front of shoe), and has a heel of moderate height—about 1 to 2 inches (2.5 to 5 centimeters).

inhospitable environment for the fungi. Washing the feet twice daily removes the dead skin that the fungi feed upon, and keeping the feet, shoes, and socks dry reduces the humidity that the fungi require. Wearing well-ventilated shoes made of porous, "breathable" materials such as leather or canvas also helps keep feet dry by allowing foot perspiration to evaporate. Dusting the feet with an over-the-counter fungicide may also help ward off athlete's foot infection.

Fungi also can work their way under the toenails, where they find an ideal hothouse climate. And because toenails are mostly dead tissue, the fungi can go unnoticed for weeks as they break down the nail. Eventually, the nail becomes disfigured and may separate from the underlying skin. By this time, the fungi are so well entrenched that they are difficult to eradicate. The most effective treatment is an oral antifungal drug, which must be taken for months and may have side effects. Even then, once the treatment is stopped, the fungi may return.

Where to go for help

Some ailments, such as corns, calluses, and mild cases of athlete's foot, respond well to simple self-care. But it is important to seek professional help for more complex problems or if you experience persistent pain, redness, or swelling of the feet. Both medical doctors and podiatrists are qualified to diagnose and treat the entire spectrum of foot problems.

Medical doctors are graduates of general medical schools who have earned the degree of doctor of medicine, or M.D., and are licensed to practice medicine in a particular state. Physicians have also completed additional years of training and have passed an examination that certifies them to practice a particular medical specialty.

People with skin infections of the foot may be treated by a dermatologist or a primary care physician, such as a family physician or an internist. Specialists in sports medicine, orthopedists, and some primary care physicians can treat structural foot problems, such as fallen arches. Orthopedists and some general surgeons treat foot patients who need either minor operations, which require only a local anesthetic, or major surgery, which requires general anesthesia.

Podiatrists are health professionals who treat problems of the foot and related structures. They are graduates of schools of podiatry, which, like general medical schools, offer four years of medical training to college graduates. The first two years of the podiatric school curriculum are devoted to general medical subjects, while the last two years of training focus on foot care. Upon graduation, the student receives the D.P.M. degree—doctor of podiatric medicine. Graduates may then choose to take additional residency training of one to three years. Podiatrists who have taken residency training in foot surgery and are certified by the American Podiatric Medical Association may perform both minor and major foot surgery in most states.

Experts agree that no matter which kind of health care professional you consult, surgery should be considered only when a foot ailment is severe and fails to respond to more conservative methods. They also stress that while surgery may provide the only permanent solution to certain foot problems, particularly structural disorders, it is not the answer for everybody. Blood circulation to the foot may be impaired, and feet heal slowly. For diabetics and others with impaired circulation, the surgery may cause problems that are more severe than the fallen arch, bunion, or hammertoe the operation was designed to correct. Finally, experts note that it is always a good idea to seek a second opinion about the need for surgery when considering an operation of any kind.

If the shoe fits. . . .

People can spare themselves a lot of discomfort and expense by taking care of their feet. And while preventing infections begins at home with good hygiene, preventing disorders such as corns and calluses begins at the shoe store.

In the best of all possible worlds, each of us would be able to select an attractive shoe that perfectly accommodates the individual contours of our feet. But because almost all shoes are mass-produced rather than custom-fitted, we can at best hope for a shoe that approximates our foot's length and width.

Nonetheless, even an approximate fit is a radical improvement over shoes of the last century. Until the end of the 1800's, there was no such thing as either a "right" or "left" shoe; the wearer had to suffer through an uncomfortable breaking-in period in which the shoes gradually took on the shape of the foot. Today, we also often assume that new shoes will become more comfortable with each wearing—but shoes that hurt in the store are likely to feel even worse after pounding the pavement. A good-fitting shoe, be it a dress shoe, athletic shoe, or boot, should neither pinch nor slip at the heel and should be wide enough to allow the toes to wiggle freely.

Other factors of shoe construction are also important. Breathable materials, including leather and porous fabrics, are preferable to synthetic materials because they allow the best air circulation, which evaporates foot perspiration. A shoe also should have a rigid back, to provide stability, and a flexible toe, to allow the spring needed in walking. Cushioned insoles of rubber, polyurethane, or thick leather absorb the shock of walking on hard surfaces.

Heels should be selected on the basis of the length of a person's calf muscle. In general, if you cannot easily touch your toes without bending your knees, you probably have relatively short calf muscles and will find that a heel of 1½ to 2 inches (3.7 to 5 centimeters) is the most comfortable height for you. People with longer calf muscles may be more comfortable wearing heels that are no higher than 1 inch (2.5 centimeters).

These rules for choosing shoes also apply to selecting footwear for children, though shoes usually are unnecessary until a child begins to walk. If an infant is wearing shoes for appearance or warmth, they should be soft and should fit loosely. In most cases, children's shoes should have flexible soles.

Men generally have relatively little trouble finding comfortable shoes. It is more difficult for women, who may find the selection dominated by shoes with pointed toes and high, narrow heels—shoes that squash and cramp the toes and pitch the body forward, creating excessive pressure on the ball of the foot. Such shoes promote the formation of corns and calluses and exacerbate bunions and hammertoes. Podiatrists often advise women who want to follow fashion's dictates to wear shoes with high heels and pointed toes only for limited periods and to exchange them for low-heeled shoes or sneakers for walking.

People buying athletic shoes should take into account the demands of the individual sport. For example, running shoes have higher heels than toes, to propel the wearer forward. The flat soles of tennis shoes, on the other hand, provide the stability needed for running from side to side and for quick changes of direction.

Since the days of the Roman Empire, when the color of a man's boot denoted his social standing, shoe styles have been used to make a statement about the wearer's status. For centuries, Chinese nobles bound their daughters' feet in bandages—stunting and deforming the feet—to enable the young women to wear a signature of their class, the tiny "lotus" slipper. In England in the 1500's, the wider the toe of a man's shoe, the more extensive his power. Among French nobility, heels rose to new heights until the French Revolution during the late 1700's, when an official edict sliced them off—along with their aristocratic owners' heads.

In the last 20 years, fashion and life style have led to the emergence of a shoe that many experts think most closely fits all the criteria of perfect footwear—the sneaker. The unprecedented popularity of the sneaker and its variants—the running shoe, the walking shoe, and the aerobics shoe—suggests that Americans have taken to heart the refrain of perhaps the only popular song to extol the virtues of proper foot care, the Beach Boys' "Take a Load off Your Feet." Their advice? "Take good care of your feet . . . nobody else will."

TUNA
SIRRELL

Every year, thousands of people are stricken with salmonellosis, a type of food poisoning. Proper food handling can help prevent it.

Food's Hidden Hazard

By Chris Anne Raymond

What's wrong with this scene? The Smiths and the Joneses are having a barbecue, but in preparing their meal they are making several mistakes that may give them salmonellosis. Can you identify what they are doing wrong? The answers are on page 132.

Answers: On the preceding page, the Smiths and the Joneses are making seven mistakes that could lead to salmonellosis. These are:

- thawing frozen raw chicken on the kitchen counter
- using a knife that came in contact with raw chicken juices to cut vegetables for a salad
- storing cooked chili in a large container
- making turkey salad from turkey that is undercooked
- mixing a batch of cookies using eggs that have cracked shells
- putting cooked hamburgers on a platter that contains raw hamburgers
- leaving barbecued chicken out in the sun.

William True of Crystal Lake, Ill., was admitted to Sherman Hospital in the nearby city of Elgin on March 30, 1985. At the time of his admission, the 53-year-old man had been suffering from vomiting and diarrhea that had begun quite unexpectedly. Given the nature and abrupt onset of his symptoms, the doctors immediately suspected some form of food poisoning. Hospital laboratory tests soon confirmed this suspicion, revealing that True had *salmonellosis,* a type of food poisoning caused by *salmonella* bacteria.

Hospital officials followed established regulations and immediately notified the Illinois Department of Public Health. Such reporting is required because public health experts know that where there is one salmonellosis case there may be others—all of them caused by the same contaminated food source. The value of the reporting system was soon apparent: Within four days of True's hospitalization, the Department of Public Health received notification that 30 other residents in three counties north and west of Chicago had fallen victim to salmonellosis.

Alarmed public health officials swung into action and soon determined that the culprit was milk produced by the Hillfarm Dairy in Melrose Park, Ill. The milk was contaminated with a type of salmonella called *Salmonella typhimurium.* The contamination occurred at the plant when raw milk tainted with salmonella inadvertently got into a batch of pasteurized milk.

By the time the 1985 Hillfarm outbreak ended, medical history had been made. More than 16,000 people in the Chicago area were diagnosed as having contracted salmonellosis. In a study released in December 1987, the Centers for Disease Control (CDC) in Atlanta, Ga.—the federal agency that tracks disease outbreaks and epidemics in the United States—estimated that at least an additional 150,000 people in four states were infected, making this the largest known salmonellosis outbreak in the nation's history. The salmonella-tainted milk probably caused 2 deaths—including William True's—and contributed to 12 others, according to the CDC study.

In contrast to the Hillfarm outbreak—which affected thousands of people—many outbreaks of salmonellosis affect only the members of one household. Take the case of a California family that we'll call the Morgans. In November 1987, Jane Morgan picked up a dozen eggs at the local supermarket. When she returned home and unpacked her groceries, she noticed small cracks in a couple of the eggshells. Since she was planning to use the eggs to make cookies later that day, Jane was unconcerned. That afternoon, she mixed the cookie dough, using the cracked eggs, and put the mixture on the kitchen counter. Then Jane was called away from the kitchen for a while. When she returned, Jane and her daughter, Suzanne, baked the cookies, tasting the dough as they dropped spoonfuls of it onto baking sheets.

The author:

Chris Anne Raymond is associate editor of the *Journal of the American Medical Association* in Chicago.

The next day, Jane and Suzanne came down with salmonellosis. The cracked eggs had been contaminated with salmonella bacteria, which quickly multiplied in the dough when Jane left it sitting on the counter at room temperature. Jane and Suzanne became infected when they ate the uncooked dough containing the bacteria.

The Hillfarm victims and the Morgans had fallen victim to one of the most common types of food poisoning in the United States. More than 40,000 cases of salmonellosis are reported each year, according to the CDC. But this figure probably represents just the tip of the iceberg. The CDC estimates that as many as 4 million Americans actually may be infected with salmonella each year. Most cases of salmonellosis go unreported because people usually mistake its symptoms—vomiting, diarrhea, nausea, and fever—for "intestinal flu."

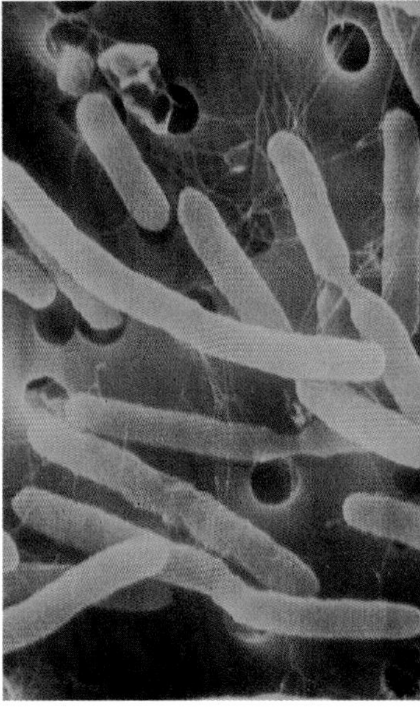

As shown above—greatly magnified and with color added—they look almost pretty. But these salmonella bacteria are the cause of salmonellosis, a form of food poisoning.

Although most cases of salmonellosis are mild, the illness can be deadly. Salmonellosis causes at least 500 deaths annually, especially among the elderly, infants, and people who have a weakened immune system, such as cancer patients. The illness also takes its toll in dollars. Experts say that salmonellosis costs more than $600 million each year in medical expenses and in time lost from work.

Unfortunately, the incidence of salmonella infection in the United States is increasing. The CDC reports that the number of laboratory-confirmed cases has doubled since the mid-1960's. From 1973 to 1984, the number of reported outbreaks nearly doubled as well, reaching 204.

The cause of this unpleasant—and potentially deadly—illness are the salmonella, a group of closely related bacteria. They are shaped like rods and are covered with *flagella*, whiplike projections that help the bacteria move. Salmonella belong to a large family of bacteria, called *enterobacteria*, that inhabit or invade the intestines. There are more than 2,000 salmonella strains, or *serotypes*. Of the 2,000 salmonella serotypes, a mere 10 account for 70 per cent of all cases of salmonellosis reported in the United States. And just 1 of these 10, *S. typhimurium*, is responsible for most of the cases.

Salmonella are found in the intestines of reptiles, birds, insects, and rodents, as well as in animal feed. Farm animals pick up the bacteria from the feed, from pests, or from the feces of other infected animals. Chickens, turkeys, and other poultry run the greatest risk of salmonella contamination, but dairy cows, cattle, and pigs also can be infected.

In the United States, 9 out of 10 cases of salmonellosis are caused by eating food that contains live salmonella bacteria.

The food may come from a contaminated animal or it may be contaminated during its preparation. Food can become tainted if it comes in contact with other contaminated food or with a food handler who is infected. Some people become infected when they accidentally come in contact with the feces or other intestinal secretions of an infected person.

Any meats—or dishes made with meat or meat juices, such as soups, chili, chicken salad, or gravy—may harbor salmonella if the foods are not cooked properly. Because the shells of eggs from an infected hen may carry the bacteria, eggs can be contaminated. Eggs with cracked shells run the greatest risk of contamination, but some scientists suspect that egg yolks also can carry the bacteria. In April 1988, the CDC reported that outbreaks of salmonellosis in the Northeastern United States seemed to be linked to eggs that were apparently clean and intact. This means that eggnog or undercooked hollandaise sauce could bring on a bout of salmonellosis if it is made with salmonella-tainted eggs. The same is true for milk and foods made with milk. One of the problems with salmonella contamination in foods is that it is virtually impossible to detect. Tainted food may look, taste, and smell just fine.

What makes meats, eggs, and milk so hospitable to salmonella is the low acidity and high protein and fat content of these foods. Foods that contain lots of salt, sugar, acid, or *benign* (harmless) bacteria are less friendly to salmonella and prevent or slow down the salmonella bacteria's growth. So soy sauces, which are high in salt; jams, which are rich in sugar; and yogurt, which contains benign bacterial cultures, are usually free from the bacteria.

Salmonella grow best between 60°F. (16°C) and 120°F. (49°C). In fact, room temperature—which ranges from 65°F. (18°C) to 75°F. (24°C)—provides the ideal temperature for salmonella to grow. For this reason, it is not a good idea to keep meat and other foods unrefrigerated for any length of time. Temperatures of 140°F. (60°C) or above kill most salmonella bacteria. Most also succumb to temperatures below 40°F. (4°C), but some salmonella strains can survive freezing temperatures.

Salmonellosis occurs after a person ingests a sufficient number of bacteria—a number that varies widely among serotypes, from fewer than 100 *S. typhimurium* bacteria to at least 10,000 *S. newport* bacteria. Most of the ingested bacteria are destroyed by hydrochloric acid secreted in the stomach to help digest food. But if enough bacteria are ingested, some survive the stomach's acid bath and pass into the small intestine. There they attach to the mucous lining and reproduce rapidly. In just six hours, 75 to 100 salmonella organisms can multiply to as many as 4 million.

Salmonellosis: a growing concern

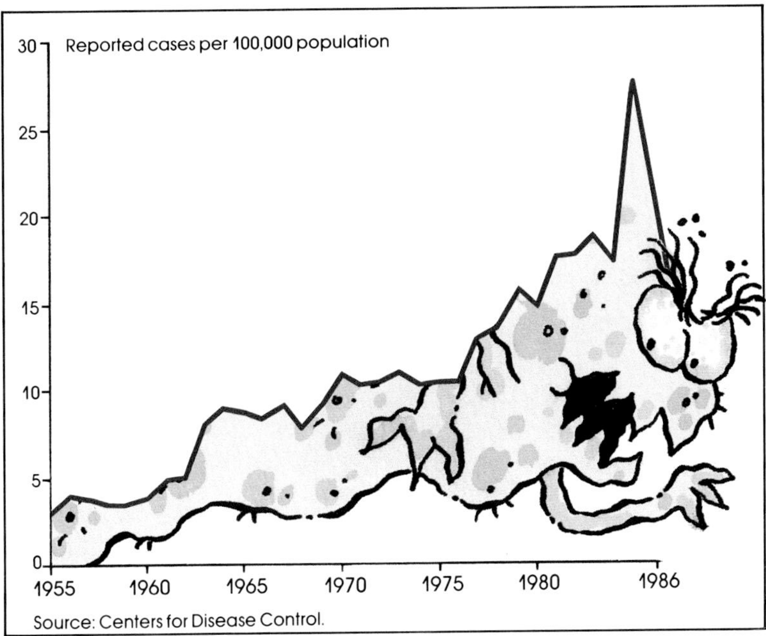

The number of salmonellosis cases in the United States has risen steadily over the past 30 years, *above left.* The dramatic jump in 1985 was due to a large outbreak that was traced to contaminated milk from the Hillfarm Dairy in Melrose Park, Ill. Although Hillfarm workers dumped the salmonella-laced milk after the contamination was discovered, *above,* thousands of people had already become ill from milk that had made its way into grocery stores.

The unpleasant symptoms of salmonellosis actually result from the body's attempt to rid itself of the foreign bacteria. When the body is infected with salmonella, its disease-fighting immune system rushes white blood cells to the digestive tract to attack the bacteria. This produces inflammation, a condition in which body tissues—in this case the lining of the intestines—become swollen. Inflammation triggers the release of *prostaglandins,* fatty acids that affect body temperature and can stimulate contractions of the smooth muscle in the walls of the gastrointestinal tract. Prostaglandins cause fever, which helps the body fight off the bacteria. Prostaglandins also cause the muscles in the walls of the intestines to contract, resulting in painful cramps and diarrhea. In addition, prostaglandins set off a biochemical chain reaction that causes the body to secrete excessive amounts of sodium, potassium, and chloride into the intestines. This also triggers diarrhea, which—though uncomfortable—helps expel the bacteria quickly.

These symptoms, as well as nausea and vomiting, begin 12 to 36 hours after eating contaminated food. The diarrhea may last three or four days before subsiding. A moderately high temperature of about 102°F. (39°C) is common the first day or two. Some people also experience headache and chills. Infants may have bloody diarrhea for as long as eight or nine days.

People have varying susceptibility to salmonellosis. Some

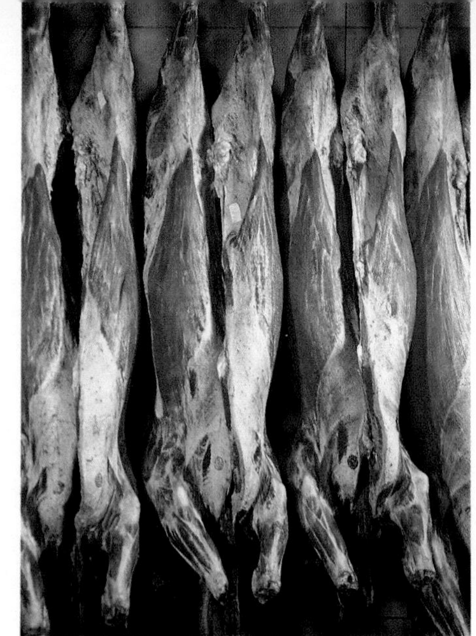

Spreading salmonella
Salmonella contamination can occur on farms and in processing plants as well as in the home. Raising chickens in close quarters, *above*, encourages the contamination of uninfected chicks. Beef carcasses, *above right*, can also spread salmonella. During butchering of infected animals, the bacteria are released from the intestines, contaminating uninfected meat, workers, and plant equipment.

may be infected but experience no ill effects, while others suffer a mild-to-moderate, short-term illness. But some people are likely to become seriously ill, because their bodies are unable to fight off the infection. These high-risk victims include elderly or malnourished individuals; people who have weakened or immature immune systems, such as cancer patients or infants; and those who have recently undergone bowel surgery. In these cases, salmonella can invade the blood, bones, and brain, leading to such serious complications as arthritis, *osteomyelitis* (inflammation of the bones), and *meningitis* (a disease that affects the lining of the brain and spinal cord).

Most mild cases of salmonellosis can be treated with bed rest. To replace water and minerals lost through diarrhea and vomiting, patients should drink plenty of liquids and eat bland foods, such as saltine crackers. Those who experience moderate or severe symptoms should contact their physician.

Except in certain special instances determined by the physician, antibiotics are not advised because they can prolong the illness by killing some of the benign bacteria along with the salmonella in the intestines. The benign bacteria compete with salmonella and often keep the numbers of salmonella low enough for the body to eliminate them. It takes the body up to five weeks to shed all the salmonella from the intestines, so anyone who has recently recovered from salmonellosis should avoid taking antibiotics.

Another reason antibiotics can be dangerous is that new strains of salmonella that resist certain antibiotics have entered the food supply. The development of these strains is fostered by the practice of adding small amounts of antibiotics to livestock feed. The antibiotics prevent disease and help the animals grow. But if an animal harbors even a few antibiotic-resistant salmonella organisms, repeated exposure to antibiotics can wipe out competing bacteria and enable the antibiotic-resistant salmonella to reproduce more efficiently.

Unfortunately, many of the antibiotics used in animal feed are also used to treat illness in people. If a person becomes infected with an antibiotic-resistant strain of salmonella and is then given that antibiotic as a treatment, the drug will destroy the patient's benign bacteria but leave the salmonella untouched. Without competition from the benign bacteria, the salmonella will reproduce freely in the intestines and cause the patient to become ill.

Although resistant strains of salmonella can cause problems for people taking antibiotics, they are probably not responsible for the increased incidence of the illness in the United States. Public health experts, in fact, are uncertain about what is behind the increase. They do not know whether the upturn is due to more reporting of the illness by the public and more accurate diagnoses by physicians or whether it stems from a genuine increase in the factors that cause contamination.

Some researchers suspect that the increase in salmonellosis is tied to a rise in the number of infected animals, but hard evidence of this is lacking. In 1987, microbiologists at the United States Department of Agriculture (USDA) conducted a survey of broiler chickens in processing plants and found that 37 per cent of the chickens were contaminated with salmonella. While this is a substantial figure, a similar study conducted in 1967 showed almost the same result. This suggests that the rise in salmonellosis may not be due to an increase in the number of contaminated chickens.

Most public health experts agree that contamination can occur in any link in the food chain—from farms to processing plants and on to restaurants, supermarkets, and homes. They are taking a close look at the first two links in the chain—the farm and the processing plant—to discover ways to control the spread of salmonella bacteria.

The farm is a logical starting point, since livestock are natural hosts for salmonella as well as for other harmful and benign bacteria. Because most salmonella infections do not cause illness in livestock, it is difficult to detect infected animals and remove them from the food chain.

Moreover, salmonella spreads rapidly on the farm. Infected animals shed the bacteria in their feces, which then infect healthy animals that come in contact with them. On poultry farms, intensive rearing practices—with chickens and turkeys raised in close quarters—encourage the contamination of uninfected animals.

Five cooking tips to prevent salmonellosis

Although the meat or eggs you buy at the store may contain salmonella, a few simple precautions in the kitchen will help make sure that the food you prepare is free of the bacteria.

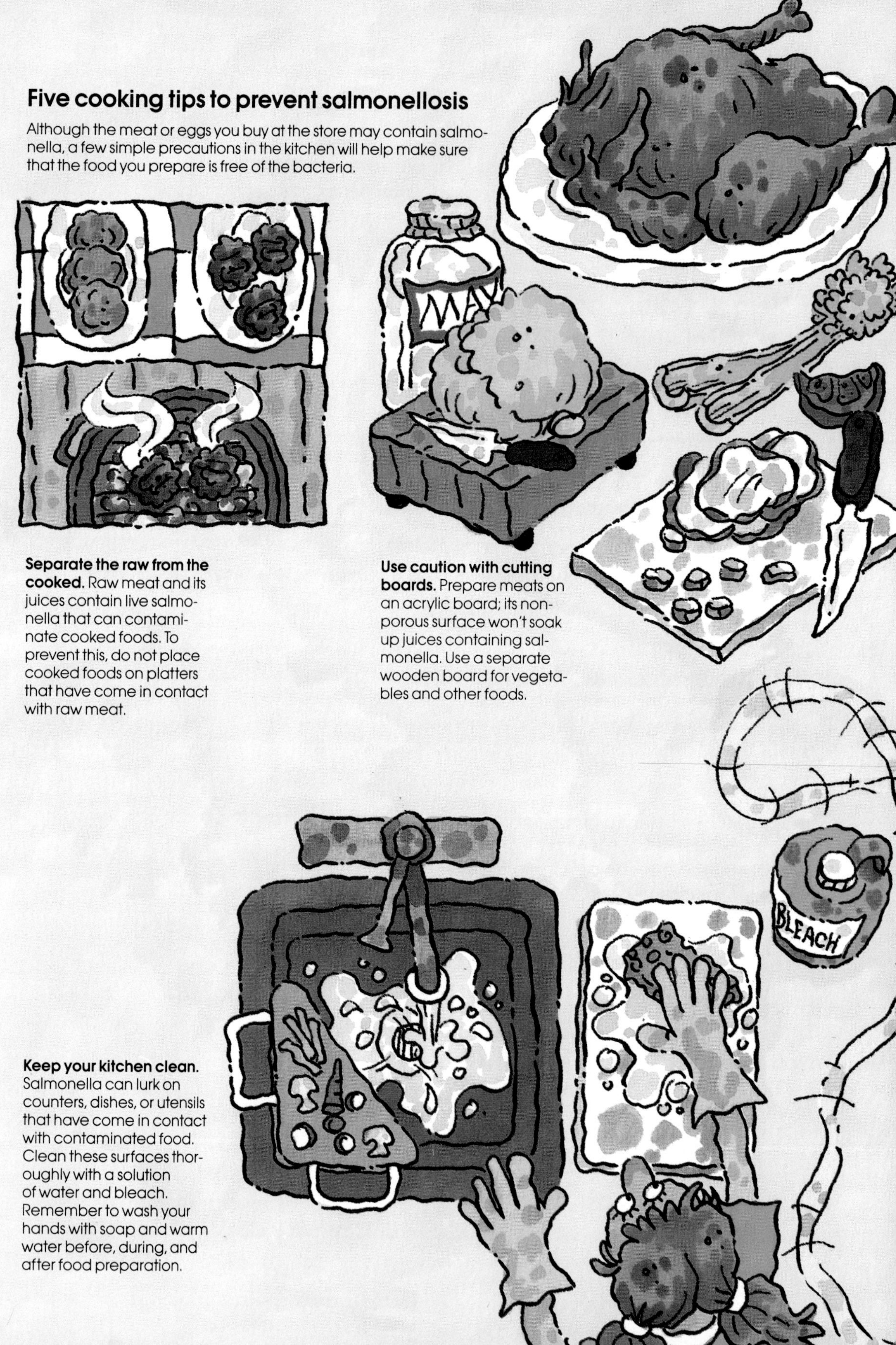

Separate the raw from the cooked. Raw meat and its juices contain live salmonella that can contaminate cooked foods. To prevent this, do not place cooked foods on platters that have come in contact with raw meat.

Use caution with cutting boards. Prepare meats on an acrylic board; its nonporous surface won't soak up juices containing salmonella. Use a separate wooden board for vegetables and other foods.

Keep your kitchen clean. Salmonella can lurk on counters, dishes, or utensils that have come in contact with contaminated food. Clean these surfaces thoroughly with a solution of water and bleach. Remember to wash your hands with soap and warm water before, during, and after food preparation.

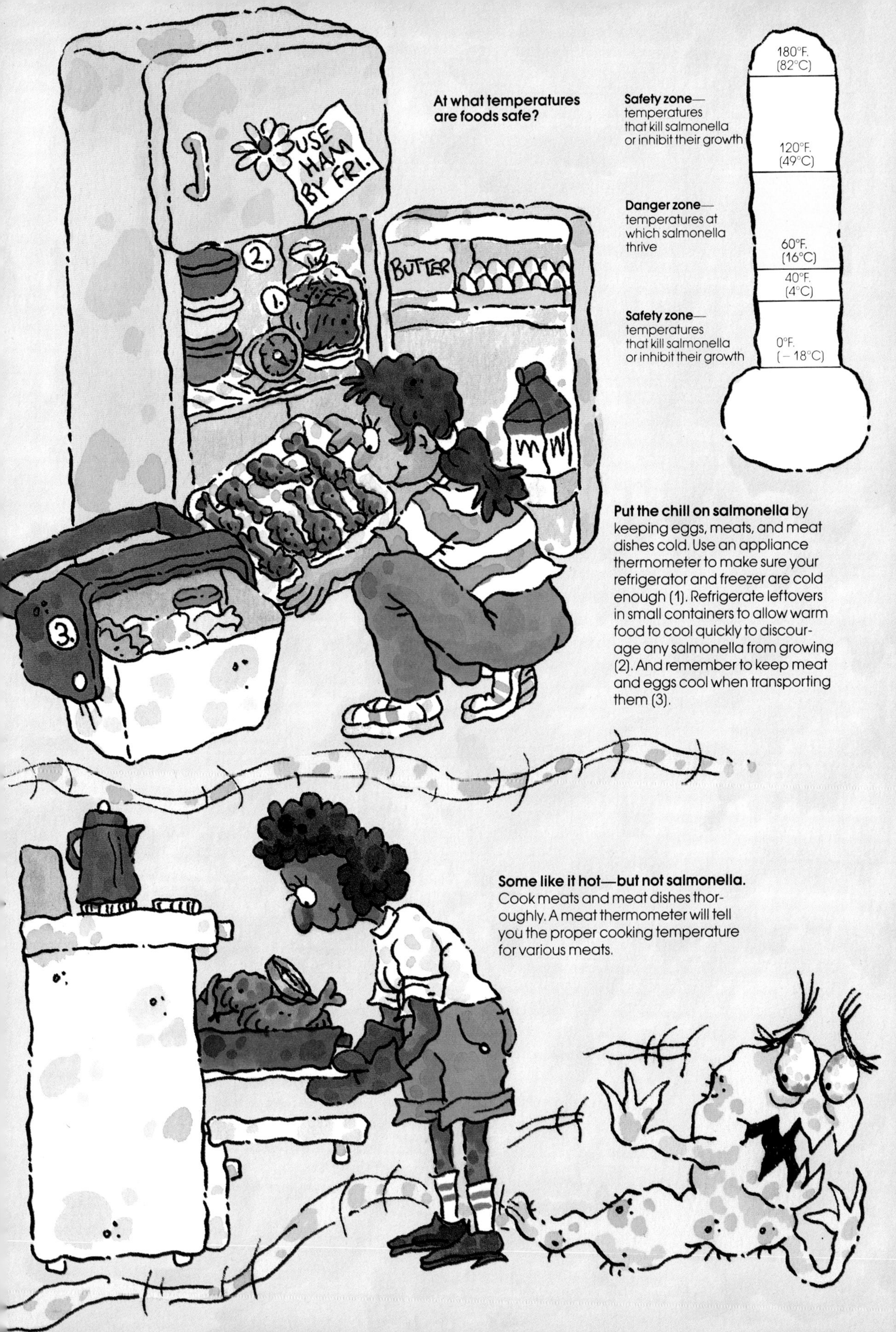

At what temperatures are foods safe?

Safety zone—temperatures that kill salmonella or inhibit their growth

Danger zone—temperatures at which salmonella thrive

Safety zone—temperatures that kill salmonella or inhibit their growth

Put the chill on salmonella by keeping eggs, meats, and meat dishes cold. Use an appliance thermometer to make sure your refrigerator and freezer are cold enough (1). Refrigerate leftovers in small containers to allow warm food to cool quickly to discourage any salmonella from growing (2). And remember to keep meat and eggs cool when transporting them (3).

Some like it hot—but not salmonella. Cook meats and meat dishes thoroughly. A meat thermometer will tell you the proper cooking temperature for various meats.

Scientists have proposed a number of ways to cut down salmonella contamination on the farm. One suggestion involves hatching chicks in a sterile environment, thereby preventing their early infection with salmonella. The drawback to this idea is that the chicks would not pick up the benign bacteria that might later protect them from salmonella or other disease-causing microorganisms. A different approach—called *competitive exclusion*—is to intentionally infect newly hatched chicks and other young livestock with benign bacteria, which would prevent salmonella bacteria from colonizing the animals' intestines. Unfortunately, pinning down the right mixture of protective bacteria and developing a cost-effective method for its commercial use have proved difficult. A third approach relies on the development of a vaccine that would protect farm animals from salmonella. At least one such vaccine was being tested in chickens in 1987.

At the next link in the food chain—the processing plant—contamination of uninfected animals is both common and difficult to control. As animals are butchered, bacteria are released from their intestines. Bacteria can also spread during the skinning and defeathering of poultry. Plant equipment and the clothing of plant workers can become contaminated, spreading bacteria to packaging.

To ensure the safety of food, USDA inspectors visually check all meat during processing for any signs of disease, such as bruises or lesions. But visual inspection is not always adequate. Inspectors usually have only a minute or two to examine a carcass, and because salmonella and other bacterial contamination cannot be seen with the naked eye, tainted meat is often missed. In 1980, the USDA developed a voluntary program, called Total Quality Control (TQC), to deal with this problem. Meat and poultry plants that wish to receive TQC certification must submit a detailed plan for monitoring the safety of each component of processing. Among the requirements is random laboratory testing of meat for bacterial contamination.

But solving the problem may take more than a voluntary program. In May 1987, the National Academy of Sciences released a study that reiterated the inadequacy of current inspection procedures in poultry plants. The study recommended that all meat and poultry plants be required to add random sampling programs to test for bacterial contamination.

What can be done in the last link of the food chain—the home—to lessen the odds of getting salmonellosis? Keeping in mind three words—hot, cold, and clean—will help prevent salmonellosis and most other types of food poisoning.

Other bacteria that cause food poisoning

Salmonella may be making all the headlines, but there are other bacteria that can contaminate our food and cause illness.

Staphylococcus aureus. An estimated 1.5 million cases of *S. aureus* food poisoning occurred in the United States in 1985, according to the Centers for Disease Control (CDC) in Atlanta, Ga. These bacteria are found in air, water, and soil, and they often grow in people's noses and on their skin. They usually are transmitted by food that has been contaminated during handling. "Staph" bacteria thrive in starchy foods, cured and cooked meats, and cheese and meat salads.

S. aureus produces a *toxin* (poison) that causes illness. People who eat food contaminated with this toxin come down with a relatively mild bout of nausea, vomiting, and diarrhea within two to six hours. To avoid *S. aureus* contamination, do not keep meats or starchy foods at room temperature longer than an hour or two, and make sure that family members wash their hands thoroughly before and after handling food.

Clostridium perfringens. Food poisoning caused by *C. perfringens* affected 10,000 Americans in 1985, according to the CDC. Like salmonella, these bacteria live in soil, animal intestines, and sewage. But *C. perfringens* is different in one important way: It prefers environments with little or no oxygen. Bacteria of this type are called *anaerobes*. *C. perfringens* occurs as active cells or as dormant spores. Spores can become active when temperatures reach 70°F. (21°C).

C. perfringens is called the "cafeteria germ," because it lurks at serving tables where foods such as gravies, casseroles, and stews are kept warm for long periods of time. *C. perfringens* produces a toxin that causes diarrhea and gas pains 8 to 24 hours after eating contaminated food. Symptoms usually persist for about 24 hours. The best protection against *C. perfringens* is to cook or reheat foods in several small dishes rather than in one large dish.

Clostridium botulinum. This bacterium causes botulism—a deadly but fortunately rare form of food poisoning. The CDC estimates that 150 to 200 cases occur in the United States annually. *C. botulinum* also lurks in soil and water, but needs just the right conditions to grow. Like its biological cousin, *C. perfringens*, it is an anaerobe and

A swollen can may be a sign that the food contains deadly bacteria.

it produces a toxin. It thrives in improperly canned foods, especially corn, green beans, peas, and other low-acid vegetables.

Most cases of botulism are caused by home-canned vegetables and fruits. High temperatures kill the bacteria, but the spores are hardier—they can survive temperatures of 212°F. (100°C).

Symptoms of botulism occur within 12 to 48 hours after eating—or even tasting—contaminated food and can linger for up to seven months. The toxin affects the central nervous system, causing double vision, drooping eyelids, difficulty in swallowing and breathing, and paralysis. Cardiac or respiratory paralysis can lead to death. There is an *antitoxin* (a drug that counteracts poison), but nerve damage caused by the illness can be irreversible. Any suspect canned goods—badly dented or swollen cans, jars with loose lids, or cans or jars that have a milky liquid or gas surrounding their contents—should be thrown away.

Campylobacter jejuni. Food poisoning from *C. jejuni* was first recognized and reported in 1978. Although about 10,000 such cases are now reported annually in the United States, the CDC believes that as many as 2 million to 3 million cases may actually occur each year. These bacteria are found in raw milk and raw meat. Symptoms appear two to seven hours after eating contaminated food, and may last one to two weeks. The infection is marked by a sudden onset of severe stomach cramps and foul-smelling diarrheal stools. It is treated with antibiotics if symptoms persist. [C. A. R.]

Baking, boiling, frying, or roasting meat and other foods to temperatures between 140°F. (60°C) and 170°F. (77°C)—or higher in the case of poultry—will kill most bacteria. Use a food thermometer and a temperature chart—usually found in cookbooks—to be sure food is thoroughly cooked. Insert the tip of the thermometer into the thickest part of beef or pork away from the bone, or into the thick part of a turkey or chicken thigh. Gravy should be brought to a rolling boil before serving.

If you are cooking with a microwave oven, follow the manufacturer's guidelines for cooking foods and then letting them stand to complete the cooking process. Since microwave ovens may cook foods unevenly, it is a good idea to bone meats prior to cooking and to rotate the food throughout cooking. Chafing dishes—containers with heaters under them—can keep cooked food at safe temperatures for an hour or two. After that, food should be refrigerated.

Any leftovers should be covered and put into the refrigerator immediately. Do not cool them first on the counter because any bacteria remaining in the food will grow at room temperature. It is a good idea to refrigerate foods in small portions that cool more quickly.

Just as heating food to the proper temperature is important, so is keeping food cold. Use an appliance thermometer to make sure that the refrigerator's temperature is no higher than 40°F. (5°C). A freezer's temperature should be no higher than 0°F. (−18°C).

The safest way to thaw frozen food is to place it in the refrigerator overnight, rather than on the kitchen counter. If something must be defrosted quickly, place it in a watertight plastic bag and put it in cold water, changing the water often to prevent the liquid from warming up. This prevents the outer portions of the food from warming enough to encourage bacteria growth while the inner portions are still thawing.

When you shop, pick up perishable items last—such as meat, eggs, or milk—and avoid running other errands on the way home. This prevents foods from warming up. Repeated handling of food can introduce bacteria, so store foods in their original wrapping unless it is torn. Freeze meats that will not be used within a day or two.

Before handling food, wash your hands with warm water and soap. All dishes, knives, and cutting boards used to prepare raw eggs, chicken, or meat should be washed thoroughly before coming into contact with cooked foods. Because the pores and crevices in a wooden cutting board can harbor bacteria, use an acrylic board for cutting up raw meat; it is much easier to clean. It is a good idea to keep one cutting board just for raw meat and another for fruits, vegetables, and other food.

After preparing meats or eggs, be sure to clean all kitchen surfaces that might have come in contact with them. This will prevent cooked foods from coming in contact with a contaminated surface. Health officials recommend using a diluted solution of household bleach to clean dishcloths, sponges, and wooden cutting boards.

Some foods need special care. Hamburger is handled more than most meats, so it is more likely to be exposed to many food-poisoning microbes. To be safe, never eat raw hamburger. Always cook hamburger or steak until its center is at least brownish-pink.

Poultry should be cooked to 180°F. (82°C). Cooked chicken or turkey should be white—not pink—and its juices should be clear—not red—when the meat is pierced. Do not store stuffing in a chicken or turkey before cooking, because salmonella grow quickly in starchy stuffings. Instead, stuff the bird loosely just before popping it into the oven so that the stuffing will be thoroughly heated. It is best to bone the bird right after cooking, but if that is not possible, refrigerate the entire carcass.

Refrigerate whole eggs and use them within five weeks. Throw away any cracked eggs. Cook eggs thoroughly and serve them hot or refrigerate them immediately. Refrigerate hard-boiled eggs and use them within a week.

Pork also must be handled properly. Smoking, curing, and aging are no guarantee against salmonella contamination. Whole hams should be kept in the coldest part of the refrigerator and eaten within a week. Canned hams also should be refrigerated. Cook fresh pork and ham to 170°F. (77°C) or until the meat is no longer pink.

It is not practical to stop eating meats, eggs, and other foods to avoid salmonellosis. But until scientists come up with a way to eliminate salmonella bacteria from the food chain, you can make sure that your food is safe to eat by paying careful attention to the proper handling and cooking of food in your own kitchen.

For further reading:

Hunter, Beatrice Trum. "Foodborne Illness: A Growing Problem." *Consumers' Research,* February 1987.

Long, Patricia. "Guess What's Coming to Dinner?" *Hippocrates,* November/December 1987.

For more information about salmonellosis, phone the USDA's Meat and Poultry Hot Line, 1-800-535-4555 (in Washington, D.C., phone 447-3333).

Cosmetic surgery can tighten wrinkled skin, straighten noses, and slim fat thighs. But it's not for everyone.

Cosmetic Surgery: New Trends, Old Concerns

By Richard Trubo

Twenty-five-year-old Melinda had been self-conscious about her nose for as long as she could remember. Because it was oversized and irregularly shaped, with a prominent bump, it always seemed to be what caught the eye of people meeting her for the first time.

Her self-consciousness only increased after she became a flight attendant for a major airline, a position that entailed meeting new people every day. Melinda never got used to the wisecracking remarks about her nose that came from the occasional tipsy passenger.

In 1987, Melinda explained all of this to a prominent New York City plastic surgeon, and asked if he would surgically reshape her nose, a procedure called *rhinoplasty.* After questioning Melinda about her medical history and her expectations for the results of the surgery, the doctor agreed that she would be a good candidate. He then discussed the cost (several thousand dollars), warned Melinda of the risks of surgery (the possibility of infection or of an allergic reaction to the anesthetic), and told her to expect some temporary pain after the operation.

Opposite page: A cosmetic surgeon cuts excess fat and skin from a patient's eyelids. A more youthful, alert appearance is the expected result.

A few weeks later, the surgeon performed the approximately

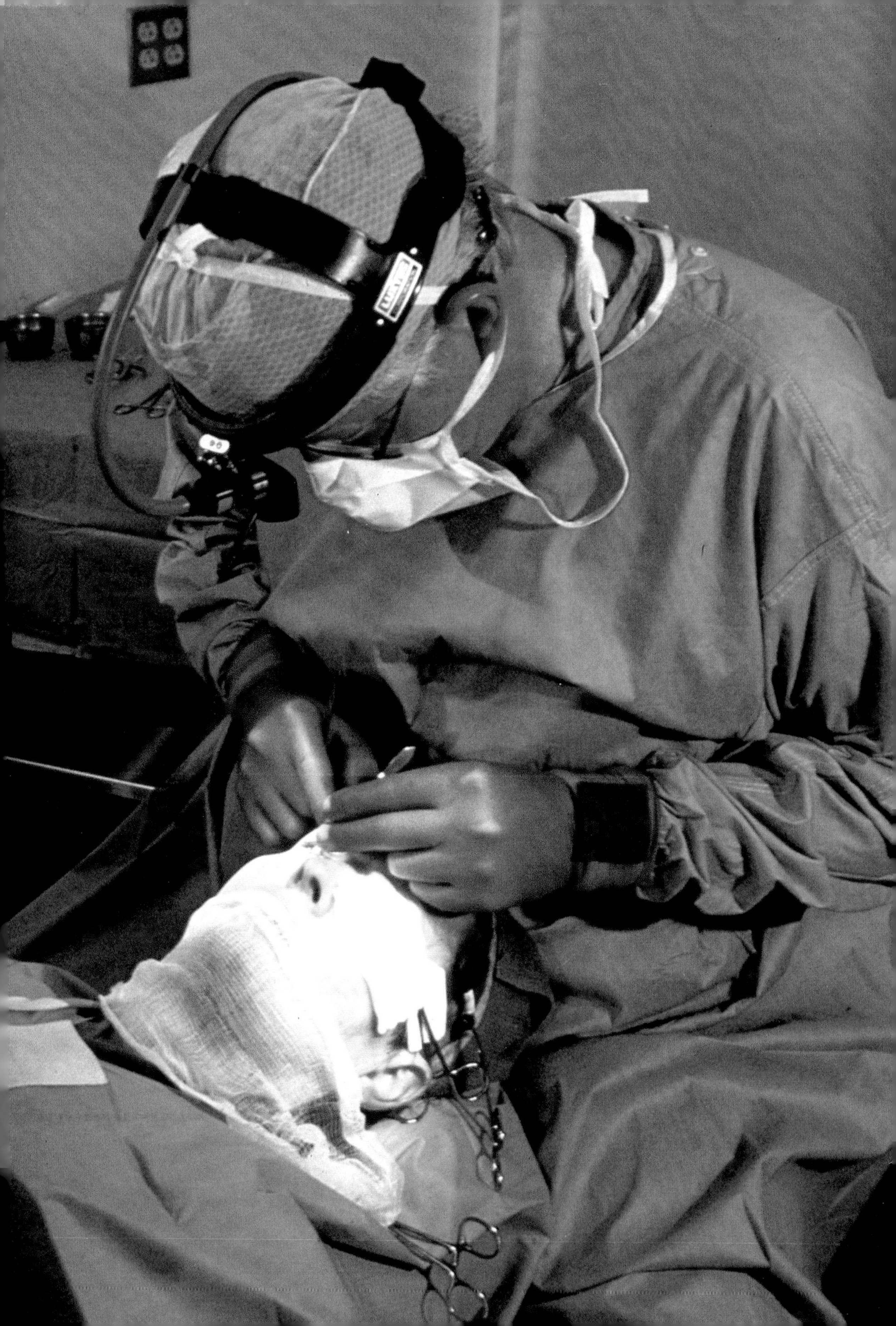

two-hour-long procedure in his office operating room. First, he gave Melinda a local anesthetic. Then, working entirely inside Melinda's nostrils so that she would have no visible scars, he sculpted her nasal bones to get rid of the bump that had troubled her for so long. He also shortened her nose, and lifted and refined the tip.

When the surgery was over, the doctor gave Melinda medication to relieve pain, and a friend drove her home. At first, she was a startling sight. It takes a certain amount of force to chip away nasal bones, and—like most people recovering from rhinoplasty—Melinda looked like she had been beaten. She wore a splint on her nose, which was to stay in place for one week, and her nose and eyelids were bruised and swollen.

After two weeks, Melinda's face had healed enough to allow her to return to work. Some swelling would remain for months, but already she was delighted with the dramatic change. Her nose was smaller, straighter, and in proportion to the rest of her features. Not surprisingly, she felt more confident at work, happy that she would never again have to laugh politely at insensitive remarks about her nose.

Like Melinda, a growing number of Americans have become sold on the benefits of cosmetic surgery in the late 1980's. Once considered an indulgence of only the wealthy, cosmetic surgery has now spread to mainstream America—and in so doing has become a booming $250-million-per-year industry. In 1986, about 600,000 cosmetic procedures were performed in the United States, twice as many as were performed in 1981.

Although the majority of cosmetic surgery patients are women, more and more men are heading for the operating room. In the 1960's, women made up almost the entire caseload of the typical cosmetic surgeon; today about 13 per cent are men, with rhinoplasty accounting for the largest number of male patients.

In addition, younger people are now becoming interested in youth-enhancing cosmetic surgery. For example, more than one-third of all face-lifts—traditionally performed on patients in their 50's, 60's, and beyond—are now performed on people who are age 50 or younger, according to a 1986 survey conducted by the American Society of Plastic and Reconstructive Surgeons.

In a culture that puts a high premium on youth and physical attractiveness, the popularity of cosmetic surgery in spite of its risks is not too surprising. Several technical and procedural advances in the field have also helped to draw an increasing number of clients into the offices of plastic surgeons. A number of these advances—a fat-suctioning technique called *liposuction*, for example, and modifications to traditional opera-

The author:

Richard Trubo is a contributing medical writer for *Medical World News*.

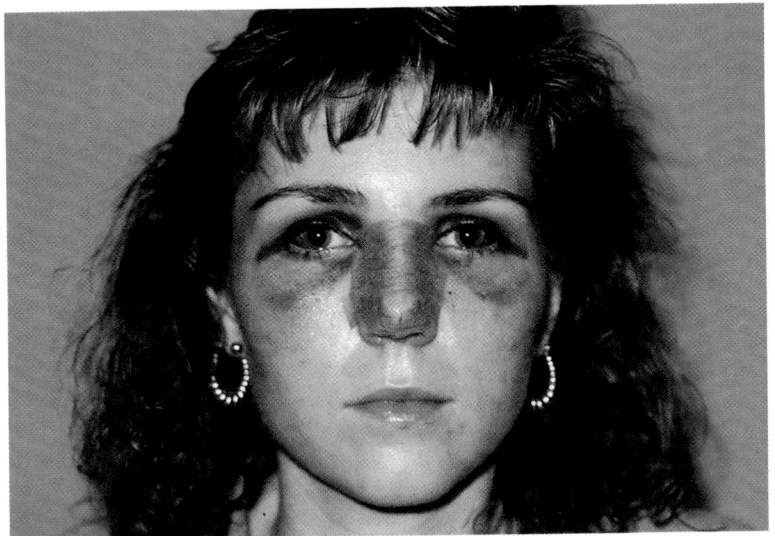

The immediate results of nose-reshaping surgery, *left,* and most other cosmetic operations are pain, bruising, and swelling. The pain, which can be controlled by medication, and the bruising will disappear in one to two weeks, but some swelling may remain for months.

tions that now produce more natural-looking results—have benefited many. Some of the new trends, however, are not without drawbacks that should be carefully considered before making the decision to have a cosmetic operation.

Sometimes called *aesthetic surgery,* cosmetic surgery is one of two fields within the medical specialty known as *plastic surgery.* The other field, *reconstructive surgery,* uses procedures similar to those of cosmetic operations. But while aesthetic surgeons enhance the attractiveness of normal features, reconstructive surgeons improve the function or appearance of parts of the body damaged by injury, disease, or birth defects (see THE SURGICAL ART OF RECONSTRUCTION on page 149).

Plastic surgery has been around for centuries, though in an admittedly primitive form compared with today's operations. (The word *plastic* comes from the Greek word *plastikós,* which means *able to be molded.*) Thousands of years ago, the ancient Assyrians implanted ivory under the skin of women's noses to change their shape. In the 1400's, Sicilians developed a technique to alter the shape of the nose by partially detaching a flap of skin from the patient's forearm and grafting the flap to the nasal area. Unfortunately, the patient's arm had to be held up to the nose with a sling until the skin became established in its new site.

The techniques of modern plastic surgery developed slowly. The greatest advances did not come until World War II (1939-1945), when devastating battle wounds motivated surgeons to refine their ability to efficiently move tissue from one part of the body to another. They began grafting not only skin but also the underlying muscle and blood vessels that sustained it. When a shellburst destroyed a soldier's nose, ear, or jaw, for example, surgeons were able to fashion a new feature using cartilage and flesh harvested from other parts of the body.

Today's cosmetic procedures are far safer and produce more natural results than those used during World War II. Nevertheless, anyone considering cosmetic surgery should bear in mind that the techniques were developed in military hospitals, not in beauty salons. As Melinda's case makes clear, the body reacts to cosmetic surgery with swelling, bruising, and pain. In some cases, there is visible scarring. There is also the slight, but nonetheless real, possibility that something could go wrong during surgery or recovery. A few people die due to complications of cosmetic surgery every year.

Many of today's advances, however, consist of refinements to tried-and-true, relatively safe procedures. Face-lifts, for example, have traditionally involved separating facial skin from underlying tissues and pulling it taut, thus smoothing out wrinkles and giving the face a more youthful appearance. But most surgeons now perform a more extensive procedure in which they tighten the underlying fat and connective tissue as well. This modification prevents healing problems that can develop when too much tension is borne solely by the skin. The new technique also avoids the unnatural, tightened look sometimes produced by traditional face-lifts.

Rhinoplasty provides a more natural appearance these days, too, one that is tailored to fit a patient's face rather than conform to a single look—an extremely upturned nose with a pinched tip—that used to make these operations so easy to spot. Today, many surgeons remove a little less of the cartilage at the end of the nose and avoid extreme upward tilts. The object is to create noses that "look as though they came from nature, not from a surgeon's hand," says Robert L. Cucin, director of the American Institute of Plastic Surgery in New York City.

Surgeons have also become more successful at hiding surgical scars. Many procedures allow incisions to be made in the natural folds of the body or inside the mouth, inside the nostrils, or—in the case of minimal lower eyelid surgery—inside the eyelid. *Keloids*, weltlike growths of scar tissue that occasionally form in incisions, can present a problem for some patients, however. Although keloids are uncommon, they are unsightly and hard to treat. When interviewing a prospective patient, a good plastic surgeon will inspect any previous scars on the patient's body for evidence of keloid formation and determine whether the individual has a family history of the growths before recommending surgery.

Another area of progress is in replacing tattooed or badly

The surgical art of reconstruction

When plastic surgery is discussed, cosmetic operations usually receive most of the attention. But reconstructive surgical procedures are actually more common than cosmetic operations, comprising about 60 per cent of all plastic surgeries performed in the United States today.

Unlike cosmetic procedures, reconstructions are often essential to the patient's health. This type of surgery can return function to a hand mangled in an industrial accident, close a gaping hole in the scalp after a skin cancer tumor is removed, or enable an infant born with a cleft palate—a gap along the roof of the mouth—to swallow food and speak normally.

Reconstruction of injured hands and severed fingers is the most common form of this type of surgery. Other common procedures involve treatment of jagged wounds caused by accidents, reconstruction after removal of tumors of the head and neck, and the revision of scars that are disfiguring or limit movement.

Some of the most dramatic reconstructive procedures involve correction of severe facial deformities such as *Crouzon's disease*, an inherited condition in which the face has a caved-in appearance. Without treatment, people with a disorder this severe may be socially shunned, but successful reconstructive surgery can enable them to lead a normal life.

The techniques used by the reconstructive surgeon to correct these problems and many other defects and injuries are often even more complex than those used for cosmetic procedures. Some repairs require not only skin grafts, but also grafts of tendons, blood vessels, muscles, bones, and nerves. The procedures can be so painstakingly detailed that the surgeons sometimes use a microscope to magnify the tissue being repaired.

Reconstructive surgery often requires more sophisticated technology than cosmetic surgery does. For example, one computer-imaging system in the early stages of development in 1988 gives surgeons a preview of the underlying bone structure of a deformed or damaged part of the body. This system typically calls for the patient to undergo a series of X rays taken from many angles, which are then fed into a specially programmed computer. The computer then produces a three-dimensional image of the bones, which the surgeon studies carefully before deciding how best to restore the flawed area.

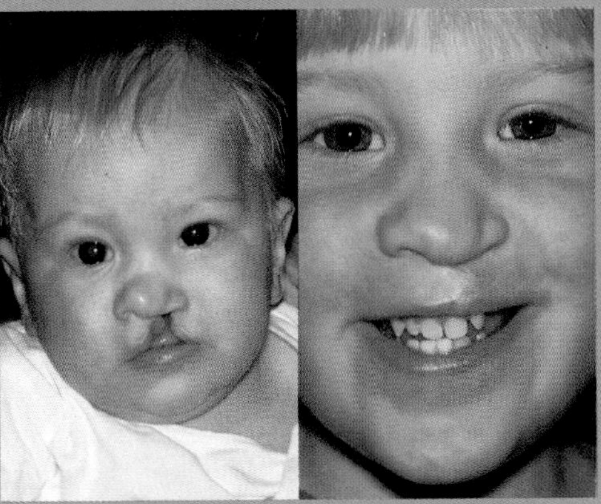

A cleft lip, *above left*, is a fairly common birth defect that can be treated by reconstructive surgery that joins the split upper lip and reshapes the nose, *above right*.

In a few procedures, however, reconstructive surgeons and cosmetic surgeons use the same techniques. Breast reconstruction after *mastectomy* (removal of the breast) is a fairly common procedure that often uses implants similar to those employed in breast augmentation. In some cases, surgeons use inflatable balloonlike implants that work on the same principle as tissue expansion.

Also, like cosmetic surgery, many reconstructive procedures can now be performed on an outpatient basis. For example, repairing a *cleft lip* (also called a harelip)—a split through the upper lip that is a fairly common birth defect in the United States—used to require a hospital stay of two to five days. But some surgeons who repair cleft lips currently discharge most of their young patients on the day of surgery, making the experience easier for the children and their families.

Finally, both cosmetic and reconstructive operations can boost a patient's self-esteem. But while a face-lift or liposuction treatment may make a person feel a little younger or a little more attractive, surgery that repairs a birth defect or restores function to an accident victim can profoundly change the patient's entire life. [R. T.]

scarred skin. In earlier procedures, surgeons removed a portion of healthy skin from elsewhere on the body, and transplanted it in place of the flawed area. But the procedure itself often created extensive scarring, and, because skin thickness and color vary at different sites on the body, the transplant often looked like an obvious patch. A new technique called *tissue expansion* is becoming a more popular means of replacing flawed skin.

In this procedure, an existing area of healthy skin is encouraged to grow, much as it would to accommodate an expanded body contour caused by weight gain. First, the surgeon implants one or more small silicone balloons under the skin next to the damaged area. During a 6- to 16-week period, the balloons are periodically injected with a saline solution, enlarging them—to the size of an orange, for example—and slowly stretching the skin until it has grown enough to cover the problem area. The balloons are then surgically removed, and the expanded skin is stretched over the flawed area and stitched into place.

Tissue expansion is used in reconstructive surgery and, in a few cases, to treat baldness. The skin-growth period can be temporarily disfiguring, however. A man undergoing tissue expansion to extend hair-growing skin on the sides of the head in order to cover a bald crown will probably want to wear a hat in public. Otherwise, according to one surgeon, the patient will look rather like someone wearing Mickey Mouse ears.

For decades, permanent implants have been used to change facial contours, but they are now made of improved materials. Hard implants made of a substance similar to plastic can be inserted through incisions made between the lips and gums to make the cheekbones or chin more prominent. The implants are manufactured in various sizes and can be carved to precise specifications.

Softer permanent implants are routinely used for *breast augmentation surgery,* which increases the size of a woman's breasts—and which is one of the cosmetic operations most likely to cause problems. The implants—flexible plastic envelopes filled with saline or *silicone gel,* a synthetic substance—are probably safer than injections of silicone, which can harden and move to other sites in the body. But at least 10 per cent of women with breast implants develop *fibrous capsular contraction,* a condition in which the scar tissue that forms around the implants contracts, squeezing the implants to such an extent that the implants—and the breasts—feel hard. As a result, the patient must undergo procedures in which the surgeon manually breaks up the scar tissue or surgically removes the implants altogether.

Another drawback of breast augmentation is that the im-

Liposuction

During *liposuction,* the physician removes excess fat from the face, hips, thighs, buttocks, or other area, using a suction tube called a *cannula.* The operation, which can be performed under general or local anesthesia, takes 45 minutes to 2 hours. The surgeon's fee ranges from $500 to $4,000.

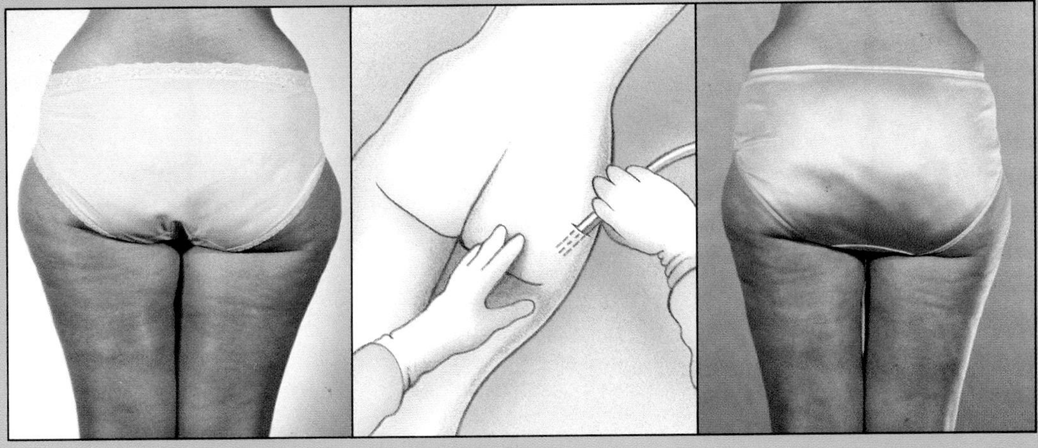

Before | Insertion of the cannula | After

plants may interfere with the ability of *mammograms* (low-dose X rays of the breast) to show early stages of breast cancer. On a mammogram of a natural breast, groups of cancer cells are visible as dense areas. But because an implant may compress natural breast tissue, making it more dense, cancerous tissue may not be as easy to see. The American Society of Plastic and Reconstructive Surgeons recommends that women with breast implants have mammograms taken by technicians with experience in X-raying surgically augmented breasts. It is equally important to tell the radiologist who interprets the mammogram about the implants' presence.

The most rapidly evolving area of cosmetic surgery has probably been in procedures for the removal and rearrangement of existing tissue. And liposuction has attracted more interest in this aspect of cosmetic medicine than any other procedure. Although introduced into the United States as recently as the early 1980's, liposuction now accounts for 17 per cent of all cosmetic operations, making it the most common procedure. (The second-most-common procedure is breast-enlargement surgery, followed by eyelid surgery, rhinoplasty, and the face-lift.)

Liposuction is used to remove localized fat deposits that are difficult to reduce through diet and exercise—most often from the thighs or the area just below the waistline. The surgeon inserts a *cannula*—a blunt-ended tube about as thick as a pen-

Eyelid surgery

This cosmetic technique removes excess fat and skin from the upper and lower eyelids. Surgery takes 1 to 2 hours and can be performed using local or general anesthetic. The surgeon's fee ranges from $1,000 to $4,000, and the results last about 10 years.

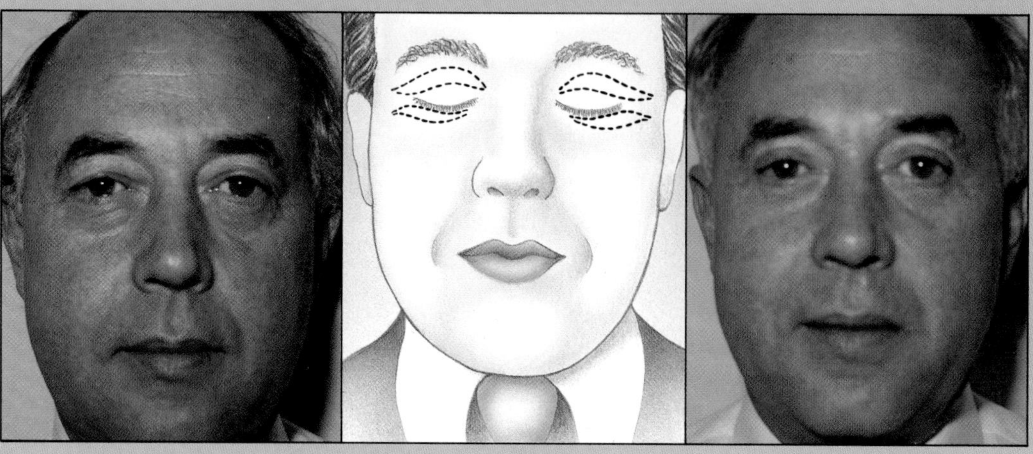

Before Incision lines After

cil—through a small incision in the skin, and vigorously thrusts the cannula into the fatty area to dislodge fat from surrounding tissue. A vacuum pump connected to the tube then suctions out an average of 2 to 7 pounds (1 to 3 kilograms) of fat. Liposuction is usually performed under general anesthesia, and the incisions leave scars as small as ½ inch (13 millimeters) long.

Although a task force of the American Society of Plastic and Reconstructive Surgeons concluded in 1987 that the procedure is normally "a safe and effective means of surgically contouring localized fat deposits," complications can occur. By 1988, 11 people had died of complications of liposuction—including shock, infection, and blood clots that blocked vital arteries and veins. Many experts say that the use of newly developed cannulae that are thinner and less destructive may reduce these risks.

Some surgeons inject the fat removed during liposuction into parts of the body that would look better if plumped out, such as facial wrinkles. The plastic and reconstructive surgeons society considers these fat transplants experimental, however, and questions their permanence. Until more is known about the effects of fat transplantation, many surgeons will continue to temporarily fill out wrinkles with *collagen*, a protein derived from cowhide that was approved for surgical use by the U.S. Food and Drug Administration in 1981.

A few surgeons use fat transplantation to augment the breasts. This, however, is a very controversial procedure that the plastic and reconstructive surgeons society has declared to

Nose surgery

This operation involves the reshaping of nasal bones and cartilage, usually through incisions made inside the nostril. The patient may receive either local or general anesthetic during the operation, which requires 1½ to 2 hours. The surgeon's fee is $1,500 to $6,000.

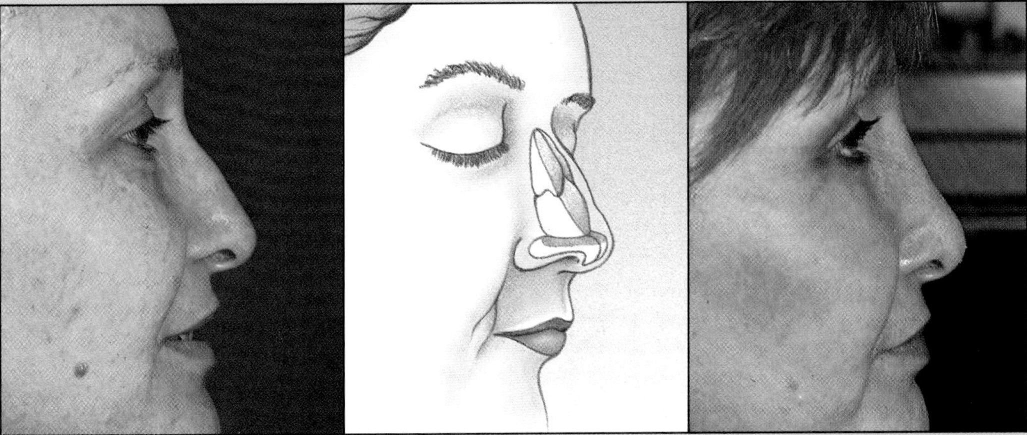

Before Tissue removed (shaded area) After

be a hazard to health. The problem is that as fat injected into the breasts is reabsorbed, it can leave lumps, internal scars, or flecks of calcium. Although these formations are probably harmless, they may be easily mistaken for cancerous tumors, causing patients to undergo unneeded X rays and *biopsies* (removal of tissue for examination under a microscope), and making accurate diagnosis of breast cancer difficult.

Another change in cosmetic surgery is the use of computer-imaging systems that give patients a preview of what surgery might do for them. These newly developed systems project a photograph of a patient's face onto a monitor, then permit the surgeon to alter the image to show how the patient might look with a smaller nose, for example, or more prominent cheekbones. After seeing the result of minimal, moderate, and drastic changes to the image on the monitor, the surgeon and patient can decide how extensive the surgery should be.

Computer-imaging systems can be very helpful, but they may occasionally mislead a patient about the certainty of the surgery's results. Nothing can unerringly predict the outcome of an operation on a particular patient because ideal results are simply not always possible. Like sculptors, plastic surgeons are limited by their own level of skill as well as by their materials—in this case, each patient's unique bone structure and the tissue's capacity for healing.

A final trend in the field is that the cost of many cosmetic

Face-lift

During a face-lift, the surgeon tightens and removes excess facial skin and tissues. The surgeon's fee for the 2- to 4-hour operation is $2,000 to $10,000. Local or general anesthetic may be used, and the results last 5 to 10 years.

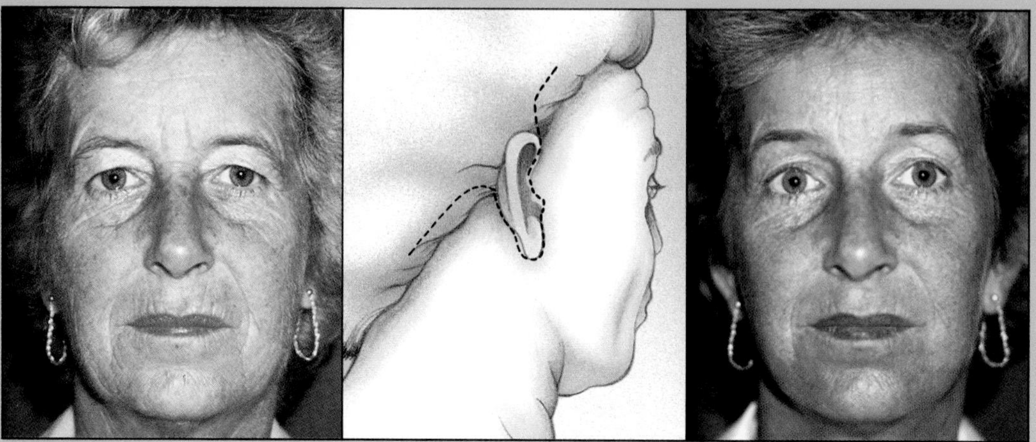

Before	Incision line	After

operations, which is rarely covered by medical insurance, has decreased as most patients elect to have *outpatient surgery*, surgery that may be performed in a hospital or other medical facility but does not include an overnight stay. The drawback to cosmetic surgery performed in an outpatient care center or a doctor's office is that it may be riskier than surgery performed in a hospital. Hospitals are obviously better equipped to handle life-threatening emergencies; they must also comply with more stringent safety regulations than outpatient facilities.

Ironically, patients' unrealistic expectations cause more serious problems than any aspect of the procedures themselves. Even the most talented surgeon using the most advanced face-lift technique can't make a 60-year-old look like a 30-year-old, though that is exactly what some patients want. Nor is there much chance that cosmetic surgery can give a patient the face or body of a favorite movie star.

Most plastic surgeons are wary of patients with unrealistic expectations as well as those who subconsciously believe that a scalpel can somehow cut away life's problems. These patients may undergo one surgical procedure, and then try another on a different part of the body, and then still another—always convinced that the next one is finally going to make life better. Such abusers of cosmetic surgery may need psychological counseling, not another operation, to help them cope with life and get off the plastic surgery treadmill.

Chin augmentation

The chin can be made more prominent by the insertion of a hard implant made of a plasticlike material. A local anesthetic is typically used during this 45-minute to 1-hour procedure. The surgeon's fee is $250 to $3,000.

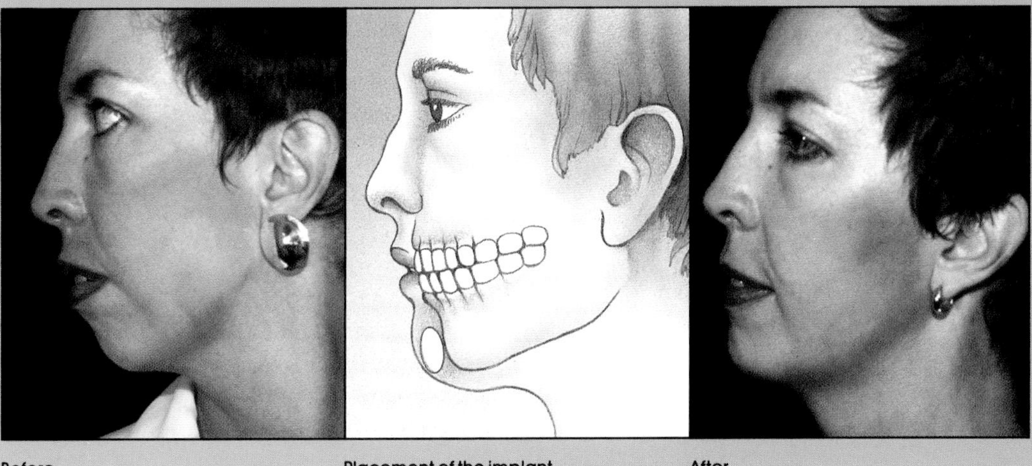

Before Placement of the implant After

Detecting these problems in people seeking cosmetic surgery is one of the hardest but most important tasks of the physician. Most doctors screen clients by asking questions about their reasons for wanting surgery and their expectations of the result. This not only helps doctors avoid patients who would never be satisfied with the surgeon's handiwork but also helps patients avoid making irreversible changes that they may later regret.

Unfortunately, not all doctors adequately screen their patients—so people considering cosmetic surgery should take it upon themselves to examine their own feelings about the operation. Patients who are most helped by feature-reshaping cosmetic surgery are those who, like Melinda, had been bothered by their appearance for many years. Someone considering a procedure solely because a spouse, parent, or friend dislikes one of their features, however, should probably avoid surgery. If not, the patient may later regret the permanent loss of a feature that had never been a personal annoyance. It is also best not to have surgery during a time of crisis such as divorce or the loss of a job. Anyone who does so may find that when the crisis is over, his or her old, familiar look—not to mention the money spent on the operation—is sorely missed.

People who feel they would be happy if surgery merely made them look "more normal"—rather than making them beautiful or handsome—may also be better candidates for feature-reshaping operations. Similarly, patients who want to look good for their age instead of 10 years younger are more likely to be satisfied with the results of a face-lift. (Some plastic surgeons suggest that prospective patients lie on their back and look at themselves in a handheld mirror to get a realistic idea of how they might appear after a face-lift. The force of gravity mimics the procedure's gentle tightening of the skin.)

From a physical standpoint, the ideal cosmetic surgery patient has good skin tone and generally good health. Any chronic illness, such as diabetes or high blood pressure, must be taken into account and may make the patient an unsuitable candidate for surgery. People under 45 get the best results from liposuction because their skin has enough youthful elasticity to shrink evenly after underlying fat is removed. In addition, a person who wants a face-lift should not smoke. The cigarette habit reduces blood flow to the face, which will slow the healing process.

Prospective patients should also take the time and trouble to find a good plastic surgeon. Badly performed operations do occur. In fact, some plastic surgeons spend a significant portion of their time repairing the botched results of other doctors' cosmetic operations. The best place to start the search for a good surgeon is with a referral from a trusted family physician, internist, or other knowledgeable acquaintance. Failing that, the professional organizations listed at the end of this article can provide referrals.

Any licensed physician can call himself or herself a plastic surgeon, whether or not he or she has training in the field. As a result of the boom in cosmetic surgery, physicians without training in plastic surgery have begun performing these sought-after procedures. For this reason, a prospective patient may want to choose a doctor who is *board certified* by the American Board of Plastic Surgery. Also, some surgeons certified by the American Board of Otolaryngology (the medical specialty that deals with the ear, nose, and throat) are trained in facial plastic surgery. Requirements for certification by these boards include several years of postgraduate medical training in plastic surgery and passing grades on a demanding series of written and oral exams. Plastic surgeons certified by the American Board of Plastic Surgery are qualified to perform any cosmetic operation, while otolaryngologists certified by the American Board of Otolaryngology specialize in surgery of the face, head, and neck.

Another criterion is the surgeon's experience in the specific procedure the prospective patient is seeking. There is little advantage in having a doctor who specializes in face-lifts if the patient wants liposuction.

Other things to consider when selecting a doctor include

whether the surgeon is on the staff of a major hospital certified by the Joint Commission for Accreditation of Hospitals (a national organization that sets basic standards for hospitals), and whether the surgeon holds a medical school faculty appointment. Both are good indicators of competence. Finally, prospective patients can contact their county medical society to find out if any of a plastic surgeon's former patients have ever made a formal complaint about the doctor.

Following this advice will help prevent one unfortunate result of the widespread acceptance of cosmetic surgery—patients rushing into operating rooms without ever giving serious thought to the consequences. Not every doctor can perform a perfectly successful cosmetic operation, just as not every would-be patient truly needs surgery. And only a good match between a competent, board-certified plastic surgeon and a patient who wants surgery for all the right reasons can produce results as pleasing as Melinda's new nose.

For a list of plastic surgeons and otolaryngologists in your area who are certified by the American Board of Plastic Surgery or the American Board of Otolaryngology, call or write:

American Society of Plastic and Reconstructive Surgeons
444 East Algonquin Road
Arlington Heights, IL 60005
(800) 635-0635

American Academy of Facial Plastic and Reconstructive Surgery
1101 Vermont Ave., N.W.
Suite 404
Washington, DC 20005
(800) 332-FACE

To find out if a cosmetic or reconstructive surgeon is board certified, call or write:

American Board of Medical Specialties
1 Rotary Center
Suite 805
Evanston, IL 60201
(312) 491-9091

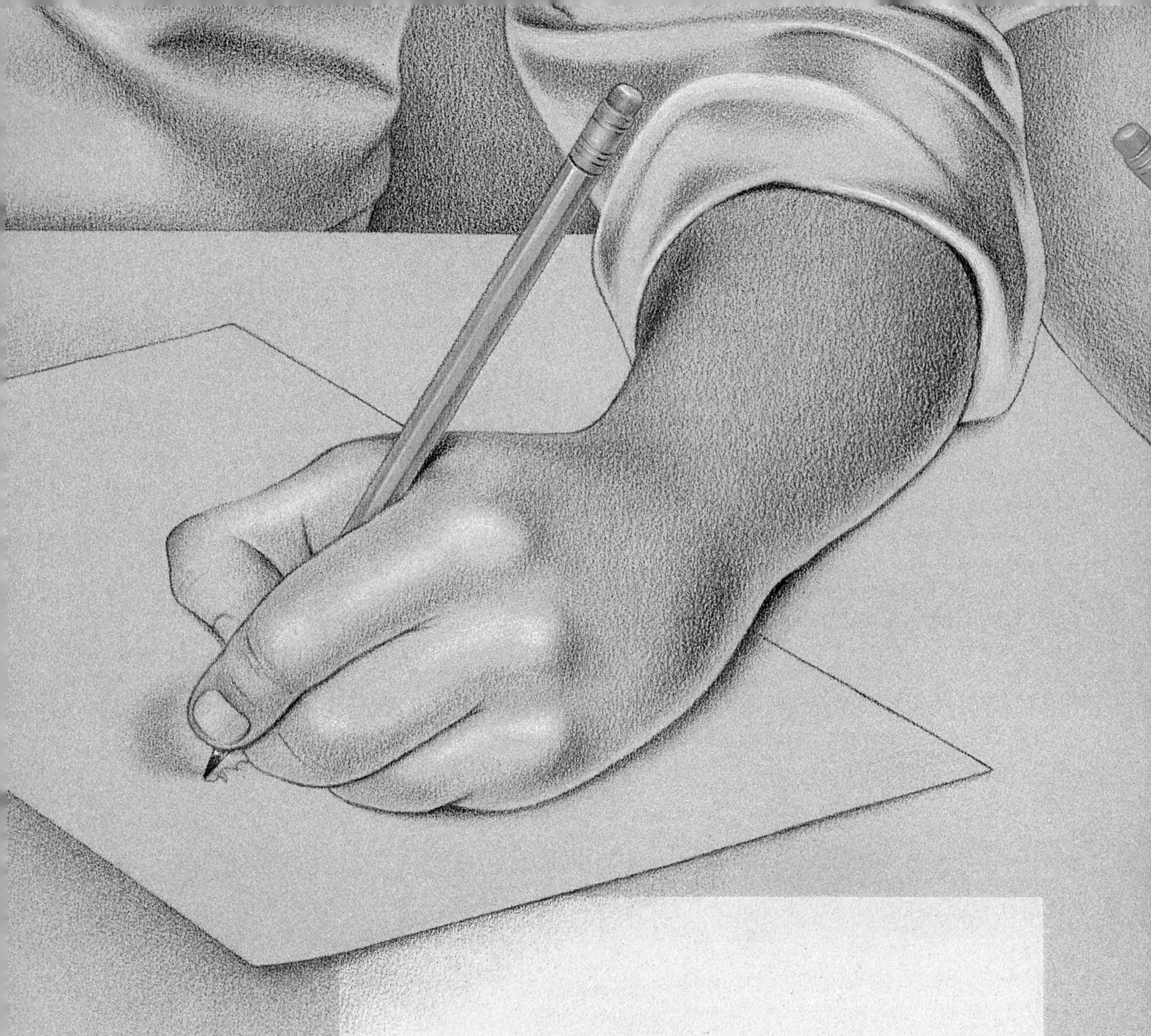

A Look at Left-Handers

By Paul Satz

Scientists are exploring claims that left-handed people are more likely to develop certain diseases—or to have certain talents—than right-handers.

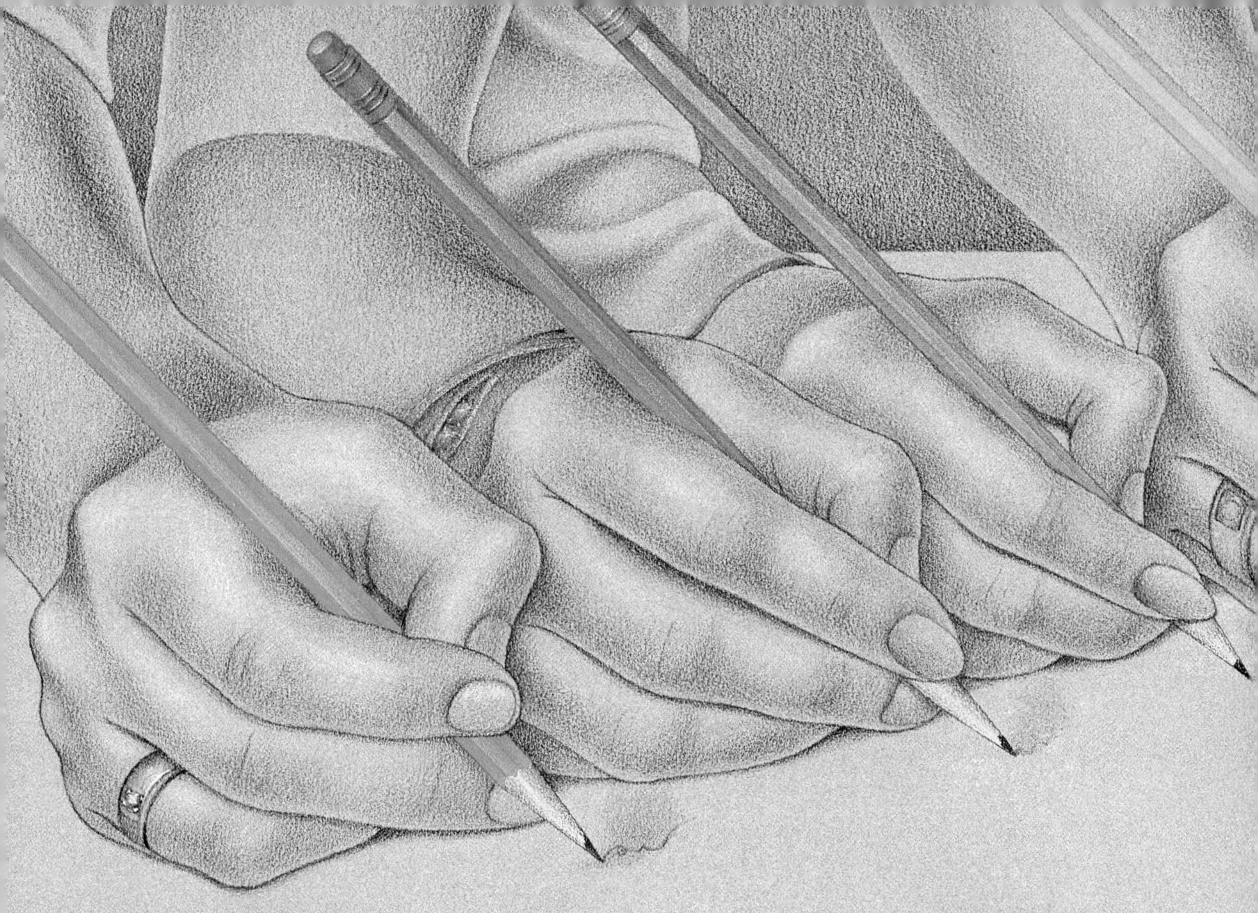

We live in a right-handed world. The overwhelming majority of people—about 90 per cent of us—find it easier to use the right hand rather than the left hand. Scientists believe that this percentage has changed little since the beginning of the human race. Historians agree, for as far as our written records show, there has never been a predominantly left-handed society.

Furthermore, as historians can tell us, left-handed people have not only been members of an ancient minority group, their inclination to use the left hand was often viewed with suspicion and fear. In centuries past, left-handedness was considered an undesirable—even sinister—trait. In fact, the word *sinister*, which has come to mean *threatening* or *evil*, is the Latin word for *left*. In the Bible, as well as in texts written during the Middle Ages—a period of history dating from the A.D. 400's to 1500's—the left hand is described as "wicked" and as an expression of "the Devil's work," while the right hand is associated with honor, power, and virtue. Although strong moral views about handedness diminished over the centuries, some bias against left-handedness survived to the 1900's—as left-handed people who were forced to learn to write with their right hand could attest.

Why, if the world has always favored right-handedness, do 10 per cent of us use our left hand to write, eat, sew, or throw a ball? This question—and other questions about left-handedness—have fascinated scientists, such as myself, for years. But though we have developed many theories as to what causes left-handedness, none has yet been proven.

Interest in the causes of hand preference has been fueled over the years by suggestions that left-handed people are more likely than right-handed people to have certain physical and mental disorders. For example, a disproportionately high incidence of left-handedness has been observed among people who are mentally retarded, and a few studies have suggested a connection between left-handedness and reading disabilities.

But left-handedness has been linked with some desirable traits as well. Some scientists have observed that there is a greater percentage of left-handers among artists, architects, musicians, and professional baseball and tennis players than among the general population. They suspect this is because left-handers, for some reason, may have greater musical and imaginative abilities and superior visual and *spatial perception* (the ability to visualize objects in space). Such a connection seems possible when one considers such famous lefties as artists Leonardo da Vinci, Raphael, and Pablo Picasso; composers Paul McCartney, Bob Dylan, and Cole Porter; baseball greats Babe Ruth and Sandy Koufax; and tennis stars Martina Navratilova, Jimmy Connors, and John McEnroe.

Such speculations about possible links between handedness and medical conditions or special skills have long intrigued scientists. To understand how left-handedness may be connected with various disorders and talents, we have turned our attention to the brain, the master control for voluntary movement and many other functions.

Glossary

Aphasia: A disorder caused by a stroke or other injury to the brain that results in the loss or partial loss of the ability to speak or understand language.

Autoimmune diseases: A group of unrelated disorders in which the body's disease-fighting immune system attacks the body's own tissues or cells.

Corpus callosum: A band of nerve fibers that joins the brain's left and right hemispheres.

Dyslexia: A reading disorder that causes a person to confuse letters, words, or numbers.

Pathological left-handers: People who would have been right-handed but suffered a physical injury to the brain—probably before the age of 6—that caused them to be left-handed.

Testosterone: A male hormone produced by the testicles in males, the ovaries in females, and the adrenal glands of both sexes.

The brain connection

We know that an individual's hand preference is controlled by the brain—except in rare cases where an impairment of a hand or arm forces a person to use the other hand. This discovery emerged from studies that demonstrated that while the brain is a single, integrated organ, it is composed of distinct halves or hemispheres—a left brain and a right brain, in a sense. These hemispheres are joined by a thick band of nerve fibers called the *corpus callosum,* which allows the two brains to share information.

Scientists have learned that though the left and right hemispheres look alike, they don't always act alike. The two hemispheres differ in the amount of control, or dominance, they have over certain functions, such as speech—an observation first made in the early 1860's by Pierre Paul Broca, a French surgeon. Broca noted that a right-handed man who injured the

The author:

Paul Satz heads the neuropsychology program at the University of California's Neuropsychiatric Institute in Los Angeles.

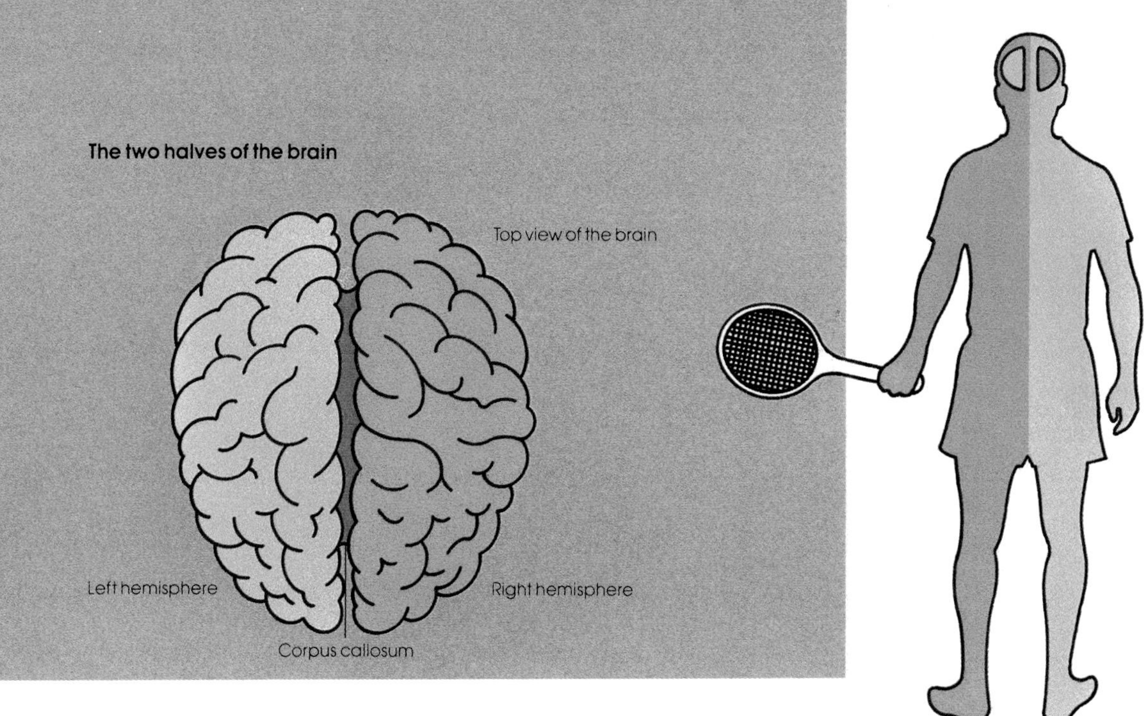

The brain is divided into halves called the right and left hemispheres. The hemispheres are connected by the corpus callosum, a thick band of nerve fibers. Each hemisphere receives information from—and controls—primarily the opposite side of the body. So the left hand is controlled by the right hemisphere and the right hand is controlled by the left hemisphere.

left hemisphere of his brain lost his ability to speak. He also examined the brains of deceased persons who suffered from *aphasia* (the loss or partial loss of the ability to express or understand speech or language), and found that the brains of these patients were damaged in the same area of the left hemisphere. He theorized that in activities such as speech and handedness, one of the hemispheres must play a greater role.

Since then, scientists have proven that the left hemisphere controls the right side of the body, including the right hand, while the right hemisphere controls the body's left side and left hand. They have also verified Broca's theory that for most people the left hemisphere seems to be the seat of language ability and speech. Studies suggest that the hemispheres have other specializations as well. For example, the left hemisphere appears to be dominant in logic and some mathematical functions, while the right hemisphere appears dominant in visual, spatial, and musical abilities.

During the 1970's, scientists discovered a significant difference in how the brains of left-handers and the brains of right-handers function. They found that while the left hemisphere controls speech in about 98 per cent of all right-handed people, the location of speech control in left-handed people is far more variable. Studies show that in some left-handers, speech control may be located exclusively in one of the two hemispheres; in others—perhaps up to 75 per cent of all lefties—speech control is shared by both hemispheres.

Left-handedness: a sign of talent?

Left-handed people have made their mark in many fields. In fact, scientists have observed a relatively high incidence of left-handedness among artists, musicians, and baseball and tennis players. Some scientists suggest that left-handers have a dominant right hemisphere, which may give them better musical, visual, and spatial abilities. Below are some famous lefties.

Artists
Leonardo da Vinci
M. C. Escher
Hans Holbein
Paul Klee
Michelangelo
Pablo Picasso
Raphael

Baseball players
Yogi Berra
George Brett
Lou Brock
Rod Carew
Steve Carlton
Ty Cobb
Whitey Ford
Lou Gehrig
Reggie Jackson
Sandy Koufax
Stan Musial
Babe Ruth, *below*
Ted Williams

Basketball players
Larry Bird
Adrian Dantley
Bill Russell

Entertainers
Dan Aykroyd
Carol Burnett
George Burns
Sid Caesar
Charlie Chaplin, *right*
Tom Cruise
Richard Dreyfuss
W. C. Fields
Greta Garbo
Judy Garland
Whoopi Goldberg, *below*
Cary Grant
Goldie Hawn
Diane Keaton
Michael Landon
David Letterman
Jay Leno
Marcel Marceau
Harpo Marx
Shirley MacLaine
Marilyn Monroe
Don Rickles
Bruce Willis
Oprah Winfrey

Football players
Gale Sayers
Ken Stabler
Phil Simms

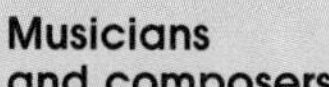

Musicians and composers
C. P. E. Bach
David Byrne
Phil Collins
Bob Dylan
Crystal Gayle
Jimi Hendrix
Paul McCartney
Cole Porter
Maurice Ravel
Lou Rawls
Ringo Starr

Rulers and royalty
Alexander the Great
Charlemagne
Napoleon Bonaparte
Prince Charles
Queen Victoria

Tennis players
Jimmy Connors
John McEnroe
Martina Navratilova

United States Presidents
Gerald Ford
James Garfield
Harry Truman

The finding that control of speech is shared by both hemispheres in most left-handed people may explain why left-handers seem to recover from brain injuries more quickly than right-handers. If one hemisphere is injured and a function, such as speech, is lost, the uninjured hemisphere is able to take over the function. This has been observed in patients suffering from aphasia caused by a stroke or some other brain injury. Left-handed aphasic patients whose speech control is located in both hemispheres seem to have less severe symptoms and seem to recover more quickly than right-handed patients.

Having found that the brains of left-handers and right-handers often function differently—at least in the control of speech—scientists began to search for detectable anatomical differences between the brains of left- and right-handed people. And at least one such difference has been found, according to a study reported in 1985 by Sandra F. Witelson, a *neuropsychologist* (a scientist who studies the psychological functions of the different parts of the nervous system) at McMaster University in Hamilton, Canada. Witelson measured the size of the corpus callosum in 42 deceased people, including strongly right-handed subjects (people who preferred to do almost all tasks with their right hand) and people who preferred to do some tasks with the left hand and others with the right hand.

Witelson found that the corpus callosum of subjects who used their left hand for many tasks was about 11 per cent larger than that of the right-handers—a difference, she says, that could mean such people may have as many as 25 million more nerve fibers in their corpus callosum than right-handers. These additional nerve fibers may improve the lines of communication between the two hemispheres, suggests Witelson, and may explain why speech control is shared by both brain hemispheres in many left-handed people.

Scientists are intrigued by evidence that the brains of left-handed and right-handed people differ in structure and function. But the existence of such differences fails to explain just what underlying factors cause people to become right-handed or left-handed in the first place—a question that has prompted a great deal of speculation among scientists. One theory proposes that hand preference is the result of childhood experience, a behavior passed down from one generation to the next. Another theory suggests that handedness is due entirely to variations in genes, just as variations in genes result in individual differences in such characteristics as height and hair color. Still others insist that left-handedness is the result of an injury to the brain, or is caused by factors that alter the development of the brain before birth.

Blaming society

Throughout history, many societies have had a strong cultural bias against left-handedness—especially in writing. Up until about 50 years ago, most left-handed children were forced to write with their right hand, and many were taught by their parents to do other tasks with their right hand, from using a pair of scissors to throwing a ball.

Scientists have found, however, that when this cultural pressure is lifted, the incidence of left-handedness increases. For example, during the 1930's, after more permissive attitudes about left-handedness emerged, the number of left-handed people in the United States and Great Britain doubled from 5 to approximately 10 per cent of the population. And in the Netherlands after World War II (1939-1945), such a change in cultural attitudes about left-handedness created an even more dramatic effect. In 1986, Dutch psychologists Leen Beukelaar and Pieter Kroonenberg studied the handwriting preference of 1,996 Dutch people. They found that while there were no left-handed writers among subjects born between 1910 and 1930, the number of left-handed writers jumped dramatically among people born after 1940.

But although the number of left-handed people increases when social pressures are lifted, social influences fail to explain the persistent dominance of right-handedness in humans throughout history. As a result, most scientists believe that some biological factor, such as genes or physical injury to the brain, causes handedness.

In the genes?

Perhaps the most plausible theory on the mystery of handedness was proposed by psychologist Marian Annett at the University of Hull in England. She suggests that genes play an important role in determining handedness. According to her theory, most people possess a gene that strongly predisposes them to have a dominant left hemisphere and, therefore, to be right-handed. But in people who lack this gene, Annett suggests, handedness is left to chance or to environmental influences—with the result that half of the people lacking the gene become left-handed.

Another researcher, psychologist Michael C. Corballis of the University of Auckland in New Zealand, proposes that a gene or genes have a less direct effect on handedness than Annett's theory suggests. Instead, according to Corballis, genes may have a general effect on the developing fetus that causes greater development on the left side of the body—an effect that would explain why the heart develops on the left side of the body. Similarly, such an effect might explain why right-handedness, which is controlled by the left side of the brain, is far more common than left-handedness.

Handedness and brain injury

Since the 1920's, many scientists have also considered the possibility that a brain injury at birth or in early childhood may result in left-handedness—an idea that may have helped promote the idea that left-handedness is somehow linked to physical abnormalities. An extreme view of this theory, suggested in 1971 by psychologist Paul Bakan of Simon Fraser University in Burnaby, Canada, is that all forms of left-handedness are caused by injury to the brain. He proposes that the left hemisphere is more vulnerable to the wide-ranging effects of stress before and during birth. When such stress occurs, says Bakan, the result is a shift in hand preference from right-handedness to left-handedness. Studies by other researchers, however, have failed to find an increased incidence of left-handedness in people who experienced complications at the time of their birth.

Other scientists, including myself, believe that brain injury causes only one type of left-handedness—*pathological left-handedness.* Pathological left-handedness is found in people who would have been right-handed but suffered some physical injury to the left side of the brain, probably before the age of 6, that caused them to be left-handed. My own theory is that only a small number of natural right-handers who suffer damage to the left side of the brain when young will become left-handed. I also believe that such a shift in handedness occurs only if the damage affects areas of the left hemisphere that control speech or movement. And since only some people who suffer such brain damage alter hand preference, I suspect that those who do change handedness may have some genetic factors that predispose them to do so.

Handedness and brain development

Some scientists have proposed that left-handedness is caused by some factor or factors that affect the development of the brain before birth. One of the chief proponents of this theory was neurologist Norman Geschwind at the Harvard Medical School in Boston. Geschwind suggested that handedness is influenced by a fetus's exposure in the womb to the male hormone testosterone.

Testosterone is produced by the testicles in males; the ovaries of females and the adrenal glands of both sexes also produce small amounts of the hormone. All fetuses are exposed to

A lefty ruler has inches marked from right to left.

Interesting facts about the left

In most languages, the word *left* is often associated with undesirable traits. The French word *gauche,* meaning *left,* also means *clumsy, awkward,* or *socially inferior. Mancino,* the Italian word for *left-handed,* can mean *deceitful* or *treacherous.* In *Old English* (English language before 1100), the word *left,* spelled *lyft,* meant *useless* or *weak.* But the Greeks have a positive view of the left. The Greek word for *left, aristos,* also means *best.* From this word comes the English word *aristocrat.*

Many common English expressions have arisen from society's negative view of the left, such as "having two left feet" to describe a clumsy person and a "left-handed compliment" to describe dubious praise.

Left-handed scissors are designed to be held in the left hand.

Southpaw, the slang word for a left-hander, was first used in the late 1800's to describe left-handed pitchers. Back then, baseball parks were designed so that home plate was west of the pitcher. When a left-handed pitcher faced the batter, his left hand, or paw, faced south. No one knows who coined the word, but some say it was a Chicago journalist, either Finley Peter Dunne in 1887 or Charles Seymour in 1890.

Even though most women are right-handed, the buttons on their clothes are sewn on the left. This custom originated when wealthy women were dressed by their maids, most of whom were right-handed. Buttons were sewn on the left so that they could be easily buttoned by a right-handed person facing them. Since men usually dressed themselves, their clothes were designed with the buttons sewn on the right.

testosterone in the womb, where it is secreted by the mother or the fetus itself. Female fetuses produce very little testosterone; male fetuses produce relatively large amounts of the hormone. But if the mother or fetus secretes excessive amounts of testosterone—or if the fetus is unusually sensitive to the effects of the hormone—the development of the fetus's brain may be affected.

One possible effect of the hormone, suggested Geschwind, would be a delay in the development of the fetus's left hemisphere. The brain would then compensate, according to his theory, by increasing the growth of the right hemisphere—which would cause the individual to become left-handed.

We don't yet have enough evidence to determine which of these theories concerning the underlying cause of left-handedness is correct. My own view, and that of many other scientists, is that in most cases, a combination of genetic and environmental factors determine whether a person will be left-handed.

When held in the left hand, the measurements on a left-handed measuring cup face the person holding the cup.

People not only have a dominant hand preference, but they also have a dominant eye, foot, and ear, which are usually located on the same side of the body as the dominant hand.

Unlike human beings—90 per cent of whom are right-handed—animals seem to be more equally divided as to which paw they prefer to use. Some studies suggest that 50 per cent of all monkeys, cats, and mice show a preference for the right paw, while 50 per cent seem to prefer the left paw. Other studies have shown, however, that a great many gorillas and chimpanzees show no preference for either paw.

A healthy child, in most cases, will not show consistent hand preference until about the age of 8.

Benjamin Franklin (1706-1790), who was reportedly *ambidextrous* (used both his left and right hands for various tasks), signed the Declaration of Independence with his left hand. He also wrote a letter stating the plight of the left hand. The letter, written as if by a left hand, said, in part, ". . . From my infancy I have been led to consider my sister [the right hand] as being of a more educated rank. I was suffered to grow up without the least instruction, while nothing was spared in her education. She had masters to teach her writing, drawing, music and other accomplishments, but if by chance I touched a pencil, a pen, or a needle I was bitterly rebuked; and more than once I have been beaten for being awkward, and wanting a graceful manner."

Leonardo da Vinci (1452-1519), a left-handed Italian painter known as the "patron saint of left-handers," often wrote backwards. The easiest way to read these writings is with a mirror.

A spiral notebook for lefties has the spiral on the right side.

Left-handedness, disease, and talent

In the early 1980's, the question of whether left-handedness is linked with certain diseases or a greater aptitude in certain fields became a hotly debated issue in the scientific community. This was chiefly due to studies by Geschwind, who suggested that prenatal exposure to testosterone not only causes left-handedness but also plays a partial role in various physical disorders and special talents.

Geschwind's suggestion sprang from the observation that people with certain disorders, such as *dyslexia* (a reading disability), share other characteristics that seem to be unrelated to the disorder. In particular, he noted a greater incidence of left-handedness, allergies, stuttering, and other problems among people with dyslexia.

Geschwind and Peter Behan, a neurologist at the University of Glasgow in Scotland, conducted a number of studies suggesting that left-handed people are more likely than right-handed people to have such disorders as dyslexia, *migraine* (a severe form of headache), and *autoimmune disease*. In autoimmune diseases, the body's disease-fighting immune system attacks the body in the same way it usually attacks the bacteria and viruses that cause illness. Among the diseases that Geschwind and Behan linked with handedness are one form of *diabetes mellitus,* a disorder in which the body cannot use sugar properly; *rheumatoid arthritis,* a condition in which the body's joints are inflamed and swollen; and *ulcerative colitis,* an inflammation of the colon. (These diseases are suspected of being caused, in part, by a malfunction of the immune system.)

Geschwind theorized that in some cases, prenatal exposure to testosterone may have effects on the body that promote both left-handedness and various disorders. He suspected that testosterone plays such a role in development because males (who are exposed to higher levels of the hormone before birth) are slightly more likely to be left-handed and are at higher risk for some autoimmune and learning disorders than are females.

Geschwind argued that one effect of testosterone would be retarding the development of the *thymus gland,* an organ that helps develop white blood cells vital to the body's immune system. He reasoned that slowing the development of the thymus gland might affect the development of the immune system, which in turn might increase an individual's susceptibility to autoimmune diseases. A second effect, he suggested, may be delaying the development of the fetus's left hemisphere, which could affect speech and language skills and lead to dyslexia and other language-related disorders during childhood.

Geschwind also suggested that the brain compensates for the delayed development of the left hemisphere by increasing the growth of the right hemisphere. This event, he argued, could account not only for left-handedness, but also might explain the superior talents many left-handers appear to have in the arts, sports, and engineering—fields that rely more on the right hemisphere's visual and spatial abilities.

But many researchers do not accept Geschwind's ideas. First of all, they say that flaws in Geschwind's understanding of the immune system weaken his argument that prenatal exposure to testosterone may be linked to autoimmune disorders. Second, Geschwind's critics also say that his studies linking left-handedness to learning problems and autoimmune disorders are inconclusive because he relied on data from questionnaires that required adults to recall details about childhood learning problems and illness. Because patients' memories about such events may not be reliable, conclusions based on such data are highly questionable.

Although some researchers continue to report associations between left-handedness and everything from hair color to homosexuality, the link between left-handedness and these other traits is not a substantial one. In general, recent studies consistently fail to demonstrate a clear-cut link between left-handedness and various disorders and talents. For example, a number of studies of children and reading and learning disorders—including one I conducted with neuropsychologists Eileen B. Fennell at the University of Florida in Gainesville, Jack M. Fletcher at the University of Houston, and Robin D. Morris at Georgia State University in Atlanta—failed to find a relationship between left-handedness and these problems. In view of this lack of evidence, many scientists are highly skeptical of the notion that left-handers are at greater risk of disease—or have greater talents in certain fields—than right-handers.

Why do the results of studies exploring possible links between left-handedness and various disorders seem to be so inconsistent, with some studies supporting these associations while others do not? In part, the answer may stem from flaws in the design of experiments, such as drawing conclusions from groups with too few subjects to be reliable. But an even more important factor may stem from society's persistent belief that left-handedness is an abnormal trait. Such an ingrained belief may, for example, cause left-handed subjects to unintentionally exaggerate childhood problems or imagine learning or health problems where none may have actually existed.

Researchers continue to work to uncover the underlying causes of left-handedness and to determine if any genuine links exist between left-handedness and various disorders and talents. Current evidence suggests that a small group of left-handers may be at slightly greater risk for dyslexia, autoimmune diseases, and other conditions than right-handers—who are also at risk. But the vast majority of left-handers are not significantly different from right-handers in talent, disability, or disease. Although it is fashionable to associate left-handedness with diseases and talents, further research is needed to help us separate fact from fiction.

For further reading:

Fincher, Jack. *Sinister People: The Looking-Glass World of the Left-Hander.* G. P. Putnam's Sons, New York, 1977.

Springer, Sally P. *Left Brain, Right Brain.* W. H. Freeman and Company, New York, 1985.

For more information on left-handedness, write to Lefthanders International, P.O. Box 8249, Topeka, KS 66608, or call (913) 234-2177.

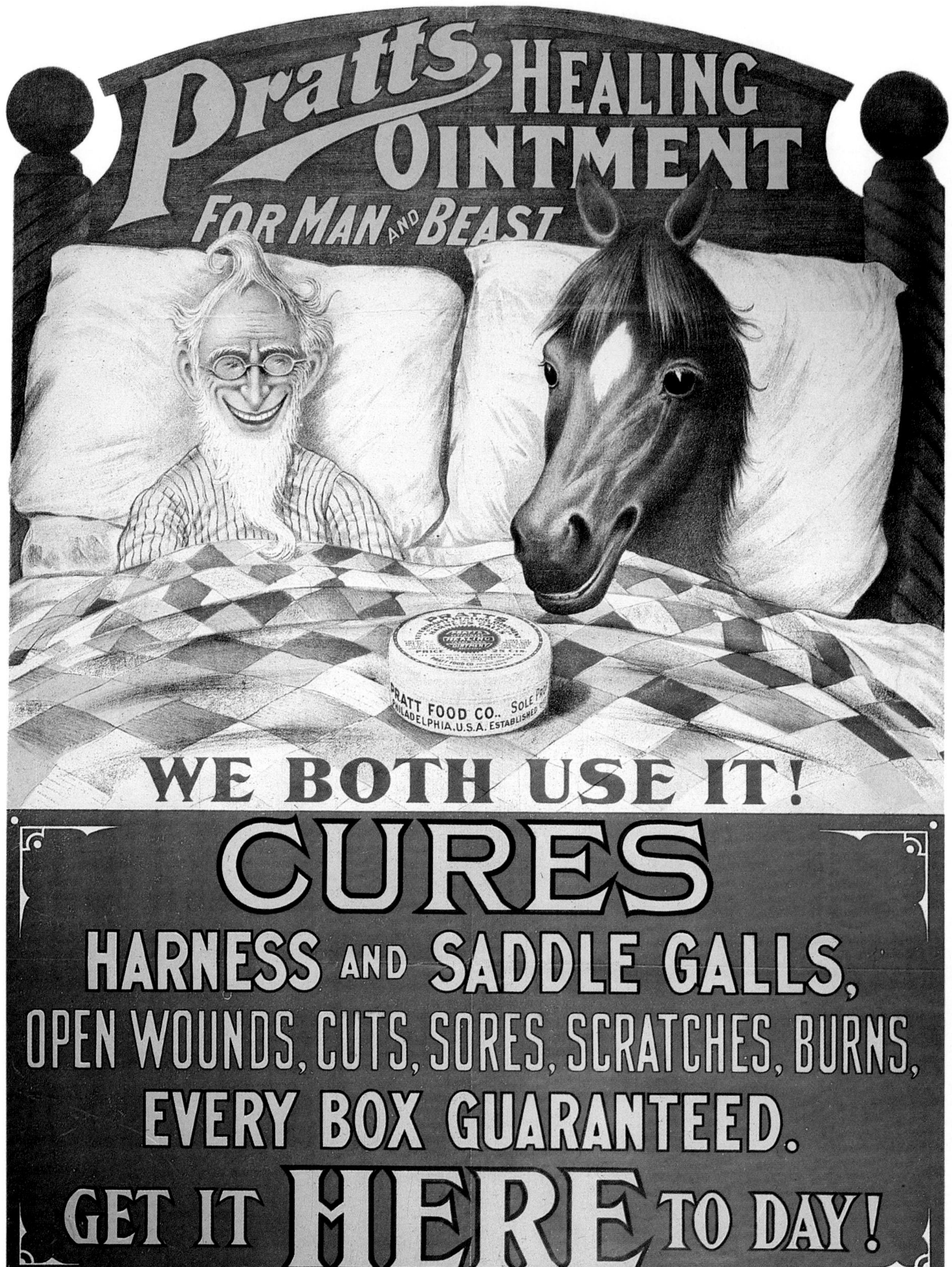
Pratts HEALING OINTMENT
FOR MAN AND BEAST
PRATT FOOD CO..
WE BOTH USE IT!
CURES
HARNESS AND SADDLE GALLS,
OPEN WOUNDS, CUTS, SORES, SCRATCHES, BURNS,
EVERY BOX GUARANTEED.
GET IT HERE TO DAY!

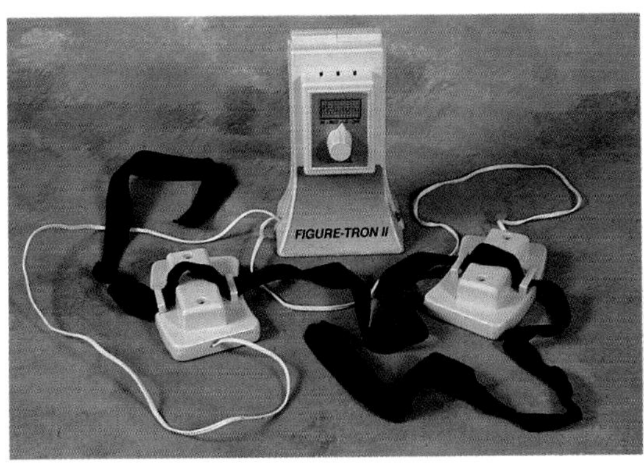

The High Cost of Quackery

By Michael Woods

Fraudulent and unproven remedies cost us billions of dollars each year—and endanger our lives.

Mention the word *quackery* today, and most people think of crooks and charlatans peddling so-called cure-alls at county fairs or along dusty country roads. In the 1790's, people with rheumatism, yellow fever, and other ailments thought two small pointed rods called "Perkins tractors" would draw disease out of their bodies. In the 1800's, ulcer sufferers sought relief from "Kickapoo Indian Sagwa—Stomach, Liver, and Kidney Renovator." And around the beginning of the 1900's, cancer patients tried "Dr. Johnson's Mild Composition Treatment," a tonic of unknown composition and dubious value.

Many of today's well-informed consumers are amazed that their ancestors were gullible enough to be hoodwinked by such obvious frauds. But the truth is that quackery has never disappeared. In recent years, for example, many arthritis patients have turned to such bogus treatments as warm cow manure, coffee enemas, and vials of "genuine" moon dust—a "bargain" at only $100 for a few spoonfuls. And some desperate cancer patients resort to a variety of worthless remedies, including asparagus oil, carrot juice, and "serums" made from human feces.

A century ago, quacks promoted fake remedies by making extravagant claims, as in the poster at left. Quackery today is often more sophisticated but no less fraudulent. In 1983, federal authorities banned sales of the Figure-Tron II, *above,* because the manufacturer claimed falsely that the device toned the body without exercise.

Medical authorities report that quackery today is thriving and even expanding, costing people their money, their health, and sometimes their lives. A four-year study by the United States House of Representatives Special Committee on Aging, completed in 1984, found that Americans spend at least $10 billion each year on fraudulent medical treatments, compared with $1-billion to $2 billion in the 1960's.

What is quackery?

Although the word *quack* is thought to have originated in the 1500's, its source is uncertain. Many people believe that the term evolved from *Kwaksalver,* a Dutch word meaning *seller of salves and medicines.* Others propose that *quack* became the name of itinerant peddlers who promoted their salves and medicines using loud, staccato tones that resembled the quacking of ducks.

Today, the terms *quackery* and *health fraud* are often used to describe the peddling of unproven or worthless medical treatments, usually with knowledge that the treatment being promoted is ineffective. Quacks have a total disregard for scientific proof of the effectiveness of their products, or they claim effectiveness on the basis of evidence that is not valid, such as testimonials of people who think the product helped them. The quack ignores the procedures, accepted by legitimate scientists, for establishing the safety and effectiveness of new therapies.

Although health fraud has been with us for centuries, the almost comic figure of the quack as a fast-talking confidence man has been replaced by a more dangerous figure. This figure, the modern quack, may appear to be respectable and well educated and often is difficult to distinguish from a legitimate medical practitioner. Many of today's quacks work in medical offices, clinics, and foundations with scientific names. Some of those promoting unproven therapies may have a medical degree and a sincere conviction in the effectiveness of their therapy. And unlike the quacks of yesteryear, who hawked their wares at county fairs or from medicine wagons, many modern quacks publish books and place advertisements in newspapers, in magazines, and on television.

But while quacks may have changed over the centuries, the basic formula of quackery has not. It is a siren song of false hope, a song that soothes and reassures the sick, the elderly, the desperate, the vain, and the gullible.

The author:

Michael Woods is science editor of *The Toledo Blade.*

Quackery's victims

For centuries, people have risked their lives and health on unorthodox treatments. Prehistoric people thought charms and fetishes could prevent and cure disease. The Roman historian

Quack cures—salesmanship and alcohol
Self-styled experts have traditionally drawn on mysterious or exotic cultures to create an air of authority, as this "Indian medicine man" did in 1945 to peddle his remedy in Tennessee, *right.* But the popularity of such cures lay mostly in salesmanship, not in the remedies themselves. Many quack tonics derived their supposed healing effects from a common ingredient—alcohol, *right below* and *right bottom.*

Pliny the Elder (A.D. 23-79) advocated eating a mouse a week to prevent toothache. And in the 1790's, George Washington was one of the purchasers of Perkins tractors, the device that supposedly drew disease out of the body.

Unlike quackery victims of the past, many people who purchase fraudulent remedies today are neither poorly educated dupes nor dying patients who turn to unorthodox therapy in desperation. In 1984, researchers at the University of Pennsylvania reported that many people who try unorthodox treatments simply want to assume greater responsibility for their own health care. According to the Pennsylvania researchers, some patients make a deliberate decision to abandon conventional health care in favor of treatments that supposedly are "natural and nontoxic," such as megavitamin therapy—which involves consuming huge doses of vitamins and minerals. Others continue to accept medical treatment, but combine it with unorthodox or fraudulent therapy, such as consuming certain foods or using enemas to "cleanse" the body.

But quacks also continue to exploit more traditional victims. People with chronic or incurable illnesses, such as arthritis, cancer, or AIDS (acquired immune deficiency syndrome) are particularly vulnerable. Also, individuals who are insecure about their physical appearance are often easily swayed by quacks' promises of treatments for losing weight, reversing baldness, or enlarging breasts. And advanced age and disabilities or illness make older people likely targets. In fact, senior citizens are now the prime targets of health fraud, according to the 1980-1984 congressional study, one of the most comprehensive examinations of health fraud in modern times.

The Oscilloclast, *above,* a desk-sized instrument manufactured in the 1920's, supposedly allowed doctors to diagnose and treat illnesses with polarized light. In fact, most of the unit's many switches connect to nothing, and the dials measure little more than the voltage used to power the impressive-looking machine.

Arthritis quackery

Experts estimate that 90 per cent of all arthritis patients try an unproven remedy at least once—treatments that waste about $2 billion each year in the United States, far more than is spent on arthritis research. And because arthritis often has symptom-free periods, people with arthritis are particularly vulnerable to quack remedies. If arthritis patients happen to try such a treatment just before a period of improvement, they may mistakenly believe that the quack remedy helped them.

Some quack arthritis treatments seem ridiculous to most of us, including "genuine" moon dust that is merely ordinary sand, or mittens and pads containing crushed rock that supposedly emits healing radioactive rays. Copper and magnetic bracelets remain the most consistently popular arthritis frauds, though they are useless, according to health authorities, in preventing or treating arthritis.

More subtle in its appeal is an unproven arthritis treatment called "diet therapy" or "nutritional therapy." Some proponents of so-called nutritional therapy argue that certain foods—such as potatoes, tomatoes, and other foods in a group of plants called the *nightshades*—cause arthritis and should be eliminated from the diet. Other people claim that certain foods—including lemon juice, honey, and herbal teas—can cure the disease. But scientists have found only one arthritic condition, caused by a metabolic disease called *gout,* whose symptoms are related to diet. Thus, experts such as those at the Arthritis Foundation (a nonprofit organization based in Atlanta, Ga.) dismiss nutritional therapy for arthritis as useless.

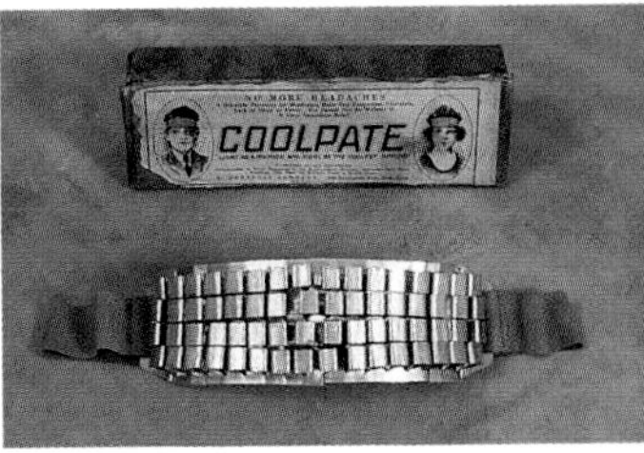

The Coolpate, *above*, sold during the 1920's, promised "no more headaches." Ailing patients were instructed to wrap the metal band across the forehead.

Quackery and cancer

Although early diagnosis and prompt treatment frequently spell the difference between life and death for cancer patients, many endanger their lives by delaying or refusing legitimate medical treatment in favor of quack remedies. The American Cancer Society estimates that about 170,000 people who died of cancer in 1987 could probably have been saved by earlier diagnosis and proper treatment.

According to a poll of more than 1,500 adults, conducted in 1986 for the United States Food and Drug Administration (FDA), 15 per cent of cancer sufferers have tried a quack product or other questionable treatment. Although the number of unproven cancer therapies is enormous, the 1984 University of Pennsylvania study classified them in six major types—diet therapy, metabolic therapy, unscientific forms of immune therapy, megavitamin therapy, mental imagery, and spiritual or faith healing.

Various forms of diet, or nutritional, therapy—a popular but unproven approach to treating cancer, arthritis, and other diseases—cost Americans $500 million each year, according to the American Medical Association (AMA), a national organization of physicians, based in Chicago. One quack cure for cancer, developed in the 1920's and still hoodwinking people today, is the "grape diet," which involves eating virtually nothing but grapes. Other such diets involve extracts of clams, large quantities of cranberry juice, and herbal teas—some of which contain chemicals that actually stimulate cancer cells.

One source of confusion among consumers regarding diet therapy is recent medical evidence that consuming high-fiber foods such as whole grain cereals, vegetables such as cabbage and broccoli, and foods rich in vitamin A and C can reduce the risk of some forms of cancer. But there is no guarantee that such foods will prevent cancer, and no evidence that these foods can cure the disease once it has developed.

Metabolic therapy, another major type of unorthodox cancer treatment, involves the use of enemas, special diets, and other techniques to "cleanse" the body of waste materials that supposedly interfere with normal metabolism. This approach not only has no proven value, it can be hazardous. Deaths have been caused by the daily enemas, consisting of strong solutions of coffee, that are included in some quack regimens.

Immune therapy, which is based on the concept of stimulating the body's own disease-fighting immune system, is another common type of cancer therapy promoted by quacks. Unlike

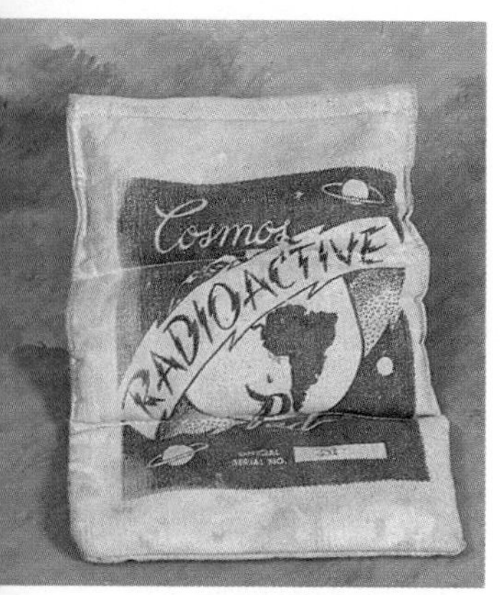

In the 1950's, the distributors of the bag of crushed uranium ore shown above capitalized on the public's fascination with radioactivity. The sellers falsely claimed that "therapeutic" radiation from the bag's contents would relieve arthritis, asthma, and sinus problems.

the legitimate immune therapy being tested in medical settings such as the National Cancer Institute in Bethesda, Md., immune therapy as practiced by quacks—which includes injections of animal fetal tissue or "vaccines" made from the patient's urine and other material—has no scientific basis.

Similarly, according to the University of Pennsylvania study, megavitamin therapy has no proven value—and large doses of certain vitamins, such as vitamin A, can be toxic. Nor is there scientific evidence that mental imagery (a technique in which the cancer patient visualizes the destruction of cancer cells in an effort to destroy the malignancy) or spiritual or faith healing are of value.

Beauty and the quack

Some quack treatments are aimed at our vanity, promising to cure every conceivable human imperfection, from obesity to baldness. Weight-loss products are by far the most popular of these remedies, according to an FDA study. These include rubberlike "sauna suits" and *body wraps* (wrapping the body in fabric soaked in a concentrated salt solution) and vibrating belts said to eliminate "cellulite" (an unscientific term sometimes used to describe dimpled fat on the waist, hips, and thighs). Fraudulent diet pills and diet plans are also prevalent. For example, the "grapefruit pill" and the "grapefruit diet" are promoted as ways to speed up the body's consumption of calories so that people can eat all they want and still lose weight, a prospect that sounds—and is—too good to be true.

Medical authorities at the FDA and elsewhere say that no scientific theory or evidence supports the effectiveness of these products. Sauna suits and body wraps may appear to remove body fat. But in reality, they only cause muscle contraction or loss of water through perspiration—a strictly temporary effect. And there is no evidence that the grapefruit pills or diet help the body burn calories.

Certain weight-loss products can even be dangerous, especially for people suffering from cardiovascular problems or other chronic illness. These include the so-called liquid-protein diet, which was associated with more than 30 deaths in 1977, when the FDA proposed that liquid-protein diet products use warning labels.

What does it take to lose weight permanently and safely? "The answer does not involve miracles or new discoveries," according to a 1985 FDA report on fad diets. Permanent weight loss requires a careful reduction in calorie intake or an increase in calorie expenditure through exercise, or both.

Insecurity about body proportions and physical appearance,

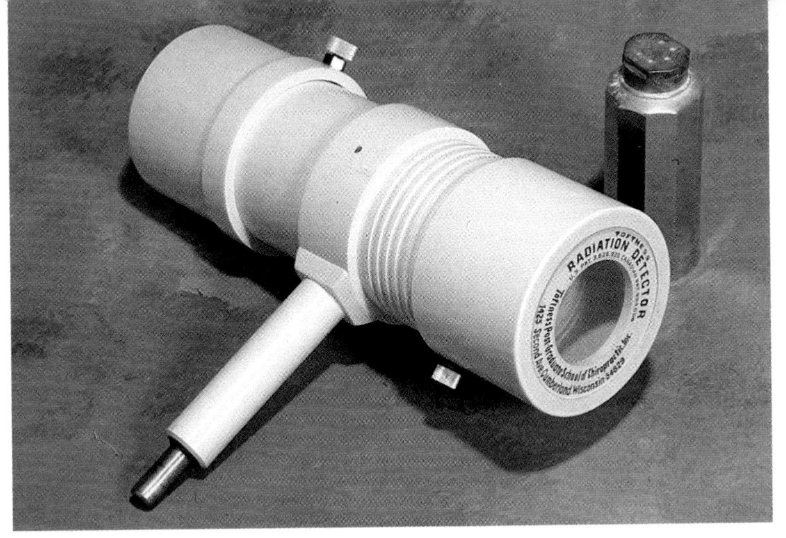

Not all frauds are marketed directly to the public. In the early 1980's, the Toftness Radiation Detector, *above,* was offered to *chiropractors* (people who treat illness primarily through manipulation of the patient's spine) as a diagnostic tool that supposedly detected electromagnetic radiation from the body. It was removed from the market in 1984.

which is normal during adolescence, has made teen-agers prime targets of fraudulent products that promise to improve the appearance. The FDA and the Council of Better Business Bureaus—an organization whose members work to protect the public from deceptive advertising and selling practices—say that teen-agers in particular are duped by phony diets, creams and mechanical devices that guarantee to enlarge breasts, and pills that supposedly produce a glowing tan.

These devices and treatments fail to deliver what they promise, or may be hazardous. The FDA reports that there is no evidence that creams or mechanical devices can enlarge the breasts. Some devices promoted as breast developers may strengthen the muscles that support the breasts, but cause no appreciable increase in bust size. Studies suggest that an additive in so-called tanning pills can cause slight visual abnormalities—a finding that concerns authorities. Although not approved by the FDA for use in the United States, the pills—which are popular in Canada, Europe, and Australia—are easily obtained in the United States through mail order.

Teen-agers are by no means alone in their concern with their appearance. "Cures" for baldness, such as creams and lotions that supposedly stimulate growth of new hair, also rank among the most popular quack products. The FDA notes, however, that most hair loss results from a condition called *male pattern baldness* that cannot be reversed by any nonprescription drug. (In August 1988, the FDA approved for sale a prescription drug called Rogaine as a treatment for some types of baldness.) And another baldness "treatment"—hair implants of synthetic fibers—can cause serious infections.

AIDS—a new target for quackery

One of the newest and most rapidly growing areas of quackery involves phony ways of treating a group of people with a new and fatal disease—AIDS. The FDA has called AIDS a "quack's

Makers of fraudulent remedies have traditionally used testimonials from "satisfied customers" as an advertising ploy. A 1912 educational poster from the American Medical Association, *above,* points out the "worthlessness of testimony": The patients who were supposedly cured of "consumption" (known today as tuberculosis) later died of that disease.

dream come true, an incurable fatal disease surrounded by fear and ignorance."

Authorities testifying at 1987 congressional hearings estimated that Americans spent $1 billion on fraudulent AIDS treatments during 1986 alone. AIDS involves impairment of the body's disease-fighting immune system, and promoters of unorthodox treatments often claim—without a shred of evidence to support their statements—that their products bolster immunity. According to physician John Renner, chairman of the Midwest Council Against Health Fraud in Kansas City, Mo., there is no scientific basis for any of the wide variety of AIDS "cures" appearing on the market, including injections of hydrogen peroxide, bathing in a solution of household bleach, massaging the skin with a dry brush, injections made from the patient's own urine, and megadoses of vitamins.

Protecting consumers against quackery

Quackery and legitimate testing of new drugs are similar in one respect: Both involve administering unproven treatments to patients. But unlike quackery, the legitimate testing of unproven treatments is carried out under strict governmental regulations and scientific review.

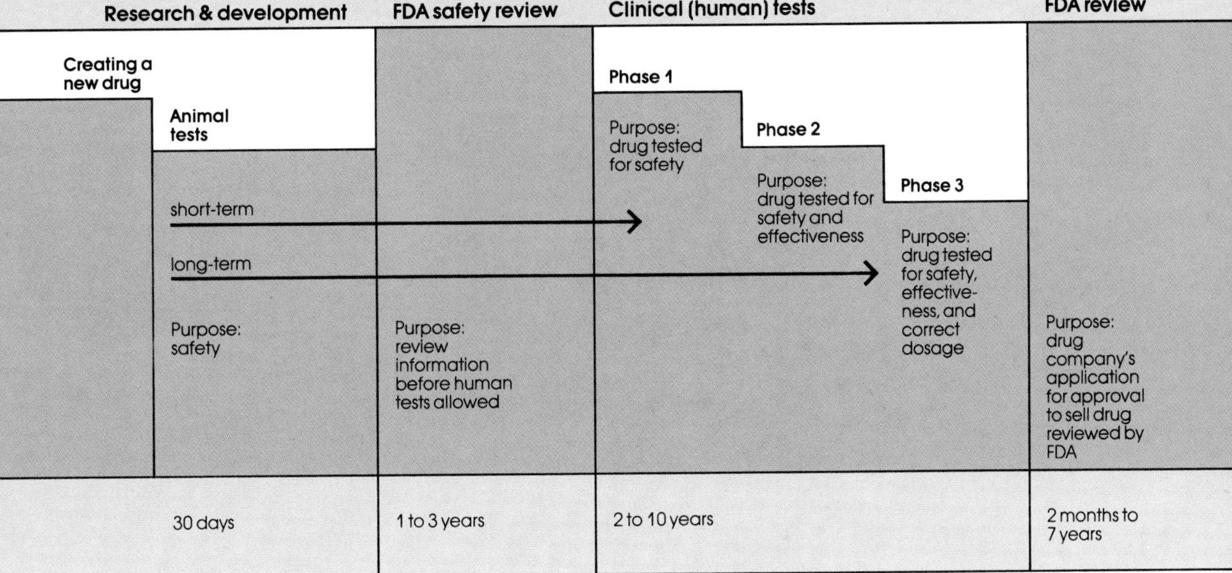

Before a new drug can legally be sold to the public, it is subjected to an average of 100 months of research and testing to determine its safety and effectiveness. This process includes both short- and long-term animal tests to determine safety, three phases of human testing to determine whether the drug is safe and effective in treating the illness for which it would be prescribed, and a review of these tests by the U.S. Food and Drug Administration (FDA) before it is approved for sale to the public. Even after the drug has been approved, it may be withdrawn from the market if new problems are uncovered.

Determining the safety and effectiveness of a potential new drug is an exhaustive process. First, the drug's sponsor—usually a pharmaceutical company—typically spends from one to three years in preclinical research, which includes testing the drug on laboratory animals. Then, if the drug shows promise and appears to be safe, the sponsor applies to the FDA for permission to test the drug on human beings. If the FDA approves, physicians at medical centers and hospitals conduct *clinical trials* (tests on human beings) in three phases.

In Phase 1 of clinical trials, researchers administer the drug to healthy volunteers to learn more about the drug's therapeutic effects and also undesirable side effects in the body. In Phase 2, they try to establish whether the drug actually is effective in treating the disease for which it is intended, and they look for short-term side effects. Some patients receive the drug, while others—called *controls*—receive either a *placebo* (a "sugar pill") or the conventional treatment for the disease. Comparisons of the results help determine the drug's effectiveness. Furthermore, the trial is usually a *double-blind* study, which means that neither the patients nor the physicians evaluating their conditions know who is getting the new drug. This feature is crucial in preventing bias that otherwise might taint the results. Patients, for example, might feel better just because they know they are receiving a promising new drug.

Phase 3 of clinical trials expands the research carried out in

Quacks often hide behind meaningless credentials. To demonstrate how anyone can acquire an official-sounding title, Victor Herbert, a New York City physician and crusader against health fraud, registered his cat, Charlie, *above*, as a "nutritional consultant" simply by paying a $50 fee.

Phase 2, clarifies the drug's benefits, helps identify less common side effects, and establishes how doctors should prescribe the drug. In Phase 3, as in earlier stages of drug testing, researchers publish their findings in medical journals, thus enabling the entire scientific community to review the experiments.

In clinical trials, most new drugs meet with failure. For every 20 substances taken to clinical trial by some large drug companies, only 1 proves safe and effective enough to gain FDA approval for marketing. The development and testing of a new drug also take time—an average of nearly nine years before FDA approval. For example, *lovastatin*, a medication aimed at reducing the risk of heart disease, was approved in 1987 after about nine years of testing.

Medical scientists throughout the world recognize such controlled clinical trials as the only valid way of determining the safety and effectiveness of new treatments. But quacks reject this process. Many rely, instead, on testimonials from patients who supposedly benefited from their treatment. But testimonials cannot establish that the product caused the improvement; many other factors may have been responsible. For example, some illnesses, such as the common cold, get better by themselves with the passage of time.

And patients using quack remedies may feel better simply because of a well-established phenomenon called the *placebo effect*. People who believe that a particular medicine will make them better often experience temporary relief of symptoms. A variety of studies over the last 40 years have established that about one-third of patients given a pill containing no medication experience remarkable relief of pain. Studies suggest that such pain relief occurs because the patients themselves secrete pain-relieving brain chemicals called *endorphins*.

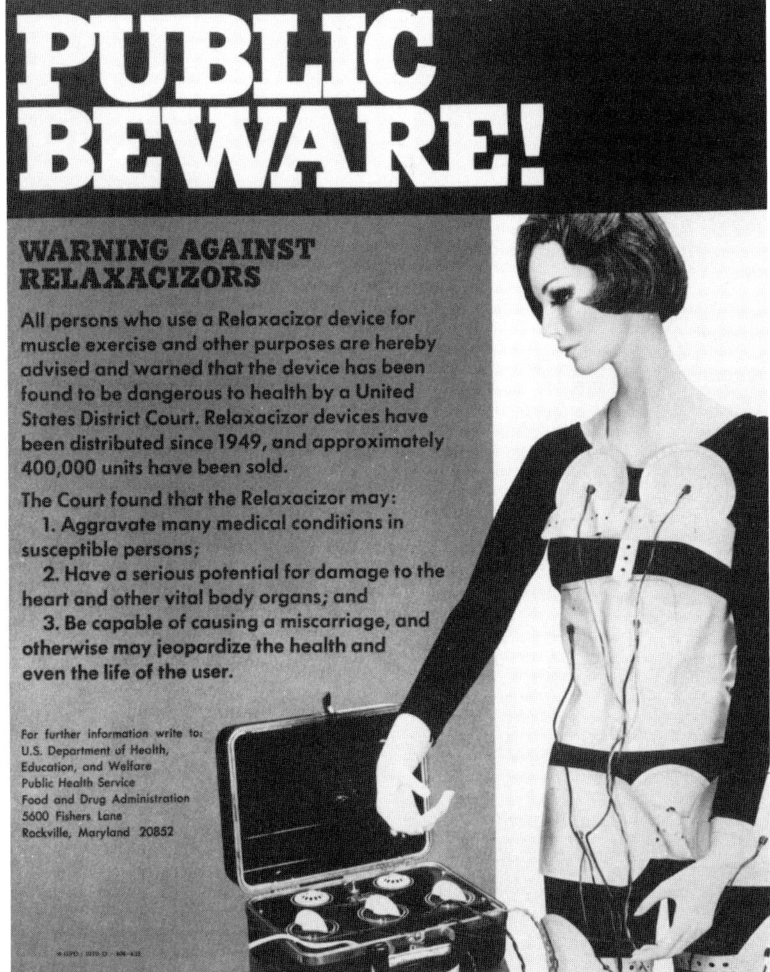

A poster published in 1970 by the FDA, *left*, alerts consumers to the perils of the Relaxacizor, a popular "electrical muscle stimulator" that supposedly strengthened muscles without exercise. Contrary to advertised claims of the product's beneficial effects, the device could injure the heart or other organs.

Some quacks, however, do cite the results of "clinical trials" in promoting their products. But their methods of testing generally have such glaring flaws—the lack of a control group of patients receiving a placebo or conventional treatment, for example—that they are meaningless.

Even legitimate drugs that have gone through the rigorous testing and evaluation process required by the FDA may be misused. Once the FDA has approved a drug for a specific use, physicians usually can legally prescribe it for any disease, even when there is no evidence that it will help treat another illness. For example, *chelation therapy*, which is used to treat lead and mercury poisoning, was approved for that purpose in 1953. But some physicians have advocated chelation therapy to stave off heart attacks—though most experts insist that it has no proven benefit in preventing heart attacks and has potentially serious side effects.

Experts say that the best defense against quackery is education. Consumer groups like the National Council Against Health Fraud, Incorporated, use a variety of attention-getting efforts—ranging from buttons, *above,* to educational programs—to alert the public to quackery and teach people how to spot and combat fraud.

Fighting quackery

A number of organizations play a role in fighting quackery. The efforts of these organizations—including government agencies, health organizations, and consumer groups—range from investigating people suspected of engaging in health fraud to educating health professionals and the public.

Government agencies. The FDA, the Federal Trade Commission (FTC), the U.S. Postal Service, and the U.S. Department of Justice fight quackery by enforcing laws meant to protect the public from health fraud. The FDA has power to seize fraudulent products and prohibit the sale of any food, drug, device, or cosmetic that is mislabeled, misrepresented, or otherwise harmful. Advertising claims in publications and on radio and television are overseen by the FTC, which can order promoters of fraudulent products to stop false or deceptive advertisements and can impose penalties of up to $10,000 per violation. In addition, most states have laws regulating misleading advertising that are usually enforced by state attorneys general. The Postal Service has the authority to protect the public from mail-order quack products. Its enforcement activities include returning to the sender products sold under false claims. Finally, the Justice Department can initiate criminal proceedings against health-fraud promoters.

Health organizations. Numerous nongovernmental health organizations are also involved in the battle against quackery. These include representatives of organized medicine such as the AMA—which was established in 1847 partly to combat quackery—and voluntary, nonprofit organizations such as the American Cancer Society in New York City and the Arthritis Foundation. These groups provide physicians and other health-care workers with scientific evaluations of the safety and effectiveness of questionable treatments, and work to educate the public about health fraud.

Consumer organizations also play a significant role in fighting health fraud. The Council of Better Business Bureaus, which has offices in many cities, can sometimes provide information about products making health claims. Another organization active in combating quackery is the National Council Against Health Fraud, Incorporated, based in Loma Linda, Calif. This organization of "quackbusters" has more than 2,300 members, including health professionals, attorneys, educators, and concerned nonprofessionals. Its activities range from educational efforts to alerting governmental agencies about health-fraud schemes.

Government agencies and others can help stop the selling of fraudulent treatments—but only if they know about it. Unfortunately, embarrassed victims of health fraud often remain silent and thereby help perpetuate the fraud.

Protecting yourself against quackery

Given the laws designed to safeguard the public against health fraud, how can quackery survive and even thrive today? The 1984 congressional study on health fraud identified several major reasons, including the lack of funds to enforce those laws. Operating on tight budgets, government agencies generally have neither the staff nor the resources needed to identify, pursue, and prosecute thousands of promoters of quack products.

But most important, perhaps, the congressional study found a lack of public awareness about health fraud—a problem that governmental groups and others hope to combat through their education efforts. In the meantime, given the magnitude of the problem—and the limited ability of government agencies to pursue quacks—the best way people can avoid becoming victimized is to educate and protect themselves. For example, antifraud experts caution against assuming that a product must be legitimate because it is advertised in a newspaper or magazine or sold through the U.S. mail. Some publications screen advertising for false or misleading claims, but others do not—and no law requires such screening. And while the Postal Service has an active program to combat mail-order frauds, it can take time to do so. Meanwhile, the product remains on sale.

Experts also advise consumers to be wary of self-proclaimed experts with meaningless "credentials." Charlie Herbert, for example, has an impressive certificate from a "nutritional" society—but most people would doubt his nutritional expertise upon meeting him, since Charlie is a cat. Charlie's owner, Victor Herbert, a lawyer and physician at the Bronx Veterans Administration Medical Center in New York City and a crusader against health fraud, obtained the document for Charlie to demonstrate that the only requirement for the official-looking certificate was a name, an address, and a check for $50.

The FDA and other authorities warn consumers to be wary. They advise people to suspect fraud when products:

- Claim effectiveness against numerous diseases.
- Use extravagant terms like "100 per cent guaranteed," "natural and nontoxic," "amazing breakthrough," or "miraculous cure."
- Offer ways of losing weight without exercise, during sleep, or while eating all you want.
- Are available from only one doctor, foundation, or clinic—especially one in another country.
- Rely on testimonials from grateful patients.

Learning to distinguish questionable therapies from legitimate medical treatment is important. Your health—and perhaps your very life—may depend on it.

Where to go for help

If you believe you have been the victim of a quack treatment or product, the groups below may be of help. Report problems immediately, indicating the date and place of your purchase.

Federal Trade Commission
Bureau of Consumer Protection
6th and Pennsylvania Ave. NW
Washington, DC 20580
(202) 362-2222

Food and Drug Administration
Health Fraud Staff, HFD-304
5600 Fishers Lane
Rockville, MD 20857
(301) 295-8070

U.S. Postal Service
Chief Postal Inspector
475 L'Enfant Plaza SW
Washington, DC 20260
(202) 268-2000
(or inform your local post office)

National Council Against Health Fraud
P.O. Box 1276
Loma Linda, CA 92354
(714) 824-4690

You can also report suspected cases of health fraud to a local Better Business Bureau and local or state health departments and consumer affairs offices.

Snow

Hyperactive children have difficulty controlling their behavior. Early diagnosis and treatment can help.

Hope for the Hyperactive Child

By Howard Wolinsky

From the time Bobby Williams was born, his parents had a sinking suspicion that there was something wrong with him. As an infant, he was in constant motion, shifting from side to side in his crib. When he began to crawl—and then walk—he was into everything, climbing onto the kitchen counters and taking apart whatever he could get his hands on.

Although Bobby seemed to be bright, his physical development lagged behind that of his peers. He had difficulty climbing stairs and was unable to ride a tricycle. Bobby also had trouble getting along with other children. His parents wondered if he had hearing problems because Bobby frequently acted as if he did not hear them. Frustrated with his behavior, the Williamses (not their real name) took 3½-year-old Bobby to a local school for a preschool screening to assess his physical and mental abilities.

As the Williamses expected, the screening showed that Bobby was physically and socially behind other children his age. But they were shocked when the psychologist who tested Bobby said that his physical and social problems might be linked to a troubling condition called Attention Deficit Hyperactivity Disorder (ADHD), *a term that describes two important characteristics of the disorder—difficulty concentrating on tasks and an abnormally high level of activity.*

Although the term *Attention Deficit Hyperactivity Disorder* was unfamiliar to the Williamses, it is a common psychological problem among children and teen-agers. Health experts estimate that ADHD—also called *hyperactivity*—affects between 3 and 7 per cent of the children and teen-agers in the United States. For reasons that are still unknown, more boys than girls suffer from ADHD.

ADHD is considered by many people to be a baffling and complex disorder. It is difficult to diagnose, and its causes are unknown. In 1987, to help doctors diagnose the condition, the American Psychiatric Association (APA) in Washington, D.C., issued a definition of ADHD. According to this definition, ADHD is a condition characterized by a cluster of symptoms, including inattention, impulsiveness, and hyperactivity. In other words, children with ADHD are unable to pay attention for more than a few minutes at a time, they repeatedly act before thinking, and they are continually talking or moving. According to the APA, a diagnosis of ADHD can be made only if a child shows this cluster of symptoms before the age of 7 and only if the symptoms are present for at least six months. In most cases, ADHD is apparent by the time a child is 3 years old. Fortunately, ADHD can be treated.

Experts stress that there is a difference between children afflicted with ADHD and highly active children brimming with excess energy. Although highly active children may be difficult to control at times, particularly during periods of stress or excitement, they do display an ability to control their own actions. But children with ADHD have much less control and find it almost impossible to respond to discipline.

Until the mid-1960's, most experts viewed hyperactivity as a temporary setback in a child's development. Since then, however, scientists have found that the symptoms of ADHD often persist beyond childhood into adolescence and adulthood.

The first signs of ADHD may appear early in life. Many children with ADHD are unusually active as infants. They also may be more irritable than most infants and have irregular eating and sleeping habits. Later, as they reach the toddler stage—from 18 months to 3 years—these children continue to be extremely active compared with other children of the same age. They also may have poorly developed muscle control.

As children with ADHD grow older, their symptoms and behavior may prompt others to label them as "immature," "rebellious," or "disruptive." Because hyperactive children have

The author:

Howard Wolinsky is a medical writer for the *Chicago Sun-Times.*

difficulty in focusing their attention for very long, they often fail to carry out requests from their parents. Many have trouble getting up in the morning, playing games, or even eating meals with the family. The disorder is more pronounced when children with ADHD start school and face many new demands to follow instructions and to control their behavior.

Much less is known about what happens to ADHD children as they mature because there are few follow-up studies of ADHD individuals past adolescence. During the teen-age years and adulthood, hyperactive behavior may diminish, but problems of distractibility and impulsive behavior often persist.

Some researchers have found a strong link between ADHD and a kind of behavioral problem called *conduct disorder*—recurring incidents of lying, fighting, or other antisocial behavior. Some studies suggest that hyperactive children are more likely than other children to have difficulties with conduct problems as they grow older—especially if the ADHD children are not treated for the disorder. In addition, hyperactive children with conduct problems often have a troubled adolescence and young adulthood, with an increased likelihood of such serious problems as drug abuse and criminal behavior.

But experts also point out that not all hyperactive children have conduct disorder—and some studies suggest that these children are no more likely than nonhyperactive children to engage in drug abuse or criminal behavior as they grow older. The best strategy for helping all children with ADHD, according to those who treat children with the disorder, is early diagnosis and treatment of the condition.

Because ADHD is such a complex problem, approximately 20 to 30 medical centers in the United States have developed special teams of medical and mental health professionals to diagnose and treat the condition. These teams usually include pediatricians, *neurologists* (physicians who specialize in disorders of the nervous system), *psychiatrists* and *psychologists* (experts in treating mental or emotional problems), and learning disabilities specialists.

Members of a team conduct a series of tests and interviews with the child and the family. First, the child receives a complete physical examination to make sure that any behavioral or physical problems are not due to some other physical disorder. Then the child and family members are interviewed, separately and together, in order to put together a complete medical, psychiatric, and social history. This information is examined for any clues that the child's problems might stem from a mental or emotional disorder. In addition, team members give the pa-

The difficult world of the hyperactive child

Because they are overactive, impulsive, and easily distracted, hyperactive children face many challenges in life. At home, these children find it hard to obey their parents because they cannot complete tasks and often do not listen. Their high activity level makes everyday pursuits—such as eating with the family—almost impossible, *below*. At school, hyperactive children are unable to concentrate or listen to the teacher for long because they cannot sit still and are distracted by classmates or noises outside the classroom, *opposite page*. Hyperactive children do not make friends easily because their impulsiveness makes them grab toys or push playmates for no reason, *opposite page, below*.

S.Snow

tient psychological tests, such as intelligence tests, to rule out a learning disorder or mental retardation.

The school psychologist recommended that the Williamses take Bobby to a special team of health professionals at the local medical center to evaluate his condition and recommend treatment. The ADHD team's pediatrician explained to the Williamses that the series of exams and interviews conducted by the multidisciplinary team are vital to making an accurate diagnosis. Because other health problems may have ADHD-like symptoms, the team must—by process of elimination—rule out these other disorders. Only then, the Williamses learned, could the team recommend the proper treatment for Bobby.

Children with such wide-ranging problems as mental retardation and hormonal disorders—and, in some cases, children who are just difficult to discipline—have been misdiagnosed as having ADHD, because their symptoms resemble those of hyperactive children. In addition, an allergy or the early stages of lead poisoning can cause hyperactive behavior. Brain disorders such as *epilepsy* may also be confused with ADHD. Although epilepsy's most notable symptom is the occurrence of periodic seizures, the disorder also can cause hyperactive behavior and unresponsiveness.

Children with learning disorders such as *dyslexia* also may be misdiagnosed as having ADHD, because both ailments interfere with a child's ability to learn. Dyslexia, which causes a person to confuse letters, words, and numbers, is believed to be caused by a brain abnormality. Although some children may have both ADHD and dyslexia, experts believe that the poor reading and writing skills of many children with ADHD may be due to their inability to sit still long enough to learn, and by their poor motor skills, which make holding a pencil difficult.

It is thus easy to see why children suspected of having ADHD must be given thorough physical examinations by a team of experts. First, a pediatrician checks the child for allergies and for vision and hearing problems. Then, a neurologist looks for problems in the brain and nervous system and may take an *electroencephalogram* (EEG), a record of the electrical activity in the brain, if epilepsy or another seizure disorder is suspected. The neurologist or pediatrician may assess the child's coordination, balance, and *gait* (the manner of walking or running) for any sign of a neurological disorder.

An examination by a psychiatrist or psychologist determines whether the child is suffering from an emotional disorder, such as depression or overanxiousness. Children who are overanxious or who have many fears or worries are often agitated and appear hyperactive.

As part of the diagnostic process, psychologists usually ask parents and teachers to fill out questionnaires concerning the child's behavior. They also conduct tests to determine the child's attention span and level of hyperactivity.

Diagnosing ADHD is difficult—not only because its symptoms resemble those of other disorders but also because its cause or causes are unknown. Because pediatricians in the early 1900's noticed that hyperactive children displayed the same restlessness and overactivity found in mentally retarded children, they suggested that ADHD was caused by brain damage. They believed that the brains of hyperactive children, like the brains of mentally retarded children, had been damaged by disease or trauma. But in the 1960's, researchers found that brain damage could not be documented in the majority of hyperactive children who were studied. They also discovered that although mentally retarded children may be hyperactive, most hyperactive children have average or above-average intelligence.

Scientists today agree that hyperactivity is probably the result of several different factors rather than one single cause. In 1982, a panel of experts at the National Institutes of Health (NIH) in Bethesda, Md., examined the results of a number of studies and concluded that ADHD probably results from a combination of genetic and environmental factors and an imbalance in the brain's biochemistry.

The idea that there might be a genetic factor behind ADHD first arose in the 1970's, primarily because hyperactivity has been found to run in families. Scientists have not yet been able to prove a genetic link, but studies with animals and human beings strongly suggest that ADHD may be a genetic disorder.

Symptoms of a hyperactive child

Children may be diagnosed as being hyperactive only if they show eight or more of the following symptoms, and only if the symptoms begin before the child is 7 years old and last for more than six months.

- Fidgets with hands or feet or squirms in seat.
- Has difficulty remaining seated.
- Is easily distracted.
- Has difficulty awaiting turn in games or other group situations.
- Often blurts out answers before the questions have been completed.
- Has difficulty following through on instructions.
- Has difficulty paying attention while doing tasks or playing games.
- Often shifts from one uncompleted activity to another.
- Has difficulty playing quietly.
- Often talks excessively.
- Often interrupts or intrudes on others.
- Often does not seem to listen to what is being said.
- Often loses things needed to complete tasks, such as pencils or books.
- Often engages in physically dangerous activities, such as running into the street without looking.

Source: *Diagnostic and Statistical Manual of Mental Disorders*, American Psychiatric Association, 1987.

If after undergoing physical and psychological tests a child is diagnosed as hyperactive, the physician may prescribe a stimulant drug, such as Ritalin. The drug helps increase the child's attention span by controlling restlessness and impulsiveness. Before drug therapy begins, the physician discusses the drug with the child's parents, and may give them a list of potential side effects. Any side effects should be reported to the doctor.

Among possible environmental causes, diet has received the most attention. One hotly debated theory is that heavy sugar consumption triggers hyperactivity. Although the theory has many adherents, there is little scientific evidence to support it.

Another popular nutritional theory that is now in disfavor is that something in the diet of hyperactive children causes allergic-type reactions that result in hyperactivity. In the 1960's and 1970's, Benjamin F. Feingold, a San Francisco allergist, advocated the theory that food dyes, artificial flavorings, and preservatives in some processed foods contributed to hyperactive behavior. In 1963, Feingold devised a diet for hyperactive children that eliminated packaged cereals, commercially baked goods, ice cream, soft drinks, ketchup, cheese, and hot dogs.

Thousands of hyperactive children were placed on the Feingold diet, and many parents and teachers claimed to see benefits. But a number of studies have been unable to prove a link between diet and ADHD. As a result, an NIH panel stated in January 1982 that although dietary restrictions might aid a "small group" of hyperactive children, scientific evidence was not strong enough to indicate that it would help all of them.

In the late 1980's, the scientific community turned its attention to possible biochemical factors behind ADHD. Some scientists strongly suspect that ADHD is the result of an imbalance of chemicals in the brain called *neurotransmitters.* Neurotransmitters are released by nerve cells and act as messengers in the brain, carrying specific nerve impulses to other nerve cells. The neurotransmitter *dopamine,* for example, stimulates a part of the brain that controls emotions and physical sensations. *Norepinephrine,* another neurotransmitter, accelerates the heart and elevates blood pressure. Many scientists believe ADHD may be caused by a defect in the production or regulation of amounts of a class of neurotransmitters called *catecholamines,* which include dopamine and norepinephrine.

Much remains to be learned about the underlying causes of ADHD. In the meantime, health care professionals are finding better ways to treat the disorder. Treatment may include medication, special education, and some form of counseling. It also may include treating any physical disorders that might contribute to the problems of a child with ADHD.

The doctors who examined Bobby Williams confirmed that the boy had ADHD. They found that Bobby's condition was aggravated by sleeping problems caused by enlarged adenoids *(tissues at the back of the nasal passage) that interfered with his breathing. Surgical removal of Bobby's adenoids helped him sleep better, which reduced his irritability during the day.*

After dealing with any physical condition that might contribute to the problems of the hyperactive child, a physician may prescribe medication to suppress the impulsiveness and restlessness of patients with ADHD. For about 40 years, *stimulants*—drugs that increase a person's mental and physical activity—have been used to treat hyperactivity. Methylphenidate hydrochloride, sold under the trade name Ritalin, is the most widely prescribed stimulant for ADHD, but dextroamphetamine (Dexedrine) and pemoline (Cylert) are also used.

More than 600,000 hyperactive children in the United States take one of these three drugs. Experts say these stimulants effectively control impulsiveness and restlessness in 70 to 80 per cent of all children with ADHD. Although these stimulants appear to calm ADHD children, they actually help make them more alert, increasing their attention span and allowing them to pay attention and direct their behavior. This, in turn, helps improve their self-image, school performance, and behavior. The stimulants used to treat ADHD are not free of side effects, however. They may cause insomnia, appetite loss, headaches, or unusual movements, such as tics.

Scientists do not understand why stimulants do not make ADHD children more frantic. Psychiatrist James H. Satterfield, executive director of the National Center for Hyperactive Children in Encino, Calif., suggests that these drugs stimulate the release of neurotransmitters in areas of the brain that inhibit or control movement and behavior more than they stimulate the release of neurotransmitters in areas that excite the brain and nervous system. As a result, the child has more control over his or her actions.

Some critics have charged that these drugs, especially Ritalin, are overprescribed and given to children who have behavioral or emotional problems but who do not have ADHD. Others charge that the drugs simply mask the symptoms of ADHD and make children listless and passive. But Satterfield and other experts say that as long as the correct doses are administered to a child who has been correctly diagnosed as having ADHD, and the child's behavior is closely monitored by parents, teachers, and the physician, side effects can be avoided.

The pediatrician treating Bobby Williams prescribed a stimulant drug to control the youngster's hyperactive behavior. This worried the Williamses, but the pediatrician assured them that properly administered drug therapy can help many children with ADHD. She carefully outlined the drug's possible side effects and advised them to watch Bobby closely for any adverse reaction. She explained that side effects often indicate that the drug's dosage needs to be adjusted. The Willamses were further reassured when the pediatrician added that Bobby would be given periodic medical checkups as well.

Most ADHD experts say that drug therapy should be only one part of a total treatment plan. While drug therapy can help ADHD children focus their attention, it does not teach them how to cope with their environment or improve their learning and social skills. So, in addition to drug therapy, these children need special attention at home and at school.

Depending on the patient's needs, a program is set up to treat learning and emotional problems. Because 10 to 30 per cent of all hyperactive children have learning disabilities, this program also may include special education. But even those children who do not have a learning problem may benefit from special education classes.

The child's program may also include individual *psychotherapy* (treatment for mental or emotional problems), *group therapy* (psychotherapy conducted with a group of patients) with other ADHD children, and *family therapy* (a form of group therapy conducted with members of the patient's family). A program is also set up for parents and may include parent-training classes, individual psychotherapy, and group therapy with other parents of ADHD children.

There is, however, considerable debate over the effectiveness of any type of psychotherapy in treating ADHD. Some mental health professionals believe that comprehensive programs of therapy help reduce tension in the family and lower the chances that other problems may develop. But in 1976, psychologist Rachel Gittelman Klein of New York State Psychiatric Institute in New York City reported that a study of 86 children with ADHD showed that those who were given Ritalin alone—without psychotherapy—showed greater improvement in their behavior than those who received only psychotherapy. This study also showed that a combination of drug therapy and psychotherapy may benefit some, but not all, ADHD children.

Gittelman Klein suggests that the combination of drug therapy and psychotherapy be used only in cases where behavior problems are not helped by stimulants alone. But Satterfield at

Because hyperactive children often have learning or reading disabilities, they can benefit from special education classes. These classes are smaller than regular classes, allowing teachers to give students more individual attention. Smaller classes also provide fewer distractions, helping these children to focus their attention. Teachers often have hyperactive children list tasks on an index card as a helpful reminder of work they must complete.

Soccer and other group sports that are directed by adults provide an excellent way for hyperactive children to learn how to interact with other children and to direct their excess energy. Such activities also give parents a much-needed break from the pressures that go along with raising a hyperactive child.

the National Center for Hyperactive Children reported in 1987 that a nine-year comparison of the effects of various ADHD treatments indicated that treatment that combined drug therapy with psychotherapy resulted in a lower rate of arrests for teen-agers with ADHD than did drug therapy alone.

The multidisciplinary team testing Bobby Williams found that a high level of tension between Bobby and his parents increased his hyperactive behavior. At the recommendation of the team's psychologist, the Williamses enrolled in a parent-training class, where a psychologist taught them what to expect from Bobby and how to communicate effectively with him. They learned how to structure Bobby's playtime around simple games, using techniques—such as describing his actions aloud to him as he did them, like play-by-play sports announcers—that would encourage him to complete games.

As a result of the Williamses' efforts, Bobby began to pay more attention to what they told him. He enjoyed receiving positive attention from his parents, and their encouragement gave him a sense that he could control his behavior.

The Williamses were fortunate that the medical center in their community had a team of ADHD experts. But parents who do not live near such a team can still arrange for their child to receive a comprehensive evaluation. The first step is to have the child examined by a family physician or pediatrician. The physician will be able to refer them to other experts—such as a psychologist and a psychiatrist—who can also evaluate the child. The average cost of a comprehensive evaluation by an ADHD team varies, but may cost about $550. In most cases, insurance will cover some—or all—of this cost.

The road for children with ADHD is perilous, but there is reason for hope. In 1988, psychologist Salvatore Mannuzza of the New York State Psychiatric Institute reported on a study in which he monitored 52 ADHD boys from the ages of 6 to 12 to young adulthood. Mannuzza found that, in young adulthood, half of the young men were leading normal lives. The individuals with ADHD were indistinguishable from others in terms of academic achievement in high school and college, emotional problems, drug abuse, and antisocial behavior.

How does the future look for Bobby? Mrs. Williams says her son's behavior has improved greatly as a result of the Ritalin and psychotherapy. Bobby is now in kindergarten. His reading and writing skills are improving and he is working hard to learn how to get along with the other children. There are still days when Bobby's behavior flares out of control, but the Williamses have learned how to cope more effectively with such incidents. Their pediatrician has assured them that Bobby will be able to be a happy, productive individual when he grows up. Bobby says he'd like to be an astronaut.

For more information on ADHD, write to The Association for Children and Adults with Learning Disabilities, 4156 Library Road, Pittsburgh, PA 15234, or phone (412)341-1515.

When Someone Aged Needs Your Support

By Larry Doyle

As the U.S. population grows older, more resources for the elderly and their caregivers are becoming available.

All Erica Block* wanted to do was make her 72-year-old mother, Carol, happy. But Erica also wanted to do what was best, and this is not always the same thing.

In 1979, Erica and her husband persuaded Carol to move from her home in New York City to their Chicago suburb, to be near them. With that decision, the Blocks joined the millions of Americans who have, to a greater or lesser degree, accepted responsibility for the well-being of an older relative. Because the Blocks lived with their four children and lacked the room to accommodate another person, they found an apartment for Carol a few miles away.

But Carol, like many older people who are suddenly dis-

*Pseudonyms are used in the case histories throughout this article.

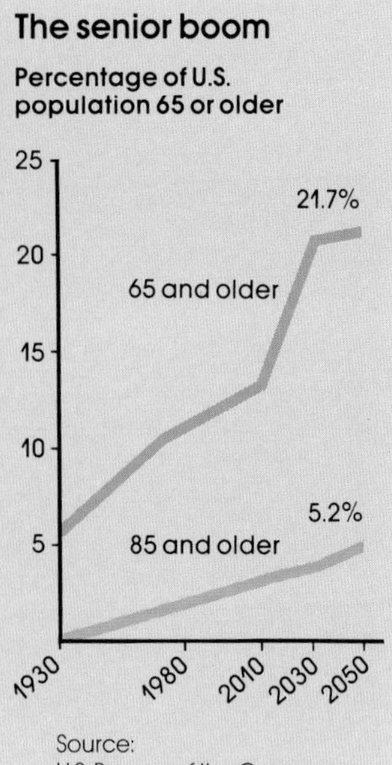

The U.S. Bureau of the Census predicts that the elderly will make up an increasingly large proportion of the U.S. population in the next 60 years, intensifying the need for resources for seniors.

placed, had trouble adjusting to her new surroundings. "After a while, she missed New York, but there was no way she could go back," Erica says. Carol began to resent her daughter and son-in-law for encouraging her to leave her home. She also developed some troubling symptoms—weakness and shortness of breath—that were eventually diagnosed as congestive heart failure, a common problem among the elderly. In simplest terms, this meant that Carol's heart was too weak to adequately pump blood throughout her body. Carol was given medication that relieved the strain on her heart but did not cure the underlying disease. She was in and out of the hospital a number of times during the next few years.

Then, in 1987, Erica's husband had a fatal heart attack—leaving Erica to take care of her mother by herself, something she had never expected. To make matters worse, Carol's health was rapidly deteriorating. In December, her doctors decided she needed nursing-home care.

"During the next two days, I called all over the place," Erica says. "I visited one nursing home I wouldn't put her in. She wanted to go to another place we looked at, but the administrators wanted to wait until her application for government financial assistance was approved. But I found a good place that would take her immediately, and in three days we had her in a nursing home."

But in March 1988, Carol was back in the hospital with pneumonia. Her mental condition had also rapidly deteriorated. "She doesn't even know she was ever in a nursing home," Erica says, her voice seemingly resigned to the possibility that she will lose her mother soon. Erica talks as if she wishes there were something she could have done differently. Money shouldn't be the point, but it has became a matter of major importance. "Whatever little savings she had will be gone very soon," Erica says. "I think that all my life I've been trying to make her happy. Why do I feel so guilty when everything I've done has been in her interest?"

Elderly Americans—a growing population

Millions of Americans can tell stories like Erica's. There are now more than 30 million U.S. citizens over 65, the age at which people are generally labeled "elderly." About 10 per cent of them are over 85—a group social scientists refer to as the "old old." And many of these elderly citizens depend on family members for varying degrees of care.

The need for family caregivers is likely to increase; the United States Bureau of the Census reports that the number of elderly citizens grows by 1,600 per day. And that's just the beginning of the wave of elderly people to come. People who are now in

The author:

Larry Doyle is a free-lance writer who lives in Chicago.

The notion that most Americans neglect their elderly parents is a myth. Millions of middle-aged Americans—like the man looking at old photographs with his father, *above left*, and the woman, *above*, styling her mother's hair—provide the elderly with companionship, help around the house, or nursing care.

their 30's—the "baby boomers" born between 1946 and 1964, a time of large population growth in the United States—will in three decades be "senior boomers."

By the year 2020, the Census Bureau predicts, there will be more than 45 million people over 65 in the United States; by 2030, 30 million of them will have reached age 75. Numbers this large are difficult to keep in perspective, so consider this example: A girl born in 1988 can expect to live to age 75. Her 75th birthday won't be very unusual, because 1 of every 7 people she meets walking down the street will be her age or older.

Advanced age by itself does not mean that a person needs care, however. But about 25 per cent of the nation's elderly require some sort of ongoing care because of chronic health problems, according to a 1985 estimate by Korbin Lui, a specialist on aging at the Urban Institute, a nonprofit corporation based in Washington, D.C., that investigates social issues. And as medical researchers have developed technologies to stave off death, the lives of the incurably ill have been prolonged. This means that increases in the average life span are not mirrored in what might be called the average "health span." "For every one year of healthy life we've added, we've also added up to four years of unhealthy life," says Robert Harootyan, a researcher for the American Association of Retired Persons (AARP) in Washington, D.C., a nonprofit organization for people who are 50 years old and over.

Elderly women learn to decorate pottery at one of the approximately 9,000 senior centers in the United States. Typically run by local government agencies, senior centers may offer free or low-cost meals, recreational activities, and information about other programs of interest to seniors.

Harootyan is optimistic that this will change. He, along with many other social researchers, believes that people who are under 50 today are taking better care of themselves, and will in 25 years constitute a society of healthy, vibrant older Americans. "But that's the future," he says. "We still have to figure out how best to care for the older people we have now and in the near future, whom we can expect to live much longer but also to have the ailments we usually associate with old age."

A nation of caregivers

As Erica Block and millions of other Americans have discovered, few situations can be as taxing as assuming personal responsibility for the care of another adult. And when the person is an elderly relative, the caregiver may feel guilty for not being able to do more—or resentful of the burden.

Nevertheless, a large number of people are willing to make whatever sacrifice is necessary to assist elderly people who need help. From the teen-ager who volunteers to mow the lawn for his arthritic neighbor to the middle-aged daughter who provides 24-hour care for a dying parent, people can and do find deep gratification in caregiving. Fulfilling these tasks can give people a sense of satisfaction, pride—and even completion,

Adult day-care centers provide part-time care for seniors with mild disabilities. In addition to offering limited medical care, adult day-care centers may provide exercise sessions like the one shown above; games, as shown at left; and other social activities.

such as when grown children tend to the needs of the parents who once cared for them.

"One of the great myths of our time is that families abandon their elderly," says Carolyn Ward of the National Council on the Aging (NCOA), an association representing thousands of professionals and volunteers involved in the care of older Americans. Ward heads the NCOA's Family Caregivers for the Aged Project, which provides guidance to people struggling to care for an aging relative. "Most older people are not just shuffled into nursing homes and forgotten," she says.

Ward's opinion is backed by research. In 1987, Robyn Stone, a researcher with the National Center for Health Services Research and Health Care Technology Assessment—a branch of the U.S. Public Health Service—reported that long-term research projects have "succeeded, in large part, in shattering the myth of family abandonment." Stone told the U.S. House of

To be old

To understand how it feels to be old, doctors, nurses, and other health-care workers at Burbank Hospital in Fitchburg, Mass., take a direct approach: For two days they adopt some of the infirmities of old age. They wear thick rubber gloves to mimic the effect of arthritis on their hands; wear dark, distorting glasses to diminish their vision; and put cotton balls in their ears to dull their hearing.

Hospital programs like Burbank's are cropping up all over the United States as hospital personnel prepare staffs for the wave of elderly patients to come. Health-care providers realize that understanding older people is essential for proper care. Family caregivers need to understand, too. Grandmother's failure to communicate clearly may not be because she is confused or disoriented; instead, she may merely be hard of hearing. Grandfather may sit in his chair all day because he's too proud to ask for help to go anywhere else.

Being elderly is different from being young, but it is not always different in the ways people assume. *Gerontologists* (experts in the study of aging) say the only rule that seems to apply is that a person's age means nothing. Christine Cassel, chief of internal medicine at the University of Chicago hospitals, says, "You can have someone who is 85 and who runs 5 miles a day and feels great, and you can have someone who is 85 and is close to death. Aging is such a diverse process; chronological age reflects neither health nor even physical age."

Nevertheless, Cassel and other experts say that a number of problems are associated with aging—problems that affect some, but not all, older people. Some of these difficulties are natural consequences of growing older, but it is important to understand that many health problems are neither inevitable nor untreatable.

Gerontologists generally group the health problems of the elderly into three rather broad categories—*mobility problems, loss of function,* and *mental or emotional problems.* These categories do not encompass every health problem, and they sometimes overlap, but they do give a general sense of the changes that come with age.

Mobility problems. Getting around is one of the biggest problems most elderly people face. The causes of mobility problems are almost as diverse as the number of people affected, and the best way to treat these problems is to find and treat the underlying ailment.

Arthritis, a term used to describe more than 100 diseases of the joints, can severely restrict movement. The two most common forms of arthritis are *rheumatoid arthritis* and *osteoarthritis.* Rheumatoid arthritis, an inflammation of joint tissues, can often be controlled by drugs that deaden pain while relieving the inflammation. Osteoarthritis, a condition in which joints literally wear out, is most common in obese elderly people. In the early stages of osteoarthritis, losing weight can alleviate the problem, just as not becoming overweight can help prevent it. For more serious cases, doctors have developed a number of helpful surgical procedures.

Osteoporosis, a bone-thinning disorder that affects 15 million to 20 million people—most of them women—in the United States, annually causes nearly 1½ million bone fractures and is a significant cause of decreased mobility. Exercise, hormone supplements, and a diet rich in calcium can help prevent osteoporosis. (See the Special Report BONE UP NOW FOR STRONGER BONES LATER.) Older people who suffer hip or leg fractures or other forms of limited mobility can benefit greatly from physical therapy.

Cardiovascular disease (heart and blood vessel diseases) can also limit mobility, because a weak or overworked heart often cannot supply the body with the oxygen needed to climb stairs, for example, or even to walk across the room. Of course, heart and blood vessel diseases also pose more serious health threats, including increased risks of heart attack and stroke. See the Special Report REDUCING THE RISK OF HEART DISEASE.

Some common-sense improvements can be made in any home to help people with mobility problems. Safety rails in the bathroom and near chairs can make getting up much easier, as can straight-backed chairs. Elderly people who have extreme mobility problems may need wheelchairs or special hydraulic beds and chairs that literally push the person to an upright position. Lifts for stairs are also available.

Loss of function. One of the least talked-about but most serious functional losses is *incontinence*, the inability to control the bowel or bladder. Incontinence does not by itself pose a significant health threat, but it does have a devastating impact on the self-esteem of an elderly person. Incontinence may also place an almost intolerable burden on the family caregiver.

Urinary incontinence in the elderly can have any of several causes, but loss of muscle tone in women and enlargement of the prostate gland in men are the most common. Simple exercises can increase tone in pelvic muscles, and enlarged prostate glands can be treated by surgery. Incontinence in people with mental disorders is often difficult to treat, but the condition can be made less traumatic if use is made of absorbent pads and disposable undergarments sold in drugstores.

Most people are well aware of the other major areas of functional loss in the elderly—impairments of hearing and sight. Both are quite common, and are perhaps a more typical consequence of aging than problems such as incontinence or arthritis.

About 18 per cent of people aged 65 to 74 and 46 per cent of those 75 or older develop *cataracts*, a hardening of the eye lens that clouds vision. Cataracts can be surgically removed, however, typically with excellent results.

Mental and emotional problems. A common belief is that older people tend to forget things—that they get confused and become senile—and that this should be expected.

"That is absolutely incorrect," according to Chicago's Cassel. "A very small percentage of older people are diagnosed with *dementia* [a loss of mental function severe enough to interfere with daily living]. And some studies show that about half of those people don't have a mental problem at all." The patients may instead be hard of hearing, depressed, or experiencing mental confusion as a side effect of a medication.

Dementia, which used to be called *senility*, is not itself a disease but a collection of symptoms that show a deterioration in the ability to think, remember, or reason. A slight memory loss, on the other hand, appears to be a natural result of aging, but it usually doesn't interfere with the ability to carry on daily activities. An estimated 2.5-million U.S. citizens suffer from *Alzheimer's disease*, a degenerative brain disorder that robs sufferers of intellect, personality, and even the ability to perform the most routine tasks. Caring for people with Alzheimer's disease is thus even more stressful than caring for disabled but mentally alert people.

About 1½ million older Americans suffer from other forms of dementia. Some are victims of stroke, *Parkinson's disease* (a disorder of the nervous system that causes trembling and body rigidity), or other diseases. Because some forms of dementia are treatable—or even curable—proper diagnosis is essential for any person whose mental function seems impaired.

Depression is a largely neglected mental problem of the elderly. Some aspects of growing old are sad—for example, the losses involved when friends and family members die. But most of the elderly are able to cope and still find pleasure in life.

If an older person does not overcome such a loss despite the passage of several months, or if he or she becomes withdrawn and abandons once-enjoyed activities, the problem may be *major depression*. This serious disorder is associated with immune-system impairment, sleep disturbances, and increased risk of suicide. Anyone concerned that a person is depressed should immediately report the problem to the patient's physician. Like most of the ailments that afflict seniors, depression is often successfully treated. [L. D.]

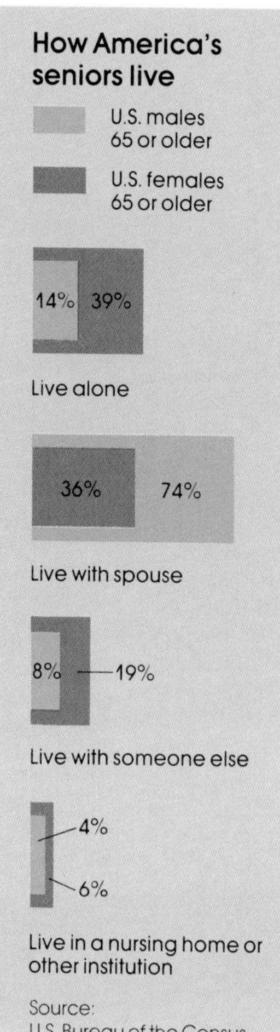

Although 25 per cent of America's elderly have chronic health problems and require ongoing care, fewer than 6 per cent live in nursing homes or other institutions. Demand is great for medical resources that allow disabled or ill seniors to live alone or with others in private dwellings.

Representatives Select Committee on Aging that perhaps as much as 80 to 90 per cent of all care for the elderly is provided by family members and friends.

A 1982 government survey found that the vast majority of family caregivers are women, usually the elderly person's daughter or wife. Although statistics do not measure such intangibles as the degree of love and respect caregivers feel, the numbers do show profound commitment and sacrifice. About 80 per cent of family caregivers provide assistance seven days a week, and 20 per cent have been caring for one or more elderly relatives for more than five years. More than 30 per cent of caregivers are themselves over 65, and 10 per cent are over 75. As Stone says, "In many cases, you have the 'young old' taking care of the 'old old.' "

Most caregivers have competing demands on their time. More than 165,000 American women simultaneously provide care to elderly relatives while raising their own children. An astonishing 40 per cent of these "women in the middle" also manage to hold down jobs.

Resources for the elderly and caregivers

As society slowly begins to adjust to the burgeoning population of senior citizens in need of care, more help for caregivers and the elderly is becoming available. Community resources can enable a senior with some disabilities to live independently; services for caregivers help lighten the burden of caring for a dependent senior who lives with a family member; and group living arrangements can provide a senior with social stimulation and, in some cases, extensive medical care.

Independent living—with a little help. The majority of seniors live alone or with a spouse in a private dwelling. Many of these people are healthy and vigorous and need make no concessions to their age. Nonetheless, there are resources available to make life easier for independent seniors.

Many communities have at least one *senior center,* a facility sponsored by a local government agency or private group that serves as a meeting place and clearinghouse for information of interest to the elderly. Some centers provide free hot meals and educational and recreational activities. Approximately 8 million seniors participate in programs offered by the 9,000 or so senior centers in the United States. State or area agencies on aging, which can be found in the government listings of a telephone directory, can direct elderly people to the senior center in their community.

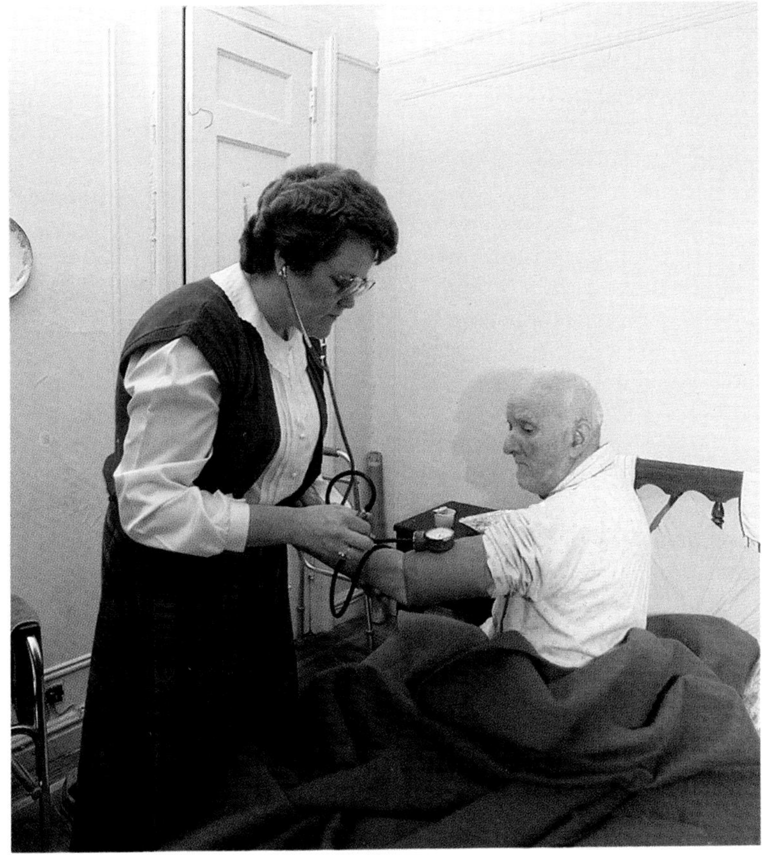

In-home care
A visiting nurse working for a community senior program checks the blood pressure of an elderly man who lives alone. In most communities, arrangements can be made to have nurses, aides, physical therapists, and other medical professionals attend to a senior's needs at home.

National special interest organizations for older Americans can be another valuable resource. The AARP, for example, offers travel and educational benefits, medical insurance, and other types of support. In addition, seniors can find meaningful outlets for their talents through volunteerism organizations such as the Service Corps of Retired Executives, the Foster Grandparents Program, and the Retired Senior Volunteer Program, all of which are based in Washington, D.C.

Some hospitals have also begun to reach out to elderly people in their community. Many hospitals sponsor health-promotion activities or health-education classes geared to helping seniors remain physically vigorous. In addition, some hospitals—along with religious groups, agencies on aging, and private businesses—offer such services as home-delivered meals (also known as "meals on wheels"), transportation to and from doctors' offices, and home medical equipment.

Nurses, physical therapists, and aides who visit or live in the elderly person's home can help ill or disabled seniors living alone. Arrangements for this type of in-home care can be made through health-care businesses, agencies on aging, or nonprofit groups like the Visiting Nurses Association, which is headquartered in Washington, D.C.

Children or other relatives of an aged person living independently can, of course, offer support and arrange any of these services. In addition, children who live far away from their aged parents may be able to assist the seniors more easily by engaging the services of a *geriatric care manager,* a specialist on aging who lives in the elderly person's area. The geriatric care manager determines the needs of the senior and contracts with others to meet them. Care managers charge an average of $250 to $500 per month for their supervision, which does not include the cost of the services they arrange. The National Association of Private Geriatric Care Managers in New York City can refer consumers to managers who meet professional and ethical standards.

Living under a family member's care. The resources available to the senior who lives independently can also be useful to more infirm seniors who are cared for by a spouse, child, or other family member. Caregivers, too, may need help in meeting the challenges of their situation. National support groups such as the Chicago-based Alzheimer's Association offer caregivers information and comfort. (*Alzheimer's disease* is a degenerative brain disorder that causes profound mental deterioration.) Another resource for caregivers is Children of Aging Parents, a self-help group based in Levittown, Pa., that provides literature, support, and guidance.

Family caregivers may also want to look into *respite services.* These include a variety of programs that provide social and mental stimulation for elderly people who might not otherwise get out of the house, and, at the same time, give caretakers a temporary respite from their responsibilities.

Adult day-care programs—which operate much like day-care centers for children—are the most common respite service. Designed for seniors who are not bedridden but are somewhat physically or mentally impaired, these programs provide transportation to and from the day-care center, meals and snacks, and social and recreational activities. Most adult day-care centers have at least one full-time social worker and registered nurse on the staff, with a physician and physical therapist sometimes available. The cost, which ranges from $10 to $70 per day, may be partially offset by financial aid from state or local health and social services agencies.

Group living options. Group living arrangements are yet another alternative for the aged. Seniors who want social stimulation or need on-premises care can choose from arrangements providing varying degrees of services.

Elderly people who do not need closely supervised medical care but do not want to—or cannot—cook and clean for themselves may enjoy life in *congregate housing*, a group of rental apartments designed for older people. In many ways, congregate housing is much like an attractive college dormitory. Meals are served in a common dining area, and recreational programs may be available. Some units offer housekeeping, grooming, and limited medical services. Residents typically pay a refundable security deposit in addition to monthly rent, which averages $900 to $1,500 for a single person, including meals and other amenities.

Another relatively new concept in group living for the elderly is the *continuing-care community*. These communities are often complete villages that include shops and recreational facilities. Long-term medical care is also available on the premises at little or no additional cost should the need arise. Medical benefits make continuing-care communities expensive, however. Most require a large and in many cases nonrefundable entrance fee—typically $35,000 to $150,000, an amount many residents raise by selling the family home. Monthly maintenance fees of several hundred dollars or more are also required.

Finally, *nursing homes* continue to be a good option for very infirm seniors. Services in nursing homes vary with the needs

Group living
Congregate housing and continuing-care communities combine the sociability of common areas, *below left*, with the privacy of apartment living, *below*. Some group living arrangements also provide residents with housekeeping services and medical care.

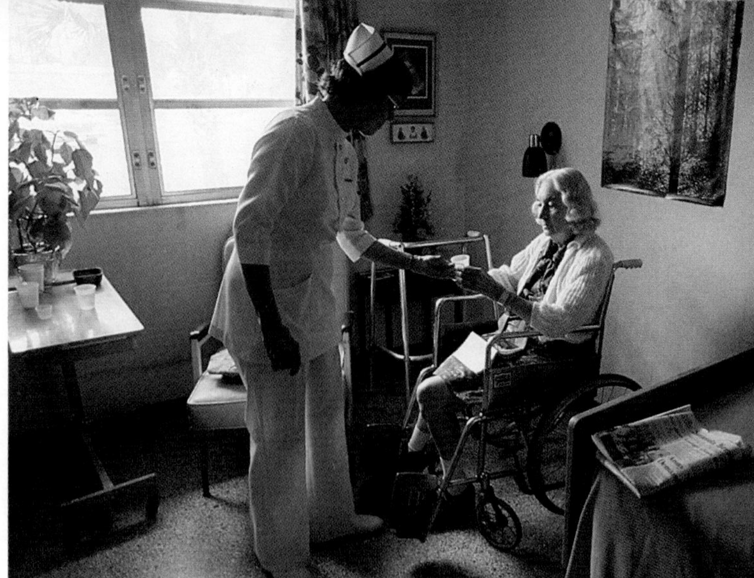

Nursing homes
For very infirm seniors, nursing homes can provide recreational activities, *above,* along with round-the-clock medical care, *above right.*

of the individual patient, ranging from *skilled care* (round-the-clock intensive medical assistance) to *custodial care* (help with grooming, bathing, and eating). Good nursing homes also provide recreational activities. The price of nursing-home care depends on the type of services required and the home's location, but average yearly costs are $22,000. The National Institute of Senior Housing, a division of the NCOA, can provide information on nursing homes as well as other housing options for the aged.

Weighing the options

Generally speaking, the best way to discover what resources for the elderly are available in your area is by contacting one of the more than 500 U.S. state or area agencies on aging. These agencies, which were created by a federal law passed in 1965, can also provide information about the availability of Medicare and Medicaid—programs funded by federal and state governments—as well as other types of financial aid for seniors.

The next step is to involve the rest of the family—and especially the senior—in the decision about the kind of care needed. The decision usually need not be made in haste, though some people wait until a situation has become a crisis before beginning to research the options. "It's never too early to discuss these things," according to the NCOA's Ward. "Although some older people are reluctant to discuss it, many families find that their older relatives are actually anxious to talk about it because they don't want to be a burden."

Working together, family members can support one another in the search for high-quality care. "We looked at, actually visited, maybe 30 different nursing homes," says Frank Stanford, a 69-year-old retired telephone repairman whose mother-in-law, Hazel, needed care. "There were some we absolutely would not put her in. But after all that, we found a place close by that we were satisfied with."

Hazel, now 93, has been in the nursing home for six years. She was joined in 1987 by Stanford's mother, Sylvia, who is also 93. Stanford says they both seem to be getting along well. "They have their ups and downs, but I'd say they are happy there," he says. "And I know that if they need any kind of medical attention, it's there for them. I know what I can't do. I'm not a doctor."

Still, the Stanfords have not abandoned their role as caregivers. "We visit them maybe three or four times a week, my sons and daughters-in-law, too," he says. "That's how we are. We're a close-knit family. That's how we got through this."

For more information, write to:

Alzheimer's Association
70 East Lake Street
Suite 600
Chicago, IL 60601

American Association of Retired Persons
1909 K Street NW
Washington, DC 20049

Children of Aging Parents
2761 Trenton Road
Levittown, PA 19056

National Association of Private Geriatric Care Managers
P.O. Box 6920
Yorkville Station
New York, NY 10128

National Institute of Senior Housing
NCOA
600 Maryland Avenue SW
West Wing 100
Washington, DC 20024

By following a few basic steps, you can help safeguard your home against fire—and increase your chance of survival if one occurs.

Fire!

By Philip S. Schaenman

The water in the pan Mrs. Freer had left on the stove to warm the baby's bottle began to heat up as she went upstairs to tuck in her 3-year-old daughter, Tricia. There was time for a short bedtime story, she thought, before the water boiled. As she read to Tricia, the little girl fell asleep—and Mrs. Freer herself started to nod off.

In the kitchen, the water in the pan soon evaporated, and the pan began to glow cherry-red. Two minutes later, heat radiating from the pan ignited a cereal box on the counter next to the stove, then a roll of paper towels and several plastic baby bottles. The flames climbed up the wooden cabinets, which added to the fuel. Black smoke rose to the ceiling and rolled into the hallway, billowing up to the smoke detector, which hung open with no batteries.

Four minutes later, the entire kitchen exploded in flames as all the flammable objects in the room ignited at the same time—a critical event that fire fighters call *flashover*. Thick smoke and hot *toxic* (poisonous) gases poured out of the kitchen and surged up the stairwell as if it were a chimney.

Mrs. Freer woke with a start, coughing. With her eyes tearing from the smoke, she ran across the hall for her infant daughter and for her sister's three children who were staying with her that night. She quickly gathered them in Tricia's room, and then struggled to remove the wooden safety bars that had been installed across the lower half of the window. Smoke continued to pour into the room through the open bedroom door.

Fire engines arrived two minutes after a neighbor had alerted them. When the fire fighters found Mrs. Freer, she was unconscious, overcome by the toxic fumes. She survived—but it was too late for the children. They died of smoke inhalation before the flames even reached the doorway of their room.

The U.S. fire problem

Home fires similar to the one that struck the Freer family (whose name was changed for this article) kill thousands of people annually. Overall, more than 2 million fires occur each year in the United States, according to the National Fire Protection Association (NFPA) in Quincy, Mass. But most Americans are unaware of the magnitude of the problem and of simple precautions that could make a significant difference in their ability to prevent—as well as survive—a fire.

About 80 per cent of fire deaths in the United States occur in the victim's home. Spectacular, large fires such as the 1980 MGM Grand Hotel fire in Las Vegas, Nev., that killed 84 people account for only a small percentage of all fire deaths. The great majority of deaths occur in the many fires that kill 1 or 2 people or an entire family, according to the U.S. Fire Administration (USFA) in Emmitsburg, Md.

The author:

Philip S. Schaenman is president of TriData Corporation, a fire-safety consulting firm based in Arlington, Va.

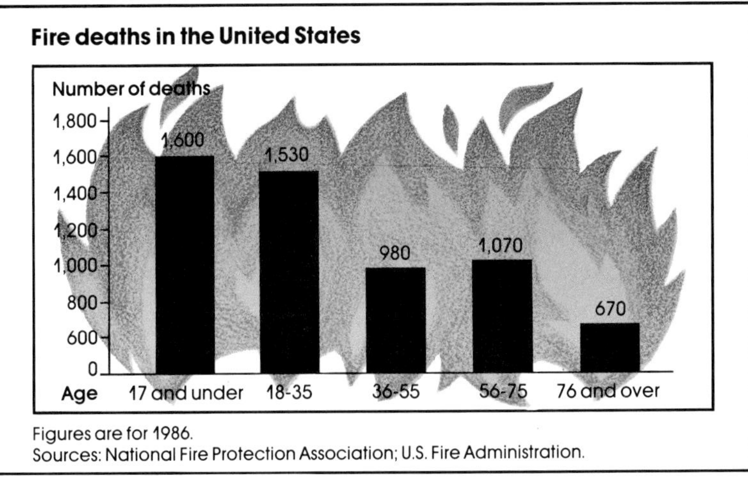

Fire plays no favorites. It kills people of all ages. Children, however, are especially vulnerable. Many become frightened during a fire and hide under a bed or in a closet where they may die of smoke inhalation or burns if not found in time.

In 1984, 1985, and 1986, about 6,000 people died each year in fires in the United States, mostly in home fires, according to the NFPA. The USFA reports that most of these deaths were due to smoke inhalation. Even in cases where victims are burned, smoke usually plays a deadly role—causing unconsciousness or disorientation, which prevents their escape.

Fire prevention officials believe that the number of fire deaths could be cut sharply if Americans learned—and followed—proper fire-safety precautions. This is not impossible. Countries such as Japan have made great strides in reducing their fire death toll.

Raising the public's awareness of fire safety is the key component in the fire prevention programs of other countries. For example, in Japan, where houses—many made of wood and treated paper—tend to be closely packed together, people are extremely aware of the potential for deadly fires. More than 1 million women and about 700,000 schoolchildren belong to fire-safety clubs that practice fire prevention and the basics of fire fighting. While the United States has one National Fire Prevention Week a year, most Japanese cities devote at least three weeks a year to fire prevention.

Does this high level of fire awareness work? The statistics suggest that it does. In 1981, New York City alone had more fire calls than the entire nation of Japan.

Home fires are so deadly because they can happen at any time, catching residents unaware. But there is another chilling reason behind the grim death toll of home fires: It can take only a few minutes for a small fire to reach flashover and turn a room into a blazing inferno. If people do not take immediate action to save themselves after a fire starts, their chances of

Stopping fires before they start

Removing fire hazards from the home is the first line of defense against fires. Here are ways to eliminate six of the most common causes of home fires.

Keep portable space heaters away from curtains, beds, and other flammable materials.

People who smoke should extinguish their cigarettes if they become drowsy, especially if they have been drinking alcohol.

Do not leave food cooking on a stove unattended.

Keep flammable items—such as cleaning fluids, paints, and old rags—away from the furnace. Have the furnace inspected annually.

Do not overload electrical outlets with too many appliances. Cords should be free of frayed spots.

Fireplaces and wood-burning stoves should be inspected yearly—or more often if used frequently—by certified chimney sweeps or other qualified service people. Have a professional installer or the local fire department check to see that wood-burning stoves are properly installed.

escaping unharmed—or alive—are sharply reduced. Flashover occurs in enclosed areas, such as a room, where heat and smoke from a small fire can quickly build up.

Prevention basics

To prevent home fires, it is useful to know what causes them. According to the USFA, the most common factors in home fires are heating systems, followed by cooking, arson, electrical systems, and smoking. Careless smoking and heating systems are the most common causes of fire deaths.

Heating fires can be caused by portable space heaters, wood-burning stoves, fireplaces, water heaters, and central heating systems. The fastest growing part of the U.S. fire problem stems from poorly maintained, improperly installed, or misused space heaters and wood stoves. All too often, portable space heaters are placed too close to drapes, beds, or other flammable materials—or flammable materials, such as clothes, are placed on top of heaters. Portable heaters fueled by kerosene or oil may spill their fuel when they are knocked over. People who do not follow manufacturers' instructions may fill kerosene heaters with the wrong kind of fuel, causing them to explode.

Wood-burning stoves are also potential fire hazards. Many people install their own wood stoves without allowing adequate space between the stove or its chimney pipe and flammable walls or ceilings. Manufacturers' specifications for installation and use must be followed to prevent problems.

Some home fires are the result of poorly maintained fireplaces. Fireplace fires usually start with the build-up of *creosote,* a black gummy substance produced by burning wood. Creosote builds up along the inner wall of the chimney and can ignite like a blowtorch. Chimneys should be cleaned at least once a year—or more often if a fireplace is used frequently—to remove the creosote. And fireplaces and chimneys should be inspected annually by certified chimney sweeps or other qualified workers to ensure that no cracks or holes have developed

Using smoke detectors
To be most effective, smoke detectors (shown in red) should be placed on every level of living space in a home. Since smoke rises, install detectors on ceilings or on walls 6 to 12 inches (15 to 30 centimeters) from the ceiling. A smoke detector with a dead battery—or no battery at all—cannot help save lives. It is important to change batteries at least once a year.

that would allow fire to escape and ignite the house structure.

Central heating systems and water heaters also cause many home fires. These fires often start when flammable objects, such as rags and paper, are stored too close to heaters. Vapors given off by gasoline and other flammable substances can ignite when heaters turn on. Central heaters also need to be professionally checked and cleaned to help prevent malfunctions.

The USFA reports that cooking-related fires injure more people than any other type of fire. Most cooking-related fires occur when people leave food cooking on the stove unattended. As in the sad case of the Freer family, a seemingly harmless pot of boiling water can turn into a deadly source of fire when the water evaporates and the pot overheats. Cooking with oil or shortening is even more hazardous. If it is not continually monitored, the oil can boil over or ignite. Most cooking fires can be prevented by simply staying in the kitchen when food is cooking on the stove.

Arson is usually thought of in connection with commercial buildings that are burned for profit, but many home fires also are intentionally set. In some cases, a house may be set on fire in order to collect on an insurance policy. Other home fires may be acts of vandalism or revenge. In many cities, more than half of all arson fires are set by young people or by children playing with matches or lighters. Often these children have an emotional problem. To combat these fires, hundreds of communities have established counseling programs for juveniles who set fires. Experts suggest that children who set fires should be referred to these programs.

Electrical systems built under modern electrical codes can stay in good condition for many years, but will deteriorate gradually over time. Very old houses often have wiring systems that were not meant for modern appliances. If an electrical system has deteriorated or if it is overloaded with too many appliances, it can overheat, causing a fire. Sparking sockets, unusually warm areas around switches or sockets, or frequent blowing of fuses or circuit breakers are signals of an electrical problem. An electrician should be called immediately.

Careless smoking is the leading cause of fire deaths in the United States. Smoking-related fires usually occur when the smoker is tired or is drowsy from drinking too much alcohol and drops a lit cigarette on a bed, couch, or chair. Since it may take a few hours for the smoldering spot to burst into flame, people are often fast asleep when fire breaks out.

To prevent such fires, people should not smoke when they are drowsy or when they are in bed or lying on upholstered furniture. Cigarette butts should be carefully disposed of, preferably after running water over them. Ashtrays should be placed

Extinguishing small fires safely

Fire extinguishers provide a line of defense against home fires. But fire-safety experts do not unanimously recommend their use, because many people are injured by fire or overcome by smoke when they try to fight a fire themselves. If used wisely and properly, however, fire extinguishers may be able to put out small fires before they cause much damage to property or life.

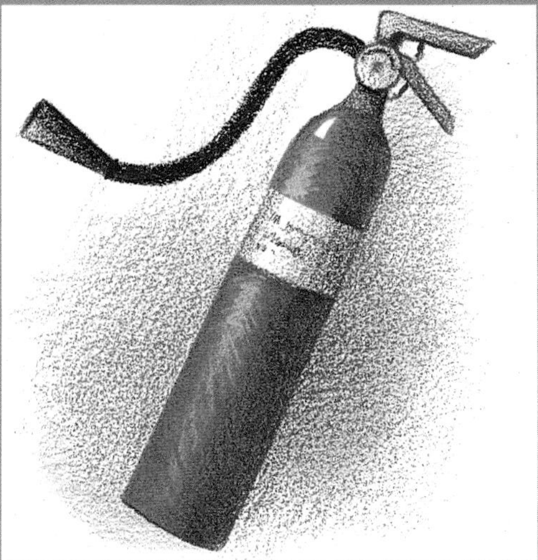

Most fire extinguishers contain pressurized gas that forces out an extinguishing agent, such as water, a chemical powder, or an *inert gas* (a gas that will not burn or react chemically when it comes in contact with any substance). In some extinguishers, such as those that contain carbon dioxide, the pressurized gas itself is the extinguishing agent.

Home fire extinguishers must be used with good judgment. The fire must be small enough to be extinguished with the contents of a small home extinguisher. Furthermore, people attempting to extinguish a fire must never let the fire get between themselves and an exit; there must always be an escape path in case the fire grows rapidly or the extinguisher does not do the job. Before using an extinguisher, it is wise to get everyone out of the house and then call the fire department. Ideally, one person should call the fire department while another uses the extinguisher.

There are several different types of extinguishers suitable for home use. The best one to use depends on the type of fire. Fires are grouped into four classes—A, B, C, or D. Class A fires are fueled by wood, paper, or other common natural and synthetic substances. Class B fires involve flammable liquids, such as gasoline or cooking oil. Class C fires are those involving electricity. Class D fires are fueled by flammable metals, such as magnesium. A class D fire is unlikely to occur in a home and cannot be put out with an extinguisher. Most fire extinguishers are marked to indicate whether they are good for class A, B, or C fires or for a combination of different types of fires.

An extinguisher that squirts water is good for only class A fires. In fact, applying water to burning oil or to an electrical fire actually does more harm than good. An extinguisher that contains carbon dioxide is good for smothering class B and C fires. Many extinguishers that shoot out powdered chemicals are good for class A, B, and C fires. Be sure to use an extinguisher only for the types of fires specified on the label.

Like smoke detectors, fire extinguishers require some simple maintenance. The pressure gauge should be read annually to make sure the pressure is high enough to force out the extinguishing agent when needed. Most extinguishers have an easy-to-read gauge with a low-pressure danger zone marked in red. If the pressure is too low, the extinguishing agent may just trickle out—or may not come out at all. There are special shops that can repressurize some extinguishers and refill them after use. The yellow pages of the telephone directory lists these shops under the heading "Fire Extinguishers."

Where should a fire extinguisher be placed? A kitchen wall away from the stove is one good location. Other areas of the home where the likelihood of a fire might be great, such as the garage or basement, are also prime locations.

But there are other ways to put out a small home fire. A pot of water is effective on class A fires. Baking soda can extinguish an oven fire or an oil fire on the stove. When heated, baking soda gives off carbon dioxide and helps smother the fire, just like a carbon dioxide fire extinguisher. A handy pot lid placed on a pan of flaming grease or oil smothers the fire by cutting off its oxygen supply, but it must be done carefully to avoid burns. [P. S. S.]

Flashover: How a fire turns deadly
Even a small fire can generate enough heat to turn a room into a roaring fire in about three minutes. For example, a fire that starts on a chair immediately begins to give off smoke, toxic gases, and heat (1). The hot smoke and gases rise to the ceiling and form a layer that grows hotter and thicker (2). Within three minutes, this layer of smoke and gases is radiating intense heat down to other objects in the room (3). These objects become so hot that they suddenly burst into flame, an event fire experts call *flashover* (4).

on a level surface to provide a stable resting place for a lit cigarette. For further protection, people can buy furniture covered with fire-resistant upholstery.

Safety devices

Once steps have been taken to eliminate situations in a home that may cause a fire, smoke detectors and home sprinkler systems can provide additional lines of defense. Smoke detectors sense smoke and sound an alarm. They give early warning of a fire, providing time to escape. An extra 30 seconds can mean the difference between having a safe path to run out of the house and facing a wall of flame or a cloud of smoke.

By 1988, about 75 per cent of all U.S. homes had smoke detectors, according to the USFA. But many of these detectors—anywhere from 25 to 50 per cent—are not in working order, according to spot checks by fire departments in various cities. Smoke detectors must be properly maintained if they are to act as sentinels against fires. A battery-powered detector should be tested once a month. For most detectors, this means pressing a specially marked button that checks the circuitry of the device and sounds a brief alarm if everything is working properly.

Detectors can be given a more complete check by periodically blowing out a lit candle near the detector to see if the smoke sets off the alarm. Once or twice a year—on dates likely to be remembered, such as a birthday—the battery in the detector should be replaced. Detectors also should be cleaned regularly to eliminate dirt or dead insects that could clog the openings that smoke would pass through.

But even a properly working smoke detector won't save lives if it is not properly installed. Since smoke rises, detectors should be placed on ceilings or walls, but not in corners where pockets of dead air form. Smoke does not penetrate these pockets as quickly as it does other areas. If they are placed on

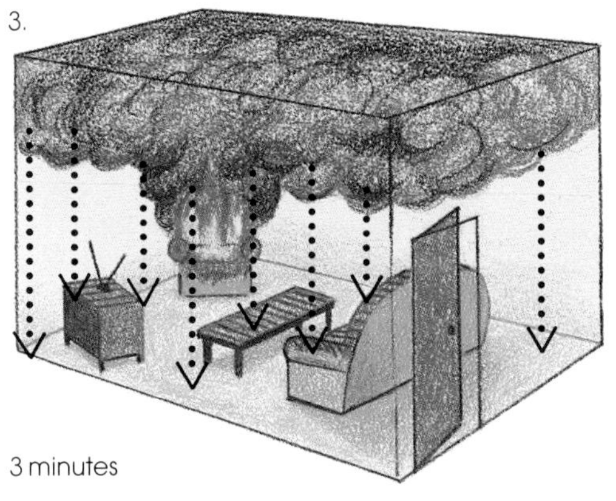

3 minutes

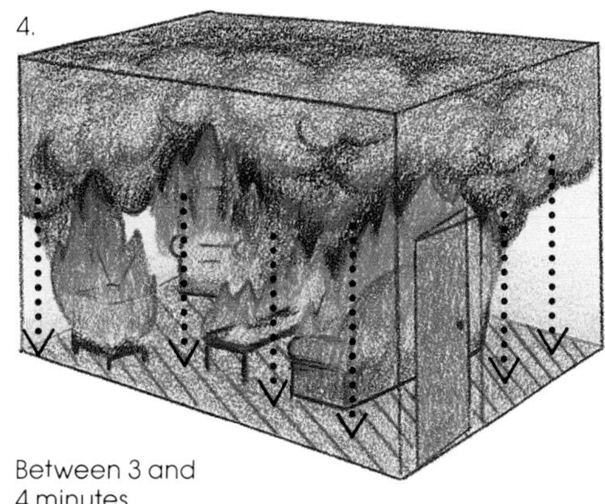

Between 3 and 4 minutes

walls, detectors should be positioned between 6 and 12 inches (15 and 30 centimeters) from the ceiling. They should not be placed too close to the kitchen, or smoke from cooking foods may set off frequent false alarms.

Ideally, there should be a detector on every floor of the house. If only one detector is to be used, it should be placed in a hallway outside the bedrooms, so that sleeping residents will be protected. Because many cities and states have laws requiring residential buildings to have smoke detectors, people should check with city or state authorities about any legal requirements for installing detectors.

Smoke detectors are one of the best bargains in safety. They usually cost between $8 and $20, and most are powered by inexpensive batteries. These batteries should never be removed from a detector except when they are being replaced. Many lives have been lost because people removed batteries from detectors to stop a detector that was triggered by smoke from burning food or to replace worn-out batteries in radios or toys, leaving the smoke detector powerless to do its job.

Home sprinkler systems offer the surest, most complete form of fire protection known today. In the mid-1970's, a fast-acting *sprinkler head* (the device from which the water sprays out) was developed for the home. Fast-acting sprinkler heads turn on early in a fire, when only a small quantity of water is often sufficient to extinguish it.

The cost of installing a sprinkler system is approximately $1,000 to $4,000, depending on the size of the home and whether the sprinklers are installed during construction of the home or put in after a house is built. A home sprinkler system significantly increases a family's chances of surviving a fire. It also reduces the chance of extensive damage to the house. Some insurance companies give people with home sprinkler

Planning an escape route

A planned escape route can help avoid the panic that costs lives in a fire. Fire experts recommend that families study a floor plan of their home to figure out two ways to exit each room in the house (1); make sure that everyone—including house guests and baby sitters—knows how to remove screens and safety bars from windows (2); practice different escape routes (3); and designate a tree or lamppost as a place to meet after escaping so that family members can make sure everyone gets out (4).

systems reductions in the cost of homeowner's insurance. Many fire experts believe that as these systems become more widely used, they will dramatically reduce the losses from fire.

Escape planning

An extremely important fire protection measure that costs nothing is an escape plan. All members of a household should know at least two escape routes if possible from every room in their home. A fire may prevent people from using normal exits, such as the front or back door. Many people panic during a fire and forget that they can escape out of a window onto the roof of an attached garage, or that by dangling from the sill of a second-story window they can get close enough to the ground to survive a fall.

It is crucial to know how to get out of windows that have safety bars or screens, or doors that have locks. It is not enough to be able to open a door or window in daylight. Family members have to be able to do it quickly and in bad visibility.

Family members should meet together to study a floor plan of their house or apartment and to figure out the various ways to escape from each part of the home. In an apartment building, it is necessary to extend the planning to include hallways and stairways outside the apartment, especially since elevators should never be used during a fire. After developing a plan on paper, it is important to practice navigating the routes as far as is practical and safe.

Families also should discuss the circumstances under which it may be better to stay in a room or apartment, rather than attempt to exit through smoke. If the door of the room is closed, a person should touch the center of the door with the back of a hand to see if it is warm. If it is cool, the door should be opened a crack. If the person sees any flames or heavy smoke, the door should be closed immediately. Keeping the door of a room closed, and stuffing towels or sheets in the cracks above and below the door to keep out smoke and hot gases may make it a place of refuge until the fire is extinguished. If it is necessary to move through smoke-filled areas, a person should crouch or crawl below the smoke layer where the air is fresher and clearer.

Children should be taught not to hide under beds or in closets when fire breaks out. Many fire fighters can tell sad stories of children who hid themselves and could not be found until it was too late.

An important part of an escape plan is to set up a meeting place outside the home—a lamppost, a tree, or some other familiar object that is well away from the house—so that everyone knows who got out. In many cases, unaware that their children have escaped by a back exit, parents rush back into burning houses and die trying to find them.

Fire!

Even with strong fire prevention efforts, a fire may still break out. Luckily, when it happened to one particular family—let's call them the Fields—they were prepared to deal with it.

Fourteen-year-old Eric Fields woke up almost immediately, thanks to the piercing wail of the smoke detector in the hallway outside his bedroom. Instead of following his first instinct—which was to leap out of bed and run to see what was happening—he rolled onto the floor while he tried to clear his mind. *Sitting up in bed or standing up can fill the lungs with smoke. The air closer to the floor is safer to breathe.*

Eric quickly crawled to the door, and switched on the light in his room. He saw only a light haze from smoke that had filtered through the space between the top of the door and the doorframe. Standing up, he touched the door with the back of his hand to see if it was hot. It wasn't, so he placed his foot near

What to do in a fire

Even with the best fire prevention, a home fire can still occur at any time. Fast action is the key to survival. Fire experts recommend that when a fire is detected, people promptly assess the situation and then take the most appropriate action. Below are some options.

The smoke alarm goes off

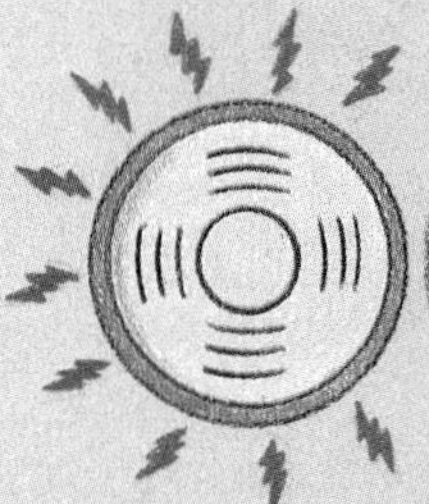

If there are no flames or smoke, get out of the house as fast as possible through the nearest exit.

If you are in a room and the door is closed, feel the door to see if it is warm. If it is not, carefully open it a crack to see if there are any flames or smoke outside the room.

If there is no safe way to escape, close the door and stuff towels or sheets in the spaces above and below it. If there is a phone in the room, call the fire department from there.

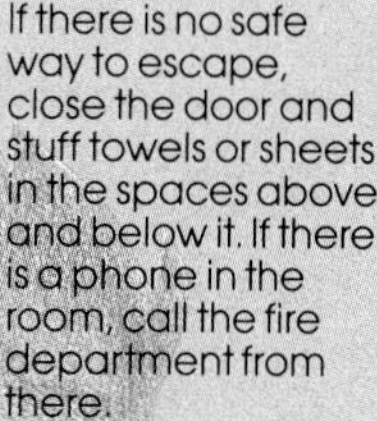

If there is some smoke, but no flames, crouch below the smoke and run—or crawl swiftly along the floor—to the nearest exit.

If you see flames, or if the smoke is too strong for you to escape, close the door quickly. If you are on the first or second floor, hang from the window sill and drop to the ground or climb out of the window onto the roof of a garage or other attached structure.

Run to a neighbor to call the fire department.

the door to brace it while he opened the door a crack, ready to slam it shut if he saw heavy black smoke or fire. But the hall was filled with only a light haze, mostly at the ceiling. Hunching over below the smoke layer, he rushed through the hallway, calling each family member by name: "Mom, Dad, Jamie, Jennifer, wake up, wake up! Fire, fire!" *Calling each person by name may help to get a response.*

Eric saw that 9-year-old Jennifer could not get out of her room. The fire was in her doorway, having started when she had moved a space heater too close to a chair next to her door. Jennifer was awake now and starting to scream. "Jennifer, go out the window," called Eric. "Get the screen off like we practiced. Get out on the sill and hang from your hands. I'll be there to catch you." Eric raced downstairs, quickly followed by his parents and younger brother, who closed their bedroom doors as they left. *A closed door can provide a temporary barrier to fire—enough to buy time and reduce losses.*

Eric and his father ran out the back door. "Go wait in front by the tree," yelled Mr. Fields to his wife and younger son. "We'll meet there after we get Jennifer." By the time he and Eric ran to Jennifer's window, she had removed the screen and was hanging from the sill, smoke billowing above her head. "Let go now, Jenny," yelled Eric. He and his father softened her fall as she hit the ground. *Each family member should know how to open windows and remove screens or other barriers to get out quickly.*

Mr. Fields and Eric picked Jennifer up and took her to the tree in front of the house. Meanwhile, Mrs. Fields had run next door to call the fire department, after telling Jamie where she was going so that the rest of the family would not think she had gone back inside the house.

Within four minutes, the fire department arrived on the scene. The Fields's home was now full of deadly smoke, and anyone remaining in the house would have been killed. It took the fire fighters only a minute to get the fire under control.

If the Fields family had not acted as surely and as quickly as they did, there would have been serious injuries and, possibly, the loss of life. Everyone can be as prepared as the Fields. By taking simple steps—maintaining smoke detectors on each level of the house, planning and practicing escape routes, and getting out quickly as soon as a fire is detected—we have every chance of surviving a fire.

For further information on fire prevention, write to:

U.S. Fire Administration, Office of Fire Prevention and Arson Control, 16825 South Seton Avenue, Emmitsburg, MD 21727; or contact your local fire department.

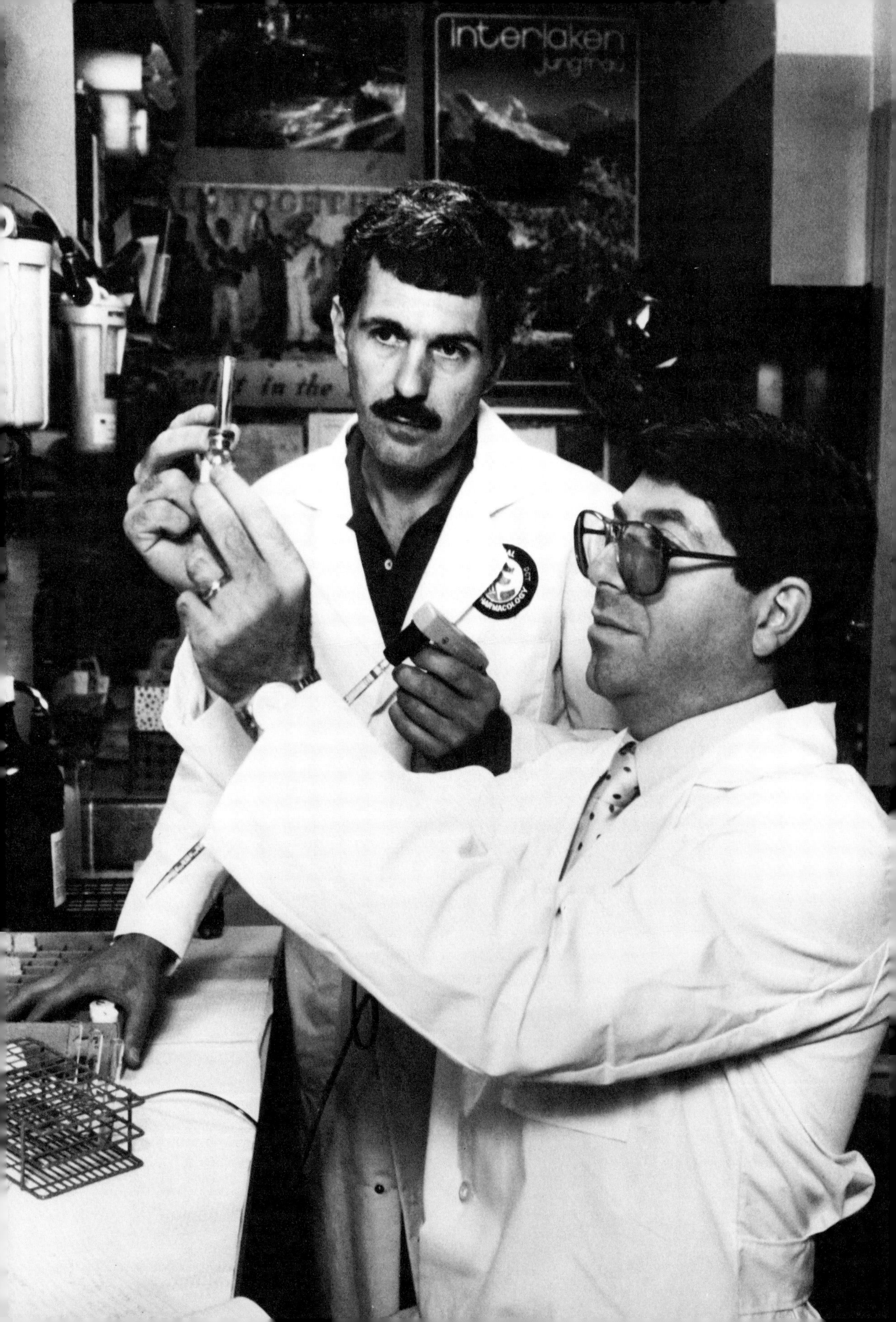
Interlaken
Jungfrau

Health & Medical File

In 41 alphabetically arranged articles, Health & Medical File contributors report on the year's major developments in health and medicine.

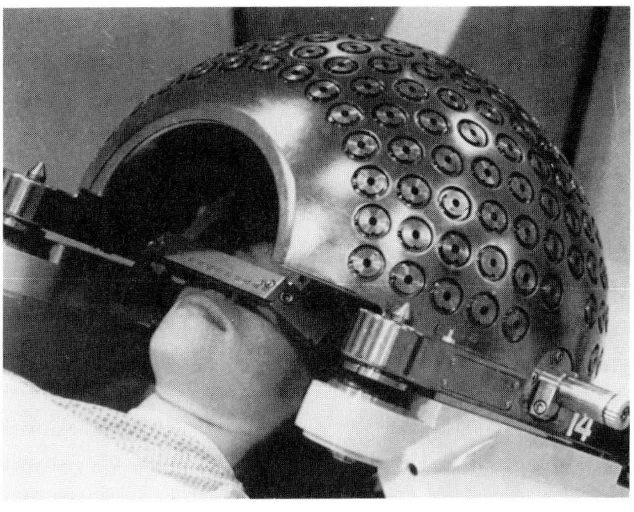

Aging

Significant progress was made in 1987 and 1988 in understanding the process of aging and the health problems of older people. Research studies provided further support for the value of exercise in maintaining good health among elderly people, particularly in the prevention of heart disease.

Important new findings also included reports about possible causes of Alzheimer's disease, a brain disorder that afflicts 2 million Americans, mostly over the age of 65. And the role of *geriatricians*—physicians who specialize in treating older people—was formally recognized in April 1988 when the American Board of Internal Medicine and the American Academy of Family Physicians for the first time offered special board examinations in geriatrics.

Benefits of exercise. A number of studies in 1988 confirmed research findings of previous years indicating that a decline in heart function in older people is due to disease and physical inactivity rather than to the aging process itself. In older people who are free of coronary artery disease, the capacity of the heart to respond to an added workload is adequate, even in people in their 80's, according to a review of research performed by cardiologist Edward G. Lakatta of the Gerontology Research Center in Baltimore, Md., and reported in 1988.

One of the tests for heart function measures *maximum aerobic capacity*—the maximum ability to burn oxygen. Research conducted in 1988 by Lakatta and cardiologist Jerome L. Fleg of the National Institute on Aging in Bethesda, Md., showed that a decline in maximum aerobic capacity is related to a decline in muscle mass due to physical inactivity. In addition, other studies have shown that muscle mass and function can be maintained through active exercise programs.

The single change in heart function that seems to be definitely age-related is a decline in the heart's responsiveness to hormones that increase the heart rate, such as epinephrine. The heart rate does not increase as much in older people as in younger people after these hormones are secreted. But the healthy older heart compensates for this by a stronger contraction of the heart muscle, resulting in an increased volume of blood pumped with each heartbeat.

Alzheimer's disease. In 1988, several potentially important contributions were made toward understanding the causes of Alzheimer's disease, the major cause of loss of

Selected chronic conditions of old age
(Per 1,000 persons aged 65 and over)

Type of chronic condition	Male	Female
Arthritis	358.6	565.8
Hypertension	329.5	440.0
Hearing impairment	371.0	242.7
Heart disease	295.5	263.3
Cataracts, glaucoma, and other vision impairment	242.0	301.0
Orthopedic impairment	137.4	197.5
Diabetes	99.2	97.6
Cerebrovascular disease	66.0	65.7

Source: National Center for Health Statistics, 1986.

A Health & Medical Annual Close-Up

THA: Help for Patients with Alzheimer's Disease?

Ever since it was hailed in 1986 as one of the best potential treatments for Alzheimer's disease, the experimental drug *tetrahydroaminoacridine* (THA) has been surrounded by controversy. Not only has research on the drug been questioned, but the first national study of THA, launched in 1987, hit a snag after just three months.

It is not surprising that THA has received so much attention. More than 2.5 million elderly people in the United States suffer from Alzheimer's disease, a progressively worsening disorder in which brain cells are destroyed. There is no cure or treatment presently available for Alzheimer's. The disease gradually impairs memory, judgment, speech, muscle coordination, and other functions until victims are unable to care for themselves. For many victims, Alzheimer's disease ends in death.

THA first made headlines in November 1986, when a team of researchers headed by psychiatrist William K. Summers of the University of California in Los Angeles reported that the drug improved memory and physical ability in people with mild to moderate symptoms of Alzheimer's disease. The researchers reported that 12 of 17 Alzheimer's patients treated with THA showed "significant" improvement. One patient was able to return to part-time work and others were able to resume simple tasks.

In theory, THA seems like a good candidate for helping Alzheimer's patients. This powerful drug blocks the action of an enzyme that destroys a brain chemical called *acetylcholine* that the brain tissues of Alzheimer's victims lack. Researchers theorized that THA might bolster the level of this chemical in Alzheimer's victims. While this action would not cure the disease, it could alleviate some of the symptoms—at least during the early stages, when the victim still has enough undamaged brain cells to produce adequate amounts of acetylcholine.

Many people with Alzheimer's disease need constant care.

Summers' study generated much publicity, but not all of it was favorable. Some scientists questioned the research methods and conclusions based on a small number of patients.

These doubts, however, did not curb the demand for THA. This demand, along with THA's potential, prompted the U.S. Food and Drug Administration (FDA) to move quickly in approving a large-scale clinical study to evaluate THA's effectiveness and safety.

The two-year study began in August 1987 under the sponsorship of the National Institute on Aging in Bethesda, Md.; the Warner-Lambert Company, a pharmaceutical firm based in Morris Plains, N.J.; and the Alzheimer's Association in Chicago. The study was to test THA in 300 Alzheimer's patients at 17 treatment centers around the United States. In October 1987, the FDA and Warner-Lambert halted the test because 20 of the first 50 patients given THA had developed signs of liver damage.

In investigating this side effect, scientists found that the indications of liver damage were linked to the amount of THA given to patients. On Feb. 3, 1988, Warner-Lambert announced that the study had been resumed but that lower THA doses were being given to patients to prevent any liver damage.

Scientists will not know for some time whether THA is an effective and safe treatment for Alzheimer's disease. But if studies prove that it is, the outcome for many Alzheimer's sufferers would be well worth the wait. ☐ Mary A. Krier

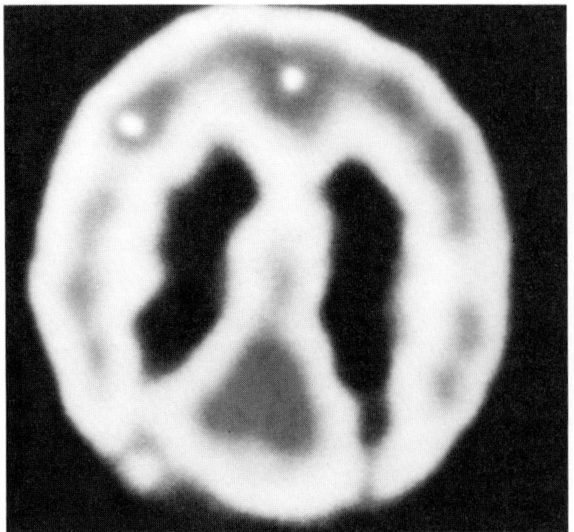

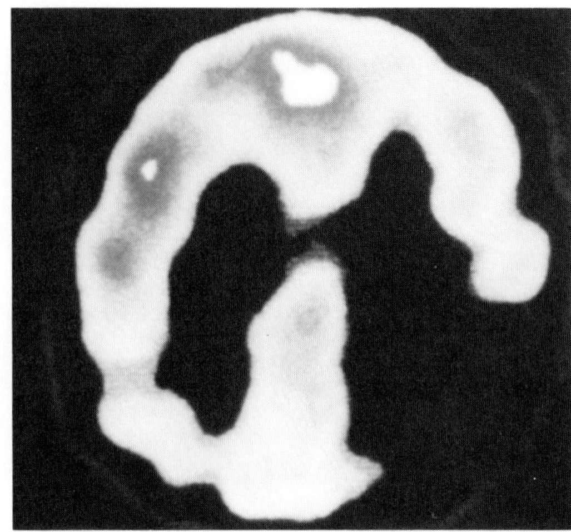

Diagnostic tool
A new tool for diagnostic imaging known as a *positron emission tomography* (PET) scan may help diagnose patients with Alzheimer's disease. The scan shown *above right* reveals that the brain of a patient suffering from Alzheimer's disease absorbs less glucose (white area) than the brain of a normal, healthy person (white area), *above.* The brain uses *glucose* (a simple sugar) as a major source of energy.

Aging (cont.)
memory and mental function in older people. One intriguing clue came from the Pacific Ocean island of Guam. Neurologist Peter S. Spencer and his colleagues at Albert Einstein College of Medicine in New York City followed up on earlier studies of an epidemic of neurological disease that occurred in the 1950's among the Chamorro islanders of Guam. Many of the victims had Alzheimer-like symptoms.

The researchers isolated an unusual *amino acid* (one of the chemical building blocks of proteins) from the seed of a cycad plant, which had been part of the diet of the Chamorros and was a suspected cause of the epidemic. They found that this amino acid produces abnormal behavior and pathological changes in the brains of animals. The researchers also found that the chemical makeup of this amino acid resembles a compound that is known to cause another neurological disease, lathyrism.

Researchers suggested that if an environmental factor caused the disease in Guam, Alzheimer's disease might similarly be caused by some as-yet-unrecognized substance that harms tissue of the brain and nervous system—perhaps in a common food source. And evidence that

Alzheimer's research
Brain damage suffered by patients with Alzheimer's disease is characterized by *senile plaque,* patches of material that contain a protein called amyloid B and occur in large numbers in areas of the brain that have deteriorated. Researchers are exploring whether amyloid B plays a role in the disease.

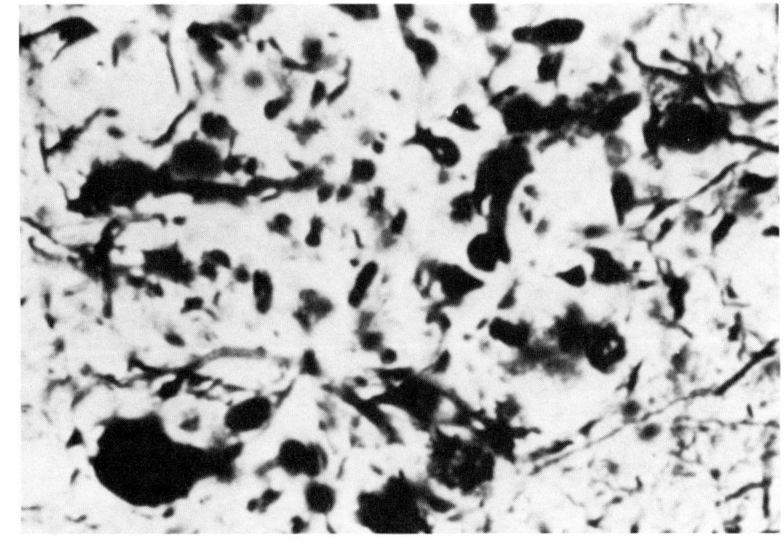

Aging (cont.)
some agent capable of being transmitted was involved in producing Alzheimer's disease was reported in July 1988 by neuropathologist Elias E. Manuelidis and colleagues at Yale University School of Medicine in New Haven, Conn.

The researchers reported that they were able to produce pathological changes in the brains of hamsters by injecting the hamsters with white blood cells from people at high risk of developing Alzheimer's disease or already showing early signs of the disease. When brain material from the injected hamsters was transplanted in the brains of a second set of hamsters, the same pathological changes occurred.

This research indicates that Alzheimer's disease may be caused by a *slow virus*—a virus that does not cause any symptoms for many years after infection. In this experiment, for example, the pathological changes observed in the hamsters may have been due to a virus carried in the white blood cells of the Alzheimer's patients. If so, the virus might also play a role in causing Alzheimer's disease.

☐ T. Franklin Williams

See also EXERCISE AND FITNESS. In WORLD BOOK, see AGING.

AIDS

The AIDS epidemic continued to exact a staggering toll in 1987 and 1988, despite progress on several fronts—including research and education. The Centers for Disease Control (CDC) in Atlanta, Ga., reported that by Aug. 1, 1988, 69,366 cases of AIDS (acquired immune deficiency syndrome) had been reported in the United States since 1981, when the disease was first identified. Also as of August 1988, 39,060 people had died of the disease.

AIDS reports. In June 1988, two groups—a presidential commission on AIDS and a panel of scientists, physicians, and public health officials appointed by the National Academy of Sciences (NAS)—called for urgent steps to halt the spread of AIDS. Both groups criticized what they saw as the U.S. government's slow response in fighting the disease. The NAS panel also charged the government with "gross inadequacy" in failing to reduce the spread of the AIDS virus by intravenous drug users. In some cities, intravenous drug users have replaced male homosexuals as the chief victims of AIDS. Both the NAS panel and retired Admiral James D.

The chart below shows the number of reported cases of AIDS and of AIDS-related deaths in the United States for every six-month period since 1981, when AIDS was first described.

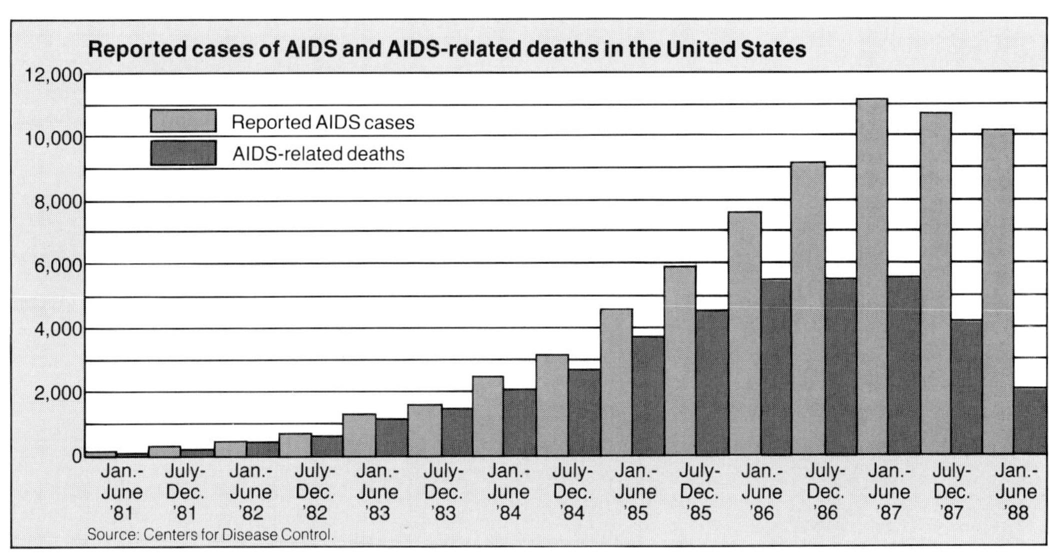

AIDS (cont.)
Watkins, the chairperson of the presidential AIDS commission, urged the passage of strong federal legislation and directives prohibiting discrimination against people infected with the AIDS virus.

AIDS drugs. In April 1988, Anthony S. Fauci, director of the National Institute of Allergy and Infectious Diseases (NIAID) in Bethesda, Md., told a congressional committee that the NIAID was too understaffed to efficiently oversee clinical trials of all the promising AIDS drugs approved for testing. Fauci described how NIAID-supervised trials of six drugs that had been assigned high-priority status were delayed for more than a year because of staff shortages. The federal budget for fiscal year 1988 allocated $467.8 million for AIDS-related research. In July, the Food and Drug Administration (FDA) announced that it would allow Americans to import small quantities of drugs that are used to treat AIDS patients in other countries but that have not been approved for use in the United States.

Drug for AIDS patients
Researchers at the National Cancer Institute in Bethesda, Md., examine a vial of trimetrexate, a drug under study as a treatment for AIDS patients with a deadly form of pneumonia. According to research published in October 1987, the drug is as effective in treating the condition as drugs currently in use and causes fewer side effects.

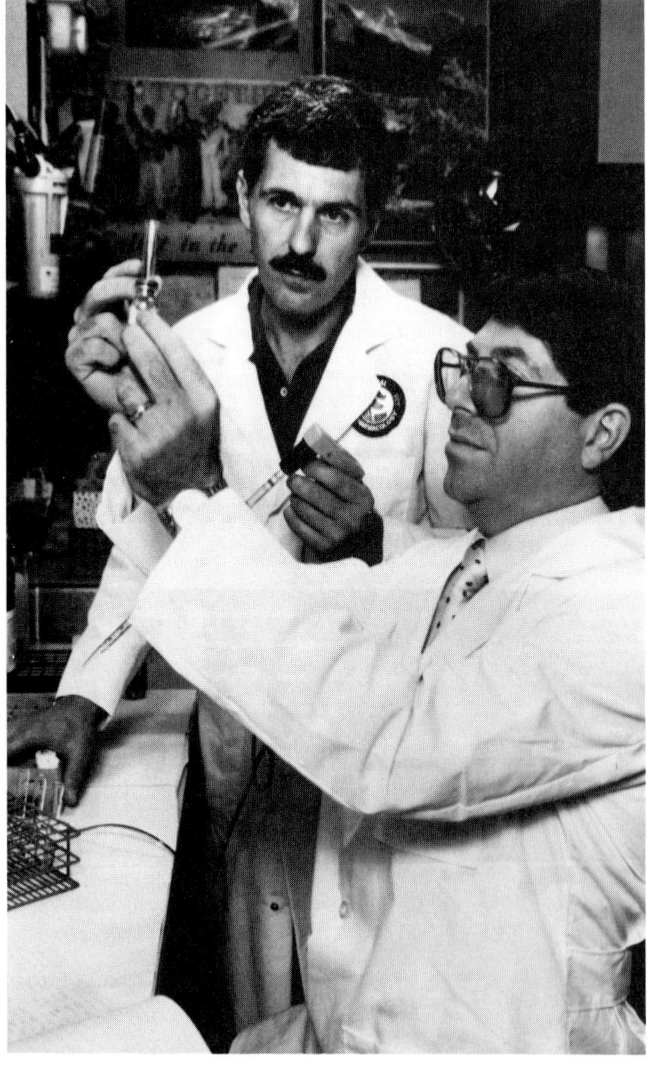

Masters and Johnson controversy. In March 1988, a book written by sex researchers William H. Masters and Virginia E. Johnson created an uproar among AIDS researchers and public health officials. In *Crisis: Heterosexual Behavior in the Age of AIDS*, the authors contended that the AIDS virus is "now running rampant" among heterosexuals in the United States, a claim strongly disputed by most AIDS experts.

To support their premise, Masters and Johnson—along with coauthor Robert C. Kolodny—cited their study of 800 sexually active heterosexual adults, none of whom fell into an AIDS risk group. That is, none of them had a recent history of intravenous drug use, or homosexual or bisexual activity, or had received a blood transfusion. According to Masters and Johnson, 6 per cent of the adults who had sexual relations with at least six partners per year for the previous five years were infected with the AIDS virus. The book also stated that kissing or dining out are "possible" means of transmitting the AIDS virus, though these theories have been rejected by most AIDS researchers.

Crisis was widely criticized by AIDS experts. Similar studies have found a 1 per cent infection rate among heterosexuals with no known risk factors.

Ethics and AIDS. The American Medical Association's (AMA's) Council on Ethical and Judicial Affairs issued a statement in November 1987 advising doctors that it is unethical to deny care to victims of AIDS if such care is "within the phy-

AIDS pamphlet
United States Surgeon General C. Everett Koop announces in May a government program to mail an educational pamphlet called *Understanding AIDS* to every American household.

AIDS (cont.)
sician's current realm of competence." The statement was issued in response to reports of doctors refusing to treat AIDS patients.

In June 1988, the AMA urged doctors to notify the sexual partners of patients infected with the AIDS virus, if other more conventional methods of alerting them proved ineffective. That is, doctors should notify the partners if infected patients refuse to do so themselves.

Education. In May 1988, the U.S. government undertook its most aggressive AIDS educational project to date, mailing a brochure titled *Understanding AIDS* to all 114 million American households. Nearly 300 public health, medical, community, and AIDS service organizations helped prepare the simply worded straightforward publication.

Second AIDS virus. The diagnosis of the first known case of AIDS in the United States caused by a second variety of the AIDS virus was reported in January 1988 by health officials at the University of Medicine and Dentistry of New Jersey in Newark. The AIDS patient was a West African who was visiting the United States.

This second virus, called *HIV-2* (human immunodeficiency virus-2), is most common in West Africa,

AIDS (cont.)
where it was discovered in 1984. At present, HIV-1 is believed to be the cause of most cases of AIDS outside of West Africa.

Some health officials warned that blood donations in the United States may eventually have to be screened for the presence of HIV-2. Blood banks now routinely test donated blood for the presence of antibodies to HIV-1.

Blood supply. In October 1987, researchers in Finland reported that some people do not form detectable antibodies for more than a year after becoming infected with the AIDS virus. This means that blood from an infected donor may appear to be safe when in fact it is not. The test used to screen the blood detects the presence of antibodies to the virus, not the virus itself.

In February 1988, CDC researchers reported that as many as 460 people per year in the United States may receive blood contaminated with the AIDS virus. About 4 million people receive transfusions of blood or blood products annually in the United States.

Grim outlook. Disturbing studies reported in 1988 predicted a grim long-term outlook for the majority of people infected with the AIDS virus. Statistics based on actual cases of AIDS reported in the United States indicate that from 20 to 30 per cent of those infected will develop the disease within five years but that the risk of developing the illness may increase with time.

In March 1988, epidemiologist Andrew Moss, an AIDS researcher at San Francisco General Hospital, reported that 50 per cent of those infected with the AIDS virus will develop AIDS and that 75 per cent will develop either AIDS or *AIDS-related complex* (ARC) within six years of infection. (ARC is a syndrome characterized by AIDS-like symptoms that often precedes the onset of full-blown AIDS.)

A CDC study published in June 1988 found that the *incubation period* for AIDS averages 7.8 years. (The incubation period is the time from HIV infection to the onset of AIDS.) Kung-Jong Lui of the CDC, who headed the study, said a person who is infected with HIV has a 99 per cent chance of developing full-blown AIDS.

Some researchers disagreed with the results of these studies. They argued that new drugs and treatment methods could help prevent some HIV-infected people from becoming seriously ill.

Vaccine studies. Research aimed at developing a vaccine against the AIDS virus accelerated in 1987 and

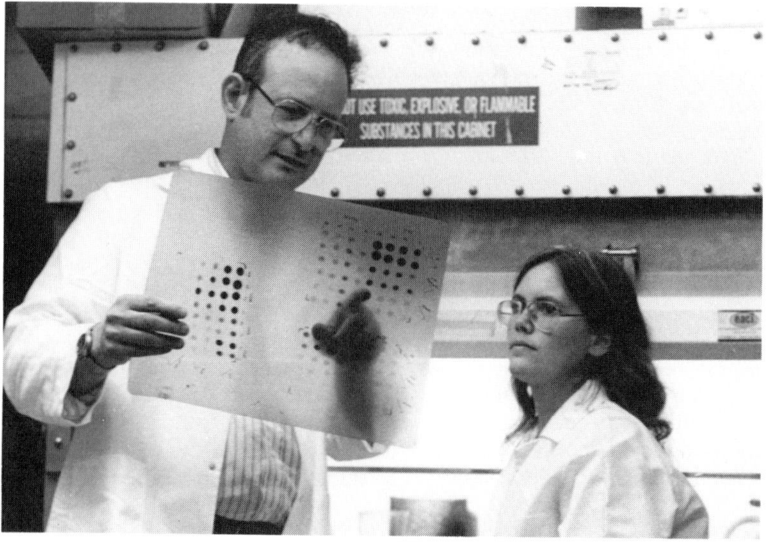

AIDS research
Scientists at the National Institute of Allergy and Infectious Diseases in Bethesda, Md., discuss an X-ray film showing the results of experiments to develop a vaccine against AIDS.

AIDS (cont.)
1988, though many scientists remained pessimistic that an effective vaccine would be developed. NIAID scientists announced in April 1988 that six volunteers inoculated with an experimental AIDS vaccine had developed an *immune response* to the virus. (An immune response indicates that a person's immune system has produced molecules called *antibodies* that help destroy invading microbes, such as viruses and bacteria.) The vaccine in the NIAID study, which uses protein similar to that found in the virus's outer coat, can stimulate an immune response without causing the disease.

Also in April, immunologist Daniel Zagury of Pierre and Marie Curie University in Paris reported that he had developed an immune response against the AIDS virus by repeatedly inoculating himself with a different AIDS vaccine than that tested by NIAID scientists. Because the volunteers in the NIAID study and Zagury and other individuals inoculated as part of his study had not been exposed to the AIDS virus itself, however, there was no proof that they were actually protected against the disease.

☐ Richard Trubo

In World Book, see AIDS.

Alcohol and Drug Abuse

A new guideline for determining whether or not a person is dependent on drugs or alcohol was set in late 1987 in a manual published by the American Psychiatric Association. The association's *Diagnostic and Statistical Manual of Mental Disorders* (*DSM-III-R*) is used by mental health professionals to diagnose mental and emotional problems.

DSM-III-R's criterion for the diagnosis of substance dependency is that the person must have experienced three or more of the following symptoms for one month or longer:

- The substance is taken in larger amounts or for a longer period than the person intended.
- The person has tried or wanted to try to cut down on the use of the substance.
- A great deal of time is spent acquiring or taking the substance or recovering from its effects.
- The person is frequently under the influence of the substance or suffering withdrawal symptoms while involved in important tasks.
- Some activities are curtailed because of substance use.
- The person continues to use the substance even though he or she knows it is causing a problem.
- The person develops a tolerance for the substance and must use increasingly greater amounts to receive the desired effect.
- Withdrawal symptoms occur if substance use is stopped.
- The person takes the substance to avoid withdrawal symptoms.

The new guideline is less strict than the previous one, which was set in 1980. The earlier diagnostic standard required that physical symptoms of addiction be present along with social or emotional problems linked to substance abuse. The new guideline implies that one can be considered alcohol- or drug-dependent even without being physically addicted.

Disease or misconduct? The question of whether or not alcoholism should be considered a disease—long the subject of controversy among some medical professionals—found its way to the Supreme Court of the United States in 1988. At issue was a Veterans Administration (VA) policy that granted extensions for educational benefits to veterans suffering from physical or mental disabilities not caused by willful misconduct.

Two veterans who had been hospitalized for alcoholism several times sued the VA when they were denied the disability extension for educational benefits. Lower courts had ruled in favor of the veterans, but these decisions had been overturned on appeal.

After hearing the two cases jointly, the Supreme Court on April 20 ruled 4 to 3 in favor of the VA.

Combating teen drinking Alcoholism, heavy drinking, and other problems associated with alcohol use continued to plague American teen-agers in 1987 and 1988. A public-service advertisement sponsored by the Ad Council and the National Council on Alcoholism stresses the need to resist peer pressures to drink.

Alcohol and Drug Abuse (cont.)
The justices voting in the majority said that the veterans did not merit disability extensions because their alcoholism was willful misconduct.

Although the high court's decision disturbed many medical professionals, it was not expected to have wide-ranging implications. Medical insurance benefits for alcoholism treatment, for example, would probably remain unchanged, according to officials of various medical insurance organizations.

Alcoholism and family history. Medical experts who view alcoholism as a disease found more scientific evidence in late 1987 to support their position. Since the 1970's, researchers have noted a correlation between alcoholism in natural parents and in their adult offspring—even when the children had been adopted at birth. These findings have led some researchers to conclude that people may inherit a tendency to develop alcoholism—just as some people inherit a tendency to develop such illnesses as diabetes or coronary heart disease.

This theory was supported in November 1987, when researchers at the San Diego Veterans Administration Hospital reported that young adult sons of alcoholics had lower than normal levels in the blood of a hormone called *cortisol* after drink-

Alcohol and Drug Abuse (cont.)
ing. Cortisol levels in the blood typically rise in response to alcohol ingestion. The findings suggested that the bodies of children of alcoholics may not react to alcohol with normal intensity, a phenomenon that might promote or allow increased alcohol use.

Another possible biological link to alcoholism was reported in autumn 1987 by medical researcher Henri Begleiter and his co-workers at State University of New York in Brooklyn. Begleiter's research indicated that an important component of the brain-wave patterns of sons of alcoholic men differs from that of the sons of men who were not alcoholics. The same researcher had previously found other differences in brain-wave patterns among the two study groups.

Depression and substance abuse. Another familial link in the development of substance abuse was reported by a group of psychiatric researchers led by Myrna M. Weissman at Yale University in New Haven, Conn. The scientists compared the behavior of children of depressed parents with that of children whose parents were not depressed. Weissman reported, among other findings, that almost 17 per cent of the children of depressed people were substance abusers. Only 7.4 per cent of the children of people who were not depressed were substance abusers.

Drug abuse among students appears to be on the decline in the United States, according to a survey of drug and alcohol abuse among about 16,000 high school seniors at 130 U.S. schools. The survey is conducted annually by social researchers at the University of Michigan Institute for Social Research in Ann Arbor.

Especially good news was the information that in 1987 cocaine use seemed to have declined for the first time in several years. In 1985, 13.1 per cent of high school seniors polled said they had taken cocaine at least once in the preceding 12 months. In 1987, the percentage had dropped to 10.3. Only 4.3 per cent of the seniors said they had used cocaine in the preceding 30 days. The use of a smokable and highly addictive form of cocaine, called *crack*, appeared to remain steady, however, with about 4 per cent reporting having smoked crack during the preceding 12 months.

The use of other illicit drugs such as hallucinogens, tranquilizers, and stimulants generally continued a slow decline begun in the early 1980's. Marijuana use also declined in 1987. In 1986, about 4 per cent of the students surveyed reported that they smoked marijuana every day. In 1987, only 3.3 per cent reported the same frequency of use.

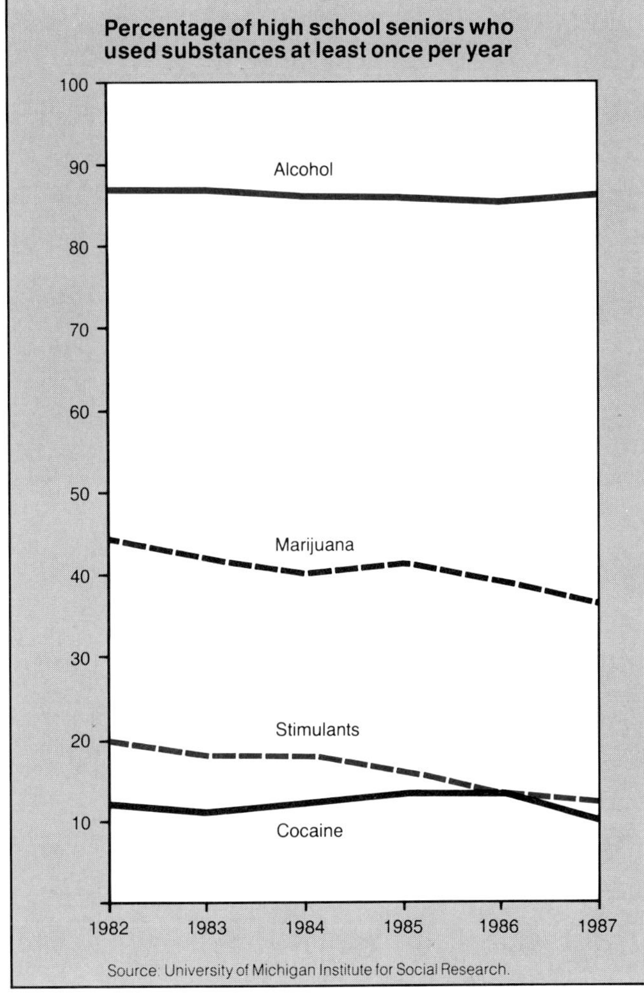

Annual surveys of substance abuse among U.S. high school seniors show that, though alcohol use is prevalent, drug abuse may be on the decline.

Alcohol and Drug Abuse (cont.)

Alcohol use among these young people remains discouragingly prevalent, however. In 1987, 66 per cent classified themselves as current users, and 37.5 per cent reported having an episode of heavy drinking within the preceding two weeks. About 5 per cent of the students said they drank some alcohol every day.

In April 1988, the National School Boards Association released a report calling for educators to take steps to combat alcohol and drug abuse among schoolchildren. The president of the association discouraged the practice of submitting entire student bodies to drug searches or tests, however.

Instead, the association recommended a three-part program to educate and assist students. The first recommendation was for each school to formulate and publicize rules forbidding the use of alcohol and drugs. Educators were also encouraged to develop curricula to teach children in every grade what substance abuse is and how to avoid it. The final recommendation of the board was to hire trained counselors to help individual students suspected of having problems with drug or alcohol abuse. These students would then be referred to treatment and rehabilitation programs.

AIDS and IV drug use. A shortage of space in drug treatment programs designed to help intravenous drug abusers may be an indirect factor in the continued spread of AIDS (acquired immune deficiency syndrome) in large urban areas in the United States, medical experts said in late 1987. Researchers estimate that AIDS, which can be spread through the use of contaminated needles, infects up to 60 per cent of the intravenous drug abusers in New York and New Jersey.

Publicly funded drug treatment programs in many cities are unable to accommodate the number of drug addicts requesting help. According to some reports, addicts in some areas of Los Angeles and Chicago must wait up to six weeks before being admitted for treatment. In New York City, the wait can be from two to four months; and in Boston, the wait may be as long as one year.

In spring 1988, a presidential commission created to formulate a national strategy for combating AIDS encouraged the Administration of President Ronald Reagan to devote $1.5 billion per year for at least 10 years to control intravenous drug abuse. ☐ Jinger Hoop

In WORLD BOOK, see COCAINE; DRUG ABUSE; MARIJUANA.

Allergies and Immunology

A new drug that may provide relief for people who are allergic to cats was being tested in 1988 at Fairfax Hospital in Falls Church, Va. The drug, CI-949, is designed to ease respiratory distress caused by CAT-1, a protein found in the dander, saliva, urine, and feces of cats.

CAT-1 causes a variety of immediate symptoms, including itching eyes, wheezing, and a feeling of tightness in the chest. Of those problems—which can usually be treated with antihistamines—CI-949 would be used only to relieve chest tightness; the drug is primarily designed to prevent delayed bronchial reactions to CAT-1.

Some people who are allergic to CAT-1, particularly if they also suffer from asthma, experience tightening of the bronchial tubes for up to 12 hours after exposure. CI-949 causes the body to release a substance called *slow-acting substance of anaphylaxis*, which causes the muscles surrounding the bronchial tubes to relax.

Testing on CI-949 was expected to continue through the end of 1988. The drug must then receive the approval of the United States Food and Drug Administration, a process that usually takes several years.

Immunity spurred by breast milk? Proteins in mother's milk may help

Breathing easy
Overreliance on *bronchodilators*—inhalant drugs that instantly open congested bronchial airways—may be contributing to a rise in asthma deaths. Doctors say that the symptomatic relief provided by the drugs may cause patients to delay seeking needed medical care.

Allergies and Immunology (cont.)
stimulate the development of an infant's immune system, a Canadian immunologist reported in March 1988. Michael H. Julius of McGill University in Montreal said human milk speeds the maturation of B cells in laboratory culture dishes and may have the same effect in the body. Julius said he had not yet identified the protein or proteins that act on B cells.

Cow's milk antibodies. Physicians have long known that mother's milk contains antibodies that protect babies from a variety of ailments, including infant diarrhea. In May 1988, researchers at the University of Maryland School of Medicine in Baltimore reported that antibodies from cow's milk can immunize people against traveler's diarrhea.

The diarrhea that afflicts travelers to less-developed countries is usually caused by the common bacterium *Escherichia coli*. Traveler's diarrhea can be prevented with antibiotics, but these can sometimes have unpleasant side effects. The Maryland researchers reasoned that antibodies produced in milk could provide equally effective protection without adverse effects.

The scientists inoculated pregnant cows for eight weeks with several strains of *E. coli*. The bacteria had no ill effects on the cows, but their immune systems formed antibodies against the bacteria. After the cows gave birth, the investigators collected their milk and separated out the antibodies. The antibodies were then processed into a powder that could be taken orally.

In a test on people, the researchers gave the powdered antibodies to 10 volunteers. Another 10 volunteers received a powder that did not contain *E. coli* antibodies. After three days, both groups were given water containing *E. coli*. None of the 10 volunteers who had received the antibodies became ill, while 9 of the 10 people who had not received the antibodies developed moderate to severe diarrhea. The scientists said these results "warrant the initiation of further studies" into the use of antibodies produced in cow's milk to prevent traveler's diarrhea.

Genetic susceptibility to autoimmune diseases. People who inherit genes for certain forms of molecules found on cells of the immune system are more likely than other people to develop several *autoimmune diseases*. That finding was reported in May 1988 by microbiologist Hugh O. McDevitt of Stanford University School of Medicine in California.

In autoimmune diseases, the body's immune system mistakes cells of the body as "foreign" invaders and attacks them just as it attacks bacteria or viruses. Rheumatoid arthritis, a chronic inflammation of the joints;

Allergies and Immunology (cont.)
rheumatic fever, which sometimes causes inflammation of the joints and heart valves; and multiple sclerosis, a degenerative disorder of the nervous system, are 3 of more than 40 known autoimmune diseases.

The molecules McDevitt and his associates studied are called *histocompatibility antigens*, which dot the surface of cells and serve as identifying markers. There are three classes, or types, of histocompatibility antigens. The researchers found that variations of one of these types, known as *human leucocyte antigens* (HLA's), are associated with at least three autoimmune diseases—rheumatoid arthritis, juvenile diabetes, and a skin disorder called *pemphigus vulgaris*.

HLA's are produced on the surface of two kinds of leucocytes, or white blood cells—*macrophages* and *B lymphocytes*, or *B cells*. Macrophages are large cells of the immune system that engulf and break down foreign substances in the body—in most cases, viruses and bacteria. B cells, another key part of the immune system, manufacture molecules called *antibodies* that help protect us against infection.

Viruses and bacteria have their own identifying antigens. When a macrophage destroys one of these microbes, fragments of the invader's antigens—called *antigenic determinants*—become linked with the antigens on the surface of the macrophage. The macrophage then "presents" the combined antigens to still other white blood cells known as *T lymphocytes* or *T cells*. The T cells recognize the invader's antigenic determinant as foreign and stimulate B cells to produce antibodies. The antibodies circulate through the body, seeking other copies of the microbe and fastening onto their antigens. Other immune-system cells then eliminate the microbes.

Research has shown that the antigens of viruses and bacteria contain a number of antigenic determinants that are identical, or nearly so, to the antigenic determinants in histocompatibility antigens. But somehow, the immune system usually ignores the body's antigens and homes in on those of the invaders.

In autoimmune diseases, however, the immune system lacks this ability to pick out and react to only foreign antigenic determinants. Without this safeguard, antibodies are likely to be made against antigenic determinants closely resembling those found on body cells. When that happens, the antibodies produced by the B cells attack not only the invading microorganism but also any cells—such as bone or nerve cells—whose antigenic determinants are similar to the germ's.

Like all proteins, histocompatibility

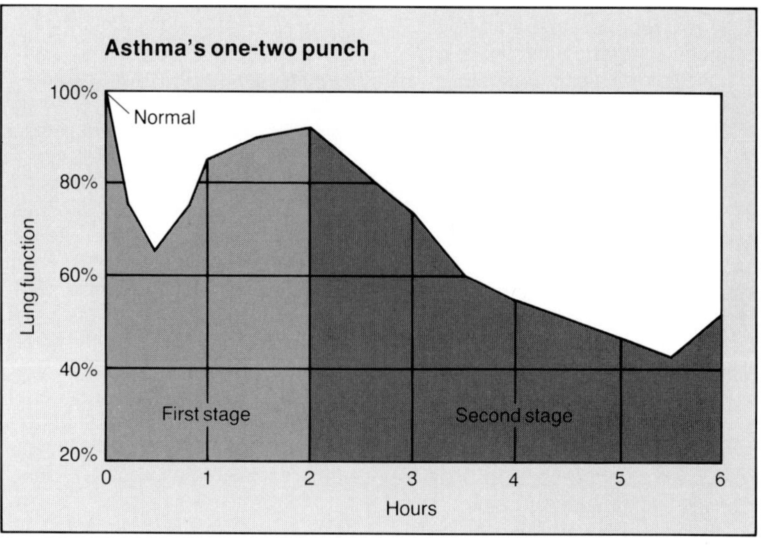

An asthma attack occurs in two stages. The first stage, marked by the swelling of air passages in the lungs, can be brought under control in an hour or so with the help of drugs called bronchodilators, which restore lung function to near-normal levels. About two hours after the onset of the initial attack, the second stage of the attack begins. In this phase, lung tissues do not respond to bronchodilators. The patient may need to be treated with steroid drugs to keep from suffocating.

Allergies and Immunology (cont.)

antigens are products of the genes. A number of genes direct the production of histocompatibility antigens, and each gene can have several possible chemical variations. These variations in genes result in different forms of antigens.

McDevitt and his colleagues discovered that certain forms of HLA's are associated with autoimmune diseases more often than other forms. Children with HLA molecules known as DR3, for example, are more than 20 times as likely to develop diabetes as are children with HLA's called DR2. The scientists found similar correlations, involving other HLA's, for rheumatoid arthritis and pemphigus vulgaris.

It may be possible to manipulate the immune system to prevent those and other autoimmune disorders, the researchers said. They speculated that another kind of T cell, which suppresses the immune response, could perhaps be alerted to stop the production of antibodies against antigens on invading microbes that closely resemble the body's own.

☐ Edward P. Cohen

In World Book, see Allergy; Immunity.

Arthritis and Connective Tissue Disorders

Methotrexate, a drug long used to treat patients with some forms of cancer as well as people with severe cases of the skin disease psoriasis, is a relatively safe treatment for patients suffering from rheumatoid arthritis (RA), a crippling inflammation of tissue around the joints. That finding was the subject of a number of studies reported at the annual meeting of the American Rheumatism Association (ARA) held in Houston in May 1988.

Research conducted in the 1980's demonstrated that methotrexate, developed in the 1940's, can reduce swelling, stiffness, pain, and inflammation in RA patients who do not respond to other drugs used to treat this condition. The United States Food and Drug Administration has not approved the use of methotrexate for RA patients, however, because of questions about the drug's safety. Some studies had indicated that methotrexate can cause serious side effects, including nausea, inflammation of the lungs, and scarring of the liver.

At the ARA meeting, rheumatologist William Shergy and his colleagues at Duke University Medical Center in Durham, N.C., reported on their study of methotrexate's effect on the liver. For their research, they removed 300 small pieces of tissue from the livers of more than 200 RA patients taking methotrexate. They found evidence of scarring in only six samples. In all cases, the scarring was mild.

Also at the meeting, rheumatologist James Brick and his associates at West Virginia University School of Medicine in Morgantown reported few side effects in nearly 100 patients who received methotrexate once a week—the standard dose. Children with arthritis may also be safely treated with methotrexate, according to research reported by rheumatologist Carol A. Wallace and her colleagues at the Seattle Children's Hospital. The researchers administered the drug to 23 children for periods of up to four years. They

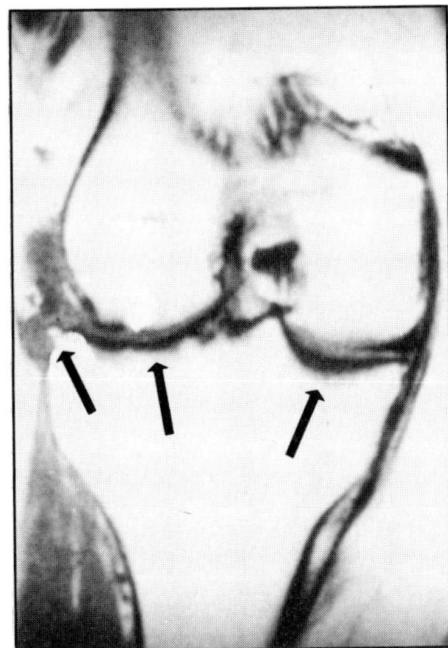

Joint disease revealed
A technique called *magnetic resonance imaging* (MRI) may provide more precise pictures of damaged or diseased joints than any other diagnostic technique. This MRI image of an arthritic knee reveals a protruding spur of bone (indicated by arrow on the left). It also shows a loss of cushioning tissue (dark area indicated by middle arrow) between two bones, compared with an area that has a normal amount of cushioning tissue (dark region indicated by arrow on the right).

Treating inflamed joints
Injections of a radioactive substance may be an effective and less costly alternative to surgery for reducing pain and inflammation in the joints of patients with rheumatoid arthritis, according to research published in February 1988. The substance, which loses its radioactivity within a few hours, destroys inflamed tissue. The procedure, new to the United States, has been used for more than 30 years in Europe.

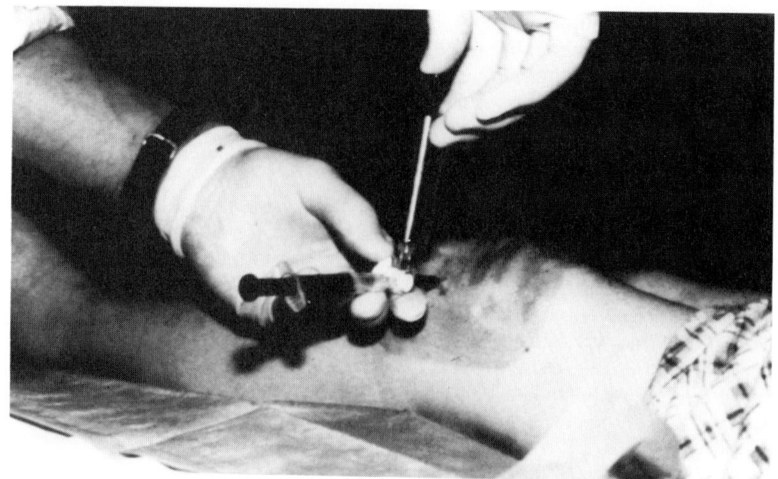

Arthritis (cont.)
reported that the children suffered no major problems.

Running limits. Runners should observe restrictions to prevent injury to their joints, particularly their knees, according to a study of 1,288 runners that was presented at the ARA meeting by rheumatologist Lawrence E. Hart and his colleagues at McMaster Medical School in Hamilton, Canada. They reported that runners increase their risk of injury if they run more than five days per week or more than 5 miles (8 kilometers) per day or 40 miles (64 kilometers) per week. Runners who compete in races are more likely to damage their joints. The researchers found that 50 per cent of the injuries suffered by the runners studied were recurrences of previous running-related injuries.

Molecular clue? The discovery of a piece of genetic material that may account for the ability of certain strains of a bacterium called *Shigella* to cause arthritis was reported at the ARA meeting in May by rheumatologists Heather Stieglitz and Peter Lipsky of the University of Texas Health Science Center in Dallas. The genetic material is a *plasmid*, a small circular molecule made up of deoxyribonucleic acid (DNA), the material that carries the instructions for an organism's life processes. The researchers found that strains of *Shigella* that do not cause arthritis lack this specific plasmid.

Shigella is a type of bacteria that can cause diseases of the intestines. Some people infected with the bacteria develop arthritis from three to seven weeks after exposure to the organism.

Scientists have found that these people are likely to have a type of immune system molecule called *HLA-B27*. People with HLA-B27 are also more likely to develop certain types of arthritis, such as arthritis of the spine. Scientists have not yet discovered the link between arthritis and HLA-B27, however.

Stieglitz and Lipsky are also unsure of the plasmid's role in triggering arthritis and its connection with HLA-B27. They theorized that the plasmid may closely resemble a still unknown protein naturally found in the body. If *Shigella* bacteria with the plasmid invade the body, the immune system may mistakenly attack the body's own tissues instead of the bacteria, causing arthritis. The researchers also suggested that HLA-B27 may somehow promote this process.

Treating anemia. RA patients suffering from severe anemia may benefit from large doses of the hormone erythropoietin, according to a report presented at the ARA meeting by rheumatologist Nancy Olsen and her colleagues at Vanderbilt Univer-

Arthritis (cont.)
sity Medical School in Nashville. Erythropoietin, which is produced by the kidneys, stimulates the production of red blood cells by the bone marrow.

Since 1987, the hormone has been used to treat RA patients with anemia who fail to respond to treatment with iron or to other standard therapy. Inadequate supplies of erythropoietin, however, have limited its use. As a result, some RA patients still suffered from anemia.

Using a synthetic version of the hormone produced by genetic engineering, Olsen and her colleagues were able to test the effectiveness of large doses of erythropoietin. In genetic engineering, bacteria or yeast cells are used as "biological factories" to produce large quantities of a protein, such as erythropoietin. The researchers found that doses of the hormone ranging from 50 to 100 per cent larger than those previously administered could increase the number of red blood cells in anemic RA patients to normal or near-normal levels.

Diagnosing with ultrasound. Ultrasound is a more effective means of diagnosing problems of the shoulder than X rays, according to a study reported in June 1988 by radiologist Jeffrey R. Crass of the State University of New York at Stony Brook. In ultrasound, reflected sound waves produce images of objects and organs in the body.

X rays have long been used to diagnose diseases of the joints, to track the development of such diseases, and to measure joints and the surrounding bone so that artificial joints can be properly fitted. X rays have been particularly useful in diagnosing problems of the *rotator cuff*, a structure composed of the tendons of a number of shoulder muscles. The rotator cuff is responsible for much of the motion of the arm in the shoulder area. Tears in the cuff caused by accidents, disease, or aging can result in pain and can severely limit the motion of the shoulder.

The standard method of diagnosing a tear is to inject dye into the rotator cuff and then photograph the shoulder with X-ray film. If there is a tear, the dye leaks from the cuff and so appears on the film.

According to Crass, ultrasound provides a more accurate and less costly way to diagnose damage to the rotator cuff. In addition, in contrast to X-ray imaging, ultrasound does not require a potentially painful injection of dye into the damaged cuff. □ John Baum

In World Book, see Arthritis.

Behavioral Disorders

See Mental and Behavioral Disorders

Birth Control

Two contraceptive devices already available outside the United States were approved for use by American women by the Food and Drug Administration (FDA) in 1988. The devices were the ParaGard, developed as the Copper T 380A intrauterine device (IUD), and the cervical cap.

The range had narrowed in recent years because of costly product liability lawsuits, heavy insurance costs, decreased public funding for contraceptive research, and increased federal regulation, which has obstructed the introduction of some devices and drugs into the United States. According to some birth control experts, the limited choice of contraceptives has contributed to higher rates of unplanned pregnancy and abortion in the United States.

ParaGard is an improved variation of copper IUD's that were withdrawn from the U.S. market in 1986 because of lawsuits. The suits claimed the devices caused pelvic infections and sterility, claims that proved invalid in most cases.

The most commonly used IUD worldwide, ParaGard, developed in the United States, is also considered the most effective IUD currently in use. For ParaGard users over age 25, the rate of pregnancy

Birth Control (cont.)
is less than 1 per cent per year.

ParaGard is a T-shaped device that can be left in place for four years. The device may be more effective than other copper IUD's because it contains more copper. For reasons not fully understood, copper improves the contraceptive action of an IUD.

ParaGard is believed to be safer than other IUD's, because it has a string composed of only one strand, rather than multiple strands, as with the defective Dalkon Shield IUD removed from the market in 1974. The string helps the wearer determine that the IUD is still in place and aids in its removal. Studies of ParaGard have revealed that IUD's with a single string may be less likely to result in infection by microbes that may use the string as a pathway to the uterus.

GynoPharma, Incorporated, the company that is marketing ParaGard in the United States, was aided in obtaining liability coverage—which had been a major obstacle—because of its educationally oriented marketing program. The company strongly cautions doctors against providing the device to women under age 25, because they usually have more sexual partners than older women and are thus at a higher risk of developing pelvic infections and sexually transmitted diseases. Such diseases can lead to sterility. The IUD is also not recommended for childless women.

Cervical cap. After seven years of negotiations and a major U.S. clinical trial, the FDA in May 1988 conditionally approved U.S. marketing of the Prentif Cavity-Rim Cervical Cap, manufactured by Lamberts Limited of Great Britain. The FDA ordered Lamberts to continue testing the device to determine whether the cap causes significant abnormalities in the cells of the *cervix* (the mouth of the uterus), which may precede the development of cervical cancer. Researchers found cell abnormalities in a few users of the cap.

The Prentif cap is a small latex device that fits over the cervix like a thimble. An advantage of the cap is that it can be left in place for up to 48 hours, twice as long as the diaphragm. Also, in contrast to the diaphragm, an additional application of spermicide is not necessary before each act of intercourse. Disadvantages of the cap are that it must be carefully fitted and that it can be difficult to insert and remove. The pregnancy rate with the cap is similar to that of the diaphragm, about 19 per cent during the first year of use. ☐ **Louise B. Tyrer**

In World Book, see Birth Control.

Birth Defects

See Genetics

Blood

Researchers in 1987 and 1988 reported on a blood-donation technique used to minimize the risk of transfusing contaminated blood during and after surgery. In this technique, called *autologous predeposit donation*, a patient whose surgery is scheduled several weeks in advance donates blood at two-week intervals for his or her own use during the scheduled surgery.

This technique has become popular because of concern about the possibility of contracting AIDS (acquired immune deficiency syndrome) or hepatitis from donated blood. The risk of contracting AIDS from transfusions, however, has become negligible, because blood banks routinely test blood for the presence of the virus that causes AIDS.

There is no suitable test for the virus responsible for a form of hepatitis called *non-A, non-B hepatitis*, however. This disease accounts for thousands of cases of post-transfusion hepatitis each year in the United States. To minimize the risk of infection by the virus, as well as the risk of *incompatibility* (poor matching of blood, leading to harmful reactions), transfusion specialists now recommend autologous predeposit donations.

Physician Jay Wasman and his

Blood (cont.)
colleagues at Case Western Reserve University Medical School in Cleveland reported in December 1987 that most of the 44 patients they studied could have donated all the blood they needed during and after elective surgery on bones and joints. Seventeen of the patients did not donate enough blood, however, and had to receive blood donated by other people.

The major limitation to autologous predeposit blood donations is the patient's red blood cell count—the concentration of red blood cells in the blood. Physicians at Johns Hopkins University School of Medicine in Baltimore reported in July 1988 that repeated donations gradually make some patients anemic, even if the patients take iron pills to replace iron lost by donating blood. The underlying cause of the anemia appears to be insufficient production of *erythropoietin*, the hormone that stimulates the body to manufacture red blood cells.

Blood specialists expect that anemia caused by donating blood will become rare in the near future because erythropoietin can be mass-produced by genetic engineering. This technique involves inserting genes that code for a substance

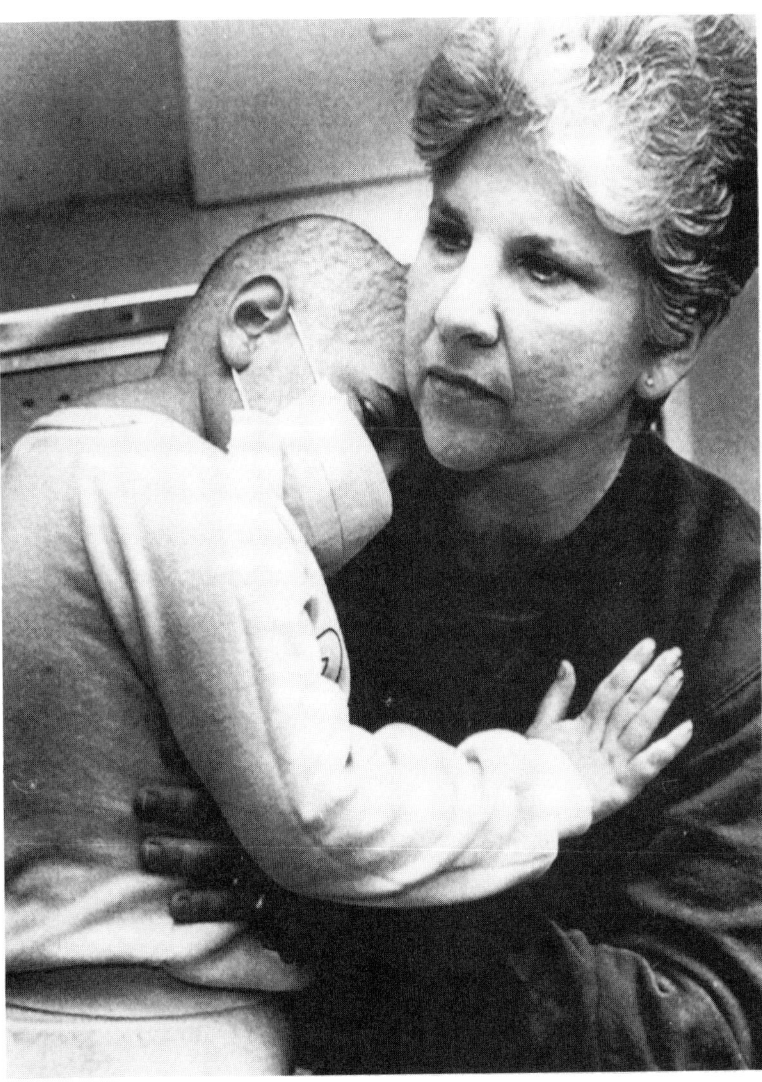

Help for leukemia
Apparently cured of *leukemia* (blood cancer), Brooke Ward, 7, of Raleigh, N.C., gets a hug from her mother before leaving Seattle's Fred Hutchinson Cancer Research Center in March 1988. Brooke was the first person to receive a transplant of lifesaving *bone marrow* (the substance that produces blood cells) through a national registry that finds suitable donors.

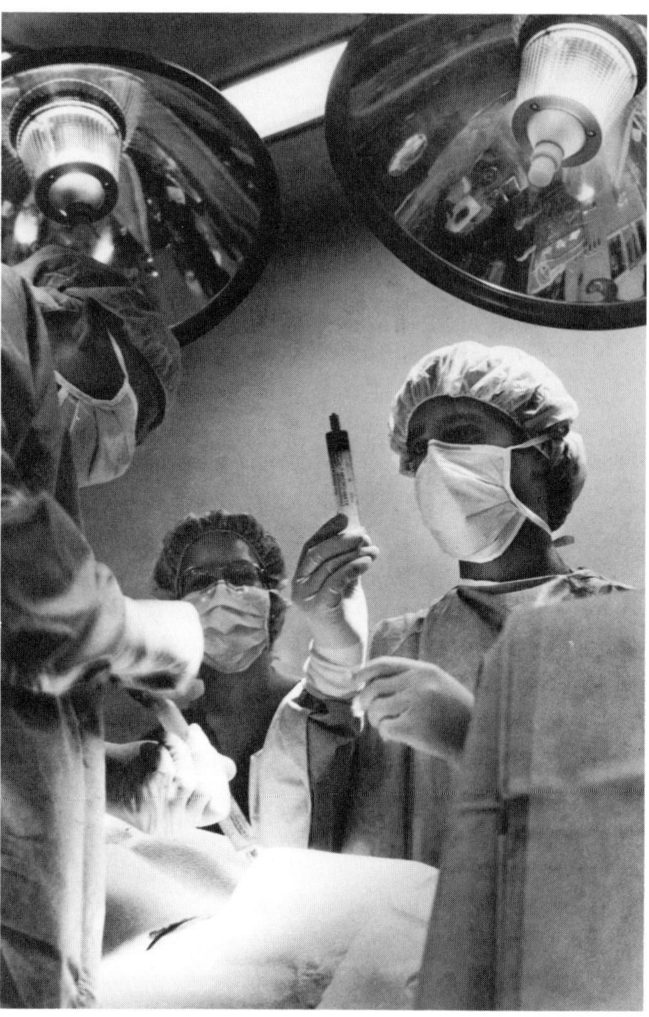

Matched marrow
A member of a bone-marrow transplant team examines marrow drawn from a donor's bones. This marrow matches that of a particular leukemia patient. So, when injected into that patient, the marrow will produce blood cells that not only are healthy but also are less likely to cause serious complications.

Blood (cont.)
such as erythropoietin into the genes of rapidly reproducing bacteria, yeast, or other host cells. These cells become "biological factories," producing this substance; and their descendants inherit the ability to produce it as well.

More white blood cells. Substances that help patients who do not have enough white blood cells and are thus at risk of serious infection were tested during the year. Though blood transfusions are helpful in patients with low red blood cell counts, they usually cannot provide long-term replenishment of white blood cells. In the mid-1980's, however, researchers used genetic engineering techniques to mass-produce the proteins that stimulate the *bone marrow* to manufacture white cells. (Marrow is the soft substance that fills the center of most bones.)

These proteins are called *colony-stimulating factors* (CSF) because they cause white blood cells to grow in colonies, or clusters, in bone marrow cells that are grown in test tubes outside the body. CSF also improves the ability of white blood cells to kill harmful bacteria and other microorganisms. Medical scientists tested recently manufactured forms of CSF that apparently could help patients who did not have enough of particular types of white blood cells called granulocytes and macrophages.

In 1987 and 1988, scientists used CSF to help patients suffering from low white blood counts caused by four different conditions. A team of researchers at Harvard Medical School and the University of California at Los Angeles announced in September 1987 that manufactured CSF increased the white blood counts of AIDS patients. The counts either became normal or rose above normal. The number of white blood cells in the patients' bone marrow also increased.

Researchers at M. D. Anderson Hospital and Tumor Institute in Houston reported in December 1987 that an artificially produced type of CSF improved white cell counts of patients suffering from bone marrow failure due to leukemia. Scientists at Duke University in Durham, N.C., announced in April 1988 that manufactured CSF improved the recovery of bone marrow function in cancer patients after the patients received bone marrow transplants. And in June 1988, researchers at the Memorial Sloan-Kettering Cancer Center in New York City reported that manufactured CSF protected cancer patients from the low white cell counts caused by anticancer drugs.

☐ Jerry L. Spivak

In World Book, see AIDS; Blood; Blood Transfusion; Hepatitis.

Bone Disorders

Lasers are of little use for most kinds of foot surgery, *orthopedists* (bone specialists) reported in February 1988 at a meeting of the American Orthopedic Foot and Ankle Society in Atlanta, Ga.

A laser produces a narrow beam of intense light that can be used to burn away diseased tissue. But the searing heat that makes the laser an ideal tool for some kinds of surgery limits its usefulness in treating bone disorders. Bones treated with lasers develop scar tissue and become structurally weaker. Participants at the meeting concluded that the laser should not be used in the surgical treatment of bunions and *hammertoes* (toes that bend upward because of a malformed joint).

The physicians said lasers can be used to treat foot ulcers and ingrown or fungus-infected toenails. They agreed, however, that laser therapy is no better than traditional treatment methods for the correction of those problems.

MRI views bones. Magnetic resonance imaging (MRI) is an extremely useful tool for assessing damage to the cartilage and ligaments of the knee, according to a February 1988 report by orthopedist David W. Jolly and his associates at Walter Reed Army Medical Center in Washington, D.C.

MRI machines use a strong electromagnetic field to produce images of the interior of the body. Although it often does not reveal bone abnormalities, MRI clearly displays the ligaments and other soft tissues in and around the joints.

Jolly and his colleagues compared MRI scans with *arthroscopy*, a diagnostic and surgical technique employing thin instruments that are inserted through incisions to view and operate on the knee. They studied 50 patients with suspected knee-ligament injuries.

MRI scans were made of the patients' knees before the patients underwent arthroscopy and a diagnosis made on the basis of these scans. In each case, arthroscopy confirmed the diagnosis that had been made on the basis of MRI.

Arthritic knees. A new technique for treating rheumatoid arthritis of the knee was reported in September 1987 by orthopedist Clement B. Sledge of Brigham and Women's Hospital in Boston. The procedure involves injecting a radioactive substance into the knee.

Arthritis is a group of more than 100 joint disorders characterized by inflammation and the degeneration of cartilage and bone. Rheumatoid arthritis, an *autoimmune disease* in which the immune system attacks

3-D imaging
Three-dimensional images of a skull, *below,* and vertebrae, *below left,* were made with the aid of new computer programs introduced in late 1987. The programs can be used to produce 3-D views of soft tissues as well as bone and can be applied to computerized tomography (CAT scans) and magnetic resonance imaging (MRI), two procedures used to see structures inside the body. So far, the programs are being used mostly for surgery.

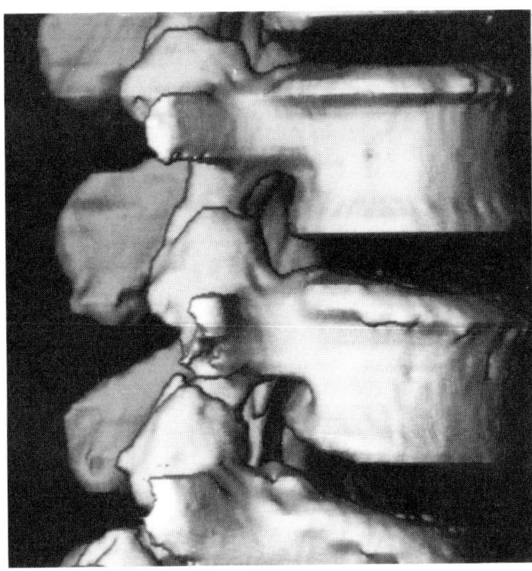

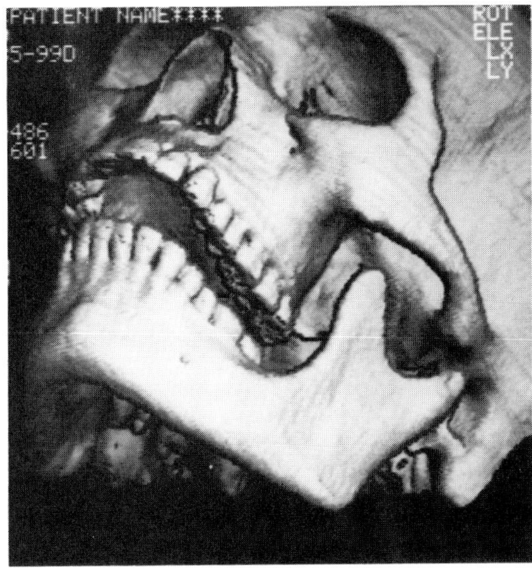

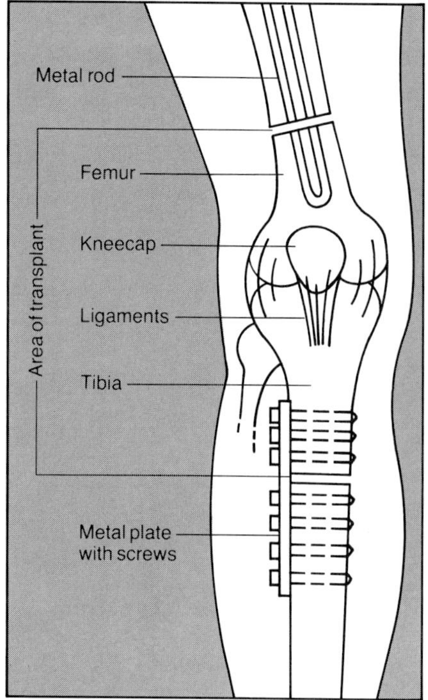

Total knee transplant
The first successful transplant of an entire knee was performed in 1987 on Susan Lazarchick of Absecon, N.J., *right.* The procedure, *above,* involved removing the knee and parts of the femur and tibia. The knee and equal segments of leg bones from an 18-year-old man who had been killed in an accident were then fastened in place with a rod and screws.

Bone Disorders (cont.)
the body's own tissues, is the most severe form of arthritis.

Between 1977 and 1985, the Boston researchers injected 135 arthritic knees in 111 patients with a single dose of a radioactive iron compound. In a two-year follow-up evaluation of 59 of the treated knees, the physicians found that 39 were greatly improved and 9 were somewhat improved. These results were the best yet reported for nonsurgical treatment of rheumatoid arthritis of the knee.

Enlarged feet. The reason pregnant women often experience enlargement of their feet was explained in February 1988 by orthopedist Richard Alvarez of the University of Vermont College of Medicine in Burlington. Alvarez and his associates examined the feet of 17 pregnant women. The physicians found that the women's feet had more fluid and soft tissue than the feet of the nonpregnant women.

Doctors had long suspected that these factors caused the problem, but they had speculated that the stretching of ligaments in the foot might also contribute to the enlargement. Alvarez and his associates, however, found no such changes in the ligaments.

☐ John J. Gartland

In WORLD BOOK, see BONE.

Books of Health and Medicine

Here are 24 outstanding health and medical books that individuals and families may find useful and interesting. These were selected from books published in 1987 and 1988.

Birth defects. *Babies with Down Syndrome: A New Parents Guide*, edited by Karen Stray-Gundersen. Chapters by parents and health professionals provide a full range of answers to questions on Down syndrome—the baby's development, potential medical problems and their treatment, and resources for families. (Woodbine House, 1987. 242 pp. $9.95 paper)

Chronic illness. *Living with Chronic Illness: Days of Patience and Passion* by Cheri Register draws on her own and others' experiences. Register discusses the effects of long-term illness on one's self-image, relationships, feelings, work, aspirations, and attitude toward life. (Free Press, 1987. 316 pp. $19.95)

Mainstay: A Companion Guide for the Well Spouse of the Chronically Ill is a personal account by Maggie Strong, whose husband developed multiple sclerosis. The book includes information on the emotional and financial impact of chronic illness on the family. (Little Brown, 1988. 323 pp. $17.95)

Drugs. *AARP Pharmacy Service Prescription Drug Handbook*. Authoritative information from the American Association of Retired Persons on medicines most frequently used by people over 50 years old. The book includes nearly 1,000 entries and a 40-page drug identification chart. Also included are explanations of many medical conditions, and guidelines for the proper use of drugs. (Scott, Foresman, 1988. 940 pp. $13.95 paper)

American Medical Association Guide to Prescription and Over-the-Counter Drugs, edited by Charles B. Clayman. Written for the lay person in clear, nontechnical language, this book covers more than 4,000 commonly prescribed and widely used over-the-counter drugs. (Random House, 1988. 576 pp. $25.00)

Ethics. *Playing God: The New World of Medical Choices* by Thomas and Celia Scully. The Scullys—he a physician and she a writer—offer practical advice in dealing with the moral issues that arise in modern medical care. They explain patients' rights, informed consent, and how to question doctors about courses of treatment. (Simon & Schuster, 1987. $19.95)

Rationing Medicine by Robert H. Blank looks at the difficult issues involved with the allocation of limited medical resources. Topics include organ transplants, the treatment of critically ill newborns, reproduction technology, and fetal health. (Columbia University Press, 1988. 290 pp. $25.00)

Setting Limits: Medical Goals in an Aging Society by Daniel Callahan. The author—director and founder of the Hastings Center, known for its work in medical ethics—argues that too large a share of health care resources in the United States are spent on extending the life of the elderly, with little thought for their quality of life. (Simon & Schuster, 1987. 256 pp. $18.95)

Exercise and nutrition. *Eat Smart for a Healthy Heart* by Denton A. Cooley and Carolyn Moore. The authors present 400 easy-to-follow recipes that are low in fat and cholesterol. The recipes, submitted by some of Houston's top chefs, follow dietary guidelines laid down by Cooley, a noted heart surgeon. (Barron's, 1987. 386 pp. $18.95)

Controlling Cholesterol by Kenneth H. Cooper is an exercise and diet guide by a leader of the health and fitness movement. (Bantam, 1988. 357 pp. $17.95)

Fatal diseases. *And the Band Played On: Politics, People, and AIDS* by Randy Shilts, a reporter for the *San Francisco Chronicle* who has covered AIDS (acquired immune deficiency syndrome) since 1982. (St. Martin's Press, 1987. 630 pp. $24.95)

Understanding Alzheimer's Disease: What It Is, How to Cope with

At the bookstore
New titles on health and medicine in 1987 and 1988 included *Health Care U.S.A.,* a directory of medical facilities; *The Last Crusade,* an account of the fight against tuberculosis; *Setting Limits,* on issues involved with caring for the aged; *The Second Medical Revolution,* a look at new trends in medicine; *The American Medical Association Home Medical Adviser,* a family health guide; and *Controlling Cholesterol,* advice on diet and exercise.

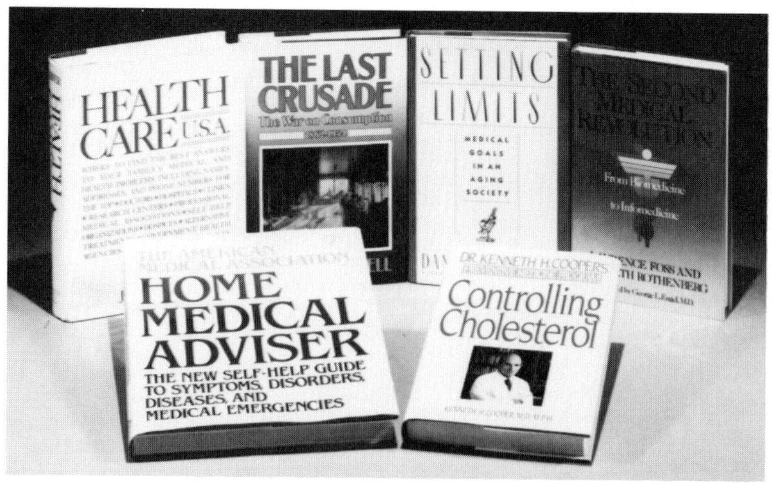

Books (cont.)
It, and Future Directions by the Alzheimer's Disease and Related Disorders Association, Miriam K. Aronson, editor. This is an in-depth guide to a degenerative brain disease affecting more than 2 million people in the United States. (Scribner, 1988. 380 pp. $15.95)

Health care. *Health Care U.S.A.* by Jean Carper. This directory includes the names and phone numbers of clinics, hospitals, and researchers specializing in more than 120 disorders as well as other pertinent information on health care. (Prentice Hall, 1987. 635 pp. $19.95 paper)

Caring for Your Own at Home: Nursing the Ill at Home by Darla J. Neidrick. Sharing her expertise as a registered nurse, Neidrick provides guidance on hygiene, diet, and other aspects of home care. (Wiley, 1988. 245 pp. $12.95)

American Medical Association Home Medical Adviser, edited by Charles B. Clayman and others. This easy-to-use guide describes the symptoms and recommended treatments for many conditions. (Random House, 1988. 320 pp. $24.95)

Your Good Health: How to Stay Well and What to Do When You're Not, edited by William I. Bennett and others. The editors, physicians at Harvard Medical School, discuss nutrition, environmental hazards, stress, and other health-related matters. (Harvard University Press, 1987. 576 pp. $24.95)

The Oral Report: The Consumer's Common Sense Guide to Better Dental Care by Jerry F. and Mary Jane Taintor. As well as explaining many technical aspects of dentistry, this book presents the major issues facing the dental health industry in the United States today. (Facts on File, 1988. 194 pp. $18.95)

Low Vision: What Can You Do to Preserve and Even Enhance Your Usable Sight by Helen K. Neal. This book offers hope to the approximately 11.4 million Americans whose eyesight is fading. (Simon & Schuster, 1987. 269 pp. $16.95)

History. *The Care of Strangers: The Rise of the American Hospital System* by Charles E. Rosenberg traces the development of U.S. hospital practice from the almshouses of the early 1800's to the establishment of modern hospitals in this century. (Basic Books, 1987. 437 pp. $22.95)

Heart of the Healer, edited by Dawson Church and Alan Sherr. Physicians and other healers relate their personal experiences and inner journeys. (Aslan, 1987. 238 pp. $14.95 paper)

The Second Medical Revolution: From Biomedicine to Infomedicine by Laurence Foss and Kenneth Rothenberg. This provocative book

Books (cont.)
examines the philosophical and clinical history of scientific medicine and critiques several modern movements in medical care. (New Science Library, 1987. 335 pp. $29.95)

The Last Crusade: The War on Consumption, 1862-1954 by Mark Caldwell. Caldwell describes society's battle against "consumption" (tuberculosis) and relates how that struggle spurred the national public health movement. (Atheneum, 1988. 336 pp. $27.50)

Disease and Discovery: A History of the Johns Hopkins School of Hygiene and Public Health, 1916-1939 by Elizabeth Fee. This book is an excellent study not only of the Johns Hopkins School but also of American public health up to the end of the 1930's. (Johns Hopkins University Press, 1987. 286 pp. $30)

Mental health. *Insanity: The Idea and Its Consequences* by Thomas Stephen Szasz. The author, a controversial antipsychiatry psychiatrist, examines the widely held belief that the mentally ill are not responsible for their actions. Szasz regards mental illness as a myth. (Wiley, 1987. 414 pp. $17.95)

☐ Margaret Moore Ovitsky

Brain and Nervous System

The discovery of a protein that is essential for proper muscle functioning was reported in December 1987 by geneticists at Children's Hospital in Boston. The researchers theorized that an absence of the protein leads to the development of Duchenne muscular dystrophy (DMD), a muscle-wasting disease. In May 1988, the scientists confirmed that theory by showing that the protein is missing in DMD patients' muscles.

The findings were hailed by neurologists, who have long treated DMD but have been unable to stop the progress of the fatal disease. For the first time, neurologists could offer DMD patients a ray of hope that a cure for the disease might be developed.

DMD, the most common and severe form of muscular dystrophy, strikes its victims in childhood and almost always causes death by the age of 30. The disease is hereditary and is caused by an abnormality on the X chromosome, one of the two human chromosomes that determine sex. Females have two X chromosomes; males have an X and a Y. (Chromosomes, of which human beings have 23 pairs, are threadlike structures in the cell nucleus that carry the genes.)

A female with one normal X chromosome and one affected with the DMD abnormality will not contract the disease, because the genes on the normal chromosome are dominant and overcome the influence of the abnormal X chromosome. DMD is therefore almost exclusively a disease of males.

A boy receives his single X chromosome from his mother. If a woman carries an abnormal X chromosome, there is a 50 per cent chance of that chromosome being passed on to any male child. A son who inherits the faulty gene will develop DMD. Because male DMD victims rarely father children, they hardly ever pass on their X chromosome to a daughter.

In 1986, the Boston researchers, led by geneticist Louis M. Kunkel, identified a gene that is missing from the X chromosome of DMD victims. By July 1987, Kunkel and his associates had mapped out the composition of the gene, and in the following December they announced the discovery of a protein, which they named *dystrophin*.

In 1988, the scientists demonstrated that dystrophin is present in normal muscle tissue, absent in the muscles of DMD patients, and present in reduced amounts in the muscles of patients with a milder form of muscular dystrophy called Becker's dystrophy.

Researchers hope to learn the exact function of the newly discovered protein. That function must be vital because the absence of the protein

Dyslexia drawing test
Drawings may be helpful in identifying children with *spatial dyslexia*—reading impairment caused by an inability to distinguish the spatial relationships of letters in words. A nondyslexic child drew a face on which the nose is a separate element, *right*. But a dyslexic child, whose spatial-perception difficulties extend to the human face, depicted the nose as a projection of the forehead, *far right*.

Brain and Nervous System (cont.)
causes muscles of patients with DMD to wither and die.

Sleepy workers. People whose jobs require them to make frequent changes in their cycle of sleep and wakefulness make more, and more serious, work-related errors than people who stay on the same shift. That finding was reported in 1988 by *chronobiologists* (scientists who study biological cycles or rhythms) at two United States institutions. And Canadian chronobiologists, reporting on animal research, said exercise might help people adjust to new work/sleep cycles.

Adapting to different hours of sleep and wakefulness—*reentrainment*, as chronobiologists call it—is necessary for people who often travel to different time zones, such as diplomats and airline pilots. It is also required for people who work irregular hours, such as physicians, nurses, and police officers. Sleep researchers had long known that sleep deprivation can impair mental and physical performance, but they disagreed on the severity of the problem.

In January 1988, chronobiologist Merrill M. Mitler of the Scripps Clinic and Research Foundation in La Jolla, Calif., reported that during reentrainment, workers often make significant and even dangerous errors. Mitler and his associates studied employee performance in a number of occupations in which work shifts are periodically changed. They noted a striking increase in the frequency of workers' performance errors during the hours of 2 to 4 A.M. The errors ranged in severity from the simple misreading of gas meters to major mistakes by nuclear-plant workers.

The work of chronobiologist Charles A. Czeisler at Brigham and Women's Hospital in Boston supported Mitler's observations. Czeisler and his associates studied the effects of changing work shifts on police officers in a large city.

When working the night shift, the researchers reported, more than half of the officers had difficulty falling asleep during their daytime off-hours, and 80 per cent fell asleep while working. Twenty-five per cent had been involved in an automobile accident or a near-collision.

Many employers are looking for ways to make shift changes less stressful. Some companies, for example, are considering shift schedules that rotate less abruptly. And groups representing hospital physicians and commercial pilots are urging major revisions in those professionals' work schedules.

The effects of exercise. Efforts to accelerate the process of reentrainment, such as giving people sedating drugs to help them sleep, have met with little success. But in No-

Brain and Nervous System (cont.)
vember 1987, chronobiologists in Ontario, Canada, reported that exercise might ease the transition to a different work/sleep cycle.

Nicholas Mrosovsky and Peggy A. Salmon of the University of Toronto accustomed hamsters to a cycle of 14 hours of light and 10 hours of darkness. At the end of 30 days, the researchers advanced the cycle by 8 hours, starting the 10 hours of darkness—followed as usual by 14 hours of light—after just 6 hours of light had elapsed.

When they advanced the hamsters' cycle, Mrosovsky and Salmon divided the animals into two groups. The hamsters in one group were exercised for one hour on a running wheel. The hamsters in the other group received no exercise.

The effect of this one short bout of activity was striking: The exercised hamsters adjusted to the new light/dark cycle in just 1.5 days, compared with 8.5 days for the hamsters that were not exercised. The scientists could not explain why exercise speeded up adaptation to the new cycle, nor could they say whether an hour of running or calisthenics would help human beings adjust to work-shift rotations or time-zone changes. Considering how many people are forced to make such adjustments, however, other chronobiologists are sure to further explore the relationship between exercise and work/sleep cycles.

Environmental toxins. Neuroscientists in 1988 were investigating the possibility that some degenerative diseases of the brain and nervous system are caused by *toxins* (poisons) in the environment. Researchers had theorized for several years that toxins are the culprits in certain neurological disorders, but evidence in support of that idea was inconclusive. In late 1987, however, neurotoxicologist Peter S. Spencer and his colleagues at Albert Einstein College of Medicine in New York City reported findings that gave a strong boost to the toxin theory.

Spencer's research team studied a neurological disorder that since World War II has stricken many of the Chamorro people of the islands of Guam and Rota in the western Pacific Ocean. The disorder is called amyotrophic lateral sclerosis-Parkinson's-dementia complex (ALS-PD) because it has features of three more common neurological diseases: *amyotrophic lateral sclerosis* (ALS, also known as Lou Gehrig's disease), a fatal disease marked by a loss of muscle control; *Parkinson's disease*, a chronic condition that causes muscle stiffness and tremors; and *Alzheimer's disease*, a brain disorder that causes *dementia*— a progressive loss of

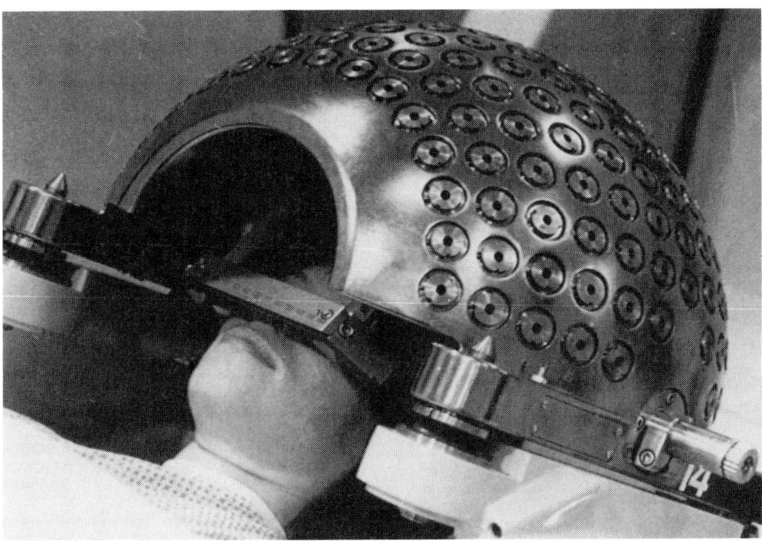

Gamma-ray surgery
A new device called the gamma knife makes it possible to treat tumors and blood-vessel abnormalities deep within the brain. The helmetlike apparatus contains 201 holes through which beams of gamma rays—a type of high-energy radiation—are focused on the trouble spot. Developed by Swedish researchers, the gamma knife was introduced in the United States in 1988 at Presbyterian-University Hospital in Pittsburgh, Pa.

Brain and Nervous System (cont.)
memory and reasoning ability.

Victims of ALS-PD, who are usually more than 45 years of age, suffer a loss of cells in the brain and spinal cord. The cells most affected are nerve cells that stimulate muscle tissue and those producing the neurotransmitter dopamine. (Neurotransmitters are chemicals that convey electrical impulses from one nerve cell to another.) In addition, the disorder causes a more generalized loss of nerve cells throughout the *cerebral cortex*—the outer layer of the brain.

Neither heredity nor infection appeared to play a role in ALS-PD, leading Spencer to theorize that an environmental factor was responsible. Spencer also noted that the incidence of the illness had declined markedly since 1955. That fact suggested that if the disease was indeed caused by something in the environment, that factor must have changed in the past 30 years.

The evidence pointed to the seeds of the cycad, a large palmlike plant. Before and during World War II (1939-1945), food was scarce on Guam and Rota, and islanders used cycad seeds to make flour and folk medicines. After the war, the use of cycad seeds greatly declined.

Spencer and his colleagues isolated a toxic compound known as BMAA from cycad seeds. The researchers fed large amounts of BMAA to monkeys and reported that the animals, after several weeks, developed neurological symptoms similar to those of ALS-PD. Microscopic examination of the animals' brains revealed that the cells had undergone changes much like those seen in ALS-PD.

Admittedly, the amounts of BMAA used in the experiments were proportionally much larger than the islanders had consumed. If smaller amounts had been ingested over a prolonged period of time, however, more gradual nerve-cell damage might have occurred, with a delay in the onset of disease symptoms. And that, Spencer believes, is what occurred with the Chamorros. Ingestion of small amounts of BMAA over a period of years probably caused a gradual death of nerve cells, resulting in the development of ALS-PD only after a critical number of cells had died.

Similar "slow toxins," progressively exerting their effects over many years, may be responsible for Alzheimer's disease, ALS, and Parkinson's disease, as well as various other neurological disorders. The search for such toxins has become a major area of investigation in neuroscience. ☐ Gary Birnbaum

In World Book, see Brain; Nervous System.

Cancer

Preliminary findings of a new study reported in June 1988 disclosed what Americans know about controlling cancer and what they are doing to prevent and detect it. The survey found that people in the United States are not getting the necessary screening tests to detect colon, breast, and cervical cancers. It also found that since 1970, smokeless tobacco use, which has been shown to cause cancer, is much higher—especially among young men—and that snuff use has more than doubled among Americans of all ages. In addition, about 40 per cent of all Americans believe there is a link between diet and cancer, but are unsure what to do about it.

The study was part of the National Health Interview Survey funded by the National Cancer Institute (NCI). A total of 48,000 people were interviewed, but the preliminary findings included the results of only 12,000 of those interviews.

"The number of people who get screening tests as often as recommended is much lower than we'd like to see," according to statistician Larry G. Kessler, who headed the study. The study showed that almost 30 per cent of U.S. women aged 18 and over did not have a Pap test for cervical cancer in the past three years. The survey also revealed that 64 per cent of women

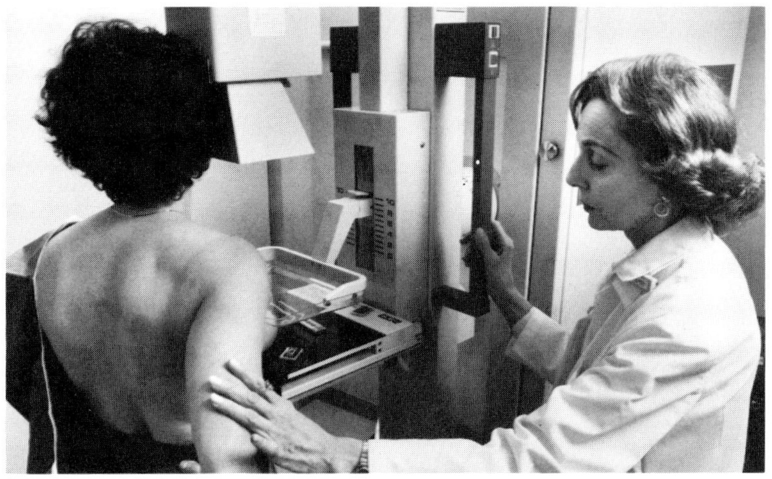

Breast cancer test
A technician positions a patient for a *mammogram* (a type of X ray) at a New York City clinic. In September 1987, the National Cancer Institute issued new guidelines for early detection of breast cancer and advised women over the age of 40 to have a mammogram every one or two years, and women aged 50 and over to have an annual mammogram.

Cancer (cont.)
aged 40 and older had never had a *mammogram* (a type of X ray) to detect breast cancer. And the study showed that 70 per cent of the men and women aged 40 and over had never had a *proctoscopy* (visual examination of the colon), and 60 per cent had never had blood stool tests for colon cancer.

Most of the people surveyed were aware of the screening tests. Up to 15 per cent, however, said they thought such tests were needed only when a problem was suspected. "The point of screening is to catch disease early, before a problem is suspected, so that chance of survival is greatest," Kessler noted.

The survey also found that almost 30 per cent of Americans aged 18 and older smoke cigarettes. The highest percentages are found among black men and low-income men. About one-third of all the male smokers are heavy smokers (25 or more cigarettes per day), compared with about one-fourth of the women who smoke.

When asked whether people should smoke in public places where it might disturb others, 80 per cent of those surveyed said smokers should not smoke in public. More than 60 per cent of the smokers agreed, but only about 30 per cent of the smokers said they refrain from smoking in public.

More than 68 per cent of those questioned believe there is a relationship between diet and cancer—a belief that is supported by a large number of research studies. Another 17 per cent believe there is a link between diet and some diseases, but no connection between diet and cancer. The rest of those interviewed do not believe there is any link between diet and cancer or any other disease.

The survey will be used by the NCI to help develop and evaluate programs that seek to bring cancer under control through early detection of the disease and changes in life style. Another survey in four or five years will monitor any changes in public opinion.

Breast cancer. The NCI announced new research findings in May 1988 on treatment for breast cancer. Based on these findings, the NCI advised doctors to consider using additional follow-up therapy after primary treatment for nearly all breast cancer patients.

In the past, most women who had breast cancer that had not spread to other parts of the body were treated with surgery or radiation therapy—or both—with no additional, follow-up treatment. About 30 per cent of patients treated for breast cancer, however, experience a recurrence of the disease. NCI sponsored three large studies to determine if additional, follow-up therapy involving *chemotherapy* (drug

Examining the Pap Test

American women received good news and bad news about the Pap smear test for cervical cancer in late 1987 and early 1988. The good news is that seven national medical organizations have finally agreed upon uniform guidelines for testing. The bad news is that this trusted cancer screen may be far less accurate than many women once thought.

Simple, inexpensive, and painless, Pap smear tests are taken during routine pelvic exams. A physician gently scrapes the cervix, removing cells that are then smeared on a glass slide. The slide is sent to a laboratory, where a pathologist or trained technician examines it under a microscope, looking for abnormal or cancerous cells. The smear is labeled *negative* if all cells are normal, *positive* if some cells are unusual or cancerous.

In November 1987, *The Wall Street Journal* reported that Pap tests were not as accurate as most women believed: As many as 20 to 40 per cent of abnormal smears are incorrectly identified as negative. In a few cases, such errors have led to life-threatening delays in the diagnosis and treatment of cervical cancer.

The medical community substantiated the story. Researchers have known since the late 1970's that preventable errors occur with some frequency. The American College of Obstetricians and Gynecologists (ACOG) attributes about half the *false negatives* (abnormal smears reported to be normal) to laboratory error. The use of high-volume labs that emphasize speed over accuracy may be a significant cause of the problem.

False negatives are also caused by physician error. A laboratory technician may be unable to correctly evaluate a slide because the doctor did not provide enough cells or those of the right type, or because the doctor failed to properly treat the smear with a special solution.

Ideally, the laboratory will reject an inadequate slide, and the doctor will ask the patient to repeat the test. In some cases, however, the patient is simply told that the smear is negative. In addition, a tiny fraction of the false negatives are not preventable. These errors are the result of the limitations of the procedure.

The Pap test made news again on Jan. 19, 1988, when seven national medical organizations including the American Medical Association, the American Cancer Society (ACS), and the ACOG held a press conference in Washington, D.C., to address the problems associated with the test. After urging women to continue having Pap smears while the false-negative problem is under study, the associations presented a joint guideline for testing frequency.

The new guideline calls for annual testing of all women except those under 18 who have never been sexually active. After a woman has had three consecutive negative test results, she, in consultation with her doctor, may elect to have the test repeated at less frequent intervals.

The joint guideline resolves a long-standing disagreement among the medical organizations. Since 1980, the groups had issued conflicting recommendations that confused women and their doctors.

Women should be careful to follow the new guideline in light of the uncertainty surrounding the test's reliability. Despite the high error rate, annual testing provides several opportunities to detect cervical cancer before it spreads.

A woman who is especially concerned about her test's accuracy should discuss this matter with her doctor and may wish to ask if the laboratory evaluating the smear is licensed, accredited, periodically inspected, and adequately staffed. □ Jinger Hoop

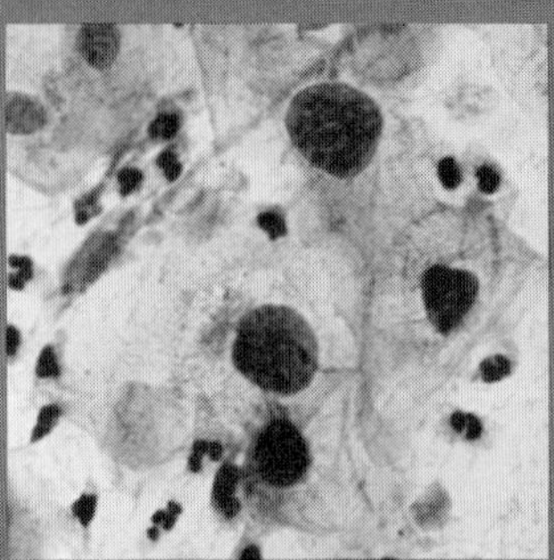

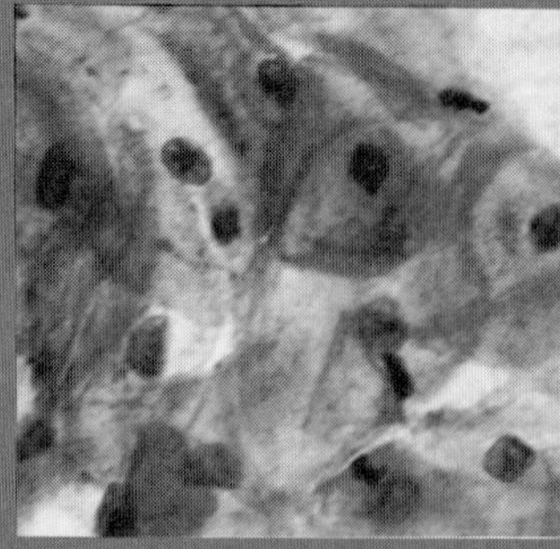

An abnormal pap smear, *left,* and a normal smear, *right.*

Cancer death rates by age
(Per 100,000 population)

Age	1950	1960	1970	1980	1982	1984
1	8.7	7.2	4.7	3.2	3.7	3.1
1-4	11.7	10.9	7.5	4.5	4.6	4.0
5-14	6.7	6.8	6.0	4.3	4.1	3.6
15-24	8.6	8.3	8.3	6.3	5.9	5.5
25-34	20.0	19.5	16.5	13.7	13.2	13.0
35-44	62.7	59.7	59.5	48.6	46.2	46.6
45-54	175.1	177.0	182.5	180.0	176.0	170.5
55-64	392.9	396.8	423.0	436.1	439.7	448.4
65-74	692.5	713.9	754.2	817.9	824.9	835.1
75-84	1,153.3	1,127.4	1,168.0	1,232.3	1,238.7	1,272.3
85	1,451.0	1,450.0	1,417.3	1,594.6	1,598.6	1,604.0

Source: Journal of the American Medical Association.

Cancer (cont.)
treatment) or hormone therapy or a combination of both could reduce the risk of recurrence.

The new studies showed that some breast cancer patients whose lymph nodes showed no sign of cancer remained cancer-free longer as a result of receiving additional therapy. *Lymph nodes* are part of the immune system and of a network of lymph vessels that remove fluid from body tissues. Cancer cells in the lymph nodes indicate that cancer has begun to spread from the breast to other parts of the body. Patients with breast cancers that have reached this stage usually receive additional therapy to eliminate cancer cells that may remain.

One of the new studies involved 679 breast cancer patients who had no cancer cells in their underarm lymph nodes, indicating that the cancer had not spread. These patients were also unable to respond to anticancer hormone treatment. The researchers found that patients receiving chemotherapy treatment using the anticancer drugs *methotrexate* and *5-fluorouracil* (*5-FU*) followed by *leucovorin* had a better survival rate four years after primary treatment than those who received no additional therapy.

A second study of 2,644 patients involved women able to respond to hormone treatment, but whose breast cancers had not spread. The study was designed to determine whether *tamoxifen*, an anticancer hormone drug, resulted in a lower rate of recurrence. After four years, disease-free survival with tamoxifen was 82 per cent, compared with 77 per cent among women in a control group who received only a *placebo* (a pill with no active ingredients).

The third study examined 422 patients with cancer confined to the breast who underwent a *total mastectomy* (surgical removal of a breast) with underarm lymph nodes removed as their primary treatment. Whether they were able to respond to hormone treatment or not, those women who received chemotherapy using a combination of four drugs had a lower rate of recurrence of breast cancer. Three years after surgery, 84 per cent of those receiving the four-drug chemotherapy treatment were disease-free, compared with 67 per cent of those who had not received chemotherapy.

Experimental treatments. Every year, about 3 per cent (about 25,000) of newly diagnosed cancer patients enter treatment trials in which physicians test new methods of treating cancer. The NCI would like to double the number of participants and in the spring of 1988 began encouraging physicians and patients to consider treatment trials.

Not every patient in a treatment trial receives the treatment being

Cancer (cont.)
tested, however. Some patients receive the best standard treatment generally available so that researchers can compare it to the new approach. Patients are assigned randomly to receive new or standard treatments.

In the past, it took physicians at least 3 to 5 years to find adequate numbers of patients for treatment studies, and another 5 to 10 years to learn whether the new treatment was more effective than standard care. To speed the process, the NCI would like to have all the needed patients enrolled within 1 year after the trials begin. The NCI has begun identifying certain studies as being particularly important for cancer treatment and has stepped up efforts to inform patients.

Early detection. To help reduce the cancer death rate, early detection of the disease is important. In September 1987, the NCI circulated early-detection guidelines for physicians. Established in conjunction with the American Cancer Society and other health organizations, the guidelines address the needs of patients receiving checkups.

The seven types of cancer covered by the NCI guidelines include:

- *Prostate cancer.* One out of 11 men will develop prostate cancer at some time during his life. For early detection, every man should have an annual prostate exam, starting at age 40.
- *Testicular cancer.* Testicular cancer is usually found in young men, between the ages of 15 and 40. If detected early, it is one of the easiest cancers to cure. Men should have a testicular exam during their regular medical checkup. In addition, men should do a testicular self-exam each month.
- *Breast cancer.* One out of every 10 women in the United States will have breast cancer sometime in her life. Every woman should have her breasts examined when she has a regular medical checkup. Starting at age 40, women should have a mammogram every one or two years; after age 50, women should have an annual mammogram. Physicians should teach their patients how to do self-examinations for breast cancer.
- *Cervical cancer.* The number of deaths due to cancer of the cervix has dropped dramatically, primarily because of the larger numbers of women who now get an annual Pap test. Every woman should have a Pap test starting at age 18 or as soon as she is sexually active. The Pap test should be done once a year until three consecutive tests are negative. After that, it is up to the physician to decide how often the test should be done.

How cancer spreads? Human breast cancer cells, *right,* secrete a substance called *autocrine motility factor* (AMF), scientists discovered in September 1987. When AMF attaches itself to the cancer cell surfaces, it causes the cell to change shape radically, *far right.* Scientists believe AMF is one of the substances that promote *metastasis*—the spread of cancer from the original tumor to other sites in the body.

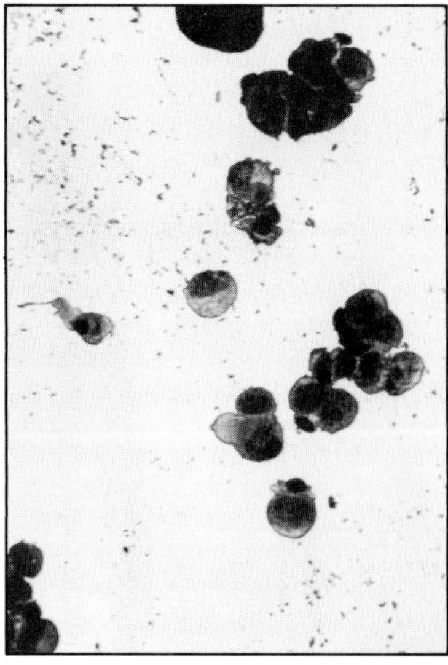

Cancer (cont.)

■ *Colorectal cancer.* This type of cancer is second only to lung cancer in the number of new cases and deaths it causes each year. Colorectal cancer is curable if detected early. Everyone should have a rectal exam during their regular checkup. In addition, persons age 50 or above should have a blood stool test annually as well as an examination of the lower part of the colon every three to five years.

■ *Oral cancer.* Individuals who are most likely to get oral cancer are cigarette smokers and people who use chewing tobacco or drink excessive amounts of alcohol. Physicians should do an oral exam during regular checkups.

■ *Skin cancer.* Excessive exposure to the sun is the main cause of skin cancer. If detected early enough, skin cancer is curable. Physicians should examine their patient's skin and show patients how to examine themselves for signs of skin cancer.

☐ Patricia A. Newman-Horm

See also EXERCISE AND FITNESS. In the Special Reports section, see THE CANCER YOU CAN SEE. In WORLD BOOK, see CANCER.

Child Development

New evidence supporting the theory that some children are born with a tendency to be extremely shy was published in April 1988 by researchers at Harvard University in Cambridge, Mass., and Yale University in New Haven, Conn. The researchers also found that this tendency, which continues as the child grows, may have a biological basis.

For their study, psychologists Jerome Kagan and J. Steven Resnick of Harvard and Nancy Snidman of Yale evaluated 400 middle-class 2- and 3-year-old children from Boston. The evaluation consisted chiefly of observing the children when they were placed in a strange room with unfamiliar women and toys and noting how long it took them to begin interacting with the new people and things.

They selected for further evaluation only children who were either consistently shy, quiet, and timid and took a long time to begin interacting or children who were consistently sociable, talkative, and spontaneous and began interacting quickly. The researchers evaluated the children three more times, including a final evaluation when the children were 7½.

The researchers found that the majority of children who were very shy at their first evaluation were still shy at 7½. They also found that the outgoing children were just as outgoing.

The cause of excessive shyness is still unknown, but the researchers found that shy children are physically different from more outgoing children. The shy children had higher heart rates. In addition, in unfamiliar situations, their pupils were more dilated, their muscles were more tense, and they had higher levels of brain chemicals that are produced by people under stress. The researchers theorized that shy children are more easily aroused physically when confronted with unfamiliar situations and objects, and, thus, tend to avoid such situations.

Although genetic factors may be involved in causing the physiological differences that lead to extreme shyness, the researchers point out that environmental factors, such as chronic stress, probably also play a role. Possible sources of stress include prolonged hospitalization, the death of a parent, quarreling between parents, or mental illness in a family member.

In addition, the researchers found that two-thirds of the shy children had older brothers or sisters, while two-thirds of the outgoing children were first-born. The researchers suggested that an older child who unexpectedly seizes a toy from or teases or yells at an infant who is easily aroused might provide the chronic stress necessary to trans-

Child Development (cont.)
form a tendency to shyness into a personality characteristic.

Using symbols. Children apparently learn to use symbols suddenly, rather than gradually throughout childhood, as many child development experts had theorized. That finding was reported in December 1987 by psychologist Judy S. DeLoache of the University of Illinois at Urbana.

The ability to use symbols is considered a hallmark of human thinking. Without it we couldn't write, create art, or follow maps. According to DeLoache, a child's ability to use symbols develops suddenly be-tween 2½ and 3 years of age.

For her experiment, DeLoache hid a tiny stuffed dog behind a small couch in a scale model of an actual room while a young child watched. The child was then taken to the actual room on which the model was based and asked to find a larger stuffed dog, which was hidden behind a real couch. To do this, the child had to understand that the model was a symbol of the room and that by remembering what had happened in the model, he or she could find the stuffed dog hidden in the full-sized room.

The experiment involved sixteen 2½-year-olds and sixteen 3-year-olds. DeLoache found that the younger children did not use what they knew about the model to find the stuffed dog. "The absence of any systematic pattern to their searching," DeLoache reported, "suggests that they were unaware they had any basis for knowing where to look for it [the stuffed dog]." The younger children gave no evidence, either in their search or in other behavior, that they realized that the scale model had anything to do with the actual room and objects, she said.

The 3-year-old children, in contrast, seemed to understand that the model was a symbol representing the real room and had little trouble finding the hidden dog. According to DeLoache, the 3-year-olds realized that an object can be understood "both as a thing itself and as a symbol of something else." The ability to think about one thing in two different ways at the same time is, DeLoache said, "a crucial aspect of mature, flexible thought."

The fact that this ability develops abruptly, "from failure to nearly universal success in the space of a few months," DeLoache said, suggests that it is not something children learn through their dealings with the real world. Instead, it appears to be an ability associated with the development of the brain.

Early learning. Research reported in June 1988 has challenged long-held beliefs about the age at which infants begin to develop an intellec-

Understanding symbols
A researcher hides a tiny stuffed dog in a model room as part of a study to determine when children learn to use symbols. The children were then asked to find a larger stuffed dog hidden in a corresponding place in a full-sized room. According to the study, the ability to use symbols develops abruptly at about age 3.

Child Development (cont.)
tual understanding of the physical world. Experiments conducted by psychologist Elizabeth S. Spelke of Cornell University in Ithaca, N.Y., suggest that infants may begin to develop this understanding much sooner than previously thought.

Swiss psychologist Jean Piaget observed the intellectual development of his own and many other infants and children and then constructed a theory of intelligence that outlines the developmental stages children seem to go through. For example, he concluded that until infants are 8 to 12 months old they have no idea of *object permanence*. That is, they do not realize that an object continues to exist even after it rolls or moves out of sight. For infants, according to Piaget, out of sight is out of mind.

According to Spelke, however, this may not be the case. She and her colleagues reported that babies only 3 months old know that a toy still exists even if it is hidden under a blanket where they cannot see it. They also seem to understand that solid objects do not pass through one another. And by the time they are 6 months old, they seem to understand that objects are subject to the force of gravity.

In order to find out what babies know about the physical world, Spelke and her colleagues measured the time the babies spent looking at various objects. Previous research had shown that infants look longer at something novel or unexpected than they do at something familiar or expected. In other words, they look longest at things they do not understand, and they spend little time looking at things they already know about.

In one experiment, the researchers showed infants a bar moving horizontally behind a block until only the ends of the bar were visible on either side of the block. Because the infants did not stare at the ends of the bar for very long, Spelke and her colleagues concluded that the infants, who had not touched the bar or block, knew that the two ends of the bar were part of the same bar even though the middle part of it was hidden behind the block.

In another experiment, the researchers showed infants a raised shelf on a table. They then placed a screen in front of the shelf. The screen did not cover the space between the base of the shelf and the tabletop. The researchers then dropped an object onto the shelf behind the screen.

According to the researchers, the infants seemed to know that the object would stop falling when it reached the unseen shelf. But the babies did not appear to realize until they were 6 months old that an object will continue to fall until it hits

Studies by a number of researchers are identifying those personality traits that seem to enable children brought up in an impoverished or disruptive environment to succeed later in life.

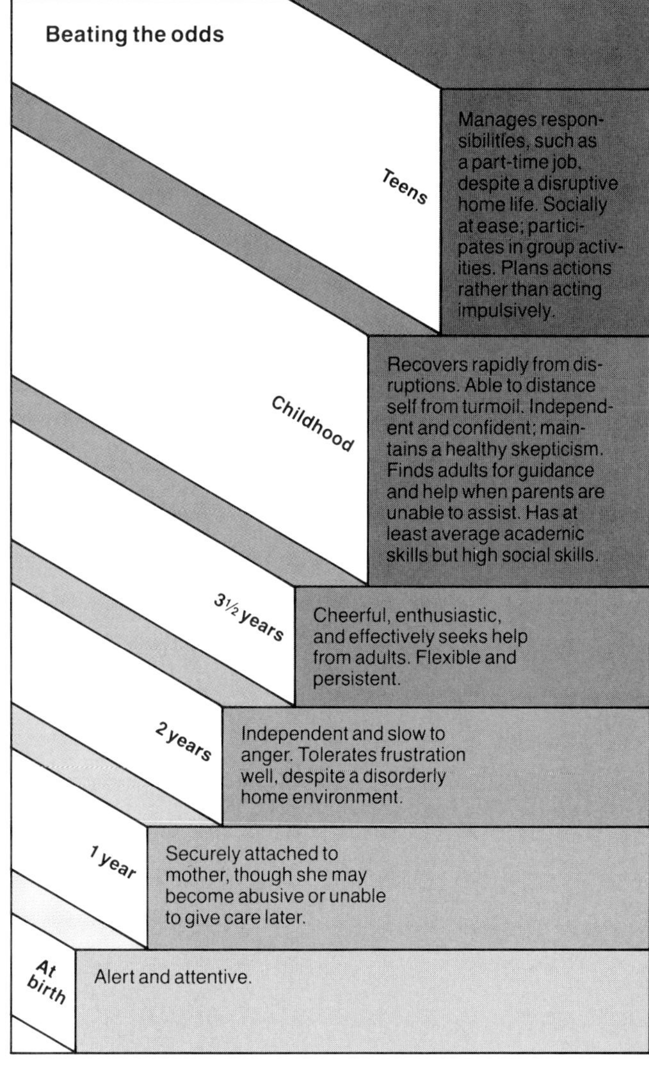

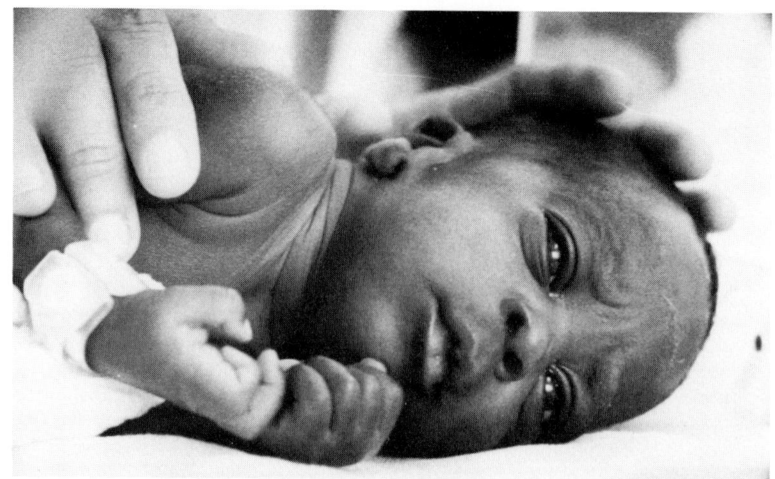

A touching matter
A premature infant in a hospital in Miami, Fla., receives a light massage. Premature infants who were massaged for 15 minutes three times a day gained weight faster, became more active, and were able to leave the hospital faster than premature infants who were not massaged, according to a study reported in early 1988. Months later, the massaged infants also performed better on tests of their mental and motor abilities.

Child Development (cont.)
a surface such as the shelf. Infants younger than 6 months did not seem to be surprised if the object—manipulated by the researchers—appeared to stop in midair before it hit the shelf.

Piaget thought that infants learned about the physical world by dealing with it—that is, by playing with blocks and dropping them—and his assessment of their knowledge was based on the ways in which they played with the objects. Three-month-old infants cannot be tested in this manner because they lack the necessary physical coordination. But, as Spelke's research suggested, they may not lack knowledge of the physical world.

"We're using methods that don't demand coordinated motor activity," she explained, "and we're finding that infants know much more than we sometimes think they do."

TV-viewing benefits. Contrary to popular opinion, time spent watching television is not necessarily harmful to children, according to a government-sponsored report issued in June 1988. The report was scheduled to be published in late 1988. By the time they graduate from high school, children in the United States will have watched an average of 18,000 hours of television. This is more time than they will have spent in school.

The report, called *The Impact on Children's Education: Television's Influence on Cognitive Development,* is the first comprehensive look at scientific research on the effect of television on children's thinking skills. It was prepared for the Department of Education's Office of Educational Research and Improvement by psychologists Daniel Anderson and Patricia A. Collins of the University of Massachusetts at Amherst.

According to the researchers, television viewing does not shorten a child's attention span, as many people have claimed. Instead, they report, children can become more attentive for longer periods by watching educational programs designed for them. The report also found that television can help children increase their vocabulary.

There are a number of studies that show that children actively engage in attempts to understand TV programs, Anderson explained. "When children talk about TV, a lot of the discussion is on what will happen next and its plausibility in real life," he said. "The most important thing is to look to the content of what the children are watching."

"We are not giving TV a clean bill of health," Anderson said. "But we are saying that, wisely used, [TV] can be used well."

☐ Robert J. Trotter

In World Book, see Child.

Childbirth
See Pregnancy and Childbirth

Contraception
See Birth Control

Dentistry

Tooth decay has declined in the United States to the extent that 50 per cent of all children under age 17 have no cavities, according to a survey reported in June 1988 by the National Institute of Dental Research in Bethesda, Md. The survey of nearly 40,000 children, conducted during the 1986-1987 school year, revealed a continuing 15-year decline in tooth decay and cavities in American children. A similar survey conducted during the 1979-1980 school year reported that only 36.6 per cent of school-age children had no tooth decay. Dental experts attribute the improvement to the widespread addition of fluoride to water supplies and to better dental care.

Anticavity vaccine. A vaccine that prevents cavity-causing bacteria in the mouth from producing an acid that destroys tooth enamel may be an effective means of preventing tooth decay, according to a study reported in July 1987 by dentists Martin A. Taubman and Daniel J. Smith of the Forsyth Dental Center in Boston. Many dentists believe that cavities are caused by a bacteria called *Streptococcus mutans*. An enzyme called *glucosyl transferase* (GTF) on the outer surface of the bacteria breaks down sugar consumed in food into an acid that eats away enamel.

Taubman and Smith used samples of GTF to create a vaccine. They theorized that the vaccine would stimulate the immune system to produce higher levels of certain *antibodies* (molecules that destroy invading microbes) to the enzyme. The antibodies would then destroy the enzyme, crippling the bacteria's ability to produce acid.

In testing the vaccine, the researchers found antibodies to GTF in the mouths of all of the 25 volunteers who received the vaccine. Further research is needed to determine whether volunteers who receive the vaccine will develop fewer cavities.

Clues to bulimia. Dentists can play an important role in identifying people suffering from *bulimia*, an eating disorder, according to research reported in April 1988 by dentist Mark Simmons, psychiatrist James Mitchell, and dental hygienist Sharon Grayden of the University of Minnesota School of Medicine in Minneapolis. People suffering from bulimia engage in eating binges during which they gorge themselves on high-calorie food. Afterward, they may make themselves vomit or take large doses of laxatives to purge themselves of the excess food.

An estimated 5 per cent of girls in the United States between the ages of 12 and 18 are believed to suffer from this disorder. Because people

Whiter smiles
Translucent ceramic braces, reportedly as effective as metal braces, are not as conspicuous as metal braces because they allow the natural color of the teeth to show through.

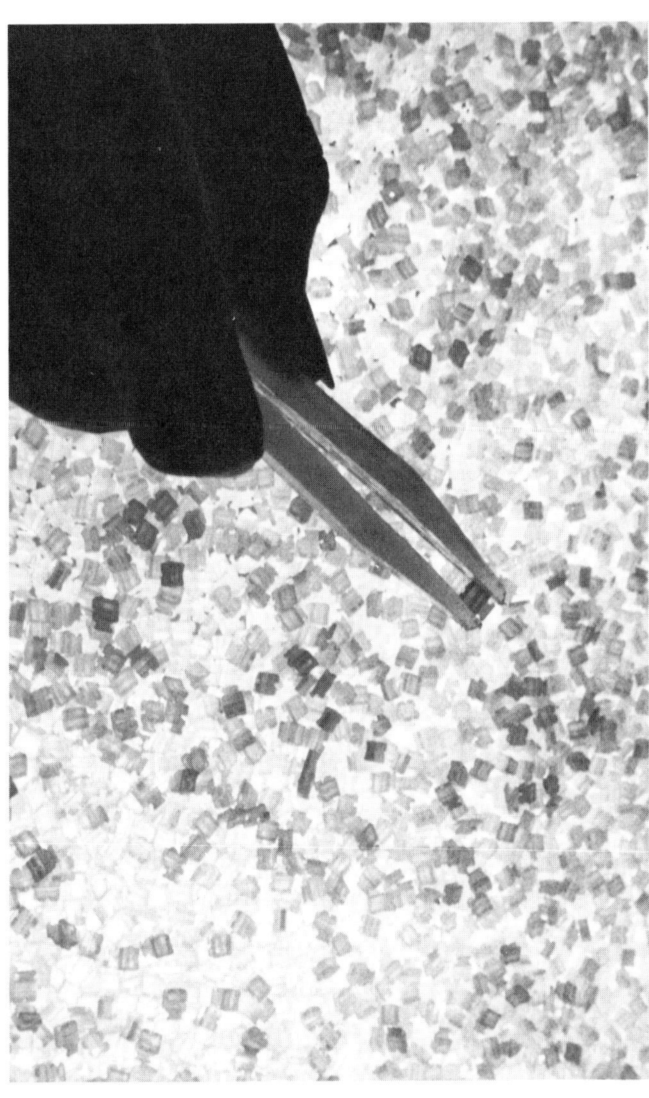

A Health & Medical Annual Close-Up

Pop Goes the Jaw Joint

It starts with a small "pop" inside the head, vaguely near the ear. The sound might come with a yawn, or a laugh, or a bite into a sandwich. The popping is more curious than troublesome, and it may even go away in a few days.

But in some people, the noise is the first sign of *temporomandibular joint dysfunction* (TMJ), a painful malfunction of the jaw joint. TMJ usually occurs in people between 20 and 40 years old, mostly women. Beyond that, few statistics exist on its prevalence—partly because TMJ is difficult to define and diagnose.

The temporomandibular joint comprises the bones, muscles, and tendons that connect the *temporal bone*, or temple, to the *mandible*, or lower jaw. When the mouth opens, muscles pull the ends of the horseshoe-shaped mandible along channels in the temporal bone. Sometimes, though, the muscles work unevenly, and the jaw is thrown off-center. In other cases, the disk-shaped cushion of cartilage between the bones pops out of place, forcing the jaw out of line.

The result of a misaligned jaw may simply be an occasional clicking or popping as the jaw moves. Many people experience this periodically without ever developing other symptoms of TMJ. But some people suffer more severe problems, such as limited jaw movement or pain—in the joint itself and sometimes in the face, neck, or shoulders. Other symptoms range from headache and earache to sinus problems and dizziness.

Some experts suggest that amid new awareness—and publicity—about TMJ, health professionals may be eager to attribute any jaw, head, or neck problems to the disorder. But many of the symptoms associated with TMJ may also be signs of other disorders, such as arthritis or sinus infections. Specialists generally agree that TMJ is present only if the patient suffers pain in the joint or limited jaw movement, or both.

Physicians cite *improper bite* and *muscle spasm* as the two factors most likely to trigger TMJ. Improper bite, in which the teeth do not meet properly, may sometimes be caused by jaw-clenching or teeth-grinding, which in turn can be a response to stress. Muscle spasm is an extreme contraction of the jaw muscle. This can occur in situations that place severe force on the muscle, such as jaw-clenching, a sudden head motion, a blow to the head, or even chewing or yawning.

Physicians suggest various methods to relieve TMJ symptoms. Pain can be eased with pain relievers, muscle relaxants, or hot compresses. In cases of severe pain, physicians may inject a painkiller into the jaw. Exercise can help restore jaw function. In many cases, symptoms subside on their own within a few days.

To treat recurrent problems, physicians try to determine the cause of the condition. They may check the patient's bite and measure the open jaw. They also look for habits that put stress on the joint, such as clenching or grinding, chewing gum or ice, or holding a telephone receiver between the jaw and the shoulder.

Different specialists may suggest different treatments. Patients who clench or grind their teeth may try relaxation techniques, therapy to reduce stress, or mouth guards that prevent clenching and grinding during sleep. People with bite problems might see a dentist for bridges or braces.

In some cases, patients will be advised to have surgery to remove bone or cartilage or to add an artificial hinge. Still, most experts are hesitant to recommend surgery. Almost all cases of TMJ, they note, subside with more moderate treatment—or without treatment at all. ☐ Beverly Merz

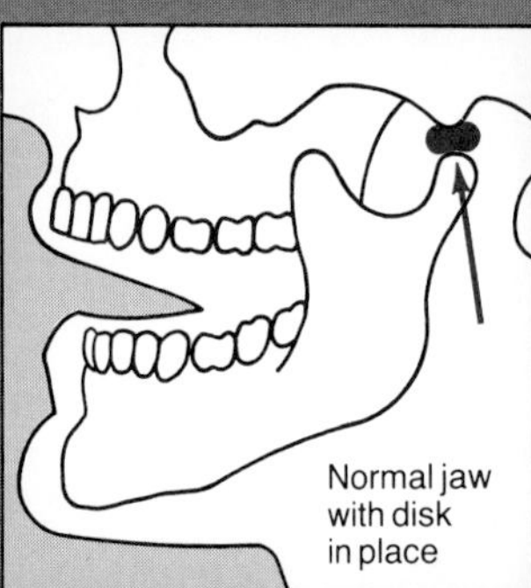

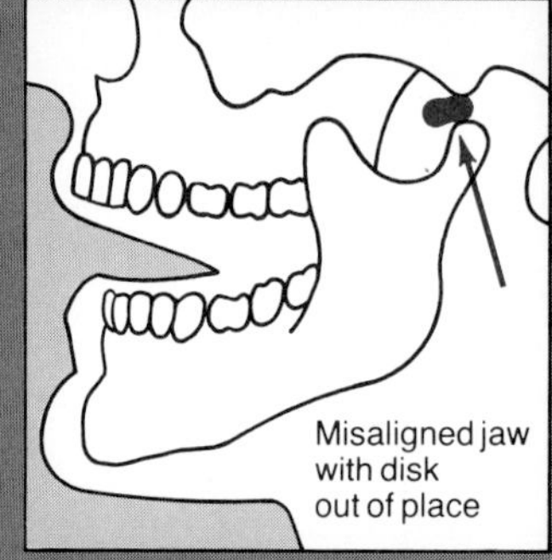

TMJ may occur when a disk of cartilage in the jaw pops loose.

Better bites
A U-shaped sensor can help dentists accurately determine a patient's bite pattern. When the patient bites down on the sensor, more than 1,500 sensing points relay information to a computer about the force of the bite as well as the order in which the teeth touch the sensor. The computer analysis of this information can help dentists diagnose and treat a variety of dental problems.

Dentistry (cont.)
with bulimia often maintain their normal weight, their destructive eating habits may continue undetected by relatives or friends for years.

The repeated vomiting that often accompanies bulimia is particularly destructive to teeth because it causes erosion of the enamel. This erosion can lead to tooth decay and tooth loss.

For their study, the researchers examined the teeth of 66 women entering the University of Minnesota Eating Disorder Program. They found that the teeth of more than half of the patients showed evidence of repeated vomiting. This evidence consisted of the erosion of enamel on the back of the upper front teeth.

The researchers also reported that the women in the study were conscientious dental patients, with more than 80 per cent having seen a dentist within the previous year. The researchers concluded that the bulimic patients' concern about dental health could enable dentists and dental hygienists to identify previously undetected cases of bulimia and refer these patients for treatment. ☐ Mark S. Simmons

In World Book, see Dentistry; Teeth.

Diabetes

Scientists in 1988 reported new insights into the treatment and causes of diabetes, a disease in which the body does not properly convert sugars, starches, and other food into the energy needed for life. Diabetes, which affects 11 million people in the United States, ranks among the nation's leading causes of death.

New drug therapy. Canadian and French scientists made encouraging advances during 1987 and 1988 in the use of the drug *cyclosporine* to treat insulin-dependent, or *Type I*, diabetes. People with Type I diabetes are unable to produce the hormone *insulin*, which helps control the level of sugar in the blood.

In October 1987, researchers at the University of Western Ontario in London, Canada, reported the results of a study in which people newly diagnosed as diabetic were given cyclosporine within six weeks of beginning regular injections of insulin to control the disease. After a year of taking cyclosporine, 25 per cent of the patients no longer needed insulin, compared with about 10 per cent of a control group that did not receive the drug. And in March 1988, a team of researchers in Paris announced that 27 of 40 children they studied no longer required insulin injections after an av-

Diabetes (cont.)
erage of 48 days of treatment with cyclosporine.

Cyclosporine is an *immunosuppressant*, a drug that suppresses the body's natural defenses. It is normally used to prevent rejection of donated organs after transplant surgery. Its effects in these diabetes studies strongly support the idea that Type I diabetes is an *autoimmune* disease, in which the immune system attacks the body's own tissues—in this case, the insulin-producing islet cells of the pancreas. The researchers found that cyclosporine treatment works best when begun immediately after diagnosis, before the immune response destroys too many of the insulin-producing cells.

The treatment has potential drawbacks, however. Continued use of cyclosporine causes such side effects as kidney damage and unwanted hair growth.

In October 1987, researchers at the Sansum Medical Research Foundation in Santa Barbara, Calif., reported a cyclosporine technique that sidesteps the drug's side effects. The researchers drew white blood cells from mice with Type I diabetes and treated the cells with cyclosporine and a protein called interleukin-2. The treated cells were then injected back into the mice. One injection of treated cells kept the disease in remission for the normal one-year life span of the mice. Since the mice never received cyclosporine directly, they suffered no side effects.

Another new drug, *metformin*, may offer advantages over other medications now used to treat non-insulin-dependent, or *Type II*, diabetes, according to a study reported by scientists of Yale University, New Haven, Conn., at the annual conference of the American Diabetes Association (ADA) in June 1988. Type II diabetics produce insulin but cannot use it properly. Many Type II diabetics take oral drugs to help control their blood sugar.

The researchers found that metformin lowered blood sugar levels while causing fewer side effects than drugs currently used for Type II diabetes. Metformin also helped correct abnormalities in blood fats and aided in weight loss. A similar study at Stanford University in Palo Alto, Calif., confirmed metformin's beneficial effects.

Insulin pill. In February 1988, researchers in Israel and France reported progress on insulin preparations that may be taken orally. Diabetics who need regular doses of insulin generally receive the hormone by injecting it under the skin. If taken orally, insulin is destroyed

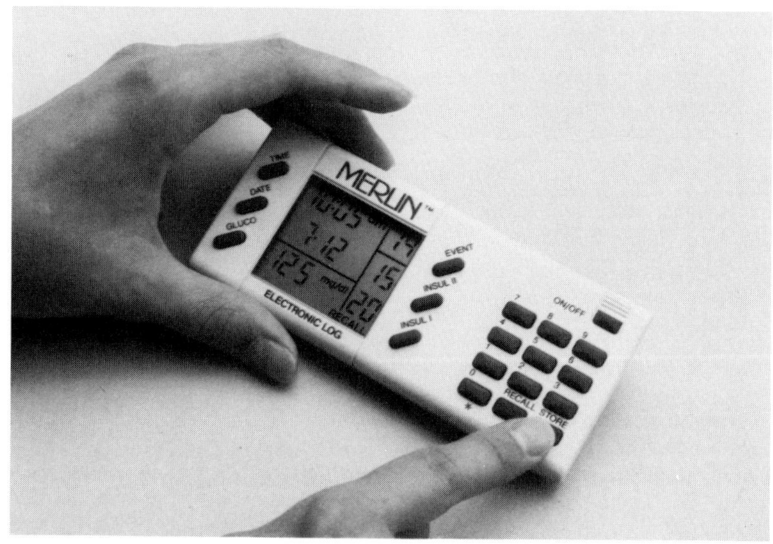

Diabetes databank
An electronic logbook, introduced in 1988 by Boehringer Mannheim Corporation in Indianapolis, helps diabetics monitor their blood sugar levels without having to keep daily written records. The diabetic enters blood test results in the calculatorlike device. The records are later transferred to a personal computer, where special software analyzes the data for dangerous changes in blood sugar.

Diabetes (cont.)

by the stomach's digestive acids. In addition, the insulin molecule is too large to pass through the walls of the intestine into the blood.

Researchers at Hadassah Hospital in Jerusalem, Israel, however, reported successful tests of an oral insulin preparation on laboratory rats. The scientists combined insulin with a compound from soybeans to inhibit the digestive enzymes that normally break down insulin. Another additive helped the insulin pass through the intestinal wall. In a separate study, scientists in Strasbourg, France, reported that insulin encapsulated in microscopic spheres of a protective material remained intact in rats' stomachs and lowered blood sugar for several hours.

Predicting diabetes. Two research teams proposed new ways to predict who will develop Type I diabetes. In October 1987, scientists at Stanford University reported evidence that a genetic error in a person's *deoxyribonucleic acid* (DNA) may increase the risk of developing Type I diabetes. DNA, the molecule that makes up the genes of most living things, determines all inherited traits. The error alters the makeup of an immune system protein called *human leukocyte antigen* (HLA). People with the altered HLA are apparently more likely to experience destruction of islet cells.

At the ADA conference in June 1988, University of Florida researchers claimed to have discovered the most accurate marker yet for predicting Type I diabetes. The marker, called a *64K autoantibody*, appeared in patients up to seven years before symptoms surfaced. Of 8,000 people in the study, all those who eventually developed diabetes had 64K autoantibodies, even if they lacked other markers associated with diabetes.

Environment as cause. Even as scientists examined genetic influences on diabetes, other studies emphasized that environmental factors may play a role in triggering the disease. In November 1987, researchers at the Joslin Diabetes Center in Boston reported that Type I diabetes has tripled among children in the Northeastern United States during the past three decades. The most likely explanation, according to the researchers, is some change in the environment. A study at the University of Pittsburgh in Pennsylvania revealed similar dramatic increases in such countries as Finland and Poland. The Pennsylvania researchers claimed that environment causes between 60 and 95 per cent of Type I diabetes cases worldwide.

□ William H. Allen

In WORLD BOOK, see DIABETES; INSULIN.

The high incidence of diabetes in certain countries suggests that environmental factors may trigger the disease. Researchers at the University of Pittsburgh in Pennsylvania, who compiled the data, estimate that such factors cause between 60 and 95 per cent of all cases of Type I diabetes (insulin-dependent diabetes, which usually starts in childhood or adolescence).

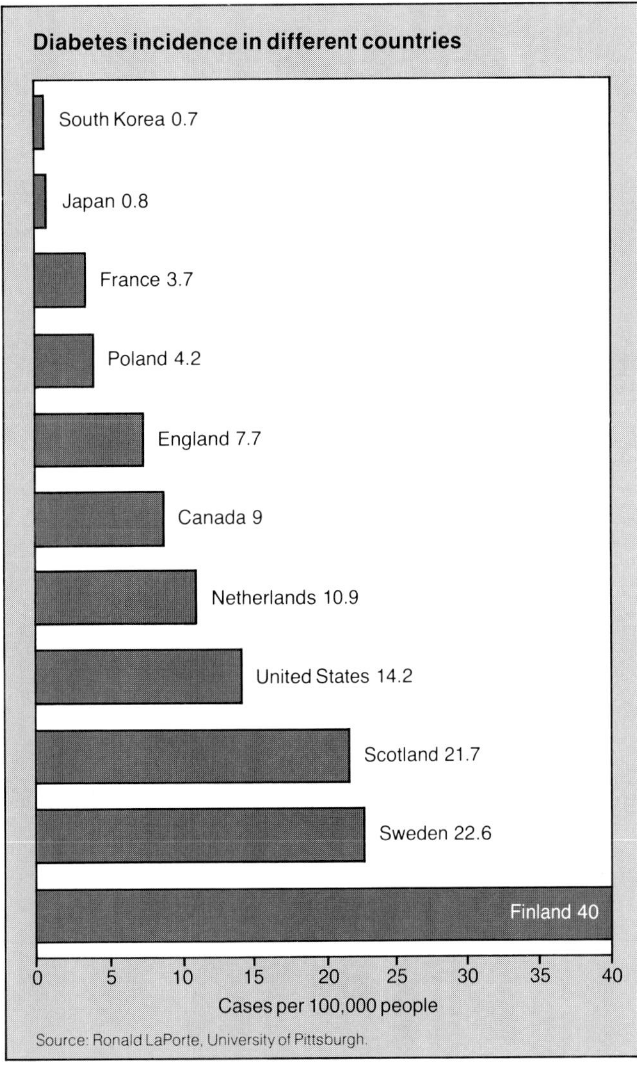

Digestive System

Researchers in mid-1988 were trying to answer a five-year-old question: How do recently discovered bacteria called *Campylobacter pylori* relate to *peptic ulcer* disease and *dyspepsia*? A peptic ulcer is an open sore in the lining of the stomach or small intestine. Peptic ulcers result from the overproduction of a digestive liquid that contains hydrochloric acid and other substances. Dyspepsia is indigestion.

In the early 1980's, physicians made the first association of the bacteria with these disorders, finding the then-unidentified bacteria on the stomach lining of patients who had chronic *gastritis* (inflammation of that lining). In 1984, microbiologist Barry J. Marshall of the Royal Perth Hospital in Perth, Australia, reported that he had grown a *culture* (a population of microorganisms) of such bacteria taken from biopsy specimens.

Since Marshall's isolation of the organism, doctors who have looked for it in patients suffering from chronic gastritis have invariably found it. To determine whether the bacteria causes gastritis, Marshall and Arthur Morris, a physician at Middlemore Hospital in Auckland, New Zealand, deliberately inoculated themselves with *C. pylori* in 1984 and 1987. In each case, the researchers suffered mild cases of gastritis a few days later.

C. pylori produce an enzyme called *urease*, which is easy to detect chemically in biopsy specimens. As a result, a chemical test based on the production of urease has become a standard technique for detecting the bacteria.

C. pylori are also present in most cases of ulcers of the *duodenum*—the part of the small intestine just below the stomach. Almost all patients who have such ulcers also have chronic *antral gastritis*—inflammation of the *antrum*, the lower part of the stomach. Researchers find the organism in the antra of most patients who have both disorders.

A compound called bismuth subcitrate prevents *C. pylori* from growing, and promotes the healing of duodenal ulcers. This substance also may diminish the frequency with which duodenal ulcer disease returns after healing.

Researchers found in mid-1987 that a combination of a bismuth compound and the drug Tinidazole was most effective in healing duodenal ulcers and decreasing the likelihood of their return. Scientists have found that this combination produces the same result in patients with stomach ulcers.

Researchers also have found *C. pylori* in patients who have dyspepsia and gastritis, but not ulcers. The bismuth compound has cured gastritis in such patients and has im-

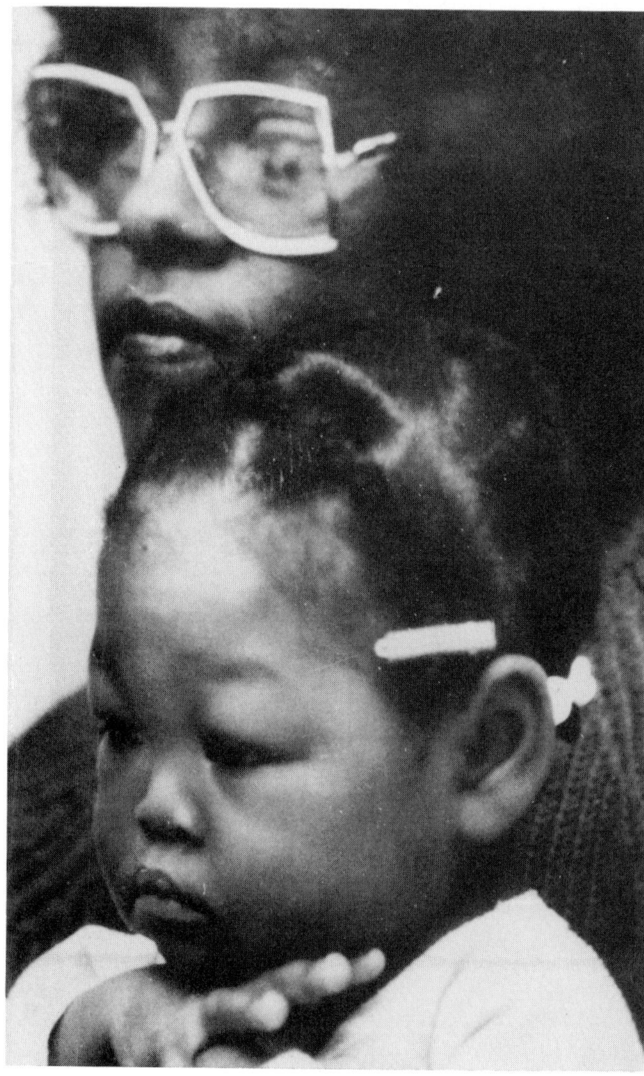

Five-organ transplant
Three-year-old Tabatha Foster, held by her mother, awaits transplant surgery on Nov. 1, 1987, at Children's Hospital in Pittsburgh, Pa. She received a new liver, pancreas, small intestine, and parts of a stomach and colon. On May 11, 1988, Tabatha died of a blood infection.

Digestive System (cont.)
proved the symptoms of dyspepsia. Researchers have found no evidence that *C. pylori* play a role in *reflux esophagitis*, inflammation of the esophagus caused by the backing up of contents of the stomach into the esophagus.

Physicians find the organism in 25 per cent of healthy individuals. The presence of the bacteria increases with the age of patients.

New treatment for gallstones. Physicians Michael Sackmann and Tilman Sauerbruch of the University of Munich in West Germany reported in February 1988 on continued success with a nonsurgical method of breaking up *gallstones*—pebblelike masses of cholesterol and mineral salts that sometimes form in the gall bladder or one of its ducts. The technique, called *extracorporeal shock-wave lithotripsy* (ESWL), uses high-pitched sound waves to break up the stones.

The initial application of ESWL, reported in 1984, was to break up kidney stones. By 1987, surgeons were using ESWL on more than 80 per cent of patients suffering from kidney stones.

In 1986, West German researchers reported on the first successful use of ESWL to smash gallstones. This application has tremendous potential because gallstones are 10 times as common as kidney stones.

The shock waves used in ESWL are waves of pressure generated inside a machine, transmitted through water inside a bag touching the patient's skin, and focused on the area containing the gallstones. The waves enter the patient's body without damaging tissue and strike the stone. After an ESWL treatment, the patient takes drugs to help dissolve the remaining fragments of stone.

Early ESWL machines did not have a bag. Instead, the patient had to be partially submerged in a tub of water. Furthermore, the original ESWL procedure could cause pain, so patients required general anesthesia. The newer machines with the bag do not require general anesthesia, so physicians expect to use ESWL as an outpatient treatment for gallstones.

Sackmann and his colleagues reported that 91 per cent of the gallstones in the first 175 patients treated with ESWL had disappeared within 12 to 18 months after ESWL treatment. The researchers had been concerned that fragments of stone passing out of the gall bladder and into the common bile duct might cause an obstruction, leading to *jaundice* (a yellowing of the skin and the whites of the eyes) or inflammation of the *pancreas* (a gland that produces substances essential to digestion). Only 2 of Sackmann's

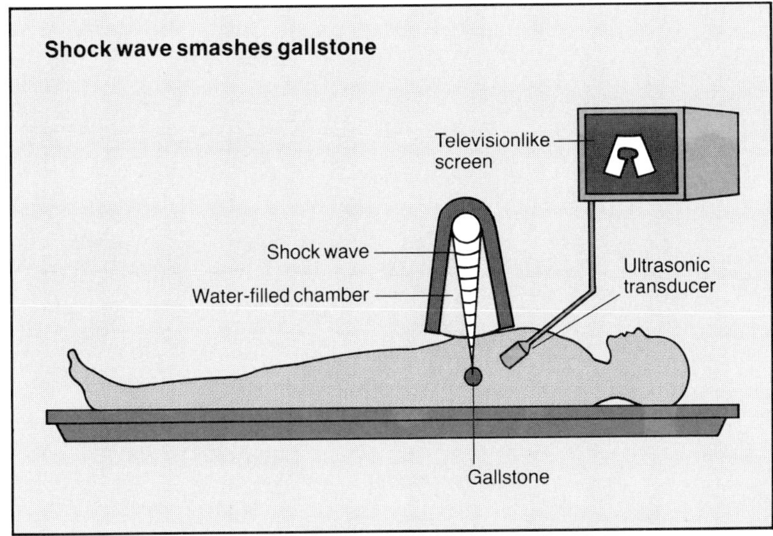

Shock waves generated in a water-filled chamber break up a gallstone in an operation performed entirely outside the body. To help surgeons focus the shock waves, a device called an *ultrasonic transducer* emits sound waves that bounce off the stone and nearby tissue. A machine translates returning waves into an image that is displayed on a televisionlike screen.

Digestive System (cont.)
175 patients had any blockage, however. And only 1 patient required the surgical removal of tissue to open the common bile duct so that the fragmented gallstone could pass through.

A second concern was—and still is—the possibility that more stones might form when drug therapy stops. The researchers base this concern on experience with patients who had not received ESWL treatments or bile-duct surgery but had received drug therapy to dissolve gallstones.

In mid-1988, medical centers throughout the United States were installing ESWL machines. Researchers expected to use these devices initially to evaluate the ESWL technique. Consequently, they planned to use the machines only on specific groups of patients.

One such group may be patients whose common bile ducts have large stones that otherwise could be removed only by surgery. Researchers already have used ESWL on several such patients.

☐ James L. Franklin

In WORLD BOOK, see DIGESTIVE SYSTEM; GALLSTONE; STOMACH; ULCER.

Drug Abuse

See Alcohol and Drug Abuse

Drugs

A drug that may help prevent heart attacks received approval from the United States Food and Drug Administration (FDA) on Aug. 31, 1987. The drug, lovastatin, was developed under the trade name Mevacor by Merck Sharp & Dohme Research Laboratories of West Point, Pa. It represents an important addition to the small group of medications that are useful in reducing blood cholesterol levels.

Each year, about 1.25 million people in the United States suffer heart attacks, resulting in about 550,000 deaths. Studies have established that high blood cholesterol is a major contributor to coronary heart disease. About 50 per cent of American adults have cholesterol levels that put them at increased risk of developing coronary heart disease. A low-fat, low cholesterol diet is the primary approach physicians recommend to reduce high cholesterol levels; many patients do not respond adequately to dietary measures alone, however, and such individuals often need supplementary drug therapy.

Lovastatin, along with a low-cholesterol diet, reduces blood cholesterol levels by decreasing the production of cholesterol in the liver. It

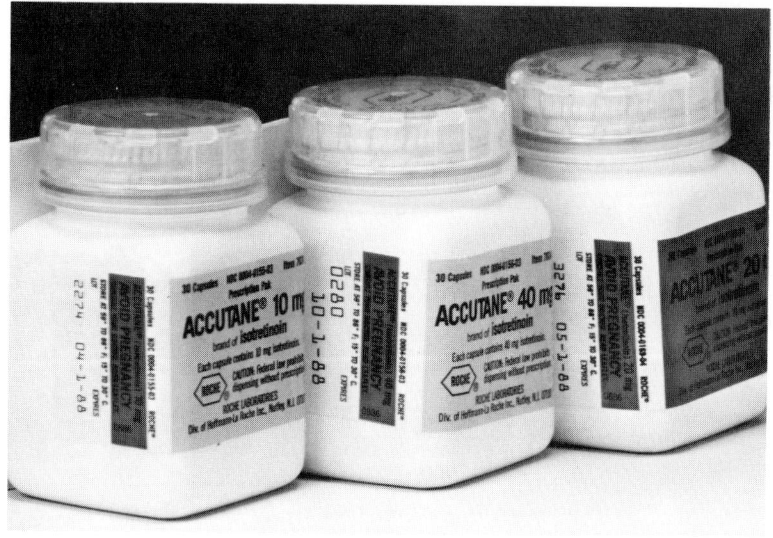

Accutane warning
A label on bottles of Accutane warns pregnant women that the drug, which is used to treat severe cases of cystic acne, has been linked to birth defects. In May 1988, the U.S. Food and Drug Administration asked the manufacturer of Accutane—Hoffmann-La Roche of Nutley, N.J.—to take additional measures in the packaging and distribution of the drug to prevent its misuse.

Drugs (cont.)
is considered more effective than other cholesterol-lowering drugs. As a result of lovastatin's effectiveness and relative safety, it quickly became the most frequently prescribed anticholesterol drug. Physicians sometimes use lovastatin in combination with other cholesterol-lowering drugs to bring about a greater reduction of cholesterol levels than can be achieved with either drug alone.

Most patients tolerate lovastatin well, and side effects are usually mild and short-lived. Because of possible side effects involving the liver, however, physicians recommend that liver function tests be performed every 4 to 6 weeks during the first 15 months of therapy and periodically thereafter.

Treating high blood pressure. Two new drugs to treat *hypertension* (high blood pressure) were approved by the FDA and introduced in late 1987. The first of these new drugs, terazosin, is sold under the trade name Hytrin by Abbott Laboratories and the Burrough Wellcome Company. The FDA licensed the second drug, lisinopril, under a marketing agreement whereby two companies will compete with each other in selling the drug. Merck Sharp & Dohme will sell lisinopril under the trade name Prinivil, and Stuart Pharmaceuticals of Wilmington, Del., will sell it as Zestril. Both terazosin and lisinopril are long-acting, allowing most patients to take them just once a day. This is important in the treatment of hypertension because many hypertensive patients fail to comply with their doctors' orders to take medication regularly.

Although hypertension can lead to heart attack, stroke, and kidney failure, it is a condition that often produces no symptoms, and many patients consequently forgo regular medication rather than experience its undesirable side effects. The once-daily dosage of the new drugs, it is hoped, will increase patient compliance.

Terazosin also has been reported to lower cholesterol levels slightly, unlike many antihypertensive drugs, such as diuretics, which may increase blood cholesterol levels. This effect is an advantage in the treatment of hypertensive patients who also have high cholesterol levels. Terazosin can cause dizziness and fainting, however. Experts stressed that specific guidelines for dosage and for monitoring the effects of the drug must be followed.

Lisinopril belongs to a new group of antihypertensive agents known as *angiotensin converting enzyme* (*ACE*) inhibitors. Blood pressure rises when the blood vessels *constrict* (become narrower). ACE inhibitors reduce this constriction by interfering with a key chemical reaction. Although these new drugs

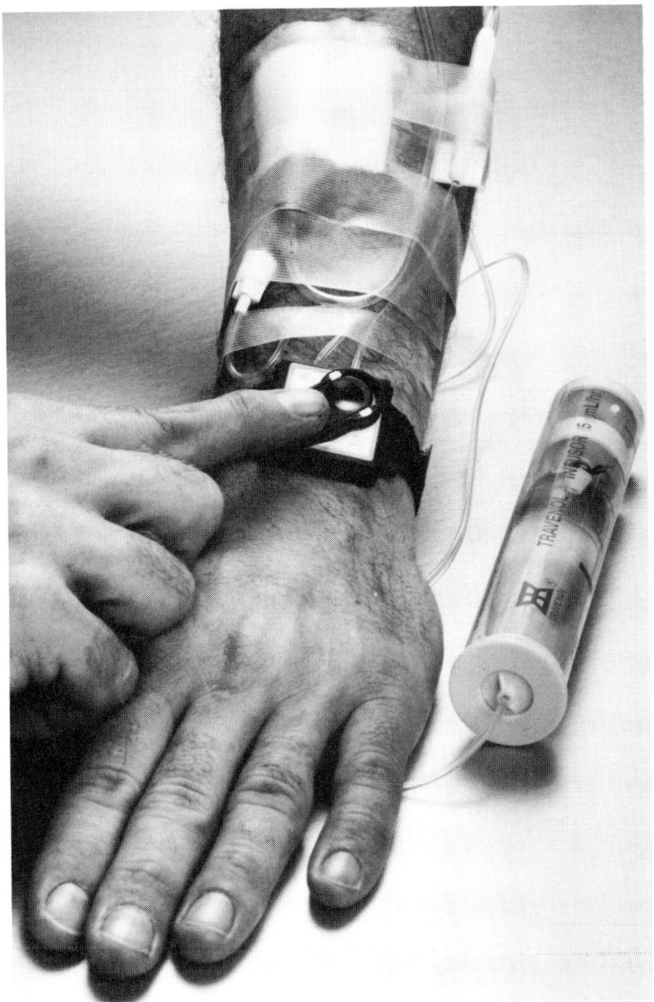

Push-button pain relief
A new intravenous device that is worn like a wrist watch allows patients to administer their own pain medication by simply pressing a button. The device is expected to ease demands on hospital staff since patients can medicate themselves. Called an infuser pump, this device is made by a division of Baxter Healthcare Corporation based in Deerfield, Ill.

Heart attack drug
Workers at Genentech, Incorporated, in South San Francisco help prepare bottles of a drug—called *t-PA* for *tissue plasminogen activator*—used to treat heart attack victims. The drug—which was approved by the U.S. Food and Drug Administration in November 1987—dissolves blood clots, like those that obstruct coronary arteries and cause heart attacks.

Drugs (cont.)

cause side effects in some patients, most patients tolerate them well. ACE inhibitors are being increasingly prescribed because they are less likely than many other antihypertensive agents to cause such side effects as fatigue, diarrhea, and loss of normal sexual function.

ACE inhibitors also may be effective in treating congestive heart failure in patients who have not responded to other treatments. (*Congestive heart failure* is a condition in which the heart cannot maintain normal blood circulation.) Lisinopril has not yet been recommended for this condition, but preliminary studies suggest that it may be effective.

Heart attack drug. A new drug that dissolves blood clots and is used to treat people who are suffering heart attacks was approved by the FDA for general use on Nov. 13, 1987. The drug, called tissue plasminogen activator (t-PA), marketed by Genentech Incorporated of South San Francisco, Calif., and sold under the trade name Activase, represents an important advance in the treatment of heart attack.

The human body produces only tiny amounts of t-PA, which can dissolve the tough fibrous material that comprises blood clots. Using genetic engineering techniques, scientists at Genentech succeeded in producing large amounts of t-PA in the laboratory.

Clinical trials showed that t-PA can break down clots that obstruct coronary arteries and cause most heart attacks. The coronary arteries supply the blood that nourishes the heart muscle. The timely use of t-PA not only can halt a heart attack but also can help limit the amount of damage to the heart muscle.

Studies have indicated that t-PA is more effective than other drugs in treating heart attacks, especially if treatment is started soon after the onset of symptoms. According to the studies, t-PA dissolved coronary artery clots in about 70 per cent of patients who were treated within six hours of the onset of symptoms.

However, t-PA is capable of causing serious bleeding as a side effect and should not be used if there is internal bleeding or a high risk of complications associated with bleeding. Although t-PA is expensive—about $2,300 per treatment—its effectiveness may make it possible to discharge patients from the hospital sooner, thereby reducing the cost of treating a heart attack.

Oral antibacterial agent. Ciprofloxacin, an antibacterial agent that represents a major advance in the treatment of many infections, was approved by the FDA in October

Drugs (cont.)
1987 under the trade name Cipro, manufactured by Miles Pharmaceutical Division, Incorporated. While many antibiotics must be given by injection, ciprofloxacin is effective when taken orally.

The convenient oral form of ciprofloxacin may make it possible to treat on an outpatient basis certain serious infections that would ordinarily require hospitalization. The use of ciprofloxacin also may permit some hospitalized patients with infections to be discharged sooner. Ciprofloxacin is used in the treatment of gastrointestinal, skin, and bone and joint infections, and infections of the urinary tract and lower respiratory tract.

New treatment for impetigo. First introduced in early 1988, mupirocin is an antibiotic that is applied to the skin as an ointment. It is used to treat *impetigo*, a contagious skin infection that occurs most frequently in children. The new drug is extremely effective against *staphylococci* and *streptococci*, the bacteria most often responsible for causing impetigo.

Comparative studies suggest that mupirocin applied as an ointment may be just as effective as an orally administered antibiotic in the treatment of impetigo and less likely to cause adverse reactions. Physicians have used other antibiotic ointments to treat impetigo, but these ointments have not been reliably effective, and as a result, orally administered antibiotics have been prescribed more frequently. The mupirocin ointment, however, appears to be more effective than other antibiotic ointments.

Antidepressant. The FDA approved a new antidepressant, fluoxetine, on Dec. 29, 1987. The new drug will be sold under the trade name Prozac by Eli Lilly & Company of Indianapolis. Fluoxetine is as effective as other medications used to treat depression, but may have fewer harmful side effects.

A side effect of the most widely used antidepressant drugs—such as amitriptyline—is an increased appetite, resulting in weight gain. Fluoxetine, however, appears to decrease appetite and cause weight loss. As a result of this finding, several studies have begun to determine if fluoxetine may also be useful in treating obesity. Fluoxetine is also less likely than other antidepressants to cause dry mouth, constipation, lowering of blood pressure, and heart disturbances. But it is more likely to cause nervousness, and insomnia.

□ Daniel A. Hussar

In World Book, see Drugs.

Ear and Hearing

A new hearing device for people with *conductive hearing loss* was introduced in September 1987 by Xomed, Incorporated, a unit of the Bristol-Myers Company of New York City. Conductive hearing loss is partial deafness that occurs when sound is not conducted properly through the middle ear.

In normal hearing, sound waves are transmitted from the outer ear to the eardrum, which sends vibrations through three tiny bones in the middle ear. The vibrations travel to the inner ear, where they stimulate the auditory nerve to the brain.

With conductive hearing loss, the bones of the middle ear are damaged, diseased, or absent. The Xomed hearing aid by-passes the middle ear, sending sound vibrations directly through the skull to the inner ear.

The device consists of a small sound processor that conveys vibrations to a dime-sized titanium-alloy disk, which is encased in a magnet and implanted in the skull just behind the ear. The sound processor, worn behind the ear, is held in place by the magnet. One of the first patients to be fitted with the instrument reported hearing many previously inaudible sounds.

Hair-cell regeneration. Animal studies published in 1988 sug-

Ear and Hearing (cont.)
gested that hair cells in the inner ear can be regenerated after being destroyed by disease, loud noises, or other causes. Those cells, which convert sound vibrations into electrical impulses and transmit them to the auditory nerve, are essential to hearing.

In birds and mammals, hair cells form during embryonic development, and scientists had thought that the cells, once destroyed, were gone for good. In June 1988, however, zoologist Jeffrey T. Corwin of the University of Hawaii in Honolulu reported that chickens develop new hair cells after being exposed to a sustained loud sound.

Corwin and a colleague, anatomist Douglas A. Cotanche of Boston University School of Medicine, said the new cells apparently arise from adjacent cells of another type that divide and differentiate into hair cells. The scientists said these findings indicate that it may be possible to induce the regeneration of hair cells in the ears of mammals, including human beings.

Bad air may harm ears. Corwin's discovery that it may be possible to regenerate the ears' hair cells should come as good news to city dwellers, in light of another recent study on hearing loss. In November 1987, researchers at Johns Hopkins School of Public Health in Baltimore reported experimental findings suggesting that air pollution—together with urban racket—may contribute to the destruction of hair cells.

The scientists exposed laboratory rats to carbon monoxide—a common component of polluted city air—and to loud noises. Rats that were subjected to both factors had greater hair-cell loss than animals exposed to just carbon monoxide or high sound levels. The researchers speculated that the carbon monoxide reduced the amount of oxygen going to the cells, making them more vulnerable to noise.

Traditional hearing aids got better than ever in 1988. One manufacturer in the United States developed the first fully computerized hearing aid, and most of the newer devices for the hearing-impaired incorporated circuitry that selectively filtered out unwanted sounds.

The computerized, or digital, hearing aid was introduced in March 1988 by the Nicolet Instrument Corporation of Madison, Wis. The device has two parts—an earpiece and a small pocket-sized computer. Sounds picked up by the earpiece are transmitted through a wire to the computer, which converts them to a digital code. After eliminating extraneous noises and adjusting the volume, the computer

Infected ears
Infections of the middle ear are one of the most common problems of childhood. Bacteria from the nose or throat travel up the Eustachian tube—which is more horizontal in children than in adults, making the trip easier—and invade the middle ear. Antibiotics will usually end the infection quickly; an untreated infection, however, can rupture the eardrum. Research has shown that the tendency to develop middle-ear infections is inherited, with children of white, European ancestry being the most susceptible.

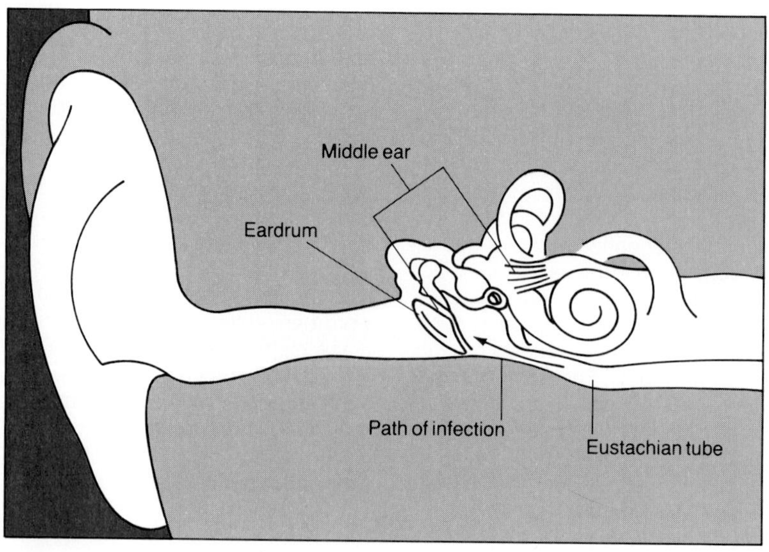

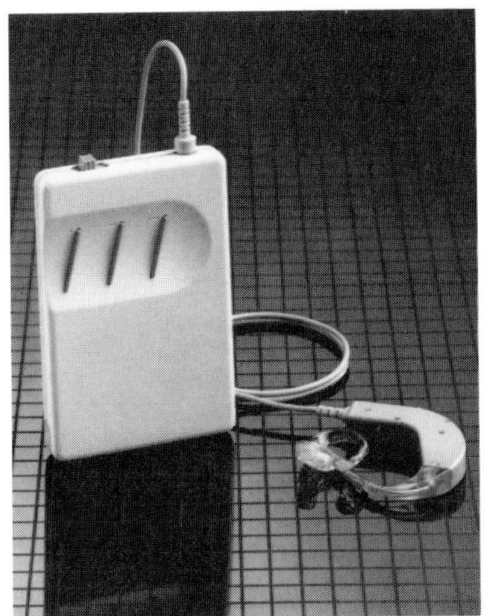

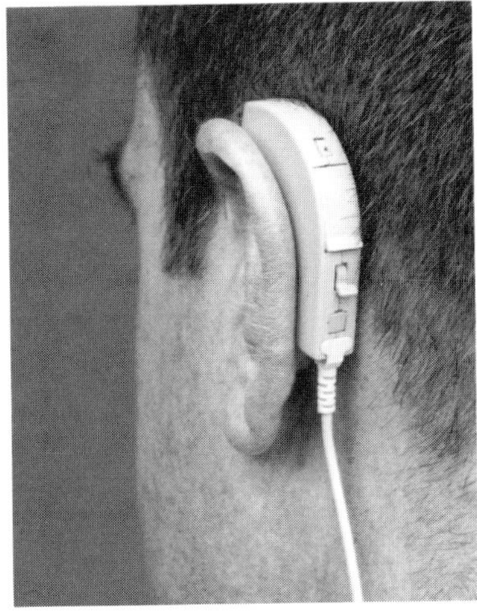

Digital hearing aid
The first fully computerized hearing aid was introduced by the Nicolet Instrument Corporation of Madison, Wis., in 1988. A small pocket-held computer, *far left,* receives sound from an earpiece and converts it to a digital code. After eliminating unwanted noises and adjusting the volume, the computer translates the code back into sound and relays it to the earpiece, which fits comfortably over the back of the ear, *left.*

Ear and Hearing (cont.)
translates the code back into sound and conveys it to the earpiece.

One bug remained to be worked out, however. Audiologists reported that the processing of sound signals in the device results in a slight lag effect. Conversing with another person while wearing the instrument is like watching a motion picture that is out of synchronization.

Sound filtration was a standard feature on many hearing aids in 1988. Several companies offered hearing aids with the Zeta Noise Blocker system, introduced in 1987 by Intellitech, Incorporated, of Northbrook, Ill. The Zeta system uses a small computer that monitors sounds and activates filters to suppress noise, while at the same time amplifying conversation.

A rival system, developed by Siemens Hearing Instruments, Incorporated, of Piscataway, N.J., employs circuits that reduce low-frequency sounds. Lower-pitched sounds tend to drown out the higher frequencies of human speech, which hearing-impaired people typically have the most difficulty picking up.

☐ David L. Dreier

In World Book, see Deafness; Ear.

Emergency Medicine

Emergency department physicians began to use a convenient and timesaving device that was introduced in the fall of 1987—a voice-activated computer. The device was designed to be used for a crucial part of a patient's care in an emergency department—the emergency physician's record of the patient's symptoms, diagnosis, and treatment. Unfortunately, this record is often written as hurried, barely readable notes on the patient's chart.

The voice-activated computer, called VoiceEM, may streamline this procedure, immediately providing a legible record while enabling emergency physicians to devote more time to working directly with patients. To use VoiceEM, the physician dictates into a telephone handset that is connected to the computer. Seconds later, VoiceEM prints the dictated record.

Kurzweil Applied Intelligence of Waltham, Mass., designed VoiceEM specifically for emergency medicine. VoiceEM recognizes common medical terms and special terms relating to emergency department procedures.

Ear thermometer. Measurement of body temperature is a routine part of nearly every visit to an emergency department. In most cases, a

Electronic typist
An emergency physician dictates a patient's record to a voice-activated computer. Seconds later, the computer prints a copy of the report. This procedure avoids delays in the typewriting of reports made on conventional dictating machines, and prevents problems that doctors, nurses, and other medical personnel have in reading handwritten reports.

Emergency Medicine (cont.)
physician or nurse takes the measurement orally—by putting a thermometer into the patient's mouth. The temperature of the mouth, however, depends upon not only body temperature but also such other factors as cigarette smoking and the consumption of hot and cold liquids.

Until recently, the only alternative to an oral temperature reading was to measure the patient's temperature rectally. Many patients, however, find this procedure physically or psychologically uncomfortable.

Two papers presented at the May 1988 annual meeting of the University Association for Emergency Medicine described another technique—inserting a probe into the *external auditory canal* (EAC), the opening that leads to the eardrum.

Physicians at the University of Virginia Medical Center in Charlottesville reported on the measurement of EAC temperature with a standard electronic thermometer available in most emergency departments. The Virginia physicians used such thermometers to measure orally the temperatures of 102 patients. In each case, they then cooled the thermometer, put a new cover on its probe, and inserted the probe 0.4 to 0.8 inch (1 to 2 centimeters) into the patient's ear.

Temperature at a touch
The FirstTemp electronic thermometer takes a patient's temperature in seconds with a gentle touch at the ear. The device detects *infrared rays,* a form of heat energy, emitted by the eardrum.

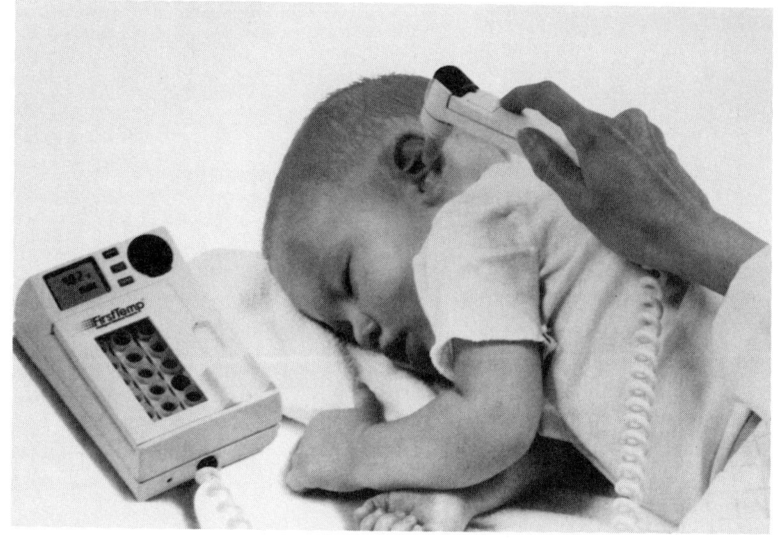

Emergency Medicine (cont.)

After comparing measurements, the physicians concluded that most EAC temperatures were as reliable as oral temperatures in adult patients. No patient reported any discomfort during the measurements of EAC temperatures.

Registered nurse Lynne A. Ward, an affiliated resident in emergency medicine at the University of Pittsburgh, described an experiment on FirstTemp, a computerized device made by Intelligent Medical Systems of Carlsbad, Calif. To use FirstTemp, a physician or nurse gently touches a handheld probe to the entrance of the EAC. Within a few seconds, FirstTemp produces a temperature reading based on *infrared energy* (a form of heat energy) emitted by the eardrum.

Ward and her colleagues compared FirstTemp with a device that measured rectal temperature in about 30 seconds. After using both devices on 150 patients, the physicians concluded that FirstTemp is a reliable device for initial measurements of the temperatures of emergency department patients.

☐ Robert D. Powers

In World Book, see Thermometer.

Environmental Health

Potentially deadly chemicals known as *heavy metals* were detected in the environment in larger amounts than previously found, according to research reported in May 1988 by geochemist Jerome O. Nriagu and other researchers at the Canadian National Water Research Institute in Burlington, Canada. On the basis of their measurements, the scientists concluded that heavy metals are a greater potential health hazard than all types of organic and radioactive waste.

Heavy metals include such elements as lead, mercury, and cadmium. When ingested through contaminated air, food, or water, these chemicals accumulate in human tissue and can eventually cause nervous-system damage and death.

Heavy metals are released into the atmosphere during coal combustion, electric generation, steel and iron manufacturing, and the operation of fuel-burning vehicles. Cities that incinerate their refuse are also responsible for a large share of heavy-metal emissions.

Dioxin regulation. The federally allowable maximum exposure level for *dioxin*, a highly toxic manufactured chemical, may be raised, according to a December 1987 document circulated by the Environmental Protection Agency (EPA). If adopted, the revised standard would be 16 times less stringent than the present maximum allowable limit for dioxin.

Although researchers know that dioxin causes cancer in animals, its effect on human beings is not clear. This has produced a scientific debate over whether dioxin is a human *carcinogen* (cancer-causing agent) and what exposure level can be considered safe. The EPA's revised standard would imply that the agency considers dioxin less deadly than it once did—but still 10,000 times more powerful than polychlorinated biphenyl compounds (PCB's), another toxic chemical for which the EPA has set exposure limits.

Establishing a health standard for dioxin is central to the regulation of large municipal incinerators, which generate dioxin during the combustion of waste. Safety levels for dioxin pollution will need to be established once the EPA sets its maximum allowable limit.

Asbestos contamination. Approximately 20 per cent of the public and commercial buildings in the United States are contaminated with asbestos, the EPA announced in March 1988. Asbestos, a group of minerals once used for insulation, is a health hazard because its tiny fibers can be inhaled, leading to lung cancer and other health problems.

Although the U.S. Congress appropriated $50 million in 1987 to

Environmental Health (cont.)

clean up asbestos-contaminated schools, the EPA did not immediately recommend a comparable program to remove asbestos from other public and commercial buildings. The expense of such a program—estimated at $51 billion—prompted the decision to delay.

Instead, the agency proposed to increase technical training of inspectors and asbestos-removal professionals through a three-year, $6-million program; devote $1.8 million to removing asbestos insulation found in buildings' heating systems; increase enforcement of current asbestos-related regulations; and study the effectiveness of the school cleanup program before initiating a program for other buildings.

Indoor radon pollution. Radon is now considered a major environmental hazard, according to an April 1988 report in *Science* magazine. Radon is a naturally occurring radioactive gas that may rise from the soil under some homes and contaminate indoor air spaces. It may also be emitted from building materials such as stone and brick and from some water supplies. Chronic, low-level exposure to radon causes an estimated 5,000 to 20,000 cancer deaths per year in the United States, according to the National Academy of Science's National Research Council (NRC) in Washington, D.C.

Home testing devices, such as an inexpensive "alpha-track" detector, can help homeowners assess their level of radon exposure. If significant levels of radon are contaminating the home, specially designed ventilation systems and other home improvements can help remove the gas. Such measures pay off in terms of health protection. The NRC found in 1988 that the health risks of radon exposure decrease over time after exposure stops.

The EPA recommends that homeowners take action if the radon level exceeds 4 picocuries of radon per liter of air. (A picocurie is one-trillionth of a *curie*, the unit for measuring the intensity of radioactivity.) Physicist Anthony V. Nero and other researchers at Lawrence Berkeley Laboratory in Berkeley, Calif., reported in 1986 that about 7 per cent of the single-family homes in the United States have radon levels that exceed this guideline.

New workplace exposure limits. The U.S. Occupational Safety and Health Administration (OSHA) announced on June 7, 1988, that it would propose new, tougher standards on workplace exposure to 402 toxic chemicals. If adopted, the regulations would cost industry an estimated $900 million, but the standards would benefit the nation by saving 500 lives per year, by reduc-

Health warnings
Employees of Chevron Corporation discuss warning signs to be placed in the company's gas stations in response to a California law mandating that all California businesses caution the public about the possible health consequences of their products. Companies not complying with the law were to be subject to heavy fines.

Radiation accident
One of 1987's worst environmental accidents occurred in September in Goiânia, Brazil. A glowing radioactive powder found by scrap-metal dealers inside an abandoned piece of medical equipment was passed from person to person in the belief that it held magical powers. More than 200 people were exposed to the substance, cesium-137, which caused severe skin burns, *above,* and, in some cases, death.

Environmental Health (cont.)
ing by 500,000 the annual number of workdays lost because of exposure to hazardous chemicals, and by reducing by 50,000 the annual incidence of cancer and cardiovascular and respiratory diseases.

OSHA's decision to propose changes in the limits for so many chemicals is a major departure from the agency's former approach to setting standards one at a time. Since 1971, OSHA has proposed new standards for only 24 other chemicals. The 1988 proposal was part of a plan to act quickly to help eliminate a 20-year backlog.

Response to OSHA's announcement was mixed. The American Federation of Labor and Congress of Industrial Organizations (AFL-CIO) felt that the proposal was not stringent enough and that it failed to address the safety concerns of millions of workers in the maritime, construction, and agricultural industries. The Chemical Manufacturers Association, on the other hand, felt OSHA's proposal was reasonable. After a period of public comment and review, employers will be given six months to comply with the new standards. □ Laura M. Lake

In World Book see Dioxin; Environmental Pollution; Radon.

Exercise and Fitness

Physical activity may help lessen the risk of death due to coronary artery disease. A seven-year study of 12,138 middle-aged men, reported in November 1987, found that those who took part in the least amount of leisure-time physical activity had a 30 per cent greater chance of dying of coronary artery disease than those who engaged in more frequent physical activity.

Coronary artery disease occurs when the coronary arteries, which supply blood to heart muscle, become narrowed by fatty deposits and thus supply less blood to the heart. The disease can lead to a fatal heart attack if a blood clot blocks the narrowed artery.

The study, led by cardiologist Arthur S. Leon of the School of Public Health at the University of Minnesota in Minneapolis, divided the participants into three groups according to the type and frequency of their physical activity. Light activity included fishing, bowling, or walking for pleasure. Moderate activity included gardening, yard work, and swimming. Jogging, tennis, and cross-country skiing were considered heavy activity.

Over a seven-year period, the researchers found that those who took part in either light or moderate physical activity for 30 to 60 minutes

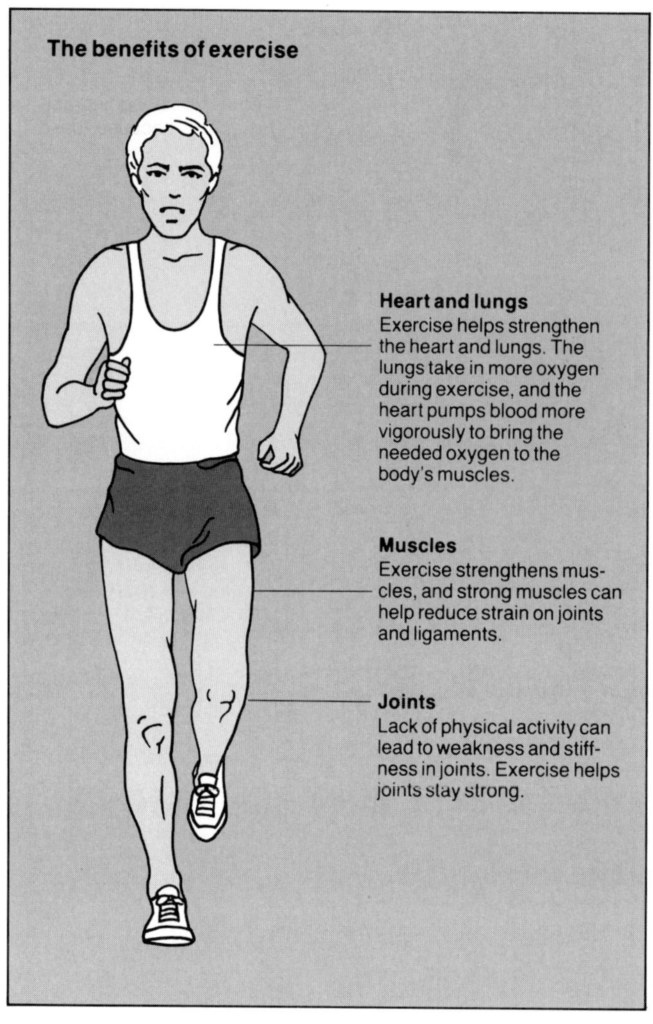

Exercise and Fitness (cont.)

a day significantly reduced the risk of dying of coronary artery disease. In addition, the benefits of heavy activity, in terms of death rate, were about the same as that of light to moderate exercise.

The researchers concluded that this was encouraging news because most people have enough leisure time to take part in physical activity lasting from 30 to 60 minutes a day. Also, since no greater gain can be expected from heavy exercise, middle-aged people can benefit from safer, light-to-moderate activity.

Risk during exercise. There is a higher risk of sudden death during exercise than during other activities, according to epidemiologist David Siskovick of the University of North Carolina in Chapel Hill. At an International Conference on Exercise, Fitness, and Health, held from May 29 to June 3, 1988, in Toronto, Canada, Siskovick reported that the risk of sudden death was, on average, five to seven times greater during the time of exercise than at any other time of day. This risk is nine times greater during strenuous exercise and three times greater during mild exercise. Siskovick also pointed out that inactive people and those who have previously suffered a heart attack are at even higher risk. Despite this caution, however, the long-term beneficial effects of exercise outweigh the chance of dying during exercise. Although exercisers may be at higher risk during the one hour they are active, they develop less risk during the other 23 hours of the day.

Effects on blood pressure. Also at the Toronto conference, physiologist James Hagberg of the University of Florida in Gainesville reviewed a number of studies suggesting that exercise helps lower high blood pressure. These studies found that about two-thirds of people of all ages who exercised regularly experienced a reduction in blood pressure. Moderate exercise was found to be as effective in lowering blood pressure as high-intensity exercise. This is especially important when strenuous exercise is inappropriate, such as for the obese, the elderly, and people with joint or muscle problems.

Speakers at the Toronto conference repeatedly noted that moderate exercise is beneficial to health, though many people feel that they must engage in high-intensity exercise to derive health benefits. If high-intensity activity seems unrealistic or too difficult, however, many people do not start an exercise program. Intense physical activity and achieving optimum physical fitness are not the same. Exercising regularly at a moderate intensity is sufficient for good health.

Studies continued to show during 1987 and 1988 that women benefit from such exercise as jogging and bicycling because these activities help maintain mineral content in bones. This is especially important for women at risk of developing *osteoporosis,* a disease that results in the loss of bone mineral.

Exercise and Fitness (cont.)

Running and osteoarthritis. Running does not lead to *osteoarthritis*, a degenerative joint disease, according to a June 1988 report in the *Harvard Medical School Health Letter*. The report cited a survey of research studies conducted by physician Harvey B. Simon of Harvard University's Medical School.

Osteoarthritis has been called "the wear and tear" disease and has prompted concern among many runners that the stress caused by running might damage joints.

Since 1986, three U.S. studies have examined leisure-time runners. In these studies, most of the runners were in their 50's and 60's—the age when arthritis normally begins to appear—and most had been running on a regular basis for 12 years.

The studies relied on questionnaires, physical examinations, and in some cases, X rays and bone scans. The researchers reported that runners had the same incidence of arthritis as people in a control group who were the same age but did not exercise by running.

Exercise and cancer. A study reported in February 1988 reaffirmed earlier findings showing a link between vigorous exercise and a lowered risk of breast cancer and can-

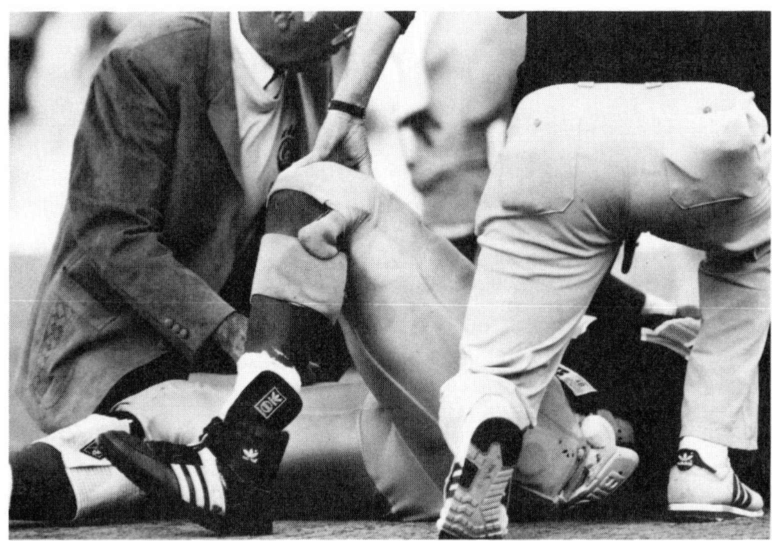

Knee braces tackled
Knee braces, such as the one worn by this football player, may not only fail to prevent knee injuries but may even help cause such injuries, the American Academy of Orthopedic Surgeons warned in November 1987.

Exercise and Fitness (cont.)

cer of the uterus. At the annual meeting of the American Association for the Advancement of Science in Boston, biologist Rose Frisch of Harvard University's School of Public Health in Boston reported the results of a study involving 5,398 women. The findings confirmed results from a 1987 study that involved 2,662 women alumnae of Harvard University. That study showed that the incidence of breast and uterine cancer was 50 per cent lower among women who were athletic in college than among women who were not athletic in college.

Frisch suggested that vigorous exercise appears to disrupt the menstrual cycle, which, in turn, seems to make women less susceptible to those cancers. The key reason may lie in the fact that *estrogen* (the female hormone) appears in two forms. One form is suspected of promoting cancer, and vigorous exercise seems to reduce the body's levels of this form.

☐ James S. Skinner

In the Special Reports section, see BONE UP NOW FOR STRONGER BONES LATER; REDUCING THE RISK OF HEART DISEASE. In WORLD BOOK, see PHYSICAL FITNESS.

Eye and Vision

Freezing part of the white of the eye can reduce the risk of blindness in certain premature babies by 50 per cent, a National Eye Institute study revealed in 1988. In February, the institute sent a special alert to 2,300 pediatric ophthalmologists in the United States, recommending the new procedure.

Very small premature infants often develop a condition called *retinopathy of prematurity*. In this disorder, blood vessels in the *retina*—the light-sensitive layer of cells on the inside back wall of the eyeball—undergo excessive growth. The vessels spread to an area at the front of the retina that usually does not contain blood vessels. This abnormal blood-vessel development can lead to bleeding, scarring, and detachment of the retina from the eyeball. The cause of the condition is not known.

Each year, retinopathy of prematurity causes some vision loss in an estimated 2,600 babies in the United States and blindness in more than 600. In many other cases, the condition does not advance and babies develop normal vision, so U.S. ophthalmologists generally have not tried to treat it.

Studies in Europe and Japan,

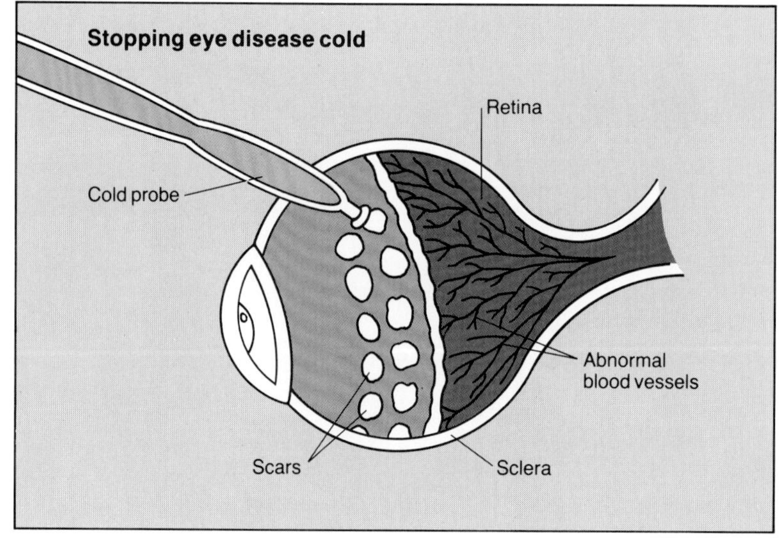

A new freezing technique has proven effective in treating *retinopathy of prematurity,* an eye condition that affects many premature infants. In this disorder, excessive blood-vessel growth in the retina (the eye's light-sensitive tissue) can cause vision loss, including blindness. The new procedure involves touching the *sclera* (white of the eye) with an extremely cold probe. Cold is transmitted through the sclera to the retina, making a tiny scar. A ring of such scars around the eyeball prevents further growth of the blood vessels.

Goggle-eyed chicken
A neurobiologist at Cornell University in Ithaca, N.Y., checks an eyeglass-wearing chicken to see how well it has adapted to looking at an out-of-focus world. Cornell scientists have found that young chickens adjust the growth rate of their eyes to compensate for the fuzziness caused by the lenses. The research may lead to new treatments for visual defects in young children.

Eye and Vision (cont.)
however, had indicated that the freezing technique, known as *scleral cryotherapy*, could prevent retinopathy of prematurity from advancing. Officials of the National Eye Institute therefore decided to test the procedure in the United States.

The institute funded a study at 23 U.S. medical centers. Physicians at the centers identified 291 babies with retinopathy. Of those, 139 babies had retinopathy in both eyes, and 152 had just one affected eye. In babies with retinopathy in both eyes, one eye was treated and the other was left untreated to serve as a control, or comparison. Thirty-three babies who had retinopathy in only one eye underwent cryotherapy, while the remaining 119 infants received no treatment and were studied as controls.

To treat the infants' eyes, the ophthalmologists touched a *cryoprobe*, a wandlike instrument cooled to −176°F. (−80°C), to the *sclera* (the white part of the eyeball). The cold was transmitted through the sclera to a spot on the retina. At each spot, a tiny amount of tissue on the retina was destroyed and converted to scar tissue. Most treatments required making a ring of approximately 50 such spots on the retina. This circle of scar tissue created a barrier that prevented the blood vessels from invading the rest of the retina.

The ophthalmologists checked the babies' eyes every three months after the operation. Among the babies with retinopathy in both eyes, 24.1 per cent of treated eyes and 45.6 per cent of untreated eyes became legally blind. Among those with retinopathy in only one eye, 5.3 per cent of the treated eyes and 15.4 per cent of the untreated eyes became legally blind.

Because the three-month results were so dramatic—an overall 49.3 per cent reduction in blindness—treatment was begun on the 119 infants serving as controls. Rather than wait for the outcome of those trials to be published, however, the National Eye Institute contacted physicians directly, urging them to send premature babies who are developing retinopathy to one of the participating centers for treatment.

Zinc and vision loss. Oral zinc supplements may help to prevent one of the leading causes of vision loss in older people—degeneration of the *macula*. That finding was reported in February 1988 by researchers at Louisiana State Eye Center in New Orleans and the University of Utah in Salt Lake City.

The macula, a small round spot in the center of the retina, is the area where vision is sharpest. Without the macula, we would not see anything in sharp focus. Deterioration of the macula usually begins at about age 55, and more than one-fourth of all

Eye and Vision (cont.)
Americans over the age of 75 have the disorder.

Macular destruction is caused in three ways: by pigment deposited in macular cells, by the formation of grainy deposits called *drusen* in the macula, or by cell death. In some cases, abnormal blood vessels grow into the macula.

Although scientists do not know exactly why the macula can degenerate with age, they do know that zinc plays a key role in the *metabolism* (chemical life processes) of the retina and that older people often have zinc deficiencies. Thus, the two research teams decided to test whether adding zinc supplements to the diet of older people would help lessen macular deterioration.

The scientists studied 174 people between the ages of 42 and 89 who had some macular degeneration but no other serious eye disease. Ninety of the patients were randomly assigned to take a 100-milligram tablet of zinc sulfate twice a day, while the other 84 were a control group and were given a *placebo*—a pill that appeared identical to the zinc tablet but contained no medication.

All the patients underwent eye examinations at the beginning of the study and at six-month intervals over the next two years. At each ex-

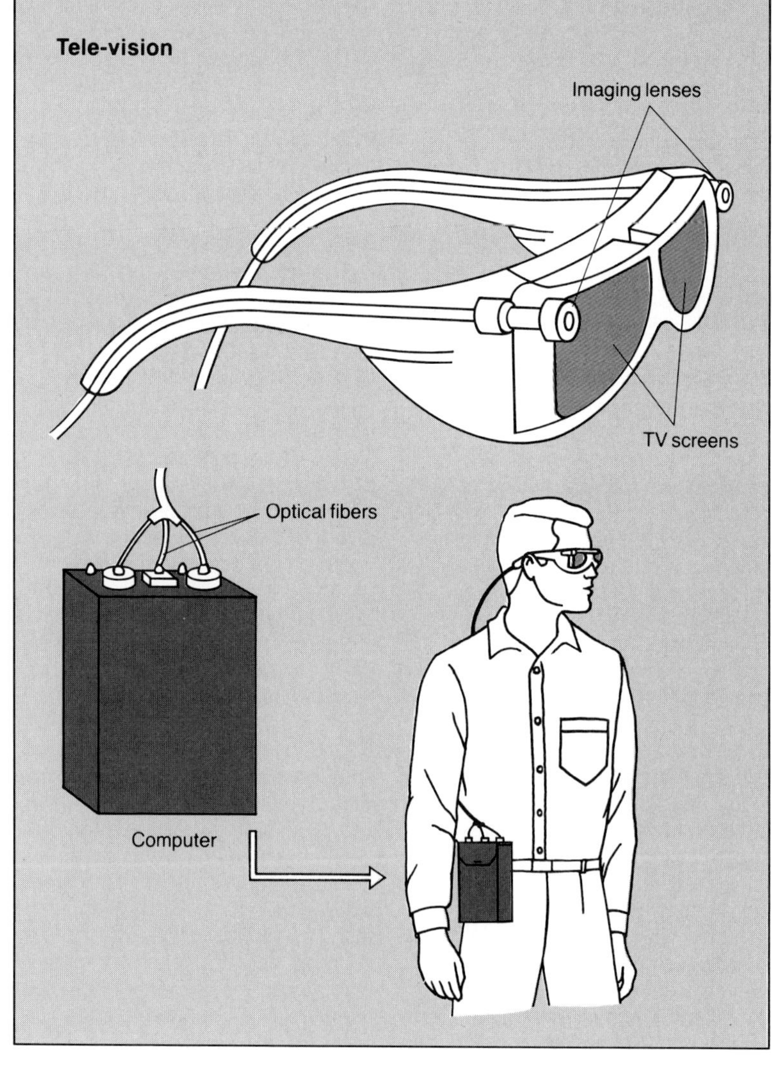

Television glasses, designed to improve the vision of people suffering from degenerative eye diseases, are being developed by scientists at the National Aeronautics and Space Administration and the Wilmer Eye Institute in Baltimore. The glasses, resembling wraparound sunglasses, will have two small imaging lenses that will transmit a picture of the scene in front of the wearer, by way of optical fibers, to a battery-powered computer in a belt or shoulder pack. The computer will convert the light images into electronic images, which will be displayed on TV screens on the inside surfaces of the glasses.

Eye and Vision (cont.)
amination, two ophthalmologists evaluated the three main types of macular loss in the patients' eyes.

Twenty-three people—10 in the group receiving zinc sulfate and 13 in the placebo group—failed to complete the study. Of those who completed the study, patients who had been taking zinc were found to have significantly less macular deterioration than patients who had received the placebo.

The researchers concluded from these results that zinc helps retard age-related degeneration of the macula. Because zinc can aggravate heart disease and cause anemia in some people, however, the scientists warned against widespread use of oral zinc until further studies are completed.

Holographic contact lenses. The clinical testing of a radically new type of bifocal contact lens for the correction of both near and distance vision began in June 1988 at 20 U.S. medical centers. The new hard-plastic lenses are called *holographic lenses* because—like instruments used in the technology of holography—they split beams of light.

Conventional bifocal contact lenses are constructed much like bifocal eyeglasses, with a close-up lens set into a distance-vision lens. Holographic lenses, in contrast, consist of a single lens. The inner surface of the lens is etched with concentric rings that split incoming light, creating two images, each with its own focal point, on the retina. The brain automatically selects one image on which to focus. The effect is similar to looking through a screened window: The viewer can choose whether to focus on the screen or on a tree in the distance.

The corrective strength of a holographic lens is determined by the number of etched rings—the more rings, the greater the correction. Because the rings are etched only two *microns* deep, they cannot be felt by the wearer. (A micron is one-millionth of a meter.)

TV glasses. Vision researchers at the Johns Hopkins Wilmer Eye Institute in Baltimore and the National Aeronautics and Space Administration (NASA) announced in April 1988 that they are collaborating to develop a new type of glasses to help patients with severe visual handicaps. The glasses will contain small television screens that display a color image of the scene in front of the wearer.

The research teams have designed the glasses to look like a pair of wraparound sunglasses with mirrored lenses. But the lenses will be false; their inside surface will be a pair of miniature TV screens. The actual lenses, about the size of the head of a thumbtack, will be mounted at the sides of the glasses.

These lenses will transmit the images through optical fibers to small television cameras carried in a belt or shoulder pack. A battery-powered computer in the pack will process the images and transmit them to the TV screens.

The glasses are being designed to help approximately 2.5 million Americans with partial vision that cannot be corrected by medication, surgery, conventional glasses, or contact lenses. These people suffer from a variety of eye conditions, including macular degeneration; *diabetic retinopathy*, in which the swelling and leakage from blood vessels cause scar tissue formation on the retina; and *retinitis pigmentosa*, a hereditary condition in which the retina gradually deteriorates.

Design of the glasses will vary to suit each patient's needs. For example, glasses for a patient with retinitis pigmentosa, in which *peripheral* (side) vision is lost, will display different images than glasses for a patient with diabetic retinopathy, which destroys central vision.

Development of the TV glasses is expected to take five years or more and to cost at least $5 million. The glasses must then be tested on patients at several medical centers in the United States and approved by the U.S. Food and Drug Administration. ☐ **Beverly Merz**

In WORLD BOOK, see EYE.

Financing Medical Care

Total health care spending in the United States in 1987 reached $498.9 billion, an increase of 8.9 per cent over 1986. The total represented 11.2 per cent of the *gross national product*—the total value of all goods and services produced—the highest percentage ever. The U.S. Department of Commerce predicted that health care spending in 1988 would reach $544 billion, or 11.4 per cent of the gross national product.

Of the 1987 total, 39 per cent, or $193.5 billion, was spent on hospital care, an increase of 7.7 per cent over 1986. Another 20 per cent, or $102.1 billion, went for physician services, an increase of 11 per cent. Nursing-home care consumed $42 billion—only 8 per cent of the total, but still a 10.2 per cent increase over 1986. The remainder was spent for drugs, nursing care, and home health care, among other health-related expenses.

Medicare. The federal Medicare program, which covers more than 31 million elderly and disabled people, received some good news in May 1988. The trustees of the Medicare Hospital Insurance trust fund, the source of funds for the program's hospital payments, reported that it was likely the fund would be solvent until the year 2005, if present trends continue. Medicare officials said they believed the fund could last until 2044, under certain economic conditions, but it could also be bankrupt by 1999 under certain adverse circumstances.

After a long and often bitter political battle, Congress passed on June 13, 1988, a significant expansion of Medicare to cover the cost of *catastrophic* illness—illness that incurs medical expenses so high that the patient's insurance coverage is exhausted.

The new benefits expand annual hospital coverage from 60 to 365 days, with only a one-time deductible of about $540. Out-of-pocket payments for physician and other services will be limited to $1,370 per year, starting in 1990, and coverage of prescription drugs will be phased in beginning in 1991, eventually covering 80 per cent of costs after a $710 deductible. The new law will also increase coverage for home health care, nursing homes, hospices, and *respite* care (temporary services to relieve family members who are caring for a disabled relative).

The benefits also affect Medicaid, the joint federal-state program that covers 22 million low-income and disabled persons. It requires states to pay certain sums on behalf of patients with incomes below the pov-

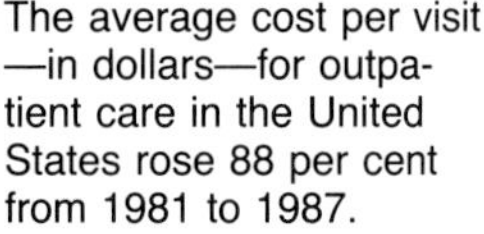
The average cost per visit—in dollars—for outpatient care in the United States rose 88 per cent from 1981 to 1987.

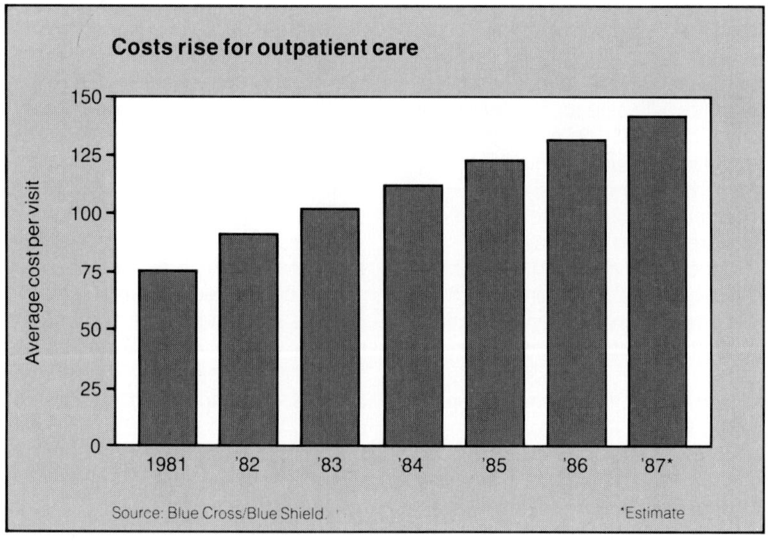

Financing Medical Care (cont.)

erty line and extends Medicaid coverage to pregnant women and women with children aged 1 year or less who have incomes below the poverty line. The poverty line was defined as an annual income of $11,650 for a family of four. The new benefits also protect the spouses of Medicaid patients in nursing homes from being forced into poverty in order to qualify.

Long-term care. The expanded benefits, however, do not address the problem of payment for long-term care in nursing homes. Medicare covers only the cost of 150 nursing-home days a year. Medicaid remains the largest insurance payer of nursing-home costs, providing 42 per cent of the total, but patients still pay the lion's share, 51 per cent, out of their own pockets.

In June 1988, the U.S. House of Representatives defeated a bill sponsored by Representative Claude D. Pepper (D., Fla.) that would have greatly expanded Medicare payments for home health care services. Despite its defeat in 1988, House Democratic leaders reportedly promised Pepper that the long-term-care issue would be a congressional priority in 1989.

Physician payments. How Medicare should pay physicians remained a hotly debated issue during 1987 and 1988. Attention focused on a "relative value scale" being developed at Harvard University in Cambridge, Mass. The scale calls for payment on the basis of the work the physician does, rather than using *prevailing fees*—the fees that are customarily charged in a particular locality. The scale was due for unveiling in late 1988, but there was no guarantee that Medicare would adopt it. Some observers predicted that Medicare would turn to fee schedules—use of fixed fees, which most physicians oppose. Either way, a new system was expected by 1990.

The rising uninsured. The number of uninsured patients who could not afford to pay for health care continued to increase to an estimated 40 million people in 1988. In 1987, Senator Edward M. Kennedy (D., Mass.) introduced a bill requiring employers to provide health insurance to all employees working more than half-time. Although the bill faced stiff opposition, it passed the Senate Human Resources Committee in February 1988 and was sent to the Senate for debate.

Passage of the bill was not expected in 1988, but support for it was surprisingly strong. Several major employers, the American Hospital Association, and the Catholic Health Association backed the bill.

Several other proposals to cover the uninsured were offered during 1988. Among these were bills from Senator George J. Mitchell (D., Me.) and Representative Fortney H. (Pete) Stark (D., Calif.), and a proposal from the Health Insurance Association of America (HIAA), representing commercial insurers.

The state of Massachusetts passed a bill on April 21, 1988, that would eventually guarantee insurance coverage for all state residents. Although estimates of the program's ultimate cost were vague, and full implementation was delayed until 1992, its passage was considered a victory for Governor Michael S. Dukakis, the Democratic Party's presidential nominee.

Private insurers had a difficult year. Eighty per cent of all large employers are now *self-insured*—funding their own programs rather than purchasing private insurance. As a result, private insurers face a dwindling market. The HIAA reported in June 1988 that commercial insurance represented 40 per cent of the private market in 1987, Blue Cross and Blue Shield plans represented 24 per cent, and self-insurance represented 36 per cent. The HIAA reported that some 180 million people in the United States had private insurance in 1987.

☐ Emily Ann Friedman

In World Book, see Medicaid; Medicare.

Genetics

About 53 of every 1,000 people will develop a genetically related disease before age 25. That finding was reported in May 1988 by Patricia A. Baird, a medical geneticist at the University of British Columbia, in Vancouver, Canada.

Baird and her colleagues surveyed the medical records of more than 1 million babies, children, and young people and noted the incidence of various genetically linked health problems. The researchers predicted that their data will help in the planning of health-care services for individuals afflicted with genetic disorders.

Although genetic factors contribute to a number of human diseases, including heart disease and many forms of cancer, genetic defects are the sole cause of a smaller group of diseases. The chart below summarizes the present status of some of the major genetic disorders.

Genetically Caused Diseases

Disease	Symptoms	Treatment	No. of cases in U.S.
Duchenne muscular dystrophy	Progressive muscle deterioration	Treatment of symptoms only; no cure	32,000
Cystic fibrosis	Lung and gastrointestinal degeneration	Treatment of symptoms only; no cure	30,000
Huntington's disease	Brain degeneration in midlife	None	25,000
Sickle cell anemia	Anemia, blood clots, damage to organs and nervous system	Drugs to ease symptoms; no cure	65,000 (mostly blacks)
Hemophilia	Uncontrolled internal and external bleeding	Controlled through injections of missing blood-clotting factors	20,000
Beta-thalassemia	Anemia; sometimes also gallstones, jaundice, leg ulcers	Controlled through blood transfusions	1,000
Phenyl-ketonuria	Mental retardation, seizures	Special diet to prevent onset of symptoms	16,000
Polycystic kidney disease	Pain, high blood pressure, kidney failure in 50% of cases	Treatment of symptoms; kidney dialysis or transplant after kidney failure	500,000
Retino-blastoma	Cancer of the eye in childhood	X rays, drugs, surgery; usually curable if caught early	10,000

Source: Federal health agencies and associations for the disorders listed above.

Sequencing human genes. Determining who will be among that 5.3 per cent of people whose genes will cause or contribute to early illness is not yet possible. If the complete sequence of human genes were known, however, scientists believe that genetic defects could be pinpointed. Individuals destined for early disease—as well as people at risk for cancer, heart disease, or other problems later in life—might then be identified at birth, or even before. Because of its potential benefits for human health, some geneticists in 1988 urged that a gene-sequencing project be started soon.

Human beings have approximately 100,000 genes, which are composed of *deoxyribonucleic acid* (DNA), the master molecule of heredity. In order to sequence all 100,000 genes, scientists must determine the exact order of their building blocks—an estimated 3 billion molecules called bases.

Many researchers think that a complete DNA sequence, in addition to serving as a diagnostic tool, would provide important insights into the structure and functioning of genes. It might also further our understanding of human evolution. Critics of a sequencing project, however, argue that, with an estimated cost of several billion dollars, it would divert funds from other biological research.

The gene for sex. The discovery of a gene that apparently plays a major role in determining a fetus's sex was reported in December 1987 by geneticist David C. Page of the Whitehead Institute for Biomedical Research in Cambridge, Mass. Page's initial findings indicated that the gene, located on the Y chromosome, causes the fetus to develop as a male. In the gene's absence, the fetus becomes a female.

Chromosomes are threadlike structures that carry the genes. Two chromosomes—the so-called X chromosome and Y chromosome—are referred to as the *sex chromosomes* because they determine gender. Biologists had known since

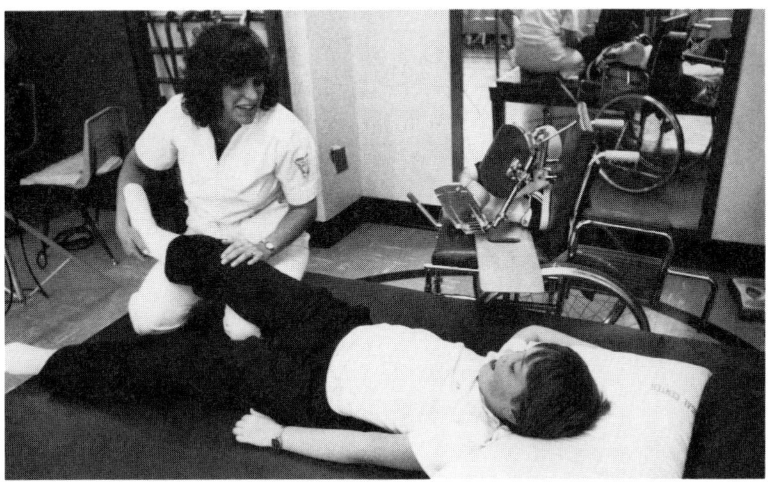

Hope for DMD victims
A boy with Duchenne muscular dystrophy (DMD)—a hereditary disease that causes muscles to deteriorate—receives physical therapy. In late 1987, researchers in the United States reported that a steroid drug, prednisone, can delay the crippling effects of DMD—the commonest and most severe form of muscular dystrophy—for an average of two years.

Genetics (cont.)
the 1950's that, in almost all cases, females have two X chromosomes, and males have one X and one Y. But they did not know how the Y chromosome causes the development of maleness.

Certain rare exceptions to the XX-XY rule provided an opportunity to learn more about the functioning of the Y chromosome. About 1 in 20,000 males is XX, and an equally small percentage of females are XY. Page and his colleagues theorized that if a gene on the Y chromosome determines maleness, XX males must have a piece of the Y chromosome containing that gene. XY females, on the other hand, must have an incomplete Y chromosome that lacks the male gene.

The researchers analyzed the DNA of about 90 XX males and XY females.As they had theorized, the DNA from all the XY females tested was missing a piece of the Y chromosome, and the same piece of the Y chromosome was present in the DNA of all the XX males. The scientists named the male gene in that chromosome segment the *TDF* gene, for *testis determining factor.* (The testes, or testicles, are the male reproductive glands.)

Page and others predicted that the TDF gene would prove to be just one of many genes involved in sex determination. A process so complicated, they said, is unlikely to be controlled by just one gene.

Page and his associates identified the protein whose production is directed by the TDF gene. It is one of a class of proteins known to control other genes by regulating the amount of *ribonucleic acid* (RNA) the genes make. (RNA is the molecule into which DNA's coded instructions are copied in the production of proteins.) So the TDF gene is probably a major regulatory gene.

Page found the gene in the DNA of many other mammals, including dogs, mice, and gorillas. That finding indicates that the gene is important in evolutionary history because it has existed for millions of years and has been passed from one species to the next.

After finding the TDF gene, Page discovered an almost identical gene on the X chromosome. Thus, rather than males having one copy of the gene that apparently creates maleness and females lacking that gene, both sexes have two copies of the gene. But how, then, is an individual's gender determined?

Page thinks the answer may lie in a phenomenon called *X inactivation*, which makes one X chromosome inactive in the cells of normal females. According to this hypothesis, only one copy of the TDF gene would function in normal females because the other X chromosome would be inactivated. Males would have two active copies of the TDF gene, one

Genetics (cont.)

on each of the X and Y chromosomes. Thus, according to this theory, sex determination depends on "dosage"—a single dose of the TDF protein for which the gene codes produces a female; a double dose produces a male.

Some biologists, however, rejected that explanation and expressed doubt that Page had found the gene for sex determination. Debate on Page's findings continued throughout the year.

Heredity and environment. Scientists have long debated whether genetics or life style plays the greater role in determining how long we live, and the answer has been elusive. But in March 1988, a group of Danish scientists reported that both factors exert a strong influence on life expectancy.

University of Copenhagen geneticist Thorkild I. A. Sorensen and his colleagues studied adoptees from 960 families. Studies of people who grow up in adoptive homes are common in genetics research. By comparing adoptees with both their biological and adoptive parents, geneticists can investigate the genetic and environmental factors contributing to various traits and diseases.

If, for example, children brought up in adoptive homes are found to die at a relatively early age of the same diseases or disorders as their natural parents, then genetics was probably the biggest factor in their death. If, on the other hand, adoptees die prematurely of the same causes as their adoptive parents, one can conclude that the home environment—including eating, drinking, smoking, and exercise habits—played a greater role in their death.

The adoptees studied by Sorensen's research team were born between 1924 and 1926, and all were adopted by people unrelated to them. The scientists compared the causes of premature death—between the ages of 16 and 58—among the adoptees and their biological and adoptive parents.

The survey revealed that the death of a biological parent before age 50 almost doubled the general, overall risk of premature death for the adoptee. The death of an adoptive parent before age 50 did not increase the general risk of death for the adoptee.

When Sorensen's group looked at specific causes of premature death, however, the picture changed considerably. The scientists found a fivefold risk for adoptees if a biological parent had died of an infectious disease, a fourfold risk if a biological parent died of heart disease or stroke, but only a slightly increased risk if a biological parent died of cancer. If the adoptive parent died of heart disease or stroke, the risk to the adoptee was roughly tripled, and—the most surprising finding—there was a fivefold increase in risk to the adoptee if the adoptive parent died of cancer.

Some of these findings seemed to contradict prevailing views about the role of genetics in disease. For example, scientists had expected a shared family environment to be more important than genetic factors in infectious disease. On the other hand, recent research has shown a strong genetic basis in most cancers. How, then, does one explain Sorensen's data?

With respect to infectious diseases, Sorensen explained that the high death rate from infections among some adoptees and their biological parents might mean that some people's immune systems are genetically weaker than other people's. Sorensen said the high incidence of cancer among adoptees whose adoptive parent had cancer could be due to such environmental factors as cigarette smoking.

Sorensen's study suggests that it is probably fruitless trying to determine whether genes or environment are the more important cause of premature death. The research indicated that most major chronic diseases result from the cumulative effect of environmental factors in people who are genetically susceptible to those diseases.

☐ Joseph D. McInerney

In World Book, see Cell; Genetics.

Glands and Hormones

An imbalance of two hormones involved in *ovulation* has been linked to functional amenorrhea, a failure to menstruate because of emotional stress, according to a study published in April 1988 by researchers at the University of California, San Diego. (Ovulation is the release of a mature egg by the ovary.)

Endocrinologists (doctors who study glands and hormones) have long attributed functional amenorrhea to a breakdown in the ability of the *hypothalamus*, a part of the brain, to direct the functions of the ovaries. Endocrinologists suspected that the problems with the hypothalamus were caused by chemicals, such as adrenalin, secreted by the brain when a person is under stress. The precise way in which this breakdown can lead to functional amenorrhea was unknown, however.

During their study of women with functional amenorrhea, the researchers discovered a peculiar pattern in the secretion of two hormones, *cortisol* and *luteinizing hormone*. Cortisol, which is produced by the adrenal glands, helps regulate the action of the hypothalamus in stimulating the development of eggs in the ovaries. Luteinizing hormone, which is produced by the hypothalamus, causes ovulation to occur. Both of these hormones are released at variable intervals rather than continuously.

The researchers found that the women in the study secreted higher-than-normal levels of cortisol but that this overproduction occurred only during the daytime. They also found that although periods of cortisol secretion occurred at normal intervals, these periods were of longer than normal duration.

In contrast, the women in the study produced lower-than-normal levels of luteinizing hormone and secreted the hormone less frequently than normal. According to the researchers, the hormonal imbalances disappeared spontaneously without medical treatment after the women's emotional stress was relieved by treatment or the passage of time.

Benefits of estrogen. The first clear evidence supporting the theory that *estrogen* (a female hormone) helps protect women against coronary artery disease and heart attack was reported in March 1988 by researchers at the University of Tennessee Center for Health Sciences in Memphis. Scientists have long known that women who have not yet gone through menopause are less likely to suffer from heart problems than are men. This difference disappears after menopause begins, a time when the level of estrogen in the body drops.

The researchers studied the med-

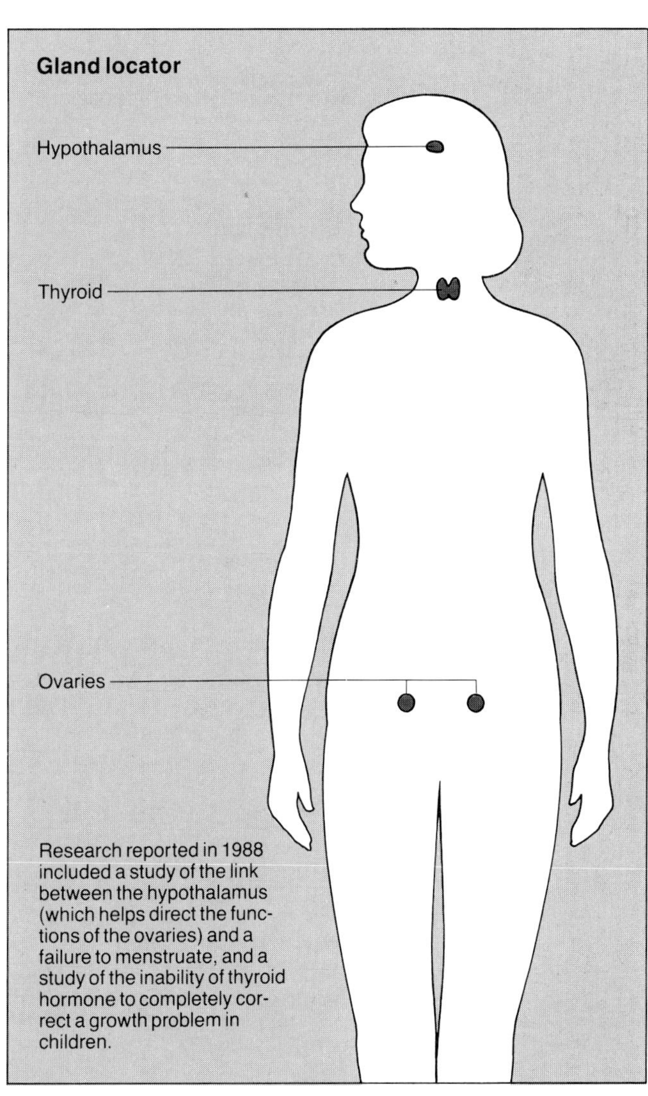

Research reported in 1988 included a study of the link between the hypothalamus (which helps direct the functions of the ovaries) and a failure to menstruate, and a study of the inability of thyroid hormone to completely correct a growth problem in children.

Glands and Hormones (cont.)
ical records of 2,188 postmenopausal women who had undergone *coronary arteriography*—a procedure in which X rays are used to photograph coronary arteries—between 1972 and 1984. They found that the women who had taken estrogen supplements had less narrowing of the coronary arteries due to a build-up of *plaque* (fatty deposits) than women who had not taken the hormone. The women in the estrogen group also suffered fewer heart attacks than the women who had not taken supplements.

Estrogen therapy also helps reduce the number of hip fractures in postmenopausal women, according to a study published in November 1987 by researchers at several medical institutions in Boston and Providence, R.I. Estrogen helps maintain bone mass. The results of both studies provided additional support for the practice of prescribing estrogen for women who have gone through menopause.

Thyroid hormone and growth. Contrary to common medical belief, treatment with thyroid hormone does not routinely enable children with juvenile acquired hypothyroidism to reach their full height. That conclusion was published in March 1988 by researchers at Harvard University in Cambridge, Mass.

Children suffering from juvenile acquired hypothyroidism grow increasingly slowly until they eventually stop growing altogether. If untreated, these children go through puberty at a later-than-normal age and are very short as adults. Doctors had previously believed that treatment with thyroid hormone would help children with this condition make up their height deficit and reach their full stature.

The Harvard study, however, revealed disappointing results with the treatment of 18 girls and 6 boys with juvenile acquired hypothyroidism. Although thyroid hormone treatment corrected some of the symptoms of hypothyroidism, such as dry skin, sleepiness, and poor performance in school, it did not correct the children's height problem.

According to the researchers, the height deficit was permanent and depended on how long the children suffered from a thyroid hormone deficiency before receiving treatment. The researchers noted that the study emphasized the importance of diagnosing and treating juvenile acquired hypothyroidism as early as possible so that children with this condition would be able to reach as much of their potential height as possible. ☐ **William Jubiz**

In World Book, see Gland; Hormone.

Health Policy

Health policymakers in the United States, joined by state and federal legislators, pondered during 1987 and 1988 how to stem the spread of AIDS (acquired immune deficiency syndrome) without harming the rights of AIDS patients. Some suggested public health measures included prohibiting discrimination against AIDS victims, alerting their sexual partners, and requiring AIDS testing for couples about to be wed.

AIDS commission report. The Presidential Commission on the Human Immunodeficiency Virus Epidemic—named after the virus that causes AIDS—presented its report to President Ronald Reagan in June 1988. The 13-member commission was established in 1987 to advise the federal government on how to check the AIDS epidemic. One of the commission's recommendations was federal legislation to prohibit discrimination against AIDS victims by the private sector. The commission proposed that a law be modeled after existing laws that prohibit discrimination against the handicapped. The commission was split on the antidiscrimination proposal, with only a slim majority of 7 voting in favor of it.

The proponents of the proposal said that measures to halt the AIDS epidemic depend to a large extent

Health Policy (cont.)
on persuading individuals at risk to come forward to be tested. They argued that testing is essential to enable public health officials to determine the extent of the epidemic. It is also necessary to warn infected individuals that they are capable of infecting others through sexual transmission or by sharing needles. But when people are wary of being tested for fear that a positive result will lead to discrimination against them in obtaining jobs, housing, or health insurance—they will refuse to come forward, it was argued.

Those who opposed the measure said that it would drive up the cost of health insurance for everyone because it would require insurers to cover the costs of AIDS treatment. The costs of treating the first 10,000 AIDS patients in the United States averaged about $147,000 per patient according to a study by epidemiologist Ann Hardy of the Centers for Disease Control in Atlanta, Ga. Opponents of the proposal also argued that businesses and landlords would face liability suits if an AIDS carrier infected others on their premises.

Antidiscrimination advocates were supported by a U.S. district court decision in California in July 1988. The court ruled that an existing fed-

Parental leave
Pregnancy in the workplace is becoming common, but more than 60 per cent of working mothers do not receive paid maternity leave, according to estimates. In 1988, legislation was introduced in 26 states to require employers to grant disability leave for pregnant female employees or parental leave for male employees about to become fathers.

Health Policy (cont.)
eral law barring discrimination against the handicapped also applied to people suffering from AIDS and those who carry the AIDS virus but do not yet show symptoms of the disease. An estimated 1 million to 1.5 million Americans have been infected with the AIDS virus but do not have symptoms of the disease. Recent studies have indicated, however, that 75 per cent of those infected with the virus will develop the disease within nine years.

The California case involved a man, identified only as John Doe, who was expelled from a hospital's alcohol rehabilitation program after he tested positive for antibodies to the AIDS virus. The man sued, contending that he had been discriminated against, citing the Federal Rehabilitation Act of 1973, which was enacted to prohibit discrimination against the handicapped. The court ruled that the law's definition of the handicapped includes people who are perceived by others to be contagious and therefore includes people who carry the AIDS virus.

Disclosure of AIDS test results. The concern that discrimination will discourage people from being tested for AIDS has also spilled over into the debate over disclosing the results of AIDS tests. For example, in a report to Congress in June 1988, the Institute of Medicine, part of the National Academy of Sciences, urged a federal antidiscrimination law for AIDS victims and also recommended stiff penalties for unauthorized disclosure of test results. The institute's report opposed several state laws that require mandatory reporting of AIDS test results to public health officials.

But on June 30, the American Medical Association (AMA), an organization of physicians, concluded that the right to privacy of AIDS carriers was outweighed by the need to warn their sexual partners of the danger of exposure. AMA President James E. Davis said it was part of the physician's "professional responsibility" to alert a spouse or known sexual partner of an AIDS carrier, despite the tradition of confidentiality between doctor and patient established by the Hippocratic oath. Davis said it was the first time the AMA had taken such a position.

The AMA recommended that doctors should first encourage the carriers to inform their sexual partners and only then alert public health officials. If either of those two options failed, doctors themselves should alert people with whom the AIDS carrier had been in contact.

The AMA said it would press for legislation to require public health officials to actively seek out people who had such contact. Some states

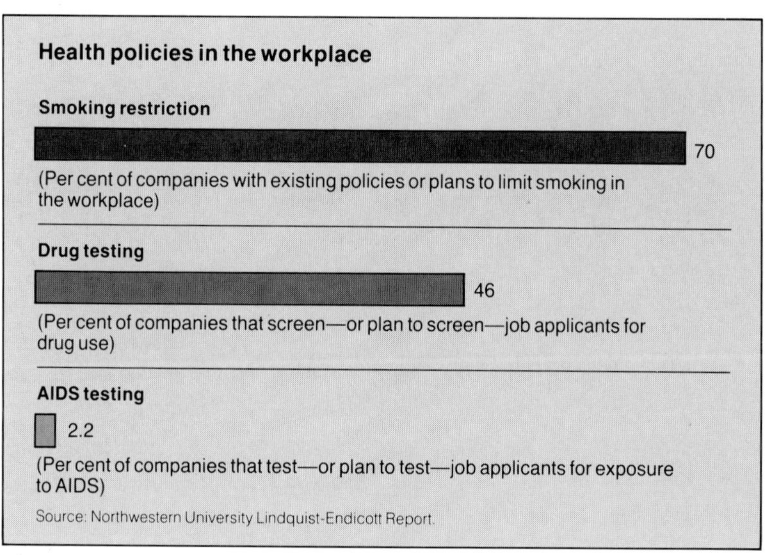

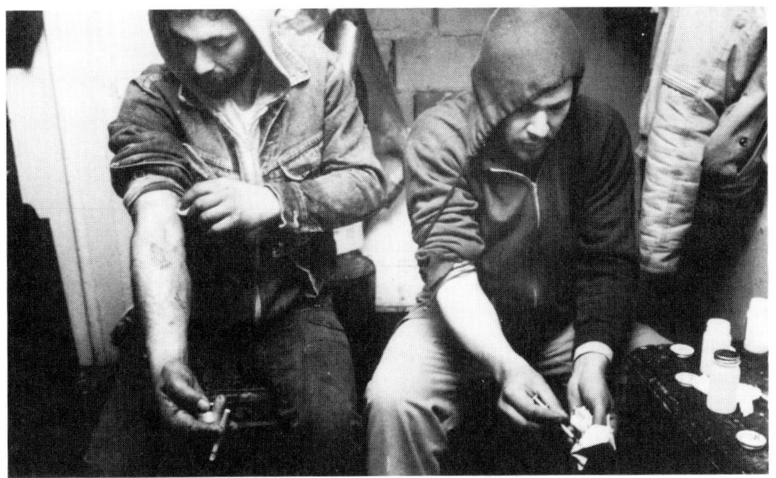

Drug addicts and AIDS
Two drug addicts in New York City prepare to inject themselves with hypodermic needles. In August 1988, New York City health officials announced a controversial plan to distribute free needles to addicts in an effort to stem the spread of AIDS (acquired immune deficiency syndrome). Many addicts have been infected by the AIDS virus due to sharing contaminated needles.

already have such efforts, known as *contact tracing* programs, and other states are considering them.

In New York, state legislators debated a bill that would require notification of contacts without divulging the identity of the AIDS carrier. The contacts would merely be notified of their exposure to the virus and the need to be tested.

Premarital screening. Other possible preventive measures also met with much debate. Two states—Illinois and Louisiana—passed laws requiring couples to be tested for AIDS before they can marry. The laws do not prohibit marriage in the event the test results are positive, but the infected person's partner is informed of the results and counseling is made available.

Critics in 1988 charged that such screening programs are a waste of time and money, diverting public health officials from helping those most at risk. "It's providing intensive, one-on-one AIDS counseling to the people who need it least," remarked Ron Sable, a physician who heads an AIDS counseling program in Chicago. ☐ Rod Such

See also AIDS. In World Book, see AIDS.

Hearing

See Ear and Hearing

Heart and Blood Vessels

Certain risk factors increase the likelihood of cardiac disorders among women who have passed through the menopause—the time of life, about age 50, when menstruation stops—according to a study published in August 1987. Generally, the rate of heart attacks among women of a given age group is about the same as the rate among men who are 10 to 20 years younger. After the menopause, however, women begin to lose this advantage. The reasons for this change have been unclear.

In the August 1987 issue of *American Heart Journal*, Boston University internist William B. Kannel reported his findings on the importance of certain risk factors for coronary heart disease in women. He based his report on the Framingham Study, which since 1948 has monitored the health of 2,873 women and 2,254 men who lived in Framingham, Mass., when the study began.

According to Kannel, the study supports the previously held idea that women have less cholesterol than men do, and that women have higher levels of the so-called "good cholesterol" or high-density lipoprotein (HDL) cholesterol. There are two main types of cholesterol—low-density lipoprotein (LDL) and HDL. The difference between the two is

A Health & Medical Annual Close-Up

Aspirin—A Role in Preventing Heart Attacks?

Aspirin, the common pain reliever found in medicine cabinets throughout the world, may be able to do more than ease a headache or reduce a fever. In January 1988, researchers at Boston's Harvard Medical School and Brigham and Women's Hospital announced evidence that aspirin can help prevent heart attacks among healthy men. Heart attacks, which are caused by the sudden blockage of one of the arteries that supply blood to the heart, kill more than 500,000 Americans every year.

But not everyone should begin taking aspirin daily. Other research, also reported in January, suggests that aspirin may cause serious health problems.

The Harvard researchers reported in *The New England Journal of Medicine* that healthy men who took aspirin every other day for more than four years reduced their risk of heart attack by 47 per cent. Although previous studies had shown that aspirin could protect heart attack survivors from a second attack, the Harvard study was the first to link aspirin to a lower incidence of heart attacks in healthy men.

The Harvard study involved 22,071 male physicians between the ages of 40 and 84. The men had no history of heart attack or stroke. Half of the men took one regular-strength buffered aspirin tablet (325 milligrams of aspirin) every other day. The rest of the men took a *placebo* (inactive substance).

The study was to end in 1990, but the preliminary results were so dramatic that the researchers halted the test in December 1987. They found that the aspirin-taking physicians experienced 5 fatal heart attacks and 99 nonfatal attacks, while the placebo-taking physicians suffered 18 fatal heart attacks and 171 nonfatal attacks.

Scientists have known for some time about the versatility of aspirin. This drug inhibits cells from releasing *prostaglandins*, powerful chemicals that cause inflammation and fever.

During the 1950's, scientists became aware that aspirin also inhibits the action of a substance called *thromboxane*. This chemical is secreted by *platelets*, disk-shaped cell fragments in the blood that play a vital role in the clotting process. Thromboxane causes platelets to clump together to form blood clots.

Clotting is one of the body's defense mechanisms. If a blood vessel ruptures, for example, platelets form clots that seal the wound and prevent excessive blood loss. But in people who suffer from *coronary artery disease*, blood clots can be dangerous. In these people, the inner walls of the arteries that nourish the heart have been narrowed by fatty deposits. If a blood clot blocks such an artery, it can cause a heart attack.

Despite the encouraging results of the research, Charles Hennekens, associate professor of medicine at Harvard Medical School who headed the study, warned that not everyone should take an aspirin every day or every other day. One reason for the warning is that the men who participated in the study were in excellent health and had been screened to make sure they did not have any condition that might be aggravated by aspirin. In some people, aspirin causes stomach upset and bleeding ulcers. Also, taking too much aspirin can cause liver and kidney problems.

An even stronger reason for

A packet of protection?

being cautious about a regimen of aspirin-taking is that the Harvard study noted a small increase in the incidence of *hemorrhagic strokes* among the aspirin-taking physicians. (Hemorrhagic strokes result from bleeding in the brain.) Although the physicians took a low dose of aspirin, it seemed to interfere with the formation of blood clots that would have sealed leaking blood vessels in the brains of the stroke victims.

A similar increase in strokes was noticed in a six-year study by researchers at Oxford University in England. This study, which was reported in *The British Medical Journal*, also in January 1988, involved 5,139 male physicians. Half of these men took 500 milligrams of aspirin per day while the rest took a placebo. Not only did the British researchers find an increase in the number of strokes but they found no evidence that aspirin reduced the number of heart attacks.

Medical experts concluded that an aspirin every other day may help men who are at high risk of suffering heart attacks—such as those who have coronary artery disease—but that regular use of the drug requires a doctor's supervision. For people who are at low risk of heart attack, regular doses of aspirin may do more harm than good.

The experts also emphasized that aspirin does not prevent or cure heart disease. Most doctors agree that the best way to cut the risk of heart attack is to stop smoking; eat a low-fat, low-cholesterol diet; and reduce high blood pressure. □ Mary A. Krier

Heart and Blood Vessels (cont.)
not in the cholesterol itself, but rather in the molecules that carry cholesterol in the bloodstream. LDL, so-called "bad cholesterol," deposits itself in cells, including cells in the walls of the arteries.

LDL deposits in the arteries promote the development of *atherosclerosis*, a build-up of *plaque*—a substance containing cholesterol, calcium, waste products from cells, and a network of fibers. When a build-up of plaque—or a blood clot that forms on the plaque—blocks an artery supplying blood to the heart muscle, a heart attack occurs.

HDL, on the other hand, does not deposit itself in plaque. In fact, HDL helps to remove cholesterol that has been deposited in cells.

Other major conclusions reported in Kannel's article:

- The risk of heart attack in women doubles at menopause.
- The presence of diabetes increases women's risk of heart attack, equalizing the rates of heart attack among men and women of any age group.
- Smoking reverses the advantage of women over men—that is, women who smoke have heart attacks as often as do nonsmoking men who are 10 to 20 years *older*.
- Whether or not women take birth control pills seems to have no influence on the risk of coronary heart disease, except among women who smoke. A woman who takes such pills and smokes has a higher risk.

Dissolving blood clots. During a heart attack, heart tissue dies unless blood flow to the tissue is restored within a short period of time. In the mid-1980's, cardiologists began to use the drug streptokinase to dissolve blood clots and restore blood flow in the coronary arteries of heart attack victims. At that time, there was evidence that restoring blood flow within a few hours resulted in less damage to the heart. Cardiologists did not know, however, whether this reduction in damage decreased the death rate due to heart attacks.

Heart and Blood Vessels (cont.)

In the November 1987 issue of the *Journal of American College of Cardiology*, researchers in the Italian Group for the Study of Streptokinase in Infarct (GISSI) reported that such a reduction in damage does reduce this death rate. (An infarct is an area of tissue that has died because of an obstruction of its blood supply.) The GISSI researchers studied 11,000 heart attack patients treated in Italy.

One randomly selected group of patients received streptokinase intravenously, while the remaining patients received ordinary care. At the end of one month, the death rate of the patients who had received streptokinase was 16 per cent lower than that of the group receiving ordinary care. At the end of one year, the death rate of the streptokinase group was 10 per cent lower than that of the conventional-therapy group. In the first few months after the first heart attack, however, the risk of another heart attack was twice as high in the streptokinase-treated group as it was in the conventional-therapy group.

To reduce the frequency of second heart attacks, surgeons perform by-pass operations or open narrowed coronary arteries with *balloon angioplasty*. In the balloon technique, a thin tube that has a deflated balloon mounted on its tip is fed into a blocked artery. The doctor then inflates the balloon to squeeze the built-up plaque against the wall of the artery. In mid-1988, researchers were conducting studies to determine whether balloon angioplasty is more effective than by-pass surgery in the treatment of heart attack survivors.

Another clot dissolver. In November 1987, the FDA approved the use of a human protein called *tissue plasminogen activator* (t-PA) to treat severe heart attacks. This protein triggers a chemical chain reaction that dissolves clots. Genentech, Incorporated, of South San Francisco uses genetic engineering techniques to make large quantities of t-PA. In this procedure, technicians insert a gene for t-PA into the genes of cells in laboratory cultures that ordinarily would not produce t-PA. The cells multiply rapidly, with each cell acting as a "factory" to produce t-PA.

Researchers at the Mayo Clinic in Rochester, Minn., reported in June 1987 that t-PA dissolved the clots of heart attack victims better than did streptokinase. The investigators gave either t-PA or streptokinase to each of 290 patients less than seven hours after the patient began to suffer a heart attack. Ninety minutes after administering the substance, the Mayo researchers took

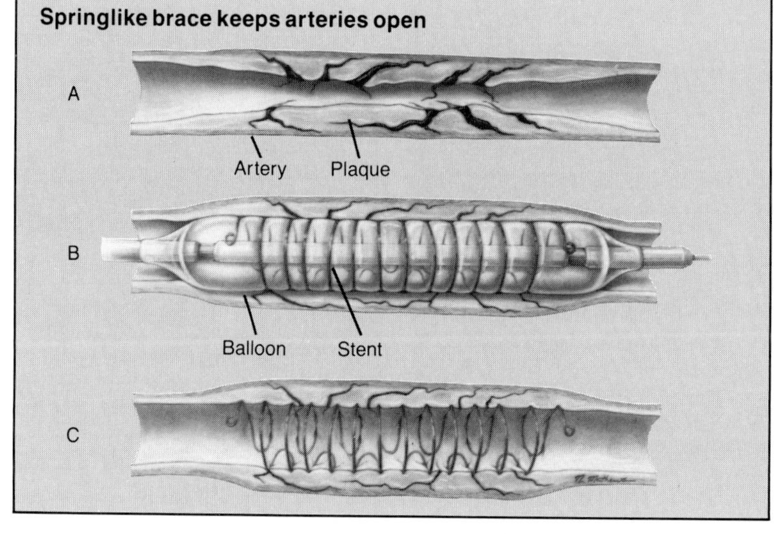

An artery serving the heart that has been partially blocked by *plaque*—a substance containing cholesterol—(A) can be held open by a *stent,* an experimental springlike brace. Surgeons guide the stent, which is mounted on a deflated balloon, to an area of plaque build-up; inflate the balloon, expanding the stent (B); and deflate and remove the balloon, leaving the expanded stent in position (C).

Smoke damage reported
By smoking, women increase their risk of heart disease, according to a November 1987 report on the health of more than 119,000 female nurses. The report left little doubt that smoking is the main cause of coronary heart disease in young and middle-aged women.

Heart and Blood Vessels (cont.)
X-ray pictures of the patient's coronary arteries.

The X-rays showed that, in the t-PA group, 62 per cent of the arteries supplying damaged areas of the heart were open. In the streptokinase group, only 31 per cent of such arteries were open.

Smoking and heart attacks. There is a strong link between smoking and heart attacks among women, according to an article in the Nov. 19, 1987, issue of *The New England Journal of Medicine*. Previous studies have shown that smoking is one of the more important heart disease risk factors in men. Recent evidence suggests that smoking makes blood form clots more readily where atherosclerosis has narrowed the blood channels of arteries.

The article in *The New England Journal* reported on the risks of coronary heart disease among women in the Nurses Health Study, an investigation of the health of more than 119,000 female nurses in the United States. The women were aged 30 to 55 when the study began in 1976. Medical personnel monitored the women's health for up to six years. Some 30 per cent of the women smoked.

The study found that the nurses who smoked more than 25 cigarettes per day had five to six times the risk of death or heart attack as the nurses who did not smoke. Among nurses who smoked more than 45 cigarettes a day, the risk was 10 times as great as for the nonsmokers.

There appeared to be no safe level of cigarette smoking. Individuals who smoked as few as 1 to 4 cigarettes per day had 2½ times the risk that nonsmokers had.

Smoking appeared to account for about half the heart attacks and deaths among the nurses. Furthermore, other risk factors such as diabetes and high levels of cholesterol multiplied the risk.

The Nurses Health Study left little doubt that smoking is the main cause of coronary heart disease among young and middle-aged women. The risk declines, however, in women who quit smoking. In fact, former smokers in the study had no increased risk.

Anticholesterol drug. A new drug called *gemfibrozil* lowered the level of cholesterol in the blood of a group of men, and thereby improved the health of their hearts, according to a November 1987 report by researchers in Finland. Several other studies, involving a total of more than 46,000 volunteers have established a link between the lowering of the cholesterol level and a decrease in heart disease. The combination of a prudent diet, exercise, and weight loss lowers the

Cholesterol levels and recommendations

Total blood cholesterol, milligrams per *deciliter* (100 milliliters) of blood	Recommendations
Desirable Less than 200	Check cholesterol every five years.
Borderline high 200 through 239 without risk factors*	Restrict total fat, saturated fats, and cholesterol in diet. Check cholesterol annually.
with risk factors*†	Check level of low density lipoprotein ("bad") cholesterol—usually follow with a strict diet, then perhaps drug therapy.
High 240 or above	

*Risk factors include family history of premature coronary heart disease, cigarette smoking, high blood pressure, low level of high density lipoprotein ("good") cholesterol, diabetes, history of stroke or blockage of blood vessels, and severe obesity.

†Recommendations are for men who have at least one risk factor, women with two or more risk factors, and men and women who have had coronary heart disease.

Source: National Heart, Lung and Blood Institute.

Recommendations issued in October 1987 by a government-sponsored panel call for physicians to monitor the cholesterol level of all United States adults and to treat people whose levels put them at high risk for heart disease.

Heart and Blood Vessels (cont.)
cholesterol level in most patients who have moderately high levels. The National Institutes of Health in Bethesda, Md., rates cholesterol levels as follows: less than 200 milligrams (mg) of all types of cholesterol per deciliter (dl, or 100 milliliters) of blood, *desirable*; 200 to 239 mg/dl, *borderline high*; and 240 or more mg/dl, *high*.

Individuals with high levels frequently need drug therapy. Unpleasant side effects such as constipation and abdominal bloating have limited the popularity of most drugs that lower patients' levels of cholesterol, however.

The Finnish researchers tested gemfibrozil in a study involving more than 4,000 men between the ages of 40 and 55. The men had high levels of cholesterol but no history of heart disease. Half the men were given gemfibrozil capsules twice a day for five years. The other half received a *placebo*, an inactive capsule resembling the gemfibrozil capsule. To prevent bias in evaluating the results of the study, neither the volunteers nor the researchers who gave out the capsules knew who received the drug.

Gemfibrozil lowered the total amount of blood cholesterol by 11 per cent and increased the level of HDL cholesterol by 14 per cent. Furthermore, the individuals who received the drug had 34 per cent less coronary heart disease than did the men who took the placebo. In addition, adverse side effects occurred much less frequently among the patients taking gemfibrozil than among patients who take other anti-cholesterol drugs.

☐ Michael H. Crawford

In the Special Reports section, see REDUCING THE RISK OF HEART DISEASE. In WORLD BOOK, see ARTERIOSCLEROSIS; CHOLESTEROL; HEART; HEART ATTACK.

Hospitals

Admissions to U.S. hospitals declined in 1987 by 0.6 per cent to 33.6 million, though this was less of a drop than the 1986 decline of 2.1 per cent. Outpatient visits continued to increase, rising 5.8 per cent in 1987 to 278.9 million visits.

Hospital *revenue margins*—the amount of revenue after deducting for expenses—shrank in 1987. Although net patient revenue rose 9.9 per cent, *net patient margin*—the excess of revenue over expenses for patient care services—sank to 0.1 per cent. Overall revenue margins were 4.7 per cent in 1987, down from 5.1 per cent in 1986.

Some areas of the United States felt the pinch more than others. Hospitals in the New England, Middle Atlantic, and West North Central regions reported net patient margin losses of 1.6, 2.8, and 0.8 per cent, respectively, and the slimmest overall revenue margins of 3.0, 2.1, and 4.7 per cent, respectively.

Hospital closings continued in 1987. A total of 79 community hospitals in 30 states shut their doors in 1987, the largest number ever recorded in a single year. In addition, 17 specialty hospitals in 13 states closed. Of the community facilities, 39 were in urban areas, and 40 were in rural areas. It was the first time that rural closures outnum-

Hospitals (cont.)
bered urban ones. Texas had the largest number of closings with 16, which may have reflected that state's overall troubled economy.

A survey conducted by the Chicago-based American College of Healthcare Executives in 1987 predicted another 700 hospital closings by 1995. A survey released in June 1988 by the accounting firm Touche Ross & Company found that nearly half of the 1,419 hospital administrators surveyed feared their hospitals were in danger of closing within five years because of declining revenue.

Hospital occupancy rates—the percentage of occupied beds—edged up in 1987, despite the decline in admissions. The increase to 64.2 per cent from 63.4 per cent in 1986, according to the American Hospital Association, was due to a decline in the number of hospital beds available, combined with a slight increase in the average length of a hospital stay. Some hospitals were overcrowded. Public hospitals in some cities reported record high use, notably by uninsured patients.

The most spectacular problem came during the winter of 1987-1988, when all hospitals in New York City, both public and private, averaged 95 per cent occupancy. Many hospitals were totally filled, causing long waits for admission.

The reasons for the sudden increase—after several years of declining occupancy—included the growing incidence of AIDS (acquired immune deficiency syndrome); increasing use of *crack*, a form of cocaine that produces severe physical and mental problems; the recent reductions in hospital beds in the city; and an increase in psychiatric admissions, with longer stays. Conditions had eased slightly by the summer of 1988, but the situation was still at a crisis point, especially in the area of psychiatric care.

Tax-exempt status. Federal, state, and local governments experienced mixed results as they moved to curtail the tax-exempt status of nonprofit hospitals. An effort to tax the property of a hospital in Vermont led to a court fight, which the hospital won, but voters in Utah approved a state referendum to take away the tax-exempt status of nonprofit hospitals. Three Pittsburgh, Pa., hospitals agreed to pay the city for municipal services, and nine hospitals in Tennessee fought tax assessments.

Congress studied the tax-exempt status of hospitals that have diversified into nonhealth activities, such as travel agencies, to determine if this may pose unfair competition for small businesses that do not enjoy tax exemption. Congressmen Fortney H. (Pete) Stark (D., Calif.) and J. J. (Jake) Pickle (D., Tex.) of the House Ways and Means Committee

AIDS hospital closes
An AIDS patient hospitalized at the Institute for Immunological Disorders in Houston—the first and only hospital devoted exclusively to treating AIDS—holds a letter informing him of the institute's plans to close. The hospital shut down in December 1987, after losing $8 million in 14 months of operation.

The cost of hospital care in the United States varies widely from city to city. California has the largest share of the 15 most expensive cities.

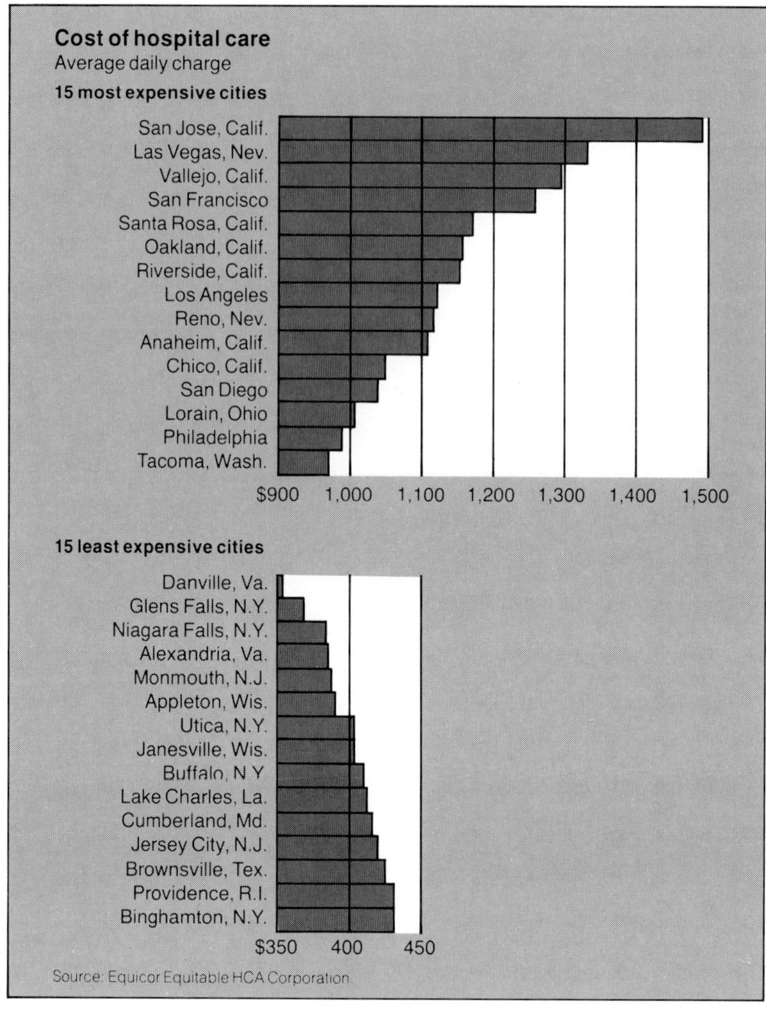

Hospitals (cont.)
proposed that hospitals "earn" their tax exemptions through specific charitable activities.

Dumping patients. The Department of Health and Human Services (HHS) was accused of being slow in issuing specific regulations against *dumping*—refusing emergency treatment to patients who cannot pay—after Congress had banned the practice in August 1986. Congressman Ted Weiss (D., N.Y.) of the House Government Operations Committee accused the HHS of neglecting the issue. The HHS finally issued regulations in June 1988, requiring hospitals with emergency rooms to examine and stabilize all patients seeking treatment, regardless of their ability to pay. The HHS rules provide for the suspension of Medicare payments and large fines if hospitals fail to comply.

On the state level, California passed an antidumping law in September 1987. Similar legislation was proposed in many other states.

The quality of care provided by hospitals continued to be a hot issue. Debate over how to measure quality was fueled in December 1987 by the HHS's second annual release of data on death rates in 6,000 hospitals. Consumer groups applauded the release of the information, but hospitals and doctors

Hospitals (cont.)
expressed skepticism about the usefulness of the data, especially because the data provided no information on the relative severity of illness among patients.

Nursing shortage. The hospital nursing shortage grew worse during 1987 and 1988. By mid-1988, the HHS reported that 75 per cent of hospitals had job vacancies for nurses, with a total of 121,000 registered nurses needed. The shortage was sparked by greater demand for nursing care, rather than a decline in the number of qualified nurses.

Nursing problems seemed to be the tip of an iceberg of labor shortages in many health care jobs, ranging from physical therapy to home health care. As the generous supply of postwar "baby boom" workers continues to shrink, the labor shortage is expected to grow worse, especially in health care.

One ray of light in the glum hospital scene was that private philanthropy to hospitals increased by 26 per cent in 1987 to $2.7 billion.

□ Emily Ann Friedman

See also FINANCING MEDICAL CARE. In WORLD BOOK, see HOSPITAL.

Infectious Diseases

A discovery that may lead to more effective treatment of an infectious disease commonly associated with AIDS (acquired immune deficiency syndrome) was reported in May 1988. The infection, which is caused by a bacterium called *Mycobacterium avium*, is rare in healthy people but is one of the leading causes of death among patients with severe immune deficiency. Medical researchers Luis Bermudez and Lowell Young of Pacific Presbyterian Medical Center in San Francisco reported that a hormonelike substance called *tumor necrosis factor* stimulated cells infected with *M. avium* to kill the bacteria. Treatment with tumor necrosis factor may thus be helpful to AIDS patients infected with *M. avium*.

AIDS-related deaths are most commonly the result of widespread infection with microorganisms such as *M. avium*. From 35 to 45 per cent of AIDS patients are infected with *M. avium*, and approximately 15 per cent die of the infection. One of the puzzling things about the disease is why it kills so many AIDS patients. In the United States, *M. avium* kills more AIDS patients than tuberculosis, a similar but usually far more common bacterial infection.

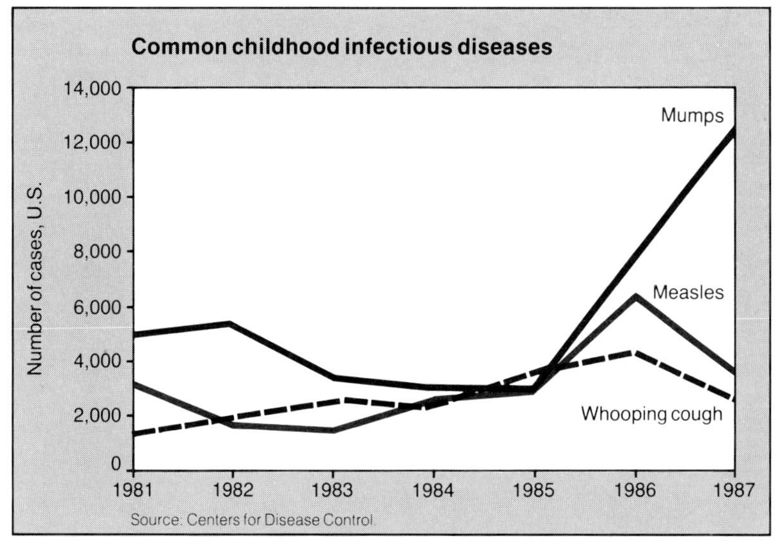

Although vaccines for many childhood diseases are readily available, measles, mumps, and whooping cough still afflict the unvaccinated children in the United States. The incidence of these diseases generally follows a cyclic pattern, with outbreaks followed by a few years of little activity.

A Health & Medical Annual Close-Up

Is Rheumatic Fever Making a Comeback?

Physicians in 1988 were concerned that rheumatic fever may be making a comeback. Rheumatic fever had been called the "vanishing disease" because it virtually disappeared from the United States during the 1960's and 1970's. But the disease suddenly reappeared in 1984 in several American cities, and an increasing number of cases have occurred every year.

Rheumatic fever primarily strikes children between the ages of 5 and 15 years. The most serious outcome of the disease is permanent damage to the heart that can lead to heart failure and death.

Rheumatic fever develops in people who have been infected by a strain of bacteria called *group A streptococcus*, which can be transmitted in airborne particles. These bacteria cause an infection known as *strep throat*, which can lead to rheumatic fever if left untreated. Not everyone who becomes ill with strep throat, however, develops rheumatic fever. In fact, one of the many puzzles surrounding the disease is that only about 3 per cent of those with untreated cases of strep throat develop rheumatic fever.

In 1980, rheumatic fever struck fewer than 1 out of 100,000 people in the United States. In the 1940's, rheumatic fever was one of the most common diseases in the United States, with as many as 338 cases per 100,000 reported at some Army bases during World War II. By the 1980's, the number of cases had declined drastically.

From mid-1984 to the end of 1986, however, physicians reported outbreaks of rheumatic fever in Akron and Columbus, Ohio; Pittsburgh, Pa.; and Salt Lake City, Utah. Another outbreak was reported in 1987 at the U.S. Naval Training Center in San Diego where 10 recruits came down with the disease between Dec. 15, 1986, and July 15, 1987.

The symptoms of rheumatic fever begin from one to four weeks after a strep throat infection. The most common symptoms are a slight fever, loss of appetite, fatigue, chest pain, and a painful, red swelling of elbow, wrist, and knee joints. Sometimes, a skin rash of distinctive red circles appears, or *nodules* (lumps) appear under the skin of the knees and knuckles.

Although the harm to joints is not permanent, the disease can scar heart valves permanently. Rheumatic fever can also lead to fatal congestive heart failure years after the original illness, as blood flow becomes progressively poorer and fluid accumulates in heart muscle. Except in the most severe cases, one attack of rheumatic fever will not lead to lasting heart damage, but additional attacks may do so.

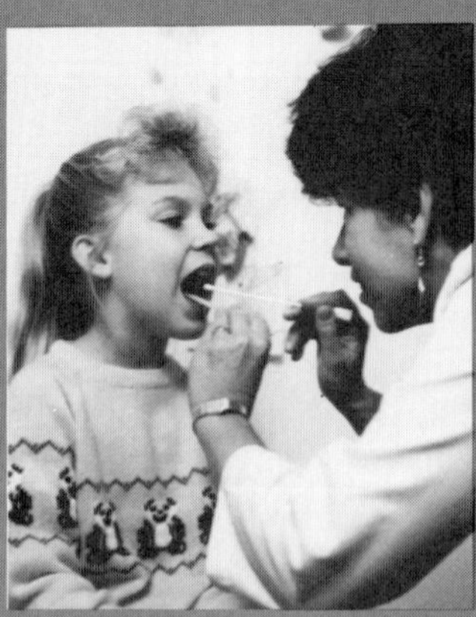

Checking for infection

Most of the deaths that occur as a result of rheumatic fever are due to this long-term damage to the heart. In 1985, about 6,600 adult Americans died of rheumatic heart disease developed in childhood, according to the American Heart Association.

Scientists are unsure how streptococci cause the heart damage and joint inflammation associated with rheumatic fever. The bacteria are incapable of causing this damage directly because once in the body, they remain in the upper respiratory tract. The most widely accepted theory is that antibodies produced by the body's disease-fighting immune system to attack streptococci also attack cells in the heart, joints, and other tissues. These antibodies recognize certain molecules called *antigens* carried by streptococci. Apparently, these streptococci antigens are similar to antigens found on cells in the heart, joints, and other tissues, so the antibodies attack cells with these antigens as well.

Heart damage, however, need not occur if the disease is properly diagnosed and the patient follows the treatment prescribed by a physician. Mild cases of rheumatic fever call for a few weeks of bed rest until tests show the illness has subsided. More severe cases are treated in the hospital. The doctor prescribes high doses of aspirin to reduce the painful inflammation of the joints. Most important, persons with rheumatic fever must take a full treatment of antibiotics, usually given orally for 10 days.

Medical experts are uncertain whether the recent outbreaks of rheumatic fever herald a return of the disease. The reported cases may prove to be isolated incidents.

No one is sure why the disease went into a decline in the first place. Some scientists have proposed that there are different strains of the streptococcus bacteria that vary in their ability to initiate rheumatic fever. When the disease went into a decline, there may have been a mild strain that was less harmful. According to this theory, the most recent cases were caused by a new strain of streptococcus that is particularly harmful.

Most medical experts believe that the best protection against rheumatic fever is early detection and treatment of strep throat infections. But because so few people with strep throat develop rheumatic fever, researchers are working on ways to improve the diagnosis of the illness and prevent its occurrence. In 1985, immunologist John B. Zabriskie of Rockefeller University in New York City reported that he identified 92 per cent of all rheumatic fever patients in a small group with a test using *monoclonal antibodies*—immune-system compounds that are genetically engineered in a laboratory. This test may also help identify people who are prone to developing rheumatic fever. Those people could then be alerted to seek medical attention immediately if a strep infection is suspected. ☐ Chris Anne Raymond

Infectious Diseases (cont.)

Scientists think that infection with *M. avium*—and other bacteria—may cause patients who have been exposed to the AIDS virus to develop symptoms of AIDS more rapidly. No one is certain why this should be so, but a possible explanation may be tied to how the human immune system responds to chronic stimulation by infectious agents.

Medical researcher John Lowenthal of Duke University in Durham, N.C., reported in April 1988 that the same factors that cause the body to produce an important immune-system substance in response to infection also stimulate a type of AIDS virus to reproduce. Thus, a bacterial infection could activate both the immune system and the dormant AIDS virus in an infected individual.

Many medical experts recommend that physicians routinely test for bacterial infection in individuals who have AIDS-related complex (the illness that often signals the onset of AIDS) or who have tested positive for the AIDS virus. If a bacterial infection is found, the physicians can quickly prescribe antibiotic treatment to kill the bacteria. Unfortunately, many of the strains of *M. avium* are difficult to eradicate.

Part of the problem of treating *M. avium* is that the organism infects and multiplies inside immune-system cells known as *macrophages*, which usually ingest and destroy bacteria but have difficulty destroying *M. avium*. Bermudez and Young showed that tumor necrosis factor can stimulate macrophages to kill the *M. avium* harbored inside them. Exploring this and other ways to stimulate the macrophages in infected patients may lead to finding better ways to fight the infection and prolong the lives of people exposed to the AIDS virus.

New childhood vaccine. A new vaccine against one of the most deadly bacterial infections afflicting children was successfully tested in late 1987 and approved by the U.S. Food and Drug Administration in early 1988. The new vaccine is safe for use in children as young as 18 months old to ward off infection by

Testing a malaria vaccine
Medical researcher W. Ripley Ballou of the Walter Reed Army Institute of Research in Washington, D.C., allows malaria-infected mosquitoes to bite his arm as part of a test of a new malaria vaccine developed by Ballou and others. Tests in human volunteers completed in late 1987 showed that the vaccine may be effective.

Infectious Diseases (cont.)

Hemophilus influenza type B (HIB), which can cause sore throat, earache, pneumonia, and *bacterial meningitis*, a potentially fatal inflammation of the membranes covering the brain and spinal cord.

Another version of the vaccine has been available for years, but it is not safe and effective in children under 2 years old—the age group most susceptible to HIB infection. The U.S. Centers for Disease Control in Atlanta, Ga., recommended that all children be given the new vaccine at 18 months of age.

Children between 2 and 5 who are at high risk of contracting HIB and who never received the previously available vaccine should also be immunized. Attendance at a day-care center is considered a risk factor for HIB, because close contact with other children increases the likelihood of being exposed to the bacterium.

Malaria vaccine update. Several groups of medical researchers reported progress in the search for a vaccine for malaria, a parasitic disease common in parts of Asia, Africa, and Latin America. Malaria is caused by *protozoans* (microscopic, one-celled animals) called *Plasmodia* and is spread from person to person by mosquitoes.

Testing of malaria vaccines developed in the United States and in Colombia produced optimistic results in late 1987. One group of scientists led by medical researcher W. Ripley Ballou of the Walter Reed Army Institute of Research in Washington, D.C., tested various doses of their malaria vaccine—the first genetically engineered vaccine ever given to human beings—in 15 subjects. After receiving the vaccine, the subjects were bitten by *Plasmodia*-infected mosquitoes. The three subjects who were given the highest doses of vaccine were completely or partially prevented from developing the disease.

A second group of researchers at the University of Maryland Center for Vaccine Development in Baltimore tested various doses of a similar vaccine on 35 subjects. Again, the three people who received the highest doses were to some degree protected from malaria.

A third vaccine, developed over several years by a research team at the Institute of Immunology at the Hospital San Juan de Dios in Bogotá, Colombia, was tested on 13 volunteers. All subjects contracted malaria after being injected with *Plasmodia*, but because those given the vaccine developed milder-than-normal cases of malaria researchers are optimistic about the usefulness of this vaccine as well.

No relief for colds. Antihistamines—drugs commonly used to relieve the symptoms of hay fever and

Infectious Diseases (cont.)
some other allergies—are of no use in treating the common cold. This finding was reported by a panel of researchers at a symposium sponsored by the Children's Hospital of Pittsburgh, Pa., in early 1988.

Many doctors prescribe antihistamines to relieve nasal congestion and other symptoms of the common cold, and most nonprescription cold medicines also contain antihistamines. But Frederick G. Hayden, an *internist* and *pathologist* (expert in the internal organs and the study of diseases) at the University of Virginia in Charlottesville, found no differences in the symptoms of 119 cold patients who were given antihistamines and 115 patients who received no medication.

William J. Doyle, an *otolaryngologist* (expert in diseases of the ear, nose, and throat) conducted a similar experiment on 40 cold patients. While those given antihistamines reported that some symptoms improved slightly, this group experienced more drowsiness than those who were given no medication.

☐ Edward P. Cohen

In WORLD BOOK, see BACTERIA; DISEASE; MALARIA.

Injury

See Emergency Medicine; Safety

Kidney

Researcher Guy Laurent of the Artificial Kidney Center of Tassin, France, reported in March 1988 on the relationship between *hemodialysis*, the filtration of waste materials from the blood by a device called a dialysis machine, and a disorder known as *carpal tunnel syndrome*. This disorder occurs when a ligament that extends across the hand becomes swollen and compresses the median nerve, which serves the first three fingers. Symptoms include numbness or pain in the wrist and hand.

Several conditions can cause carpal tunnel syndrome. Laurent's work suggests, however, that patients who undergo hemodialysis are at risk for the condition.

One effect of hemodialysis is the accumulation of a waste product called *amyloid* in bones throughout the body and in tissues located at the joints. Amyloid is composed of a protein called *beta-2 microglobulin*. Build-up of amyloid in bone can lead to fractures and arthritis; an accumulation of amyloid in the lining of the carpal tunnel (the space containing the median nerve) can bring on carpal tunnel syndrome.

Laurent found that 48 of 68 hemodialysis patients, or 71 per cent, who had surgery for carpal tunnel syndrome had amyloid deposits. By contrast, amyloid deposits occur in less than 10 per cent of patients with the syndrome and normal kidney function.

Some authorities suspect that the rate of accumulation of amyloid in bones and tissues may depend upon the filter material used in the dialysis machine. For example, the levels of amyloid are higher in patients dialyzed with filters made of a substance called *cuprophane*, than in individuals dialyzed with filters made of more *biocompatible* materials. (A biocompatible material has very few undesirable effects on living tissue.)

Hemodialysis and bone disease. One common complication experienced by patients with chronic kidney failure is a bone disorder called *renal osteodystrophy*. Until the early 1980's, *nephrologists* (kidney specialists) thought the condition was solely caused by hormonal and metabolic changes resulting from the failing kidney. Now, however, researchers have evidence that one change in bone—a softening of the bones called *osteomalacia*—may be due to the accumulation of aluminum in the bodies of chronic hemodialysis patients. Nephrologist M. W. Turner of McGill University in Montreal, Canada, reported in January 1988 that a build-up of aluminum in the bones caused osteomalacia in 25 per cent of 59 hemodialysis patients who had undergone bone biopsies.

Kidney (cont.)

Since the early 1980's, nephrologists have become increasingly aware that chronic exposure of hemodialysis patients to aluminum can interfere with the normal process of bone formation, in which calcium is deposited in bones. As a result, such patients develop osteomalacia.

The main source of the aluminum is an aluminum-containing *phosphate binder*, a drug that hemodialysis patients take to bind phosphorus chemically so that the phosphorus can be excreted in the feces. Because elevated phosphorus levels in the blood can contribute to bone disease in kidney patients, such patients take phosphate binders to remove phosphorus from the body.

In addition to bone loss, an accumulation of aluminum also can cause disease in other parts of the body, including the blood and the brain. To prevent aluminum-induced disorders from worsening, nephrologists are discontinuing the use of phosphate binders containing aluminum, and instead prescribe equally effective calcium preparations.

☐ **Stephen M. Korbet**

In WORLD BOOK, see BONE; KIDNEY.

Mental and Behavioral Disorders

In addition to its devastating physical assaults, AIDS (acquired immune deficiency syndrome) has a cruel psychological component that may afflict many more AIDS patients than was previously thought, according to a May 1988 report. Neurologist Richard Price and his colleagues at Memorial Sloan-Kettering Cancer Center in New York City found that in the later stages of AIDS, many patients show numerous signs of mental deterioration, a syndrome Price and his co-workers termed *AIDS dementia complex* (ADC) in 1986. Symptoms of ADC may show up even before other signs of AIDS appear and, in some cases, may be the only sign of AIDS. Price's most recent estimate of the frequency of ADC is that 90 per cent of AIDS patients may suffer some form of the syndrome.

Many people develop depression and other emotional problems after learning they have AIDS. But unlike this normal psychological response to the realization that one has a fatal illness, ADC is the result of various infections that attack the brain and nervous system because AIDS impairs the body's disease-fighting immune system. ADC can also be caused by the AIDS virus infecting brain tissue.

Symptoms of ADC include forgetfulness, inability to concentrate, impulsiveness, and impaired decision-making abilities. Personality may also change, making the patient apathetic or moody. Psychotic behavior, including paranoia and hallucinations, may also result.

At present there is no cure for ADC, but now that physicians and caretakers of AIDS patients are aware of ADC, they can be better prepared to deal with its effects. Psychotherapy helps some patients cope with their condition, and there is hope that zidovudine, one of the drugs used to treat AIDS, may help reverse ADC's effects on the brain and nervous system.

How trustworthy is expert testimony? Psychologists and psychiatrists give expert testimony in up to 1 million legal cases every year. Their testimony is used to help judges and jurors decide whether a defendant is sane or insane, for example, and whether a defendant is likely to commit violent acts. But expert testimony may not be truly useful, according to research reported in July 1988. The new findings suggest that judgments about these matters made by professionals are no more accurate than those made by untrained people.

The researchers, psychologist David Faust of Rhode Island Hospital in Providence and Jay Ziskin, a psychologist and lawyer in Marina Del Rey, Calif., examined 1,400

Warning signs of stress and ways to cope

Symptoms of stress	How to deal with stress
Intestinal problems	Keep your sense of humor
Rapid pulse	Exercise regularly
Frequent illness	Follow a sensible diet
Insomnia	Delegate responsibility
Persistent fatigue	Limit your intake of caffeine and alcohol
Irritability	Take refuge in family and friends
Nail-biting	Stand up to the boss
Difficulty concentrating	Change jobs
Increased use of alcohol and drugs	Meditate
Hunger for sweets	Get a massage

Source: American Institute of Stress.

Mental Disorders (cont.)
studies of the accuracy of the testimony of psychologists and psychiatrists. They concluded that these experts did not agree among themselves about the current mental and emotional states of defendants and generally failed to provide trustworthy answers to difficult criminal-justice questions.

One study cited by the researchers examined the case of a group of military recruits who were kept in the United States armed services despite recommendations by psychiatrists that they be discharged due to severe psychiatric problems. Two years later, most of these military personnel were still on active duty and were considered as well adjusted as a similar group who had originally been judged free of mental-health problems.

Other experiments showed that office workers and high school students were as able as mental-health professionals to correctly diagnose brain damage and predict whether or not a person was likely to behave violently. Another study cited by the researchers found that experts' predictions of future violent behavior were incorrect at least twice as often as they were correct.

"If lay persons are as accurate as the expert or equally accurate with or without the expert's help, the expert is not needed," according to Faust and Ziskin. They concluded that "the involvement of experts wastes many hours of already too-scarce court time and costs taxpayers millions of dollars."

Suicide prevention. As difficult as predicting human behavior may be, it is still the goal of many types of behavioral research and, in the case of suicide prevention, could produce lifesaving results. Harriette Mogul, director of health services at Barnard College in New York City, reported in July 1988 that it might be possible to identify suicide-prone college students. (Suicide is the second leading cause of death—after accidents—among this age group.)

Mogul's conclusion was based on data collected from a comprehensive medical-history questionnaire completed by female college students before enrollment. She analyzed the questionnaires of students who committed suicide and compared them with those of students who did not. The comparison showed that the probability that a student would commit suicide could be predicted on the basis of such factors as drug abuse, eating disorders, emotional and sexual problems, and feelings of anxiety, inadequacy, frustration, loneliness, uncontrollable anger, and sadness.

Possible cause of schizophrenia. Stress or trauma to a developing fetus in the womb may be a cause of

Mental Disorders (cont.)

schizophrenia, a devastating mental disorder characterized by loss of contact with reality and unpredictable disturbances in thinking, feeling, and behavior. This theory was proposed by psychologist Sarnoff A. Mednick and his colleagues at the University of Southern California in Los Angeles.

Mednick studied the medical records of Finnish psychiatric patients born during the nine months after a severe influenza epidemic that struck Helsinki, Finland, in 1957. The researchers compared the incidence of schizophrenia among these patients with the incidence among patients born during the six-year period before the epidemic.

Nearly 36 per cent of the patients whose mothers were in their fourth to sixth month of pregnancy during the epidemic were diagnosed as schizophrenic by the time they were 26 years old. Only 22 per cent of the other patients were similarly diagnosed by age 26.

There is no direct evidence that the pregnant women were actually infected by the virus, Mednick said. But the researcher proposed that a risk factor for schizophrenia may be some kind of trauma to the fetus during the fourth to sixth months of pregnancy. In the case of the Fin-

Autistic child
In 1988, medical researchers found new evidence that *autism,* a severe psychological disorder characterized by an avoidance of human contact, may be caused by physical abnormalities in the brain. Their inability to make sense of what they see and hear may cause autistic people such as the boy at right to seem to withdraw into a world of daydreams.

Mental Disorders (cont.)
nish patients, the trauma might have been fever, the mother's infection with the virus, or use of over-the-counter flu medication. Any of these factors might have interfered with the fetus's developing brain.

Autism and brain dysfunction. More evidence that there is a physical cause for *autism,* a rare, severe psychiatric disorder, was published in May 1988. A group of researchers headed by Eric Courchesne, a *neuropsychologist* (expert in the psychological functions of the nervous system) at the San Diego Children's Hospital found that portions of the brains of patients with autism are underdeveloped.

The new evidence supports research conducted in the early to mid-1980's that focused attention on physical factors linked to autism instead of factors such as poor parenting. Autism has long been considered a mysterious disorder because its symptoms, which typically appear by age 3, are so unusual. Babies with autism usually dislike being held or cuddled, and autistic people are socially withdrawn, often seeming to live in a world of daydreams. They may never learn to speak and may continually repeat unusual movements such as hand fluttering or rocking back and forth.

On the basis of the newly reported work and that of researchers who earlier found other abnormalities in the nervous system of autistic people, Courchesne theorized that the brains of patients with autism may be overwhelmed by and unable to make sense of sensory stimulation. Thus, the withdrawn behavior of autistic people may be a means of coping with an environment that seems to bombard them with confusing information.

☐ Robert J. Trotter

In World Book, see Autism; Mental Illness; Schizophrenia; Suicide.

"With all I've learned about psychology recently, establishing who's naughty and who's nice is not as simple as it used to be."

Nervous System
See Brain and Nervous System

Nutrition

Eating too much of the wrong kinds of food has become a major health problem in the United States, according to a 712-page report issued on July 27, 1988, by U.S. Surgeon General C. Everett Koop. The report, the most comprehensive one ever issued by the U.S. government on nutrition and health, said that 5 of America's 10 leading causes of death—heart disease, cancer, stroke, diabetes, and *atherosclerosis* (the progressive clogging of the arteries)—have been linked to diet.

Americans are too fond of eating foods that are high in animal fats, such as red meats and dairy products, the report noted. The report recommended replacing such foods with low-fat dairy products and lean meats, fish, and poultry. It also noted that people should eat more fruits, vegetables, and whole-grain products—foods that are high in complex carbohydrates and fiber.

Salt should be used more sparingly, the report said. It also advised that people should limit alcohol intake to two drinks a day.

Vitamin B_6 and immunity. Elderly people who are more susceptible to infections may suffer from a vitamin B_6 deficiency, according to an October 1987 report by researchers at Oregon State University in Corvallis.

Nutrition (cont.)
The researchers believe that such a vitamin deficiency in the elderly may slow down or prevent their immune system from fighting off viruses and bacteria.

Scientists have long known that elderly people are more likely to become ill with infections than younger people. Many researchers suspect that this may be due to deficiencies in one or more of the nutrients vital to the immune system, such as proteins, minerals, and vitamins.

To test this theory, the Oregon researchers conducted a two-month study on the effect of vitamin B_6 supplements on the immune systems of 15 volunteers between the ages of 65 and 81. The volunteers were screened to make sure they were not suffering from any disease or disorder that might have weakened their immune system. Of the volunteers, 11 were given 50 milligrams of vitamin B_6 each day—a dose considerably larger than the U.S. Recommended Dietary Allowance of 2 milligrams per day for this vitamin. The others received a *placebo* (inactive substance).

The researchers studied the responsiveness of the volunteers' immune systems by checking the activity of their *lymphocytes*—white blood cells that are part of the im-

Demystifying food labels

Food manufacturers often make special claims about their products. Below are some common claims for meat and poultry products and what they mean according to the United States Department of Agriculture (USDA).

Natural: Meat or poultry product that is minimally processed. Contains no artificial flavors, colors, or preservatives.

Imitation: Product made to resemble or substitute for another product but does not contain the specific ingredients required for that product by the USDA.

Unsalted or no salt added: Product processed without salt. May contain other sources of sodium, however, such as monosodium glutamate.

Sodium free or salt free: Product contains 5 milligrams (mg) or less sodium per serving.

Very low sodium: Product contains 35 mg or less sodium per serving.

Low sodium: Product contains 140 mg or less sodium per serving.

Reduced sodium: Product contains 75 per cent less sodium than traditional product.

Lower or less salt or sodium: Product contains at least 25 per cent less sodium than traditional product.

Lean or low fat: Product must contain 10 per cent or less fat.

Lite, lighter, leaner, or lower fat: Product must contain 25 per cent less fat than similar products on the market.

Nutrition (cont.)

mune system. Some lymphocytes produce *antibodies*—proteins that destroy infectious organisms or render them harmless—while other lymphocytes destroy such organisms directly. The scientists added substances to blood samples taken from the volunteers—to simulate what might happen if a lymphocyte came in contact with a disease-causing organism.

The researchers found that the lymphocytes of volunteers who received the vitamin B_6 supplements, especially in those who had the lowest vitamin B_6 levels in their blood at the start of the study, showed a significantly greater response than the lymphocytes of the volunteers who were given the placebo. According to the researchers, this result indicates that vitamin B_6 supplements may improve the functioning of the immune system in the elderly.

Coffee and heart disease. The controversy over whether coffee can increase the risk for heart disease heated up in 1987 when researchers at Northwestern Medical School in Chicago reported in November that people who drink six or more cups of coffee per day are almost twice as likely to die of heart disease as people who drink less coffee. Heart disease occurs when the *coronary arteries*—the arteries that feed oxygen-rich blood to the heart muscle—become clogged with fatty deposits, leading to a heart attack or other heart problems.

To determine the relationship between coffee drinking and heart disease, the researchers studied the coffee habits and cause of death of 1,910 men between the ages of 40 and 56 who had worked for the Chicago Western Electric Company and had participated in a 20-year health study that began in 1957 and 1958. They took into account other factors that also could have increased the men's risk of developing heart disease, such as age, weight, smoking habits, levels of blood *cholesterol* (a white fatlike substance found in the blood and other body tissues), blood pressure, and alcohol intake. But even when all these factors were considered, the researchers found that the men who were heavy coffee drinkers still had a higher death rate from heart disease than the men who drank less coffee.

The researchers were not sure what caused this increased risk. They suspected that coffee may promote high levels of a type of cholesterol that is carried through the bloodstream by proteins called low-density lipoproteins (LDL). Because LDL cholesterol is deposited in cells, it is considered a major factor in heart disease. Although the link between high levels of LDL cholesterol and coffee drinking was not

Fake fat

In January 1988, the NutraSweet Company of Deerfield, Ill., unveiled Simplesse, a low-calorie fat substitute that gives food the creamy texture of fat but contains no fat or cholesterol. Made from the protein found in egg whites and skim milk, Simplesse is expected to replace fat in such foods as mayonnaise, *below*.

Nutrition (cont.)
examined by the Northwestern study, other studies provide evidence of such a link.

Lactose intolerance. People who have difficulty digesting milk or milk-based foods because of an intolerance for *lactose*, a milk sugar found in cow's milk, may benefit from eating other foods along with foods containing lactose, according to a January 1988 report from researchers at the University of Minnesota in St. Paul. Some people lack an enzyme called *lactase* that helps the body digest lactose in the intestines. When these people eat dairy products, their intestines cannot digest the lactose, resulting in cramps, gas, and diarrhea.

The researchers gave different test meals to 12 lactose-intolerant people. When the volunteers ate a nondairy meal with a food supplement containing lactose, they experienced fewer—and less severe—symptoms of intestinal distress than when they ate just the lactose supplement. ☐ Jeanine Barone

In the Special Reports section, see FIBER: A RECIPE FOR GOOD HEALTH? and REDUCING THE RISK OF HEART DISEASE. In WORLD BOOK, see NUTRITION.

Occupational Health

See Safety

Pregnancy and Childbirth

Chorionic villus sampling (CVS) is a reasonably safe method of diagnosing genetic defects in fetuses during the first weeks of pregnancy according to two studies reported in 1988. During CVS, a special tube is inserted into the uterus and a small amount of tissue is removed from the *chorionic villi*—fingerlike projections of a membrane that surrounds the fetus. The tissue is analyzed for abnormalities in the fetus's chromosomes, such as those that cause Down's syndrome.

CVS can be done as early as the 7th week of pregnancy. Results are usually available within a few days. In contrast, amniocentesis, the most commonly used method of prenatal diagnosis, is usually not performed until the 16th week of pregnancy, and the results are not available for two to four weeks.

Concerns about the safety of CVS had led the Food and Drug Administration to restrict the number of centers performing the procedure. Reports on the first study, issued in February 1988 by researchers at several institutions, including the National Institutes of Health in Bethesda, Md., indicated that only 7 of 940 women who underwent CVS suffered a miscarriage attributed to

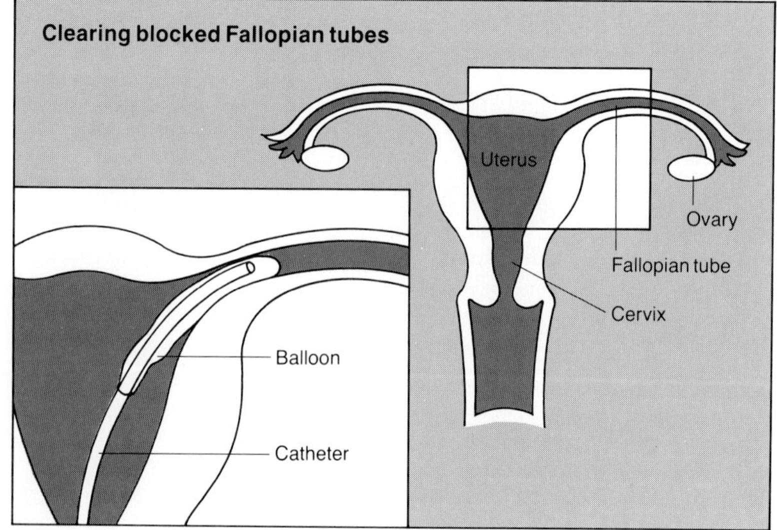

Infertility treatment
A technique developed to unclog coronary arteries is being used to open blocked Fallopian tubes, a major cause of infertility in women. In the procedure, a *catheter* (a slender tube) with a small balloon is inserted through the uterus into the blocked Fallopian tube. As the balloon is inflated, the Fallopian tube is stretched and the obstruction is dislodged and washed out.

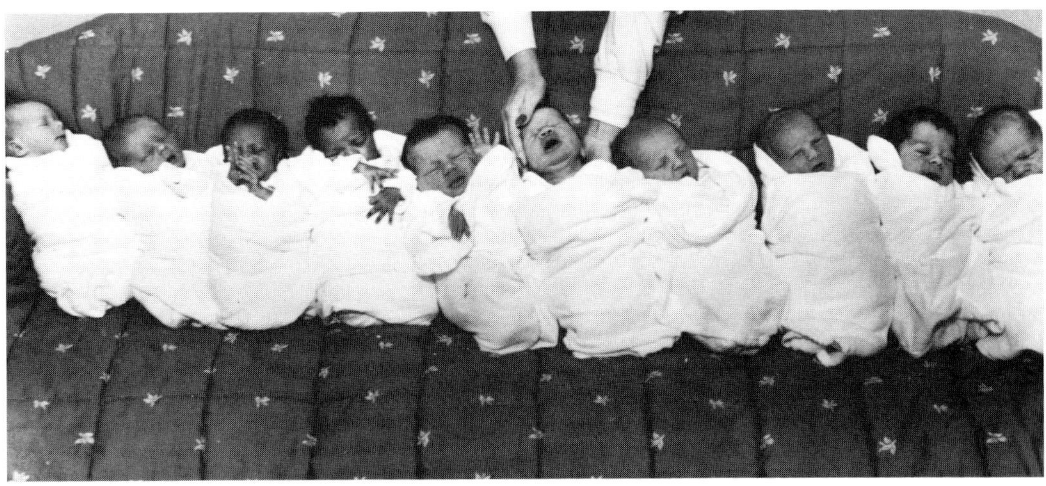

Minnesota twins
Five sets of twins, born in one 24-hour period in St. Paul, Minn., in winter 1988, make a group appearance. According to a study published in early 1988, the rate of multiple births in the United States reached 21 per 1,000 live births in 1985, the highest rate in 30 years.

Pregnancy and Childbirth (cont.)
the procedure. This miscarriage rate of 0.6 per cent was only slightly higher than the rate attributed to amniocentesis.

The second study, reported in May by researchers working under the direction of the National Institute of Child Health and Human Development in Bethesda, involved 3,000 pregnant women who underwent either CVS or amniocentesis. As in the first study, the researchers found only a slightly higher risk of miscarriage in the CVS group.

Miscarriage rate. Nearly one-third of all pregnancies end in miscarriage, according to a study published in July 1988 by a team of researchers headed by Allen Wilcox of the National Institute of Environmental Health Sciences in Research Triangle Park, N.C. The study has provided the most precise information to date on the rate of miscarriage. Estimates of the miscarriage rate have varied widely because many pregnancies end before women are aware that they are pregnant.

For their research, Wilcox and his colleagues tested the urine of 221 women who were trying to become pregnant for the presence of human chorionic gonadotropin, a hormone produced by embryos beginning about eight days after an egg is fertilized by sperm. They found that at least 31 per cent of all the pregnancies of the women in the study ended in miscarriage. They also found that 22 per cent of the women in the study who had miscarriages never had any signs of pregnancy.

Toxoplasmosis testing. Prenatal testing and prompt treatment with antibiotics of pregnant women infected with a parasite that can cause severe birth defects reduces the chances that the infected women will transmit the parasite to their unborn children. That conclusion was reported in February 1988 by a team of researchers headed by obstetrician Fernand Daffos of the Hospital of Notre Dame in Paris. The researchers also found that the antibiotic treatment reduces the severity of the problems caused by the parasite, *Toxoplasma gondii*, in infected fetuses.

Toxoplasmosis is contracted by eating the eggs of the parasite in undercooked meats or by handling the feces of cats in cat litter or when gardening. Cats are the natural host of the parasite. Fetuses infected with the disease may be born with such defects as *hydrocephalus* (excess brain fluid), blindness, or damage to the nervous system.

As many as 1 in every 1,000 babies born in the United States has toxoplasmosis. Routine screening of pregnant women for the presence of the parasite, common in France and

Pregnancy and Childbirth (cont.)
other European countries, is rarely done in the United States.

Daffos and his associates studied 746 pregnant women infected with *T. gondii*. All the mothers were treated with spiramycin, an antibiotic, throughout their pregnancy.

The researchers were able to detect 39 of the 42 fetuses who were infected by their mother. Most of the women with infected fetuses decided to end their pregnancy. The women with infected fetuses who decided to continue the pregnancy were given other antibiotics in addition to the spiramycin.

The researchers found that the percentage of fetuses who developed the infection was 70 per cent lower than expected, based on previous studies. In addition, 11 of the 15 infected fetuses were born without any physical signs of the disease. All 15 infants had normal nervous systems at birth and at age 30 months.

Caesarean sections. Ultrasound can be a valuable tool in helping obstetricians determine whether a woman who has given birth by Caesarean section can safely give birth vaginally in later pregnancies. That conclusion was reported in January 1988 by obstetrician William Michaels and colleagues at Providence Hospital in Southfield, Mich. (A Caesarean section is an operation to remove a baby from the uterus by cutting through the mother's abdominal and uterine walls.)

During labor, the uterus of women who have previously had a Caesarean section may rupture along the scar left by the incision. If this occurs, the fetus is expelled into the mother's abdominal cavity, resulting in the death of the fetus—and many times of the mother. Currently, there is no sure way of predicting which women will develop a rupture of the surgical scar.

Michaels and his colleagues studied 58 women who had undergone a Caesarean section. Using ultrasound, they examined the women's lower uterine segment—that part of the uterus that thins out as the pregnancy progresses and where the incision is made for a Caesarean section. They determined that 13 of the women had defects in the uterine wall that could cause a rupture if they tried to give birth vaginally.

When the 58 underwent Caesarean section, the researchers found thinning of the uterine wall in 12 of the 13 women diagnosed as having the problem. The remaining patient diagnosed as being abnormal had a normal uterus.

☐ Deborah Turner

In World Book, see Childbirth.

Respiratory System

Lung surgeons in 1987 and 1988 improved techniques used to transplant lungs and also to prevent the body from rejecting transplanted lungs. There are two major ways to transplant lungs—the single-lung transplant and the combined heart-lung transplant.

The first successful human lung transplant—a single-lung replacement—was performed in 1963. The patient lived for only 18 days after the operation, but this surgery showed that a transplanted lung could function normally. During the next 20 years, surgeons developed techniques to extend the lives of patients receiving a single lung.

Chest surgeon Joel D. Cooper and his colleagues in the Toronto Lung Transplant Group at the University of Toronto and Toronto General Hospital in Canada described highly successful techniques in the February 1987 *Journal of Thoracic and Cardiovascular Surgery*. The surgeons discussed five single-lung transplants that they performed during a period of about 2½ years. Four of the patients, including the first one, were still alive at the time of the report.

The physicians said that their success was due to a careful selection of patients, advanced techniques for anesthetizing patients, the use of

Oxygen with a twist
What looks like a fashionable bar is actually an oxygen counter in a Tokyo department store. For about 70 cents, a customer can buy a three-minute supply of the gas. Many Japanese say they find such an "oxygen break" refreshing.

Respiratory System (cont.)
three particular drugs to prevent rejection, and a procedure known as an *omentopexy*. This procedure solved a problem that plagued early single-lung transplants: air leaks where the transplanted lung was joined to a *bronchus* (one of the two large tubes between the windpipe and the lung). In an omentopexy, the surgeon wraps this area in a piece of the *omentum*, a tissue normally found in the abdomen.

The omentum contains many blood vessels, so it may prevent leaks by increasing the supply of blood to the bronchus. This supply is disrupted by transplant surgery.

By supplying nutrients to the bronchus, the omentum may promote the healing of the connection between the bronchus and the transplanted lung. Surgeons have found new blood vessels supplying the bronchus three or four days after a transplant operation that includes an omentopexy. The omentum also fights infections well, a capability that may help stop the spread of infection when air leaks develop.

The drugs used to prevent rejection are cyclosporine, azathioprine, and antilymphocyte globulin. Corticosteroids also are useful for this purpose, but doctors try to avoid prescribing them during the first three weeks after surgery because

Respiratory System (cont.)
they interfere with surgical healing. Typically, long-term therapy to prevent rejection calls for the use of prednisone (a corticosteroid) and cyclosporine.

Drug fights rejection. Surgeons in California reported in September 1987 on a new way to prevent the most common long-term complication of combined heart-lung transplant surgery—*bronchiolitis obliterans*. In this disorder, small air passages called *bronchioles* become inflamed and scarred. In some cases, an accumulation of mucus, fibrous material, and dead cells clogs one or more bronchioles, blocking the air flow.

Symptoms of bronchiolitis obliterans include coughing, shortness of breath, and abnormal exhalation due to obstruction. Physicians suspect that this disorder represents an attempt by the body to reject transplanted tissue.

Bronchiolitis obliterans afflicted 50 per cent of 26 long-term survivors of heart-lung transplants performed by the heart-lung transplant team at Stanford University Medical Center in Stanford, Calif. To slow the rate of decline of lung function in their heart-lung transplant patients, the team added the drug azathioprine to the standard medications cyclosporine and prednisone.

The use of azathioprine also had a secondary benefit. The California surgeons found that they could decrease the dose of cyclosporine, thereby decreasing the drug's side effects, including high blood pressure and kidney poisoning.

Marijuana smoking studied. The smoking of marijuana cigarettes increases the tendency to develop symptoms of respiratory disorders, according to an article in the Dec. 12, 1988, *British Medical Journal*. Internist John W. Bloom and his colleagues at the University of Arizona College of Medicine in Tucson reported that young male marijuana smokers could expel much less air from their lungs in certain measured periods of time than could smokers of tobacco cigarettes.

In related research, internist Henry Gong, Jr., and his co-workers at the University of California School of Medicine in Los Angeles had reported in July 1987 on respiratory damage due to smoking tobacco and marijuana. The researchers examined the windpipes, bronchi, and bronchioles of volunteers through a *bronchoscope*, a thin tube inserted into the nose and down to the lungs. This instrument contains lenses and a hair-thin strand of glass that enable researchers to view the inner surfaces of the airway.

The physicians examined the airways of nonsmokers, tobacco-only smokers, smokers of tobacco and marijuana cigarettes, and heavy smokers of marijuana. They observed that 91 per cent of all the smokers' airways were abnormal.

There were two main types of abnormality—a bright redness of the lining of the airway, and tiny craterlike pits in the surface of the lining. Biopsies of these abnormalities revealed that disorganized growths of cells were more numerous in marijuana smokers than in tobacco-only smokers and nonsmokers.

Researchers do not know how such abnormalities affect the long-term health of heavy smokers of marijuana. They are concerned, however, that the abnormalities may lead to chronic lung disease or even lung cancer.

Another team of researchers at the University of California School of Medicine in Los Angeles compared chemical effects of marijuana smoking with effects of tobacco smoking. Physicians led by Tzu-Chin Wu reported in the Feb. 11, 1988, *New England Journal of Medicine* that the smoking of marijuana causes the blood to absorb nearly five times as much carbon monoxide as is absorbed when an individual smokes a comparable amount of tobacco. And the body retains 33 per cent more tar from marijuana smoke than from tobacco smoke.

☐ **Robert A. Balk**

In World Book, see Heart; Lung; Tissue Transplant.

Safety

Transportation safety drew an unusual amount of attention in 1987 and 1988, largely because of a series of highly publicized accidents in the air and on the road. In a spectacular incident on April 28, 1988, an Aloha Airlines Boeing 737 jet lost a large section of its *fuselage* (body) while flying over Hawaii. Although the plane landed safely, 65 passengers were injured, and a stewardess died. Investigators found that the 19-year-old craft, which had made 89,193 previous flights, showed signs of metal fatigue, but they were not able to determine whether the structural problems occurred before or after the incident.

The Aloha accident spurred demands for closer inspections of older aircraft. After the incident, the Federal Aviation Administration (FAA) ordered such inspections. The FAA also prohibited airlines from flying Boeing 737's with 50,000 or more flights higher than 23,000 feet (7,000 meters), pending further inspections.

Airline crackdown. Prior to the Aloha Airlines incident, the United States government had been conducting extensive investigations into the maintenance practices of several other airlines. A principal target was Northwest Airlines, the owner of a jetliner that crashed near Detroit on Aug. 16, 1987, killing 156 people. It was the second worst air crash in U.S. history. In March 1988, the FAA accused Northwest of 139 safety violations involving crew scheduling, plane maintenance, and other matters.

Other targets were Continental Airlines and Eastern Airlines, both owned by the Texas Air Corporation. On April 13, the FAA proposed fines of approximately $823,000 against Eastern for safety violations and ordered the firm to inspect its 267 planes.

The FAA also said it feared that the company's union problems might have a negative impact on public safety. Inspections by federal authorities caused Continental to temporarily remove more than 14 per cent of its planes from service, some because of safety problems.

School bus hazard. One of America's worst highway crashes emphasized the potential hazard of outdated public school buses that are often sold to churches and other private groups. On May 14, near Carrollton, Ky., a school bus owned by the First Assembly of God Church in Radcliff, Ky., was rammed head-on by a pickup truck driving on the wrong side of the road.

Twenty-five young people and two adult chaperones were killed and 18

Portable floatable pillow
A man shows how to use the Aqua Buoy, a portable flotation device that provides assistance when needed. It consists of a wristband that contains a folded nylon pillow and a carbon dioxide cartridge. When a lever on the band is hit, the pillow inflates. Aqua Buoy U.S.A. of Pompano Beach, Fla., began marketing the device in April 1988.

A Health & Medical Annual Close-Up

Stop Sign for Off-Road Vehicles

The love affair between teenagers and motorized three-wheelers was thwarted in 1988 after a four-year controversy over safety. On April 28, United States District Court Judge Gerhard A. Gesell in Washington, D.C., approved an agreement between manufacturers and the government that banned sales of the vehicles in the United States.

The agreement, which had been announced in December 1987 by the U.S. Department of Justice, also requires manufacturers to provide information and driver training to buyers of four-wheel off-the-road vehicles. The major manufacturers are all Japanese firms.

From 1982 through 1987, nearly 1,000 people were killed and about 300,000 were injured in accidents involving all-terrain vehicles (ATV's). About half of the victims were under age 16, according to the U.S. Consumer Product Safety Commission (CPSC).

The issue began to attract government attention in 1984, as parents and consumer groups complained that the vehicles were unsafe. Critics also raised concerns about environmental issues, including motor noise and soil erosion caused by the vehicles.

By 1987, the CPSC estimated that ATV accidents were killing 20 people and injuring some 7,000 others each month. By then, casualties from ATV's were far higher than for any other consumer product, according to research provided to Congress.

CPSC engineers contended that the three-wheel design was unstable. Industry officials, however, maintained that injuries and deaths resulted from driver carelessness, not design flaws. Most of the estimated 2.5 million ATV's in use today are three-wheelers.

In December 1986, the CPSC concluded that three-wheel ATV's presented an "unreasonable" risk and should no longer be sold. The commission recommended that manufacturers set up recall and refund programs. Claiming to lack sufficient resources to pursue the case further, the CPSC asked the Justice Department to bring court action.

To the disappointment of consumer advocates, the eventual settlement made no provision for recalls or refunds. The failure to authorize refunds, which could have reached $2-billion, drew strong condemnations from state attorneys general, consumer advocates, and members of Congress who considered refunds the best way to take the vehicles off the road and thus reduce injuries. Manufacturers refused to discuss refunds with the Justice Department, according to congressional aides.

The companies began voluntarily to phase out production of three-wheelers during 1987, and sales of four-wheelers began to exceed sales of three-wheelers. Buyers of four-wheelers sign statements saying they have read warnings about vehicle use.

In addition, manufacturers are required to spend about $8.5 million on advertisements and improved labeling to warn the public of ATV hazards. They must also set up a toll-free hotline to handle consumer inquiries, a driver-training program for anyone who has bought an ATV since 1986, and printed materials for distribution to consumer groups and potential buyers. Finally, manufacturers and the CPSC are discussing setting performance standards to ensure that future ATV designs will be safe. □ Arthur E. Rowse

Regulations in 1988 restricted sales of all-terrain vehicles.

Safety (cont.)
other passengers were hospitalized with serious injuries when the bus exploded in flames, trapping many passengers inside. Police said the driver of the truck, Larry W. Mahoney, had a blood alcohol level of 0.24 per cent, more than twice Kentucky's legal limit. While recuperating in the hospital, Mahoney was charged with 27 counts of murder.

The crash focused attention on safety standards for school bus fuel tanks since investigators determined that all the fatal injuries were due to smoke and fumes caused by the fire. The bus had been built before 1977 federal regulations went into effect requiring that fuel tanks be wrapped in crash-resistant steel cages and fuel lines be made of metal rather than rubber. Investigators, however, did not conclude that such improvements would have prevented the deaths that occurred in this accident. Even so, many school districts around the United States looked into their own situations and found that they were still using buses that did not meet the 1977 standards.

Airbags. A 20-year-old struggle between auto manufacturers and safety advocates over the installation of airbags underwent a dramatic change in 1988, when the Chrysler Corporation announced that it would make airbags standard equipment on all cars built in the United States by 1990. Chrysler's program began on May 15, 1988, with the installation of airbags on the driver's side of the Chrysler LeBaron coupe and convertible, Chrysler Fifth Avenue, Dodge Daytona, Dodge Diplomat, and Plymouth Gran Fury. Chrysler's action was expected to spur other U.S. automakers to follow suit.

An airbag is designed to inflate in about one-twentieth of a second when a head-on collision activates sensors on the front of the car. The bag pops out of the steering wheel, forming an air-filled cushion between the driver and the steering wheel and windshield—the parts of the car that often cause injury.

Federal regulations require auto manufacturers to offer either airbags or *automatic seat belts*—wrap-around safety belts that tighten automatically when a person closes the door—in 25 per cent of 1988 models, 40 per cent of 1989 models, and 100 per cent of 1990 models. Although the technology for airbags has existed for many years, U.S. automakers, afraid that the extra costs and publicity would hurt sales, persuaded government officials to impose delays on the deadline for installing them.

Safety experts estimate that airbags could save at least 10,000

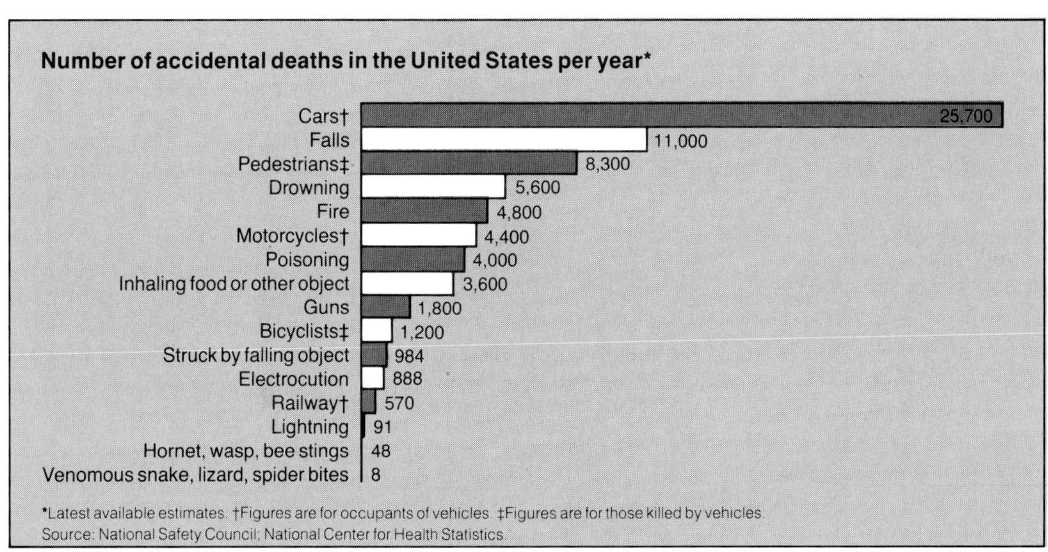

*Latest available estimates. †Figures are for occupants of vehicles. ‡Figures are for those killed by vehicles.
Source: National Safety Council; National Center for Health Statistics.

Detecting toxic gas
A fire fighter tests the air for poisonous gas with a portable toxic-gas detector developed by the Argonne National Laboratory near Chicago. The device, first demonstrated in 1988, can analyze air samples in four minutes. It is expected to be used by health and safety inspectors, petroleum and chemical firms, and the United States Coast Guard.

Safety (cont.)
lives a year. But airbags do not solve the entire safety problem. They protect only the driver—not the other front-seat passenger—and they do not help in crashes where the car is hit from the side. Auto manufacturers recommend that occupants of cars with airbags also wear shoulder belts for maximum protection.

New auto standard proposed. In January 1988, the National Highway Traffic Safety Administration (NHTSA) proposed a new safety standard to protect occupants of vehicles when the side of the car is hit. According to the NHTSA, about one-third of all vehicle fatalities occur in such collisions. The proposal, similar to one prepared in 1979 but dropped in 1982, would strengthen a 1973 standard for the stability of car doors. The standard would not apply to small trucks and minivans.

Highway deaths. In May 1988, the U.S. Department of Transportation (DOT) reported on the effects of the 1987 federal law permitting states to raise speed limits on rural interstate roads from 55 miles per hour (mph), or 88 kilometers per hour (kph), to 65 mph (105 kph). DOT reported that in the first nine months of 1987, highway deaths in the 37 states where speed limits were raised above 55 mph rose 18 to 23 per cent over the same period in 1986, and rose 17 per cent in states that retained the lower speed limit. Arizona, California, Louisiana, and New Mexico accounted for 70 per cent of the increase among states that raised their limits.

When Congress voted in 1987 to allow a 65-mph speed limit, some federal officials warned that the measure would result in increased deaths on the road. The DOT says, however, that it is still too early to determine if the higher speed limit causes more fatalities.

Defective cars. In March 1988, the U.S. Circuit Court of Appeals in Washington, D.C., rejected the government's charge that some 1.1 million "X" cars produced by the General Motors Corporation had defective brakes that sometimes locked, causing the vehicles to spin out of control. The case had been filed in 1983 after the government said it had received more than 4,000 complaints from drivers.

In September 1987, the Ford Motor Company acknowledged a safety defect in the fuel lines of some 4.3 million 1986, 1987, and 1988 cars, vans, and light trucks. Faulty fuel lines had caused 230 engine fires. The recall was the third largest in U.S. history.

Rail safety. As a result of a number of train crashes, including the collision between an Amtrak train and

Informative windshield
To keep automobile drivers from diverting their attention from the road to look at the dashboard, engineers at General Motors (GM) Delco Electronics Corporation developed a device that projects a display indicating the car's speed, fuel level, turn signals, and headlights directly onto the windshield. GM plans to install the device in some of its 1989 models.

Safety (cont.)
three Conrail locomotives in January 1987, the U.S. House of Representatives voted in May to require—for the first time—licenses for train engineers, and to give the government more power to penalize train employees who violate safety regulations. A measure to require drug tests for certain railroad workers was stripped from the legislation.

Asbestos ruling. In April, a group of Californians lost a landmark suit contending that all asbestos manufacturers should jointly pay for removal of the substance from homes. People who inhale asbestos fibers often develop severe lung disease, including lung cancer. A California court ruled that only homeowners who could identify a specific manufacturer could sue.

Lead warning. In December, the U.S. Environmental Protection Agency (EPA) reported that the water dispensed from many water coolers in schools, businesses, and other public places has high concentrations of lead. The EPA said its tests showed lead levels in some water coolers to be 40 times higher than the EPA standard. The suspected source of the poisonous substance was lead solder in the coils of the water coolers.

Dangerous darts. On May 25, 1988, the Consumer Product Safety Commission took the first step toward removing lawn darts with long metal tips from store shelves when it voted to ban sales of the toy. This type of lawn dart injures an estimated 670 people annually and has been responsible for the deaths of three children. Darts with blunt plastic tips were not included in the ban. The matter was expected to go before the commission again in late 1988. After a second approval of the ban, the commission would set a date for the ban to go into effect.

Factory safety. To quiet charges that it relies too heavily on the injury and illness records of employers rather than on visual inspections of plants, the Occupational Health and Safety Administration (OSHA) on March 23, 1988, ordered its inspectors to also examine hazardous factory areas. Since 1982, OSHA has exempted plants in high-hazardous industries from undergoing plant inspections if their records showed injury rates below the nationwide average for manufacturing. Some government officials and unions had complained that the practice encouraged employers to underreport injuries to avoid plant inspections.

☐ Arthur E. Rowse

In the Special Reports section, see Fire! In World Book, see Safety.

Sexually Transmitted Diseases

Genital ulcers caused by such sexually transmitted diseases (STD's) as syphilis, genital herpes, and chancroid seem to increase the chances of contracting and transmitting the virus that causes AIDS (acquired immune deficiency syndrome). That finding was reported in a number of studies published in 1987 and 1988. Researchers theorized that the ulcers provide an easy point of entry for the virus.

Health experts in Nairobi, Kenya, reported that people suffering from genital ulcers were four times more likely to become infected with the AIDS virus than people without ulcers. Also, researchers in Zimbabwe found that the wives of men with a history of genital ulcers were nearly three times more likely to become infected with the AIDS virus than women whose spouses had no such history.

A similar relationship between evidence of syphilis and transmission of the AIDS virus was reported among people in New York City and Miami, Fla., prostitutes in five United States cities, and homosexual men in London and San Francisco. In addition, researchers in Seattle and San Francisco found that homosexual men who had been infected with herpes simplex virus type 2, another cause of genital ulcers, had a higher incidence of infections with the AIDS virus than those who had no history of herpes infection.

The studies suggested that the ulcers alone—independent of other factors that increase the risk of becoming infected with the AIDS virus—contribute to the spread of the AIDS virus. For example, people with genital ulcers were found to be more susceptible to the virus regardless of how many or how few sexual partners they had.

Increase in genital ulcers. Alarming increases in the number of cases of STD's that cause genital ulcers were reported in 1987 by the Centers for Disease Control (CDC) in Atlanta, Ga. According to the CDC, the incidence of syphilis rose by 30 per cent in 1987, with nearly 35,000 cases reported, compared with 27,000 cases in 1986. It was the largest yearly increase in more than 30 years.

Three areas—New York City, Los Angeles County, and the state of Florida—accounted for more than 75 per cent of the increase. Nearly all the cases occurred among heterosexuals, with blacks experiencing a disproportionately greater increase than whites.

Researchers found that in several cities, many people infected with syphilis were exchanging sexual services for drugs. Health experts

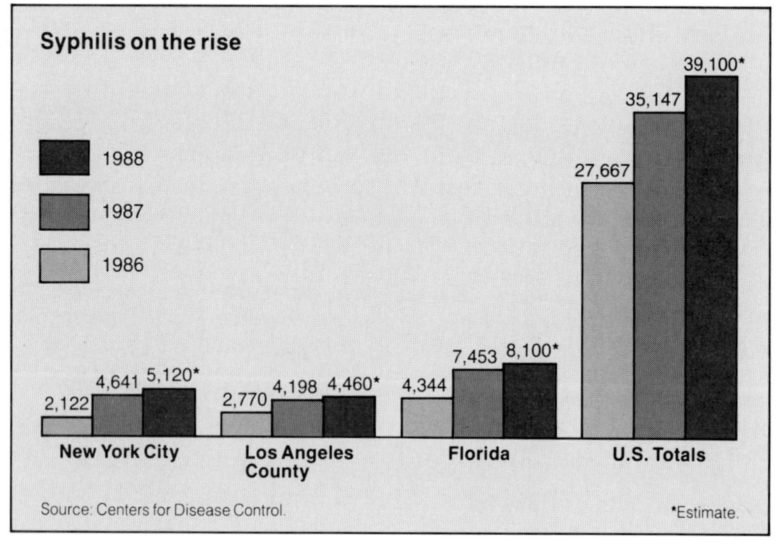

A surge in syphilis
The number of reported cases of syphilis in the United States rose dramatically in 1987 and 1988. Only three areas—New York City, Los Angeles County, and Florida—accounted for most of the increase.

Sexually Transmitted Diseases (cont.)
feared that the combination of syphilis, intravenous drug use, and multiple sexual partners would speed the spread of the AIDS virus among heterosexuals, especially in areas where relatively large numbers of people are already infected with the AIDS virus.

The CDC also reported outbreaks of chancroid, another venereal disease that causes genital ulcers, in 1987 in several of the areas where cases of syphilis have skyrocketed. The spread of chancroid has also been linked to prostitution and drugs. Genital herpes, however, continued to be the main cause of genital ulcers in the United States. In 1987, ulcers caused by genital herpes accounted for more than 15 times as many visits to U.S. physicians' offices as all reported cases of syphilis for that year.

Chlamydia screening. Routine testing of all women of reproductive age who seek family-planning services is a useful and cost-effective way of identifying women infected with *chlamydia trachomatis*. That conclusion, based on a study of family-planning clinics, was reported in January 1988 by the San Francisco Health Policy Group.

Chlamydia, the most common bacterial STD among U.S. women, often produces no symptoms. If untreated, it can cause such severe and costly complications as pelvic inflammatory disease, infertility, and ectopic pregnancy. In the United States, between 10 and 25 per cent of sexually active women of reproductive age are infected with chlamydia trachomatis.

Condoms and STD. Condoms are an effective means of controlling the spread of STD's, according to a report issued in early 1988 by the CDC. The study noted that abstinence or an exclusive sexual relationship between uninfected persons are the only totally effective ways to avoid STD. But condoms, if properly used during each act of sexual intercourse, can greatly reduce the risk of infection.

According to the study, the failure of condoms to protect against STD occurs more often because the condom is not used properly than because of defects in condoms. The most common causes of such failure include not using a condom with each act of sexual intercourse, not putting the condom on before any genital contact occurs, and not completely unrolling the condom.

□ Willard Cates, Jr.

See also AIDS. In World Book, see Venereal Disease.

Skin

The startling announcement that a skin cream containing all-*trans* retinoic acid, or tretinoin, had reversed a type of skin damage caused by overexposure to the sun was made by Ortho Pharmaceutical Corporation of Raritan, N.J., in January 1988. Since 1971, Ortho Pharmaceutical had sold a tretinoin cream under the trade name Retin-A as a prescription drug for the treatment of acne.

Tretinoin reversed *photoaging*, premature aging due to exposure to the sun. Photoaged skin is wrinkled, rough, and mottled.

Two studies announced in 1986 by dermatologist Albert M. Kligman of the University of Pennsylvania in Philadelphia had provided a strong indication that the drug also could smooth wrinkles caused by sun exposure. Kligman's first study showed that the application of tretinoin to photoaged skin of hairless mice partially reversed photoaging. The second study recorded the partial reversal of photoaging in human volunteers.

This study excited dermatologists, but it was not conclusive because the investigation was not a *double-blind* study. In a double-blind experiment on a drug, the volunteers are divided at random into two equal groups—an *experimental group* and

Treatment for wrinkles
Fine lines caused by overexposing skin to the sun, *top,* became smaller, *bottom,* when treated with a substance called tretinoin, according to a January 1988 report by researchers at the University of Michigan in Ann Arbor. This substance is sold in the United States as Retin-A, a prescription drug for the treatment of acne.

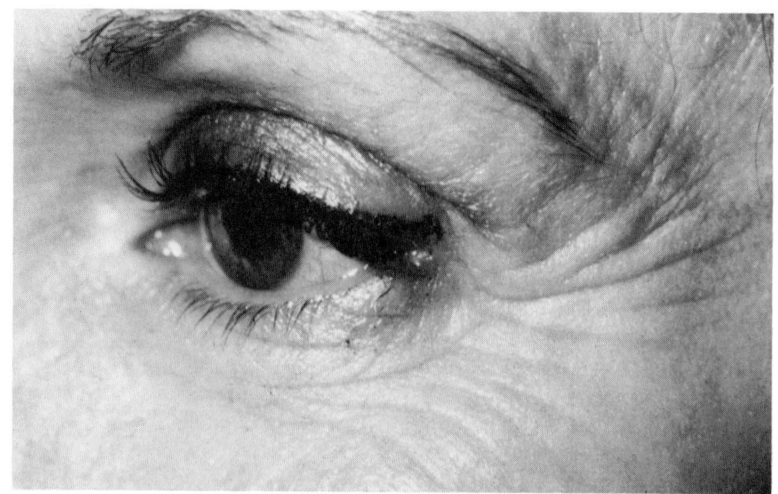

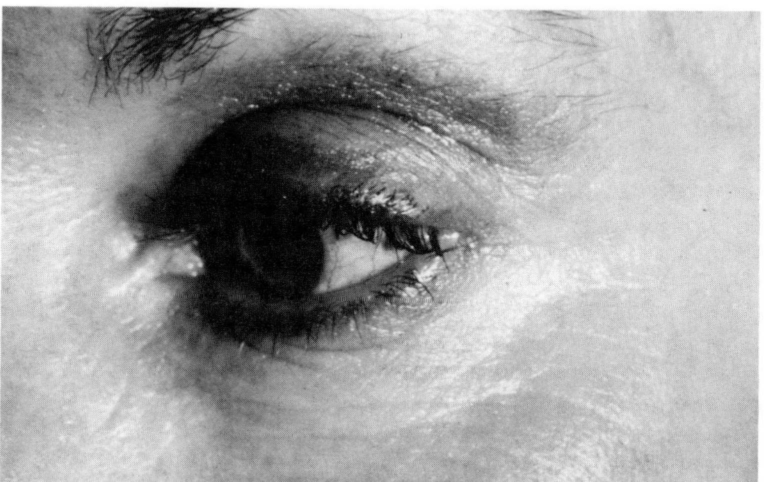

Skin (cont.)
a *control group*. The experimental group receives the drug, while the control group receives a *placebo*—an identical-looking preparation that contains none of the substance being tested. Neither the volunteers nor the investigators who distribute the preparation know which volunteers are given the drug and which are given the placebo. This procedure minimizes the influence of factors other than the presence or absence of the drug in the preparations on the outcome of the study.

In 1987, dermatologist Jonathan S. Weiss and his colleagues at the University of Michigan in Ann Arbor conducted a double-blind study showing that tretinoin reverses photoaging. The researchers tested 30 volunteers whose facial skin had been wrinkled by excessive exposure to the sun for long periods of time. The results of this experiment were the basis of Ortho Pharmaceutical's January 1988 announcement. The researchers published their results the next day in the *Journal of the American Medical Association*.

The volunteers in Weiss's test were white people from 35 to 70 years old. During the experiment, half the volunteers applied a cream containing 0.1 per cent tretinoin to their faces. The other half used a placebo. After 16 weeks, Weiss and

Skin (cont.)

his colleagues observed that the faces of 14 of the 15 patients treated with retinoic acid were less wrinkled, and that the color and surface texture of their skin had improved. No one in the control group showed any kind of improvement. When the researchers examined treated skin under a microscope, they observed such improvements as a smoother and more compact outer layer, and a thicker underlying layer. Unwanted side effects of the cream included burning, tingling, and itching of the skin.

Impressive as Weiss's experiment was, dermatologists did not accept its conclusions as scientific proof. Scientists do not accept the conclusions of even the most carefully conducted double-blind experiment as proof until other researchers perform the same experiment and obtain essentially the same results. By the summer of 1988, no one had duplicated Weiss's experiment, so dermatologists were not certain that the reported effect actually occurs; and, if it does, that it persists after treatment is discontinued.

Baldness remedy tested. The application of a substance called *minoxidil* to balding regions of men's scalps stimulated the regrowth of hair, reported dermatologist Judith A. Koperski in September 1987. Minoxidil is normally used to treat high blood pressure, and its side effects on hair growth were discovered by chance in 1980. Koperski conducted a 30-month study of the substance at Stanford University in Stanford, Calif.

At the beginning of the test, the male volunteers had an average of 119 hairs in a circular area 1 inch (2.5 centimeters) in diameter on the crown of the head. After 12 months, the average count was 353 hairs. This average declined to 250 after 30 months.

A hair count of 250 falls far short of what most people would consider to be cosmetically acceptable regrowth. Furthermore, several other studies showed that only 10 per cent of volunteers investigated regrew a cosmetically acceptable amount of hair. Nevertheless, minoxidil is the first preparation that has been scientifically proven to promote regrowth of hair.

Since 1986, minoxidil—as a treatment for baldness—has been available commercially in Canada, where the Upjohn Company of Canada sells it under the trade name Rogaine. In August 1988, the United States Food and Drug Administration (FDA) approved Rogaine for sale in the United States.

☐ Tania J. Phillips and Jeffrey S. Dover

In World Book, see Skin.

Smoking

Smoking has long been known to promote lung cancer and heart attacks, but only in the past few years has it been listed by the American Heart Association as a risk factor in stroke. In 1988, new research revealed evidence of a strong link between smoking and stroke, which kills 152,000 people in the United States each year and is the third leading cause of death.

In January, Boston University researchers who analyzed data from the landmark Framingham Heart Study reported that smoking increased the risk of stroke by 60 per cent in women and 40 per cent in men. The Framingham Heart Study, named for a city in Massachusetts, spanned 26 years and had 4,255 participants.

Women and heart disease. In March, scientists from Harvard University Medical School in Boston, presented the results of a study of 120,000 female nurses—the largest ever to examine the effects of smoking on heart disease risk in women. The researchers concluded that women who smoke half a pack of cigarettes per day double their risk of stroke, while those who smoke about two packs or more per day have a six times greater risk.

The researchers found that even

Smoking (cont.)
those who smoked one to four cigarettes per day were more than twice as likely to have a heart attack as nonsmokers. Smoking was a factor in half of all the heart attacks among the women and 90 per cent of the heart attacks among the heavy smokers—those who smoked 45 or more cigarettes per day.

Successful liability case. In June 1988, for the first time, a tobacco company was held legally liable for the death of a smoker. A federal jury in Newark, N.J., found the Liggett Group, Incorporated, partially responsible for the death of Rose Cipollone, a woman who died of lung cancer in 1984 at the age of 58 after smoking over a pack of cigarettes daily for 40 years.

The jury awarded $400,000 to Cipollone's husband, Antonio, finding that Liggett failed to caution about the health risks of smoking its cigarettes before a 1966 federal requirement put warnings on cigarette packages. But the jury found that Mrs. Cipollone was 80 per cent responsible for her own death. In addition, the jury rejected charges of conspiracy and misrepresentation of health risks after 1966 against Liggett and the other defendants in the case—Lorillard, Incorporated, and

Doctor's orders?
A 1951 ad for L&M cigarettes, made by Liggett & Myers Tobacco Company, was introduced as evidence in the first trial to find a tobacco company partly to blame for a smoker's death. In June 1988, a jury in Newark, N.J., awarded $400,000 in damages to the husband of Rose Cipollone, who died of lung cancer in 1984. The jury found that in its advertising prior to 1966, Liggett had wrongly implied that cigarette smoking was safe.

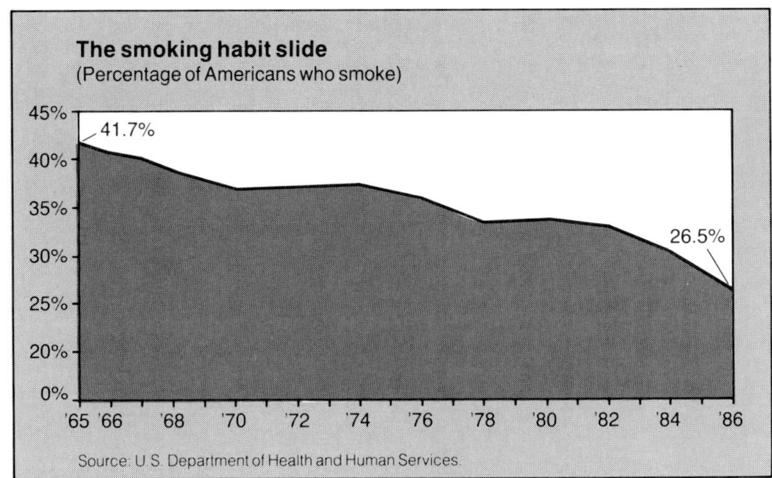

The percentage of Americans who smoke has been on a general decline since 1965, one year after the surgeon general issued the first official warning linking cigarette smoking to several diseases, including lung cancer. In 1965, 41.7 per cent of adult Americans smoked, but by 1986, the percentage had declined to 26.5 per cent, according to one government survey.

Smoking (cont.)
Philip Morris Companies, Incorporated—whose brands she had smoked after 1966, when the warnings were first put on packages.

Both the tobacco industry and antismoking activists claimed victory in the Cipollone case. Antismoking forces noted that the case marked the first time in more than 300 similar lawsuits filed since 1954 that a tobacco company had lost a single claim or paid any damages.

Fewer smokers. As social pressures to ban smoking in public places rose, the smoking habit continued its 20-year slide in popularity during 1987 and 1988. In September 1987, officials at the Centers for Disease Control (CDC) in Atlanta, Ga., reported the results of a 1986 survey showing that 26.5 per cent of Americans smoke cigarettes. This was the lowest level of smoking ever reported in the United States, down from 30 per cent in 1985.

In 1964, when the surgeon general issued the first official U.S. government warning linking smoking to cancer, a survey found that 40 per cent of the adult population smoked. Officials in 1988 predicted that the proportion of smokers would drop to 10 to 15 per cent over the next several years. The 1987 CDC survey estimated that about 47 million American adults are still smokers.

The preliminary results of another survey, conducted by the National Center for Health Statistics in 1987, showed that about 30 per cent of all Americans aged 18 and older smoke cigarettes. This survey questioned 48,000 Americans about their smoking habits and by August 1988, findings from 12,000 of the interviews had been released.

Smokeless skies. On April 23, 1988, a new federal regulation went into effect banning smoking on all airline flights scheduled to last two hours or less. The regulation carried fines of up to $1,000 for smoking on such flights and $2,000 for tampering with smoke alarms or smoking in an aircraft lavatory.

The new rules applied to about 13,600 flights per day in the United States, accounting for about 80 per cent of all flights on U.S. carriers. On the same day, Northwest Airlines became the first commercial airline to prohibit smoking on all flights within the continental United States.

Nicotine a drug addiction. In May 1988, Surgeon General C. Everett Koop, in his annual report on the health consequences of smoking, warned that nicotine is just as addictive as heroin and cocaine. Smokers compulsively take *nicotine*, a harmful drug in tobacco, for its mood-altering effects, the report said. They develop a tolerance to the drug and suffer withdrawal

Addictive nicotine
Surgeon General C. Everett Koop announces findings in May 1988 asserting that nicotine in tobacco is just as addictive as heroin and cocaine. Koop called for new regulations on the sale of tobacco products.

Smoking (cont.)
symptoms when they try to quit smoking, relapsing at the same rate as alcohol and heroin abusers. The report was a significant reversal of the findings of the surgeon general's 1964 report, which found smoking merely "habit-forming."

The new report summarized more than 2,000 scientific studies on nicotine and its effects on smokers. The report concluded that nicotine meets the standard criteria for an addictive drug. Koop called for stronger federal government action to regulate tobacco products, including a ban on vending machine sales, the licensing of tobacco retailers, and an added warning on packages to the effect that tobacco products are just as addictive as the other drugs.

"Our nation has mobilized enormous resources to wage a war on drugs—illicit drugs," Koop said. "We should also give priority to the one addiction—tobacco addiction—that is killing more than 300,000 Americans each year."

☐ William H. Allen

See also CANCER. In the People in Medicine section, see FAMILY DOCTOR TO AMERICA. In WORLD BOOK, see SMOKING; TOBACCO.

Stroke

Women who smoke have a much higher risk of stroke than do nonsmoking women, according to a report published in April 1988 by a team of scientists and physicians from Harvard University Medical School and Brigham and Women's Hospital in Boston. The team began the study in 1976 by sending health questionnaires to 121,700 female nurses between the ages of 30 and 55. The team then sent each woman a follow-up questionnaire every two years through 1984.

When the questionnaires sent in 1976 were returned, researchers selected the 118,539 women in the study who had said in 1976 that they had not had a stroke and did not have heart disease or cancer. Next, the investigators divided the women into five groups: those who had never smoked; former smokers; light smokers (1 to 14 cigarettes daily); moderate smokers (15 to 24 cigarettes daily), and heavy smokers (25 or more cigarettes daily). Finally, the investigators tallied the number of women who had suffered strokes in each group between 1976 and 1984, and calculated the risk of stroke for each group.

They found that the risk of stroke for former smokers was 1.5 times greater than the risk for women who had never smoked; for light smok-

Stroke (cont.)
ers, the risk was 2.2 times greater; for moderate smokers, 2.7 times greater; and for heavy smokers, 3.7 times greater.

Defect linked to strokes. A study reported in May 1988 may help scientists and physicians to determine the cause of stroke in relatively young people who seem to be at low risk for stroke. A team at the Hopital Pitie-Salpetriere in Paris had noticed a certain heart defect in some patients who suffered a type of stroke in which a blood clot blocked an artery supplying blood to the brain.

This defect is a partial opening in a passage between the two upper chambers of the heart. Normally, this passage closes before birth.

The Paris team decided to determine whether this defect was present in people who had strokes for unexplained reasons. The researchers studied 60 patients under the age of 55 who had suffered a stroke, but whose heart still apparently functioned normally.

The researchers divided these patients into three categories. In the first category were people whose strokes had known causes, such as a blood clot traced from a leg vein to an artery feeding the brain. The

Plaque-removal surgery under evaluation

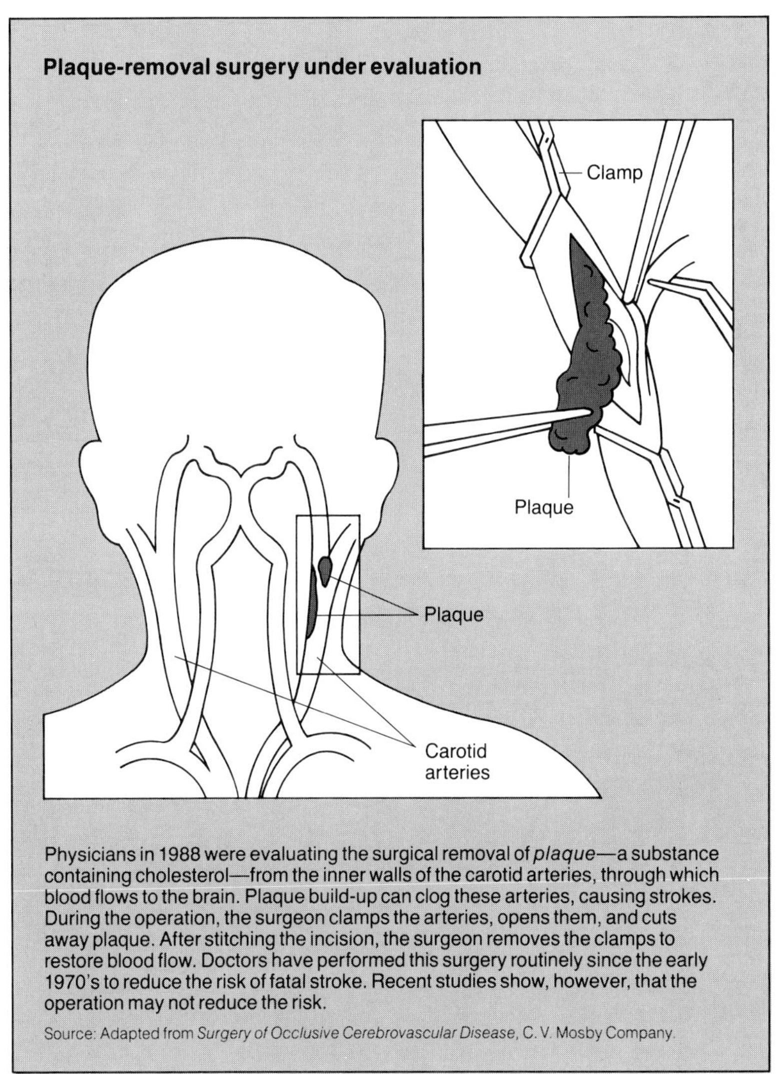

Physicians in 1988 were evaluating the surgical removal of *plaque*—a substance containing cholesterol—from the inner walls of the carotid arteries, through which blood flows to the brain. Plaque build-up can clog these arteries, causing strokes. During the operation, the surgeon clamps the arteries, opens them, and cuts away plaque. After stitching the incision, the surgeon removes the clamps to restore blood flow. Doctors have performed this surgery routinely since the early 1970's to reduce the risk of fatal stroke. Recent studies show, however, that the operation may not reduce the risk.

Source: Adapted from *Surgery of Occlusive Cerebrovascular Disease*, C. V. Mosby Company.

Stroke (cont.)

second category was made up of individuals whose strokes had no known cause, but who also belonged to groups with a significant risk of stroke—for example, women who used oral contraceptives. In the third category were patients whose strokes had no known cause and who were not in risk groups.

The researchers then used *echocardiography* to examine all the patients. In this technique, a small, microphonelike device held against the patient's chest projects sound waves into the heart. The waves reflect from various parts of the heart and strike microphones that are connected to a computer. The computer translates the reflected waves into an image of the heart.

The scientists found the heart defect in 21 per cent of the patients with a known cause of stroke, in 40 per cent of the high-risk patients with no known cause of stroke, and in 54 per cent of the patients with no known cause of stroke who were not in a high-risk group. The researchers speculated that clots form in defective hearts as blood passes from one upper chamber to the other. □ Beverly Merz

In WORLD BOOK, see HEART; STROKE.

Teeth

See Dentistry

Urology

Major technological advances occurred in 1987 and 1988 in *urology*, the branch of medicine dealing with the kidneys, ureter, bladder, and the male sex organs. Two of the most important advances help urologists to diagnose cancer of the prostate gland and to treat kidney stones.

Detecting prostate cancer. Urologist Thomas A. Stamey of Stanford University in Stanford, Calif., reported that a new ultrasound technique for the detection of prostate cancer at an early stage became more accurate and more versatile. Urologists have begun to use this technique to supplement the traditional methods of rectal examinations and blood tests.

In the ultrasound technique, the urologist inserts a small probe into the rectum. The probe emits high-frequency sound waves, some of which bounce off tissue in the body and return to the probe. The probe translates the returned waves into electric signals, which in turn create a televisionlike image of the tissue. By examining the image on a screen, a urologist can find signs of small tumors that might not be found by rectal examination.

Ultrasound images have become

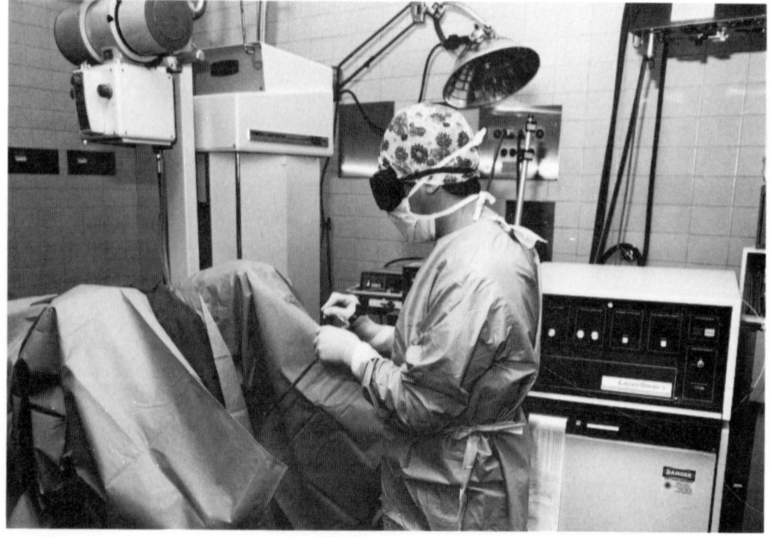

Laser breaks kidney stone

A surgeon uses a laser to break up a kidney stone lodged in a patient's *ureter*—one of a pair of tubes that drain urine from the kidneys to the bladder. The doctor inserts a tube containing a flexible but glasslike fiber into the ureter, then turns the laser on. Laser light travels through the fiber and strikes the stone.

Urology (cont.)

so detailed that urologists have begun to use them to guide a very thin needle into areas showing signs of tumors. A urologist uses this needle to remove tissue that is tested for the presence of cancer cells.

The needle is part of an instrument called the Biopty gun, which was introduced in late 1987 by the Bard Corporation of Covington, Ga. The Biopty gun is built into the probe, allowing the urologist to remove a tissue sample through the rectum. The Biopty gun causes little or no pain.

Before the development of the Biopty gun, the urologist had to admit the patient to a hospital for surgery. Now, in most cases, the urologist can remove the tissue sample during an office visit.

A new blood test became a valuable tool in the diagnosis of prostate cancer in 1987 and 1988. The test measures the amount of a substance called *prostatic specific antigen* (PSA) in the blood. This test also helps urologists determine the effectiveness of the surgical removal of a cancerous prostate gland. Both healthy and cancerous cells of the prostate gland produce PSA, but no other kind of cell produces it. The presence of elevated PSA in the blood following the removal of the prostate gland for cancer may indicate a poor prognosis.

The PSA test supplements the traditional blood test for prostate cancer, the measurement of a substance known as *prostatic acid phosphatase* (PAP). Testing the blood for both PAP and PSA is more effective than testing for PAP alone.

Breaking up kidney stones with shock waves in many cases no longer requires X-ray examinations, general anesthesia, and partially submerging the patient in a large tub of water. In the treatment involving the tub, a machine generates mechanical shock waves that travel through the water and into the kidney stone. The waves break the stone into fragments, which then leave the body in the urine.

Urologist John Wickham reported in the May 1988 issue of *Urology Times* that a new machine with no tub broke up stones effectively in treatments conducted at the Institute of Urology of Shaftesbury Hospital in London. Treatment with the machine is painless, so the patient can be handled as an outpatient. The machine does not require X-ray examinations because it uses ultrasound to help the urologist locate the stone. □ Dennis A. Pessis

In World Book, see Kidney Stone; Prostate Gland; Ultrasound.

Venereal Diseases

See Sexually Transmitted Diseases

Veterinary Medicine

A dietary deficiency of vitamin E may cause blindness in dogs, according to veterinary researchers Ron Riis of the New York State College of Veterinary Medicine and Ben Sheffy of the James A. Baker Institute for Animal Health, both in Ithaca, N.Y. Riis and Sheffy's nutritional study of dogs fed a diet low in vitamin E revealed that these dogs developed eye lesions that caused difficulty with night vision, which eventually progressed to blindness.

Ellis Loew, a *physiologist* (expert in the normal functions of animals) at the New York State College performed laboratory tests on the dogs under study and found that the retinas of their eyes had been damaged. Further studies indicated that the damage caused by vitamin E deficiency may be halted if the condition is detected in its early stages and the animal is given increased amounts of vitamin E.

Studies are planned to learn whether vitamin E deficiency affects older dogs more seriously than it does younger ones, and to determine the optimum dietary intake of vitamin E for dogs.

Pet identification. A simple, safe, and permanent means of identifying pets became available to many U.S. pet owners in 1988. The device is a *microchip*, a thin piece of copper

I.D. microchip
Veterinarian Thomas J. Lane of the University of Florida in Gainesville uses an electronic transponder to locate and "read" an identification microchip that had been injected under a dog's skin. Microchip identification, which is permanent and safe, became available to pet owners in 1988.

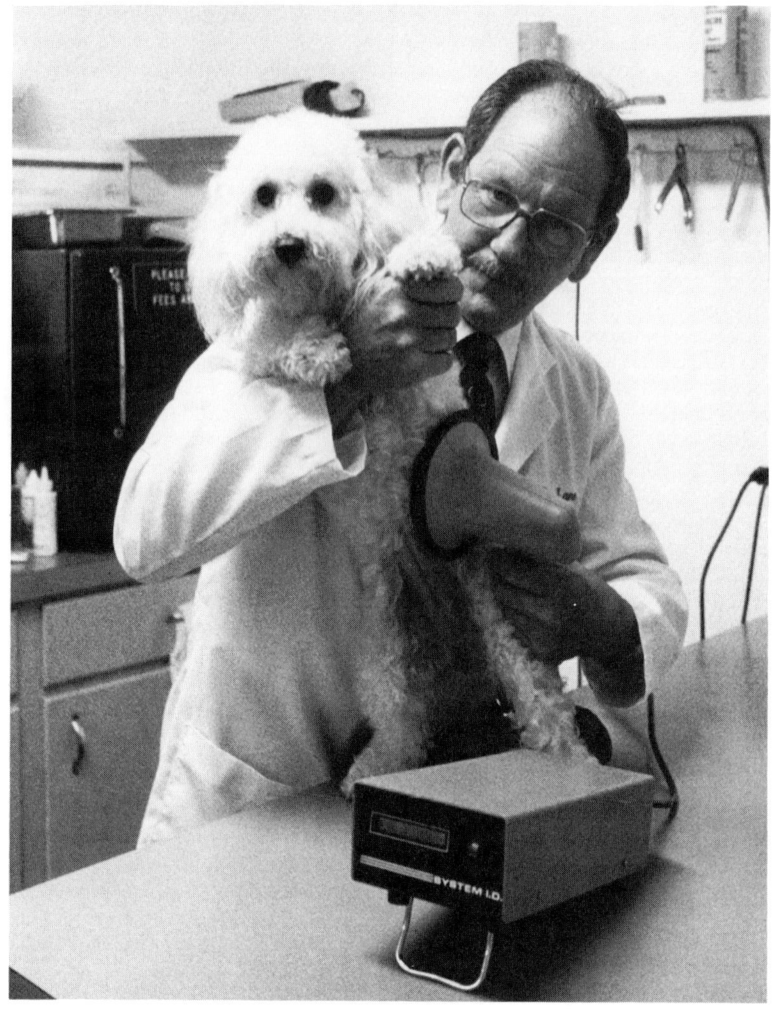

Veterinary Medicine (cont.)
wire, imprinted with an identification code, that is coiled and encased in a tiny glass capsule. A veterinarian injects the microchip under the animal's skin, where it remains for the rest of the pet's life.

Animal welfare agencies that are frequently called upon to handle lost animals can easily locate and "read" the microchip using an electronic device called a *transponder*. A nationwide phone network can then match the code with the name and address of the pet owner as well as the name, age, and sex of the animal.

Microchips have been safely implanted in more than 1,000 animals, including horses and alligators and other wild animals. To date, there have been no reports of rejections. The future success of microchip identification will depend upon whether the technology becomes widely accepted by pet owners and animal welfare agencies.

A hearing aid for dogs was developed in 1988 by a veterinarian and an *audiologist* (expert in the study of hearing) at Auburn University in Auburn, Ala. Like people, dogs sometimes lose part or all of their hearing as they age. A canine hearing aid can allow a hearing-impaired dog to respond to its owner's calls and to avoid dangers by re-

Cloning cattle
Three cloned bulls, genetically identical animals derived from a single embryo, are a striking result of rapidly developing animal-breeding technologies. The Brangus bulls were cloned from a single 5-day-old embryo in a complicated series of procedures that involved transferring genetic material from the embryo into specially treated egg cells, and implanting these eggs in the wombs of three surrogate cows.

Veterinary Medicine (cont.)
sponding to sounds—such as the squeal of automobile brakes—in its environment.

The researchers reported, however, that all hearing-impaired dogs are not necessarily good candidates for the hearing aid. Because the device works as an amplifier that boosts sounds so that they can be heard by the damaged ear, the hearing aid can help only those dogs who still have some hearing. In addition, the dog's outer ear must be completely free of any infection, growths, or other abnormalities that would prevent comfortable fitting of the hearing aid.

The dog's owner must also be willing to spend three to four weeks training the dog to tolerate the device. The unfamiliar presence of something within the ear canal as well as the sudden amplification of all sounds may unnerve some dogs so much that they cannot tolerate the hearing aid.

By mid-1988, only about 20 dogs had been successfully fitted with hearing devices. Canine hearing aid programs may eventually be established by many veterinary colleges in the United States, however.

☐ Thomas J. Lane

In World Book, see Cat; Dog; Veterinary Medicine.

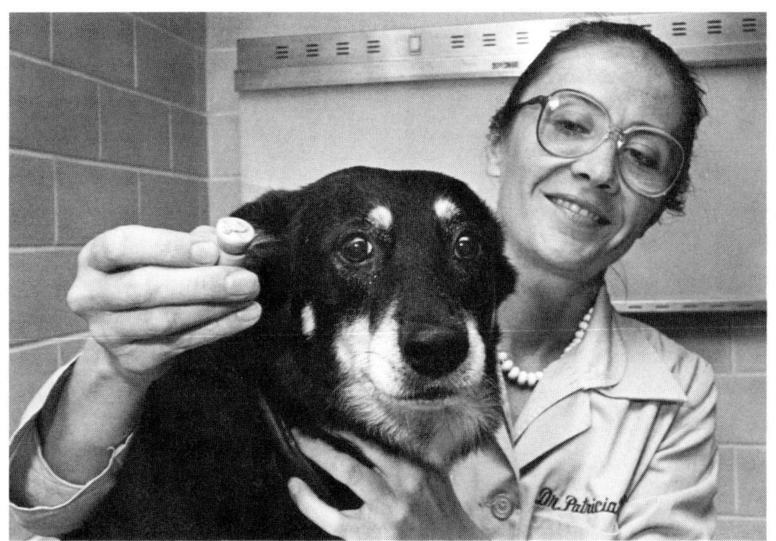

Helping hounds' hearing
Veterinarian Patricia Luttgen of Texas A&M University in College Station prepares to fit an aged dog with a newly developed canine hearing aid. By mid-1988, about 20 dogs had been fitted with the device, which was developed at Auburn University in Auburn, Ala.

Weight Control

Family history may be the most important risk factor for obesity, according to a February 1988 report by researchers at the National Institutes of Health (NIH) in Bethesda, Md. (*Obesity* is generally defined as being 20 per cent or more above the ideal weight for people of the same sex, age, and height.)

The researchers studied American Indians of the Pima tribe, who live in southern Arizona. About 85 per cent of the Pima Indians are obese, and by age 35 a high proportion of the population develop obesity-related *diabetes*—a serious disorder in which the body cannot make use of sugar in a normal way.

The researchers carefully measured the metabolic rates of some Pima Indians and found that they burned an average of 80 calories less per day than was normal for people of the same weight and height. A metabolic rate this slow would cause a weight gain of 9 pounds (4 kilograms) per year while eating a normal diet.

The slow metabolic rate among the Pima Indians led the scientists to propose a "thrifty-gene" theory, which suggests that natural selection may have caused the Pima to utilize food in a very efficient way. The Pima endured frequent periods of famine and drought during their history; presumably Pima with a faster, less efficient metabolic rate—who needed more calories than average—died, while those with a slower metabolism survived.

The offspring of these people may have inherited a genetic predisposition for a slow metabolic rate. While this type of natural selection would be beneficial when food is scarce, modern Pima, who live in a society in which food is plentiful, are plagued with obesity and the medical problems it causes.

Heredity versus environment. The NIH study indirectly verified the findings of previously published research indicating that heredity may be a more important factor than environment in determining whether or not a person will become obese. A 1986 study of Danish adults who had been adopted as children showed a correlation between the weight of the adoptees and that of their natural parents, but no correlation between the adoptees' weight and that of the adoptive parents with whom they lived.

Another study published the same year examined the relative weights of male twins at age 20 and age 45. The researchers concluded that heredity accounted for 80 per cent of the variation in the men's weight.

Most researchers agree that weight problems cannot be entirely

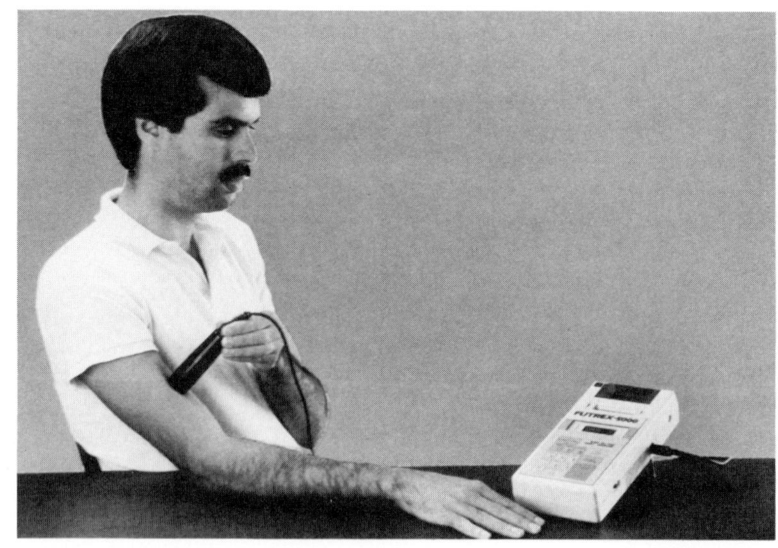

Infrared fat analyzer
A new device for measuring a person's body fat percentage, the Fitness & Body Fat Analyzer, was introduced in late 1987. A wand, which emits a beam of infrared light, is held to a person's upper arm. The device measures the amount of light reflected by the tissue and uses this measurement to calculate the person's overall percentage of body fat. The device then prints out diet and exercise tips.

Weight Control (cont.)
blamed on inherited metabolism, however. A significant percentage of obese people overeat and are also physically inactive. A 1985 study, for example, showed that the most accurate predictor of whether or not a child will become obese during adolescence is the amount of time the child spends viewing television between the ages of 6 and 11. Watching TV may be linked not only to inactivity but also to increased snacking.

Obesity among teen-agers has increased by 39 per cent since the 1970's, and the problem now affects 21.9 per cent of 12- to 17-year-old Americans. Before the mid-1980's, effective treatments for obese adolescents were not available.

In 1988, however, studies of two programs designed for obese teenagers reported some success. An after-school program called Weight Winner combined behavior modification and aerobic exercise to help 12 obese girls aged 12 to 15 improve their exercise and eating habits and decrease their body weight by 11 per cent. Shapedown, another program found to be effective in helping obese teens lose weight, utilized a variety of learning techniques to help the teen-agers make gradual improvements in their diet and exercise habits—as well as their communication skills and emotional health.

More gastric bubble problems. The gastric bubble—a balloonlike device that is placed inside the stomach as an aid to weight loss—continued to undergo scrutiny in 1987 and 1988, and on May 15, 1988, it was taken off the market. A research team at the Mayo Clinic in Rochester, Minn., had reported that the balloon had high rates of accidental deflation and of causing damage to the stomach lining. Two other studies by researchers in Pennsylvania and Arkansas confirmed the high rate of complications connected with the procedure. The Pennsylvania researchers also found that the balloon was ineffective as an aid to weight loss, though the Arkansas researchers reported that the gastric bubble produced satisfactory weight loss during the first four months after implant.

Suction-assisted lipectomy, also known as *liposuction*, continued to be a popular fat-removal technique in 1987 and 1988. Liposuction involves suctioning fat from under the skin using a vacuum-powered tube. Many weight-control experts agree that liposuction is valuable as a method of shaping the body, provided that only small quantities of fat are removed from truly conspicuous areas of fat accumulation.

But because liposuction is a relatively new procedure, its effect on a patient's overall fat distribution is unknown. Some experts believe liposuction may cause permanent—and perhaps harmful—changes.

There are two types of fat distribution in obese people—*lower-body obesity*, in which fat accumulates in the hips, buttocks, thighs, and lower abdomen; and *upper-body obesity*, in which fat accumulates in the back, shoulders, and upper abdomen. Of the two, lower-body obesity may be more difficult to eliminate through dieting, though one 1988 study challenged this assertion. Upper-body obesity is linked to obesity-related health problems such as high blood cholesterol levels, diabetes, and high blood pressure.

Removing too much fat through liposuction on a patient with lower-body obesity may, if the person later gains weight, cause the patient to develop fat accumulations in parts of the body that were previously slender. Some patients may develop upper-body obesity and its attendant health problems. Thus liposuction may inadvertently change cosmetically objectionable obesity into medically harmful obesity.

☐ Stephen P. Nozetz

In the Special Reports section, see Cosmetic Surgery: New Trends, Old Concerns. In the Health Studies section, see Weight Control and Your Health. In World Book, see Weight Control.

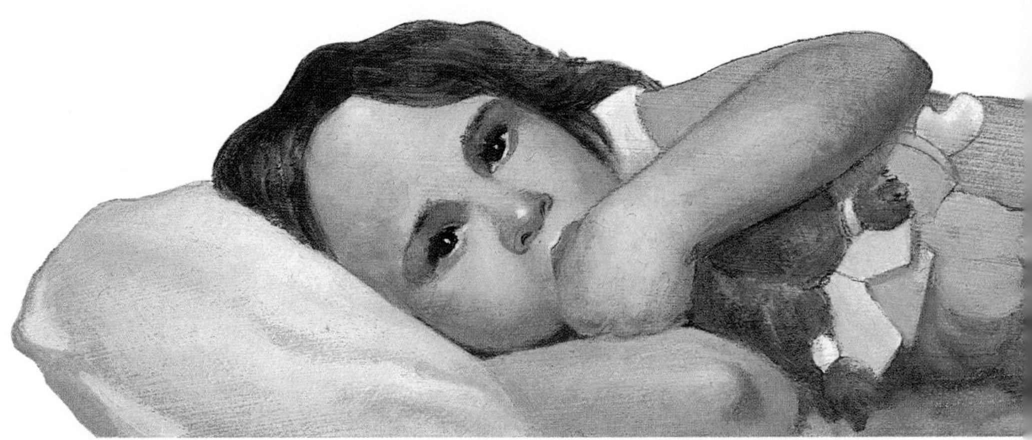

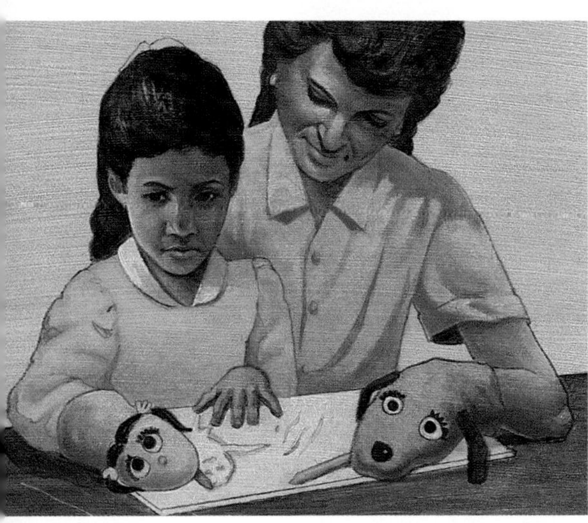

People in Health Care

Two articles provide a glimpse of health care professionals in action.

Family Doctor to America

By Frank Cormier and Margot Cormier

Surgeon General C. Everett Koop treats the nation's health problems with a prescription of straight talk and solid facts.

C. Everett Koop's tough stands on such topics as smoking and AIDS (acquired immune deficiency syndrome) have made him the most celebrated—and controversial—surgeon general ever. In his eight years in government, he's fought with the White House, gained and lost enemies and allies, and turned a low-profile job into a powerful platform.

In the 119 years since the first surgeon general of the United States was named, the office has been heard from only rarely. The job even has been vacant for long stretches with no one seeming the wiser. Although the title sounds grand, the job offers few powers and, by federal standards, a tiny budget.

Despite these limitations, America's current, and 13th, surgeon general, C. Everett Koop, has done more to expand the impact and visibility of the office in the past eight years than virtually all his predecessors combined. He did so by exercising the only power he had in abundance—the power to jawbone against threats to the public health.

"I am not in the least bit hampered in what I want to do, even though I have no power and I have no money," Koop has said. "Whatever I accomplish, I accomplish on the basis of moral suasion."

By any standard, Koop has accomplished much since he entered the government in 1981. At that time, the 64-year-old Koop presented both the reputation and the look of a stern moralist. Bespectacled and weighing more than 200 pounds, Koop had the bearing of a 6-foot 1-inch block of granite and

KOOP

sported square-cut gray chin whiskers that would have done credit to his Dutch forebears.

It was his energetic crusade against abortion, as well as his national standing as a pediatric surgeon, that brought Koop to the attention of newly elected President Ronald Reagan in 1981. While many of Reagan's followers saw Koop as a prospective surgeon general who shared their views, other legislators objected to the political implications of his appointment and questioned his qualifications for the post.

That was eight years ago. Since then, Koop has used his limited powers as the nation's chief health spokesman to advocate sex education and the use of condoms as primary weapons in the battle against AIDS (acquired immune deficiency syndrome, a fatal illness primarily transmitted through sexual activity and intravenous drug use). He has brought such explosive issues as smoking and the rights of disabled children into the legislative arena. In general, he has redefined and revitalized this once-quiet post. In the process, he has both alienated many of his original supporters and won applause from the very people who tried to block his nomination.

The surgeon general's responsibilities are, in brief, to promote the highest level of health attainable for Americans and to develop cooperation on health projects with other nations. Traditionally, the surgeon general offers advice on such questions as nutrition, immunization, and disease prevention. More recently, thanks in part to Koop, the office addresses such concerns as sexually transmitted diseases, environmental hazards, and the health needs of the aged and disabled.

One of the position's few formal responsibilities is to act as personnel chief of the commissioned officer corps of the U.S. Public Health Service (PHS). The corps consists of about 6,000 physicians, nurses, and other health specialists who staff health centers on Indian reservations and work in offices throughout the many institutions that make up the PHS. The corps is organized along military lines so that it can be dispatched quickly to sites of disasters or epidemics.

As surgeon general, Koop has the rank and pay ($88,552 in 1988) of a three-star Navy admiral, and he relishes wearing dress uniforms—though his efforts to encourage other corps officers to wear uniforms met with mixed results. But despite his rank, Koop has no responsibility for the medical activity of the corps. That job, along with responsibility for the other agencies of the PHS, falls to the assistant secretary for health in the U.S. Department of Health and Human Services (HHS).

Koop's statement that he has no power or money is close to the truth. His office is allotted just six full-time positions, for his

The authors:

Frank and Margot Cormier are free-lance writers based in the Washington, D.C., area. Frank Cormier is a former White House correspondent for the Associated Press.

personal staff, and the budget amounts to hundreds of thousands of dollars, not millions. By contrast, the far-flung PHS is a multibillion-dollar operation encompassing such agencies as the National Institutes of Health (NIH), the Centers for Disease Control, and the Food and Drug Administration.

Koop earmarked much of his small budget for travel around the United States to preach on health topics. But he has found funds from other agencies to finance many of his projects. His periodic warnings against smoking, for example, are paid for by HHS's Office of Smoking and Health. When he prepared a report on AIDS, the money came from the PHS.

Koop's role as a preacher of good health practices is the culmination of a lifetime commitment to deeply held beliefs, both medical and religious. The only child of a banker, Charles Everett (Chick) Koop was born in New York City on Oct. 14, 1916. By age 6, he wanted to be a surgeon, and at 13, with his mother's help, he was capturing, anesthetizing, and "operating" on stray cats. "I'd just take out something they didn't need, like one ovary," he explains. He would then suture his "patients" closed and release them in the neighborhood.

As a high school student, Chick Koop spent Saturdays at a New York City hospital, where he borrowed a white coat and wandered uninvited into operating rooms as though he were a medical student-observer. Koop entered Dartmouth College in Hanover, N.H., at age 16, got a summer job in a hospital, and, at the suggestion of a friendly orthopedist, performed his first surgical amputation while an undergraduate.

Koop meets with members of the commissioned officer corps of the Public Health Service, *below*. The corps consists of about 6,000 physicians, nurses, and other health specialists who staff Public Health Service offices and clinics. It is organized as a military operation so that it can be dispatched quickly to sites of epidemics or disasters.

He received his B.A. degree in 1937 and moved on to Cornell Medical College in New York City. In 1938, while still in medical school, he married Elizabeth (Betty) Flanagan, the daughter of a Connecticut country doctor. Three years later he completed his M.D. degree. He did his internship and residency in Philadelphia hospitals while receiving graduate training in surgery at the University of Pennsylvania School of Medicine.

When Koop completed his medical education in 1947, the couple—who by then had a 2-year-old son, Allen—decided to remain in Philadelphia. Koop wanted to specialize in cancer surgery, but a professor asked him instead to set up a surgery department at Children's Hospital in Philadelphia. Thus it was largely by happenstance that Koop became a specialist in pediatric surgery. He was the sixth pediatric surgeon in the United States—today there are nearly 500—and the first to confine all his surgery to children.

Koop went on to spend his entire surgical career at Children's Hospital, serving as chief surgeon for 33 years while also teaching surgery at the University of Pennsylvania School of Medicine. A second son, Norman, was born as Koop began his work at Children's Hospital, and son David and daughter Elizabeth arrived within the next five years.

Koop welcomed every opportunity to break new ground in the field of children's surgery. "It was almost like we were beginning to invent the wheel," he said later. "Everything you did then was brand new." He developed dozens of new surgical and diagnostic procedures, ranging from repairing intestinal obstructions to correcting birth defects thought untreatable. He improved preoperative and postoperative care for children and established America's first intensive surgical care unit for newborns. His work helped reduce mortality rates in child surgery that had reached a shocking 90 per cent for some procedures—such as the *colostomy,* the creation of an opening in the colon, an operation that involves very little risk today.

Koop earned national attention in 1977 by successfully rebuilding the chest of a baby born with its heart outside its body. He also became something of a specialist in separating Siamese twins, gaining celebrity status in 1974 by leading a 23-member surgical team that separated 13-month-old girls who shared an intestinal tract and rectum as well as other organs.

Koop's single-minded dedication to his practice would later carry over to his work as surgeon general; even now, he typically rises at 5 A.M. and works a 12-hour day. As the Koop children were growing up, Betty Koop was the mainstay of the family as her workaholic husband concentrated on surgery.

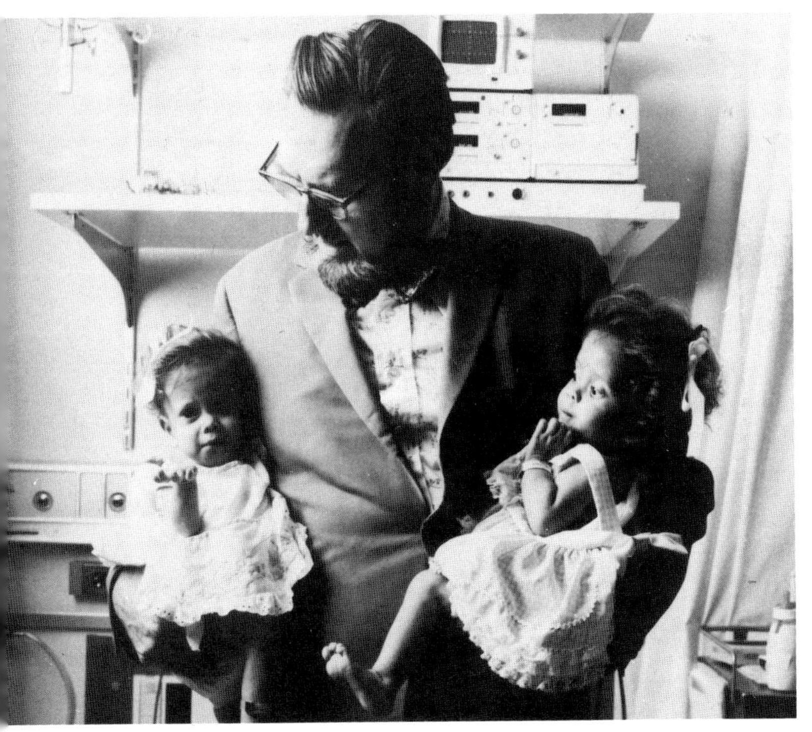

As a pioneer in the field of children's surgery, Koop earned celebrity status with his operations to repair birth defects. He successfully separated three pairs of Siamese twins, including the set he holds in this 1974 photograph, *left.* A 1980 portrait, *below,* shows Koop at Children's Hospital in Philadelphia, where he spent his entire surgical career after completing his medical training in 1947. During more than three decades as chief surgeon there, Koop developed dozens of new procedures, established America's first intensive surgical care unit for newborns, and helped bring down high mortality rates of surgery on children.

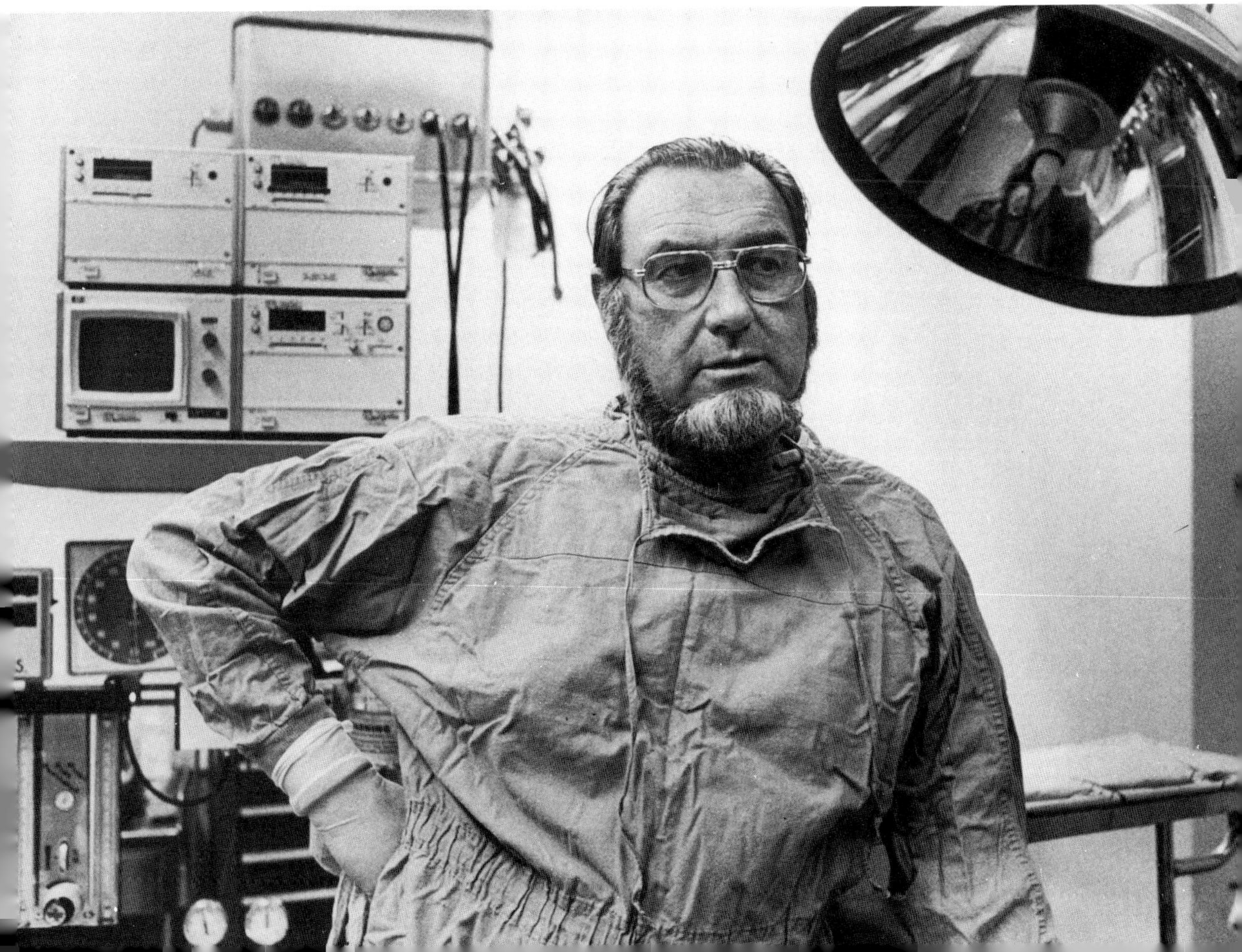

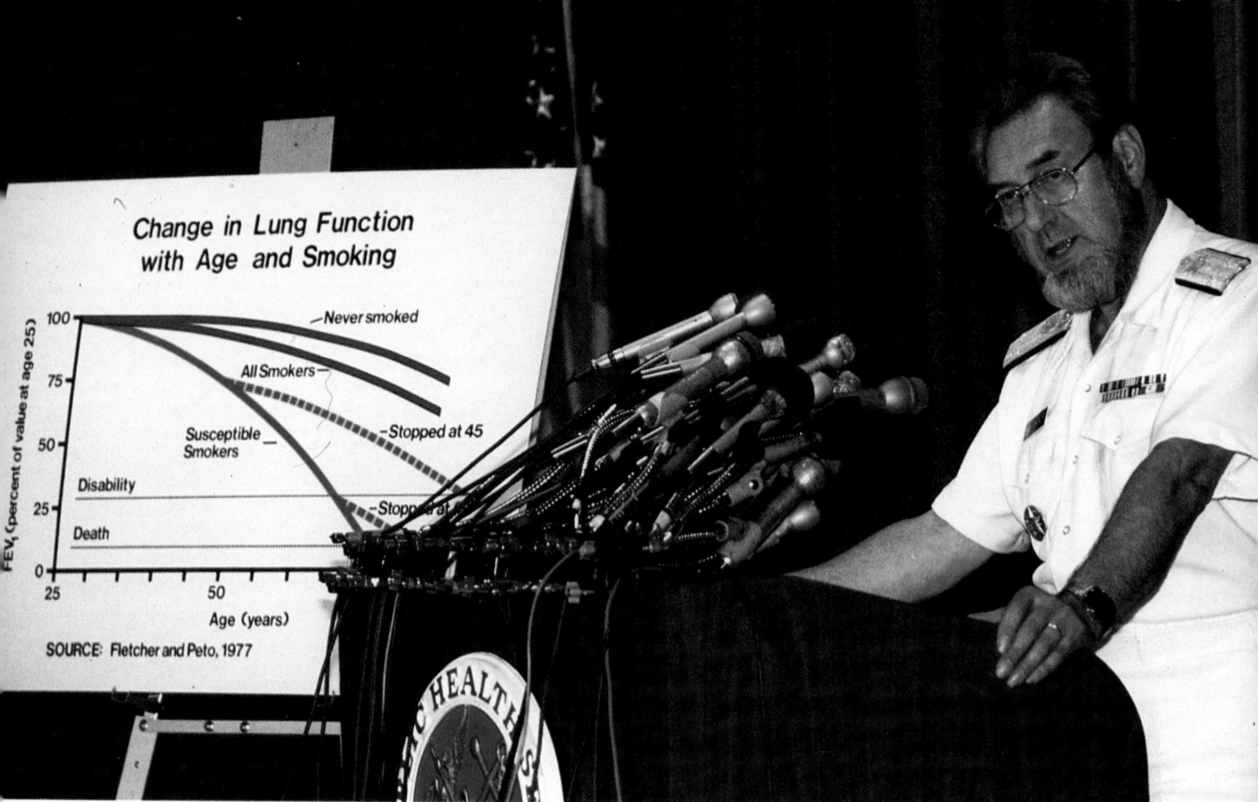

Following the lead of his best-known predecessor, Surgeon General Luther Terry—who in 1964 issued the first report on smoking and health—Koop established himself as a crusader against smoking. His frequent pronouncements on the harmful effects of smoking led to stronger health warnings on cigarette packs and legislation to ban smoking in many public places.

Koop's dedication to his profession is matched only by his dedication to his faith. Soon after he began practicing medicine, the Koops joined Philadelphia's 10th Presbyterian Church in Rittenhouse Square. "From then on," he explained in a 1982 interview, "there was never any question. I knew I was to practice my Christianity through my surgery. Everything I value or do I consider to be a gift from God." He shocked colleagues by praying at the bedsides of sick and dying children and by attributing all manner of developments to "the will of God."

The faith of the Koops sustained them when 20-year-old son David, a premedical student at Dartmouth, died in 1968 in a rock-climbing accident. For some time, Koop found it almost impossible to console grieving parents of his young patients. He and Betty told how they came to terms with the tragedy in their 1979 book, *Sometimes Mountains Move.*

By then, Koop had already begun to invest his own time and money in a crusade against abortion. In 1976, he published a book against abortion titled *The Right to Live: The Right to Die.* In 1979, he and theologian Francis A. Schaeffer toured 20 cities with a multimedia presentation that included a $1-million movie, *Whatever Happened to the Human Race?* Koop, who co-wrote a book of the same title with Schaeffer, presented abortion as a precursor of infanticide and euthanasia.

Largely because of Koop's stand on abortion, the Reagan Administration knew it faced serious obstacles in trying to install him as surgeon general. In the meantime, Koop was appointed in February 1981 to an HHS position as deputy assistant secretary for health, a job that did not require Senate confirmation.

Koop's impending nomination as surgeon general drew fire from both within and outside the government. *The New York Times* editorialized that he was chosen "for his political compatibility" and called him "Dr. Unqualified." Others less kind referred to him as "Dr. Kook." Representative Henry A. Waxman (D., Calif.), chairman of a congressional subcommittee that deals regularly with the surgeon general's office, was aghast at the prospect of Koop becoming the nation's voice on public health issues. "Dr. Koop scares me," Waxman told reporters at the time. "He is a man of tremendous intolerance." And for the first time in its 109-year history, the American Public Health Association, a national organization of health professionals, objected to a prospective surgeon general, on grounds that Koop lacked the training and experience required.

On Sept. 16, 1981, Reagan appointed Koop to the PHS commissioned officer corps and nominated him for the post of surgeon general. At the October hearings on the nomination, Koop noted his extensive international public health experience, which included teaching and volunteer work in developing countries. And he countered concerns about his political views by saying he would not continue to speak on the antiabortion circuit. "It is not my intent to use any post that I might have in government as a pulpit for ideology," he declared.

By a vote of 68 to 24, the Senate confirmed Koop's nomination on Nov. 16, 1981. He was sworn in on Jan. 21, 1982, nine years after the last full-time surgeon general stepped down.

Koop drew attention early in his tenure when he was drawn into the case of "Baby Doe," a boy born in Bloomington, Ind., in 1982. The infant had Down's syndrome, a genetic abnormality that causes mental retardation, as well as a correctable physical defect that prevented him from swallowing food. The child died of lack of nourishment after the parents and physicians chose to forgo surgery. When the Reagan Administration and the medical community clashed over new federal rules that required medical treatment in such cases, Koop helped draft compromise regulations to curb medical personnel from denying food or treatment to severely handicapped infants. "I have spent my whole life taking care of children with congenital defects," he told *U.S. News and World Report* in 1982, "and the majority have become very worthwhile citizens."

Koop's regulations were later struck down by the courts, but his stand was applauded by many who had battled to get him his job. And Koop argues now that handicapped infants are more protected today than before his efforts because "a lot of things that the regulations called for are still being done."

On the question of smoking, however, Koop demonstrated he would not automatically follow the inclinations of the Reagan Administration. Koop, who had himself quit smoking a pipe 10 years earlier, established himself as the most determined antismoking crusader to hold the office since Surgeon General Luther L. Terry issued his historic 1964 report on the perils of smoking—a report that prompted a law requiring a health warning on all cigarette packages. President Reagan had promised in his 1980 campaign that members of his Cabinet would "be far too busy with substantive matters to waste their time proselytizing against the dangers of cigarette smoking." Although not a Cabinet member, Koop nevertheless provoked Cabinet-sized headlines with a February 1982 report linking 30 per cent of cancer deaths to smoking.

Koop succeeded in winning Reagan's endorsement of legislation mandating stronger health warnings on cigarette packs. And the surgeon general later succeeded in placing health warnings on smokeless tobacco products such as snuff and chewing tobacco.

In December 1986, Koop broadened his antismoking efforts to embrace the perils of "passive smoking"—the inhalation of smoke by nonsmokers, which he said could cause cancer and other ills. Congress subsequently banned smoking on many airline flights, and local authorities curbed smoking in many public places. In May 1988, Koop renewed his attack by declaring that nicotine in tobacco products is comparable to heroin or morphine and should be labeled an addictive drug.

Even as Koop fought against tobacco, he was beginning an even more controversial battle. On Oct. 22, 1986, he issued a 36-page report outlining his views on combating the deadly AIDS virus. At the time, an estimated 1.5 million Americans had been infected, 15,000 had died, and the toll was growing.

Koop wrote the report himself and released it without going through the customary bureaucratic clearance process. "I said I was going to, and no one said not to," he told *Washingtonian* magazine in 1987. "That's the way I've done a lot of things in this job." Startling many who had expected him to advocate sexual abstinence or use vague and euphemistic warnings, Koop bluntly recommended that schools teach children about the use of condoms and that AIDS-related sex education should "start at the lowest grade possible." He also rejected suggestions to quarantine victims or require people to have their

In 1988, over White House objections, Koop spearheaded an unprecedented, $17-million mass mailing of an eight-page brochure on AIDS to every household in America. The pamphlet discussed the causes and prevention of AIDS in frank, clear terms.

blood tested for signs of the AIDS infection, saying, "It is time to put self-defeating attitudes aside and recognize that we are fighting a disease—not people."

Gary L. Bauer, Reagan's chief domestic policy adviser, was aghast at Koop's report. "I don't see why a third-grader needs to know anything about condoms or sexual practices," he said. Secretary of Education William J. Bennett, in a White House-approved speech, denounced "condom-mania" and called Koop's sex-education policy "clinically correct but morally empty." Koop lamented that Bennett "just can't see that as a public health officer I don't have the luxury of preaching a sermon."

Critics of Koop's stand on AIDS education argued that sex should be discussed only in the context of marriage and that children should be taught abstinence. In a 1987 interview with *People Weekly,* the surgeon general acknowledged: "Abstinence is the only sure method of preventing AIDS. But abstinence, I think we all know, is not a realistic goal." Although he championed monogamous relationships, Koop emphasized he had to deal with the practical, not the ideal.

Koop's AIDS stand met with disfavor among many of the people who had supported him earlier. He acknowledges being surprised at the intensity of disapproval, even hatred, directed at him for his controversial stand on AIDS—hatred that has forced him periodically to seek police protection against death threats. But undeterred by disapproval and threats, Koop ram-

rodded the preparation of an eight-page, $17-million brochure, *Understanding AIDS*, that was mailed in mid-1988 to every American household. The White House had killed PHS plans for the unprecedented mass mailing a year earlier, but Congress ordered Koop to proceed, with or without White House clearance.

In a personal message on the cover of the pamphlet, Koop wrote: "Some of the issues involved in this brochure may not be things you are used to discussing openly. I can easily understand that. But now you must discuss them. We all must know about AIDS. Read this brochure and talk about it with those you love. Get involved."

Facing page: Koop often brings work home, where a photograph of his son David—who died at age 20 in a 1968 rock-climbing accident—is prominently displayed.

Koop's stands on AIDS and smoking have been applauded by many, including congressmen who led the fight against his nomination in 1981. The once-skeptical Waxman, now a Koop ally, told *Washington Monthly* in 1987, "I just have the very highest regard for Dr. Koop. He's a man of tremendous integrity. He's done everything a surgeon general should do, and more, to protect the health of the public."

Koop took that duty to perhaps its broadest extreme yet in July 1988, when he issued a 712-page report citing dietary excess as a major national health problem. In particular, the report linked overconsumption of fat to heart disease, diabetes, high blood pressure, and other illnesses, and cited reduction of fat intake as America's top dietary priority.

Chick Koop's term as surgeon general expires on Nov. 16, 1989—well into a new administration. He has no intention of quitting before then; nor does he plan to retire after November. "I will work," he vows. "I will do something where I make a difference." He expects to remain in the national capital. "My skills really are in Washington now," he says.

Koop may also have the last word in the battle with his critics. "I have four books rattling around in my head, and they're going to come out," he says. At least one will tell about his years in government, based on the diary he's kept as surgeon general. But it won't be a "kiss-and-tell" book. "It's not going to destroy anybody," he says. "I'm not interested in that."

Instead, Chick Koop is pleased to have transformed what he calls "a cul-de-sac job," a job divorced from policy, into a focal point of controversy—and action. "I was essentially making policy by consensus or embarrassment. That's an interesting way to do it," he concedes. "But it works."

A Place to Heal

By Thomas H. Maugh II

The Child Sexual Abuse Treatment Center in Los Angeles helps repair the damage caused by child molestation.

Previous pages: Children's Institute International (CII) comprises two buildings in downtown Los Angeles—a modern facility that houses 42 abused infants and toddlers, left, and a converted mansion where older children come for individual, group, and family therapy, right.

Eight-year-old Rita's life had been the stuff nightmares are made of. Shortly after Rita* was born, her father left home to marry a woman addicted to alcohol and drugs. For years, Rita was shuttled between the homes of her mother and father. Her stepmother had three serious alcohol-related automobile accidents while Rita was in the car, and the child spent many months recuperating from each wreck. But these were the least of her problems.

When Rita was only 2 years old, her mother began sexually abusing her. As Rita grew older, the abuse worsened. By the time her father discovered the molestation when she was 8, Rita was having sex regularly with her 10-year-old brother and had begun sexually abusing her stepmother's two younger children in the same way that her mother abused her.

Rita's father reported the abuse to the Los Angeles Division of Children's Services, and Rita and her brother were placed in foster homes. Rita was also enrolled in an innovative therapy program at the Child Sexual Abuse Treatment Center, a division of Children's Institute International (CII) in Los Angeles.

CII—a private, nonprofit agency founded in 1906 as a home for unwed mothers—has been devoted since the 1970's to treating children who have been neglected, abused, or molested. There are few such agencies in the world, and CII is one of the largest and oldest in existence. CII's mission is to provide children like Rita with the expertise and care that will help them recover from their tragic beginnings.

To provide such treatment takes money, and CII operates on an annual budget of $5 million, which is provided by grants, foundations, individual donations, and contracts with the city and county of Los Angeles. First lady Nancy Reagan is an especially visible supporter. She is a member of the Colleagues, a philanthropic organization that has raised more than $3.5 million for the center.

CII's full-time and part-time staff of more than 100 includes psychologists, pediatricians, licensed clinical social workers, nurses, and day-care workers. Trained volunteers and professional trainees help the professional staff give the children the individual attention and support they need. CII occupies two adjacent buildings—including a 32-room mansion formerly owned by silent-film star Mary Miles Minter—in the Wilshire district of downtown Los Angeles. There, CII provides a broad range of services. These include a state-of-the-art emergency-care facility; a center for the diagnosis of child sexual abuse; day care for abused, neglected, abandoned, and underprivileged children; and individual and group counseling for molestation victims. In 1988, the institute established its own foster home agency. The agency recruits and trains foster parents to care for some of the abused children who have been treated at the institute.

The author:

Thomas H. Maugh II is a science writer for the *Los Angeles Times*.

*Pseudonyms are used in the case histories throughout this article.

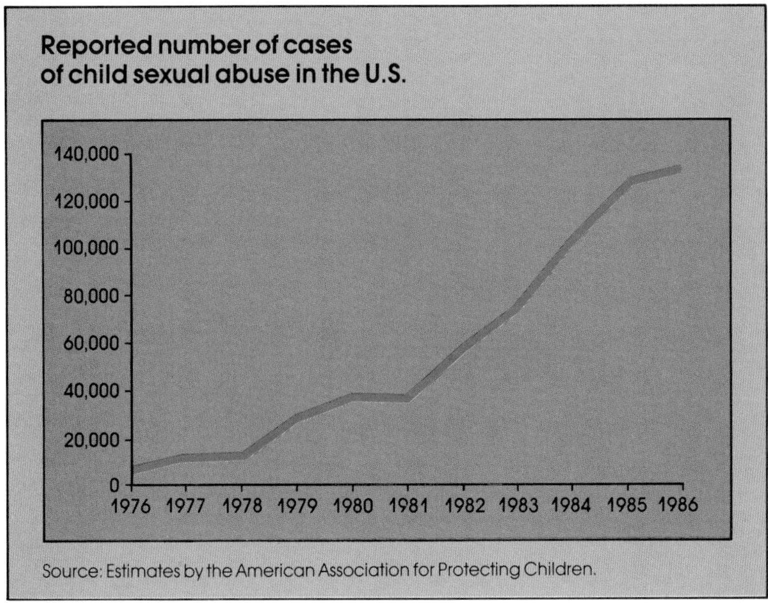

The number of reported cases of child sexual abuse increased twenty-fold from 1976 to 1986. The sharp rise may not mean that greater numbers of children are being abused, however. Instead, increased public awareness of the problem may have led to a greater likelihood that molestation is reported to the authorities.

CII uses a variety of approaches to help molestation victims. These include encouraging the children to express their anxieties and fears and helping them to develop such important "life skills" as making friendships. And through all of its programs, CII brings hope and understanding to children who, in some cases, have never had either, and strength and support to families on the verge of collapse. In 1987, nearly 1,600 children and their families participated in CII treatment programs. About 500 of them received treatment for sexual abuse. The institute also trained more than 3,500 social workers, psychologists, police officers, physicians, and nurses in dealing with abused children.

The children helped by CII represent only a fraction of the total number of abused children in the United States. No one is sure precisely how pervasive the problem is in our society, because many molestation victims never report the crime. The American Association for Protecting Children—a research, training, and advocacy group based in Denver—estimates that there were 132,000 reported cases of child molestation in the United States in 1986, the latest year for which statistics are available.

About 25 per cent of all women and 16 per cent of all men in the United States suffered some form of sexual abuse during childhood, according to Donald C. Bross, director of the National Association of Counsel for Children, a Denver-based coalition devoted to improving the legal representation of children.

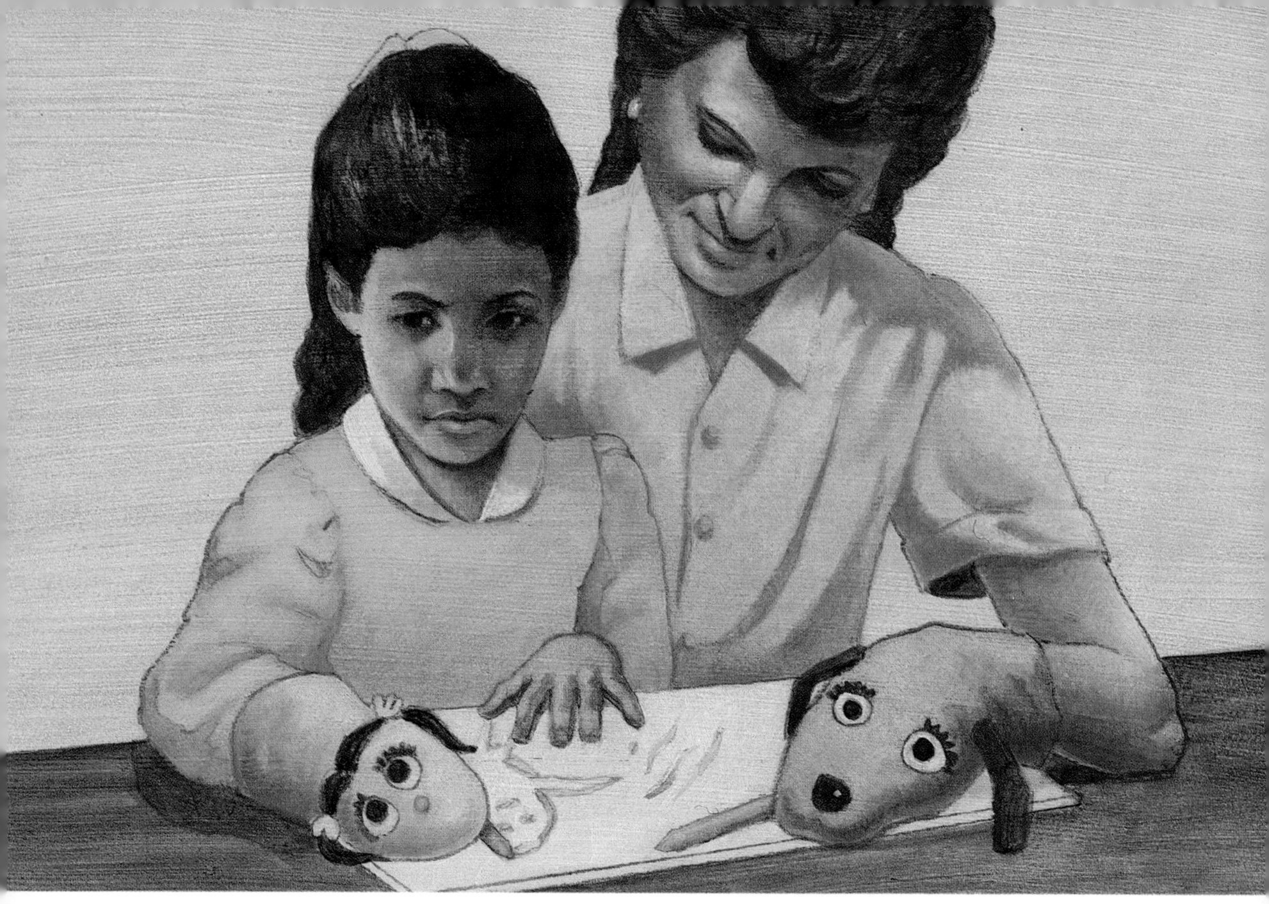

At CII's Child Sexual Abuse Diagnostic Center, a counselor uses puppets and markers to help a child suspected of being sexually abused talk about her experience.

Other experts estimate the percentage of child-molestation victims in the U.S. population to be anywhere from 6 to 62 per cent among females and 3 to 31 per cent among males.

Children between the ages of 8 and 12 are the age group most likely to be molested, though even babies are sometimes abused. And child abuse cuts across all social and economic boundaries. President Ronald Reagan's son Michael, who grew up amid the opulence of Beverly Hills, Calif., revealed in 1987 that as a child he was molested by a counselor at a summer camp. Television talk show host Oprah Winfrey, raised in poverty in Mississippi, told her viewers in 1985 that she had been a victim of repeated child molestation.

Most molesters are male, but they are rarely the stereotypical social misfit. The abuser is usually "the last person you would suspect—a parent, a concerned adult, a neighbor, a teacher, a scout leader, a minister," says clinical psychologist Toni Cavanagh Johnson, a clinical supervisor at CII's Child Sexual Abuse Center. Molesters who are not related to their victims are often "quite good with kids," Johnson says, "which is understandable, because they usually have to gain children's trust before they can take advantage of them."

"We should *not* assume that only youth counselors or day-care workers or teachers molest children," cautions Gene G. Abel, a psychiatrist at Emory University School of Medicine in

Atlanta, Ga., who treats child molesters. Statistics show that the typical molester is a parent, stepparent, or other adult living with the child. Despite many parents' fears that their children may be molested in day-care centers, molestation is far more likely to occur in the home, according to a 1988 study by sociologist David Finkelhor of the University of New Hampshire in Durham.

Mental health experts do not agree on the reasons for molestation. The traditional explanation, says Johnson, is that molesters are people who cannot relate to other adults sexually, or who become emotionally childlike, with a sexual interest in children, when under stress. This explanation is only a theory, however. We have no scientific evidence to explain why molesters abuse children, according to the Clearinghouse on Child Abuse and Neglect Information, which operates under the direction of the U.S. Department of Health and Human Services.

Studies have shown that as many as 80 per cent of perpetrators had themselves been sexually abused as children. Of course, not all abused children will later inflict their suffering upon the next generation. "But many do," says Mary M. Emmons, executive director of CII. "And early effective help is the key to breaking this terrible cycle of abuse."

Five-year-old Mary was in desperate need of such help when Johnson first saw her in the spring of 1987. The preschooler had *gonorrhea,* a sexually transmitted disease, which she contracted after being molested by her 10-year-old brother, Bobby. A chronic truant who couldn't read and wouldn't speak to his mother, Bobby had caught the disease from a 12-year-old girl.

Bobby had molested his sister for a year without their mother, a single parent, ever recognizing in Mary the classical symptoms of sexual abuse—nightmares, bedwetting, excessive masturbation, and an unusual level of sexual interest in other people. Only when Mary's gonorrhea was diagnosed by a physician was the sexual abuse revealed. The case was referred to local authorities, who sent the family to CII.

Johnson and her colleagues conducted typically thorough admission processes during which Mary, Bobby, and their mother were interviewed separately and then together. "We're looking into what happened to the child, the child's response, the parent's response, the legal system's response," she says. The children and their mother then took a battery of psychological tests designed to detect such factors as overwhelming stress, depression, and family disruption. With this information, "we can design a treatment program that has very focused goals for that family," Johnson says.

After the initial screening, Mary and Bobby were enrolled in two of the eight therapy groups for children at the center, and their mother was enrolled in a group organized to teach parents how to help their children. Each of the therapy groups is directed by one or two trained therapists.

Mary's group was designed to help victims of incestuous molestation by a brother or sister. The group met in 14 weekly sessions that coincided with the semesters of the school year. The therapist's main goals during these weekly sessions are to get the children to talk about their experiences, to show them that others have gone through similar things, and, most important, to help the victims realize that the abuse was not the children's fault.

"Many perpetrators are very good at making children think they are to blame. When children live with that, it can be very destructive," Johnson says. Without treatment, they may become depressed, fearful, or overly aggressive.

The group sessions provide a caring, nurturing environment—unlike the home environment of some of the children. For each session, the leader chooses a topic such as guilt, anger, or fear and develops a highly structured activity, such as playing a game or modeling with clay, that may prompt the children to talk about their experiences.

"There is not a tremendous need to discuss the nitty-gritty issues of the molestation," Johnson says. "The details are not all that important. You just want them to talk about the incident in general terms and to express their feelings about what happened. This helps make the pain go away." When necessary, the children are given additional individual counseling.

Bobby—along with Rita—was enrolled in a group that was part of the center's Support Program for Abuse-Reactive Kids (SPARK). *Abuse-reactive* refers to children who react to sexual abuse or other family problems by molesting other children. While treating children in the SPARK program—who range in age from 4 to 13—the center attempts to counsel every other member of the immediate family. "I see that as essential," Johnson says. "This is not an isolated kid that popped out of nowhere; the behavior is a family issue that needs to be treated in the family."

Although the SPARK program is organized in the same manner as programs for victims of abuse, the themes of the sessions are quite different. "Whereas in groups like Mary's we are talking about shame, anger, and fear, in the SPARK program we consistently work on changing the child's sexual behavior," she says. "We emphasize that the behavior is wrong and unacceptable, and that the kids need other avenues to act out their feelings."

The sexual activity of child perpetrators is usually an expression of anger, anxiety, and confusion. Many of the children, like Rita, have been molested themselves, according to Johnson's 1988 study of 60 abuse-reactive children.

Others, like Bobby, were not sexually abused but are exposed to other family problems. If an abuse-reactive child has never been sexually abused, Johnson says, "we always find that there has been a tremendous amount of sexual anxiety and confusion in the family." For example, the parents may have had a very difficult sexual relationship, or a succession of boyfriends or girlfriends. Thus, says Johnson, "when you look at the child's family, it no longer seems confusing why the child has become sexually aggressive. But of course you can't go the other way and say that if certain things happen in the family, the child will become a molester."

Clay modeling and drawing can be helpful for children in SPARK groups as well as for those in the groups for victims of sexual abuse. The children are asked to make or draw something that reminds them of themselves. When Rita first came into the program, for instance, she molded a clay figure whose legs and arms were twisted and shriveled; she even made a tiny wheelchair for it. "Clearly, she thought of herself as being very

Young victims of sexual abuse meet weekly for group counseling with a therapist. Clay modeling helps the children express their feelings about what happened to them.

Preteens who molest other children—behavior typically sparked by having been victims of sexual abuse themselves—are counseled in group sessions led by a team of therapists. Clay modeling and drawing help these children express themselves—but the major focus of therapy is setting limits on the children's behavior.

handicapped," Johnson says, "but the clay figure helped her to start talking about it."

At any one time, as many as 150 children are enrolled in various therapy groups at the Child Sexual Abuse Treatment Center. On average, a child victim stays in treatment about nine months. The staff does not talk about "cures," and there are few hard and fast rules about determining when a child is ready to leave the program. The best measure of progress, says Johnson, is when the child is no longer exhibiting symptoms of distress—such as bedwetting, nightmares, fears, and phobias—and is able to make and sustain friendships, participate in school activities, and get along with the family. Most of the children treated at the Child Sexual Abuse Treatment Center eventually reach this point.

Long-term success is extremely difficult to measure, but the short-term results of the two programs can be impressive. Mary, for example, is now in kindergarten and shows none of her former symptoms. Her brother, Bobby, is attending school regularly, passing all his subjects, and reading at the third-grade level. Most important, he is not a gang member like many of his peers. The childen's mother is seeking to improve her situation by going to a junior college to learn to become a teacher's aide. "Their success is the kind of thing that keeps us at CII going," says Johnson.

Helping abused children who are asked to testify in court about incidents of child abuse—an experience that can be frightening for a child—is another challenging task for the therapists and volunteers at the center. One of the most innovative programs at CII, called Kids in the Court System, is designed for children aged 4 to 12 who must make such court appearances. The aim of this program, says staff psychologist Sandra M. Ballester, "is to educate children and families about the court to prevent the child from experiencing further trauma as he or she becomes involved in the legal system." Ballester and trained volunteers use dolls and mock trials to demonstrate how a courtroom session is conducted and to show the role of each participant. The children's individual cases are not discussed, because that could invalidate their testimony.

Counseling for the whole family is an important part of the CII treatment program. While their children are being counseled, parents meet in separate groups directed by therapists.

CII's Kids in the Court System program reduces the stress children feel when compelled to testify in court. A trained volunteer uses dolls and felt figures to show the child how a courtroom session is conducted. Later, the volunteer or a psychologist will accompany the child to court and provide emotional support.

The therapists' biggest challenge, however, is treating infant molestation victims. Children over the age of 2 have a good chance of recovering from sexual abuse with effective therapy, but younger children may be harder to help, Johnson says. "The emotional damage may occur, in part, because the very young child is unable to understand what has happened or talk about it. Because people have only fragmentary memories of the things that happen to them when they are infants, victims of molestation at that age may never be able to clearly recall and talk about the abuse."

One of these young victims was Emma, aged 18 months, who came into the center's care after her mother was arrested for drug abuse. Emma clasped her legs firmly together when anyone picked her up and screamed hysterically when her clothes were removed to change her diaper or give her a bath. She had to be anesthetized for examination by a physician, who found that she had been raped repeatedly. The molester was her mother's boyfriend.

Or consider Tony, a 3-year-old who was so withdrawn that he had effectively "checked out of life," says developmental specialist Sheila Anderson, director of CII's Infant Shelter Care Program. Tony had undergone physical and sexual abuse by his mother's boyfriend.

Tony and Emma spent several months at CII's Colleague Infant Care Center, an emergency shelter where 42 abused, abandoned, or neglected infants and toddlers are housed and cared for while the courts decide whether to return them to their parents or place them in foster care. The center "tries to provide care in a familylike way," says Anderson, by dividing the children into three groups of 14. Separate sleeping quarters, kitchen area, and yard are provided for each group. The groups share a large play area, but playtimes are staggered so that each group gets to use the area all by itself.

Each group has four full-time caregivers—who are well-trained in child development and health care—per eight-hour shift, plus a varying number of professionals and professionally directed volunteers who work with each child in a family-sized grouping of three. A caregiver's most important job is simply to gain the trust of the children. Most abused or neglected children are so leery of adults that they do not even make eye contact, Anderson says. They may generalize from their experiences and conclude that all adults will treat them in the same manner as their abuser. Abandoned toddlers may also lose

Sexually abused infants and toddlers live at CII's Colleague Infant Care Center while the courts decide whether to place them in foster homes. During their stay at the center, trained caregivers and community volunteers give the children love and direction, encouraging them to form trusting relationships with others.

Has it happened to a child you know?

A concerned adult can be an active force for the well-being of a molested child, according to *Please, No, Not My Child . . .*, a manual published by CII for parents of abused children. Parents and other adults have an extremely important role in the uncovering of sexual abuse as well as in its treatment.

Experts advise that if a child tells you that he or she has been sexually abused, believe what you hear. Children rarely fabricate such tales. Unfortunately, some adults, recoiling from the thought that sexual abuse has occurred, may deny or ignore the problem. This attitude can be very destructive because treating the incident as a shameful secret may be more devastating to the child than the abuse itself.

Because many abused children are too frightened or confused—or simply too young—to put the experience into words, parents should also be alert to changes in a child's behavior that may indicate sexual victimization. The child may suddenly become fearful of certain people or places or of being separated from the parents. He or she may also begin having nightmares or incidents of bedwetting. Unexplained moodiness, along with sexualized behavior—such as excessive masturbation, a sexual interest in others, and using new terms to describe the genitals—are other indicators that something may be wrong. A child therapist can help you determine the cause of these behaviors.

In a few cases, molestation leaves physical signs. A child who complains of pain in the genital or anal areas—which may be most apparent when using the toilet or being picked up—may be a victim of sexual abuse. Redness, rashes, tears, swelling, bleeding, or discharges in the genital or anal area are important signs as well. The anxiety that abuse provokes may also cause generalized medical problems such as stomach pains, headaches, and asthma. You should immediately bring physical symptoms to the attention of a physician, who can gently examine the child, looking for signs of abuse.

If you discover that the child has been molested, the first thing to do is try to get control of your own feelings. You may be filled with outrage, shock, and disbelief, but you must make every effort to be calm with your child, because he or she is probably already very anxious. The more matter-of-fact you are, the more information your child will be willing to share with you. Be especially careful never to give the impression that you are blaming the child for what happened. Emphasize that—no matter what the child did, said, or felt—the incident was not his or her fault. Tell the child that he or she did not cause the abuse or deserve it in any way.

The molestation—which is a crime—should then be reported to your state's agency on child abuse, which in most cases is a division of the state department of social services, protective services, or child and family services. If you are unable to reach this agency, call the local police.

Once the appropriate authorities have been contacted, do not make efforts to put the molestation behind you immediately. Children need to be given the opportunity and the permission to express their feelings as they come up. Counseling with a child therapist will probably be very helpful.

The long-term effects of child molestation vary from child to child and are difficult to predict. But there is absolutely no evidence that molestation by itself leads to homosexuality, sexual problems, or future sexual abusiveness. Rather, it appears that ignoring the abuse or treating the child insensitively may cause problems later in life. Thus, parents have a great deal of influence over their child's fate. [T. M.]

much of their language ability because of the trauma of being abused as well as the distress they feel at being separated from their parents.

The children in the Infant Care Center, especially those too young to talk, often reenact their traumatic experiences using dolls or other toys. Two-year-old Charlie, for example, would place a doll on an imaginary toilet, then shake the doll violently, slap it, and throw it down. The caregivers take advantage of such situations by allowing the children to vent their feelings and then trying to change the children's behavior by letting them know that there are other ways to treat the toy. Charlie was shown that the doll could be cuddled and gently put to bed. More important, Charlie himself was treated lovingly by the caregivers. If the toddler had been older, he would also have been gently asked what he thought the doll might feel about being abused and what he himself feels when he is treated cruelly.

At the shelter, Charlie, Emma, and Tony were able to form relationships with adult staff members and volunteers, which helped the children come to terms with their experiences and begin to mend. Today, the boys are two of CII's success stories. Both are doing well in foster homes. Emma's story also has a happy ending. Her mother testified in court against her boyfriend and has been reunited with Emma.

And Rita recently graduated from her SPARK group after two years of therapy. "I had just about decided she was ready to leave the program," Johnson says, "when Rita came in one day and said 'I feel good now. I feel normal, like other kids.' " In her last session, Rita took the clay figure of the little girl with twisted legs and shriveled arms and made them whole.

For further information:

Literature and referrals concerning all types of child abuse can be obtained by calling Childhelp USA's National Child Abuse Hotline at (800) 422-4453.

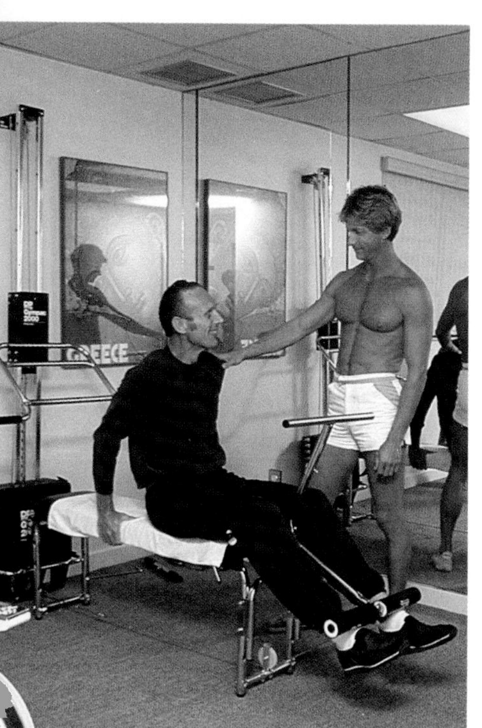
GREECE

Health Studies

The World Book Health & Medical Annual takes a wide-ranging, in-depth look at a crucial issue related to personal health and fitness.

Weight Control and Your Health

by Kelly D. Brownell

As many as 34 million U.S. adults face the health risks and social pressures that come with being overweight. This report looks at why people gain weight, how to lose it, and how to keep weight at a healthy level.

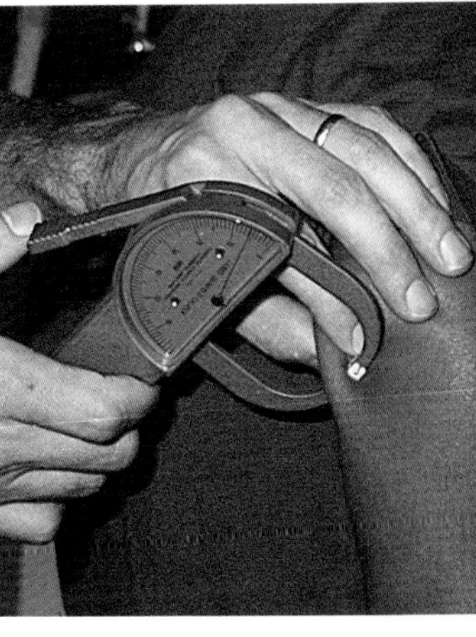

Weight Control and Your Health

By Kelly D. Brownell

We are a society preoccupied with thinness. Survey after survey shows that most adults in North America think they weigh too much. Each year, Americans spend about $10-billion on diet books, diet products, and diet programs, according to *The Wall Street Journal.* Magazines and newspapers contain advertisements for a variety of unproven or fraudulent "remedies," from pills that supposedly melt fat to magic blankets that purportedly extract fat while you sleep. But even if such remedies don't make good health sense, a concern with weight does. Roughly 34 million U.S. adults—about 20 per cent of those aged 19 or older—are overweight. The proportion is about the same in Canada. Because overweight people show increased risk for illnesses ranging from diabetes to heart disease, this disorder may be one of our culture's most significant health problems.

How fat is too fat?

Notions of what body shape and size is desirable have varied widely from place to place and era to era. In some countries, where few people can afford ample food, being overweight is a sign of prosperity. Anthropologist Peter J. Brown of Emory University in Atlanta, Ga., found that 47 of 58 cultures he looked at viewed plumpness as an ideal of feminine beauty.

In contrast, our own society's image of the ideal female has become progressively thinner during the last few decades. Canadian researchers who analyzed weight data from Miss America Pageant contestants found that while average weights of U.S. women under age 30 increased by an average of about 0.3 pound (0.14 kilogram) per year between 1959 and 1978, weights of the pageant contestants *decreased* at almost exactly the same rate.

Defining ideal weight, overweight, and obesity

Popular ideals of body shape reflect cultural aesthetics, not necessarily good health. From a health standpoint, people are considered *overweight* if they weigh more than an ideal weight for their height as noted in a standard height-weight table.

Height-weight tables were developed by life insurance companies to determine the weights at which people live longest. An individual's *ideal weight,* therefore, is the weight at which a large group of insured adults of that person's sex and height were found to have the longest life span. The most widely used tables come from the Metropolitan Life Insurance Company, which published its first tables in the early 1940's and revised them in 1959 and 1983.

Height-weight tables provide a rough idea of what healthy

Detail from *The Garden of Love* (1637), a painting by Peter Paul Rubens; Prado Museum, Madrid, Spain.

The ideal female form of the year 1637, above, *was rounded and fleshy. Today's fashion models,* right, *prize extreme thinness.*

people weigh. The figures in the tables, however, are simply averages based on large groups of people. Since healthy individuals vary widely, the tables cannot state precisely what any one person should weigh or how much weight is too much.

To provide a guideline, a panel of experts brought together in 1985 by the National Institutes of Health (NIH) in Bethesda, Md., declared that a weight of 20 per cent above the midpoint of the ideal range constitutes a health hazard. A weight of 40 per cent or more over ideal constitutes "severe" overweight; about a third of overweight Americans—some 12.4 million U.S. adults—fall into this category. For people who suffer from diabetes, high blood pressure, or heart disease, health risks appear at even lower levels of overweight.

But measurements of body weight alone do not determine whether a person is obese. *Obesity* is an excessive accumulation of body fat. What constitutes an excess varies among individuals, but in general, fat should account for 20 to 27 per cent of body tissue in women and 15 to 22 per cent in men.

Measuring fat

Usually a high weight reflects a high level of fat. But that's not always the case, because a given volume of muscle—a nonfat tissue—weighs more than the same volume of fat. For example, a football player with a large amount of muscle may be "overweight" according to the tables but still have a smaller proportion of body fat than a "normal weight" person in poor physical condition.

People can measure their weight merely by standing on a scale. Measuring body fat accurately is more difficult. In the simplest method, the thickness of folds of skin at various points on the body is measured with a device called *skinfold calipers.* One such site is the underside of the upper arm. Experts use measurements from as many as eight sites to estimate the level of fat in a person's body.

An obese person has too much body fat, top. *But a muscular person,* above, *may weigh as much and not be obese.*

A more accurate method, *hydrostatic* weighing, involves weighing a person underwater and calculating the percentage of body fat using the person's land weight (measured above water) and underwater weight. Fat tissue is less dense than nonfat tissue; measured underwater, a pound of comparatively buoyant fat weighs less than a pound of nonfat tissue. Thus, if two people who weigh the same have a different proportion of fat, the person with more fat will weigh less underwater.

Where overweight begins

For adults of average frame size, without shoes or clothing

Men			Women		
Height	Ideal Weight (in pounds)	Overweight (in pounds)	Height	Ideal Weight (in pounds)	Overweight (in pounds)
5′1″	131	157	4′9″	112	134
5′2″	133	160	4′10″	114	137
5′3″	135	162	4′11″	117	140
5′4″	138	165	5′0″	119	143
5′5″	140	168	5′1″	122	146
5′6″	143	172	5′2″	125	150
5′7″	146	175	5′3″	128	154
5′8″	149	179	5′4″	131	157
5′9″	152	182	5′5″	134	161
5′10″	155	186	5′6″	137	164
5′11″	159	190	5′7″	140	168
6′0″	162	194	5′8″	143	172
6′1″	166	199	5′9″	146	175
6′2″	170	203	5′10″	149	179
6′3″	174	209	5′11″	152	182

Height-weight tables reflect the average weights at which large groups of people lived longest. Because healthy individuals can vary widely, height-weight tables cannot specify a precise ideal weight for any one person. In these tables, "overweight" reflects an arbitrary standard of 20 per cent above ideal weight.

Source: Based on 1983 Metropolitan Height and Weight Tables and NIH recommendations.

Risks of obesity

Overweight or obesity carries significant physical risks. In ad-

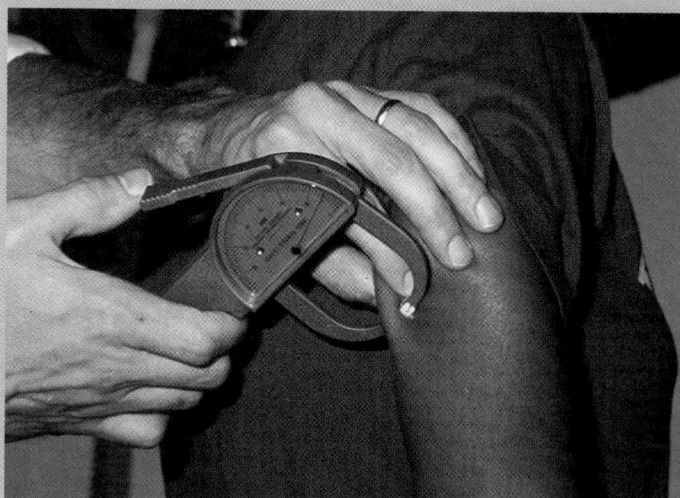

Using skinfold calipers, a physician measures the thickness of a fold of skin in order to estimate body fat.

dition, obese people often suffer from certain social and psychological pressures.

Physical consequences

Several major studies indicate that death rates increase as the degree of overweight increases. In an American Cancer Society (ACS) study of 750,000 people, those under age 60 who weighed 40 per cent or more above average had a death rate more than double that of those of average weight. The 1979 Build Study, a life insurance study of more than 4 million men and women, reported a similar relationship between weight and death rates and also showed that the probability of dying increases even more among people who have been overweight for a longer time.

The role of weight becomes even more important as people get older. The Framingham Heart Study, which monitored the long-term health of about 5,000 people in Massachusetts, showed that the risk of death within a 26-year period increased by 1 per cent for each 1 pound (0.45 kilogram) of excess weight for men aged 30 to 49. For men aged 50 to 62, the risk of death increased by 2 per cent per extra pound.

Research has linked overweight and obesity to a variety of health problems. Experts point out that overweight does not necessarily cause these conditions; it may simply reflect other factors, such as poor diet or lack of exercise, that are the real causes. But in any case, overweight signifies an increased risk of developing these problems.

Hypertension (high blood pressure). The National Health and Nutrition Examination Survey (NHANES), a federal survey conducted in the 1970's on a sample of U.S. residents, showed that overweight people as a group were 2.9 times more likely than nonoverweight people to have hypertension. Overweight people aged 20 to 44 were 5.6 times more likely to have hypertension than were nonoverweight people of the same age. Untreated hypertension significantly increases the risk of heart attack, stroke, and kidney disease.

Diabetes. Overweight people in the NHANES study were 2.9 times more likely than nonoverweight people to have diabetes, a disease in which the body cannot use sugar properly. Complications of diabetes, one of the leading causes of death in the United States, include heart disease, stroke, blindness, and kidney failure.

Hypercholesterolemia (high blood cholesterol). In the NHANES study, overweight people aged 20 to 44 were more than twice as likely as nonoverweight people in the same age group to have high levels of

The most accurate way to measure body fat is to weigh a person underwater and compare that weight with weight on land.

Increased risk of health problems with obesity

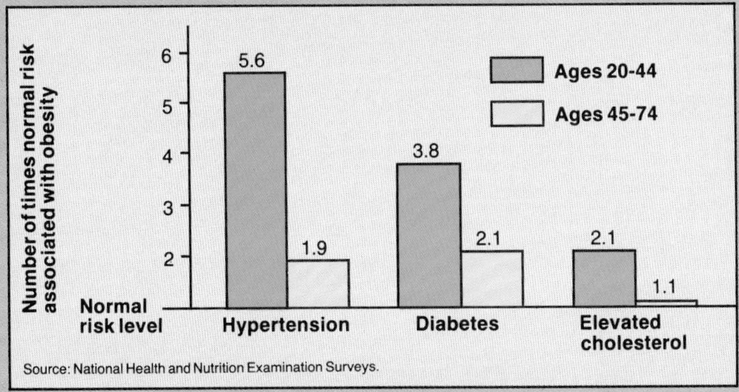

Increased likelihood of developing health problems is especially high among obese people aged 20 to 44.

blood *cholesterol* (a fatty substance in the blood and body tissues). After age 45, the risk was the same for overweight and nonoverweight people. High blood cholesterol levels have been linked with high risk for coronary artery disease.

Coronary artery disease. Obesity is a significant factor in *coronary artery disease* (CAD), the leading cause of death among American adults. CAD, a progressive narrowing of the blood vessels that carry blood to the heart muscle, can lead to heart attacks and other problems. The NHANES study found that three conditions that heighten the risk of CAD—hypertension, diabetes, and hypercholesterolemia—increase with obesity. In addition, the Framingham study linked increased CAD with increasing levels of obesity alone, regardless of other risk factors.

Cancer. ACS studies of 1 million people between 1959 and 1972 showed that obese men had higher death rates than nonobese men from cancer of the colon, rectum, and prostate. Obese women had higher death rates from cancer of the gall bladder, *biliary passages* (ducts connected to the liver and gall bladder), breast, uterus, and ovaries.

Other risks. Studies have also linked overweight to a variety of other diseases, including liver and gall bladder problems, gout, and trauma to the joints. In addition, overweight people are more likely to experience complications during pregnancy or surgery.

Disease and fat location. Placement of fat may be almost as important as the amount of fat. In general, people with *upper-body obesity* (fat at the waist or abdomen, or an apple-shaped figure) are more likely to suffer from heart disease, stroke, and diabetes than those with *lower-body obesity* (fat on the hips, thighs, and buttocks, or a pear-shaped figure), according to various studies.

Fat distribution can be calculated by dividing the waist measurement (measured at the narrowest point) by the hip measurement (measured at the widest point). A figure of more than 1 for men or 0.8 for women represents significant risk, even if a person is not overweight.

Psychological consequences

Given the pressures on obese people in a society that values thinness, psychologists long assumed that obese people were especially likely to show psychological disturbances. As it turns out, obesity seems to have no effect on standard measures of such traits as anxiety or depression. Researchers at the University of Pennsylvania, in Philadelphia, found that obese people who do have psychological problems tend to develop disturbances related directly to their weight, such as disparaging feelings about their bodies. Studies repeatedly show, however, that obese people are no more likely than normal-weight people to have psychological problems in general.

Researchers offer several interpretations of these results. One is that obesity does cause distress, but that for most obese people, this distress does not affect facets of their lives not directly related to weight. Another possibility is that psychological tests do not accurately measure the problems obese people experience—for example, low self-confidence from failure to control weight. And, of course, it's possible that obesity indeed has no connection to psychological problems.

Some psychologists believe our society's dislike of obesity may be responsible for the increasing prevalence of eating disorders, particularly *anorexia nervosa* (a disorder characterized by self-starvation) and *bulimia* (a disorder involving binge eating, followed by purging with laxatives or self-induced vomiting). People who develop these disorders are rarely overweight, but they have an intense fear of becoming so. Studies suggest that women in professions that emphasize thinness (such as dancers and models) and upper-class women, who tend to be thinner than average, are at greatest risk for developing anorexia. Other studies indicate that only 5 per cent of people with bulimia are overweight, but that as many as 88 per cent were dieting rigorously when the disorder first appeared.

Social consequences

Overweight people face a strong social prejudice against obesity. For example, a 1980

The importance of fat distribution

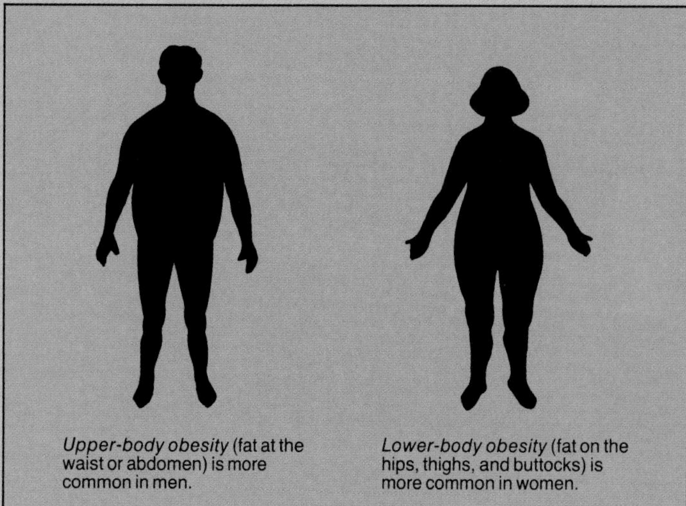

People with upper-body obesity are more likely to develop heart disease or diabetes than those with lower-body obesity.

survey by the State of Maryland Commission on Human Relations found that obese people in that state suffered from lower pay, inequitable hiring standards, and other discriminatory treatment not based on job-related criteria. Other studies have shown evidence of discrimination against the obese in such areas as college admissions and housing applications.

Bias against obesity begins in childhood. In a 1967 study, children as young as age 6 described silhouettes of obese children as "dirty," "lazy," "stupid," "ugly," "cheats," and "lies." In similar studies, children and adults who were shown line drawings of an obese child, a normal-weight child, and children with deformities and handicaps rated the obese child as least likable. Not only were these attitudes common regardless of age, sex, race, and economic status, but they also appeared among obese people themselves.

Some social scientists have suggested that such biases stem from the importance our society places on self-denial and self-control. According to these theories, Americans see obesity as the result of overindulgence and lack of willpower, which in turn indicate a sinful or immoral nature.

Whatever the reason, many people believe that obese people are responsible for their own condition. What we now know about the causes of obesity indicates that this blame is unfair and misplaced. To understand why, we need to look at how and why the body stores fat.

How the body stores fat

Our bodies need energy to operate. That energy comes from the proteins, carbohydrates (starches and sugars), and fats in our food. For the most part, proteins provide the material used to build, maintain, and repair body tissues; carbohydrates and fats provide energy for activity.

If the body takes in more energy than it needs, it stores the excess in *adipose tissue,* which consists of fat cells. Fat cells have tremendous storage capacity; each cell can expand to 100 times its normal volume in order to store fat. When adults gain weight, they usually do so by increasing the size of their fat cells. Some scientists suggest that when people reach extreme levels of overweight, they may also manufacture new fat cells.

Scientists suggest that human beings developed the ability to store extra fat to protect themselves against an uncertain food supply. In a time of famine, a person can survive by turning stored fat back into energy. Without that reserve, the body would need to draw energy from other tissues and would eventually destroy vital organs.

Anthropologist Brown of Emory University points out that obesity was rare for most of human history because regular food shortages made ongoing weight gain impossible. The prevalence of obesity increases in modernized societies that have a constant supply of food.

In addition to providing an energy reserve, fat also acts as a protective cushion for vital organs as well as insulation against cold. Having too little fat, in fact, may be a sign of major illness.

How the body handles calories

The amount of energy available in any particular food is measured in calories. To measure calories in food, scientists use a device called a *bomb calorimeter,* which consists of a small chamber that rests in a container of water. When food is burned inside the chamber, the water heats up. The temperature increase of a measured amount of water indicates the number of calories in the food.

People have commonly believed that 3,500 calories equals 1 pound (0.45 kilogram) of body weight—that is, a person who eats 3,500 calories too much will gain 1 pound. That notion is not exactly true. To begin with, we now know that how the body handles calories varies from individual to individual. Studies have shown that not every person needs the same number of calories. Some people eat a great deal and do not gain weight; others eat a "normal" amount, or even less, and still gain weight.

Furthermore, not all calories are alike. Calories that come from fat in food can become stored fat with practically no extra effort from the body. But if extra calories come in the form of carbohydrates or proteins, the body must convert those substances into fat in order to store them. Like all bodily functions, that conversion requires energy. In other words, the body uses calories to store calories.

Who stores fat

Women tend to store more fat than men do. Researchers suggest that women's bodies might store extra fat to prepare for pregnancy. Pregnancy requires up to 80,000 more calories than the body would normally use over a nine-month period.

A woman's need to maintain a reserve of extra fat may also explain why women and men store fat in different places. Men tend to store fat in the abdomen, while women tend to store fat in the hips, thighs, and buttocks. Also, upper-body sites add and release fat more frequently than do lower-body sites. This suggests that women may have developed lower-body fat sites for long-term energy storage.

Some groups of people show statistically higher rates of obesity than others. For example, the prevalence of obesity increases with age. Age itself does not cause obesity, but older people tend to be less physically active and more susceptible to conditions that restrict activity, such as arthritis. This, in turn, may encourage weight gain.

Similarly, the NHANES surveys show that obesity is more common among white men than black men from ages 20 to 34, but it is more common among black men aged 35 to 54. Black women have a much higher prevalence of obesity than white women at any age. Women living below the poverty line are much more likely to be obese than women of higher economic status, regardless of race; at the same time, men living in poverty are slightly less likely to be obese than men of higher economic status. The reasons for these racial and socioeconomic differences remain unknown.

To measure calories with a bomb calorimeter, a scientist puts some food in a small chamber that rests inside a container of water.

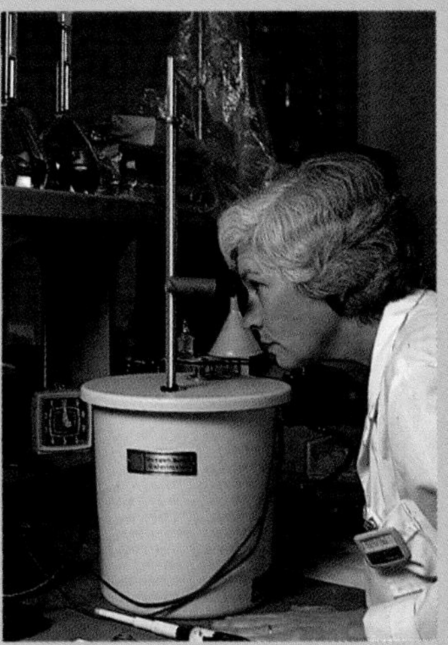

As the food is burned, the scientist watches a temperature gauge to see how much heat—or energy—the water absorbs.

Causes of obesity

People have traditionally assumed that individuals are overweight because they cannot control their eating. Since a person gains weight by eating more than his or her body needs, then in one sense it's accurate to say that obese people "overeat." But many factors besides willpower affect a person's chances of becoming obese.

No one can pinpoint any single cause of weight gain. In any individual, body weight reflects many physical, behavioral, and cultural factors.

Physical factors

Even if two people eat the same amount of calories, several physical factors can cause them to gain different amounts of weight. These include individual differences in how the body uses energy, hereditary factors, and certain physical disorders.

Energy use. The body uses energy not only to power physical activity but also to carry out the daily chemical processes required for living. The process by which the body transforms calories from food into energy is called *metabolism*. The number of calories individuals "burn" at rest—their *metabolic rates*—can vary, because different people require different amounts of energy. People with lower metabolic rates require fewer calories, and thus less food.

In a recent study of how energy use affects weight gain, physiologists at an NIH laboratory in Phoenix measured metabolic rates and overall energy use of a group of Pima Indians. They chose this group because

Pima Indians have a high rate of obesity; 80 to 85 per cent of Pima adults are obese.

The researchers determined metabolic rates in 126 people by monitoring their breathing as they lay still for a 40-minute period. By measuring the oxygen consumed and the carbon dioxide produced, the scientists calculated metabolic activity.

The researchers then monitored the subjects' weight and metabolic rates over four years. They found that the people who gained substantial amounts of weight over time had shown lower metabolic rates at the start of the experiment. After the weight gain, however, their metabolic rates rose to levels similar to the rates of those who had not gained weight.

In a related experiment, 95 individuals each spent 24 hours at rest in a *respiratory chamber,* an enclosed room equipped to measure how much energy a person uses overall. Two years later, the researchers found that the people who had originally shown low levels of energy use were four times as likely to have gained substantial amounts of weight as the people who had shown high energy use.

Heredity. Obesity runs in families. Studies from the early 1970's indicate that while only 7 per cent of children of nonobese parents are overweight, 40 per cent of those with one obese parent and 80 per cent of those with two obese parents are also obese. Obesity also appears as a predominant characteristic of certain racial and social groups, such as the Pima Indians.

Traditionally, scientists believed obesity in families was due in large part to family influence on eating habits, though centuries of selective breeding of livestock, and more recent studies of laboratory animals, demonstrated that genes help control weight in animals. Until recently, however, no method existed to study the influence of heredity on human obesity.

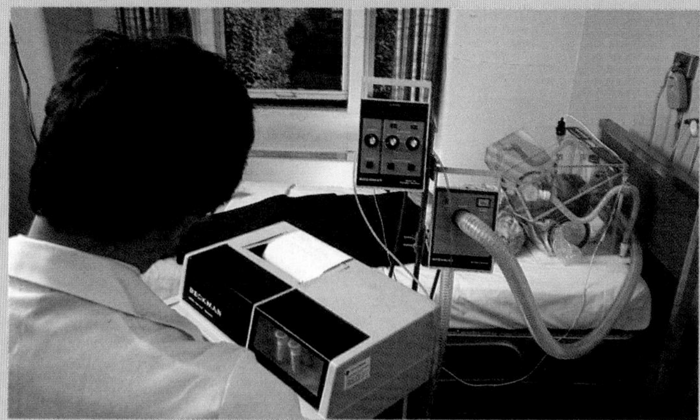

A scientist measures a woman's metabolic rate by placing her under a ventilated hood and analyzing the air she breathes.

Today, studies of adoptees and twins suggest that genes play an important role in obesity in human beings. In 1986, psychiatrist Albert Stunkard of the University of Pennsylvania, along with researchers in Denmark, found that the adult body size of people who had been adopted as children closely resembled that of their biological parents and bore no relationship to that of their adoptive parents. In a separate study that same year, Stunkard compared identical twins with nonidentical twins. He found that identical twins (who have identical genes) were twice as likely to have similar body weights as nonidentical twins (who have fewer of the same genes).

Glandular disorders. Problems with certain *glands* (organs that produce chemicals called hormones) can cause weight gain. These conditions include disorders of the thyroid or adrenal glands, which regulate metabo-

A man bicycles inside a respiratory chamber, a room used by researchers to measure how much energy a person uses.

lism, and tumors in the hypothalamus, which controls signals for hunger. Such conditions are rare, and the resulting weight gain is often mild. Obesity itself can create changes in hormonal functions, but such changes are a result of obesity, not a cause.

Behavioral factors

Many people find eating enjoyable. In addition, various behavioral factors, including habits and feelings, can affect a person's choice of what foods to eat and how much.

Eating habits. The body uses a network of electrical and chemical signals to monitor energy needs. When the body senses it needs energy, it responds with hunger pangs, which signal us to eat. When the body senses we have eaten enough, we experience a feeling called *satiety,* which makes us want to stop eating.

The satiety response is not instantaneous; it may take up to 20 minutes between the time we have taken in enough food and the time we feel satiated. During that time, we may continue to eat. Thus, people who eat rapidly may regularly be eating more than they need.

Other eating habits can override feelings of hunger and satiety. For example, some people always eat at regular mealtimes or eat everything set before them, even if they are not hungry. In the 1960's, some psychologists suggested that obese people might overeat because they are more sensitive to these external signals than to their body's internal ones.

More recent studies show, however, that these habits are as common among nonobese people as among the obese. Still, even if such habits do not cause obesity, they might contribute to it. In other words, behavior that thwarts the body's satiety signals may lead to weight gain in people who are inclined to obesity, while the same habits may cause no trouble for people without such a predisposition.

Smoking habits. Quitting smoking can promote weight gain for physiological reasons. Tests on smokers and animals exposed to *nicotine* (the addictive element in tobacco) show that when individuals stop their intake of nicotine, they increase their preference for sweet-tasting, high-carbohydrate foods. Former smokers don't necessarily eat more, the studies show, but the change in diet tends to cause weight gain.

In addition, recent studies suggest that quitting smoking may lower metabolism, which would also contribute to weight gain. Whatever the reason, the average weight gain is 7 pounds (3.2 kilograms), but individuals vary widely.

Psychological influences. Many studies suggest that some people learn to use food to allay anxiety, loneliness, or anger. Psychologists suggest that children whose parents comfort them with food may overeat as adults when they are unhappy.

Cultural factors

The sedentary nature of our culture may contribute to the prevalence of obesity. People are less physically active today than ever, due partly to such labor-saving devices as automobiles and washing machines.

In addition, our environment provides countless temptations to eat, ranging from advertisements for food to a wide variety of restaurants and food stores. In fact, our culture's "cafeteria diet," which allows unlimited ac-

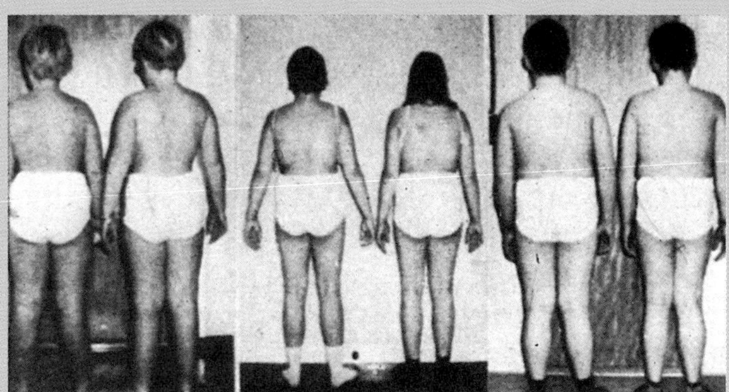

Pairs of identical twins, above, *who share the same set of genes, show highly similar patterns of body size.*

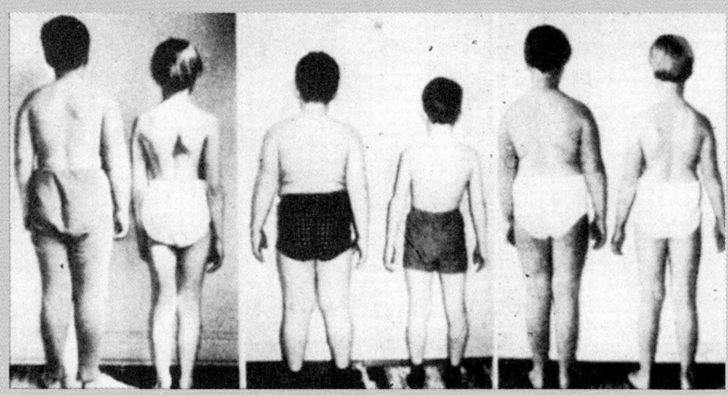

Nonidentical twins, above, *who share fewer of the same genes than identical twins, show greater variation in body size.*

cess to many good-tasting, high-fat foods, may be partly responsible for the prevalence of obesity.

Weight loss methods

Although heredity and other factors may make some people more likely to gain weight, this predisposition does not mean that they are doomed to be overweight. They may simply need to take special care to control their weight.

Among severely obese people, any weight reduction can reduce health risks substantially. Surgeon George Blackburn of Harvard Medical School in Boston found that a weight loss of even 10 per cent yielded significant health benefits for severely obese patients. Other studies have shown that a weight loss of 10 to 25 pounds (4.5 to 11 kilograms) can improve such conditions as hypertension and diabetes in some patients. For that reason, physicians often consider weight loss to be the first line of treatment for people with these problems.

At lesser degrees of overweight, or in the absence of other health problems, the need for weight loss is not as clear. People in this group, however, often seek to lose weight for cosmetic or social reasons, regardless of health needs.

Remedies for obesity range from diet plans to commercial weight-loss programs to drugs or even surgery. Some of these methods are sensible; others are useless or even harmful. But health experts agree on one point: For most people, the best approach for successful weight loss and long-term weight control is some combination of changes in diet, exercise habits, and attitudes. Medical experts advise checking with a physician to find out what combination of these approaches is most appropriate.

Diet

The American obsession with thinness has led to an epidemic of dieting. Estimates of the number of dieters vary, but a 1983 Rand Corporation study provides typical figures: Only 22 per cent of the 5,800 Americans studied were overweight, but 41 per cent—mostly women—perceived themselves as overweight. More than half of the latter group were trying to lose weight, mostly by dieting. Market research tends to place the numbers higher: A poll reported in *Newsweek* noted that 27 per cent of American men and 38 per cent of American women were dieting during any given two-week period in 1985.

Children are not immune to the epidemic of dieting. A 1986 survey of schoolgirls in San Francisco found that almost half of the 9-year-olds and 81 per cent of the 10-year-olds dieted to control their weight.

Diet books regularly hit the best-seller lists. What is common to most popular diets is the promise that weight loss will be rapid, permanent, and best of all, easy. Consumers should be skeptical of any diet that makes such claims. Moreover, fad diets can be harmful or even fatal. For example, in the late 1970's, the U.S. Food and Drug Administration attributed more than 60 deaths to a diet consisting solely of a liquid protein formula.

The type of diet favored by nutritionists produces gradual weight loss of 1 to 2 pounds (about 0.5 to 1 kilogram) per week. Such a diet reduces total food intake but ensures good nutrition by requiring a variety of food types.

One such method limits the dieter to a specific level of calories per day, typically 1,200 for women and 1,500 for men. At the same time, dieters apportion those calories among the four basic food groups—vegetables and fruits, breads and cereals,

Bookstores offer a large selection of diet plans. A few are sensible; many are useless; some can be dangerous.

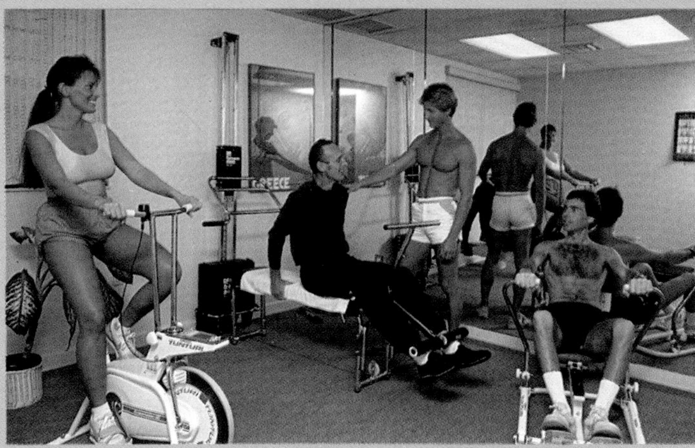

Dieters who exercise are more likely to lose fat tissue instead of muscle and to maintain weight loss over time.

meats and proteins, and dairy products. A similar method is an *exchange* plan, such as the diet recommended by the American Diabetes Association and the American Dietetic Association. An exchange plan eliminates the need to count calories by specifying serving sizes for foods. A dieter eats a certain number of "exchanges," or measured servings, from each of several food categories daily.

Both of these approaches are valuable. But anyone—especially people with medical conditions in which diet is important, such as diabetes—should consult a physician before beginning a diet.

Exercise

Although studies have shown that obese people are less physically active than normal-weight people, it is not clear whether inactivity leads to obesity or vice versa. Obese people may be inactive because their excess weight makes exercise physically difficult as well as frustrating or embarrassing.

Exercise has long been recommended as a weight-loss method because it uses calories. Exercise does burn calories, but discouragingly few compared with the number of calories that can be consumed in a single meal. And although some advocates of exercise claim that exercise temporarily increases metabolic rate, recent research indicates that this effect occurs only when exercise is intense and prolonged. In other words, the amount of exercise an obese person is capable of doing safely will probably not increase metabolism.

Still, exercise does offer long-term benefits that help in weight control. Exercise combined with a weight-reduction diet can help maintain muscle tissue during weight loss. Several studies indicate that weight lost by a combination of diet and exercise consists of a higher proportion of fat, and less muscle, than weight lost through diet alone.

Exercise may also counter some of obesity's ill effects. Even without weight loss, exercise can reduce high blood pressure and cholesterol levels and improve heart conditions and diabetes. And exercise is one of the few factors shown to predict successful long-term maintenance of weight loss. Studies indicate that people who exercise during a weight-reduction program are more likely to keep lost pounds off. Overweight people should consult a

Approximate calories used in physical activity

Activity	**Body weight (in pounds)**				
(10 minutes, continuous)	**100**	**125**	**150**	**175**	**200**
Sleeping	8	10	12	14	16
Reading or watching TV	8	10	12	14	16
Writing	12	15	18	21	24
Typing (electric)	15	19	23	27	31
Standing	10	12	14	16	19
Dressing or washing	21	26	32	37	42
Walking, 2 miles/hour	23	29	35	40	46
Walking, 4 miles/hour	42	52	62	72	81
Walking downstairs	46	56	67	78	88
Walking upstairs	118	146	175	202	229
Running, 5.5 miles/hour	73	90	108	125	142
Cycling, 13 miles/hour	71	89	107	124	142
Making beds	25	32	39	46	52
Washing windows	29	35	42	48	54
Shoveling snow	53	65	78	89	100
House-painting	23	29	35	40	46
Baseball (not pitcher)	31	39	47	54	62
Basketball	46	58	70	82	93
Bowling	45	56	67	78	90
Dancing (vigorous)	39	48	57	66	75
Football	55	69	83	96	110
Golfing	26	33	40	48	55
Swimming (crawl)	32	40	48	56	63
Tennis	44	56	67	80	92

Source: K. D. Brownell, University of Pennsylvania.

physician to determine what level of exercise they can handle safely.

Behavior-related approaches

Nearly every weight-control program includes some behavior-related techniques for encouraging weight loss. These may range from simple motivational aids—such as keeping food out of sight or posting inspirational photographs on the refrigerator door—to a comprehensive program for long-term changes in life style.

The most comprehensive behavioral approach is a program of *behavior modification* or *behavior therapy*. Psychologists use behavior modification to treat problems ranging from drug dependencies to phobias. Methods include positive reinforcement, which rewards desirable behavior; record-keeping, which enables a person to identify personal attitudes and patterns; and stimulus control, which involves altering the environment to promote or discourage actions.

Some techniques in a comprehensive program for weight control

Life style techniques
Keep an eating diary
Examine patterns in your eating
Prevent automatic eating
Keep a weight graph
Follow an eating schedule
Eat in one place
Do not clean your plate
Put your fork down between bites
Pause during the meal
Shop on a full stomach
Shop from a list
Buy foods that require preparation
Keep problem foods out of sight
Keep healthy foods visible
Remove serving dishes from the table
Leave the table after eating
Serve and eat one portion at a time
Prepare in advance for special events

Exercise techniques
Keep an exercise diary
Increase walking
Use stairs whenever possible
Know the calorie values of exercise
Always warm up and cool down
Experiment with jogging
Experiment with cycling
Experiment with aerobics

Attitude techniques
Distinguish hunger from cravings
Confront or ignore cravings
Set realistic goals
Counter food and weight fantasies
Ban perfectionist attitudes
Beware of attitude traps
Focus on behavior rather than weight
Be aware of high-risk situations
Outlast urges to eat
Cope positively with slips and lapses

Relationship techniques
Identify and select partner
Tell your partner how to help
Reward your partner
Do shopping with your partner
Have partner do shopping for you
Exercise with partner
Refuse pressures to eat

Nutrition techniques
Watch caloric intake
Be aware of calorie values of foods
Know the four food groups
Eat a balanced diet
Increase complex carbohydrates
Limit fat to 30% of total calories
Make low-calorie foods appetizing
Increase fiber in diet

Source: K. D. Brownell, LEARN Program for Weight Control, 1987.

As applied to weight control, behavior modification focuses on encouraging gradual but permanent changes in eating and exercise habits. It may be used in conjunction with a diet or other weight-control methods, not only to enhance weight loss but also to discourage weight regain later.

In general, behavior-modification programs work best for people who need to lose moderate amounts of weight—about 40 pounds (18 kilograms) or less. Studies show that on average, such programs produce a weight loss of about 20 pounds (9 kilograms) during a 16-week program. Programs that include a broad range of methods—such as exercise and family involvement as well as behavior-modification techniques—produce losses of 25 to 30 pounds (about 11 to 14 kilograms) over 16 weeks.

An example of a comprehensive program is one developed by the author at the University of Pennsylvania. Participants adopt changes in five areas indicated by the acronym LEARN. *Life style* includes habits related to food and eating. *Exercise* covers physical activity. *Attitudes* involve goals, ways of thinking, and behavior. *Relationships* refer to the involvement of friends and family. And *Nutrition* covers diet. (Examples of specific techniques for change in these areas appear above.)

Another psychological aid to weight loss is group support. This method allows overweight people to meet, share their experiences, and encourage one another. Programs such as Overeaters Anonymous and Take Off Pounds Sensibly (TOPS) provide group support at little or no cost.

Some commercial programs—such as Weight Watchers, NutriSystem, and Diet Center—offer services and products ranging from group support to diet foods. These programs vary in cost and in the amount of involvement by trained health professionals. Little information is available on their effectiveness because independent researchers have not yet studied many of these groups.

Drugs

Amphetamines, drugs that increase physical and mental activity and suppress appetite, were popular as diet aids in the 1960's. The medical community restricted the use of amphetamines in the early 1970's, however, because of high rates of abuse. These drugs are no longer used to treat obesity.

Other prescription drugs—notably *phentermine, diethylpropion,* and *fenfluramine*—can promote weight loss. Proponents of drug therapy maintain that side effects are minimal, ranging from dry mouth to insomnia or drowsiness. But many physicians consider drugs unsuitable for weight control, primarily because patients maintain their reduced weight only as long as they continue taking the drug—and long-range effects are unknown.

Over-the-counter diet preparations take several forms. Some are simply low-calorie candy; a person who eats the candy before a meal will supposedly be less hungry and thus less likely to overeat. Other preparations, called *bulk producers,* are meant to create a feeling of stomach fullness. Still other diet aids contain anesthetics that theoretically dull the taste buds and reduce the pleasure of eating. These approaches may help some people, but none has gained wide acceptance by health professionals.

Some over-the-counter products include the drug *phenylpropanolamine,* which has a modest effect on weight loss. But some health experts caution that this drug may cause some potentially dangerous side effects, including sudden increases in blood pressure.

Aggressive approaches

For some severe cases of obesity, physicians may recommend any of several extreme treatments. These include medically supervised modified fasts and surgery.

Modified fasts limit a patient's food intake to as little as 400 calories per day, typically for 12-week periods. The patient consumes only small amounts of meat, fish, fowl, or a protein supplement, along with a precise combination of vitamins and minerals. Some dieters find these programs attractive because the method eliminates the need to make choices about food. Also, many dieters claim that hunger diminishes after the first few days of the fast.

Studies of these diets show that weight loss is both rapid and substantial, averaging 44 pounds (20 kilograms) over a 12-week period. But people who lose weight on these diets tend to gain it back quickly. In a recent study, only 19 per cent of fasters—and only 13 per cent of those who had no behavior-modification training—were still within 5 pounds (2.3 kilograms) of their end-of-fast weight after three years.

Side effects of a properly supervised fast are generally minimal, and might include dizziness, sensitivity to cold, and bowel problems. Since improper fasting can lead to serious illness or death, fasts should be followed only under close medical supervision and through a reputable program. About 2,000 U.S. hospitals and clinics offer such programs. The best ones offer weekly contact with a specially trained physician, as well as nutrition education, exercise, and behavior modification.

Surgery. Experts say that the only viable surgical method used for weight control is *vertical banded gastroplasty,* commonly called stomach stapling. Permanent surgical staples or sutures are placed in a line across the stomach to reduce its capacity. As a result, patients feel full after eating smaller amounts of food.

The procedure is typically reserved for people who weigh at least twice their ideal weight, have medical complications of obesity such as diabetes or hy-

Reducing stomach capacity with surgery

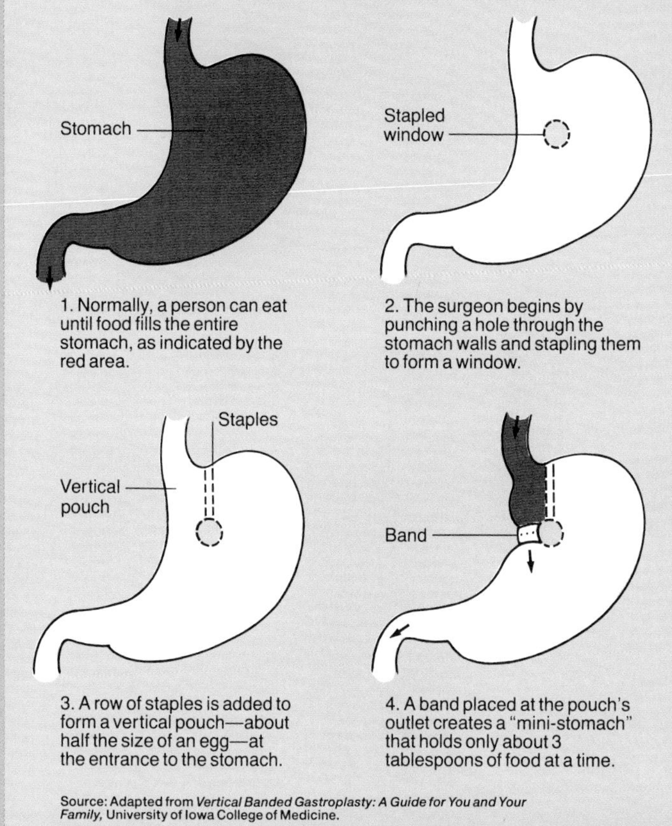

Severely overweight patients may undergo vertical banded gastroplasty *to reduce the stomach's capacity for food.*

pertension, and have had no success with less aggressive weight-loss methods. On the average, patients lose about 60 per cent of excess weight within a year after the surgery, according to Edward E. Mason, the Iowa surgeon who developed the procedure in the early 1980's. While most patients experience a slight increase in weight two or three years after the surgery, most of the loss is permanent.

The procedure involves a hospital stay of about five days, and patients can be active as soon as they leave the hospital, though they should avoid heavy exertion for about six weeks. Severe complications or death are rare and often related to heart problems and other conditions common among severely obese people. Side effects are generally minor; the most common is vomiting when patients eat too fast for their newly limited stomach capacity.

Other forms of surgery aimed at reducing stomach capacity, including *horizontal gastroplasty* and the *gastric by-pass,* are still used occasionally. But these procedures have shown more of a tendency than vertical gastroplasty to interfere with the stomach's function.

The *gastric bubble,* a balloon implanted and inflated in the stomach, was taken off the market in May 1988. Studies showed no indication that the bubble helped weight loss significantly, and in rare cases it caused severe complications.

Another surgical approach, *intestinal by-pass surgery,* involves by-passing part of the intestinal tract to speed food through the digestive system, thus reducing the number of calories absorbed by the body. The method is no longer used because of side effects, including diarrhea and dehydration, as well as more serious complications such as protein malnutrition and diseases of the liver, kidneys, or bowel.

Maintaining weight loss

Keeping weight off can be more difficult than losing it to begin with. If we define "cure" of obesity as a reduction to ideal weight and maintenance of that weight for five years, the cure rate for obesity is lower than that for most forms of cancer.

No data are available for people who try to lose weight on their own, but estimates of successful weight loss and maintenance in any circumstance rarely go above 5 per cent. For example, physician Alvan Feinstein of Yale Medical School in New Haven, Conn., estimated in 1984 that only about 12 out of 100 patients who seek medical help to lose weight actually succeed in reducing, and only 2 of those 12 maintain the weight loss for more than a year or two.

Such figures may be misleading because they generally reflect only people who have sought professional therapy for weight loss. Such people may have particularly extreme problems, and people who don't require therapy to lose weight may be better able to maintain their weight loss. On the other hand, people who seek help might reflect a *higher* rate of success because professional treatment might be more effective—or because those seeking help are exceptionally motivated to lose weight.

People who want to keep lost weight off typically must reduce daily calorie intake permanently. Since our environment is filled with signals to eat, ranging from luscious depictions of foods in advertisements to the easy accessibility of food, even a dieter with great determination may find it difficult to resist overeating. In addition, the same habits that first led to overweight, such as eating to combat anxiety or failing to get enough exercise, can cause weight regain.

The set point theory

Physiological factors may make maintaining a low weight difficult. Over the last decade, scientists have proposed a concept called the *set point theory* to explain the tendency toward weight regain. This theory suggests that the body regulates weight at a particular level—a set point—just as a thermostat regulates room temperature.

According to this theory, when weight goes too far above or below the body's set point, the body works to bring weight back to the set level. In other words, some obese people who try to lose weight may be fighting against their own bodies.

Specially bred rats used in obesity studies, such as the rat at left, can grow to twice the weight of a normal rat, right.

Numerous studies indicate how strongly the body will attempt to maintain a level of weight. For example, researchers at Rockefeller University in New York City studied obese people who had lost substantial amounts of weight—an average of 124 pounds (56 kilograms) each. The people were still overweight by an average of 86 pounds (39 kilograms). But as they lost weight, their calorie requirements dropped by an average of 28 per cent to a level even lower than that of normal-weight people.

Effects of weight regain

Regaining lost weight seems to make it harder to lose weight again. Researchers at the University of Pennsylvania, one of five universities involved in a research effort called the Weight Cycling Project, tested the effects of *yoyo dieting* (repeated weight loss and gain) on rats. The researchers overfed a group of rats to make them obese. The rats then underwent a series of diet changes that made them lose weight, regain it, and lose it again.

On their first weight-loss diet, the rats took 21 days to reach normal weight, and they regained the weight within 45 days. But the second time they dieted, the rats took 46 days to lose the same amount of weight, even though they ate exactly as many calories as they had on the first diet. Furthermore, the rats needed only 14 days to regain the lost weight once more. In other words, on the second diet cycle, the rats took twice as long to lose weight and only one-third the time to regain it.

Studies with human beings show similar results. Harvard Medical School researchers examined records of 140 dieters who had lost weight at their clinic, regained it, and returned for a second try. The records showed that the dieters lost an average of 2.3 pounds (1 kilogram) a week on their first diet but only 1.3 pounds (0.6 kilogram) per week on the second.

One explanation is that the body interprets a diet as a famine and protects itself by using and storing calories more efficiently. In effect, the body learns to live on less food. This ability lasts even after the dieter has regained the lost weight.

Other studies done as part of the Weight Cycling Project linked repeated dieting to additional disturbing consequences. Yoyo dieters seem to lose their pounds as muscle tissue and regain them as fat, thus increasing their overall body fat. They also tend to store regained fat in the abdomen, increasing their risk of heart disease and diabetes. And one study of 1,701 men over a 25-year period found that those who showed the greatest up-and-down weight swings also had the highest risk of sudden death from heart disease.

The finding that repeated, unsuccessful dieting makes later weight loss more difficult has several implications, according to weight control experts. First, dieting should be taken seriously; people should begin a diet only if they are willing to change their habits permanently. Second, dieters should seek the approach that offers them the best chance of long-term maintenance as well as initial success.

Weight control for young people

Obesity in children and adolescents can pose particular problems. Not only do obese children face social troubles and health risks in childhood and later in life, but obesity in some children persists into adulthood.

Obesity in childhood

Factors such as heredity and energy use contribute to obesity

Increase of obesity among children

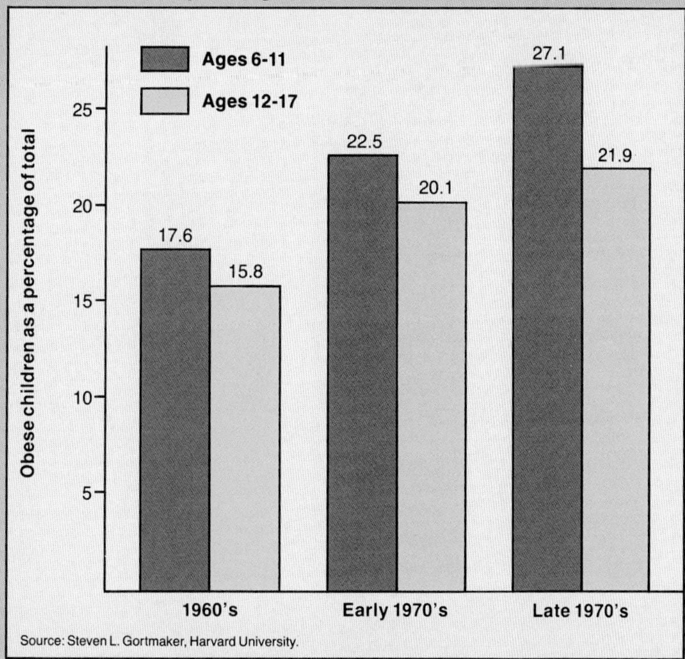

A study of national survey data from the 1960's and 1970's shows steady growth in the percentage of children who are obese.

early in life. In a 1988 study of babies born to both overweight and lean mothers, researchers in Cambridge, England, found that half the babies born to overweight mothers became overweight by their first birthday. None of the babies born to lean mothers were overweight at 1 year old. Energy use, measured when the babies were 3 months old, was about 21 per cent lower among the infants who later became overweight.

The prevalence of obesity among children in the United States has grown dramatically in the last two decades, according to pediatric researcher William H. Dietz of Massachusetts Institute of Technology in Cambridge, Mass., and sociologist Steven L. Gortmaker of Harvard University School of Public Health in Boston. Using data from U.S. government surveys, they found that between 1963 and 1980, obesity increased 54 per cent among children aged 6 to 11 and rose 39 per cent among those aged 12 to 17.

The most likely explanations for this alarming increase are changes in what children eat and how much they exercise. High-calorie food is more widely available today. And children, like adults, are more sedentary.

In 1985, Dietz and Gortmaker found that obesity in children increases in proportion to the amount of television they watch. The researchers suggested that watching television promotes obesity in three ways. First, children get constant messages to eat from commercials advertising sugar-coated cereals, candy, soft drinks, and fast food. Second, children may snack as they watch television. Finally, the more time children spend watching television, the less time they might be expending energy in more active play.

Consequences of childhood obesity

Overweight children are more likely than normal-weight children to have two risk factors for heart disease—high blood pressure and high levels of blood cholesterol. They also show greater risk of respiratory disease, diabetes, and orthopedic problems. In addition to health risks, obese children are likely to encounter social pressures related to their weight. Often shunned or teased by classmates as well as adults, overweight children face special problems in everyday activities from shopping for clothes to playing games.

Obesity in children does not automatically lead to adult obesity, but obese children are more likely to become obese adults. Studies suggest that children who are overweight as early as age 1 are at slightly higher risk for excess weight gain throughout life.

Whether obesity actually develops may depend on each individual's food intake and exercise patterns. The likelihood of childhood obesity lasting into adulthood increases with age, however. Various studies indicate that 40 per cent of obese 7-year-olds and 70 per cent of obese adolescents become obese adults.

Treatment for obese children

Children require different weight-loss programs than adults do because children have different physical needs. A child's weight-reduction program must ensure enough nutrients for growth and development, and it must decrease body fat without reducing muscle tissue.

In general, weight programs for children should focus on long-term efforts to control weight gain rather than attempts to lose weight quickly. Often children may need only to hold weight constant while they grow in height. In any case, parents should consult with a physician before placing a child on a weight-loss program.

Diet. Adult diets can be dangerous for children. In 1987, pediatricians at one New York hospital reported treating seven infants for *failure to thrive* (stunted development). In each case, well-meaning parents had restricted the child's food intake or fed the child low-calorie or

Studies show that obesity in children increases in proportion to the amount of television they watch.

low-fat foods in hopes of preventing obesity. Nutritionists warn that such diets for children under age 2 can be harmful.

Even among older children, dieting by adult standards may be inappropriate. Some experts suggest that parents who enforce diets for their children may prevent the children from learning how to regulate their own food intake.

When weight loss is necessary for a child, experts recommend reducing calorie intake by 20 to 30 per cent, primarily through cutting down on dietary fats. Such a diet can lead to losses of up to 1 pound (0.45 kilogram) per week. Parents should ask their pediatrician for guidelines on developing a reasonable eating plan for an overweight child.

Dietz and other researchers are testing the effects of modified fasting programs on severely overweight adolescents. Such extreme treatments, however, are still only experimental.

Exercise. Regular exercise not only burns calories, but it may also improve a child's self-confidence and motivation to adhere to a diet. Experts suggest that the more enjoyable the exercise, the more likely the child will sustain increased activity over a long term.

Psychologists Leonard H. Epstein and Rena Wing of the University of Pittsburgh monitored weight loss among groups of children and adults who followed various exercise programs. They found that people who followed scheduled routines of traditional exercise, such as calisthenics, were most likely to improve their fitness in the short term. But those who were allowed to integrate their own choice of calorie-burning activities into their normal day were more likely to maintain weight loss over several years. For example, such "life-style" exercise might include walking or bicycling to school daily instead of riding in a car or bus.

Ideal weights for children (in pounds)

Height (in inches)	**Boys (age in years)**											
	7	**8**	**9**	**10**	**11**	**12**	**13**	**14**	**15**	**16**	**17**	**18**
43	41	40										
44	43	43										
45	45	45	45									
46	48	47	47									
47	50	49	49	49								
48	52	52	52	52								
49	54	54	54	54	54							
50	57	57	57	57	57	57						
51	60	60	60	60	60	60						
52	62	63	63	63	63	63	63					
53		66	66	65	65	67	67					
54		68	68	69	68	69	69	70				
55		71	71	72	72	72	73	73				
56			75	75	76	76	77	77	78			
57			78	79	80	80	82	82	82			
58				82	83	84	84	85	85			
59				86	87	87	88	88	89	89		
60					90	91	92	93	94	96		
61					94	95	96	97	98	101	105	
62					99	100	101	103	103	107	111	116
63						106	105	107	108	111	115	120
64						109	110	111	113	115	119	124
65							114	116	118	120	125	129
66							117	121	123	126	129	132
67								127	127	131	134	136
68								131	132	135	139	141
69								135	136	138	141	144
70								140	142	143	145	147

Height (in inches)	**Girls (age in years)**											
	7	**8**	**9**	**10**	**11**	**12**	**13**	**14**	**15**	**16**	**17**	**18**
43	40	40										
44	42	42										
45	44	45										
46	46	47	47	47								
47	50	49	50	50								
48	52	52	52	52	52							
49	53	54	55	55	56							
50	56	57	58	58	60	60						
51	59	60	60	61	62	62						
52	63	63	63	64	64	66						
53		66	67	67	67	68	70					
54		68	70	70	71	71	73					
55			73	74	74	75	77	78				
56			76	78	78	79	80	84				
57				81	82	82	84	89	93			
58				84	87	86	88	93	96	100		
59				87	91	90	93	97	101	104	105	
60					95	96	97	101	105	108	109	111
61					97	101	101	105	108	112	113	114
62						105	106	108	112	114	115	116
63						110	111	112	115	116	118	118
64						114	115	117	118	120	121	122
65							120	120	121	124	125	126
66							124	125	126	128	128	131
67							127	129	131	133	133	134
68								131	133	134	136	138
69								133	135	136	138	140
70								134	136	138	140	141

Source: World Health Organization and Leonard Epstein, University of Pittsburgh.

Behavior-related approaches. The principles of behavior modification used for adults can be applied to children, but methods are different. This is partly because goals of weight loss or good health are rarely sufficient motivation for young children to change eating and exercise habits. In addition, since children are often fully or partly dependent upon their parents for food selection and scheduling of activity, life-style programs must involve the parents.

Epstein and Wing recommend specific ways parents can help children of different ages. Parents of children under 5 generally regulate their children's eating and activity level. When children enter school, parents need to teach their children how to respond to the new influences on eating habits that come with contact with other children. By age 9, as children take more control over their eating, parents should focus on teaching them to make good eating decisions.

For example, to help children learn good dietary habits, Epstein and Wing developed an eating program that children can understand and adopt easily. The children learn to identify foods according to the colors of a traffic light. "Red-light" foods—foods that are high in fat and low in nutrients—should be avoided; "yellow-light" foods, such as most protein sources, dairy foods, and grains, may be eaten in moderate amounts; and "green-light" foods, such as vegetables and diet soda, may be eaten as often as desired.

Professional assistance. If a moderate, long-term program of medically supervised diet, exercise, and behavioral change is not sufficient, a professional who specializes in childhood weight problems may be able to help. Such expertise may be difficult to locate, but parents can begin by contacting local hospitals, psychologists, and dietitians for recommendations.

For more information:

These organizations provide material on weight control and health:

American Diabetes Association
1660 Duke St.
Alexandria, VA 22314

American Dietetic Association
208 S. LaSalle St., Suite 1100
Chicago, IL 60604-1003

Overeaters Anonymous
P.O. Box 92870
Los Angeles, CA 90009

TOPS (Take Off Pounds Sensibly)
P.O. Box 07360
Milwaukee, WI 53207

Weight Watchers International
500 N. Broadway
Jericho, NY 11753

The following books also provide additional information:

Bennett, William, and Gurin, Joel. *The Dieter's Dilemma: Eating Less and Weighing More*. Basic Books, 1982.

Brody, Jane. *Jane Brody's Nutrition Book*. W. W. Norton, 1981.

Brownell, Kelly D. *The LEARN Program for Weight Control*. University of Pennsylvania, 1988. (For information, write the author at 133 S. 36th St., Philadelphia, PA 19104.)

Epstein, Leonard H., and Squires, Sally. *The Stoplight Diet for Children*. Little, Brown, 1988.

The author:

Kelly D. Brownell is a professor in the Department of Psychiatry at the University of Pennsylvania School of Medicine in Philadelphia. He is codirector of the Obesity Research Clinic and author of six books.

Weight loss programs for children combine such approaches as exercise, above left, *and parental education,* above right.

Here are your

1989 World Book Health & Medical Annual Cross-Reference Tabs

For insertion in your World Book

Each year, The World Book Health & Medical Annual will add a valuable dimension to your World Book set. The Cross-Reference Tab System is designed especially to help students and parents alike link the Health & Medical Annual's Special Reports and other major articles to the related World Book articles they update.

How to Use These Tabs

The top Tab on this page is ASPIRIN. Turn to the A volume of your World Book and find the page with the ASPIRIN article on it. Affix the ASPIRIN Tab to that page.

Note that several Tabs—for example, LYME DISEASE and LEFT-HANDEDNESS—go on World Book pages where there is no such article. Put these Tabs in the correct volume and in proper alphabetical sequence. LYME DISEASE thus would go in the L volume, on the same page as the LYMPHATIC SYSTEM article.

Put all of the Tabs in your World Book volumes, and your new Health & Medical Annual will be linked to your encyclopedia set.

Health & Medical Annual Close-Up
ASPIRIN
1989 Health & Medical Annual, p. 296

Special Report
CANCER
1989 Health & Medical Annual, p. 24

People in Medicine
CHILD ABUSE
1989 Health & Medical Annual, p. 352

Special Report
FIBER, DIETARY
1989 Health & Medical Annual, p. 86

Special Report
FIRE PREVENTION
1989 Health & Medical Annual, p. 212

Special Report
FOOD POISONING
1989 Health & Medical Annual, p. 130

Special Report
FOOT
1989 Health & Medical Annual, p. 116

Special Report
HEADACHE
1989 Health & Medical Annual, p. 10

Special Report
HEART
1989 Health & Medical Annual, p. 70

Special Report
HYPERACTIVE CHILD
1989 Health & Medical Annual, p. 184

Special Report
LEFT-HANDEDNESS
1989 Health & Medical Annual, p. 158

Special Report
LYME DISEASE
1989 Health & Medical Annual, p. 38

Special Report
OLD AGE
1989 Health & Medical Annual, p. 198

Special Report
OSTEOPOROSIS
1989 Health & Medical Annual, p. 54

Health & Medical Annual Close-Up
PAP TEST
1989 Health & Medical Annual, p. 256

Special Report
PLASTIC SURGERY
1989 Health & Medical Annual, p. 144

Special Report
POLIOMYELITIS
1989 Health & Medical Annual, p. 100

People in Medicine
PUBLIC HEALTH SERVICE
1989 Health & Medical Annual, p. 340

Health & Medical Annual Close-Up
RHEUMATIC FEVER
1989 Health & Medical Annual, p. 304

Health Studies
WEIGHT CONTROL
1989 Health & Medical Annual, p. 366

Index

This index covers the contents of the 1987, 1988, and 1989 editions of *The World Book Health & Medical Annual.*

Each index entry gives the edition year and a page number—for example, 89-123. The first number, 89, indicates the edition year, and the second number, 123, is the page number on which the desired information begins.

There are two types of entries in the index.

In the first type, the index entry (in **boldface** type) is followed immediately by numbers:

Dentistry, 89-263, 88-248, 87-247

This means that *The Health & Medical Annual* has an article titled Dentistry and that in the 1989 edition the article begins on page 263. In the 1988 and 1987 editions, the Dentistry article begins on pages 248 and 247, respectively.

In the second type of entry, the **boldface** title is followed by a clue word instead of by numbers:

Gastric bubble: Health Studies, 89-380; ils., 87-322; weight control, 89-337, 88-320

This means that there is no *Health & Medical Annual* article titled Gastric bubble, but that information about this procedure can be found in the Health Studies section of the 1989 edition on page 380. There are illustrations of the device on page 322 of the 1987 edition, and text information in the Weight Control articles in the 1989 and 1988 editions.

Sometimes information appears only as an illustration:

Spine: ils., 89-60

This means that there are pictures of the spinal column on page 60 of the 1989 edition.

The "See" and "See also" cross-references direct the reader to other entries within the index:

Deoxyribonucleic acid. See **DNA.**

A

B

C

D

G

H

I

J

K

L

M

N

O

T

U

V

W

X

Y

Z

Acknowledgments

The publishers of *The World Book Health & Medical Annual* gratefully acknowledge the courtesy of the following artists, photographers, publishers, institutions, agencies, and corporations for the illustrations in this volume. Credits should read from top to bottom, left to right, on their respective pages. All entries marked with an asterisk (*) denote illustrations created exclusively for *The World Book Health & Medical Annual.* All maps, charts, and diagrams were prepared by *The World Book Health & Medical Annual* staff unless otherwise noted.

4 © Dan McCoy, Rainbow; © Thomas S. England, Photo Researchers
5 Donna L. Nelson*; AP/Wide World; © Julie Brown, Custom Medical
8 Roberta Polfus*; Porterfield/Chickering, Photo Researchers; London School of Hygiene & Tropical Medicine, Science Source from Photo Researchers; James D. Wilson, Woodfin Camp, Inc.; Migraine Art pictures published by permission of the British Migraine Association and Boehringer Ingelheim
9 Joe Rogers*
10-14 Migraine Art pictures published by permission of the British Migraine Association and Boehringer Ingelheim
17 © Dan McCoy, Rainbow
20 © Eric Nelson, Custom Medical; World Book photo; © Arthur Sirdofsky, The Stock Shop; Joel Saper, M.D., Michigan Headache Institute; Ed Gallucci, The Stock Shop
21 Joel Saper, M.D., Michigan Headache Institute
24 © Arnold H. Crane from Marilyn Gartman
25 Steven Spicer*
28 The Skin Cancer Foundation
29 Katherine M. Ozanich, M.D.
30 Brent Jones*; Steven Spicer*; Brent Jones*; Steven Spicer*; Brent Jones*; Brent Jones*
32 Steven Spicer*
35 NASA
36 © Bruce Byers, FPG
38-42 Bob Fuller*
43 Bob Fuller*; Centers for Disease Control, Atlanta, Ga.
45 Willy Burgdorfer, M.D., Rocky Mountain Laboratories; Bob Fuller*
46-48 Bob Fuller*
49 Joe McNally, Wheeler Pictures
50 Samuel L. Howard
51-52 Bob Fuller*
54 Roberta Polfus*
57 © Jacques Chenet, Woodfin Camp, Inc.
58 Roberta Polfus*
59 Art—Roberta Polfus*; photos—From "Effect of pH on Bone Resorption by Rat Osteoclasts *in Vitro*" by Timothy R. Arnett and David W. Dempster, *Endocrinology* 119:119-124, Copyright © 1986 by The Endocrine Society
60 © Ira Wyman; From *The Journal of Bone and Mineral Research,* Copyright © 1987 by the American Society of Bone and Mineral Research; © Ira Wyman; From *The Journal of Bone and Mineral Research,* Copyright © 1987 by The American Society of Bone and Mineral Research
61-66 Roberta Polfus*
70 © Bill Longshore, Science Source from Photo Researchers; © Robert Rathe, FPG; © Pete Saloutos, The Stock Market
71 © Thomas S. England, Photo Researchers
73-75 Don Wilson*
78 © Thomas S. England, Photo Researchers; Don Wilson*; Peter Kondos, M.D., University of Illinois Medical Center
81-83 Don Wilson*
86-97 Art—Catherine Twomey*; photos—Ralph Brunke*
100 UPI/Bettmann Newsphotos
103-104 FPG
105 Sister Kenny Institute; Brown Bros.
107-109 March of Dimes Birth Defects Foundation
110 UPI/Bettmann Newsphotos
111 March of Dimes Birth Defects Foundation
112 UPI/Bettmann Newsphotos
113 Ruth Massey, UNICEF
116-126 Joe Rogers*
130 Terry Sirrell*
133 London School of Hygiene & Tropical Medicine, Science Source from Photo Researchers
135 Terry Sirrell*; © 1985 Chicago Tribune Company. All rights reserved
136 John Colwell from Grant Heilman; Grant Heilman
138-141 Terry Sirrell*
145 James D. Wilson, Woodfin Camp, Inc.
147 Russell W. H. Kridel, M.D.
149 David E. Schuller, M.D., The American Academy of Facial Plastic and Reconstructive Surgery
151 Art—Catherine Twomey*; photos—Louie Patseavouras, M.D., The American Academy of Cosmetic Surgery
152-153 Art—Catherine Twomey*; photos—Robert L. Cucin, M.D.
154 Art—Catherine Twomey*; photos—Ferdinand F. Becker, Jr., M.D., The American Academy of Facial Plastic and Reconstructive Surgery
155 Art—Catherine Twomey*; photos—Stephen X. Giunta, M.D.
158-161 Roberta Polfus*
162 Bettmann Archive; Culver; © LGI
166 Ralph Brunke*; Ralph Brunke*; © Gerald Cubitt, Bruce Coleman Ltd.
167 Ralph Brunke*; Ralph Brunke*; © Gerald Cubitt, Bruce Coleman Ltd.
170 Granger Collection
171 FDA (Kent DuFault*)
173 Bettmann Archive
174-175 Bakken Library (Kent DuFault*)
176-177 FDA (Kent DuFault*)
178 FDA Archives
180 Linda Creighton, *U.S. News & World Report*
181 FDA
182 World Book photo
184-196 Scott Snow*
198 Porterfield/Chickering, Photo Researchers
201 Alan Carey, The Image Works; David Wells, The Image Works

202 Jeff Lowenthal, Woodfin Camp, Inc.
203 Alan Carey, The Image Works
204 Jeff Lowenthal, Woodfin Camp, Inc.
207 C. Vergara, Photo Researchers
209 Friendship Village, Schaumburg, Illinois
210 Kevin Horan, Picture Group; Michal Heron, Woodfin Camp, Inc.
212-224 Donna L. Nelson*
226 Bruce Hoertel
227 AP/Wide World
229 © Ira Wyman, Sygma
230 National Institute of Neurological and Communicative Disorders and Stroke; Laboratory of Neuroscience, National Institute of Aging; National Institute of Neurological and Communicative Disorders and Stroke
232 Bruce Hoertel
233 AP/Wide World
234 National Institute of Allergy and Infectious Diseases
236 The Advertising Council/ National Council on Alcoholism Inc.
239 © Vince Zuber, Custom Medical
241 David W. Stoller, M.D., Radiology Dept., University of California at San Francisco from *Medical World News*
242 Joseph D. Zuckerman, M.D.
245 AP/Wide World
246 Larry Barns, Memorial Sloan-Kettering Cancer Center
247 Diagnostic Imaging
248 *Atlantic City Press*
250 World Book photo
252 Anneliese A. Pontius, M.D., Harvard Medical School
253 AP/Wide World
255 Jon Riley, Medichrome
256 © Martin M. Rotker, Phototake
258 Lance Liotta, M.D., National Cancer Institute
260 Judy S. DeLoache, University of Illinois at Urbana-Champaign
262 Susan Greenwood, NYT Pictures
263 Unitek Corporation/3M
265 Tekscan, Inc.
266 Boehringer Mannheim Corporation (Ralph Brunke*)
268 AP/Wide World
270 Hoffmann-La Roche Inc.
271 Baxter Healthcare Corporation
272 Genentech, Inc.
275 Nicolet Instruments
276 Ben Casey, MLS/A; Intelligent Medical Systems
279 Terrence McCarthy, NYT Pictures; Agence France-Presse
281 © Frank Siteman from Marilyn Gartman; David Madison
283 Claude Levet, Cornell University
289 Muscular Dystrophy Association
293 Steven Spicer*
295 Linda M. Baron, NYT Pictures
296 AP/Wide World
298 Nancy Mathews, Emory University
299 Dan Miller*
301 UPI/Bettmann Newsphotos
304 Lynn Johnson, Black Star
306 Walter Reed Army Institute of Research from *Medical World News*
310 © David M. Grossman, Photo Researchers
311 © Sydney Harris
312 © Mick Stevens
313 Steve Leonard
315 Minneapolis *Star Tribune*
317 AP/Wide World
319 Aqua Buoy, U.S.A.
320 © Ellis Herwig from Marilyn Gartman
322 Argonne National Laboratory
323 Delco Electronics Corporation
326 *Medical World News*
328 *Time* Magazine
330 UPI/Bettmann Newsphotos
332 Department of Urology, Presbyterian-St. Luke's Hospital
334 Thomas J. Lane
335 Granada Corporation; Texas A&M University
336 Futrex, Inc.
338 Guy Wolek*; Guy Wolek*; Linda Creighton, *U.S. News & World Report*
339 Guy Wolek*; John Troha, Black Star*
341 John Troha, Black Star*
343 Linda Creighton, *U.S. News & World Report*
345 The Children's Hospital of Philadelphia
346 © Judy Sloan, Gamma/ Liaison
349 AP/Wide World
350 Linda Creighton, *U.S. News & World Report*
352–364 Guy Wolek*
366 © Werner Bertsch, The Stock Shop; © Yoav, Phototake; © Christy Volpe from Marilyn Gartman; © Yoav, Phototake
367 Photri from Marilyn Gartman; © Julie Brown, Custom Medical
368 SCALA/Art Resource; Daniel Simon, Gamma/Liaison
369 Photri from Marilyn Gartman; © Christy Volpe from Marilyn Gartman
370 © Julie Brown, Custom Medical; © Yoav, Phototake
373 © Henry Schleichkorn, Custom Medical
374 © Yoav, Phototake; Tim McCabe, U.S. Department of Agriculture
375 Albert J. Stunkard, M.D., University of Pennsylvania
376 Todd Winters*
377 © Werner Bertsch, The Stock Market
380 © Yoav, Phototake
382 Brent Jones
384 SHAPEDOWN-Balboa Publishing